"*Fundamental Photoshop* provides a complete referenc
artist. More than just a 'glorified manual,' it gives the reader a comprehensive
view of working with images ranging from basic skills, to explaining creative
approaches, color theory, and calibration and output issues. Of particular interest is
the 'Photoshop in Action' section, which uses real-world examples to explain how
Photoshop is used professionally."

Bruce Wands, Chairman of the Computer Art Department
School of Visual Arts, New York City

"As a photographer, I'm in awe of the incredible powers of Photoshop. As a
Photoshop user, I'm in awe of the learning curve—all those layers, levels, nooks
& crannies. What's a user to do?? When I hit a wall, I turn to THE best source of
information available—*Fundamental Photoshop*! It's like having an expert
instructor sitting on my keyboard, ready to help me navigate through complex
waters.

When I need to get it done & I'm out of answers, *Fundamental Photoshop*
pulls me through. It's extremely user-friendly, with clear, concise, well-organized
and easy to use information plus great illustrations & step-by-step exercises.

Take my Nikon, take my Kodachrome—but don't take my *Fundamental
Photoshop*!"

Ira Wexler, Photographer/Author
The Business of Commercial Photography
(published by Watson Guptil/Amphoto, 1995)

"*Fundamental Photoshop* is an informative text filled with practical and easily
understood facts concerning every aspect of the program. A source worth its
weight in gold! A must for every Photoshop owner!"

Raymond A. Mastrobuoni, I.B.D. I.S.P, Vice President
Cartier Inc.
Visual Merchandising and Store Planning

"When you start to understand the full power of Photoshop it can be
overwhelming, until you fully understand how to use that power—and you will
with this book."

Homer Wright, VP Creative Director
Grey Advertising

"Terrific...A boon for beginners and a bible for professionals. This book will become as indispensable to anyone in the graphic arts industry as a set of magic markers and a layout pad."

Steve Alburty,
Writer /Former MIS Director
Chiat/Day Inc. Advertising

"This book should be a fundamental part of any computer artist's library. It covers all the essential ins and outs of Photoshop more succinctly and vividly than other books of its kind."

Sally Face, Manager of Computer Systems
BBDO New York

"Photoshop is one of the most powerful programs available to desktop publishers today, with a daunting array of features geared to varying areas of professional publishing. *Fundamental Photoshop* presents the features of the program in logically organized chapters and provides examples each step of the way. It is a well-organized, easy-to-follow guide to this sometimes difficult program."

Wendy Allen, Director of Electronic Publishing Systems
New York Times Women's Magazines

"Oh, no—not another Photoshop book! Oh, YES! If you only have time for one Photoshop book, *Fundamental Photoshop*, with its clarity, information, and pertinent examples, is the one to get."

Donald Gambino, computer artist, consultant, and educator

"*Fundamental Photoshop* is an unusually informative and highly readable introduction to the magic of Adobe Photoshop. It is of value to newcomers as well as experienced users in learning to effectively use Photoshop's power for image processing, photo retouching, and electronic painting. Particularly helpful are the clear illustrations, easy-to-understand explanations, and detailed step-by-step exercises. This is a truly comprehensive, single-source reference to Photoshop that will be of long-time value."

Burton Holmes, President of Burton Holmes Associates
Corporate Marketing Communications

FUNDAMENTAL

Photoshop 5
4th Edition

FUNDAMENTAL

PHOTOSHOP 5
4th Edition

Adele Droblas Greenberg

Seth Greenberg

Osborne/**McGraw-Hill**

Berkeley   New York   St. Louis   San Francisco
Auckland   Bogotá   Hamburg   London
Madrid   Mexico City   Milan   Montreal   New Delhi
Panama City   Paris   São Paulo
Singapore   Sydney   Tokyo   Toronto

Osborne/**McGraw-Hill**
2600 Tenth Street
Berkeley, California 94710
U.S.A.

For information on translations or book distributors outside the U.S.A., or to arrange bulk purchase discounts for sales promotions, premiums, or fund-raisers, please contact Osborne/**McGraw-Hill** at the above address.

Fundamental Photoshop 5 4ᵗʰ Edition

1234567890 DOC 901987654321098

ISBN 0-07-882579-2

Publisher: Brandon A. Nordin
Editor-in-Chief: Scott Rogers
Acquisitions Editor: Megg Bonar
Project Editor: Jennifer Wenzel
Editorial Assistant: Stephane Thomas
Technical Editor: Jeff Kryvicky
Copy Editor: Claire Splan
Proofreader: Rhonda Holmes
Indexer: Valerie Robbins
Computer Designers: Roberta Steele and Jean Butterfield
Illustrator: Lance Ravella
Cover Design: Curium Design

Dedication

Dedicated to our daughter, Angelique, and the rest of our family

About the Authors...

Adele Droblas Greenberg is a New York–based artist, retoucher, and desktop/prepress/multimedia consultant. She teaches at Pratt Institute and Columbia University. She is also the former training director at a New York City prepress house.

Seth Greenberg is a computer consultant, database/multimedia programmer, and freelance writer. He has also worked as a television producer and scriptwriter, and he has written for several magazines.

Contents At A Glance

Contents

Acknowledgments

A book as extensive as Fundamental Photoshop could not have been written without the help of numerous people.

Above all we'd like to thank the editorial, production, marketing, and sales staff at Osborne/McGraw-Hill, particularly Publisher Brandon Nordin, Editor-in-Chief Scott Rogers, and Acquisitions Editor Megg Bonar. We owe a debt of gratitude to Scott for his dedication, perseverance, help, and enthusiasm during the writing, editing, and production stages of Fundamental Photoshop. We'd like to also express our thanks and gratitude to Jennifer Wenzel, Cynthia Douglas, Betsy Manini, Stephanie Thomas, Claire Splan, Rhonda Holmes, Valerie Robbins, and the entire talented staff of the Osborne Production Department, for their work on Fundamental Photoshop.

A special thanks goes out to Jeff Kryvicky for the excellent job he did as the technical reviewer for *Fundamental Photoshop*. We thank Jeff for all his long hours of hard work, and for the helpful suggestions he gave us while we were writing this book.

We'd also like to thank the many artists whose excellent work appears in the color insert and the "Photoshop In Action" sections in this book.

Thanks to everyone at Adobe Systems, especially John Leddy, Product and Marketing Manager of Adobe Photoshop, for his support and help. We'd also like to thank Jolene Woo and Jill Nakashima from Adobe Public Relations, Christie Cameron, Photoshop Beta Coordinator, and Michelle Garrett of Cunningham Communication, Inc. We'd like to thank the Photoshop programmers who created and developed such an outstanding product. Their accomplishments make our work look like magic.

We're grateful to our friends, clients, and students who kept asking us to put our consulting and training skills down on paper and provide a book for them.

We thank the many corporations who graciously provided assistance: Affinity, Agfa, Alien Skin, American Databankers Corp., Andromeda Software, Inc., Apple Computer, Arrivo, ArtBeats, Avid Technology, ColorBytes Inc., Corel, Dana Publishing, DataStream Imaging Systems, Daystar, DPA Software, D'Pix, Eastman Kodak, EFI, Extensis, Flamenco Software, Gryphon Software, HSC Software, IBM, ImSpace, IN Software, IOMEGA, Iris Graphics, Ken Hansen Photography, Knoll Software, LetraSet, Light Source, Linotype-Hell, Logitech, Macromedia, Media Lab, MetaCreations, Monaco Systems, Nikon, NIQ, PANTONE, PhotoDisc, Pixar, PixelCraft, Strata Inc., Sun Microsystems, SyQuest, Tektronix, 3M, Toshiba, TRUMATCH, Vertigo 3D Software, Vivid Details, Wacom Technology, and Xaos Tools, Inc.

We'd also like to thank everyone else who helped us along the way and everyone else who helped make this book a bestseller.

Introduction

Photoshop's Beginnings

In the late 1980s Thomas Knoll, a University of Michigan graduate student, created a computer program whose primary purpose was to open and display different graphics files on a Macintosh Plus. This was the humble beginning of the program that was eventually to become Photoshop.

Thankfully for Photoshop users, Tom found that working on a computer program proved to be much more fun than writing a thesis paper. With the encouragement of his brother John Knoll, a special effects supervisor at George Lucas's Industrial Light and Magic Company, Tom began adding image-editing capabilities to his program.

Adobe took Tom's creation under its wings. Soon Tom's brother John was creating filters for the program, and through the collaborative efforts of the Knoll brothers; Adobe's programmers; Photoshop evolved into a software package that began revolutionizing the color publishing world.

As Photoshop grew in power and popularity, its users sought help. As consultants, trainers, and Photoshop users, we were encouraged to write an easy-to-understand book that would cover the program's fundamentals, yet go well beyond the basics. The result is *Fundamental Photoshop*.

About This Book

Whether you are a Photoshop beginner or an experienced user, we're sure you'll find *Fundamental Photoshop* to be unique as both an instruction book and a reference book. We not only cover virtually every command and dialog box in the program, but we also have you try them out. The book is filled with features, hints, tips, step-by-step tutorials, and full-fledged Photoshop projects. You can create these projects with your own images, with those provided by Adobe in the Photoshop package, or with the practice images that appear in the book (see the Disk Offer section for more information).

As you read through the book, you'll learn how magazine and book covers, advertisements, and images for television series, films, Web sites, and multimedia productions were created by some of the top Photoshop artists in the country.

Photoshop Portfolio

This book contains a 16-page portfolio of color images that showcases the power of Photoshop. Please refer to Appendix D for detailed descriptions of how each of the images was created.

How This Book Is Organized

The book is divided into four major parts. Chapters 1 through 7 are introductory chapters that guide you through the fundamental tools and basic features of the program. Chapters 8 through 11 bring you to an intermediate level. Chapters 12 through 20 lead you to more advanced levels, and Chapter 21 and five appendixes conclude *Fundamental Photoshop*.

- Chapter 1 begins with an overview of the entire Photoshop design process, from digitizing images to having them output at a prepress house. The chapter concludes with a guide to Photoshop 5's new Color management system. Follow along in this important section to setup Photoshop's RGB, CMYK and Grayscale setup dialog boxes. This chapter helps ensure that your monitor is calibrated and that when you start your Photoshop work the colors on your screen are displayed as accurately as possible.

- Chapter 2 brings you into the world of Photoshop by introducing you to the basics with a tour of the program's menus, tools, palettes, and preferences.

- Chapter 3 introduces you to Photoshop's 5's new type capabilities. This chapter also emphasizes the importance of thinking like a painter and understanding the concepts and features of a pixel-editing program.

- Chapter 4 provides an introduction to the selection tools, including Photoshop 5's new Magnetic Lasso tool. You may be surprised to see that even with the program's basic selection tools, you can create attractive montages, collages, and vignettes.

- Chapter 5 provides an introduction to color theory. Understanding color theory is one of the prerequisites to successfully using Photoshop for color publishing. This chapter takes a thorough look at the difference between the RGB (red/green/blue) and CMYK (cyan/magenta/yellow/black) color models. Also discussed are the HSB (hue/saturation/brightness) and Lab color models.

- Chapter 6 covers Photoshop's painting tools and shows you how to create custom brushes and use Photoshop's blending modes.

- Chapter 7, which concludes the first section of this book, is an introductory look at image-editing techniques. In this chapter you'll learn how to use the Blur/Sharpen, Dodge/Burn/Sponge, and Rubber Stamp tools. You'll also get a chance to try out Photoshop 5's new History palette and History brush.

- Chapter 8 covers digitizing images, cropping images and rotating, and changing brightness and contrast. We round out the chapter by covering Image | Rotate Canvas and Edit | Transform Commands so that you not only learn the basics of scanning, but can create a design project with the images you scan.

- Chapter 9 shows you how you can use Photoshop's Actions and History palettes. The History palette provides you with virtually unlimited undoes; the Action palette allows you to record and play back Photoshop commands. You'll also learn how to use Photoshop 5's File | Automate | Batch command to apply actions to multiple files.

- Chapter 10 covers the Photoshop fascinating filters such as Unsharp Mask, Gaussian Blur, Motion Blur, Lighting Effects, Emboss, and Spherize. If you like special effects, you'll especially enjoy this chapter.

- Chapter 11 provides an overview of third-party filters that add to the functionality of Photoshop and allow you to create special effects with a few clicks and drags of the mouse.

▢ Chapter 12 provides an in-depth discussion of switching modes—in particular, converting an RGB color file to a CMYK color file, and converting from RGB mode to Grayscale mode. This chapter also leads you step-by-step through the process of creating a duotone and a mezzotint.

▢ Chapter 13 introduces you to Photoshop's powerful Pen tool. Here you'll be able to try your hand at creating paths and Bézier curves. You'll also learn how to use Photoshop 5's new Magnetic Pen and Freeform Pen tool. The chapter concludes with step-by-step instructions for creating clipping paths, which allow you to silhouette images that you place in other programs.

▢ Chapter 14 provides an in-depth discussion of creating masks and using channels, including Photoshop's versatile Quick Mask. You'll also learn how to save and load selections. The chapter includes a look at using Photoshop's Apply Image and Calculations commands. The chapter concludes with step-by-step instructions for creating spot colors using Photoshop 5's new Spot Color Channels.

▢ Chapter 15 provides a thorough look at Photoshop's powerful layering features and the program's Layers palette. You'll learn techniques for creating, viewing, hiding, moving, linking, blending, merging and flattening layers.

▢ Chapter 16 leads you through the more advanced features of layers. You'll learn how to use composite controls and clipping groups. The chapter features a detailed discussion of Photoshop's powerful layer masks which allow you to seamlessly blend layers together. You'll also learn how to use Photoshop's adjustment layers, which allow you to color correct with limitless "undos" and "redos."

▢ Chapter 17 shows you how to create special effects using Photoshop 5's new Layer Effects commands. You'll also learn how to create special effects using a variety of filters and layer blending modes. The Chapter concludes with a look at creating effects with Photoshop and other programs. 3-D programs, morphing and paint programs, and other 2-D programs are all discussed in this chapter.

◻ Chapter 18 takes you step-by-step through the retouching and color-correcting processes. It shows you how to correct old and damaged photographs, as well as how to use the Curves and Levels dialog boxes and Photoshop 5's new Color Sampler tools. Photoshop 5's intriguing new Channel Mixer is also covered in this chapter. For many readers, this may be one of the most interesting chapters in the book.

◻ Chapter 19 explains the printing process and includes instructions for calibrating your system to a proof.

◻ Chapter 20 explains how to output your Photoshop work to the Web, to multimedia programs, and to digital video. The chapter focuses on creating images in GIF and JPEG formats.

◻ Chapter 21 covers copyright issues involving digital images and shows you how to embed digital watermarks in your images.

◻ Appendix A provides a discussion of file formats and techniques for exporting and importing to Photoshop and other applications.

◻ Appendix B shows you how to use Photoshop's File Info command, which allows you to tag files according to the International Press Telecommunications Council standard.

◻ Appendix C provides you a listing of company names and addresses mentioned in this book.

◻ Appendix D describes how the images in the Photoshop Portfolio were created.

◻ Appendix E concludes the book with encouragement and a few final thoughts.

 NOTE: *For updated information on Adobe Photoshop, visit Adobe's Web site at www.adobe.com or our own Web site at www2.infohouse.com/~addesign.*

Although this book concentrates on the Mac and PC versions of Photoshop, users with Silicon Graphics and Sun Computers can also benefit from this book.

The keyboard shortcuts for both of these computers have a META key, which is similar to the ALT key. See your Quick Reference card for more details on keyboard shortcuts.

Disk Offer

Fundamental Photoshop was carefully designed so that you can easily re-create the sample projects in the book using your own images or Adobe Photoshop Sample files. For more practice you may want to download many of the images that appear in the book from Osborne/McGraw-Hill's Web site at www.osborne.com. If you don't have access to the Web, you may also purchase images used in the book on three disks. The disks contain color renditions of the images that appear in black and white in the book. If you would like to purchase these disks, please make out a check or money order for $12.95 payable to "AD Design" and send it to:

Fundamental Photoshop
P.O. BOX 3117
Westport, CT 06880

Please specify whether you would like a Mac or PC disk and which edition (first, second, third or fourth) of the book you are using.

Note for Those Updating from Previous Versions of Photoshop

The fourth edition of *Fundamental Photoshop* has been completely updated for Adobe Photoshop 5. If you're still using a previous version of Photoshop or if you just upgraded, here are a few notes:

- Many keyboard commands have been added or changed in Photoshop 5.
- The Batch command has been moved from the Actions palette to the File | Automate Submenu. See Chapter 9 for details.

- Photoshop's Color Settings dialog boxes have been revised. You now work in an RGB color space—not the same color space as your monitors. See Chapter 1 for details.

- Using Type in Photoshop 5 has been improved. The Type Tool dialog box has been greatly enhanced. Type can now appear in your image as you type it in the Type Tool dialog box. Photoshop 5 features Vertical type tools which allow you to create type vertically. In order to paint over type created with the Type Tool, you must render it (Layer | Type | Render Layer). See Chapter 3 for details regarding this and the other features mentioned above.

- The "Float" menu command and float mode no longer exist. The keyboard command COMMAND-J (Windows users: CTRL-J) copies a selection into a new layer. (Although you won't see the word "float" in Photoshop 5, moving a selection and copying a selection still float the selection above the background pixels. This subject is covered in Chapters 3 and 4.

- Edit | Transform commands replace Layer | Transform. The transform commands work with paths, selections, layers and masks in Quick Mask mode. The transform commands are covered in Chapters 8, 13, and 15.

- Actions have been beefed-up. Actions in Photoshop 5 now record more commands than in Photoshop 4. See Chapter 9 to learn more about actions.

- The Filter | Fade command now allows you to fade back your last paint stroke; also fade out Image | Adjust commands.

- You can now create spot colors in Photoshop. See Chapter 14 for details.

- The History palette provides multiple undoes. The old Take Snapshot command in previous versions has been replaced. You can now take a Snapshot using the History palette. If you wish to paint back the snapshot version or fill with the snapshot version, you must click in the History palette to set the state that you wish to paint back from; then paint it back on screen with the History brush. You can also fill an image with a History state, and use the Eraser tool to paint a history version over your image. See Chapters 7 and 9 for specifics.

- ◻ The Move tool now includes an Auto Select Layer feature which allows you to select layers without switching the target layer in the Layers palette. See Chapter 15 for details.

- ◻ You can now use the Select | Transform command to reshape a selection without affecting the underlying pixels. See Chapter 4 for details.

These are only a few enhancements awaiting you. Read on for more.

CHAPTER 1

The Photoshop Studio and Color Management System

Photoshop is truly magical. It can pluck a pyramid from the sands of Egypt and gently drop it down on the Champs-Elysées, looking so real that even a Parisian might not think anything is out of place. Photoshop can make the wrinkles of age vanish magically—or create them where they haven't yet appeared. It can transform a scan of a torn and discolored photograph so that it looks like a flawless image taken by a master photographer. And Photoshop can turn your blank computer screen into an artistic masterpiece—a blend of photorealistic images, fantastic designs, patterns, and colors.

As you'll see in the many professional art and design samples throughout this book, especially in the color inserts, the Photoshop design process can take many forms and can lead in a multitude of directions. Photoshop is an electronic passport to high-end color desktop publishing as well as prepress, multimedia, animation, digital photography, and painting.

Photoshop transports you to these ports of call in many different ways. Once an image is input into Photoshop from a scanner, digital or video camera, video recorder, or Photo CD image, it can be retouched, painted, color corrected, sharpened, rippled, or distorted. An image can be cut apart, juxtaposed, or blended into another. It can then be output to the Web, to a slide recorder, a video recorder, a black-and-white or color printer, or an imagesetter to create the final film, which is used to make plates for a printing press. Figure 1-1 illustrates the various input and output devices that cooperate in the Photoshop design and production process.

Although you undoubtedly are eager to jump right in and start turning your artistic visions into reality, take some time first to get acquainted with the Photoshop design process and the digital technology involved in computer image editing. This chapter provides a brief overview of the entire process—inputting, editing, and outputting images—and covers the basics of computers, storage devices, monitors, video display and accelerator cards, scanners, Photo CDs, digital and video cameras, and color printers.

You may want to consider purchasing much of the equipment reviewed in this chapter, but keep in mind that some of it is best left to the professional prepress houses, service bureaus, and electronic imaging centers that can afford state-of-the-art, high-end technology. For a fee, these electronic production companies will digitize your photos, slides, and artwork on drum scanners, providing you with high-quality images without your having to spend a fortune. A service bureau can also output your work to a color printer or imagesetter in preparation for the project's final destination, usually the printing press.

This chapter's overview of studio equipment begins with a discussion of computers and computer peripherals, and then branches out to input and output

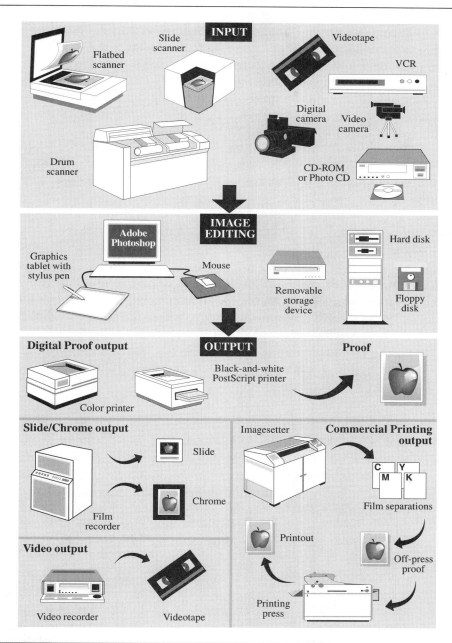

FIGURE 1-1   The Photoshop design and production process

devices. The chapter concludes with Photoshop installation tips and a vitally important section on choosing color settings. Getting started with the correct color settings and a sound knowledge of equipment requirements will help you to complete your design work efficiently and effectively.

Personal Computer Systems

The focal point of the Photoshop studio is your computer. To a significant degree, Photoshop's performance depends on the speed and power of your computer.

Following are the system requirements specified by Adobe for running Photoshop on Macs and PCs:

 NOTE: *The interface and commands for both Macs and PCs are virtually identical.*

☐ On the Power Macintosh or PowerMac OS clones, 32MB of application RAM (random access memory), 64MB recommended. For all Macs, at least 80MB of hard disk space available. System software should be System 7.5 or higher.

☐ On PCs running Windows 95 or Windows NT (4.0 or higher), at least 32MB of RAM (64MB recommended) and at least 80MB of free hard disk space. The PC should be able to display at least 256 colors.

If your computer meets these minimum requirements, youG17ll be able to run Photoshop and perform the exercises in this book. However, if your computer system barely squeaks by, be warned: Photoshop is a very enticing program. The more you learn about it, the more potential you'll see for its use. As you master Photoshop, you'll probably want to add more horsepower to your system to accelerate its performance and increase its ability to utilize Photoshop's power. And if you are buying a new computer just for Photoshop work, by all means consider purchasing the most powerful system you can afford, with the most amount of memory.

You might wonder why Photoshop is so demanding. The answer is that a large, high-quality color image can easily consume over 20 million bytes, or 20MB, of storage space. When such a large file needs to be loaded, color corrected, and edited, a computer that typically is adequate for other tasks may bog down under the stress of working with Photoshop.

The CPU

To evaluate Photoshop's performance on your system, or to decide what system to buy, you should have a basic knowledge of what controls a computer's operating speed. Perhaps the most important component is the computer's microprocessor, or CPU (central processing unit). The microprocessor is a chip that is often called the "brains" of a computer. Its job is to process the steps of a computer program and send instructions along the various data highways connected to its circuitry. In any microprocessor, regardless of whether it is driving a Macintosh or a PC, two main factors determine performance: the speed of the chip and the amount of data the chip can process.

Available CPUs run at various speeds and process various amounts of data. The primary CPU for the Macintosh and Mac clones is the PowerPC 600 series. The PowerPC 604 and 750 (known as the G3) chips can send over 64 data channels at once—the equivalent of a 64-lane highway, with carloads of information running through the CPU. This highway is called a *64-bit data bus*. The bigger the data bus, the better the performance. The 68040 CPU (on many older Macs which can't run the current version of Photoshop) can process 32 bits of information at a time. Apart from its 64-bit data bus, the PowerPC's RISC-based (Reduced Instruction Set Computing) architecture allows it to process instructions simultaneously and handle data more efficiently than the 68040.

 NOTE: *RISC chips are often compared to CISC (Complex Instruction Set Computing) chips. Instead of maintaining a set of complex instructions, RISC chips are programmed with fewer, simpler instructions—those that are most commonly used. When the RISC chip performs a task, it can do so at lightning speed because it breaks the chore into smaller, simple ones that it can perform simultaneously.*

Among PC-compatible computers, the Pentium II and Pentium II Xeon are the most sophisticated. Although the Pentium is not considered a RISC chip, it does feature a 64-bit data bus and is very fast. If you are considering purchasing a new PC, your best bet for Photoshop is the latest Pentium chip running Windows NT.

The speed of the microprocessor measures how quickly it handles a computer program's instructions. The speed, usually called its clock speed, is measured in megahertz (MHz, which equals 1 million clock cycles). A 400MHz Pentium chip is faster than a 300MHz chip. But clock speed isn't everything. The sophistication and architecture of the chip make a difference. On the Mac, a 300MHz PowerPC

750 runs faster than a Mac with a 200MHz PowerPC 604. On PCs, a 200MHz Pentium II runs faster than a 200MHz Pentium.

 NOTE: *Don't rely on clock speed alone. G3 chips running at slower clock speeds often outpace Pentium chips with higher clockspeeds, in some Photoshop operations. You might also find that an operating system such as Windows NT provides a speed boost when using some applications.*

If you already own a computer, there are sometimes ways of improving the clock speed of your machine. Apple has traditionally provided motherboard upgrades (which should be installed by authorized Apple dealers) so that many of its older computers—especially the Power Macs—can be improved to function like the faster models. Currently, manufacturers such as Newer, Maxpower, and Sonnet offer CPU upgrades that boosts older PowerPCs to the lightning fast G3 chip. Many PCs sold in years past were outfitted with an empty microprocessor socket to allow an upgrade to faster Pentium chips. If you are interested in investigating upgrades, contact an authorized Apple or PC vendor.

If you can't wait for an upgrade, or if none is available, a variety of manufacturers sell accelerator boards that take over the processing chores for slower computers. Many vendors and mail-order suppliers sell these boards, which generally are easily installed in a slot on your computer's motherboard.

 CAUTION: *Before buying any accelerator equipment, be sure to verify that it will run with Photoshop and any of the other peripherals connected to your system.*

Multiprocessor Systems

If you're really looking for the ultimate in speed, you may wish to invest in an Apple, Mac-compatible, or Pentium computer with two or more CPUs built in. Photoshop is one of the few software applications that can take advantage of computers with more than one CPU. Speed-up is most notable in filter operations (blurring and sharpening, for instance) and converting RGB color images to CMYK color images. Computers with four processors can make many operations two to four times as fast as a computer with one processor.

 NOTE: *The Pentium II Xeon can accept four or more processors. Apple's forthcoming G4 processor will be capable of multiprocessing, although the G3 isn't.*

Frequently, however, when you want to speed up your computer, you do not have to do anything as drastic as adding another CPU. Instead, adding memory often provides a noticeable increase in Photoshop's performance.

RAM

Much of Photoshop's speed is based on how much work it can accomplish directly in your computer's RAM (random access memory). RAM is the area of memory your computer uses when you are first working on a file, before you store the data on your hard disk or on a floppy disk. Once a file is saved, when you reload it, Photoshop will keep as much of the file in RAM as it can.

If you do not have enough RAM available for Photoshop's operations, it turns to your hard disk and grabs as much free space as it can to complete its chores. Memory accessed from the hard disk when RAM is insufficient is called *virtual memory*. Operations that take place purely in RAM are always going to be faster than those using virtual memory. The computer can interact faster with data it accesses from electronic chips than from a spinning mechanical disk.

As a rule of thumb for estimating RAM requirements, Adobe suggests having three to five times your file size available in RAM, plus an additional five to ten megabytes. The more RAM available, the less often Photoshop will need to rely on virtual memory. Despite the safety net of virtual memory, you should be aware that certain Photoshop special effects will not operate at all unless sufficient RAM is available.

When upgrading your system's memory or purchasing a new computer, remember that not all computers are expandable to the same degree. The less expensive Macs and PCs generally will not allow as much memory expansion as the more expensive models. If you can't add any more RAM to your system, your hard disk becomes a crucial element in the Photoshop studio.

Hard Disks

Since Photoshop must work with your hard disk when RAM is insufficient, the disk's speed and size have a direct effect on Photoshop's productivity. In Photoshop, a hard disk used for virtual memory is called a *scratch disk*. If you don't have enough room on your hard disk, Photoshop may not be able to complete the command you are trying to execute. You will receive a screen alert with the message "Scratch Disk Full." It is imperative that you have sufficient hard disk space, or you may not have enough room to save the file you are working with.

If you are planning to add another hard disk to your system, purchase the largest and fastest one that you can afford. Usually, the larger the hard disk, the faster its seek time (the time it takes the drive's read/write head to jump to a specific spot on the disk's platter). Hard disk seek time is measured in milliseconds (ms). A 9 ms hard disk is faster than a 12 ms hard disk. Most hard drives over 1 gigabyte have seek times less than 10 ms and usually can transfer several megabytes of data per second from the drive to the computer.

AV Drives

A hard disk is really not too different from a runner who has to sprint around a stadium track a few times. Every so often, the runner has to stop and catch his or her breath. You may not realize it, but every now and then, your hard disk catches its breath in a process known as *thermal calibration.* Most drives are programmed to calibrate themselves on a regular basis to compensate for heat changes. If you are involved in multimedia production, this can create data problems because the recalibration can take place while you're copying very large digital files, particularly digital video. If you will be integrating your Photoshop work into digital video, you should investigate purchasing an AV (audiovisual) drive. These drives are designed to handle large streams of data without calibrating in the middle of file transfer. Many AV drives sold today work in both AV and non-AV environments.

Raid Arrays

If you require the ultimate in speed from your hard drive, you may wish to purchase an array of hard disks, called a *Raid array.* Raid systems can cut read/write times in half and double transfer rates. A typical Raid system splits the data onto two or more hard disks in a process called *data striping.* By reading and writing from multiple drives, access times and transfer rates are significantly enhanced. All you see on your desktop is one hard drive; software handles the tricky process of juggling data between drives.

Raid systems are divided into different levels, from 0 to 5. Level 0 provides the speedy process of data striping. In Raid Level 1 systems the data is saved to both disks in a process called *mirroring.* Although data transfer times are not as quick as Level 0 systems, Level 1 provides data redundancy: If one drive fails, the other is immediately available, with no loss of data. Many SCSI Raid systems include accelerator boards, which further speed up the data transfer process.

Removable Hard Disks

Before you add another hard disk to your system, you might consider offloading data to a removable hard disk to free up space on your system's internal hard disk. Removable hard disks are not only valuable for backing up data but have become essential to many Photoshop users because graphics files are often too large to fit on a floppy disk. When graphic designers need to send a large file out to a service bureau or deliver it to a client, they usually save it on a removable hard-disk cartridge. These cartridges slide in and out of a drive mechanism much as video cassettes do in a VCR, and thus are easily transported from computer to computer.

The most popular removable hard drives are manufactured by Iomega and Syquest. Iomega's 100MB Zip drive has become the most popular removable drive in the United States. In fact, many computer manufacturers provide models with internal Zip disks built into the computer. The drive costs less than $120, and cartridges for the drive are less than $20. The newer and faster ZipPlus is a bit more expensive. Photoshop users, however, would probably be better off with Iomega's Jaz drive, which can store 2GB on a removable cartridge. The 2GB model retails as low as $500; the 1GB model retails for about $299. The Jaz drive is also quite a bit faster than the lower-capacity Zip—almost as fast as many high-capacity hard disks.

If you are purchasing an Iomega or Syquest removable cartridge that you will be sending to a printer, prepress house, or service bureau, check to see that the service bureau can accept the type of drive you are going to buy. Most will accept Zip and Jaz cartridges and 44MB, 88MB, 200MB, and 270MB Syquest cartridges.

Optical and DAT Drives

When you need to store many large files for archival purposes, you may wish to purchase an optical drive. Although slower than hard disks, optical drives often store between 500MB and 1GB. The chief appeal of opticals is that the cost per gigabyte is much lower than that of hard disks or removable hard disks, and the storage media lasts longer than most others.

Another economical choice for storing large amounts of data is a digital audiotape (DAT) drive. These tape drives store several gigabytes of data on tapes that cost approximately $10 each. Many DAT drives are available for under $2,000. Unlike hard drives, which can quickly access data anywhere on a spinning platter, the DAT has to wind and unwind to read and record data. This makes DAT drives inappropriate for most operations except regular backups of files.

CD-ROM Recorders

One of the most economical ways of archiving data so that it can be easily accessed and shipped is to save it on a CD-ROM disc. Current discs can store 650MB and generally cost under $4 each. Since CD-ROMs discs last longer than any media, they're best used for important digital files that you never want to erase. We store data on our CD-ROM, which allows us to free up storage space on our more expensive removable Jaz and Syquest cartridges. We've started to use a CD-ROM to store all text and digital files from our book, as well as to master a CD-ROM interactive multimedia-training disc.

Data is written to CD-ROM by a CD-ROM recorder. In recent years, prices on many desktop CD-ROM drives have dropped drastically, to well below $1,000—and the reliability of the recording devices has improved remarkably. Most software included with CD-ROM recorders allows you to save files so that they can be read by Macs, PCs, or both. Additionally, software allows you to write discs in multiple "sessions." This means that you can save data to a disc in one recording session, then add data to the disc at a later session. The newest CD-ROM drives, often called CD-RW drives, allow you to create erasable versions of your work on CD-RW discs. Unlike older drives, these allow you to re-record over previous data.

If you are shopping for a CD-ROM drive, purchase the fastest one that you can afford. Most inexpensive models are two-speed recorders. If you'll be doing a lot of archiving onto CD-ROMs, shop around for at least a four-speed recorder, which writes data twice as fast. Also investigate the new DVD drives which allow you to save 5.2MB of data and record over data already written to a DVD disc.

File Compression

If you are short on hard disk or archival storage space, one scheme for managing large files is to save them in compressed format. Various types of data compression exist. Some compression methods result in data loss; others compress without sacrificing picture quality. If you plan to compress your files, you should know whether your compression software will remove picture information during the compression process.

On the Mac, programs such as Stuffit Deluxe and Disk Doubler can compress files without losing data. On the PC, PKZIP and Stacker are two popular programs that offer compression without data loss. Stacker automatically compresses every file on a hard disk, as opposed to PKZIP, which compresses only the files that you select.

Photoshop can save files using JPEG and LZW compression formats. JPEG results in data loss; LZW does not. These options are discussed in more detail in Appendix A.

MAC to PC Links

As the popularity of the Windows version of Photoshop grows, many design studios need to share graphics files between their Macs and PCs. Sharing files is easy if your Macs and PCs are networked together: You can simply store graphics files on file servers and load them onto either the Macs or the PCs. If your Macs and PCs aren't on the same network, several solutions exist: If you need to load PC files on Macs, you can use Apple's PC Exchange Control Panel, which allows you to mount PC disks, and removable cartridges. The Control Panel is part of the System 7 and 8 operating system, and can be turned on and off using Apple's Extensions Manager.

If you to need to load Mac files onto a PC or mount Zip and Jaz cartridges onto your PC, your best bet is DataViz MacOpener. The product costs less than $100 and is quite simple to use and install. We have a Jaz drive connected to our PC and another one connected to one of our Macs. With MacOpener installed on our PC we simply place the Mac cartridge in the PC Jaz drive. The cartridge mounts on screen like any other Mac or PC disks. We've found it particularly helpful because we don't need to purchase one set of Jaz cartridges that only run on one computer.

Color Video Monitors

As you create and edit images, your window into the color digital world is your video monitor. Your monitor's screen size, sharpness, and color accuracy are all critical factors when working with Photoshop. When purchasing a monitor, it's important to understand that the color you see on screen is created from red, green, and blue color phosphors. The phosphors on one monitor may not match another monitor and the colors you see on screen may not match the colors generated on a scanner or another monitor. Scanners create colors using red, green, and blue colors, but they create them differently than monitors. When an image is printed, the colors are often created from cyan, magenta, yellow, and black inks.

 NOTE: *To ensure that the colors you see on screen match the color output on printers, follow the steps for setting up Photoshop's color setting options described at the end of this chapter.*

When purchasing a monitor, try to do as much research as possible, and get the best monitor you can afford. Although using a full- or two-page monitor is not a necessity in Photoshop, the larger your monitor, the more efficiently you'll be able to work. Even if you are working on small images, you will certainly want to magnify them. You will often want to have a palette of colors or brushes open while you paint or edit, or to have several images open at the same time. You may even wish to view the same image at various sizes in separate windows. All of these factors make screen real estate an important commodity.

If you think that 19- or 21-inch color monitors are beyond your budget, consider purchasing a 17-inch model. Many 17-inch monitors cost about half the price of 19-inch monitors and will probably pay for themselves in convenience and ease of use. The difference between 13- and 17-inch monitors may not seem like much, but because monitor size is measured diagonally, a 17-inch monitor actually provides approximately 85 percent more viewing area than a 13-inch one.

 TIP: *If you really want more work space, check with your computer manufacturer to see if your model can drive two monitors at once. Most Mac-compatible systems can support two monitors right out of the box.*

If you are planning to buy a new monitor, you'll find that many of the major desktop publishing vendors, such as Apple, NEC, Radius, and Sony, offer models that will suit your needs. Clone manufacturers, such as Power Computing and Dell, often include 15-, 17- or 19-inch models in their package choices.

Most graphics monitors provide a resolution of at least 72 pixels per inch (ppi). A *pixel* is the smallest visible element on screen. At 72 pixels per inch, the resolution on a 14-inch monitor is 640 by 480 pixels. Most 19-inch monitors display 1,024 by 768 pixels. Radius's 20-inch IntelliColor for both PCs and Macs boasts a resolution as high as 1,600 by 1,200 pixels. Most newer monitors allow you to switch from one resolution to another. Switching to a higher resolution adds more pixels to the screen and thus increases the viewing area of images (although the images are smaller).

A good monitor should not flicker. Most high-end models refresh the screen fast enough so that flickering is not a problem. Higher-quality monitors are also *non-interlaced,* which means that lines of information are scanned one row after another, rather than the odd lines first, then the even. Non-interlaced monitors are sharper and produce less flickering. The dot pitch on monitors is also a factor governing image quality. *Dot pitch* is the distance between the holes in the *shadow mask,* which is a metal plate with holes in it that focuses the beams from the electron guns at the back of the CPU. The smaller the dot pitch, the sharper the monitor. You'll generally see graphics monitors featuring dot pitches of .31 mm (millimeters) or less.

When analyzing an image on a monitor, study the uniformity of the colors displayed. Different areas of the screen should generally appear at the same levels of brightness. Images should look sharp, not blurry. A straight line that traverses the screen should look straight, not bent. Circles should look like perfect circles.

Any new color monitor you buy should be capable of displaying over 16 million colors. The number of colors a monitor displays is closely tied to the video display card inside your computer, as explained next.

Video Display Cards

The video display card, one of the circuit boards found in a computer, controls how many colors the monitor displays and often controls how fast the monitor redraws images on the screen. Some computers, including the newer models from Apple, have a video card built in, and no extra hardware is needed to drive the monitor.

The minimum number of colors displayed by most color computers and most video display cards is 256. But for most Photoshop users, 256 colors just isn't enough. In order to view digitized images of color photographs on screen and see them as realistically as possible, millions of colors are needed. The reason so many colors are needed is simple: The human eye can discern millions of colors.

 NOTE: *Many artists who design for the World Wide Web or multimedia only need to output images with 256 colors or less. For more information about Web and multimedia design, see Chapter 20.*

In order to view millions of colors, you will need a 24-bit video display color card. If you own a Mac or Mac clone, chances are you can add chips, called *video RAM,* to get 24-bit color on a 14- or 16-inch monitor. On top-of-the-line Power Macs, you can add enough video RAM to view millions of colors on a 20-inch monitor. When buying a PC, you can often specify how much video RAM you want included on your PC's video card. For instance, on most Dell computers, purchasing a video card with 2MB RAM provides 24-bit color on a 17-inch monitor.

If you're wondering how 24-bit color translates into 16 million colors, you need to know something about computer technology. This knowledge will be helpful because you will see the term "bit" used in several Photoshop dialog boxes. A *bit* is the smallest element the computer uses to describe data. The bit has two states: on or off. The total possible combinations for 8 bits of data yield 256 colors ($2 \times 2 \times 2 \times 2 \times 2 \times 2 \times 2 \times 2 = 256$).

A 24-bit color system divides the 24 bits into 8 bits for red values, 8 bits for green values, and 8 bits for blue values. This produces 256 possible values of red, 256 of green, and 256 of blue. By making combinations of all the possible values of red, green, and blue, the computer can create over 16.7 million colors ($256 \times 256 \times 256 = 16,777,216$).

If you do need to buy a 24-bit card, make your purchase carefully. Not all 24-bit cards will work with all monitor sizes. One 24-bit card may produce millions of colors on a 13-inch monitor, but not on a 19-inch monitor. One reason for this is that video cards need more memory to address larger screens.

Accelerated Video Display Cards

If you decide you need a 24-bit video card, your next decision should be whether to buy an accelerated video display card. Acceleration is desirable because it reduces the amount of time required to update the thousands of pixels on a large color screen.

In addition to producing 16.7 million colors, accelerated 24-bit video cards speed up screen operations by adding an extra microprocessor, called a *coprocessor*, to your computer. This accelerates the entire procedure of working with graphic images. When your computer has a graphics coprocessor, its microprocessor can take a break from handling time-consuming screen processing operations.

Manufacturers of 24-bit cards for both PCs and Macs include Matrox, Radius, TrueVision, and NEC.

 NOTE: *If you do plan to purchase an accelerated video card, be aware that it's hard to predict how much these will speed up screen display when you are working with Photoshop. They will undoubtedly accelerate screen redraw and scrolling, but they may not affect specific Photoshop functions.*

Graphics Tablet with Stylus Pen

Often overlooked in the array of sophisticated graphics peripherals is the value of a graphics tablet and stylus pen. The stylus pen is a pressure-sensitive device that replaces the mouse. A stylus can simulate the pencil, pen, and paintbrush more accurately than the mouse, and thus many artists find it easier to use. The fine point of the stylus pen also enables you to more precisely retouch photographs in Photoshop. Figure 1-2 shows artist C. David Piña using a Wacom tablet and stylus pen with Photoshop to work on the main title design for the 63rd Annual Academy Awards show.

The stylus must be used in conjunction with a graphics tablet. Wacom manufactures a tablet that includes a plastic overlay. You can slide art under the overlay and trace it much more accurately than you can with a mouse. One of Wacom's latest models simultaneously sketches on paper with pencil lead while it sends digital signals to your computer. Other manufacturers of tablets with stylus pens include CalComp and Kurta.

Input Devices

Input devices digitize images so they can be edited and color corrected in Photoshop. These devices include scanners, Photo CDs, digital cameras, and video cameras. Chapter 7 covers the digitizing process in detail. Although the use of

©A.M.P.A.S.® main title design by C. David Piña

FIGURE 1-2   A Wacom tablet and stylus pen, courtesy of Wacom Technology Corp.

Photo CDs and digital photography is growing, the most common technique for digitizing images is with a scanner.

Scanners

Scanners are used primarily to digitize photographs, flat art, and slides. Although the price of many scanners fits the budget of many Photoshop studios, the quality of low-cost scanners may not suit your needs. Depending on the type of work you do, you may find it necessary to send your files to a prepress house or service bureau to get the final quality you desire.

Even if you aren't going to purchase a scanner or actually do the scanning yourself, you should know the basics of how scanners work. This will give you an idea of what quality you can expect from various types of scanners.

Flatbed Scanners

Most scanners sold today are flatbed scanners. In many ways, a flatbed scanner resembles a copy machine. Art or a photograph is placed under the scanner's cover, and the digital reproduction process begins. Some of the better-known manufacturers of flatbed scanners are Agfa, Hewlett-Packard, Howtek, La Cie, Microtek, Sharp, Nikon, and Umax.

Flatbed scanners are sometimes called CCDs. CCD stands for *charged coupled device,* a component in the scanner's head that sends thousands of beams of light across the object being scanned. Photoelectric cells on the head detect red, green, and blue components of light that are reflected back to the CCD. The reflected information produces high and low voltages, depending on the lightness and darkness of the image. This information is digitized so it can be saved to disk.

There are several factors to consider when evaluating what scanner to use or buy. The first is resolution, or how many pixels per inch (ppi) the scanner can create. The greater the number of pixels, the sharper the image. Many low-priced scanners scan at least 600 ppi. Some use interpolation to make the resolution appear as high as 1,200 ppi. When a scanner interpolates, it does not really produce a sharper representation of the actual scanned image. It merely adds more pixels and then colors the new pixels with the average color of surrounding pixels. For more information about scanning resolution, see Chapter 8.

One of the primary factors that determines scanned image quality is dynamic or density range. A scanner's *dynamic range* measures its ability to capture gradations from the lightest to darkest parts of an image. The greater a scanner's dynamic range, the sharper the image. To provide better dynamic range, the scanner needs to utilize more bits to store the information. Most low-end scanners are 24-bit scanners. They scan at 8 bits per each red, green, or blue component. Technically, this should produce over 16.7 million colors; however, 2 bits are needed to handle noise and calibration, so this decreases the dynamic range.

Midrange scanners are often 30-bit scanners. The Agfa Arcus II, shown in Figure 1-3, which sells for about $2,000, is a 36-bit scanner. A high-end scanner such as the Scitex Smartscan sells for about $80,000. This scanner not only has a better dynamic range than lower-bit scanners but also has its own image-processing system. The Smartscan operator can make color adjustments before and during the scanning process.

Slide Scanners

If you can obtain your images as slides, you're likely to improve the quality of your digital images. Slides are brighter than prints and have a higher dynamic range; thus the originating image for the scan is better than an opaque object.

In many slide scanners, the CCD is stationary, and light is redirected back to the photo sensors through a combination of mirrors and lenses. The optical system

FIGURE 1-3   Agfa's Arcus II scanner, courtesy of Agfa Corp.

of slide scanners is often better than that of flatbeds; many slide scanners have resolutions in the 5,000-6,000 ppi range. Some of the better-known manufacturers of slide scanners are BarneyScan, Kodak, Nikon, and Polaroid.

Though slide scanners can be expensive, several models fall into the price range of flatbed scanners. Nikon's LS-10 Coolscan, shown in Figure 1-4, retails for about $1,000. The internal model will fit in the drive bay of various Macs and PCs.

Rotary Drum Scanners

For most color professionals, the best way to ensure the highest digital quality is to scan with a drum scanner, shown in Figure 1-5. Instead of utilizing a CCD to sense light, the drum scanner uses a photomultiplier tube, often called a *PMT*. In PMT technology, the image being scanned rotates on a drum while a stationary source transmits light using photomultiplier tubes.

The rotary drum's sophisticated photoreceptors and advanced optics make the drum scanner much more sensitive to highlights and shadows than most CCD scanners. Service bureaus typically charge from $25 to $100 for images scanned on drum scanners. These scanners cost from $25,000 to several hundred thousand dollars and require trained operators to get the best scanning results.

FIGURE 1-4   Nikon's LS-10 Coolscan slide scanner, courtesy of Nikon

| **FIGURE 1-5** | Dupont Crosfield drum scanner, courtesy of Dupont Crosfield |

If you need to digitize photographic images, you may be able to avoid scanning altogether and take advantage of the most recent and one of the more important developments in digitizing images: the Photo CD.

Photo CDs

Since Eastman Kodak developed the Photo CD in 1992, it has become a serious and high-quality alternative to scanning. For a nominal fee per photo, a Photo CD service bureau can digitize your photographic film directly to a Photo CD disc. Kodak's Photo CD Master discs can hold 100 high-resolution 35mm images. Kodak's Pro Photo CD format allows the following film formats to be digitized on a Photo CD: 120mm, 70mm, 35mm, and 4-by-5 inch. The Photo CD image can be opened directly into Photoshop for image editing and color correcting.

Virtually all new computer systems are sold with built-in CD-ROM players. However, if you are in the market for one, prices range from $200 to $500, with the fastest models generally being the most expensive. Speed is important because a large color image can take many times longer to load on a CD-ROM than on a hard drive. Today, most computers are sold with at least 24-speed CD-ROMs—approximately twenty-four times the 1-speed CD-ROM data transfer rate of 150KB per second.

Video and Digital Cameras

If your Photoshop work requires that you take your own photographs, you may want to investigate using a video or digital camera in order to digitize your images instantaneously. This eliminates delays caused by film processing, test shoots, and scanning prints or transparencies.

Many video cameras require that a video card be installed in your computer to digitize the video signal from the camera. There are also many systems that come with software that allows you to control the video digitizing process directly from Photoshop.

Although capturing an image from video is both convenient and quick, the resolution of images produced on most video digitizing systems is not higher than 640 by 480 pixels (72 ppi). This is because they use the NTSC (National Television System Committee) standard.

The alternative to a video camera is a digital camera. Many of these cameras look like standard 35mm cameras, but they store images to the camera's memory or to a small attached hard disk. Besides providing higher resolution than a video camera, the digital camera is easier to carry around. Kodak, for instance, has released several digital cameras similar to the DCS 420 digital camera, shown in Figure 1-6, which uses a 35mm Nikon body as the optical power behind its digital camera system. The price for this camera runs from about $8,500 to $10,000.

Leaf Systems, a Scitex company, has developed a digital camera back that attaches to high-end cameras, such as the Mamiya RZ 67 and Hasselblad's 500 EL and 553 RLX. Images taken by these cameras can then be downloaded to a Mac or PC. On the lower end of the scale, both Kodak and Apple are marketing digital cameras that retail for less than $1,000. These cameras can be great for creating inexpensive brochures and Web graphics. They are covered in more detail in Chapter 8.

Video Capture Cards

Another method for capturing video images is to use a video card, such as those manufactured by Apple, Radius, and TrueVision. These allow you to use your computer to directly input from and output to videotape. Most cards allow you to

FIGURE 1-6   Kodak DCS 420 digital camera, courtesy of Eastman Kodak Company

capture directly from a video camera as well. Recently, several computer manufacturers, such as Apple and Compaq, have begun including video capture cards in their computer models. If you do purchase a new computer for its video capabilities, be aware that most video boards built into computers are not designed to produce the highest quality full-screen, full-motion video.

Output Devices

Once you start working in Photoshop, you'll undoubtedly want to print your color images for final output or as a proof—a sample of your final printed version. Proofs created from the desktop before the film negative stage are often called *digital proofs.* To print a proof on paper, you can use either a black-and-white or color printer. Output devices generally used for producing color proofs include inkjet printers, thermal wax printers, dye-sublimation printers, color laser printers, and imagesetters. Most manufacturers of printers produce models that accept data from both Macs and PCs.

NOTE: *Many manufacturers of new printers include ICC (International Color Consortium) profiles with their printers. ICC profiles can be read by Photoshop and help ensure that the color output by the printer matches the color you see on screen.*

When outputting, it's always important to consider the quality of the color and the sharpness of the output. Printer resolution is usually measured in dots per inch (dpi). The greater the number of dots, the better the quality.

 NOTE: *If your final output will be slides, you'll need to buy a film recorder or send your files to a service bureau that can output to a film recorder. If your final output will be videotape, you may need a special video card to output to a VCR.*

Inkjet Printers

Low-end inkjet printers are the most inexpensive way of producing color files. These printers create colors by spraying ink from cartridges, usually using a process called *dithering*. The dithering process typically uses dot patterns of cyan, magenta, yellow, and often black inks (CMYK) to create the illusion of millions of colors. In many inkjet printers, the dot patterns are easy to see and the color is not always highly accurate. Cost per page for inkjet printers is usually less than 30 cents. Although many new inkjet printers output at 300 dpi, the dithering and color quality of most inexpensive inkjets is not precise enough to provide highly accurate representations of screen images.

Recently, technology has led to a new crop of mid-range inkjet printers that provide much better color fidelity than low-priced inkjets. Epson's Stylus COLOR 3000, which retails for about $2,000, has received excellent reviews. We've know several artists who claim that this is the best color printer you can buy in its price range. If you want more speed and even better color fidelity, Epson's Stylus Pro 5000, which retails for less than $10,000, provides color quality that matches many printers that cost twice as much.

On the high end of the scale for inkjet printers are the Scitex IRIS and IRIS Series 3000 printers. These printers cost from $40,000 to over $100,000 and are usually found at service bureaus and ad agencies. The IRIS produces images that are near photographic quality by varying the dot size as it produces an image. In terms of color output, the IRIS provides higher quality than thermal wax and most dye-sublimation printers. The smallest printout from an IRIS printer is approximately 11 by 17 inches. The IRIS can also print poster-size images. The IRIS 3024 prints images as large as 24 by 24 inches; the 3047 prints images 34 by 44 inches.

Thermal Wax Printers

Thermal wax printers are a large step up in quality from low-end inkjet printers, and thus are a popular choice for producing samples for clients or internal evaluation of layout and design. In the thermal wax printing process, ribbons coated with cyan, magenta, yellow, and black waxes are heated and transferred to paper. During the printing process, heat from the printer's head fuses dots of color to the page. The dot combinations produce the color. The cost per page averages between 50 cents and a few dollars.

If you're interested in a thermal wax printer, you might want to investigate the Tektronix Phaser III PXI. This printer prints on plain paper instead of coated, and the cost per page is about 25 cents. The printer will print on paper as large as 12 by 18 inches, thus allowing bleeds for work on 11-by-17-inch paper. Other well-known manufacturers of thermal wax printers include QMS and Océ.

Dye-Sublimation Printers

Dye-sublimation printers produce stunning, photorealistic-quality images by printing colors created with dyes that sublimate, or turn into gas, when a heated printhead hits a colored ribbon. The gaseous colored inks are absorbed on special, expensive paper needed to output the print job. By properly controlling heat, the printhead applies pigments in specific amounts to produce many thousands of colors. Images are not created from a pattern of dots that produce an illusion of color; rather, the printer fills specific amounts of colored ink into each dot. The result is an image that is very detailed, with smooth transitions. Even though most dye-sublimation printers print at about 300 dpi, the quality resembles resolutions of 1,500 dpi.

Dupont, 3M, Kodak, and Tektronix all make dye-sublimation printers that cost from $6,000 to $20,000. The cost to output a print is between $3 and $5 when all consumables (paper and other supplies) are added together. Apart from the high cost of each printed page, the main disadvantage of dye-sublimation printers is that text can appear a bit fuzzy.

Color Laser Printers

Recent advances in printing technology, particularly by Apple and Hewlett-Packard, have made color laser printers an attractive alternative to high-priced color printers. Color laser technology uses toner colors of cyan, magenta, yellow, and black to create colored images. Although the quality is not as high as with dye-sublimation printers, color laser printers output faster, and the price of consumables is less expensive.

Imagesetters

One of the last stops for the Photoshop design project that is headed for a commercial printer is the imagesetter. An imagesetter is a high-end output device used by prepress houses to record images on paper or film at resolutions from approximately 1,200 to 3,500 dpi. From film, the prepress house can provide a proof, giving an accurate preview of the final color output. The imagesetter output is then delivered to a commercial printer, who creates printing plates from the film. These plates are used on the press to produce the final product.

 NOTE: *Chapter 19 takes you step by step through the process of printing composite proofs and separations with Photoshop.*

Installing and Optimizing Photoshop

Now that you've had a brief look at some of the important elements involved in

Adobe Photoshop® 5.0

the Photoshop design process, you're ready to start installing Photoshop. We won't repeat the thorough explanations provided by Adobe in the Photoshop package. Installation is simple and involves merely running the installation program from the installation CD. If you haven't installed Photoshop, use the guide included with the software and begin the installation process.

1

If you are running Photoshop on a Mac, you must use System 7.5 or greater. On the PC, you must use Windows 95/98 or Windows NT (4.0 or greater). In order for both systems to display type without jagged edges, Adobe Type Manager must be installed. Both Mac and PC versions of Adobe Photoshop come with complete instructions for installing Adobe Type Manager.

The Read Me File

Read Me

Before running Photoshop for the first time, double-click on the Read Me file that is installed along with the program. This file explains any changes to the program that are not included in the Photoshop manual.

Installing Plug-Ins

Your next step is to install any Photoshop plug-ins created by third-party software vendors. Plug-ins are programs that work within Photoshop, often created to run scanners or to output images to printers more efficiently. On both Mac and PC systems, all plug-ins that you wish to use in Photoshop should be copied to the Plug-ins folder. Plug-ins for scanners and digital cameras should be placed in the Import/Export folder within the Plug-ins folder.

 NOTE: *Photoshop automatically recognizes all plug-ins in the Plug-ins folder. Photoshop also recognizes any plug-in that is in a folder within the Plug-ins folder. On the Mac, you can "hide" Plug-in subfolders so that Photoshop won't load their plug-ins. To hide a subfolder in the Plug-in folder, type ¬ (OPTION-L) in front of the subfolder's name.*

Allocating Memory for Photoshop on the Mac

System 7.5 and 8 Mac users should be aware that Photoshop won't access all free memory in your computer unless you allocate it to Photoshop. Just because 90MB of RAM is available on your Mac doesn't mean Photoshop will grab extra memory when you're working on a large color image. You need to allocate the amount of memory you want to reserve for Photoshop. On the Mac, allocating memory is handled from the Finder.

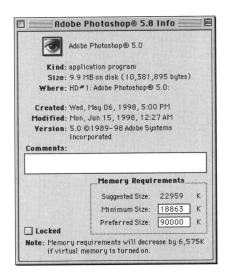

To allocate memory to Photoshop in System 7.5 or 8, first make sure that Photoshop is not running; otherwise, you will not be able to edit its memory size options. Next, click once on the Photoshop program icon, which is in the Adobe Photoshop folder. When you select Photoshop, the program's icon will turn darker. Then choose Get Info from the File menu. In the lower-right corner of the Adobe Photoshop Info window, you will see a number indicating the current size of memory allocated to Photoshop. The suggested size on a Power Macintosh system is 22,959K, about 23MB. Notice that there are two editable fields: Minimum Size and Preferred Size. You should allocate as much memory as you can afford in the Preferred Size field (but leave some memory left over for System operations). When Photoshop loads, it checks to see if you have enough memory free to use your preferred memory setting. If your system does not have this much memory available, Photoshop will at least use the memory setting in the Minimum Size field (provided you have enough memory available).

After you've set the memory allocation, close the Adobe Photoshop Info window. The next time you use Photoshop, it will open into the memory partition size that you designated.

Later in this chapter, the section "Resetting the Scratch Disk for Both Macs and PCs" describes another memory allocation adjustment that can aid Photoshop's performance.

Memory Control Panel Settings

Memory

If you don't have too much memory to spare, Mac users might wish to turn down the disk cache in their System folder as low as possible. Photoshop can not use any of the memory allocated to the disk cache.

Access the disk cache by double-clicking on the Memory control panel in the Control Panels folder. In the Memory window that appears, as shown in the following illustration, make sure that the Off radio button for Virtual Memory is selected. Photoshop has its own virtual memory system. If you leave System 7.5 or System 8's virtual memory on, the two systems may conflict.

The On radio button under 32-Bit Addressing should also be selected in this window to ensure that your Mac can access the extra memory beyond 8MB.

Allocating Memory for Photoshop on the PC

For Windows users, memory allocation is handled automatically within Photoshop. Thus, to change or view memory allocation, you will need to load Photoshop. To load Photoshop, double-click on the Adobe Photoshop icon.

When Photoshop first loads, it automatically grabs a percentage of free memory. If you wish to increase the percentage, choose Preferences from the File menu. In the Preferences submenu, choose Memory & Image Cache.

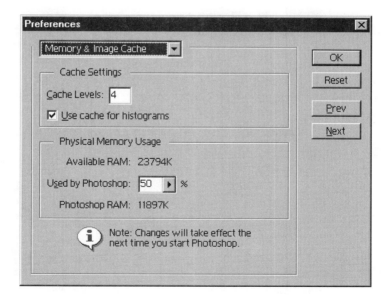

TIP: *If you are using large images, raising the Cache Levels setting can produce speed improvements, particularly in screen redrawing. However, a large cache setting causes Photoshop to use more RAM and hard disk space.*

Resetting the Scratch Disk for Both Macs and PCs

Your last installation step is to check the memory allocated to your scratch disk. In

Adobe Photoshop® 5.0

order to do this, you'll need to load Photoshop. To start Photoshop, double-click on the Adobe Photoshop icon in the Adobe Photoshop folder. After the program loads, you may want to reset the scratch disk that Photoshop uses for virtual memory.

As mentioned earlier in this chapter, when Photoshop needs more memory than it can find in RAM, it will start using your hard disk as virtual memory. By default, Photoshop designates your startup drive as the first scratch disk (you can designate up to four different scratch disks). If you have another hard disk connected to your computer that is faster or has more space available, you may want to set it as the first scratch disk.

If you wish to reset the scratch disk, choose Preferences from the File menu. From the Preferences submenu, select Plug-ins & Scratch Disks.

```
┌─────────────────── Preferences ───────────────────┐
│                                                    │
│  ┌ Plug-Ins & Scratch Disks    ⌘7 ♦ ┐    ┌──OK──┐ │
│                                          ├─Cancel┤ │
│   ┌ Plug-Ins Folder ──────────────────┐            │
│   │ HD#1: Adobe Photoshop® 5.0:Plug-Ins:  │Choose...│ │
│   └────────────────────────────────────┘  ┌─Preu──┐ │
│                                            ├─Next──┤ │
│   ┌ Scratch Disks ───────────────────┐            │
│   │   First: │HD#1          │ ♦        │            │
│   │  Second: │HD#2          │ ♦        │            │
│   │   Third: │HD#3          │ ♦        │            │
│   │  Fourth: │None          │ ♦        │            │
│   │                                    │            │
│   │      Note: Scratch disks will remain │           │
│   │      in use until you quit Photoshop.│           │
│   └────────────────────────────────────┘            │
└────────────────────────────────────────────────────┘
```

In the Preferences dialog box that appears, click on the First, Second, Third and/or Fourth pop-up menus and choose the desired drive. Your first scratch disk should be the fastest and emptiest hard drive connected to your system.

NOTE: *When setting scratch disks and allocating memory, you should have at least as much free scratch disk space as RAM allocated to Photoshop. Otherwise, you may receive a "Scratch Disk Full" error message, even though you have enough memory to complete the command you execute.*

If you wish to boost the performance of Photoshop, be sure that the free space on your hard disk is as contiguous as possible. If you've been accessing your hard disk frequently during your computer sessions, available free space may be spread over many different sectors. Packages such as Norton Utilities include optimization programs that will reallocate the files on your hard disk so the free space is as contiguous as possible.

 TIP: *If you are not going to be copying and pasting to other applications, you can free up a bit more memory if you turn off the Export Clipboard option. You can access this by selecting General Preferences in the File menu, then clicking on the More button.*

The Photoshop Color Management System

To ensure that the colors you see on screen match printed colors and colors displayed on other monitors, it's important to understand how Photoshop 5 manages colors. Unlike previous versions, Photoshop 5 embeds industry standard ICC (International Color Consortium) color profiles in images. The profiles are designed to help provide consistent colors no matter what scanner or monitor is used. Working with devices such as scanners and monitors that use profiles help provide a workflow that results in consistent color. To help provide better color workflow, Photoshop 5, unlike previous versions, does not use your monitor's color space as the image-editing color space. Instead, Photoshop 5 allows you to choose an RGB color space that is separate from your monitor's RGB color space. This helps ensure that the colors of your Photoshop file remain consistent when loaded on another system regardless of what monitor is being used.

The following sections provide detailed descriptions of how to set up Photoshop's color management options. Nevertheless, you may wish to start using Photoshop immediately and delve into the subject of color management at a later time. If you do, we recommend that you return to this section before you begin to share files with other Photoshop users or begin to work on projects that will be output on a printing press.

If you're in a hurry to get started, here are the major steps you need to take to set up your system. Each of the steps is discussed in detail later in the chapter.

1. Calibrate your monitor using Photoshop 5's new Adobe Gamma utility. Mac users updating from a previous version of Photoshop should not use the old Gamma Control Panel.

   Review the settings in the RGB Setup dialog box (File | Color Settings | RGB Setup). If you are creating images for the Web or multimedia, the default setting (sRGB) will probably be sufficient. If you are creating images that will be printed on a commercial printing press, you should change the RGB color space to SMPTE–240M.

2. If you will be working with CMYK images, review the settings in the CMYK Setup dialog box (File | Color Settings | CMYK Setup).

3. If you will be using grayscale images on the Web or in multimedia, set the Grayscale Behavior in the Grayscale Setup dialog box to RGB. If you will be working with images that will be printed, choose the Black Ink settings.

4. If you will be loading images created by other Photoshop 5 users, review the settings in the Profile Setup dialog box (File | Color Settings | Profile Setup). To see what color settings are used by files you are loading, and to prevent Photoshop from automatically converting these files to your current color settings, set the Profile Mismatch Handling Section to the Ask When Opening option for RGB, CMYK and Grayscale images.

If you follow the steps listed above, you'll be off to a consistently colorful future when using Photoshop. For a more detailed description of Photoshop's color management system, read on; otherwise, you may wish to skip ahead to Chapter 2.

Understanding ICC Profiles

As discussed earlier in this chapter, colors that you view on screen may not match printed colors or colors other Photoshop users view on their screens. To address these issues, software and hardware manufacturers formed the ICC (International Color Consortium). The ICC created a series of specifications for creating *profiles* to describe colors and specifications for embedding *tags* in files with profile information in it. For instance, software included with a scanner may be able to embed a scanned file with a profile that describes the scanner's color properties (and possibly its idiosyncrasies). If the scanner's software tags the file with an ICC profile, Photoshop can read the ICC color tag.

When you save files, Photoshop can embed the file with a color tag. One aspect of the tag describes the color space you are working in so that other Photoshop users can load the file and view colors that match yours no matter what monitor they are using.

When you follow the steps for calibrating your monitor and choosing an RGB color space (described later), Photoshop can properly tag the files you create. Your first step to ensure color consistency is to calibrate your monitor.

Calibrating Your Monitor

In order for the colors you see on screen to match those on the printed page as closely as possible, your monitor needs to be properly calibrated. When you calibrate your monitor, Photoshop saves a file on disk that describes the color characteristics of your monitor.

Gamma is the relationship between the picture data input from your software and the color values that are output on screen. For example, if the stored color values saved to disk for an image are set for a light shade of yellow, the screen may display it darker despite the fact that the values are correct on disk. Adjusting a monitor's gamma can help you distinguish between light and dark shades in an image. Many color monitors also display color casts and color shifts toward red or blue. These color shifts can be corrected by calibrating your monitor.

Another variable that must be factored into the calibration equation is room lighting. Bright light, shifts in sunlight, and even color reflection from objects near a monitor can change the way color is perceived on screen.

 TIP: *Manufacturers such as Kodak and Radius create hardware and software calibration devices. Mac users may get better results calibrating their monitors with third-party calibration hardware and software than with Adobe's Gamma utility. If you use a third-party utility you may need to specify your monitor in Apple's Colorsync Control Panel because Photoshop obtains its monitor information on the Mac from Colorsync.*

Photoshop 5 ▶ In Action

The Calibration Process

The windows in the second floor needed to be removed.

Some of the windows on the side needed to be removed.

Artist: Yusei Uesugi   **Client: Lucasfilm Ltd.**

The images on these two pages will give you an idea of the image-editing power of Photoshop.

Yusei Uesugi of Industrial Light & Magic, a division of Lucasfilm, creates mattes (backgrounds) for films. Often, he must take a dull vintage image, such as the one shown above used for a scene in the television program "Young Indiana Jones," and transform it into a lively background. This image was captured on film, transferred to video, and then digitized into Photoshop, where the image-editing process began.

Photoshop 5 In Action

Photoshop was used to delete the windows and create the movie marquee and the awning.

The windows on the side were deleted. More light was added to the center of the image, and the movie posters were added.

A new wall was painted in to separate the theater from its surroundings.

In Photoshop, Yusei removed the windows on the side of the building and on the second floor. He also created the marquee and movie posters near the entrance with Photoshop's painting tools.

After the editing was completed, a printout of the image was used by a model maker to create a model. Yusei then took photographs of the model, which provided him with various angles and light settings so that versions of the image could be created for different scenes.

The versions of the image were digitized into Photoshop for some touching up and so that more details could be added. The result shown above appears to be a photograph taken of an actual location.

Preparing for the Calibration Process

Before you begin to calibrate your monitor, take these steps:

1. Make sure your computer's screen display has been turned on for half an hour or more. This stabilizes your monitor.

2. Adjust the room lighting, if necessary, so it is at the level you will maintain while working on the computer. Remember that if you are working near a window, colors may appear different depending on the amount of sunlight entering your room.

3. Adjust your monitor's brightness and contrast controls to the desired levels. Once the brightness and contrast are set, you may wish to put tape across the monitor's knobs so they can't be changed.

4. Set your monitor's background color to gray. This will prevent background colors from altering your color perception while you are calibrating and while working in Photoshop. For instance, if the background color on your screen is blue, yellows might appear to have a greenish shade around them.

   Mac users with System 8: Open the Desktop Pictures Control Panel. Click on the Pattern button. Then click the right arrow to reach the gray pattern (Pattern 24). Then click the Set Desktop button.

   Mac users with System 7: Open the Background or Desktop Patterns Control Panel to change your background screen to gray.

   Windows users: Choose Settings in the Start menu. Then click on the Control Panel choice. Next, double-click on the Display icon in the Control Panel folder. In the Appearance section, change the Desktop Item to gray.

5. Once you have set your monitor's background color to gray, you need to access the calibration program.

   Mac users: Open the Control Panels folder by choosing Control Panels from the Apple menu. If you see Adobe Gamma in the Control Panels submenu, click on it. If don't see Adobe Gamma, open your Control Panels folder (in the System folder), and double click on the Adobe Gamma icon. If you don't see the Adobe Gamma icon in your Control Panels folder, open the Calibration folder (in the Goodies folder). Double-click on the Adobe Gamma file to run the Gamma utility.

Windows users: The Adobe Gamma calibration program can be found in the Calibrate folder (in the Goodies folder). To load the program, double-click on it.

 CAUTION: *Photoshop 5 does not support settings saved by the "old" Gamma Control Panel or settings created by the Photoshop for Windows Monitor Setup utility.*

After you've followed all the preparatory steps outlined in the previous section, you're ready to begin the actual calibration process. Fortunately, the process is identical for both Mac and Windows, and leads you step by step through the calibration process. To use the step-by-step version of the utility, select the Step by Step option in the Adobe Gamma dialog box. Then click the Next button.

Your next step is to load a monitor profile, if a profile hasn't been previously designated. Mac users who have designated a monitor in their ColorSync Control Panel will see the name of their monitor in the Adobe Gamma Assistant dialog box. Windows users can click the load button and load a profile from the Windows/System/Color folder.

 NOTE: *Windows 98 users: If you have already set a default profile within Windows 98, the Adobe Gamma utility should load the ICC monitor profile that you have set as your default profile.*

After loading a profile, Mac and Windows users should now click the Next button. In the dialog box that loads, follow the instructions to set brightness and contrast settings. Click Next to continue.

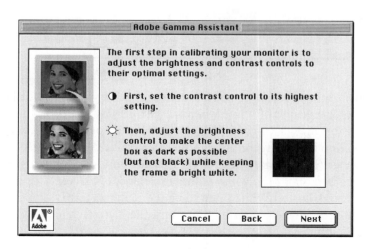

On the next screen, the Gamma Assistant designates the phosphors your monitor uses to create colors. Many Apple, SuperMac, and Radius monitors that were manufactured by Sony use Trinitron as their Phosphor settings. If your monitor is not on the list, try to obtain the proper red, green, and blue *chromacity* coordinates from your monitor's manufacturer. These can be entered by choosing Custom in the Phosphors pop-up menu.

The manufacturer may be able to give you a custom setting to enter. Click Next to continue to the next screen to determine how bright the midtones are on your screen. Adjust the slider as described in the dialog box. You can turn off the single Gamma settings and make the adjustments to red, green, and blue gamma settings. The Gamma pop-up menu should automatically enter 1.8 for Mac users and 2.2 for Windows users. (Note that the Gamma pop-up menu does not appear on all Windows systems.)

 NOTE: *Most monitors change over time. For best results you should check calibration periodically.*

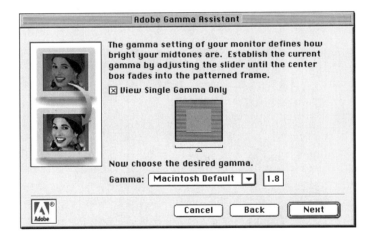

On the next screen, the Gamma Assistant chooses a white point. The white point is the color measure of white when the intensity of red, green, and blue are equal. For instance, setting 6500°K is the color temperature of cool daylight (K stands for Kelvin, a temperature measurement scale). If you wish to have Photoshop measure the white point, click Measure and follow the instructions in the next dialog box. Once the white point is selected, click Next. Most users should leave the Adjusted White point to be the Same as Hardware. Click Next to go to the final screen where your monitor's profile is given a name. Click Finish to save the profile on disk.

Your next step is to choose an RGB color space.

Understanding RGB Color Space

As discussed earlier, your monitor creates colors by combining red, green, and blue color values. A computer monitor cannot actually display every single RGB color. The phosphors, white point, and internal dynamics of your computer monitor determine exactly which colors in the RGB color gamut (range of colors) you can see.

Various manufacturers and professional organizations have established standards for different types of digital and video color work. The standards use the monitor's phosphor settings and white point to define an RGB color space. For instance, the color space of broadcast television in the U.S. is different from the color space of European television. The color space for High Definition Television is different from both the American and European broadcast standards.

If you are creating images for video as opposed to print, you'll want your monitor to display colors specifically geared towards your final output. Furthermore, since different monitors can display different RGB color spaces, it makes sense to attempt to work in a specific color space rather than the color space provided by your monitor manufacturer.

Monitor vs. RGB Editing Color Space

When you ran the Adobe Gamma utility, Photoshop saved a profile that described the color space, or color characteristics of your monitor. Your next step in setting up Photoshop's color settings options is to choose an RGB editing or workspace.

In previous versions of Photoshop you did not pick an RGB editing space. You edited your images in the same RGB space provided by your monitor. This presented problems with color consistency. Since every monitor displays colors differently, the colors in Photoshop files appeared differently on different monitors. Also, not all monitors display all colors that can be printed. For instance, if you create an RGB color file in Photoshop 4 and create several color swatches with a percentage of cyan higher than 80%, you won't see the difference on screen. If you place the Eyedropper tool over the images, the Info palette readout for CMYK colors will show that the percentage is no higher than about 80%. In Photoshop 5, if you choose an RGB gamut with a wide enough color space, you will see higher percentages of cyan on screen.

 NOTE: *You might find it easier to conceptualize RGB color space as the colors that fit within a triangular shape. The larger the color space, the larger the triangle.*

Thus, the key to successful color work in Photoshop 5 is to choose an RGB color space that encompasses the colors you need to use. Once you choose a color space, you can have everyone in your work group choose it as his or her common color space for work.

The next section describes how to choose an RGB color space and the choices Photoshop provides. It also describes the necessity of choosing the Display Monitor Compensation option in the RGB Setup dialog box. When you choose Display Monitor Compensation, Photoshop translates the monitor color space into the RGB working space.

Choosing an RGB Color Space

Choosing the proper RGB color space is a simple procedure, but it's particularly important for those Photoshop users who will be outputting images for print. The colors you see on screen are determined by the RGB color space you choose. The colors created when converting to CMYK Color mode from RGB Color mode are influenced by RGB color space.

To choose an RGB color space, choose File | Color Settings | RGB Setup.

In the RGB Setup dialog box, shown in Figure 1-7, choose a color space in the RGB pop-up menu and make sure that the Display Monitor Compensation option is selected. Here is a description of each color space as well as the Display Monitor Compensation option:

- **sRGB** (Standard RGB) is Photoshop's default setting. sRGB was chosen because a variety of hardware and software manufacturers, most notably Microsoft and Hewlett-Packard, endorse it. Some digital imaging industry experts expect it to be the default color space of desktop scanners and low- to mid-range printers. Since the sRGB color space is supposed to represent the standard PC monitor, it's probably a good choice for those Photoshop users who primarily create graphics for the Web. Photoshop artists who will be working with images that will be printed should choose an RGB color space that provides a wider gamut of colors. For instance, high percentages of printable cyan cannot be represented by the sRGB color space.

- **Apple RGB** was the color space for the previous version of Photoshop. The color space is based on Apple's 13-inch monitor with Trinitron phosphors. The color gamut is not larger than that of sRGB, but can be useful for creating images for Mac intranets, multimedia, or Web sites particularly devoted to Mac users.

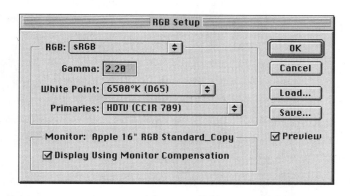

FIGURE 1-7   The RGB Setup dialog box

☐ **CIE RGB** is the color space specified by the Commission Internationale d'Eclairage. This option provides a large color gamut, but high values of cyan are not displayed. If you choose this option, you'll find that many images are not displayed properly because Photoshop cannot handle images with such a wide color gamut.

☐ **ColorMatch RGB** is a color space based on Radius PressView monitors. If you are working with PressView-based equipment, ColorMatch should provide a wide enough gamut to handle your prepress needs. ColorMatch RGB is also a suitable color space for prepress work

☐ **NTSC (1953)** is the color space for the original NTSC television standard. It generally is not used because it has been replaced by the SMPTE-C standard.

☐ **PAL/SECAM** is the color space used for European broadcast TV. If your work will be output to video for European broadcast television, you probably should choose PAL/SECAM.

☐ **SMPTE-240M** is a recommended color gamut for High Definition Television. Although created for television, SMPTE-240M is the recommended choice for those Photoshop users outputting to print. (This is the setting that we are using for Photoshop.) The gamut is wider than sRGB, though smaller than Wide Gamut RGB. The downside of SMPTE-240M is that this color space includes more colors that are beyond the CMYK printing gamut than sRGB or ColorMatch RGB.

- **SMPTE-C** is the color space used for U.S. broadcast TV. If your work will be output to video for broadcast television, you should consider SMPTE-C.

- **Wide Gamut RGB** provides a very broad range of colors. The color space is probably too broad for most Photoshop users because the color space encompasses many colors that cannot be printed as well as colors that cannot be displayed properly on computer monitors.

- **Monitor RGB** uses the same color space defined by your monitor as the image editing workspace. This is not recommended because colors will appear differently on different monitors.

- **Custom** allows you to create your own RGB color space. This can be handy if you know your scanner's RGB color space and wish to re-create that color space in Photoshop. You may also see postings at different Web sites for custom RGB color spaces that attempt to improve on the prebuilt color spaces in Photoshop. When you choose the Custom choice, you can choose a gamma, a white point, and Primaries for your color space.

- **Display Using Monitor Compensation** should be selected before exiting the dialog box. When this option is selected, Photoshop uses your monitor profile (set when calibrating the monitor) to adjust the screen colors for the RGB color space. When you choose this option, it's like applying corrective lenses to your monitor's viewing space. Colors are most accurate when this option is turned on.

Before continuing, here are a few important points to remember about choosing an RGB color space.

- It's best to choose one RGB color space and not change the settings. If you change RGB color space and load an image you saved in another color space, the color values may change when you load the image, and re-save it. See the section below on the Profile Setup dialog box to have Photoshop alert you when one color space is being loaded into another.

- If you change the settings in the RGB Setup dialog box while an image is open, the colors may change on screen but the actual image data in the file is not changed. If you wish to change the color profile of an image on screen, use the Profile to Profile command, described later in this chapter.

- For the most accurate color, make sure the Display Using Monitor Compensation option is selected.

- Photoshop's default RGB color space setting, sRGB, will be adequate for many users. However, if you will be working on projects that will be output for print, you will probably want to use SMPTE-240M or ColorMatch.

CMYK Setup

The CMYK Setup dialog box is used to set options for CMYK color images. Like the RGB Setup dialog box which sets an RGB color space, CMYK Setup sets a CMYK color space for images that will be printed. In CMYK images, colors are created from different combinations of cyan, magenta, yellow, and black (the same colors used by printing presses to create color). If you are not going to be creating CMYK color images or converting RGB color images to CMYK color, you do not need to change any of the settings in the CMYK Setup dialog box.

The CMYK Setup dialog box options are crucial to users converting from RGB to CMYK, the different settings discussed in detail in Chapter 12. However, it's a good idea to gain a general idea of how the options affect images when you first start using Photoshop. To open the CMYK Setup dialog box, shown in Figure 1-8, choose File | Color Settings | CMYK Setup.

The two most important functions of the CMYK Setup dialog box are:

1. To allow you to choose settings for images converted from RGB Color mode to CMYK Color mode. Different settings result in different colors when converting images.

2. To allow you to choose ICC profiles for the color space of CMYK images.

The CMYK Setup dialog box is divided into three sections: Built-in, ICC, and Tables. Each section is described below:

- **Built-in**   If you choose Built-in, the display of CMYK colors is controlled by the Ink Settings and Dot Gain options. If you are converting from RGB to CMYK, the Separation Options determine how much cyan, magenta, yellow, and black are used to create the colors in your image.

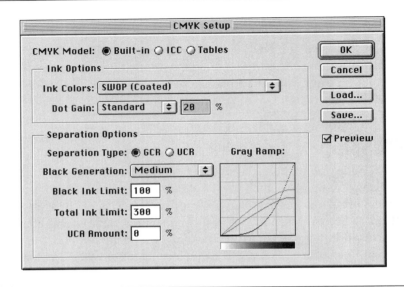

FIGURE 1-8 The CMYK Setup dialog box

□ **ICC**   If you choose ICC, the CMYK color space of an image is determined by an ICC profile. The profiles are primarily for various printing and proofing devices.

□ **Tables**   If you choose Tables, you can load a pre-saved color table to define the CMYK color space. You can create a color table by clicking Save in the Built-in section of the CMYK Setup dialog box, then load the table in the Tables section. Tables are sometimes provided by prepress houses to help clients convert RGB color images to CMYK.

 NOTE: *See the section below on the Profile Setup dialog box to have Photoshop alert you when a CMYK image with a color space other than the one specified in the CMYK Setup dialog box is being opened.*

Grayscale Setup

If you will be working on grayscale images for print, the Web, or multimedia, you should understand how the Grayscale Setup dialog box, shown in Figure 1-9, affects how grayscale images appear on screen. To open the Grayscale Setup dialog box, choose File | Color Settings | Grayscale Setup.

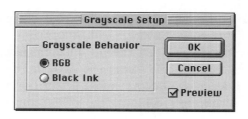

FIGURE 1-9   The Grayscale Setup dialog box

The Grayscale Setup dialog box options are simple to use and understand. If you will be working with grayscale images on the Web or in multimedia, choose RGB in the Grayscale Setup dialog box. The RGB option specifies that the grays in the image be created from equal values of red, green, and blue.

If you will be working with Grayscale mode images for print, choose the Black Ink option. When you choose Black Ink, Photoshop compensates for dot gain when converting to Grayscale mode. In Grayscale images, Photoshop adjusts the screen display to compensate for dot gain. (Briefly put, dot gain is the spreading of ink on press which causes the image to darken when printing. Dot gain and converting to Grayscale mode are discussed in detail in Chapter 12.)

 NOTE: *The dot gain percentage Photoshop uses is determined by the Dot Gain setting in the CMYK Setup dialog box, so you may need to open the CMYK Setup dialog box (File | Color Settings | CMYK). Choosing from the Ink Colors pop-up menu in the CMYK dialog box changes the dot gain setting, or you can enter a number into the Dot Gain field. If you are unsure what setting to use, consult your pre-press house or printer.*

In the dialog box, selecting the Preview check box provides a live preview of how changing settings affects an image on screen.

Using Profile Setup for Loading Images

Since many users will be loading images created by other Photoshop users, Photoshop's Profile Setup dialog box provides a means of warning you when images with different color profiles are being loaded. It's important to understand the settings in this dialog box. Here's why: If another Photoshop user loads an image that you created onto his or her system, Photoshop may automatically convert the image into a different color space. This may cause a shift of colors on screen. For instance, if you create an image using the SMPTE-240M color space, and another Photoshop user loads it into the sRGB color space, he or she may not see the colors on screen as you intend them to be viewed. The Profile Setup dialog box, shown in Figure 1-10, allows you to choose whether or not images should be converted to the color space you specified in the RGB Setup, CMYK Setup and Grayscale Setup dialog boxes. The dialog box is divided into three sections: Embed profiles, Assumed Profiles, and Profile Mismatch Handling.

The Embed Profiles section determines whether RGB, CMYK, Grayscale, and Lab mode images are embedded with profiles. To maintain a consistent color workflow, most Photoshop users will want to keep embedding on. To turn profile embedding off for RGB, CMYK, Grayscale, and Lab mode images, simply click the appropriate check box.

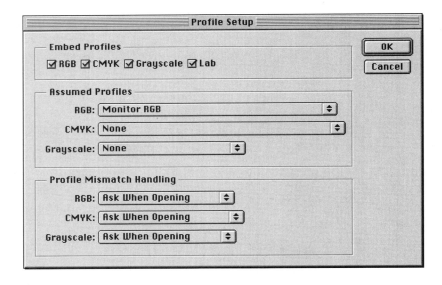

FIGURE 1-10   The Profile Setup dialog box

NOTE: *The following file formats support profiles: EPS, JPEG, PCT, PDF (for RGB and grayscale images), PSD, and TIFF. Also note that embedding profiles in images increases file size.*

The Assumed Profiles section determines how Photoshop handles images that aren't tagged with an ICC profile. For most users this will be images created in previous versions of Photoshop. The default setting, Monitor RGB, tells Photoshop to assume that all RGB images were created using the Monitor as the RGB color space. (The previous version of Photoshop used the monitor as the RGB color space).

If desired, you can choose a profile in one of the pop-up menus so that Photoshop assumes a specific profile exists (when none really does). You can have Photoshop assume that no profile exists (choose None), or you can have Photoshop ask when opening the image which profile is the assumed profile (choose Ask When Opening).

 NOTE: *If you choose the Ask When Opening option in the Assumed Profiles section pop-up menus, a dialog box appears allowing you to choose an Assumed profile when the image is loaded.*

The Profile Mismatch Handling section allows you to specify what Photoshop will do when an image tagged with a color space is loaded into another color space. For instance, if your RGB Color Setup is set to SMPTE-240M and you load an image tagged with sRGB, you can have Photoshop convert automatically to SMPTE-240M or provide a dialog box asking whether you want the image converted to the color space.

Choose the Ask When Opening option to have a dialog box displayed when profiles don't match. This dialog box is shown in Figure 1-11 and can be very handy when working with files from different sources. If you force this dialog box to be displayed you'll always know the color profile of the images that you load into Photoshop.

Choosing one of the Convert options in the Profile Mismatch Handling section of the Profile Setup dialog box converts the image to the color space specified in the RGB, CMYK or Grayscale setup dialog box. If you choose Ignore, Photoshop ignores the embedded color profile in the file and does not convert it when the file is loaded.

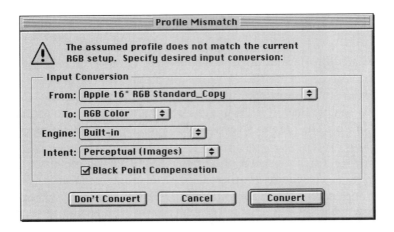

FIGURE 1-11 The Profile Mismatch dialog box alerts you to the color profile of images being opened

Using Profile to Profile to Convert Opened Images

If an image is already open on screen, Photoshop's Profile to Profile command provides a means of converting the image to a color space specified in the Color Setup dialog boxes. The most likely use of Profile to Profile is to convert the color space of an image that wasn't converted when you opened it.

You can also use the Profile to Profile dialog box, shown in Figure 1-12, to change the color space of an image to a color space that is not set in any of the color settings dialog boxes. This can be dangerous because when you save the file it ignores the screen colors and saves the file with the color settings specified in the Color Setup dialog boxes.

To open the Profile to Profile dialog box, choose Image | Mode | Profile to Profile.

To convert an onscreen image to any of the color settings specified in the Color Setup dialog boxes (RGB Setup, CMYK Setup, Grayscale Setup), click on the To pop-up menu and choose a color space currently specified in the appropriate color setup dialog box. If you wish to change to another color space, choose the color space from the list of choices.

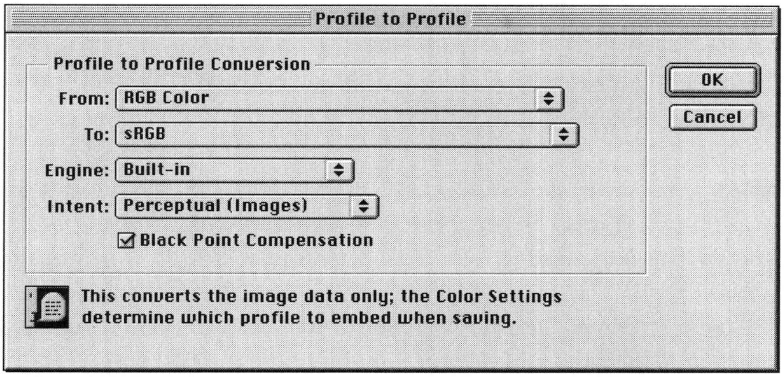

FIGURE 1-12   The Profile to Profile dialog box

In the Engine section, choose a color management system. Choosing Built-in uses Photoshop's internal color management system, and is usually the best choice. The rendering intents are described below:

- **Perceptual**   Choose Perceptual to maintain color relationships among the colors even if the colors change during the separation process. This is the most common choice because it generally provides the most attractive color. Perceptual is often used for Photographic images.

- **Saturation**   Choose Saturation to maintain the saturation relationship among the colors. Use this if you are printing color charts and graphs.

- **Colorimetric**   Choose Relative Colorimetric to prevent the colors that are within the profile gamut from changing. Choose this option if you are printing logos or other items where the color values should be precise. Note that this choice may result in the clipping of colors that cannot be printed. The Absolute Colorimetric choice is not recommended.

In the dialog box, choose Black Point compensation to convert the darkest neutral color in the image of the source color space to the darkest neutral color of the destination color space. Otherwise, black will be used.

After you've made your choices in the popup menu, click OK to convert the image.

Conclusion

Now that you've established your color settings for Photoshop, you're ready to start exploring the magical world of digital image editing. Chapter 2 provides you with a "get acquainted" look at Photoshop's menus, tools and palettes.

 NOTE: *In most cases, Photoshop "remembers" the changes you make in a dialog box so that the next time you open that dialog box, you see the previous settings used. If you wish to revert all Photoshop settings to their original factory-installed settings, Mac users should drag the Adobe Photoshop 5 Prefs file found in the Adobe Photoshop Settings folder into the trash. Windows users should delete (Adobe Photoshop 5 Prefs PSP) located in the Photoshop Settings folder. If you wish to revert the Color Setup dialog boxes and Actions palettes to their defaults, delete the Color Settings and Action file.*

CHAPTER 2

Getting Started in the World of Photoshop

If you begin to use Photoshop, mouse in hand but without any "basic training," it won't take long for you to figure out how to fill your screen with assorted shapes, text, and rainbows of brilliant colors. But without a foundation of knowledge about Photoshop's simple tasks and operations, your creativity will soon give way to frustration: How do you access the tools in Photoshop's tools palette? How do you separate a palette from its palette group? How do you decide at what resolution to create a file?

Although it's tempting to dive right into Photoshop and start grabbing every tool in sight, the best way to learn how to use this powerful program is to start with the basics. You need to become acquainted with the overall structure of the program and find out how the program works. That's the goal of this chapter. You'll begin with an introductory tour of the program's menus, windows, and palettes; then you'll create a new file and try out several of the tools in the Toolbox. By the end of the chapter, you'll have a good idea of what's going on behind the scenes in Photoshop.

What's behind the scenes in Photoshop? Pixels. Every Photoshop image is composed of a grid of tiny squares called *pixels*. When you paint, retouch, cut, paste, or alter any image in Photoshop, you are changing pixels. A pixel is the smallest picture element in your image—in fact, the word was created from the two words "picture" and "element." In an image with a resolution of 72 pixels per inch, there are 5,184 pixels in every square inch of the image (72 pixels per row in an inch $\times$ 72 pixels per column in an inch = 5,184). Generally, the more pixels per square inch, the sharper an image is and the smoother the blend between colors when the image is printed.

 NOTE: *Choosing the correct number of pixels per inch in an image is discussed later in this chapter. The subject is covered in more detail in Chapter 8.*

Drawing programs such as Adobe Illustrator, Freehand, and CorelDRAW utilize lines to create shapes; each shape you draw and each letter you type is an object, separate from other objects. In these programs, when you want to move or resize an object, you can often simply click on it and drag it with the mouse.

This is not so in Photoshop. When you work in Photoshop, you have to think like a painter. When you draw a line, create a shape, or type text, you are filling in pixels on screen, painting on an electronic canvas. As you create an object or text, it "dries" on the canvas, almost as if it's embedded on the screen. If you wish to move the object, you'll need to use the proper tool, which essentially cuts the object out of its background so it can be lifted and moved to replace other pixels. To delete the object, you may have to paint over it—usually with a white background color.

 NOTE: *In Chapters 4, 6, 15, and 16 you'll learn how layers can provide you with more freedom to move images on screen.*

Once you begin to think like a painter, what at first may have seemed to be a peculiarity of Photoshop will begin to feel more natural.

Touring Photoshop

When you are ready to begin your tour of Photoshop, launch the program by double-clicking the Photoshop icon.

Adobe Photoshop® 5.0

After Photoshop is loaded, its menu bar, Toolbox, and three palette groups (Navigator/Info/Options, Color/Swatches/Brushes, Layers/Channels/Paths/History/Actions) appear on the screen. Unlike many programs, Photoshop does not automatically open a new document for you to work in. You'll learn how to do this later in this chapter, in the section "Creating a New File."

Photoshop has nine pull-down menus available in the menu bar. The more familiar you are with how Photoshop divides its power, the more likely you are to take the right path when you begin to work with the program.

A Tour of Photoshop Menus

Most of the commands in the File menu are for storing, loading, and printing files. The New, Open, Save, Save As, Page Setup, Print, and Quit (Windows users: Exit) commands work very much as they do in other Macintosh and Windows applications. The Save As command allows you to save your file in different formats so that it can be output to service bureaus, the Web, and multimedia programs. Revert is covered later in this chapter, as is the Save a Copy command. The Import command allows you to digitize images from scanners, digital cameras, and video capture boards directly into Photoshop. The Export command allows you to export a file in GIF format (for Web images) and to export Photoshop paths to Illustrator. You can obtain and enter information about your file by choosing the File Info command. In the File menu you'll also find the Color Settings commands, which allow you to set up Photoshop so you can properly convert a file from RGB (red/green/blue), the standard computer color monitor display mode, to CMYK (cyan/magenta/yellow/black), the mode used for four-color process printing. The File menu also provides quick access to Adobe's Web site (www.adobe.com); simply choose File | Adobe Online.

The Edit menu is generally used for duplicating or moving parts of images to other areas of a document or to other files. It also features an Undo command that allows you to void the action of your last command. Mac and Windows users will recognize standard Edit menu commands: Undo, Cut, Copy, and Paste. Photoshop's Edit menu allows you to paste an image into a selection or define a custom pattern that can be used in place of a painting color. The Define Pattern command allows you to designate a selected area as the basis of a pattern that you can paint (with the Pattern Stamp tool) or fill on screen. Creating patterns is discussed in discussed in Chapter 7. The Fill and Stroke commands are discussed in Chapter 4. Free Transform and Transform allow you to a scaled, rotate and distort selections. These commands are also discussed in Chapter 4.

The Image menu allows you to change a color image to grayscale and then from grayscale to black and white. The Image menu also allows you to convert a file from RGB to CMYK or to convert an image to Index Color mode, a step you might take as you prepare an image for the Web or for a multimedia program. Changing modes is covered in Chapter 12. Using the Image menu, you can manipulate the sizes of files and canvases and analyze and correct colors in an image. For example, you can adjust its color balance, brightness, contrast, highlights, midtones, and shadows. Image menu commands are covered in Chapters 8, 14, and 18.

The Layer menu features commands that allow you to create and manipulate layers. (A layer is somewhat similar to a sheet of clear plastic in an invisible plane above your image.) Some of the commands in the Layers menu are also found in the Layers palette—New Layer, Duplicate Layer, Delete Layer, and Layer Options. These commands are covered in Chapters 15 and 16. Chapter 16 also covers how to blend layers together using Layer Masks and how to use Adjustment Layers—useful when color correcting. The Layer | Effects commands,

2

which allow you to bevel and create drop shadows out of images and type in layers, are discussed in Chapter 17. The Layer | Type commands are covered in Chapter 3.

The Select menu allows you to modify a selection or select an entire image. (In Photoshop, before you can change any part of an image, you often need to isolate or select it.) Select | Deselect deselects an image on screen. Select | Reselect reselects the previous selection on screen. Select | Grow expands a selection, and Select/Inverse reverses a selection so that everything that isn't selected will be selected. The Select | Modify submenu commands allow you to turn a selection into one that borders the previous selection, smooth a selection, or expand or contract a selection. Select | Feather blurs the edges of a selection. Transform Selection allows you to scale, rotate, or skew a selection by clicking and dragging the mouse. The Select commands are covered in Chapter 4.

The Filter menu creates effects similar to those of a photographer's filter that is placed in front of a camera lens to produce a special effect. By applying a Photoshop filter in one of the Filter submenus, you can sharpen, blur, distort, stylize, and add lighting effects and noise to an image or part of an image. Photoshop features over 50 different filters, which are covered in Chapters 10 and 11.

The View menu allows you to change the view of your document (zoom in or out or fit your view on screen). You can also create a new window to view the same image simultaneously at different magnifications; when an image is edited, both windows are updated. With the View menu you can show or hide Photoshop's rulers, guides, and grid. The View menu also allows you to temporarily hide the edges of a selection or a path outline. The View menu's Preview command is a powerful feature that provides a preview of how your document will look when in CMYK mode. The Gamut Warning command alerts you if you have chosen any colors that are beyond the printable spectrum of colors.

The Window menu allows you to move from one open document to another. It will also allow you to open and close Photoshop's various palettes. The Window menu is discussed later in this chapter.

The Help menu allows you to quickly access information about Photoshop features and commands. In many respects, the Help screens are like having the Photoshop User manual a few mouse clicks away. (Mac users: Choose Help | Contents to see the help choices on screen.) Added to Photoshop 5's Help menu are several "wizards" that, step by step, walk you through the process of resizing an image or creating a transparent background for an image you will be outputting to the Web or multimedia. The Resize Image Wizard is discussed in Chapter 8. The Export Transparent Image Wizard is used for silhouetting an image for print (*clipping paths*) and is covered in Chapter 13. Exporting transparent images for the Web is discussed in Chapter 12.

 TIP: *Both Mac and Windows users can access help by choosing Help/Help Contents. Windows users can also access Photoshop's help contents by pressing F1. Windows users can obtain context-sensitive help by pressing SHIFT-F1. After the question mark appears on screen, click on a menu command or palette. If you need help with dialog box commands, press F1 with the dialog box open on screen.*

Photoshop's Roving Menus

If you get tired of always dragging your mouse to the top of the screen to access Photoshop menus, you can use the program's "context-sensitive" menus instead. Context-sensitive menus pop up on screen whenever Mac users click the mouse while pressing the CONTROL key and whenever Windows users click the right mouse button. The contents of the menus change depending on which tool is activated and where you click on screen. The menus even change when you click on a palette.

Creating a New File

In this section, you'll create a new file so that you can explore and become familiar with the Photoshop document window and get started using the Toolbox. Without a document on screen, you won't be able to use Photoshop's palettes or any of its tools. You'll create a document 7 inches wide by 5 inches high, which will provide a comfortable working area on most monitors.

1. To create your new document, select New from the File menu. The New dialog box appears. The settings in the New dialog box will either be Photoshop's default settings or the settings that were last used. As you work in Photoshop, you'll find that the program often retains the dialog box settings that were last used.

 NOTE: *If you copy or cut a selection, the dimensions of the selection will appear in the New dialog box. If you wish, you can override this by pressing OPTION (Windows users: ALT) when choosing File | New.*

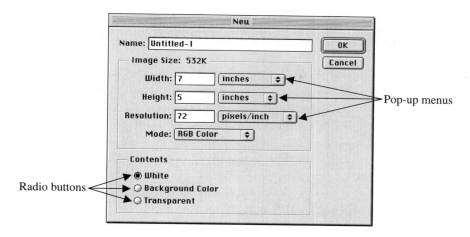

Pop-up menus

Radio buttons

2. In the Name field, you can enter a window title for your document before you save it. Naming your document before it is saved can be helpful when you have more than one unsaved document on screen. At this point, leave your document untitled.

3. If the Width and Height measurement units are not set to inches, change them by selecting Inches in the pop-up menus to the right of the Width and Height fields. A pop-up menu is represented by a box containing a down-pointing arrowhead and is outlined with a drop shadow. To access a pop-up menu, Mac users can click anywhere on the pop-up menu and select Inches from the list. Windows users must click on the down arrow in the pop-up menu and then choose Inches.

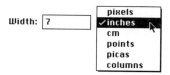

4. If Width is not set to 7 and Height is not set to 5, enter these values now. Click on the Width field to select it, and type **7**. Press TAB to move to the Height field and type **5**. (Note that you can move among the fields in a dialog box by either clicking on the field or pressing the TAB key to move the cursor from one field to the next.) If you make a mistake, press DELETE (Windows users: BACKSPACE) and then retype your entry.

Notice that the Resolution field is set to 72 pixels per inch (ppi). Photoshop uses 72 as the default ppi because many monitors display 72 pixels for every inch of screen area. In other words, you are setting the resolution of your document to be about the same as the resolution of your monitor.

 NOTE: *Most IBM PC–compatible monitors display 96 ppi; many Macintosh monitors display 72 ppi. Monitors that display 640 by 480 pixels output at 72 pixels per inch.*

5. If necessary, change the Resolution setting to 72. Press TAB to move to the Resolution field, and type **72**. If you make the Resolution, Height, or Width settings larger, the size of your file will also grow. Try to avoid large images when practicing; they're cumbersome to work with and they slow down your computer.

You should only raise the Resolution setting when necessary. For instance, when creating a file that will be printed on a commercial printing press, resolution should generally be 1.5 to 2 times the screen frequency measured in lines per inch (lpi). For more information about screen frequency, see Chapter 8.

 NOTE: *If you are creating an image that will eventually be output to the Web or to a multimedia program, the image resolution need not be greater than the resolution of a computer screen (usually 72 ppi or 96 ppi). Setting the resolution higher does not result in better quality; it only results in files that consume more memory.*

 NOTE: *If you create a file with a resolution higher than your monitor's 72 (or 96) pixels per inch, Photoshop displays the image larger than actual size, because it needs the extra screen area to display the extra pixels. For example, on a 72-ppi monitor, Photoshop displays a 300-ppi file approximately four times larger than its actual size, because there are about four times as many pixels on the 300-ppi grid as on a 72-ppi grid. In other words, because your monitor can only display 72 dots per inch, Photoshop stretches the image across a wider screen area in order to display it.*
If you create a Web image at 96 ppi per inch and view it on a monitor set to 72 ppi (640 by 480 pixels), the image appears larger than the size at which you created it. Although the screen resolution of most PCs is 96 ppi (Macintosh screen resolution is usually 72 ppi), most Web designers still create images at 72 ppi to ensure that they can be adequately viewed on all monitors.

2

 TIP: *If you are viewing a high-resolution image on screen and wish to see the image at its actual printing size, choose Print Size from the View menu.*

The Mode option should be set to RGB Color (red/green/blue). Photoshop uses RGB Color as the default display mode because RGB is the standard color model used by video monitors to display colors. In RGB mode, colors are created from red, green, and blue values. When the Mode is set to RGB Color, all painting and editing features of Photoshop are available. The other Mode options are Bitmap, Grayscale, CMYK Color, and Lab Color. For a full discussion of the different modes in Photoshop, please refer to Chapter 12.

6. If necessary, set the Mode option to RGB Color by clicking on the Mode pop-up menu and choosing RGB Color from the Mode list.

7. To ensure that the background of your new document is white, click on the White radio button in the Contents group. If you choose the Background Color option instead, the background color that was last used in Photoshop will be used for your new document. If you choose Transparent, you'll be working in a layer with a background that is clear, without any color values. A checkerboard grid pattern represents the clear area. Note that you can change how the transparent background appears by changing Transparency settings in the Transparency & Gamut dialog box. To access this dialog box, choose File | Preferences | Transparency & Gamut.

8. Click OK to close the New dialog box.

 NOTE: *If you're confused about the difference between a white background and a transparent background, think of a transparent background as a clear layer above your electronic canvas. Imagine you have created a black, doughnut-shaped object on a transparent background. If you copy the doughnut with the transparent background into a document that has a colored background, the color will show through the doughnut hole. Had you created the same doughnut with a white background, you would see white in the middle of the doughnut hole even after copying it into a colored document.*

A new Untitled document window appears. If you wish to magnify the screen, select Zoom In from the View Window menu or press COMMAND-+ (Windows users: CTRL-+). To zoom out, select Zoom Out from the View menu, or press COMMAND-MINUS (-) (Windows users: CTRL-MINUS). You can press the plus and minus keys either on the keyboard or on the numeric keypad with NUM LOCK on (Mac users: Press SHIFT-CLEAR/NUM LOCK on the numeric keypad to activate the numeric keypad).

The Photoshop Window

The Photoshop window, shown in Figure 2-1, conforms to Mac and Windows conventions. You can scroll, zoom, resize, and close it as you would in most Windows or Mac applications. You can move the window by clicking and dragging in the title bar. In the window's title bar are the document's filename, mode, and the magnification percentage.

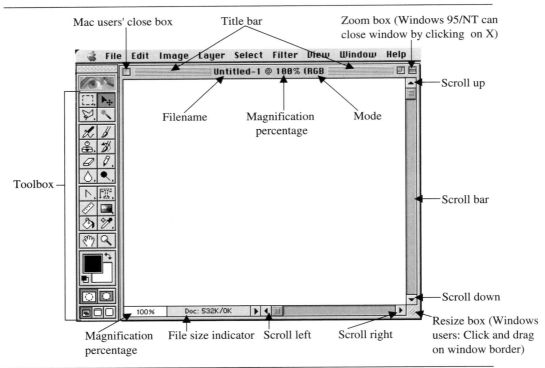

FIGURE 2-1   The Photoshop Window

2

The File and Memory Indicators

In the bottom-left corner of the window, next to the magnification percentage indicator, is the file size indicator. The numbers show you how much memory you are using and whether or not Photoshop needs to use a scratch disk.

Take a moment to see how this setting can be changed by clicking on the arrow to the right of the two numbers. When you click on the arrow, a pop-up menu appears. Here is a description of the choices:

☐ When the pop-up menu is set to Document Sizes, the left number indicates the document size without any layers. You can also think of this number as the size of the image when all layers are flattened, or when the document is output to a printer. The number on the right indicates the file size when all layers, alpha channels, and data are included. (This number originally reads 0 when you begin with a blank canvas or solid-colored background canvas.) The number is often larger than the amount of space actually consumed on your hard disk, because Photoshop can compress information when it saves to disk.

☐ When the pop-up menu is set to Scratch Sizes, the first number indicates how much memory all open documents are consuming (as well as any memory being used by the Clipboard). The second number reveals the amount of RAM available to create and edit your images. More specifically, this number is the available memory minus the memory Photoshop needs to work. When the first number is larger than the second number, Photoshop needs to rely on your scratch disk, because additional memory is needed. When the scratch disk is used, Photoshop performance slows.

☐ When the pop-up menu is set to Efficiency, the number on screen represents the percentage of work handled in RAM (as opposed to the scratch disk). If the number is 100%, Photoshop is not using the scratch disk.

☐ When the pop-up menu is set to Timing, you can have Photoshop time how long it took to display the last action taken.

☐ When the pop-up menu is set to Current Tool, the name of the current tool appears at the bottom of the active window.

The Magnification Ratio

At the bottom left-hand of the document window you will find the document's magnification percentage. You can change the magnification percentage by simply editing this number, then pressing RETURN. For instance, if you click and drag over the number and then type **200** and press RETURN, the magnification of your image changes to 200%—two times its normal viewing size.

Viewing Photoshop's Rulers

No matter what magnification ratio you are working in, it's generally a good idea to display Photoshop's horizontal and vertical rulers on screen. That way, you won't lose sight of how large or small your file's dimensions and images are. To make the rulers visible if they're not already on screen, choose Show Rulers from the View menu.

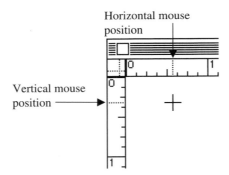

The rulers continually indicate your position in the window with a mark that glides along each ruler as you move the mouse. If you haven't noticed the marks, keep an eye on either the horizontal or the vertical ruler and move the mouse diagonally across the screen until you see them.

Using Guides

If you are moving images or lining up objects on screen, you can drag nonprinting guides out of Photoshop's horizontal or vertical rulers. The guides can be moved using the Move tool or locked using the View | Lock Guides command. To create a guide, simply position the mouse a little above the horizontal ruler or a little to the left of the vertical ruler. Press the mouse button. With the button still pressed, begin to drag the mouse. You'll see the mouse pointer change to a two-arrow icon. As you drag, a guide will appear. Drag the guide to where you want to position it on screen. If you want the guides to temporarily disappear, choose View | Hide Guides.

Here are a few tips and pointers about using guides:

- If you wish to reposition a guide after you create it, activate the Move tool, then click and drag on the guide.

- Double-click on a guide to open the Guide Preferences dialog box.

- By default, the View Menu's Snap to Guide command is set on (indicated by a check mark next to the menu command). When this option is on, selections and image areas that you move on screen jump to the nearest guide when you move the object to within a few pixels of the guide. To turn this feature off, choose View | Snap to Guide. The check mark will disappear when the option is off.

- To change the color of grid lines or make them dashed, choose Guides and Grids from the File | Preferences submenu.

- To line up a guide on a ruler tick mark, press and hold SHIFT when dragging a guide.

- To convert a vertical guide to a horizontal one (or vice versa), press OPTION (Windows users: ALT) when dragging a guide.

- To remove all guides from the Screen choose View | Clear Guides.

- If you resize an image or resize or rotate the work canvas, Photoshop guides maintain their relative positions in the image, if the guides are not locked.

Using the Grid

Photoshop's Grid option can also be a handy aid in lining up objects onscreen, and a balancing aid when composing an image. To see the grid onscreen, choose View | Show Grid. By default, the grid is set to a matrix of 1-by-1-inch squares, with 16 smaller squares within each larger square. If you wish to change the size of the grid squares or their subdivision of smaller squares, choose File | Preferences Guides and Grid. (Shortcut: double-click on the ruler.)

 NOTE: *Like Photoshop's guides, Photoshop grid lines attract objects that you drag near them. This feature of snapping to the grid can be helpful when you want to align objects on grid lines. If you wish to turn this feature off, choose View | Snap to Guides. This removes the check mark next to the menu command.*

The Photoshop Toolbox

Along the left side of the window is Photoshop's Toolbox. The Toolbox contains the essential tools for painting, selecting, and editing graphics. Each tool is depicted by an icon. Understanding the purpose and power of each tool is the key to learning Photoshop. Just as an artisan must know the right tool to use for each job, so must the Photoshop user.

There are over 36 tools in the Photoshop Toolbox (shown in Figure 2-2), each providing a specific utility to aid you when you're creating, editing, and color-correcting images. The first time you load Photoshop after it is installed, the Marquee is the selected tool. Thereafter, when you load Photoshop or create a new file, the last tool used remains selected. When a tool is selected, its Toolbox location turns gray. When you select a tool, the choices available in the Options palette change to options specific to the selected tool. This section introduces you to the tools as well as the other icons that share the Toolbox.

Before starting your tour of the Toolbox, notice the tiny arrow that appears in several Toolbox locations. When you see the arrow, it means that several tools share one location. To see all the occupants of a Toolbox location, move the mouse pointer over the Toolbox location and press and hold the mouse button. To select one of the tools, keep the mouse button pressed and drag over to the tool you wish to select. When you release the mouse, the tool is selected and it appears in the Toolbox.

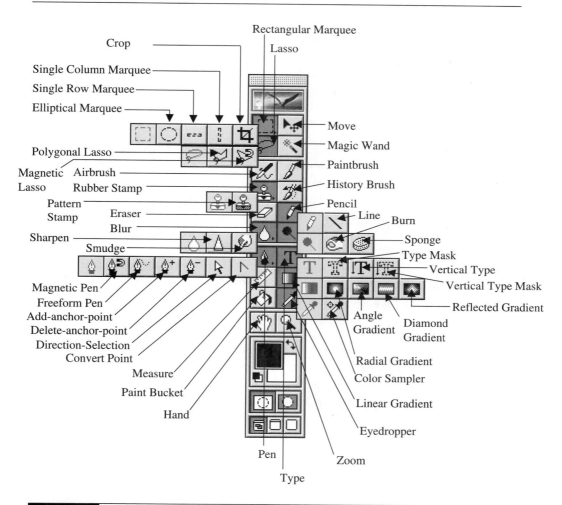

Crop

Single Column Marquee

Single Row Marquee

Elliptical Marquee

Rectangular Marquee

Lasso

Move

Magic Wand

Paintbrush

Polygonal Lasso

Magnetic Lasso   Airbrush

Rubber Stamp

History Brush

Pattern Stamp

Eraser

Pencil

Line   Burn

Sharpen

Blur

Smudge

Sponge

Type Mask

Vertical Type

Vertical Type Mask

Magnetic Pen

Freeform Pen

Add-anchor-point

Delete-anchor-point

Direction-Selection

Convert Point

Reflected Gradient

Measure

Paint Bucket

Hand

Angle Gradient

Diamond Gradient

Radial Gradient

Color Sampler

Linear Gradient

Eyedropper

Pen

Type

Zoom

FIGURE 2-2   The Photoshop Toolbox

TIP: *To select a tool that has multiple tools in its Toolbox location, press SHIFT and the keyboard shortcut for that tool. For instance, pressing SHIFT-M allows you to select the different selection tools. Pressing SHIFT-P allows you to select the different Pen tools.*

TIP: *If you keep the mouse pointer over a tool for a few seconds, a yellow bar appears over that tool, displaying its name and the letter to press on your keyboard to select it. If you wish to turn these "tool tips" off, choose File | Preferences | General. In the Preferences dialog box, turn off the Show Tool Tips option.*

The Selection Tools

The first tool on the top row and the two tools in the second row of the Toolbox are the selection tools. If you wish to make changes to an object, you'll usually need to select it with one of these tools first. At the top left Toolbox location are the Marquee tools, which allows you to create differently shaped selections. If you position the mouse pointer over the Marquee's Toolbox location, then press and hold down the mouse button, options for the Marquee tool appear. These options allow you to change the Marquee so that it creates rectangular or elliptical selections. It also allows you to create 1-pixel-wide vertical and horizontal selections. The last choice in the group of options allows you to change the Marquee into a cropping tool, which is described later in this section. If you want to switch any option for the Marquee tool, keep the mouse button pressed and simply drag the mouse pointer to the option.

If you choose the Elliptical tool Marquee the icon in the Toolbox changes to a circle. If you choose the Single Row or Single Column tool, the icon in the Toolbox changes to a thin horizontal or vertical rectangle. If you wish to quickly switch from the Rectangular to the Elliptical Marquee tool, press OPTION (Windows users: ALT) and click on the Marquee in the Toolbox.

Below the Marquee tool is the Lasso tool, which can be used as a freehand tool; you use it to outline irregularly shaped selections. The Lasso tool can be activated by pressing L. Two other Lasso tools share the standard Lasso tool's toolbox location: the Polygon tool, and the Magnetic Lasso tool. The Polygon Lasso tool allows you to create straight-edged polygon selections by clicking on different points on screen. Each time you click, Photoshop adds to the selection, creating a blinking selection line from one mouse click location to the next. The Magnetic Lasso automatically snaps to high contrast edges as you drag the tool over an image. To end the selection when using either the Magnetic or Polygon Lasso tool, click again at the point you first clicked on or double-click anywhere in the image window on screen.

You can access the Lasso tool by pressing L on your keyboard. If you wish to toggle between the Lasso tools, press OPTION (Windows users: ALT) and click on the Lasso in the Toolbox. The Lasso tool is discussed in Chapter 4.

2

The Magic Wand selects according to similarity of colors. It can be helpful when you wish to select an area that has a different color than other areas in your image. For instance, in Chapter 4, you'll see how the Magic Wand can be used to select just the river section of a nature scene.

Several of the selection tools also allow you to create shapes. You will learn how to use the selection tools for this in Chapter 4.

The Cropping Tool

 The Cropping tool is used to cut out a portion of an image and remove the rest. It can also be used to resize an image. As mentioned earlier, you access the Cropping tool by selecting the Marquee tool, holding down the mouse, and dragging to the Cropping tool when it appears. You can also activate the Cropping tool by pressing C on your keyboard. The Cropping tool is covered in Chapter 8.

The Move Tool

 The Move tool is used to move selections or layers. If you're working in a layer, you can click and drag with the Move tool to move all objects in a layer at one time. You can activate the Move tool by pressing V on your keyboard. For more information about the Move tool, see Chapter 15.

 TIP: *You can activate the Move tool when using most other tools by pressing COMMAND (Windows users: CTRL). However pressing COMMAND (Windows users: CTRL) will not activate the Move tool when you are using the Hand or Pen tool.*

 TIP: *Selecting the Pixel Doubling option in the Move tool Options palette makes the Move tool move objects faster.*

The Measure Tool

 The Measure tool allows you to click and drag over an image area to measure the distance between two points. As you click and drag, a nonprinting line appears in your image. The distance, angle, and X and Y position of the nonprinting line appear in the Info Palette History palette. Using the Measure tool, you can even drag the nonprinting line on screen to compare measurements of different image areas.

The Eyedropper and Color Sampler Tools

The Eyedropper picks up colors from your image and changes the foreground or background color to the color you click on with the Eyedropper. Press OPTION (Windows users: ALT) to change to the background color. You can also use the Eyedropper to take color readings as you color correct an image.

If you click and hold the mouse button on the Eyedropper, it changes to the Color Sampler tool. Using the Color Sampler tool, you can click on four different points in your image and view their color values in the Info palette. You can also move the four points on screen to analyze the colors of other image areas. To access the Eyedropper, press I. To toggle between the Eyedropper and Color Sampler tool, press SHIFT-I.

The Painting Tools

The painting tools are the Airbrush, Paintbrush, Eraser, History Brush, Pencil, Line, Gradient, and Paint Bucket tools. In Photoshop the painting color is called the foreground color, and the background color (often white) is the color that can be used to erase parts of an image or to delete an entire object.

The Paint Bucket, Paintbrush, and Airbrush tools all paint with the foreground color. The Eraser paints with the background color and can erase parts of an image so that a transparent background can show through the image. The Pencil tool (which shares its Toolbox location with the Line tool) simulates drawing with a pencil, in either the foreground or background color. The Gradient tool can create blends with either the foreground or background color and create a blend from a transparent background to the foreground color and vice versa. When you click and hold the mouse on the tool, you can choose to create different styled gradients: Linear, Radial, Angled, Reflected, Diamond. You can also create and edit gradients by choosing Edit in the Gradient Options palette. Perhaps the most unusual tool is the History Brush which is used in conjunction with the History palette. Using the History Brush, you can paint over your image to return it to a previous History state. The History brush is discussed in Chapters 7 and 9.

The painting tools are covered in Chapter 6. The keys for activating the different painting tools are listed here:

Tool	Key
Paint Bucket	K
Gradient	G
Pencil/Line	N
Eraser	E
Airbrush	A
Paintbrush	B

The Editing Tools

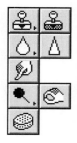

The editing tools are the Rubber Stamp, Pattern Stamp, Blur, Sharpen, Smudge, Dodge Burn, and Sponge.

The Rubber Stamp is a cloning tool. You can use it to sample an area and clone (copy) it elsewhere, pixel by pixel, by clicking and dragging the mouse. You use this tool frequently when retouching images or creating special effects. Press S to activate the Rubber Stamp tool. The Pattern Stamp tool shares the Rubber Stamp tools' Toolbox location. You can use this tool to add patterns to images by clicking and dragging. Both the Rubber Stamp and Pattern Stamp tools are covered in Chapter 7.

 NOTE: *You cannot access the Pattern Stamp tool unless you define a pattern. To define a pattern, select an area on screen with the Rectangular Marquee tool, then choose Edit | Define Pattern.*

The Blur, Sharpen and Smudge tools appear in one Toolbox location; the icon in the Toolbox changes to reflect which tool is selected. You can choose among the three tools by clicking and holding down the mouse in the Blur/Sharpen/Smudge Toolbox location. Blur softens hard edges, and Sharpen brings out more detail. The Smudge tool allows you to create a watercolor effect. It smudges a color to make it look as if water has been applied to it. You can toggle between the Blur and Sharpen tools by pressing OPTION (Windows users: ALT) and clicking on the Toolbox location, or by pressing SHIFT-R. You can also access the Blur/Sharpen/Smudge tool by pressing R on your keyboard.

The Dodge, Burn, and Sponge tools change the color and/or gray tones in an image. Like Blur and Sharpen, Dodge, Burn, and Sponge share a Toolbox location. To choose a tool, press and hold the mouse over the Toolbox location, then drag over the tool you wish to select. Dodge and Burn, traditional darkroom tools, are used to correct an exposure by lightening and darkening specific areas. Sponge allows you to saturate or desaturate (intensify or reduce intensity of) the color in an image. You can activate and step through the Dodge/Burn/Sponge tools by pressing OPTION (Windows users: ALT) and clicking on their Toolbox location. Press O on your keyboard to activate the Dodge/Burn/Sponge tools.

The Path-Creating and Path-Editing Tools

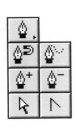

The Pen tool allows you to create paths. Although Pen paths can be used to create outlines for filling and stroking, paths are commonly used to create shapes for masks. A mask can be used to create an electronic stencil on screen that protects image areas from being changed while you edit in an unprotected area. To use the Pen path as a mask, you can convert the path to a selection. Photoshop also allows you to turn a path into a *clipping path* so that the mask can be used to create a transparent background when the image is imported into Illustrator, PageMaker, or QuarkXPress.

Sharing the Pen tool's Toolbox location are other tools that allow you to create and edit paths. They are the Magnetic Pen, Freeform Pen, Add Point, Delete Point, Direct Selection, and Convert Point tools.

The Magnetic Pen tool helps create masks by snapping to image edges as you drag the tool over an image. The Magnetic Pen tool bases its image-embracing decisions on image contrast. The Freeform Pen tool allows you to create a path by clicking and dragging on screen as if you were sketching over an image. The Add Point and Delete Point tools allow points to be added and subtracted from paths. The Corner tool can change a soft curve into a sharp corner or vice versa. The Direct Selection tool (arrow) allows you to select paths so that they can be moved and edited.

If you wish to switch from the Pen tool to a path-editing tool, press OPTION (Windows users: ALT) and click on the tool in the Pen tool's Toolbox location.

You can also toggle between the tools by pressing P on your keyboard or by clicking and dragging from one tool to the other in the Toolbox.

 NOTE: *The Pen tool and the path-editing tools work virtually identically to the pen and path-editing tools in Adobe Illustrator. You'll learn all about making and editing paths in Chapter 13.*

The Type Tools

The Type, Vertical Type, Type Mask, and Vertical Type Mask tools share a Toolbox location. To see the Type tools, move the mouse pointer over the Type tool's Toolbox location and press the mouse button. You'll use the Type tools and Type Mask tool to add text to your images (the Vertical Type tool creates text vertically on screen, rather than left to right). The Type and Vertical Type tools create type in a new layer on screen. The Type Mask and Vertical Type Mask tools create a selection out of the text you type in the Type tool's dialog box. To create type on screen, you can fill the selection with color. The Type tools are covered in the next chapter and in exercises throughout this book. You can activate the Type tool by pressing T on your keyboard.

The Hand Tool and Zoom Tool

The Hand and Zoom tools are often used in conjunction with each other. The Hand tool allows you to scroll through a document to view areas that don't fit in the Photoshop window. It allows more control than the window's scroll bars because you can click on the document and scroll in any direction. You can activate this tool by pressing H on your keyboard. When any tool is activated, you can temporarily access the Hand tool by pressing and holding the SPACEBAR on your keyboard.

The Zoom tool increases or decreases the magnification of an image. Activate this tool by pressing Z on your keyboard. If you press OPTION (Windows users: ALT) with the Zoom tool selected, you can zoom out. If you have any tool selected, you can temporarily access the Zoom tool: to zoom in, press COMMAND (Windows users: CTRL) and hold down the SPACEBAR while you click on your document; to zoom out, press OPTION (Windows users: ALT) and hold down the SPACEBAR while clicking on your document. After zooming, you may need to use the Hand tool to reposition the area you zoomed in to. You will use the Hand and Zoom tools in the next chapter and throughout the book.

 TIP: *Dragging with the zoom tool zooms in on the area that you click and drag over.*

The Color-Control Icons

 Just below the Hand and Zoom tools are several color-control icons that allow you to view and switch colors.

The Foreground Color and Background Color icons display the current foreground and background colors. If you click on either icon, Photoshop's Color Picker dialog box appears, allowing you to change either the foreground or background color. The Color Picker is explored in Chapter 5.

 Clicking on the Switch Colors icon changes the foreground color to the background color and vice versa. You can also press X on the keyboard to switch between foreground and background colors.

 The Default Colors icon restores the default colors for the foreground color (black) and the background color (white). Pressing D on the keyboard also restores the default colors.

The Mode Icons

 The right-hand icon represents the Quick Mask mode, which allows you to easily create, view, and edit a mask. This lets you view your work through a tinted overlay and edit areas in a cutout (similar to a rubylith—a red film that is used to shield objects in print production). The area outside the cutout is normally protected; the area inside is unprotected. If you're unfamiliar with the concept of a mask, think of a painter laying down masking tape around an area so that he or she can paint there without harming surrounding areas. In Photoshop, working in the cutout allows you to refine your work without affecting areas beyond the cutout.

Clicking on the Quick Mask mode icon (or pressing Q on the keyboard) turns on the masking function. Once you enter the Quick Mask mode, you can create a mask and edit its shape with the selection tools, as well as the painting tools. The left-hand Standard mode icon, the default, takes you out of the Quick Mask mode. Creating quick masks is discussed in Chapter 14.

The Screen Display Icons

 The three Screen Display icons at the bottom of the Toolbox change the window display mode. The left-hand icon represents the standard window. Clicking on the middle icon zooms the window out to occupy the full video screen. Clicking on the right-hand icon also zooms out to full-screen size and hides the menus as well. The keyboard shortcut for switching from one screen display to another is F.

Photoshop's Floating Palettes

Now that you're familiar with the Toolbox, take a quick look at Photoshop's other floating palettes. Unlike other windows, palettes always float above your active window. This means that they are always accessible and never drop behind any open document windows. (Windows that are not palettes can drop behind other windows.) When more than one document is open, clicking on a Photoshop window causes it to jump in front of all other document windows on the screen.

Photoshop's palettes are accessed by clicking on the Window menu, then choosing Show Tools, Show Brushes, Show Options, Show Color, Show Swatches, Show Layers, Show Channels, Show Paths, Show Info, Show Navigator, Show History, or Show Actions. The design of Photoshop's palettes and their ability to lock together into specific groups provide quick and easy access to commands and options that are frequently used. Each palette can be moved by clicking and dragging its title bar. This lets you keep particular palettes handy at all times.

 NOTE: *If a palette is already open on screen, the menu choice for that palette switches from Show to Hide. For instance, Show Info changes to Hide Info.*

By default, many Photoshop palettes are organized into palette groups. A palette group is essentially one window with several palettes in it. For instance, the Navigator, Info, and Options palettes open together in one palette group; the Color, Swatches, and Brushes palettes in another. The individual palettes in each group are easily distinguished by a palette tab with the palette's name on it.

NOTE: *By default, palettes for Photoshop tools appear in the Navigator/Info/Options palette group. If the Navigator/Info/Options palette group isn't open, you can open the palette for a specific tool by double-clicking on the tool. You can also press ENTER after you select a tool.*

To bring a palette to the front of a palette group, simply click on its tab. You can also click and drag on a palette tab to move the palette from one group to another, as shown in Figure 2-3. By dragging on a palette's tab you can also pull it out of a group to use it alone on screen. Custom palette groups can also be created. For instance, if you wish to use the Info and Actions palettes together in a palette group, you can drag the Color palette out of its palette group, then drag the Brushes palette out of its palette group. Once the two palettes are separated, you can drag one palette into the other to create the new group. The next time you choose Show Actions or Show Info from the Palettes submenu, your new palette group will open (with both palettes in it).

a)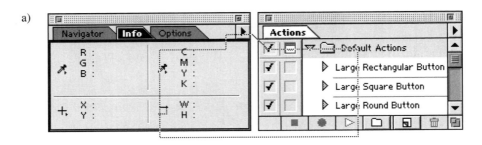

b)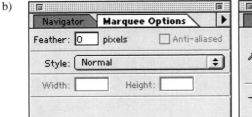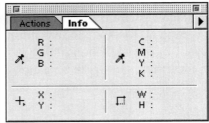

FIGURE 2-3   (a) Click and drag on a palette tab to separate it from its palette group; (b) The Info palette moved from its palette group

NOTE: *The Actions, Channels, Layers, Navigator, History, and Paths palettes can be resized. To resize a palette on a Mac, click and drag on the Resize box in the lower-right corner of the palette. On a PC, click and drag on the palette's border.*

Certain features are common to all the palettes. In Figure 2-4(a) you can see the palette tabs of the Brushes and Options palettes; the palette group's Close box, which closes the palette (Windows 95 and Windows NT users, click on the X in the upper-right corner); its title bar, which you click and drag to move the palette; and the Expand/Collapse box. The Expand/Collapse box allows you to shrink a palette so that it occupies less room on screen, thus letting you view more of your image. To shrink the palette to its smallest size, press OPTION (Windows users: ALT) and click on the Expand/Collapse box, or double-click on the palette's tab. After a palette shrinks, you can expand it again by clicking once on the Expand/Collapse box or by double-clicking on the palette's tab. Below the Expand/Collapse box is the palette's pop-up menu arrow. When clicked, it displays a menu of options for that palette, as shown in Figure 2-4(b).

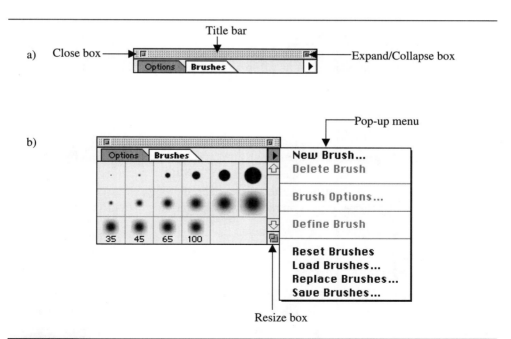

FIGURE 2-4   (a) The Brushes palette, collapsed; (b) the Brushes palette, expanded, with its pop-up menu displayed

Let's start our examination of the palettes by looking at one of the most frequently used palettes—the Brushes palette.

The Brushes Palette

You'll use the Brushes palette, shown in Figure 2-4(a), primarily to choose the size of a brush and whether you want it to be soft- or hard-edged.

In the Brushes palette pop-up menu are commands for loading, saving, creating, and deleting brushes. To see these commands, click on the pop-up menu arrow in the Brushes palette. Using the commands in the Brushes palette's pop-up menu is covered in Chapter 6.

The Options Palette

The Options palette provides options for the currently selected tool. For instance, the Options palette for the Paintbrush tool allows you to set the opacity of the painting color and to choose a painting mode, which can change the resulting color when one color paints over another. By default, the Options palette opens in a group with the Brushes palette. If the Options palette isn't open on screen, you can double-click on any tool to open the palette for that tool, or press ENTER after selecting the tool.

The Options palette pop-up menu allows you to reset the palette's tool or all tools to their defaults.

The Color Palette

In the Color palette you can change foreground and background colors by using sliders based on color models such as RGB and CMYK, or by clicking on the color spectrum bar at the bottom of the palette. The Color palette pop-up menu can be used to switch to sliders based on different color models. This topic is discussed in Chapter 5.

The Swatches Palette

The Swatches palette is used for quickly picking a foreground or background color by clicking on a swatch. The Swatches palette pop-up menu allows swatches to be added to the palette, saved on disk, and reloaded. This topic is discussed in Chapter 5.

The Layers Palette

A layer is like a clear plastic overlay that can be placed over the background electronic canvas. Objects in one layer can be easily moved independently of objects in another layer. This provides an extremely efficient means of compositing images together and previewing their effects.

The Layers palette allows you to create new layers, move from layer to layer, rearrange layers, and group and merge layers. The Opacity pop-up slider in the Layers palette provides a simple means of blending one layer with another. The palette's blending mode pop-up menu provides special effects for blending layers together. For instance, using the Darken mode, you can replace lighter image areas in one layer with darker image areas from another layer.

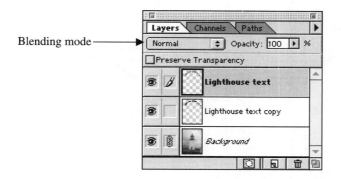

Layers are covered in detail in Chapters 15 and 16.

 NOTE: *In the Layers palette, the word "Background" appears as your base layer if you create a new file with the Contents radio button set to White or Background Color. If you choose the Transparent Contents radio button instead, "Layer 1" appears as the first layer. In all layers other than the Background, areas without color are transparent.*

The Info Palette

If you move the mouse pointer over colored or gray areas, the Info palette functions as a densitometer (an instrument used by printers to measure color density), displaying color values as you move over them. By default, the Info palette displays the RGB (Red, Green, and Blue) and CMYK (Cyan, Magenta,

Yellow, and Black) color components. For instance, a dark red might be displayed as R 205, G 40, B 19 in the RGB section of the palette; in the CMYK section of the palette, it might be displayed as C 1%, M 93%, Y 100%.

The display of the color components can be changed by clicking either of the two Eyedropper icons. After you click the Eyedropper, you can choose to display color components according to HSB and Lab color modes (discussed in Chapter 5) or Grayscale. You can also display Total Ink coverage (Chapter 12) and Layer opacity (Chapter 15).

The Info palette also displays the X-coordinate (horizontal) and Y-coordinate (vertical) of the mouse pointer. Move the mouse pointer across the screen, and you'll see the X and Y values in the palette change. If you wish to change the measurement units for the mouse coordinates displayed in the Info palette, access the Info palette's pop-up menu or click on the tiny + in the palette. The mouse coordinates can be displayed in inches, points, pixels, centimeters, or percentages.

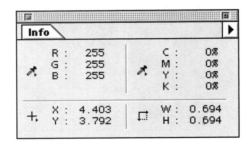

 NOTE: *When you use the Color Sampler tool, the Info palette displays the color values of the sampled areas.*

The Paths Palette

The Paths palette allows you to edit and control paths created with the Pen tool. The Paths palette's pop-up menu can be used to outline or fill paths with colors and to change paths into selections. You can also assign names to paths and duplicate and delete paths using different palette options. The Pen tool and Paths palette are covered in Chapter 10.

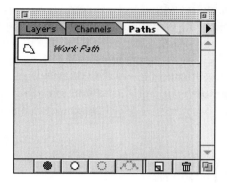

The Channels Palette

A channel is similar to a plate in commercial printing. The Channels palette allows you to easily view a channel or edit an image in a channel.

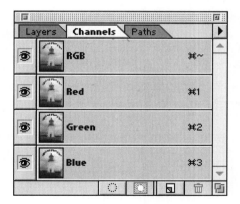

The Channels palette displays different channels depending on the current file's image mode. If you are working in an RGB color file, the Channels palette displays the separate channels for each of the Red, Green, and Blue color components of the image along with the RGB composite. If you are viewing a CMYK color file on screen, the Channels palette displays the separate channels for Cyan, Magenta, Yellow, and Black along with the CMYK composite. If you wanted to alter only the Yellow component of a CMYK image, you could click on Yellow in the Channels palette and then make your changes.

The Channels palette pop-up menu allows you to create and name alpha channels to use as masks. See Chapter 14 for an in-depth discussion of using channels and masks.

The Navigator Palette

The Navigator palette allows you to quickly zoom in and out to specific image areas. The palette features a miniature version of your image and a view box that shows you the area of your document that appears on screen. As you drag the view box on screen, the image on screen changes to display only the area within the view box. To change the zoom percentage, you can click and drag on the sliders in the palette, click on a mountain icon at either end of the slider, or enter a specific zoom percentage by editing the number in the lower-left corner of the palette. Using the palette, you can zoom from .19% to 1600%. To learn more about the Navigator palette, see Chapter 3.

 TIP: *To zoom out while dragging the view box, press COMMAND (Windows users: CTRL).*

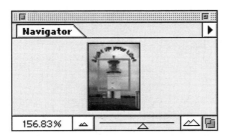

The Actions Palette

The Actions palette allows you to record Photoshop actions and play them back. Using the palette, you can create a sequence of actions that can be played back and applied to different images. Actions can easily be edited by dragging an action up or down in a palette. You can even assign actions to function keys. The Actions palette is discussed in detail in Chapter 9.

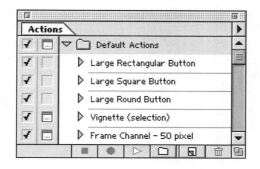

 TIP: *You can hide all palettes by pressing TAB. Press TAB again to view the palettes. SHIFT-TAB hides all but the Toolbox.*

The History Palette

The History palette is Photoshop's answer to user requests for multiple undoes. As you work with Photoshop, the History palette lists all of the changes you've made to an image while working on it. (The number of steps is limited by the amount of Scratch Disk space available and the Maximum History states setting in the History Options palette.) If you wish to revert to a previous stage, you simply click on the step in the History palette. At crucial image-editing stages, you can also use the palette to take a *snapshot* of your image. You can then quickly return to the snapshot version of the image by clicking on the snapshot in the palette.

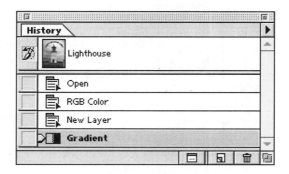

The History palette further encourages experimentation when used with the History Brush. After you click on the History Brush column alongside a historical step in the palette, you can paint away effects with the History Brush using different blending modes. Chapter 9 provides an in-depth look at the History palette and History Brush.

Storing and Retrieving Files

Although Photoshop requires you to think like a painter, it doesn't allow you to work exactly like one—when your work is done you can't just turn out the lights in the studio and go home for the day. If you wish to return to your Photoshop work for another session, you need to save your file.

Saving a File

Saving a file in Photoshop is quite similar to saving a file in any other Mac or Windows program.

1. To save your work after you've made changes to it, select Save from the File menu. The Save As dialog box appears the first time you save your file. In the text box labeled "Save this document as," you'll see the highlighted word "Untitled-1." This is the text box where you name your document.

2. Type a filename for your file. (When Untitled-1 is highlighted, you can replace it with the name of your file when you type.)

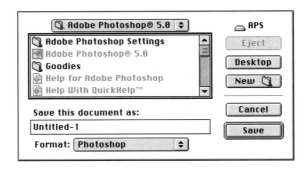

Notice that the Format box (Windows users: Save As) displays Photoshop; this is the default file format. If this field contains another format name, you or someone else changed it at some point.

3. To change the file format back to Photoshop (if necessary), click on the Format (Windows users: Save As) pop-up menu and choose Photoshop. Look at the folder icons in the dialog box to see where you're saving your file. Make sure you are saving it in a location that you will remember.

4. When you're ready to save, click the Save button (Windows users: OK). After Photoshop saves your file, the filename appears in the title bar of your document window.

 NOTE: *As you work on any Photoshop file, you can save as often as you like by choosing Save from the File menu or by pressing COMMAND-S (Windows users: CTRL-S). Be aware, though, that the Save command always replaces the previous version of your file. If you wish to make a copy of your file, you should use the Save a Copy command or the Save As command.*

 CAUTION: *System crashes, however rare, do occur. To avoid losing hours of your hard work in the electronic void, save your work frequently.*

Using Save As

The Save As command opens the Save As dialog box so that you can save your file under a new name. This lets you create different versions of a file or save it to another hard drive or storage device as a backup.

1. To save another version of your file, choose Save As from the File menu. The Save As dialog box appears, where you'll see the original filename waiting to be renamed.

2. Enter a new filename for your file. Click the Save button (Windows users: OK).

TIP: *Mac users who are working with PC files may wish to save their files with PC file extensions. To add file extensions, choose File | Preferences | Saving Files. In the Append File Extension pop-up menu, choose either Always or Ask When Saving. You can also add an extension by pressing OPTION when clicking in the Format pop-up menu.*

As you work on new versions of your practice file, you can continue to use Save As to rename your file so that you can always return to any previous version of your file.

 NOTE: *If you use the File | Save a Copy command to save your file under a new name, Photoshop leaves you in your original document, not the copy. As you'll learn later in this book, File | Save a Copy allows you to flatten layers (Chapter 15) and save a file without its alpha channels (Chapter 14).*

Using the Revert Command

A command almost as useful as Save As is the File menu's Revert command. Although Save As can be used to save different versions of your file, Revert always returns you to the last saved version.

1. To start the process of reverting to the previous version of a saved file, choose Revert from the File menu. The Revert alert box appears.

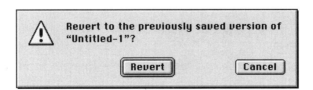

2. If you wish to revert to the last saved version, click Revert. In a few seconds, the document on screen is replaced with the previously saved version.

 CAUTION: *The Revert command is irreversible. Once you revert, you can't undo it.*

2

Once you've saved your file and determined that the image on screen is exactly the way you want it, you'll probably want to output it to your printer. The next section covers printing and Photoshop's page preview feature.

Page Preview and Printing

Before you print, it's often a good idea to preview your output, particularly because graphic images take a long time to be processed by most printers. Although Photoshop does not provide a print preview of your image, it does let you preview page orientation and other specific printing options such as crop and registration marks. For a detailed discussion of the options in the Page Setup dialog box, see Chapter 19.

To preview your file, click on the file size number in the lower-left corner of the Photoshop window. A preview of your page's orientation—landscape or portrait—pops up in the lower-left corner of the window.

The preview can also show labels, crop marks, registration marks, calibration bars, negatives, and emulsion type. These are all options that can be selected in the Page Setup dialog box accessed through the File menu.

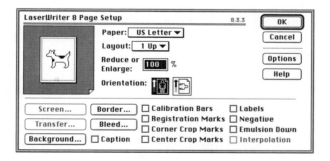

If you click on the file size number with the OPTION (Windows users: ALT) key pressed, Photoshop will display information about your file's size, resolution, and number of channels.

```
Width:      504 pixels (7 inches)
Height:     360 pixels (5 inches)
Channels:     3 (RGB Color)
Resolution:  72 pixels/inch
```

To print your document, select Print from the File menu. The Print dialog box appears and contains standard Mac/Windows print options. In addition, Photoshop allows you to print a color image as a grayscale, RGB, or CMYK image (in the space pop-up menu). The Print Selected Area option will only print an area that is selected on screen. If no area is selected, this option will be dimmed. For more information about printing, see Chapter 19.

Using Preferences to Change the Defaults

Before quitting Photoshop, you might wish to take a look at how to change some of the program's default settings. Changing the defaults lets you customize your Photoshop environment to make it more comfortable for you to use and possibly to save you some time. The defaults can be accessed from the Preferences command in the File menu.

Unit Preferences

To change the Photoshop ruler's measuring units, select Units & Rulers from the File | Preferences submenu. In the Preferences dialog box, you can change the measuring units to pixels, inches, centimeters, points, picas, or percentages.

If you are using points, you can choose either the PostScript (72 points/inch) or Traditional (72.27 points/inch) setting by clicking on the appropriate radio button in the Unit Preferences dialog box, shown in Figure 2-5.

 REMEMBER: *To display the rulers in your document window, select Show Rulers from the View menu.*

The Column Size settings allow you to specify a column width and gutter as a measuring unit. This measuring unit is named Columns. In the New, Image Size, Canvas Size, and Cropping Tool dialog boxes, Columns can be used in place of inches, points, pixels, or centimeters. This can be helpful when working with images that will be placed in columns in page-layout programs such as QuarkXPress and Adobe PageMaker.

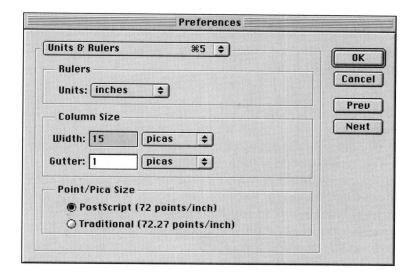

FIGURE 2-5   Unit Preferences dialog box

General Preferences

Most of Photoshop's Preferences options are found by choosing File | Preferences | General. These general preferences cover a wide variety of settings, from how the screen displays imported images to whether your computer beeps when it has completed a task.

Although most preferences are simple in concept, some might be confusing until you've had a chance to work more with Photoshop. Don't worry—these options will be covered in detail as you work through the chapters in this book.

 TIP: *If you would like all palettes and dialog boxes to return to the positions you left them in, make sure that the Save Palette Locations option is selected in the Preferences dialog box. To access the dialog box, choose File | Preferences | General.*

NOTE: *Photoshop 5.0 files can be read by Photoshop 4.0. However, if you wish to ensure that Photoshop 5.0 files can be read by Photoshop 2.5, choose Saving Files from the File | Preferences submenu. In the Preferences dialog box, select Include Composited Image with Layered files.*

Conclusion

By now you should have begun to feel at home in Photoshop. In Chapter 3, you'll build on this foundation by taking a thorough look at how to create type in Photoshop. Chapter 3 will also set you on your way to using layers and a variety of Photoshop's tools and palettes.

If you wish to exit Photoshop now before going ahead to Chapter 3, select Quit (Windows users: Exit) from the File menu. If you made changes to a file that you haven't saved, an alert box will appear, asking if you wish to save the changes. Click the Save button if you do, or click Don't Save if you don't. Click Cancel if you change your mind and want to go directly on to the next chapter.

CHAPTER 3

Type Basics

Undoubtedly, you've heard the expression—"a picture is worth a thousand words." When it comes to graphic design, words (although you probably won't need a thousand) can also add some worth to a picture. Words can add interest and convey a message. They can reinforce a point or put the punch in the punch line of a humorous image.

In Photoshop you add words to your images by using its Type tools. Once you master its Type tools, you'll not only be able to add text to your images, but you'll soon be able to create amazing type effects. For instance, you can blend type over any background, place images in type, create drop shadows from type, and turn your type into shiny, chromelike letters. This chapter provides an introduction to the basics of working with type in Photoshop. You'll learn how to create text with the Type and Type Mask tools. By the end of this chapter, you'll be manipulating type in two different layers to create type drop shadows. But before you begin exploring the world of Photoshop type, you should be familiar with some fundamental concepts about how type is created in Photoshop, as opposed to how it is created in drawing, or vector, programs such as Adobe Illustrator.

 NOTE: *Creating special effects with type is demonstrated throughout* Fundamental Photoshop.

Raster Versus Vector Programs

Any image created in Photoshop is composed of a grid of tiny rectangles called "pixels." Your computer scans this grid of pixels from top to bottom in a procedure called "raster scanning." Thus, programs like Photoshop are often referred to as *raster programs*. When you are dealing with type, the differences between raster and vector (drawing programs) become quite important.

As discussed in Chapter 2, working in Photoshop is often similar to working with paint on a canvas. When you create and edit images in Photoshop, your work "dries" on an electronic canvas. In drawing programs such as Adobe Illustrator, objects float above the background—you can easily move text by clicking and dragging it around on screen. You can even click between letters and edit text as you would in a word processing program. In Photoshop, type works a bit differently. As you'll see later in the chapter, when you create type in Photoshop you use either one of Photoshop's Type tools or one of its Type Mask tools. The Type Mask tools create type from a selection on screen. The Type tools create text in a new layer.

Text created with the Type Mask tool selection becomes locked down on screen after you deselect. If you make a spelling mistake, you can't click between two letters and press the DELETE or BACKSPACE key. Instead, corrections are often made by first painting over text with white or the background color. When you use the Type tool to create type, your type is automatically placed on a layer. Again, you can't edit the type by placing the cursor next to the letter you want to edit. To edit the type, you need to double-click in the type layer in the Layers palette. This opens up the Type Tool dialog box, where you can edit your text. When you click OK in the dialog box, the changes are automatically updated. Although you can edit the type created with the Type tool, you must render it (rendering type is covered later in this chapter) in order to apply effects to it. Once the type is rendered, it is locked down onto the screen and you can't re-edit the type in the Type Tool dialog box.

Type for Print, the Web, or Multimedia

An important consideration when using type in Photoshop is that it is resolution-dependent. This means that quality is based on the resolution of the image. If you're designing for the Web or multimedia, this presents little or no problem. Most Web images and multimedia productions are created at 72 pixels per inch. When your audience views the images on a computer monitor with a resolution of 72 pixels per inch, the text looks fine. It looks pretty much the way you viewed it when you created it.

 REMEMBER: *If you create an image at one resolution and view it on a monitor set to a higher resolution, the onscreen image looks smaller. If you create an image at one resolution and view it on a monitor set to a lower resolution, the onscreen image looks larger. To make an image's size appear on screen as it would when printed, choose View | Print Size. For more information about resolution, see Chapters 2 and 8.*

If you are creating type that is going to be output on a commercial printing press, life is not so simple. For instance, if you create type in an image that has a resolution of 300 pixels per inch, there will always be 300 picture elements per inch, whether you output it on a 600 dpi laser printer or a 2,540 dpi typesetter. If you enlarge the image, the resolution may shrink, depending on how you enlarge it. (Chapter 8 covers how resolution changes when you enlarge or shrink images.)

If you are using a drawing program such as Adobe Illustrator, Macromedia Freehand, or CorelDRAW, you don't have to worry about resolution. You don't set the resolution of the image when you create it. When you print, you can specify that you want the image output at 1,200 or 2,540 dpi. In a drawing program, the higher the output resolution, the better the quality. In Photoshop, if you created an image at 1,200 pixels per inch or greater, the file size on disk would be enormous. To avoid this problem and ensure that type quality is the highest possible, many Photoshop artists export their files to Adobe Illustrator, CorelDRAW, QuarkXPress, or Adobe PageMaker, and complete the type work in these programs. However, when artists create type to make artistic type effects for print, multimedia, and the Web, they often turn to Photoshop.

Working with Type in Photoshop

Creating type in Photoshop is quite easy. But before you start, you need to choose the best tool for the job. Photoshop features two categories of type tool: Type and Type Mask. The two categories accomplish pretty much the same thing. They allow you to set type on screen, yet they produce the results in different ways. Here's how they work:

- **The Type and Vertical Type Tools**   When you enter type with the Type tools, Photoshop automatically creates a new layer and places the type in the layer. As you create type in the Type Tool dialog box, the type appears on screen filled with the current foreground color. If the Preview option is selected in the Type Tool dialog box, you can even click and drag to move the type in the document window while the dialog box is open.

After the type appears on screen, and the Type Tool dialog box is closed, you can reopen the Type Tool dialog box by double clicking on the Type tool icon in the Layers palette. After the Type Tool dialog box opens, you can edit the type. You can also press CTRL, while clicking on the text (Windows users: right-click on the text), then choose Edit Text in the menu that appears on screen. However, if you wish to paint over the type or apply a special effects filter to it, you need to render the type by choosing Layer | Type | Render Layer. After the type is rendered, you can no longer edit the individual letters using the Type Tool dialog box.

The Type Mask and Vertical Type Mask Tools   When you enter type with the Type Mask tools, Photoshop creates an outline selection on screen that is shaped like text. The text is not automatically painted with the foreground color. To color the text, you can fill it or paint over it. When you fill or paint, the text selection functions like a stencil, or mask, on screen—meaning only the masked text area is filled or painted.

You're probably wondering what the advantages and disadvantages of each tool are. The main advantage of using the Type tool is that the text is automatically created in a layer, and the type can be re-edited before it is rendered, allowing you to easily move and manipulate the text independently of other layers. As mentioned earlier, if the Preview option is selected in the Type dialog box, you can click and drag your type to reposition it on screen while the dialog box is opened.

When you create type with the Type Mask tool, a text selection is created on screen. In order for your text to remain on screen, you need to fill it with a color. When you deselect it, the text is locked into place on the background pixels of the layer that you are working in. Once the text is locked down, it cannot easily be moved.

NOTE: *The last selection you created by the Type Mask tool can be returned to the screen by choosing Select | Reselect. Selections can also be saved and reloaded using alpha channels. Saving selections to alpha channels is covered in Chapter 14.*

Using the Type Dialog Box

Even though the Type tool and Type Mask tool are not difficult to use, you may be surprised when you first try to enter text, because Photoshop (unlike many other programs) does not allow you to type directly on screen. Text must be typed into the Type Tool dialog box, as shown in Figure 3-1. In the exercises in this chapter, you'll activate the Type Tool dialog box, enter text, and edit the text with the Eraser tool. When using the Type Tool dialog box, you can either change settings before you type, or, if you want to change the individual characteristics of words or letters, select them in the dialog box with the mouse before changing settings. Before you begin, here's a review of the Type Tool dialog box which allows you to set the type size, style, tracking, and kerning.

FIGURE 3-1   The Type Tool dialog box with entered text

☐ To change typefaces, click on the Font pop-up menu and choose a font.

☐ To change styles, click on the pop-up menu to the right of the font.

☐ To change type sizes, enter a number in the Size field.

☐ To change the color of text with the Type tool (not the Type Mask tool), click on the color swatch (set to the current foreground color). This opens Photoshop's Color Picker (described in Chapter 5).

☐ To change leading (space between lines), enter a number in points in the Leading field.

☐ To manually change kerning (space between two letters), first turn off the Auto Kerning by removing the check mark. Then click between two letters, and enter a value in the Kerning field. Positive values increase the space between letters; negative values decrease the space. If Auto Kern is on, Photoshop automatically kerns according to the kerning specifications built into the typeface.

☐ To change tracking (space between text), select the letters that you want to change and enter a value in points in the dialog box. The greater the number, the greater the distance; to decrease the distance between letters, enter a negative number. Note that the Tracking field is dimmed until you click and drag over type in the dialog box.

 NOTE: *Kerning and tracking are measured in units that are 1/1000 of an em space. An em space is a typographical unit of measure roughly equal to the size of the letter "M" in the currently selected typeface. It can also be thought of as the distance that is equal to the height of the type.*

- To raise or lower the text above or below other letters, enter a value in the Baseline field; to shift the baseline lower, enter a negative number. The baseline of the type is established by the dash on the I-beam cursor when you click on screen with the Type or Type Mask tools.

- To align text flush left, center, or flush right from the point in the document where you click to the end, click the appropriate alignment icon above the Preview check box.

- To preview the text on screen while entering type into the Type dialog box, make sure that the Preview check box is selected. When the Preview check box is selected (and while the Type dialog box is open), you can position the type in the document window by clicking and dragging on it.

- To create anti-aliased type, make sure that the Anti-Aliased check box is selected. When the text box is selected, Photoshop softens type edges to enhance the appearance of smoothness.

- To rotate vertical type, click the Rotate check box. This option is only available when creating vertical type.

Entering Type with the Type Mask Tool

The following exercise demonstrates how to use the Type Mask tool. Afterwards, you'll learn how to zoom in to see the actual pixels that compose the text.

 NOTE: *Before beginning this next series of exercises, check to see that black is the foreground color icon and white is the background color icon in the Toolbox. If black is not the foreground color and white is not the background color, click on the Default Colors icon or press D on your keyboard. This will ensure that your text is black and the Eraser tool erases with white. You should also have a new 7-by-5-inch RGB file with a resolution of 72 ppi on screen and the contents set to white.*

1. Before you can create any text in Photoshop, you must first activate a type tool in the Toolbox. Start by activating the Type Mask tool. If the Type Mask tool is not displayed in the Toolbox, click on the Type tool and hold down the mouse button. When the Type Mask tool appears, drag the mouse over it to select it. Note that the Type Mask tool is the dotted "T" in the Toolbox location.

 TIP: *You can toggle between the Type Mask tool and the Type tool by pressing SHIFT and pressing the letter T on your keyboard or by pressing OPTION (Windows users: ALT) and clicking on the Toolbox location.*

2. Move the mouse pointer toward the document window. When the pointer appears over the document window, it changes to a cursor called the I-beam.

3. To enter text in the upper-left corner of the window, move the I-beam to this part of the screen.

4. Click the mouse where you want the text to appear. As soon as you click, the Type Tool dialog box appears.

5. Click on the Font pop-up menu and choose Times or any other font from the list.

6. Press TAB to move to the Size field and type **100**. (Make sure "points" has been selected from the pop-up menu.) This sets your font size to 100 points, or about 1.5 inches high. Make sure alignment is set to left. Leave the Anti-Aliased and Auto Kern check boxes selected. You'll learn why this option is important in the section "Examining Pixels."

7. Click on the text box at the bottom of the dialog box. A blinking cursor will appear; this is where you enter your text. Type **noah** (or your own name, in lowercase letters) in the text box.

8. In the Type Tool dialog box, check to make sure you haven't made any typos. If you made a mistake, this is your chance to fix it. The simplest way to replace a character is to position the cursor to the right of the character you want to change, and press DELETE (Windows users: BACKSPACE). Then type the correct character.

9. When you're done, click OK. (Windows users: Don't press ENTER or you'll create a new line. Mac users, though, can press ENTER instead of clicking OK.)

An outline of your text appears in the document window surrounded with a marquee (represented by a series of dotted lines), as shown here:

The marquee indicates the text is a *mask*, meaning that it works like a stencil. When you paint with a painting tool, only the area within the selection is affected. If you execute Photoshop's Fill command (Edit | Fill), only the area within the selection is filled.

CAUTION: *If you wish to delete the text, you might think you can simply press the* DELETE *key, but doing that fills a selection with the background color. At this point, if you need to delete the selection on screen, you can choose Select | Deselect. This removes the marquee selection from the screen.*

Moving the Selection Marquee

Before you fill the text outline with color, you can safely move the selection around on screen. To move the text selection, position the I-beam directly over the center of any of the letter outlines. Notice that the I-beam changes to an arrow with a tiny rectangle next to it. Once you see the arrow, click and drag—the text selection moves as you drag the mouse. You can also move the text selection by pressing the UP, DOWN, LEFT, or RIGHT ARROW keys on the keyboard. Try it. Each time you press an arrow key, the text selection moves up, down, left, or right one pixel.

At this point you may be tempted to immediately fill the text with color. If you fill the text with color or paint over the text, the paint "dries" onto the background canvas. This is fine if you don't want to move your text after you've filled it with color. If you do try to move the selection after you fill the text with color, Photoshop only moves the selection and leaves a copy of the filled letters in the background. How do you avoid this situation? You can make the text "float" above the image background, by copying the selection on screen (before filling it) and moving the selection (this technique is described in the next section). Alternatively, you can copy it into a new layer before filling the selection.

NOTE: *Here are a few points to be aware of when moving and filling text created with the Type Mask tool:*

1. If you try to move a filled text selection by clicking and dragging in the selection with the Type Mask tool, only the selection moves. The original filled text is left behind.

2. If you move a filled text selection with the Move tool, the filled type and the selection marquee move. However, Photoshop leaves behind a copy of the text filled with the background color. This will not happen if you are in a layer other than the Background. Note that clicking and dragging with COMMAND (Windows users: CTRL) pressed temporarily activates the Move tool when the Type Mask tool is selected in the Toolbox. Also note that if your background color is the same as the color in the Background layer you won't see any change on screen.

3. You can copy a filled text selection, and move it by pressing COMMAND-OPTION (Windows users: CTRL-ALT), then clicking and dragging your text selection.

Copying and Filling a Selection Marquee

If you copy a text selection on screen before you fill it with color, Photoshop won't leave a painted copy of the text behind when you move it with the Move tool. To copy the text on screen (before you fill it with color), press and hold OPTION-COMMAND (Windows users: ALT-CTRL); then click and drag the text to move it. After you've executed these steps, you can fill the text, then move it without leaving a copy behind.

NOTE: *If you want to isolate your text selection so you can move it at any time, you can copy the selection to a layer by choosing Layer | New | Layer Via Copy. After you copy the text to a new layer, you can fill the text using the Edit | Fill command (make sure the Preserve Transparency option is selected) or you can paint over the text using a painting tool (make sure the Preserve Transparency option is selected in the Layers palette). For more information about working with layers, turn to Chapters 15 and 16. If you know beforehand that you are going to move the text after filling it with color, you may want to use the Type tool instead of the Type Mask tool.*

One of the easiest ways to fill a text selection with color is to use the Edit | Fill command. When you fill, only the contents of the text selection are affected. Try it by following the next steps, and you'll see the masking powers of the Type Mask tool in action.

 NOTE: *In order to perform the following steps, you must have a text selection on screen.*

1. With your text selection on screen, choose Edit | Fill. In the Fill dialog box, choose Foreground Color in the Use pop-up menu. Make sure that the Mode pop-up menu is set to Normal, and change the Opacity percentage, if desired. Click OK.

After you apply the Fill command, notice that the color only fills inside the letters. The masking effect of the type prevents the color from splashing anywhere else.

 TIP: *A shortcut to filling with the foreground color is pressing OPTION-DELETE (Windows users: ALT-DELETE).*

NOTE: *You can also fill a text selection by painting over it with any of the painting tools. In addition, you can fill the text with a photograph by pasting one into the selection. You'll learn how to paste a photograph into a selection in Chapter 16.*

 CAUTION: *If you create type with the Type tool, then create type with the Type Mask tool, you will not be able to fill the type created with the Type Mask tool until you render the Type layer. Don't worry if this sounds confusing—it will be covered in more detail later in this chapter.*

2. To deselect the type, choose Select | Deselect, or press COMMAND-D (WINDOWS USERS: CTRL-D). This deselects the text and removes the marquee selection from the screen.

 CAUTION: *In previous versions of Photoshop, you could deselect text by simply clicking away from the text. In the current version, clicking away from the text reopens the Text dialog box. If you wish to deselect, choose Select | Deselect or press COMMAND-D (Windows users: CTRL-D).*

After you've finished experimenting with filling and moving your text, you may want to zoom into the text to see how Photoshop makes the text out of pixels.

Zooming In

There are several ways to zoom in to magnify text on screen so that you can see the matrix of pixels that combine to make the letters you typed. The traditional way is to use the Zoom tool. The most efficient way to zoom, however, is to use Photoshop's Navigator palette.

Using the Zoom Tool

  The Zoom tool allows you to point to an area in the document window and magnify it by clicking the mouse. Each time you click the Zoom tool, the magnification grows. After you zoom, you can then use the Hand tool if you need to scroll the document in any direction. To use the Hand tool, simply click and drag on screen. Be aware that the Hand tool does not move objects on screen, it only provides a fast way of scrolling.

TIP: *You can zoom in to a specific area on screen by clicking and dragging over that area with the Zoom tool. You can quickly access the Zoom tool from another tool by pressing COMMAND-SPACEBAR (Windows users: CTRL-SPACEBAR), then clicking the mouse. To zoom out, press COMMAND-OPTION-SPACEBAR (Windows users: CTRL-ALT-SPACEBAR), and then click the mouse.*

3

Zooming with the Navigator Palette

The fastest and most versatile way to zoom in and out is to use the Navigator palette. Unlike the Zoom tool, the Navigator palette allows you to zoom in or out to any percentage between 0.19% and 1600%. To open the Navigator palette, choose Window | Show Navigator. In the Navigator palette, you'll see a tiny version of your document window. You can zoom in or out by clicking and dragging the slider at the bottom of the screen. Drag to the right to increase the zoom. As you drag, Photoshop zooms in. In the Navigator palette, you'll see a rectangle indicating the visible area on screen. You can click and drag to move this rectangle over the area that you want to zoom to. Try dragging the slider to the right, and then drag the rectangle in the Navigator palette over text in the palette screen. Drag all the way to the right until the percentage indicator reaches 1600%.

 TIP: *When using the Navigator palette, you can zoom in and out by typing a number in the lower-left corner of the palette, then pressing ENTER. Alternatively, you can click on the tiny mountain icon in the lower left of the palette to zoom out and click on the larger mountain icon in the lower right of the palette to zoom in. If you want to make the preview area larger on screen, enlarge the size of the palette.*

Examining Pixels

Once you zoom in on your text, you can begin to see how Photoshop creates images. Notice that your zoomed text looks jagged (as in Figure 3-2); this is because the letters are made of pixels. The jaggies are the pixel edges. Notice how different combinations of pixels form the various letters. As discussed earlier, all images in Photoshop are basically created the same way, from pixels. You might notice that some of the hard edges in the zoomed text are blurred or partially filled in. Photoshop tries to eliminate the jaggies as much as possible; this blurring effect is called *anti-aliasing*.

 NOTE: *If you created your file at a resolution of 72 pixels per inch, each linear inch of your image is composed of 72 pixels. At this resolution there are over 5,000 pixels in every square inch of your image (72×72).*

Editing Pixels with the Eraser Tool

Since letters created with the Type Mask tool or rendered text created with the Type tool are locked together on a grid of pixels, there's no way of slipping a cursor between them to delete or edit them. To delete and edit in Photoshop, you

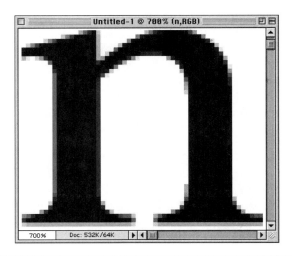

FIGURE 3-2   Jagged edges displaying pixels in text

need to white out the pixels of any letter you wish to remove (paint them with the background color—in this case, white) and then make your changes.

The following steps show you how to use the Eraser tool to white out the lowercase "n" from the word "noah," and then replace it with an uppercase "N." (You can do the same with the first letter of whatever text you typed on the screen.) To follow along with the exercise you need to have a word created with lowercase text. If you use the Type tool, make sure you render it by choosing Layer | Type | Render Layer.

 NOTE: *If you create type with the Type tool (as opposed to the Type Mask tool), you can edit letters after typing them on screen. Using the Type tool is covered later in this chapter.*

 NOTE: *If you need to review how to enter text with the Type Mask tool, turn back to the section called "Entering Text with the Type Mask Tool."*

1. Click the Eraser tool in the Toolbox. (If the Options palette isn't open, open it by choosing Window | Show Options so that you can see the Eraser tool's options.) The mouse pointer changes to a small eraser, and the Options palette displays Eraser options. By default, the Eraser Options palette is
    set to erase by painting with a paintbrush stroke. In order to better see the Eraser's pixel-by-pixel erasing effects, switch tool types in the Eraser Options palette by clicking on the pop-up menu and choosing Block. When you erase with a Block, you erase blocks of pixels, and you erase with 100 percent of the background color (in this case, white).

2. Position the Eraser over any part of the "n" in noah (or the first letter of your text). Click the mouse and Photoshop replaces the black in that pixel with white.

3. Click over different parts of the letter to create a speckled effect. At first glance it seems the Eraser is merely removing black from each individual pixel. You are, however, actually painting with the default background color of white. This may seem like a slow way of deleting, but it's actually one of the strengths of Photoshop: You can edit any object at the smallest possible level—the pixel. In most other programs, you can edit text, but not pieces of type.

4. Continue whiting out the lowercase "n" until you have deleted it. To work a little faster with the Eraser tool, keep the mouse button pressed as you move the Eraser back and forth over the letter, much the same as you would use a rubber eraser on paper.

 TIP: *If you accidentally erase part of another letter in your text, choose the Undo command from the Edit menu. This cancels your last action.*

Now that you've removed the lowercase "n," you can use the Type Mask tool to enter a capital "N" and move it to the left of the letters currently on screen. It will be easier to perform this task if you can see all the letters of the name on the screen. Instead of zooming out and scrolling, here is a shortcut you can use to make an image fit on screen: Double-click on the Hand tool. The magnification ratio will change to 100%. Or click on the Fit on Screen button in the Hand or Zoom tool's Options palette. You can also press COMMAND-ZERO (Windows users: CTRL-ZERO.) Now follow these steps:

 NOTE: *Double-clicking on the Zoom tool makes the image 100%, but does not resize the document window.*

1. To enter the capital "N," activate the Type Mask tool, and then click below the letters on screen. The Type Tool dialog box opens. In the dialog box, type **N**. Click OK.

2. Move the I-beam over the letter selection. When the I-beam changes to the arrow pointer, click and drag the letter to the left of the other letters, as shown here:

3. When you're happy with the position of your new capital letter, fill the letter with the foreground color by choosing Edit | Fill.

4. Next, lock down the text on screen by deselecting. To deselect, choose Select | Deselect or press COMMAND-D (Windows users: CTRL-D). The letter locks down on the screen.

Type Selection Tips

The foregoing should give you an idea of how type works in Photoshop, but occasionally you may wish to move individual letters. Here are a few tips for selecting letters. (Selecting is covered in detail in Chapter 4.)

- You can select individual letters and move them on screen by first selecting the letter with the Lasso tool.

- If you want to add a type selection to the selection on screen, press and hold down the SHIFT key before you click on screen to create type with the Type Mask tool.

- If you want to delete a character in a text selection that already exists on screen, press and hold down OPTION (Window users: ALT), then click and drag around the letter with the Lasso tool. The character will disappear from the screen.

- If you want to create a selection based on the overlapping areas of a selection on screen and type, press SHIFT-OPTION (Windows users: SHIFT-ALT) before you click on screen to create type with the Type Mask tool.

- Text selections can be converted to paths and then edited. After editing, the path can be turned back into a selection, filled, and stroked. For more information about working with paths, see Chapter 13.

- After you've filled text on a transparent layer and deselected, you can select an individual letter by clicking and dragging around the letter with the Lasso tool. To move the letter, use the Move tool.

Using the Type Tool and Rendering Type

The Type tool creates text and places the text in the new layer. Having text in a layer can simplify image manipulation because you can easily move objects in one layer independently of objects in another layer. Type created in the layer can easily be re-edited by double-clicking on the Type icon in the Layers palette. As mentioned earlier, if you want to paint over the type or apply effects to the type, the layer must first be rendered by choosing Layer | Type | Render Layer. The following steps demonstrate how you can create text over another image, move the text around, and then experiment with a special effect. In the next section, you'll create a drop shadow from the text.

1. Start by opening an image on screen. To open an image, choose File | Open, select the image in the dialog box, and click Open (Windows users: OK).

2. Select the Type tool. If the Type Mask tool is selected in the Toolbox, click and hold down the mouse button until the Type tool appears. When you see the Type tool, click and drag over it to select it. Alternatively, you can select the Type tool by pressing SHIFT-T on your keyboard.

3. Move the Type tool pointer to the middle of your document, and then click. In the Type Tool dialog box, enter a word and set the size to at least 45 points.

4. After you click OK, observe the Layers palette. Notice that a "T" appears in the palette. This means that a new Type layer has been created. In the Layers palette, the paintbrush icon and eye icon next to it mean that the layer is in view and can be edited. For an in-depth discussion of working with layers, see Chapters 15 and 16. If you need to edit the text, simply double-click on the "T" to re-open the Type dialog box. (Do not double-click on the thumbnail version of the text in the Layers palette. This opens the Layer Options dialog box, which is covered in Chapter 16). In your document you'll see that the text is created over the background image. You can now move the text by clicking and dragging it with the Move tool when the Preview checkbox is selected.

5. To reposition the text in the middle of the screen, first select the Move tool by clicking on it in the Toolbox (it's the tool in the upper-right corner); then click and drag in the middle of the text (in the document, not in the dialog box).

6. To create an interesting effect, you can make the text translucent. To do this, lower the opacity in the Layers palette or click on the Opacity arrow, then drag the slider to the left. As you decrease the opacity, the text becomes more and more translucent.

> **NOTE:** *You can also create blending effects by selecting a blending mode in the pop-up menu in the Layers palette. To see the different modes, click on the down arrow to the right of the word Normal. Modes are discussed in Chapters 6 and 15.*

3

At this point, the type has not been rendered onto its layer. This means that you cannot apply any special effects to the type. For instance, try activating the Paintbrush tool and painting over the type. Nothing will happen. To solve this problem, render the type by choosing Layer | Type | Render Layer. Now you can paint over the layer. However, if you start painting after rendering the layer, you will paint over the entire layer, not just the type.

To ensure that you paint only over the type, select Preserve Transparency in the Layers palette. When the Preserve Transparency option is selected, any editing you do only affects areas that are already painted or filled with color. If you'd like to try this, change the foreground color, activate the Paintbrush tool, and paint on and around the letters. As you paint, the transparent area is not affected, only the text is affected. If you deselect the Preserve Transparency option, when you paint, the entire layer is affected.

Duplicating Layers to Create Text Drop Shadows

After you've created a layer with text in it, you can duplicate that layer to create a drop shadow. Figure 3-3 shows an image with text (created with the Type tool)

FIGURE 3-3   Text drop shadow in image created with layers

and a drop shadow created by duplicating a layer. The following steps show you how to create a drop shadow by hand. The next section, "Using the Vertical Type Tool," discusses how to create a drop shadow using Photoshop's Layer Effects menu.

1. Start by either opening an image or creating a new file.

2. Open the Swatches palette if it isn't already open, and then click on any colored swatch to pick a foreground color. This is the color that will be automatically applied to your text.

3. Use the Type tool to create some type on screen. If you wish, type **Shadow**.

   After you've created some type with the Type tool, you should see the word you typed in the Layers palette.

 NOTE: *Before creating the shadow, you may want to alter your text using one of the Edit | Transform commands. You can apply these commands to type before it is rendered. For more information on using these commands, see Chapters 8 and 15.*

4. Duplicate the layer by choosing Layer | Duplicate Layer. In the As field of the Duplicate Layer dialog box, you can enter a name for your layer. Type **Text**. Don't change the Destination option.

   Notice that the Text layer is selected and the paintbrush icon and eye icon are activated in the palette. In the other layer, Shadow, there is no paintbrush icon, but the eye icon is activated. This means you can view this layer, but not edit it. Note that you can only edit one layer at a time.

5. Your next step is to offset the Shadow layer to create the shadow effect. First, click on the Shadow layer in the Layers palette to activate it. Then select the Move tool in the Toolbox. With the Move tool activated, click and drag the text a little to the right and down. As you click and drag, you'll be moving the text in the Shadow layer.

 CAUTION: *Normally, clicking and dragging with the Move tool in a layer only moves the currently selected layer. However, if the Auto Select Layer option is activated in the Move tool's Options palette, clicking and dragging in a transparent area of the active layer may actually move another layer. This option activates any layer that has non-transparent areas if you click and drag over them. For more details about using layers, see Chapter 15.*

6. Your next step is to fill the shadow text with black. However, you can't fill the text unless it is rendered. To render the text, choose Layer | Type | Render Layer. Next choose Edit | Fill. In the Use pop-up menu, choose Black. Make sure the Preserve Transparency option is selected, and then click OK. If the Preserve Transparency option is dimmed in the Fill dialog box, it means that the Preserve Transparency option is selected in the Layers palette. When the Preserve Transparency option is selected, it means that Photoshop only fills the areas of your layer that aren't transparent.

 TIP: *If you want your shadow to be soft-edged rather than hard-edged, you can blur the edges of the shadow layer. First, turn off the Preserve Transparency option in the Layers palette (this allows the transparent area bordering the text to be changed). Next choose Filter | Blur | Gaussian Blur. In the Gaussian Blur dialog box, the more you move the slider to the right, the softer the shadow will become. When you're happy with the preview, click OK. The type layer must be rendered (as described in step 6) to execute the Blur filter.*

Using the Vertical Type Tool

Photoshop's Vertical Type tool creates type vertically in a new layer. We used the Vertical Type tool and Photoshop's Layer | Effects commands to create the image in Figure 3-4. We used filters to create the background, then used a layer mask to blend the photo onto the image. Filters are covered in Chapter 10; layer masks in Chapter 16. If you wish to create an image using the Vertical Type tool and Layer | Effects commands, here are the steps we used:

1. We loaded a digital image on screen.

2. We selected the Vertical Type tool and typed text on screen. Since we used the Vertical Type tool, we could experiment with fonts and sizes by double-clicking on the "T" layer in the Layers palette. This re-opened the Type Tool dialog box, allowing us to edit the text. With the dialog box opened (and the Preview check box selected), we could even move the text on screen. We finally settled on the Present font.

3. To add interest to the type, we applied several Layer | Effects commands. To apply a drop shadow, simply choose Layer | Effects | Drop Shadow. Click OK to apply the default settings.

NOTE: *The Layer | Effects commands are discussed in detail in Chapter 17.*

4. We created a new layer by choosing Layer | New | Layer and then used the Paintbrush tool to draw a shape around the word "Vacations" (in the layer below). We then applied the Layer | Effects | Bevel and Emboss command to give the shape a three-dimensional look.

 NOTE: *Since the photograph of the two people was a Grayscale image, we used the Paintbrush with the Color mode selected in the Paintbrush tool's Options palette to colorize the image. For more information on using the Paintbrush tool and different color modes, turn to Chapter 6.*

FIGURE 3-4 Image created with both the Type and Vertical Type tools

Photoshop 5 ▶ **In Action**

The type was created in Photoshop.

Dashes were created using Adobe Illustrator. The dashes behind the type were erased with the Eraser tool.

This cutout area was created using the Pen tool. Turn to Chapter 13 for more information on using the Pen tool.

Artist: Christopher Ching   **Promotional Material**

Christopher Ching, a New York City artist, created this image for a self-promotion package. To create the image, he first created a watercolor painting the old-fashioned way. Next, he scanned the watercolor using Photoshop. Once the watercolor was digitized, he used the Pen tool to mask the cutout area in the image. After Christopher created a path, he selected the area and deleted it. With the Burn tool, he created the shadow in the cutout area and at the bottom of the image. He also used the Burn tool to create the shadow below the figure.

Finally, Christopher used the Type tool to create the text in the balloons. He used Adobe Illustrator to create the dashed balloons and imported them into the Photoshop file. In order for the dashed balloons not to cover the text, Christopher used the Eraser tool to erase part of the dashes where the text appears.

Importing Type from Adobe Illustrator

Despite the versatility of Photoshop, you might find that you can create and control type more efficiently in a drawing program like Adobe Illustrator. For instance, in Illustrator you can quickly create type on a curve or within objects and edit the text you create. Figure 3-5 shows text on a curve created in Illustrator and imported into Photoshop.

Here are the steps for importing text from Illustrator into Photoshop:

1. Begin by loading Illustrator and creating some text.

To create type on a curve in Illustrator, you first need to create a curve. You do this by creating an oval with Illustrator's Oval tool. Next, activate the Path Type tool (you may need to click and keep the mouse button

FIGURE 3-5 Text created in Adobe Illustrator and imported into Photoshop

3

pressed, then click and drag to activate the Path Type tool). With the Path Type tool selected, click on the edge of the curve and begin typing. If you wish, you can change the alignment to center, which will center the text on the curve.

2. Now you need to save your file. You can save your Illustrator file either in Illustrator format or in EPS format. After you save your file, you may want to quit Illustrator, depending upon how much RAM your computer has (the more RAM, the more programs you can have open at one time).

3. Load Photoshop, if it is not already loaded.

4. You can import text from Illustrator into Photoshop in one of four ways—use either the File | Open command, the File | Place command, drag and drop, or copy and paste.

   ☐ If you want to import your Illustrator text into a new Photoshop file, use File | Open. When you use the File | Open command, a dialog box appears asking you to determine the width, height, resolution, and so on, in order to rasterize your text. (For more information on the Rasterize Generic EPS Format dialog box, see Chapter 7.) After the Illustrator text is rasterized, it is opened in a new Photoshop file, in a layer with a transparent background (unless you created a background in Illustrator).

   ☐ If you are going to place your Illustrator text over a photograph in Photoshop, you'll want to use the File | Place command because the text is placed in a new layer in the currently opened document. When the text is placed on screen, you can scale it if you wish. You also need to activate the text by double-clicking on it.

   ☐ If you wish to drag and drop your text from Illustrator into Photoshop, both Illustrator and Photoshop should be opened on screen. Select the text in Illustrator using the Selection tool, then click and drag it over to the Photoshop window.

   ☐ If you wish to copy and paste text from Illustrator into Photoshop, select the text in Illustrator with the Selection tool; then choose Edit | Copy. Open or activate Photoshop. In Photoshop choose Edit | Paste.

Exporting Text to Other Programs

As mentioned at the beginning of this chapter, if you want your text to look sharp when printed, you may want to export your Photoshop images to other programs. If you want to export a Photoshop image into Adobe Illustrator, QuarkXPress, or Adobe PageMaker, you should save the file in Photoshop as EPS or TIFF format. For more information about file formats and exporting and importing files, see Appendix A.

CHAPTER 4

Creating and Understanding Selections

It is virtually impossible to complete any Photoshop project without using at least one of the selection tools. The selection tools, which can be found at the top of Photoshop's Toolbox, are used primarily for outlining and isolating specific areas in images so they can be moved, copied, retouched, or color corrected.

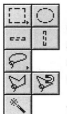 The selection tools are integral to the creation of photomontages (multiple photographs from different images) and collages (various images and graphics blended together). These tools also allow you to quickly turn scanned images into line art and to create special effects such as vignettes (pictures that gradually fade off into the surroundings).

In this chapter you'll have a chance to try each of the selection tools. More importantly, you'll be introduced to the concept of selections and why they're so important in Photoshop. Along the way you'll learn how to fill and stroke (outline or frame) a shape with the foreground and background colors. As you work through the chapter you'll use many of the commands in Photoshop's Select menu, as well as create simple collages and a vignette.

If you follow the exercises in this chapter, you'll be able to create selections and shapes—the stepping stones to image creation and editing. The exercises will also help you understand what a selection is. If you are learning how to work with selections, it might be a good idea to practice working with simple images in this book before you move on to more complicated real-life jobs.

Before you proceed, it's important to remember that you are using a pixel-based (sometimes called *raster*) program, not an object-oriented (sometimes called *vector*) drawing program. As discussed in the previous chapter, in object-oriented drawing programs you can select an object with the mouse and delete it. In Photoshop, your electronic canvas is filled with either colored or "transparent" pixels. To delete a selected object on a white or colored background, you have to paint over it with the background color, in much the same way you use a liquid white-out product to correct typing mistakes. If, however, you are working on a layer (other than the Background), selecting an object and deleting it causes the transparent background or the layer beneath it to show through the hole you have created in your electronic canvas. (For a complete discussion of layers, see Chapters 15 and 16.)

Because Photoshop is pixel-based, you need to take special care when selecting and moving objects. If you don't understand the fundamentals of these actions, you may get some surprising and unwanted results. But once you've learned the basics of how to create and use selections, you'll be on your way to creating successful Photoshop design projects.

Introductory Exercises: Creating, Filling, Moving, and Floating a Selection

It doesn't matter what shape a selection is; Photoshop treats them all the same. Once you select an area on the screen, Photoshop directs its attention to the selection. You can execute virtually any image-editing command, and only the selected area will be affected.

Before beginning to work with the selection tools, create a new document to use for the following introductory exercises.

1. Select New from the File menu.

2. When the New dialog box appears,

   a. Check to see that the Width and Height measurement units are set to inches. If they aren't, click on the pop-up menu for each field and change the units to inches.

   b. In the Width field, type **5.5**, and in the Height field, type **3.75**. The flag that will be created in a later exercise will fit snugly in the document window with these dimensions.

   c. Resolution should be set to 72 pixels per inch. If it isn't, press TAB to move to the Resolution field and enter **72**.

   d. If Mode is not set to RGB Color, click on the pop-up menu and change the setting. Because having a white background will make it easier to create the white stripes of the flag, set the background Contents radio button to White.

 REMEMBER: *When you create a new file with the Contents radio button set to White or Background Color, Photoshop creates a base layer called Background. When you choose the White Contents radio button, working in the Background is like painting on a white canvas. If you choose the Background Color Contents option, working in the Background is like painting on a colored canvas. If you choose the Transparent option in the New dialog box, Photoshop creates a base layer called Layer 1. Working in this layer is equivalent to painting on a sheet of clear acetate, rather than on a white or colored canvas.*

   e. Click OK to open the new document window.

 TIP: *It is a good idea to add Photoshop's rulers and Info palette to the window before you start learning to create selections on screen. These features help you judge the size of the selections that you create.*

1. To make the rulers visible, select Show Rulers from the View menu.

2. To open the Info palette, select Show Info from the Window menu.

Let's start with the Marquee tool, because it is used very often. Besides allowing you to create rectangular selections, the Marquee tool can create elliptical selections and 1-pixel-wide selections. These options will be discussed later in this chapter.

 NOTE: *The selections you create with the Marquee tool share the same characteristics as all selections, no matter what selection tool created them.*

Creating a Selection with the Rectangular Marquee and Normal Option

 The Marquee tool's Rectangular option allows you to create and select squares and rectangles.

1. Before you create a selection, take a look at the Marquee Toolbox location which houses the Rectangular, Elliptical, and Single Column Marquee tools, as well as the Cropping tool. If the Rectangular Marquee tool appears in the Toolbox, double-click on the Marquee tool to open the Marquee Options palette. If the Rectangular Marquee tool does not appear in the Toolbox, click in the Marquee Toolbox location and hold down the mouse button. When the Marquee tool icon appears, click and drag over it to select the tool. You can now open the Marquee Options palette by pressing ENTER on your keyboard.

Marquee Options

Feather: 0 pixels ☐ Anti-aliased

Style: Normal

Width: Height:

4

2. In the Marquee Options palette, check to see that Normal is selected in the Style pop-up menu; if it isn't, click on it. If the Feather value in the palette is not set to 0, change it to 0 now.

When the Rectangular Marquee tool is selected, the Normal setting allows you to create rectangular selections of any size. This is the default setting, and it will be selected unless you changed it previously. If another option is selected, such as Fixed Size, the tool will create rectangles that are always the same size. The Constrained Aspect Ratio forces the width and height of a selection to be created at a specific ratio. Don't worry about the other options in the Marquee Options palette; they will be covered later in this chapter.

 REMEMBER: *The Options palette settings for all of the tools in Photoshop retain the last settings used. They do not automatically return to their default settings. To reset a tool palette to its default settings, click on its pop-up menu arrow and choose Reset Tool. To reset all tools to their default settings, choose Reset All Tools from the pop-up menu.*

3. Move the mouse pointer to the document window. Notice that when the pointer moves over the document area, it changes to a crosshair, as shown here. Now you can start using the Rectangular Marquee tool to create a selection.

4. Position the crosshair at the 1-inch mark both vertically (y-axis) and horizontally (x-axis). To make sure you are positioned at 1 inch both vertically and horizontally, refer to the Info palette. As you move the mouse, the X and Y readings next to the crosshair icon show your horizontal (X) and vertical (Y) positions. The X and Y readings next to the anchor icon indicate your original X and Y positions.

NOTE: *You can change the measurement units in the Info palette by first clicking on its pop-up menu arrow, then choosing Palette Options. In the Info Options palette, click on the Ruler Units pop-up menu and choose Inches. As a shortcut, you can also click on the small crosshair in the lower left of the palette and choose inches from the pop-up menu.*

5. When the Info palette shows both X and Y reading 1, click and drag diagonally down from left to right to make a rectangular selection about 2 inches by 2 inches, as shown in Figure 4-1. Refer again to the Info palette; notice the width (W) and height (H) readings of the selection you are creating. When your selection looks like Figure 4-1, release the mouse.

6. Your selection is represented on screen by a blinking marquee, which appears as a series of dashed lines. Your selection is now an isolated area that you can work with as an independent object, separate from the rest of the screen.

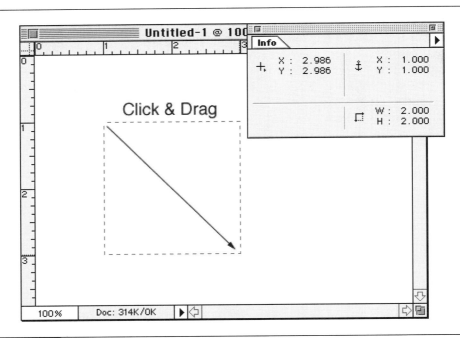

FIGURE 4-1   Clicking and dragging with the Marquee tool to make a rectangular selection

7. Click again anywhere in your document outside your rectangular selection. Photoshop thinks that you're finished working with the selection or that you want to create another selection, so it deselects your original selection, and the marquee disappears.

A marquee created by a selection tool is really nothing but tiny, blinking lines on the screen. The marquee is used to isolate part of an existing onscreen image or to create a shape. The next sections introduce you to techniques for editing the selection marquee and creating shapes by filling selections with colors.

Filling a Selection with the Foreground or Background Color

If you wish to fill a colored area on screen using Photoshop's selection tools, you must first create a selection and then make it come to life by either filling it with a color (in the foreground or background) or stroking it (putting an outline around it). You will see how to do this in the following exercise.

 To make it easier to follow the instructions in this exercise, start with the foreground and background colors at their default settings (black foreground and white background). Check the Foreground Color and Background Color icons in the Toolbox. If the foreground color is not black and the background color is not white, click the Default Colors icon to reset the colors to their defaults (you can also press D on the keyboard).

 NOTE: *Until you have become familiar with Photoshop, you might find it helpful to refer to Figure 2-2 in Chapter 2 for the locations and names of all Toolbox icons.*

To fill a selection with the foreground color, you can either choose Fill from the Edit menu or hold down the OPTION key and press DELETE (Windows users: ALT-BACKSPACE). To fill a selection with the background color, press DELETE or choose Edit | Clear. When you fill selections using these commands, you apply opaque foreground and background colors. The Edit | Fill command also allows you to fill with the foreground or background color, allowing opacity and painting/editing modes to be changed. These and other Edit | Fill options are also discussed in Chapters 6 and 7.

NOTE: *If you have a layer on screen and the Preserve Transparency option is selected in the Layers palette, the Edit \ Fill command fills the nontransparent areas of the layer.*

 TIP: *If you wish to fill a selection in a layer (other than the Background layer) with the background color, press COMMAND-DELETE (Windows users: CTRL-BACKSPACE). If you wish to fill the nontransparent areas of a layer with the foreground color, press OPTION-SHIFT-DELETE (Windows users: ALT-SHIFT-BACKSPACE). To fill the nontransparent areas of a layer with the background color, press COMMAND-SHIFT-DELETE (Windows users: CTRL-SHIFT-DELETE). Note that if you have a selection on screen, the selection will be filled instead.*

Start by creating a rectangular selection and filling it with the foreground color, then with the background color.

1. Notice that the Marquee tool is still selected—it's the last tool you used and Photoshop keeps it active. To create the rectangular selection, click approximately 1 inch from the upper-left corner of the screen and drag down diagonally approximately 2 or 3 inches. Release the mouse button.

2. To fill the selection with the foreground color, press the OPTION (Windows users: ALT) key. Hold it down, and press DELETE (Windows users: BACKSPACE).

   Your rectangular selection immediately turns black. Notice that the selection marquee still surrounds your rectangle.

3. Now fill with the background color by pressing DELETE. (Windows users: BACKSPACE).

   The rectangle disappears but the selection remains. This often gives new Photoshop users the mistaken impression that the DELETE key (Windows users: BACKSPACE) deletes objects. Actually, however, the DELETE key (Windows users: BACKSPACE) fills with the background color and could therefore be considered a painting tool. You have just painted your black rectangle white. (If you're still skeptical about this concept, be patient. When you press DELETE (Windows users: BACKSPACE) with a background color other than white, you'll be convinced.)

NOTE: *If you were in a layer other than the Background, DELETE (Windows users: BACKSPACE) would cut a hole in the layer, allowing either the layer below or the transparent background to show through the deleted area.*

Changing the Foreground and Background Colors

Photoshop provides a variety of ways to choose colors for the foreground and background. The simplest method of picking colors is from the color bar spectrum found at the bottom of the Color palette.

 NOTE: *If you don't see a spectrum of colors at the bottom of the Color palette, click on the Color palette's pop-up menu arrow and choose Color Bar. When the Color Bar dialog box opens, choose RGB Spectrum or CMYK Spectrum in the Style pop-up menu. Then click OK.*

1. To display the Color palette, select Show Color from the Window menu.

 2. Notice the two squares in the upper-right corner of the Color palette. The top square is the Foreground selection box and represents the foreground color. It overlaps a second square, the Background selection box, which represents the background color. A white band surrounding the selection box indicates that that color is active and ready to be changed. Click on the Foreground selection box so that you can change the foreground color. (At this point, don't worry about any other items in the Color palette—they will be introduced to you in Chapter 5.)

3. To change the foreground color to red, position the mouse pointer over a red area in the color bar. The mouse pointer changes to an eyedropper. Click on the red area. The Foreground selection box and the Foreground Color icon in the Toolbox both change to red.

4. Now change the background color to blue. Point to and click on the Background selection box, which is currently white. The white band jumps to and surrounds this box.

5. Point to the color bar and click on a blue area. Again, notice the change in both the Background selection box in the Color palette and the Background Color icon in the Toolbox.

TIP: *If the Foreground selection box is activated, pressing OPTION (Windows users: ALT) and clicking in the color bar changes the background color. If the Background selection box is activated, pressing OPTION (Windows users: ALT) and clicking in the color bar changes the foreground color.*

Now you're ready to create an object and fill it with the new background and foreground colors.

6. Using the Marquee tool, create a rectangular selection. To apply the background color, press DELETE (Windows users: BACKSPACE). The rectangle fills with blue.

7. To apply the foreground color, press OPTION-DELETE (Windows users: ALT-BACKSPACE). The rectangle changes to red.

8. To remove the marquee from the selection, position the crosshair anywhere inside the document window and click. Alternatively, to deselect, choose Select | Deselect.

The marquee disappears, indicating that the rectangle is no longer selected. If you wish to continue experimenting with the colored rectangle on screen, you must select it again, as described in the following exercise.

Selecting a Rectangle with the Rectangular Marquee

Often when working with images, you'll want to select an area on screen and edit using one of Photoshop's many image-editing tools. As a simple experiment, try selecting the rectangle on screen. To select the rectangle from the previous section, position the Marquee crosshair so that it touches the top-left corner of the object, as shown here:

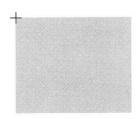

Click and drag diagonally down to the bottom-right corner, and release the mouse button. After selecting, you may find that you didn't quite grab the area on screen that you wanted. When this happens, you can turn to Photoshop's Select | Transform command.

Transforming a Selection

Once you create a selection on screen, you may wish to edit it: make the selection larger or smaller, rotate it or move it, or even change its shape to distort it. Fortunately, Photoshop 5 allows you to transform a selection—without altering the area within the selection. Before moving on, try the following steps to transform the selection on screen. (If you don't have a selection on screen, click and drag with the Rectangular Marquee tool.)

1. To transform a selection marquee on screen, choose Select | Transform Selection. Handles (tiny squares) appear around the selection, as shown in Figure 4-2. Now try the following steps:

   a. To resize the marquee, click and drag on any of the handles on the edge of the wireframe on screen. To constrain the aspect ration, press SHIFT while you click and drag on a corner handle.

   b. To rotate the selection marquee, click on or near the edge of the transformation box and drag, but don't click on a handle. If you wish to change the center point for the rotation, click and drag on the center point icon, then rotate the selection.

   c. To distort the selection, press COMMAND (Window users: CTRL) and click and drag on a handle.

2. To complete the Transformation, press ENTER on your keyboard.

If you wish to undo the transformation, Choose Edit | Undo, or click above the Free Transform Selection state in the History palette.

 NOTE: *Don't confuse the Select | Transform Selection command with Photoshop's Edit | Transform commands. The Edit | Transform commands transform image areas on screen, not the selection marquee. See Chapters 8 and 15 for more details about Edit | Transform.*

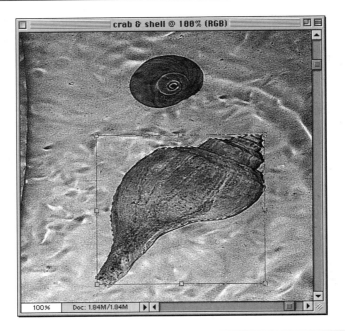

FIGURE 4-2   Art being transformed with Select I Transform Selection

Now that the rectangle is selected, you can change it—by filling it with either the foreground or background color or by moving it to another location, as described in the next section.

Moving a Selection

Once you have created a selection, you may want to move it to the perfect location on screen. In this exercise you'll move a selection using the mouse.

1. Make sure you have a rectangle selected on screen and the Rectangular Marquee tool activated.

2. To move the rectangle with the mouse, start by positioning the crosshair over the middle of the rectangle. The crosshair changes to an arrow pointer with a small rectangle at the end of it.

3. Once the arrow pointer appears on screen, click and drag it to move the rectangle about 1 inch to the right and about .5 inches down.

Notice that just the selection moved and not the filled rectangle. Click Undo, or reselect the rectangle with the Rectangular Marquee tool.

 NOTE: *You can also move a selection marquee using Select | Transform Selection.*

 NOTE: *Clicking away from a selection causes it to be deselected. If this occurs, you can reselect it by choosing Select | Reselect.*

4

Here's how to move both the selection and the filled rectangle inside it:

4. With the Rectangular Marquee tool activated, press and hold the COMMAND key (Windows users: CTRL) while you click inside the selected rectangle and drag. Notice that as you press and hold the COMMAND key (Windows users: CTRL), a small scissors icon replaces the small rectangle icon at the bottom of the arrow pointer. You can also use the Move tool to move both the selection and the filled rectangle inside it.

As you move the object, you will see that Photoshop leaves a duplicate of the rectangular selection in its original position, filled with the background color, as shown in Figure 4-3. Note that if the Background color in the Toolbox and the document color are both white, you will not see a change.

You may find it annoying that Photoshop leaves the background color on the portion of the screen from which an object was moved. (If you are working in a layer other than the Background, moving a selection causes the transparent background or the layer beneath it to show through.) Most of the time, when you move an object you won't want a hole left behind filled with the current background color. Figure 4-4 shows the effects of moving a rectangular selection (with the Move tool) in a scanned image. Here, too, Photoshop has cut a hole in the image.

A simple way to avoid this is to copy the selected area before you fill it with a color. In the preceding chapter, you were introduced to this concept when you created and moved text. The next exercise reviews this technique so that you can move a selection without affecting the underlying pixels.

However, before proceeding note that you can now freely move the selection on screen by clicking and dragging it, or by using the keyboard: Press any directional arrow key three or four times. With each key press, the object will move one pixel up, down, left, or right. This time, Photoshop does not rip a hole out of the background.

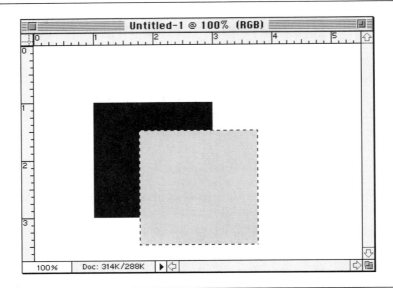

FIGURE 4-3   Moving an object leaves the current background color in the object's original position

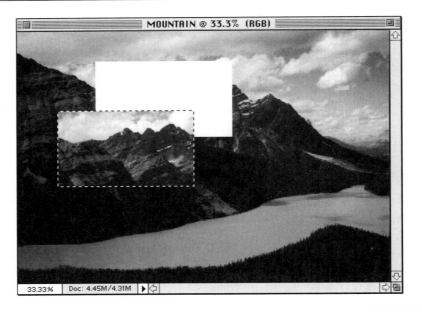

FIGURE 4-4   Cutting and moving a portion of an onscreen image leaves the background color behind

REMEMBER: *When you move a selection for the first time with the Move Tool, Photoshop creates a "hole" in your image. You can click in the History palette, choose Edit | Undo File | Revert command to restore your original image.*

Clearing the Screen

In order to give yourself more room to work, try deleting everything on screen. In Photoshop, one method of clearing the screen is to execute the Select | All command, which selects the entire screen. Once the entire screen is selected, it can then be "erased" by filling it with white. The Select | All command is also helpful when you wish to apply a Photoshop command to everything on screen.

1. Change the background color back to white by clicking once on the Default Colors icon.

2. To select the entire screen, choose All from the Select menu or press COMMAND-A (Windows users: CTRL-A).

3. Press DELETE (Windows users: BACKSPACE). The entire screen fills with the background color, white.

 NOTE: *If you do this in a layer other than the Background, the layer will be cleared and images in the underlying layers will then be visible.*

4. Notice the marquee surrounding your screen, indicating that the entire screen is still selected. To deselect it, choose None from the Select menu or press COMMAND-D (Windows users: CTRL-D).

Duplicating and Moving a Selection

In this exercise you'll create a rectangular selection and then duplicate it so you can move it, fill it with a color, or delete it without affecting the underlying pixels.

1. Start by resetting the foreground color to red and the background color to blue. If you don't change the background color, you won't see the effects of floating a selection.

2. If the Rectangular Marquee tool is not selected, select it now.

3. Click on the upper-left corner of your window and drag diagonally about 2 or 3 inches to the right to create a rectangular selection. Do not deselect.

4. To duplicate and move the selected area, hold the OPTION-COMMAND keys (Windows users: ALT-CTRL) while you click and drag inside the rectangular selection on screen. (Note that you can also activate the Move tool, then press OPTION (Windows users: ALT) while clicking and dragging).

5. Fill the object with the foreground color by pressing OPTION-DELETE (Windows users: ALT-BACKSPACE).

6. Position the pointer in the middle of the rectangle and drag about 1 inch down and to the right. Do not deselect.

This time, when you moved the selection, the background did not change.

7. Once the selected area has been moved on screen, you can delete it by pressing DELETE. Do this now. Notice that the selected area was deleted, and Photoshop didn't fill the deleted area with the background color. Once you move a selected object, it's almost as if the object is floating above the background pixels. Thus, pressing DELETE only affects the selected "floating" area.

Changing Selection Opacity

If you move a selection on screen, you may wish to create a blend between the selection you move and the pixels beneath it. In Photoshop 5, you can change the opacity of a selection that you move by using the Fade command.

After moving the selection with the Move tool (or by pressing OPTION (Windows users: ALT while dragging), simply choose Filter | Fade. In the Fade dialog box, lower opacity by dragging the Opacity slider to the left. In the Fade dialog box, you can also choose a blending mode from the Mode pop-up menu. The blending modes create special effects by blending the pixels in the moved selection with pixels in the underlying area. (Blending modes are discussed in Chapter 6 and Chapter 15).

 TIP: *You can also access the Filter | Fade command after painting with a painting tool, filling a selection using the Edit | Fill command, color correcting with an Image |Adjust command, and after applying one of Photoshop's Edit | Transform commands to a selection. The Edit | Transform commands are discussed in Chapter 8 and in Chapter 15.*

Working with Copy and Paste

In the upcoming exercises in this chapter, you will use the Edit | Copy and Edit | Paste commands to copy a selection from one file into another. When you copy or cut a selection and paste it into another file, Photoshop automatically creates a new layer with the selection in it, and de-selects.

 NOTE: *When using the Paste command to work with text, bear this in mind: Although you can copy and paste text directly into Photoshop from Adobe Illustrator, you cannot paste text from most other applications directly into a Photoshop document. Instead, you must paste it into the Type Tool dialog box.*

Storing and Purging the Contents of a Selection in the Clipboard

Before you begin to experiment with Photoshop's Paste commands, you need to understand how Photoshop handles memory when you cut or copy the material you want to paste. When Photoshop's Edit | Cut and Edit | Copy commands are executed, Photoshop automatically copies the contents of a selection in the active layer to an area of the computer's memory called the Clipboard. The Clipboard is a temporary storage area for copied or cut items. Every time a selection is copied into the Clipboard, that selection replaces any existing Clipboard contents; only one item at a time can be stored in the Clipboard. When the Paste command is executed, the contents of the Clipboard are copied into the active document and placed in a new layer.

 NOTE: *If you wish to copy an image from Photoshop's Clipboard to another Mac or Windows application, you must first select the Export Clipboard option in the General Preferences dialog box. To open the dialog box, choose General from the File | Preferences submenu. In the General Preferences dialog box, click the Export Clipboard check box. Mac users note that Photoshop places a 4MB limit on PICT images that can be exported from the clipboard. You can disable this limitation by installing the Disable Clipboard Size Limit plug-in. The plug-in is located in the Optional Extensions folder, located on the Adobe Photoshop CD ROM.*

It is important to realize that when the contents of a large selection are being held in the Clipboard, there is less memory available for Photoshop to use. In this situation, you might receive an unexpected out-of-memory message. To prevent this from happening, make sure that you allocate as much RAM as possible to Photoshop and that your scratch disk's storage capacity is as large as possible. Ideally, of course, the best solution is to purchase more RAM or a larger hard disk. For more information about allocating memory, RAM, and hard disks, see Chapter 1.

If you think the contents of the Clipboard are consuming too much memory (and you no longer need to store that information), there is an easy way to remove the memory used by the Clipboard: Choose Purge from the Edit menu. In the Purge submenu, choose Clipboard.

Handling Different Resolutions During Paste Operations

When you paste a selected area from one Photoshop file into another file with a different resolution, you may be surprised at the consequences. The contents of the selection you paste will take on the resolution of the file into which you paste it. Thus, if the selection's resolution is higher than that of the target file, the selection will enlarge when pasted. If you paste a selected area with a low resolution into a higher-resolution file, the selection will shrink when pasted.

To understand this phenomenon, remember that there are more pixels per square inch in a high-resolution file than in a low-resolution file. For example, if you select an area 72 pixels by 72 pixels in a file that has a resolution of 72 pixels per inch, the selection is 1 inch. But if you paste the selection into a file with a resolution of 300 pixels per inch, the selection shrinks to about one-quarter of an inch in the new file. The selection is still composed of 72 pixels by 72 pixels, but the pixels must diminish in size when they are placed in an image where a square inch comprises 300 pixels by 300 pixels.

 NOTE: *If a selection's size increases or decreases after pasting, you can resize the pasted area by using the Edit | Transform | Scale command. (See Chapter 8 for more information.) However, be aware that this command adds or subtracts pixels in the image which can degrade image quality.*

Creating the Telephone/Dock Collage

The telephone/dock collage shown in Figure 4-5(a) was assembled primarily by using the Marquee selection tool. To create the image in Figure 4-5(a), we scanned a photograph of a dock [Figure 4-5(b)] and one of a telephone booth [Figure 4-5(c)] at the same resolution. Next, we selected the telephone booth with the Rectangular Marquee tool (as seen in Figure 4-6), copied it, and pasted it into the dock document. Note that Photoshop automatically placed the telephone image into a new layer in the dock document after the paste command was executed.

 TIP: *As you create a rectangular selection, you can move it without releasing the mouse by pressing SPACEBAR. After you create the selection, keep the mouse button down. Press SPACEBAR and continue to drag the mouse. As you drag, the selection moves. Note also that you can drag a selection border from one open Photoshop document to another.*

When the telephone booth was in the dock document, we scaled it using the Edit | Transform | Scale command. (For more information on using the Scale command, see Chapters 8 and 15.) Once the telephone booth was scaled, we moved it into position using the Move tool.

For the final touch, we used the Eraser tool to erase the extra areas (seen in Figure 4-7) around the telephone booth from the original file that we did not want included in the collage.

The Flag Collage

The flag collage shown in Figure 4-8 was assembled primarily by using the Marquee selection tool. The highway in the upper-left corner of the flag was taken from a larger scanned image by selecting it with the Marquee tool; once selected, it was then copied and pasted over the flag graphic.

You might be surprised to learn that the flag was created with a selection tool, but all of Photoshop's selection tools provide a dual function: They can be used to create, as well as select, shapes.

(a)

(b)

(c)

FIGURE 4-5   (a) The telephone/dock collage; (b) the dock image used to create the collage in (a); (c) the telephone booth image used to create the collage in (a)

FIGURE 4-6   A rectangular selection over the telephone booth

Composing the Flag

Now you are ready to create the flag portion of the image shown in Figure 4-8. For this project you will need a 5.5-by-3.75-inch file on screen. If you are working in the original file, clear the screen to its original state by clicking on the snapshot labeled New, at the top of the History palette. If you don't have the original practice file open, create a new one with these dimensions and set the background Contents to White. Make sure all objects are cleared from your screen.

Bear in mind that the resolution of your file is set to 72 ppi (unless you or somebody else has changed it). This resolution will be fine for practicing and producing comps (samples or simulations of the completed art design) to test designs and techniques. A resolution of 72 ppi is also suitable for Web graphics and most onscreen and video presentations. For professional output of the collage,

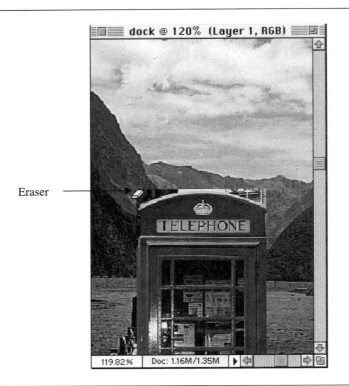

Eraser

Using the Eraser tool to erase unwanted areas

you may want to use a higher resolution such as 300 ppi. If you do this, make sure you have enough memory to handle the file. A 5.5-by-3.75-inch RGB color file at 300 ppi will consume 5.31MB, versus 314K at 72 ppi. Remember, as mentioned in Chapter 1, that Photoshop generally requires memory at least three times your file size to be free on either your hard disk or in RAM.

If you do create the flag collage or any of the other projects in this chapter at a resolution higher than 72 ppi, you will need to convert the pixel measurements in order to compensate for the fact that more pixels per inch will be used. For instance, in the next exercise the height of the flag stripes is 21 pixels at 72 ppi. To convert to 300 ppi, divide the 21 pixels by 72 (72 pixels = 1 inch) to get the precise size of the object in inches. Then multiply by 300 to calculate how many pixels there will be at 300 pixels per inch: (21 ÷ 72) × 300.

FIGURE 4-8   The flag collage

 TIP: *Use the following formula to convert a measurement from one resolution to another: (Measurement in pixels ÷ Original ppi) × New ppi.*

Creating the Red Stripes

To create rectangles with specific measurements, use the Fixed Size option from the Style pop-up menu in the Marquee Options palette. This option allows you to type in specific measurements for rectangular objects.

 TIP: *The Fixed Size option in the Style pop-up menu is a time saver because it allows you to create objects at precise sizes with one mouse click. It's much easier to use Fixed Size than to create shapes with the Normal option while checking against the ruler and/or the Info palette.*

1. Start by selecting the Rectangular Marquee tool in the Toolbox. To specify the size of the stripes, first double-click on the Marquee tool (if the Marquee Options palette is not already open); or press ENTER to open the palette.

2. In the Marquee Options palette, choose Fixed Size from the Style pop-up menu.

3. Notice that the Fixed Size option only allows measurements to be entered in pixels. Because a pixel is the smallest element possible on screen, it is the most precise way of measuring.

   The red stripes you are creating are approximately .3 by 5.5 inches. To set the length of the stripe to approximately 5.5 inches, type 396 (72 × 5.5 = 396) in the Width field of the Fixed Size option. (Remember that there are 72 pixels per inch in a file that has a resolution of 72 ppi.)

4. To set the Height of the stripe to approximately .3 inches, type 21 (72 × .3 = 21.6). Make sure that the Feather pixel value is set to 0.

5. To create the selection, move the center of the crosshair to the 0 points on the ruler (at the top-left corner of your document) and click on the screen. A rectangular selection appears, 5.5 inches long; this is the first stripe.

6. Change the foreground color to red using the Swatches palette. You'll use the red foreground color to fill the stripes.

7. To color the stripe red, press OPTION-DELETE (Windows users: ALT-DELETE). At this point your document should look like Figure 4-9.

   TIP: *Pressing OPTION-DELETE (Windows users: ALT-DELETE) is a shortcut for filling with 100% of the foreground color.*

8. Because the background color of your file is white, you won't need to create a white stripe. What you need is the ability to create a duplicate of the red stripe's selection to use as a white placeholder between the red stripes. Photoshop allows you to move a selection marquee without grabbing the underlying pixels. With the Rectangular Marquee tool selected, click on the middle of the selection marquee and drag. As you drag, press and hold the SHIFT key to constrain the selection until you have reached the bottom border of the first red stripe. Release the mouse button, but don't deselect! The selection marquee creates a placeholder that will act as the white stripe. Your screen should now look like Figure 4-10.

   NOTE: *As you're working, you may find it helpful to view Photoshop's grid on screen. First set the grid preferences by choosing File | Preferences | Guides & Grids. In the dialog box, set the Gridlines to appear every 21 pixels, and set the Subdivisions to 1. As you work you can turn the Grids on and off from the View menu.*

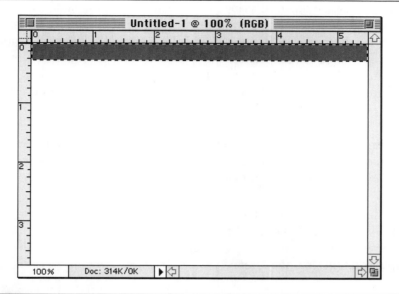

FIGURE 4-9   Creating the first stripe of the flag

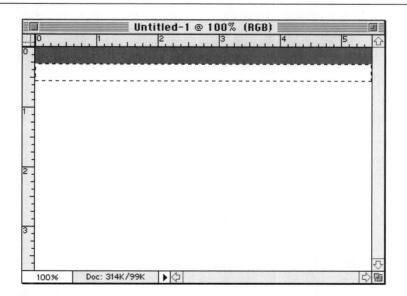

FIGURE 4-10   Moving the selection marquee to create a placeholder for the second stripe

9. Now, to create the third stripe (the second red stripe), move the selection you just created. Use the Rectangular Marquee tool to move the marquee down until the top of it touches the bottom border of the white stripe. Click on the middle of the selection marquee and drag. As you drag, press and hold the SHIFT key to constrain the selection until you have reached the bottom of the white stripe (the second stripe). Release the mouse button, but do not deselect.

 TIP: *If you wish to temporarily hide a selection (but keep the selection selected), press COMMAND-H (Windows users: CTRL-H). To bring back the selection marquee, press COMMAND-H (Windows users: CTRL-H) again.*

10. With the Foreground color set to red, press OPTION-DELETE (Windows users: ALT-DELETE) to fill the selection with red, completing the third stripe. With the third stripe complete, choose Select | Deselect to remove the selection from the screen.

Now that you have three stripes created, you can speed things up by selecting a white and red stripe together (because the flag ends on a red stripe) and then duplicating them.

11. To select both the second (white) and third (red) stripes, switch from Fixed Size to Normal in the Marquee Options palette by choosing Normal in the Style pop-up menu.

12. With the Rectangular Marquee activated, select the second and third stripes.

13. With the Rectangular Marquee activated, press and hold OPTION-COMMAND (Windows users: ALT-CTRL), then click on the middle of the marquee on screen and drag down. As you drag, press and hold the SHIFT key to constrain the selection. Drag the duplicated stripes into position under the first set of stripes to create your fourth and fifth stripes. Release the mouse, but do not deselect.

 REMEMBER: *You can press COMMAND-H (Windows users: CTRL-H) to temporarily hide a selection but still keep it selected.*

When you dragged with the Marquee tool activated and with the OPTION-COMMAND keys (Windows users: ALT-CTRL) pressed, Photoshop copied your selection and its contents and put it into float mode—above the underlying pixels.

REMEMBER: *Here is a shortcut for duplicating a selected object and moving it: With the Rectangular Marquee tool activated, press and hold OPTION-COMMAND (Windows users: ALT-CTRL) while you click on the middle of the object and drag. As you drag, Photoshop duplicates the object without changing the background pixels. You can also use the Move tool to duplicate a selected object. With the Move tool activated, press and hold OPTION (Windows users: ALT) while you click on the middle of the object and drag.*

14. To save your work, choose Save from the File menu. Name your file Flag, then click Save (Windows users: OK).

15. Continue creating stripes by duplicating them with the Rectangular Marquee tool activated and with the OPTION-COMMAND keys (Windows users: ALT-CTRL) pressed, until you have created seven red stripes and six white ones. The first and last stripes should be red.

16. Save your work again.

NOTE: *Throughout the next sections, you will save your file after you have successfully finished each segment of the flag collage. If you keep saving, you will always be able to use the Revert command to return to the last correct version of the file.*

Creating the Blue Rectangle of the Flag

Next you'll use the Marquee tool's Rectangular shape and Fixed Size option to create a blue rectangle and move it to the top-left corner of the screen.

1. In the Marquee Options palette, click on the Style pop-up menu and choose Fixed Size.

2. The blue rectangle you are creating is approximately 2.5 by 2 inches, so enter **180** (2.5 × 72) in the Width field, and **147** (21 pixels × 7 stripes) in the Height field.

3. Click the mouse on screen, then click and drag to move the selection to the upper-left corner of your screen. Notice that when you move the selection, you do not affect the stripes beneath it.

4. Change the foreground color to blue, then press OPTION-DELETE (Windows users: ALT-DELETE) to fill the selection.

5. Choose None from the Select menu to deselect and lock the blue rectangle in place. Your flag should now look like the one shown in Figure 4-11.

You have now completed the flag, so save your work. Your next step is to place a scanned image into the flag's blue rectangle.

Placing a Photograph into the Flag File

In this section, you will copy an image in one file and paste it into another. This example uses a scanned image of a highway, which you will place in the Flag file.

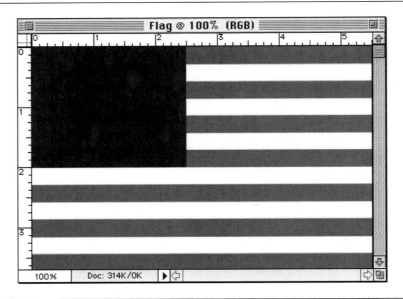

FIGURE 4-11   Adding the blue rectangle to the flag

CAUTION: *No matter what digitized image you use, its resolution should match the resolution of your Photoshop collage file. The digitized image you place into the collage will enlarge if its resolution is higher or shrink if its resolution is lower.*

1. To open a digitized image in Photoshop, choose Open from the File menu. If you don't see the file you are looking for, try selecting the Show All Files check box. Select the filename, and then click Open (Windows users: OK). The image will load on screen.

2. If the Marquee Options palette is not displayed on screen, double-click on the Marquee tool. To create a selection that is the proper size for the blue rectangle of the flag, make sure that the Style pop-up menu is set to Fixed Size. Enter **168** in the Width field and **134** in the Height field. Then click on screen to make the selection appear. If you wish, move the selection by clicking and dragging with the mouse. Click and drag the selection to the part of the image that you wish to copy into the Flag file, as shown in Figure 4-12.

3. To copy the area into memory so that you can paste it into the Flag file, choose Copy from the Edit menu. Photoshop stores the selection in the Clipboard.

4. Close the image file; the Flag file will still be open.

5. To paste the selection from the Clipboard into your Flag file, select Paste from the Edit menu.

 TIP: *COMMAND-C (Windows users: CTRL-C) is the keyboard shortcut for Edit | Copy. COMMAND-V (Windows users: CTRL-V) is the keyboard shortcut for Edit | Paste.*

6. When you use the Paste command, Photoshop automatically puts the pasted image into a new layer, so you can easily click and drag it without worrying about altering the underlying pixels. To move the image, use the Move tool to click and drag it into position—into the top-left corner of the flag, as shown in Figure 4-13.

FIGURE 4-12 Selecting an image from a photograph to be copied and pasted into the flag's blue rectangle

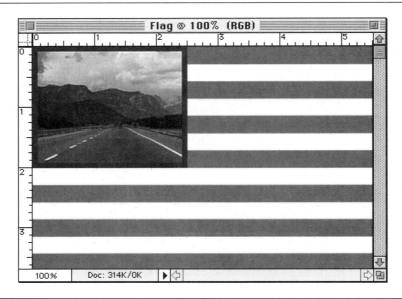

FIGURE 4-13 Pasting and moving the photograph into position

4

 NOTE: *If you wish, you can scale the selection by using the Edit |*
Transform | Scale command. For more information about the Scale
command, see Chapters 8 and 15.

To see the new layer, open the Layers palette (if it is not already open). In
the palette, notice that there is a new layer called Layer 1. When you are
working on this layer, the title bar reads "(Layer 1, RGB)." Also notice that
in the Layers palette the eye icon indicates the visible layers, and the
paintbrush icon indicates the layer that is currently being edited. You will
learn more about layers and layer masks in Chapters 15 and 16.

 NOTE: *Instead of copying and pasting, you can also drag a selection from*
one file directly to another. You'll do this later in this chapter.

7. To conserve memory, you may want to flatten your file—collapse all
layers to the background. To flatten your file, choose Flatten Image from
the Layers palette pop-up menu.

Placing Text on the Flag

In Chapters 2 and 3 the issue of type quality was discussed, and here it's worth
repeating that type quality in Photoshop is dependent on file resolution. If you
work in a file with a resolution of 72 ppi, sending it as output to a high-resolution
printer will not improve its quality. If you need to produce a Photoshop project
with very high-resolution text, it's often best not to create the text in Photoshop.
Save the file so that it can be exported to a drawing program such as Adobe
Illustrator or a page-layout program such as QuarkXPress. In these programs, text
is created as a separate object that is printed at the resolution of the output device.
If you wanted Photoshop's text to match the quality of text as output from these
programs, you would need to create an image at an extremely high resolution. For
example, if you wanted your text output at 1,270 ppi, your file's resolution would
need to be 1,270 ppi. Obviously, the file size would be gigantic. Saving files so
they can be output to other programs is covered in Appendix A.

In this exercise, high-resolution text isn't necessary, so you can use Photoshop's
Type tool to generate the words for the flag collage.

Before you begin adding text, make sure that the Foreground color is still
set to blue.

1. Select the Type tool.

2. Click about an inch above the middle of the screen.

3. If you wish to make the text appear as it does in the example in Figure 4-8, enter the following specifications:

   Click on the Font pop-up menu and change the font to Times. If Times is not installed on your system, pick another font. In the Size field, type **70** points. In the Leading field, type **125**. In the Alignment group, click on the Align Right (the last icon in the group). In the text box, type **USA's** and press RETURN (Windows users: ENTER). Then type **HIGHWAYS** (underneath USA's). In the Style options, make sure the Anti-Aliased check box is selected. Click OK.

 REMEMBER: *If you wish to change the spacing between letters, select the text in the Type Tool dialog box, then enter a value in the Tracking field.*

4. When the text appears on screen, use the Move tool to click and drag USA's and HIGHWAYS into position, as seen in Figure 4-8. As you move the type, the underlying pixels will not be affected because the text is in its own layer.

 TIP: *If the Preview option is selected in the Type Tool dialog box, you can move the Type with the Type Tool dialog box open.*

5. When you are satisfied with the position of the text, save your file.

 TIP: *When you save your file, Photoshop can create a thumbnail image preview that is displayed in the Open dialog box. To have Photoshop create the thumbnail, make sure that the Thumbnail check box is selected in the More Preferences dialog box (File | Preferences | Saving Files). If the Icon check box is also selected (Macintosh only), Photoshop creates a preview of the image seen in the file's icon. Windows users can decide whether they want image previews by clicking in the Image Previews pop-up menu.*

That's it! You've just completed the flag collage.

In the next sections, you'll create more collages and will learn more about the options available in the Marquee Options palette. You will also begin to explore the other selection tools—the Elliptical Marquee, the Lasso, and the Magic Wand.

Introductory Exercises: Filling and Stroking Selections in a Layer

The introductory exercises in the next sections demonstrate how to create perfect squares and circles. You will be using these shapes to produce the cab and wheels of a truck. To build these objects, you'll use the Constrained Aspect Ratio option found in the Marquee Options palette. Before beginning this section, close any other documents you might have open on screen. This will keep memory usage to a minimum.

In this section, you will work in a layer that has a transparent background. This means that any layers beneath the layer in which you are working can be seen through areas in your file that are not filled with color.

1. Start by creating an RGB color file 7 inches wide by 5 inches high to use for the introductory exercises. This size will give you sufficient room to practice.

   In the New dialog box, choose the Transparent radio button in the Contents group. After you click OK, notice that the screen is filled with a checkerboard-like pattern. This indicates that the background of your file is transparent. Notice also that the title bar of your document window includes the words "Layer 1." If the Layers palette is not open, open it now by choosing Show Layers from the Window menu. As mentioned earlier, the words "Layer 1" appear in the Layers palette instead of the word "Background" if you choose the Transparent Contents radio button in the New dialog box.

 NOTE: *The color and size of the grid that indicates you are working in a layer with a transparent background can be modified. To change the transparent background, choose Transparency and Gamut from the File | Preferences submenu. To change the size of the checkerboard pattern, choose a size from the Grid Size pop-up menu. To change colors, click on the Grid Colors pop-up menu.*

2. From the View menu select Show Rulers, and from the Window menu select Show Info. Use the rulers and the Info palette to help you measure when completing the exercises in this section.

3. Use black as the foreground color and white as the background color. Check to see that these are your current settings; if they aren't, click on the Default Colors icon in the Toolbox.

Using the Rectangular Marquee and the Constrained Aspect Ratio Option

We'll start by exploring the Constrained Aspect Ratio option, which creates selections according to proportions specified in the Marquee Options palette.

1. To open the Marquee Options palette, double-click on the Marquee tool. In the Style pop-up menu, choose Constrained Aspect Ratio. Leave both the Width and Height fields set at 1, the defaults.

These settings will constrain the mouse selection so that the width and height are always drawn at a 1:1 ratio—in other words, you'll be creating a square. The width and height of the rectangular selection will always be equal to each other.

2. To create the square, move the crosshair to the upper-left corner of your document. Click and drag down diagonally from left to right. As you drag, notice that your selection is a square. Release the mouse.

Now try creating another rectangular selection. No matter how hard you try, you will not be able to create anything other than a square selection. The selection can be any size, but it will always be a square because the width to height proportion has been constrained to a 1:1 ratio.

Although the Constrained Aspect Ratio option is often used to create squares, you can use it to create rectangles at other proportions. For instance, if you need to make rectangles in which the height is twice as long as the width (1:2), you can set the aspect ratio accordingly.

3. To make a rectangle with a 1:2 ratio, leave Width set to 1, and change Height to 2 in the Marquee Options palette.

4. Click and drag to create a selection.

No matter how large your selection, the height will always be double the width. Here are some rectangles with 1:1, 1:2, and 2:1 ratios, respectively:

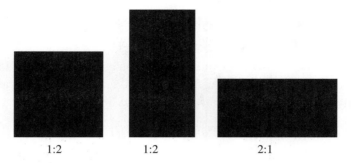

1:2   1:2   2:1

Using the Elliptical Marquee Tool

The Elliptical Marquee tool functions similarly to the Rectangular Marquee, except it creates round rather than rectangular shapes. To use the Elliptical Marquee tool, click in the Marquee Toolbox location and keep the mouse button pressed. Then drag over the Elliptical Marquee tool to select it. Alternatively, you can OPTION-click (Windows users: ALT-click) on the Rectangular Marquee icon in the Toolbox. In the Marquee Options palette's Style pop-up menu, the Normal, Constrained Aspect Ratio, and Fixed Size options work exactly as they do with the Rectangular Marquee tool.

The Elliptical Marquee Tool and the Normal Option

The Marquee tool's Elliptical shape allows you to create elliptical selections. Since you haven't used the Elliptical Marquee before, start with it set to the Normal option so that you can see how the tool works without any constraints.

1. Start by checking to see that Normal is selected in the Style pop-up menu. If it is not, select it now.

   Drawing an ellipse with the mouse is not too different from drawing a rectangle, primarily because you can click and drag diagonally to create the shape. The perimeter of the ellipse starts where you click, and the shape grows according to the size of the angle and distance you drag.

2. To draw an ellipse, click on the upper-left corner of your screen and slowly drag diagonally toward the lower-right corner. When you have an elliptical selection on the screen, release the mouse button.

3. To practice a bit more, try drawing another ellipse. This time, drag only about one-half inch down and then drag across to the right, almost to the edge of the screen. This produces a cigar-shaped ellipse.

The Elliptical Marquee Tool and the Constrained Aspect Ratio Option

As with the Marquee tool's Rectangular shape, you can utilize the Style pop-up menu's Constrained Aspect Ratio to create selections with the Elliptical Marquee tool according to specific proportions. With this option selected and a 1:1 ratio specified, the Marquee tool's Elliptical shape creates a perfect circle.

Try creating a circular selection with the Elliptical Marquee tool:

1. In the Marquee Options palette, select the Constrained Aspect Ratio in the Style pop-up menu. If Width and Height are not set to 1, type **1** in both the Width and Height fields.

2. Click and drag diagonally down from the upper-left corner of your screen toward the bottom-right corner. Your selection will be a perfect circle.

3. Try creating another selection, but this time, use a different ratio. Here are some ellipses with 1:1, 1:2, and 2:1 ratios:

| 1:1 | 1:2 | 2:1 |

 TIP: *If the Constrained Aspect Ratio option is not activated, you can still create a perfect square or perfect circle by clicking and pressing SHIFT after you start dragging the mouse.*

Using Edit | Fill and Edit | Stroke

To fill the circular selection with white, you'll use the Edit | Fill command, which allows you to fill with the background color, as well as the foreground color. The Fill command also allows you to fill a selection with black, 50% gray, white, a pattern, or the currently set History state in the History palette. (The Pattern and History options are covered in Chapter 7.) The Fill dialog box also provides settings for blending modes and changing Opacity. (Changing Opacity and using the blending modes are covered in Chapter 6.) After using the Edit | Fill command, you'll use Edit | Stroke.

The Stroke command in the Edit menu allows you to put a border or outline around a selection, using the current foreground color. You cannot stroke with the background color. The Stroke dialog box allows you to enter the stroke width in pixels; acceptable values are integers between 1 and 16, inclusive. You can designate whether you wish the stroke to be along the outside of the selection marquee, inside it, or in the middle. You can also create a stroke with a tint (a percentage of the foreground color) and apply a blending mode. Working with tints is discussed in Chapter 6. The blending modes are covered in Chapter 5.

In this exercise, you will fill a selection with white, then stroke the selection.

1. Before you fill or stroke an object, you need to create a selection on screen. Select the Elliptical Marquee tool, then click and drag to create a circle about 2 inches in diameter.

2. If the foreground and background colors are not set to black and white, click on the Default Colors icon to change them.

3. To fill the selection with white, open the Fill dialog box, shown below, by choosing Fill from the Edit menu. In the Use pop-up menu, choose either Background Color or White. Leave Opacity set to 100% and Mode to Normal.

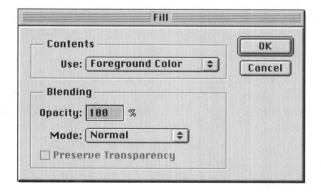

 CAUTION: *Do not select the Preserve Transparency check box; otherwise, the transparent area in the selection (in this case, the entire selection) will not be affected.*

TIP: *Press and hold SHIFT, then press the DELETE key (Windows users: BACKSPACE) to open the Fill dialog box.*

4. To stroke the selection, open the Stroke dialog box, shown below, by choosing Edit | Stroke.

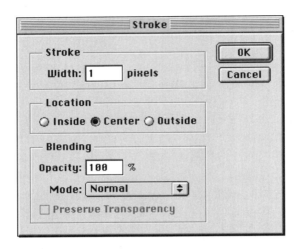

5. To set the size of the stroke, type **5** in the Width field. Set Location to Center, Opacity set to 100%, and Mode set to Normal (these are the defaults). Then click OK. The circle appears, with a 5-pixel outline. In the middle of the circle's 5-pixel stroke, you'll see the selection marquee still blinking. The stroke was created in the center of the selection. Click away to deselect and see the stroke.

Before closing this file, take a look at some aspects of working in a layer. In a layer, you can move all of its contents by clicking and dragging with the Move tool. Try this out by activating the Move tool, then clicking and dragging with the Move tool on the circle. The circle moves, but you didn't have to select it. This does not mean that you don't need the selection tools anymore. If you had two circles in the same layer and wanted to move them independently of one another, you would need to select the one you wanted to move first.

Now that you've covered all the tools and commands you'll need to create the truck collage, you can close this practice file.

Selecting to Create a Clock Collage

The clock collage shown in Figure 4-14(a) was created using the Elliptical Marquee tool. We started by scanning two photographs at the same resolution. First, we scanned the clouds [Figure 4-14(b)], and then the clock with the signs of the zodiac [Figure 4-14(c)]. After both images were digitized, we selected the clock with the Elliptical Marquee tool. After the elliptical selection was created, we moved it into position, as seen in Figure 4-15. Next, we copied and pasted the oval selection into the cloud image. When we pasted the oval selection, Photoshop automatically placed the zodiac sign clock image into a new layer in the clouds document. Note that instead of copying and pasting, we could have dragged the clock image with the Move tool and dropped it into the clouds document.

Finally, we moved the clock into position using the Move tool.

The Truck Collage

Making the truck collage shown in Figure 4-16 will give you additional experience with the selection tools and their Options palettes. This collage project is divided into two parts. In the first part, you will create a truck on which you'll paste a scanned image of some fruit. Then you will go through a few introductory exercises designed to introduce you to the selection tools and options that you'll be using for the first time. In the second part of the truck collage project, later in the chapter, you'll outline and fill parts of a scanned image to create a landscape background.

Creating the Truck

Start the truck collage by creating a new file designed to tightly fit the truck you are creating.

1. To create a new file, choose New from the File menu. Enter the dimensions of the file as Width **5** and Height **3.5**. Set Mode to RGB Color and 72 ppi for the resolution. Before clicking OK, set the Contents radio button to Transparent. When the new document appears, you'll see the words "Layer 1" in the Layers palette, rather than the word "Background."

(a)

(b)

(c)

FIGURE 4-14 (a) The clock collage; (b) the clouds image used to create the clock collage in (a); (c) the zodiac signs clock image used to create the clock collage in (a)

REMEMBER: *If you wish to create this collage at a resolution higher than 72 ppi, you'll need to convert the pixel measurements in the text to compensate for the resolution change. See the Tip in the section "Composing the Flag" earlier in this chapter for the conversion formula.*

NOTE: *You can change the way transparent layers appear onscreen by changing the settings in the Transparency & Gamut dialog box. To open this dialog box, choose File | Preferences | Transparency & Gamut.*

FIGURE 4-15   An oval selection around the zodiac sign clock image

FIGURE 4-16   The truck collage

2. Since the file's dimensions are small, you'll probably want to zoom in to make your work area bigger. To magnify the document window, press COMMAND-+ (Windows users: CTRL-+), the keyboard equivalent of the Zoom In command found in the View menu. The magnification ratio in the Window title bar now reads 200%. You can also use the Navigator palette to adjust the document's magnification ratio.

3. You'll be needing both the rulers and the Info palette for measuring, so open them (if they are not already open) by choosing Show Rulers from the View menu, then choosing Show Info from the Window menu.

Moving the Zero Point

When you create the truck, give yourself some breathing room by creating it one-half inch from the top and one-half inch from the left side of your document. You will measure distances from the truck's origin, not from the zero point, or origin, of the rulers. To help you measure in these situations, Photoshop allows you to move the zero point of both the vertical and the horizontal screen rulers so that you can measure from anywhere on screen.

Before moving the zero point, make sure that the 0 and half-inch marks appear on both the horizontal and vertical rulers. In order to move the zero point, you'll need to be able to view this part of the ruler. If you can't see it, scroll left and/or up until you can see these marks on both rulers.

To move the zero point, select the crosshair at the intersection of the horizontal and vertical rulers in the top-left corner of your screen, as shown in the top illustration here. Click and drag diagonally down to the half-inch mark on the vertical ruler and the half-inch mark on the horizontal ruler. As you drag, horizontal and vertical guides will appear at what will be the new zero point, as shown in the bottom illustration here.

Check the Info palette to make sure that the X and Y positions of the mouse both read .5 inch. When they do, release the mouse button to set the origin of both horizontal and vertical rulers.

If you released the mouse at the wrong point, you can return the zero point to its original position and try again—just double-click on the crosshair in the top-left corner of the screen.

To see the effects of the relocated zero point, move the mouse across the screen and watch the X and Y coordinates in the Info palette. Notice that the values read zero when you are at one-half inch from both the top and the left side of the screen. You will start creating the trailer of the truck at this new zero point.

Creating the Truck Trailer

Both the truck trailer and the poster area within it will be created using the Marquee tool's Rectangular shape. Later in this exercise you will paste an image into the poster area.

To make the truck's trailer, you'll need to create a rectangle that is twice as wide as it is high.

1. Select the Rectangular Marquee tool, then press ENTER to display the Rectangular Marquee Options palette. In the Shape pop-up menu, choose Rectangular. In the Style pop-up menu, choose Constrained Aspect Ratio. In the Width field type **2**, and in the Height field type **1**.

2. Use the rulers and the Info palette as guides to position the crosshair so that the X and Y coordinates both are close to 0. Click and drag diagonally to the right until the width is approximately 2.75 inches. The height of the trailer will be set automatically to about 1.375 inches, because you are using a Constrained Aspect Ratio of 2:1.

3. At this point, release the mouse button.

4. Next, fill the selection with black. If the Foreground color is not set to black, press D on your keyboard to set the Foreground to its default color. To fill with the foreground color (black) press OPTION-DELETE (Windows users: ALT-DELETE).

5. Click away from the truck to deselect so that you don't inadvertently move it.

6. Before continuing to create the poster border on the truck's trailer, save your file. By doing so, you can use the Revert command if you make a mistake in the following steps. Name the file **Truck**.

   Now you are going to create a smaller rectangle inside the truck's trailer. This rectangle will be used as a border for the fruit image you'll be pasting into the file.

7. Double-click on the Rectangular Marquee tool and set the Style pop-up menu in the Marquee Options palette to Normal.

8. Move the crosshair so that the x-axis is at approximately .250 inches and the y-axis is at about .125 inches. Click and drag diagonally to create a rectangle within the larger black rectangle.

4

To create a placeholder for the poster on the trailer, fill this rectangle with white. Don't deselect, because you're going to add a finishing touch by filling the area with white and then stroking the selection with a 4-pixel-wide gray border.

9. To fill the selected area with white, open the Fill dialog box by choosing Fill from the Edit menu or by pressing SHIFT-DELETE. In the Fill dialog box, choose White in the Use pop-up menu. Leave Opacity set to 100% and the Mode set to Normal. Make sure Preserve Transparency is not selected. Then click OK.

10. Because the Stroke command paints with the foreground color, you need to start by setting the foreground color to light blue. If the Color palette is not on screen, open it by choosing Show Color from the Window menu. Set the foreground color to a light blue by clicking on a blue area in the color bar.

11. To create the stroke, select Stroke from the Edit menu. In the Stroke dialog box, type **4** in the Width field. In the Location group, click on the Inside radio button—you want the stroke to be placed on the inside of the selection marquee (extending 4 pixels in from the selection), not on the outside of the selection (extending 4 pixels out from the selection) and not centered (placed directly on the selection marquee). Keep the Opacity set to 100% and the Mode set to Normal. Make sure the Preserve Transparency option is not selected. Click OK.

12. Choose Select | Deselect to deselect and save your work before continuing.

Before pasting the fruit into the poster area, proceed to create the chassis, cab, and wheels of the truck.

Creating the Chassis and the Cab

The truck's chassis consists of two long, filled rectangles, as shown below. Use the Marquee tool's Rectangular shape to create the rectangles, then fill them with shades of blue. To make the cab, create a square selection and fill it with black. To add a transparent window to the cab, create a rectangular selection with the Marquee tool, then press DELETE or choose Edit | Clear. The truck should now look like this:

Creating the Smoke Stack

To make the truck's smoke stack, use Figure 4-16 as a guide. Create two rectangles, a large one on the bottom (standing on its end) with a smaller one on top. Fill both with black.

Creating the Wheels

Now you are ready to create the first back wheel. After you create one wheel, you'll duplicate it to make the other three wheels.

1. Select the Elliptical Marquee in the Tool palette. In the Elliptical Marquee Tool Options palette set the Style pop-up menu to Constrained Aspect Ratio. Type in **1** for both the Width and Height fields. Make sure that the Feather pixel value is set to 0.

2. Position the crosshair in the back of the truck chassis at the spot where you want the midpoint of the wheel to be. To draw a circle from the midpoint out, press OPTION (Windows users: ALT) and hold the key while you click and drag to create a small circle. Fill the selection with the background color, white, by choosing Fill from the Edit menu. In the Use pop-up menu, choose Background Color or White. Then click OK.

3. To create the black tire, you will stroke the circle with the foreground color. Make sure that the foreground color is black, and then choose Stroke from the Edit menu. In the Stroke dialog box, set the width to 9 pixels. The Opacity should be 100%, and the mode should be Normal. Make sure Preserve Transparency is not selected and that Location is set to Inside. Click OK. The circular selection will now look like a wheel.

   Now you'll duplicate the wheel three times and drag each duplicate into position. Before you start to drag, you'll create a guide and then press the SHIFT key to constrain the wheel to moving in a straight line.

4. To create a guide below the wheel, click on the middle of the top ruler and drag down to the bottom of the wheel.

5. With the wheel selected and the Elliptical Marquee tool still activated, press and hold COMMAND-OPTION (Windows users: CTRL-ALT), then click and drag to duplicate the wheel. Next, press and hold SHIFT and drag to the right. As you drag, the wheel is constrained to move on a horizontal line. Position the wheel using Figure 4-16 as a guide. Repeat this procedure to create and position two more wheels.

6. Before continuing, save your work.

   You have just finished creating the truck. Now you're ready to paste an image of some fruit in the poster placeholder.

Creating the Poster

To create the proper selection size for the poster, use the Fixed Size option in the Marquee Options palette.

1. Select the Rectangular Marquee tool in the Toolbox.

2. In the Style pop-up menu, select Fixed Size and type **145** in the Width field and **65** in the Height field. Make sure that the Feather pixel value is set to 0.

3. Click on the truck's trailer to make the selection marquee appear. This is the selection size you will eventually use for the scanned image. Click and drag the selection into the middle of the poster area of the truck, as shown here:

Keep this portion selected, because later you will copy an image into this area. Notice that the selection was made slightly smaller than the poster area to provide a white border for the scanned image.

Select the fruit image to copy into the poster, or use any suitable image. The image you see on the truck in Figure 4-16 is one that was scanned from a photograph.

 REMEMBER: *The resolution of your scanned image should match the resolution of your file.*

4. To open a file, choose Open from the File menu. Locate the file and double-click the filename. If you don't have a suitable file, use one from the Samples folder.

5. Once the image opens on screen, you'll only need to click to create a selection, because the Fixed Size option is in effect. Click on the middle of the screen to create the 145-by-65-pixel selection. Adjust the position of the selection until you have framed the desired area.

6. To copy the selection, choose Copy from the Edit menu.

7. Select Close from the File menu.

8. You are now back in the Truck file; notice the selection marquee is right where you left it, in the border area of the truck's trailer. When you paste, you will be pasting the image directly into the selection marquee. Choose Paste from the Edit menu. Your image will look like this:

9. Save your work and close the Truck file.

Photoshop 5 > In Action

The boxers were selected with the Lasso tool so that they could be pasted into the image.

Parts of the letter M were selected with the Magic Wand tool and then moved.

Artist: Marc Yankus　　　　**Client: Data Communication**

The Perspective command in the Edit/Transform submenu was applied to the circuit board.

Marc started this image by creating a rectangular selection with the Marquee tool. Once the selection was on screen, he filled it with a blend using the Gradient tool. His next steps were to scan in a circuit board, select it with the Marquee tool, and then paste it into the image. Next, he applied the Perspective command from the Edit/Transform submenu. This created a sense of depth in the image.

Once the circuit board was placed, the boxers were scanned in, selected with the Lasso tool, copied, and pasted into the image. Finally, the letters *IBM* were scanned, copied, and pasted into the image. Then Marc used the Magic Wand tool to select parts of the letter *M* and break them away from the rest of the letter.

TIP: *When a selection tool is activated you can drag a selection marquee from one file to another. As an alternative to step 5 above, you could have first created the correctly sized selection marquee in the truck file, then dragged it into the fruit file before executing Edit\ Copy and Edit \ Paste*

Next, you'll perform several introductory exercises before moving on to the second part of the truck collage, in which you will create a background landscape from a scanned image and then paste the truck over it.

Using the Lasso, Polygon Lasso, and Magnetic Lasso Tools

 The Lasso tools—Lasso, Polygon Lasso, and Magnetic Lasso—are frequently used for selecting by tracing over image areas on screen. Although not as precise as the Pen tool, the Lasso tools can often create intricate selections. When you use the Lasso tools you click to begin a selection and drag to complete the selection. If you don't return to the starting point of your selection, each of the tools always closes your selection. They will not allow you to leave an open curve or angle on screen.

In general the Lasso tool is used to create freeform selections. The Magnetic Lasso tool, the newest member of Photoshop's Lasso family, is used to create precise selections because it automatically snaps to an image's edge. The Polygon Lasso tool is used to create selections shaped like polygons.

The Lasso, Polygon Lasso and Magnetic Lasso tools all reside in the same Toolbox location. To select the Lasso Toolbox location, press L on your keyboard. To switch from tool to tool, you can press SHIFT while pressing L on your keyboard.

The Lasso and Polygon Lasso Options Palettes

Before you test each of the Lasso tools take a look at the Lasso Options palette or the Polygon Lasso Options palette. As usual, you can open the palette by double-clicking on the tool or by pressing ENTER after selecting the tool. Note that the Lasso Options palette and the Polygon Lasso Options palette are the same.

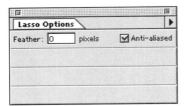 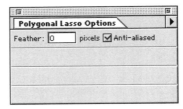

 The Anti-Aliased check box is selected by default. Leave it selected, because this option softens the hard edges of pixels by partially selecting them. This will cause selection edges to appear less jagged when filled with a color. (Review Chapter 2 for a discussion of pixels.)

 The Feather Radius option provides a means of softening the inside and outside edges of a selection. The value that you type here determines the width in pixels of the feathered edge. You won't use feathering in this exercise, but you will later in this chapter when you create a vignette. If this value is not currently set to 0, type **0** in the field now.

 NOTE: *In order to complete the next group of exercises, you will need a new document open on screen. Create a new file, 7 by 5 inches, to give you sufficient room to practice with these tools. You can set the background Contents to either White or Transparent.*

Creating Freeform Shapes with the Lasso

In this section, you'll try your hand with the Lasso tool by creating a freeform, kidney-shaped selection.

1. With the Lasso tool active, move the pointer into the middle of the document window. As you move the mouse, the pointer changes to a Lasso icon. Position the Lasso in the upper-left corner of the screen.

 NOTE: *If you press the CAPS LOCK key, the mouse pointer will turn into a crosshair. The crosshair is provided as an alternative to the Lasso pointer, because it allows you to select more precisely. The crosshair will also appear if the Tool Cursors setting for Other Tools is set to Precise in the General Preferences dialog box.*

2. To create the kidney shape, click and drag as shown in Figure 4-17. As you drag the mouse, be careful not to release the mouse button. If you do, the Lasso tool will finalize the selection by connecting the starting and ending points. If this happens, click outside the selection to deselect it and start over again.

3. When you've completed the kidney shape, release the mouse button.

Tracing with the Magnetic Lasso Tool

 The Magnetic Lasso tool is a true time saver. It helps you create intricate selections by automatically snapping to image edges that you trace over. Before you try out the tool, load an image that includes an area that you wish to select. Then activate the Magnetic Lasso tool in the Toolbox, by clicking and dragging to it or by pressing SHIFT-L until the Magnetic Lasso tool is selected.

After you select the Magnetic Lasso tool, press ENTER to view the options in the Lasso Options palette. As you'll see from the choices, the Magnetic Lasso tool

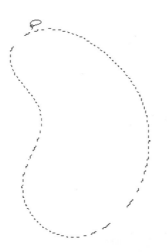

FIGURE 4-17   Creating a freeform selection with the Lasso tool

is the most sophisticated of the Lasso tools. Here is a description of the different tool options that are specific to the Magnetic Lasso.

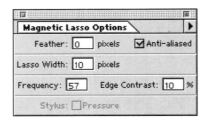

☐ **Lasso Width**   Controls image edge detection. The Magnetic Lasso tool uses the value in the Lasso Width field to determine how far from the point to look for image edges. When the value is set to 10 pixels (the default setting), the Magnetic Lasso tool detects image edges up to 10 pixels away. If you are trying to trace over an image that includes twists and turns, you'll probably want to lower the value. Acceptable values are between 1 and 40 pixels.

 NOTE: *Stylus users should click the Stylus Pressure option in the dialog box. Adding pressure to the stylus decreases Pen Width.*

☐ **Frequency**   Controls how fast the Magnetic Lasso tool adds fastening points. Higher values drop fastening points faster. Enter values between 1 and 100%.

☐ **Edge Contrast**   Controls how the Magnetic Lasso tool reacts to different contrast values along image edges. Enter higher values to have the Magnetic Lasso tool recognize edges that contain more contrast. Enter lower percentage values to detect lower contrast.

 TIP: *When selecting high contrast images, choose a large Lasso Width and large Edge Contrast. For images that don't display much contrast along image edges, choose a smaller width and lower contrast.*

To trace an image with the Magnetic Pen tool, start by clicking to establish a magnetic point, then move the Magnetic pen along the edge of the object (you don't need to keep the mouse button clicked). The Magnetic Lasso starts creating a selection based upon the image's edge contrast and the tool's settings in its

Options palette. If the selection jumps off the edge you are tracing, simply click the mouse to establish another fastening point segment, then continue to move the mouse along the object. If you wish to delete the previous segment, simply press DELETE.

To end the selection created with the Magnetic Lasso tool, double-click or press RETURN (Windows users: ENTER). If you wish to close the selection with a straight segment, press and hold OPTION (Windows users: ALT) while you double-click.

 TIP: *To temporarily activate the Lasso tool while using the Magnetic Lasso tool, press OPTION (Windows users: ALT) while you click and drag. To temporarily activate the Polygon Lasso tool while using the Magnetic Lasso tool, press OPTION (Windows users: alt) and click.*

Figure 4-18 show an image being selected with the Magnetic Lasso tool. Figure 4-19 shows the image after we selected it and placed it into another background.

FIGURE 4-18   Magnetic Lasso tool selecting image

Photoshop 5 In Action

Artist: Larry Hamill   **Client: Stock image**

To create this revealing image, artist/photographer, Larry Hamill, photographed a wall with paint peeling off of it. Larry then scanned the photograph into Photoshop. He applied the Image | Adjust | Levels command to help increase the contrast of the wall.

Next, Larry used the Lasso tool to make a selection on top of the wall, in the torn paint section. Larry then pasted several images of circuits into the selection. Larry then rotated the circuits 90 degrees counter clockwise and enlarged them. Next he applied, Photoshop's Spherize filter (Filter | Disort | Spherize) to the circuits.

To complete the image, Larry scanned several old engravings and pasted them on top of the wall in another layer. He applied the Darken mode on the engravings so that only the black area and not the white area would show through.

FIGURE 4-19   Selected area after being placed in new image

Constraining the Lasso Selection Using the Polygon Lasso Tool

The Polygon Lasso tool allows you to create polygons by clicking at different points on the screen. As you click, the Lasso connects the points with selection lines. (You can also make the Lasso work in this mode; press OPTION (Windows users: ALT) while you use the Lasso tool.)

 NOTE: *When working with the Polygon Lasso tool, it's often a good idea to use the crosshair pointer to make more accurate selections.*

Try out the Lasso's constraining option by creating a simple triangle.

1. Activate the Polygon Lasso tool.

 NOTE: *Instead of using the Polygon Lasso tool, you can use the Lasso tool and press CAPS LOCK to activate the crosshair pointer. Press OPTION (Windows users: ALT) to constrain your selection. Keep OPTION (Windows users: ALT) pressed as you create the triangle.*

2. Move the crosshair down to about 1 inch from the top side of your file and 4 inches to the right of the left edge. Click the mouse button. Next, move the pointer diagonally, about 2 inches to the right and about 3 inches down. Click again.

   You now have a straight line connecting your first and second mouse clicks.

 NOTE: *To delete a segment created with the Polygon Lasso tool, press DELETE.*

3. Move the mouse horizontally to the left about 4 inches and click. Now return to your original starting point. When you see a small circle appear next to the Polygon Lasso tool icon, your ending and starting points have met. Click to close the selection. Your screen will look like Figure 4-20.

 TIP: *If you wish to end a selection created with the Polygon Lasso tool without returning to the selection's starting point, double-click, or COMMAND-click (Windows users: CTRL-click).*

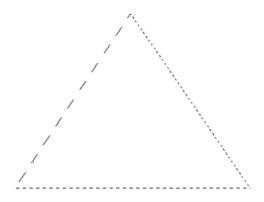

FIGURE 4-20   Constraining a selection with the Polygon Lasso tool

TIP: *To temporarily activate the Lasso while using the Magnetic Lasso tool, press OPTION (Windows users: ALT) while you click and drag.*

Don't deselect yet, because you'll need to use this triangular selection in the next exercise, in which you'll start working with the Magic Wand.

Introductory Exercises: Using the Magic Wand Tool and Various Select Commands

In order to complete the next group of exercises, you'll need a new document open on screen. If you don't have a document open from the previous section, create a new file, 7 by 5 inches, to give you sufficient room to practice with the Magic Wand. You can set the background Contents to either White or Transparent.

In order to see the Wand's color-selecting capabilities in action, you'll need to fill a triangular selection (the one you just created in the preceding section) with a color. If you don't have a triangular selection onscreen, use the Polygon Lasso tool to create one.

If the Color palette is not on screen, open it by choosing Show Color from the Window menu. Change the foreground color to orange by clicking on an orange area in the color bar in the Color palette. Fill the selection by pressing OPTION-DELETE (Windows users: ALT-DELETE). Click away from the object to deselect, and release CAPS LOCK.

Use the Marquee tool's Elliptical Shape option to create a circle in the middle of the triangle. Set the style to Normal in the Marquee Options palette, if necessary. Change the foreground color to yellow, and fill the circle with yellow.

You now have two shapes and two colors with which to test the Magic Wand tool's powers.

Using the Magic Wand

 Of all Photoshop's selecting tools, the Magic Wand is usually considered the most powerful, because it can create selections that would be nearly impossible to reproduce by hand. This tool works by selecting a color range with one click of the mouse. It is normally used to select areas according to similarity of color.

Before you begin to use the Wand, examine the Magic Wand Options palette. Open it in the usual way, by double-clicking on the Magic Wand in the Toolbox. If the Options palette is already open, you can click on the Wand in the Toolbox instead, or press W on your keyboard.

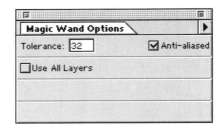

☐ Notice that Anti-Aliased is also an option in the Wand's dialog box. It functions exactly as it does in the Type and Lasso Options dialog boxes.

☐ The value you see in the Tolerance field controls the color range that the Wand will select. The greater the Tolerance setting, the broader the color range. The smallest value you can enter is 0; the largest is 255. The default value is 32. If the Wand's Tolerance is set to 0, it selects an area of contiguous pixels that are only the same color as the pixel that you click on. If you increase the Tolerance setting, the Wand expands the selection to include a greater range of color, using the color you clicked on as its starting point. A very high Tolerance setting creates a selection over a color range that can vary greatly from the color originally clicked on.

☐ If Select All Layers is chosen, the Magic Wand tool analyzes not only the pixels you click on but the pixels in all visible layers. For more information about layers, see Chapters 15 and 16.

Change the Tolerance setting in the Magic Wand Options palette so you can begin testing the Wand. For this exercise, you should have the yellow circle and orange triangle from the previous exercise on screen. If you don't, create an orange triangle, then create a yellow circle over it.

1. In the Tolerance field, type **0**.

2. Point to the yellow circle you just created. Notice that the mouse pointer changes to a wand icon when you move it over the document area. (If the mouse pointer is a crosshair and not a wand icon, CAPS LOCK is on.)

3. Click on the circle. The Wand selects only the circle. Click on the triangle and the Wand selects only the orange area of the triangle. Since the Tolerance value is set to 0, in both cases the Wand only selects one color.

4. Now change the Tolerance setting in the Magic Wand Options palette to see how it affects the selection. Type **255** in the Tolerance field.

5. Click again on the yellow circle. This time the Wand selects both the circle and triangle because the high Tolerance setting allowed more colors to slip into the selection.

Even with this less-than-intricate selection, the Wand still proves to be a time-saver: If you had to reselect the triangular selection on screen, you'd have to use the Lasso tool to click precisely over your original mouse clicks.

 NOTE: *The Select menu's Color Range command provides another means of creating a selection based on color. This advanced selection command is covered in Chapter 14.*

Using the Layer | Matting Commands

When using the Magic Wand, you might encounter a mysterious halo of color that seems to tag along with your image. When you select an area with the Magic Wand, the Lasso, or the Elliptical Marquee, Photoshop may include extra colored pixels along the edges of the selection; these can become noticeable when a selection is pasted or moved. It is especially apparent when a light image is moved onto a dark background or a dark image is moved onto a light background. The extra colored pixels are often the result of Photoshop's Anti-Aliasing feature, which partially blurs fringe pixels. In that process, extra pixels around the perimeter are added to the selection. Photoshop's Layer | Matting command allows you to remove the unwanted pixels.

DEFRINGING A PASTED IMAGE   With the Layer | Matting | Defringe command, you can remove the unwanted color from fringe pixels. The Defringe command replaces the colors on the fringes of a selection with a color that is closest to the fringe from within the selection. In order for the Defringe command to be accessible, the area you want to defringe should be in a selection that you've moved or in layer with a transparent background. When you select Defringe, a dialog box appears, allowing you to specify the pixel width of the fringe area to be colored. The following illustration (a) shows an image (courtesy of Stacy Kollar photography) that was copied and pasted without Defringe. Illustration (b) shows the same image after the Defringe command was applied.

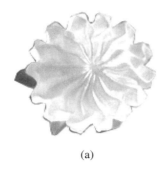   

(a)   (b)

If you wish to try out the Defringe command, open any file. Activate the Magic Wand tool and set the Tolerance in the Wand Options palette. Make sure the Anti-Aliased check box is selected. Click on an object in your file to select it. Now, copy and paste the object into a new file with a white background. Zoom in, and you'll most likely see a thin border of darker or lighter pixels lining the image edges. To remove these pixels, choose Defringe from the Layer | Matting submenu. In the Defringe dialog box, enter **3** as the Pixel Width. After you click OK, the colored fringe will be gone.

   TIP: *Select | Modify | Contract can also be useful when trying to remove fringe pixels from a selection.*

USING BLACK-AND-WHITE MATTE   If you select an image in a black background, choose Black Matte from the Layer | Matting submenu to remove extraneous black fringe pixels. If you select an image in a white background, choose White Matte from the Layer | Matting submenu to remove the extraneous white fringe pixels.

If you'd like to experiment more with the Magic Wand, try filling various selections with different colors and then testing the Wand's selections. When you're finished, proceed to the next section, where you'll learn several very helpful selection tips for all of the program's selection tools.

Adding to and Subtracting from Selections

Even though you've learned to use all of Photoshop's selection tools, your selection knowledge won't be complete until you know how to change your selections by adding to them, subtracting from them, and intersecting them.

If you've used other Mac or Windows programs, you can probably guess that you add to a selection by SHIFT-clicking. Just hold down the SHIFT key when you make a new selection, and Photoshop adds to a previous selection. However, unlike many Mac and Windows programs, you cannot subtract from a selection by pressing SHIFT and clicking on a selection.

Suppose you want to remove part of a selection but leave other areas selected. To subtract from a selection, press and hold OPTION (Windows users: ALT) while you click and drag over or within the selection.

Try removing a corner from a rectangular selection using the Lasso tool. First, create a rectangular selection on screen. Then activate the Lasso tool. While holding down OPTION (Windows users: ALT), click and drag to create a curved selection over any corner of the rectangle on screen. When you release the mouse, the corner is subtracted from the selection.

You can also create a selection that is the intersection of two selections. To try this, press both OPTION and SHIFT (Windows users: ALT and SHIFT) and then click and drag to make a selection that overlaps the rectangular selection on screen. Fill with the foreground color, and you'll see that Photoshop paints the intersection— that is, only the common areas of the two selections.

Using Select | Grow and Select | Similar

The Select menu includes two commands that can help when you are selecting with the Magic Wand. Execute the Select | Grow command, and the selection on screen will expand as if you had doubled the Tolerance range in the Wand's dialog box. Execute the Select | Similar command, and the selection will jump over areas beyond the Wand's tolerance to select areas that fit within its tolerance. For instance, if an image contained a black bridge over a river, which prevented the Wand from selecting the entire river, the Select | Similar command would cause the selection to jump over the bridge and select the rest of the water.

Expanding and Contracting a Selection

The Select menu has two other commands that can help you manage selections. The Select | Modify | Expand and Select | Modify | Contract commands allow you to make a selection grow or shrink by a specified number of pixels. As with Select | Grow and Select | Similar, these commands are used after a selection is created. For instance, if you have selected an area and wish to expand it by one pixel, choose Select | Modify | Expand. The Expand Selection dialog box opens. Enter **1** in the Pixel field. After you click OK, the selection will grow one pixel outward.

To shrink a selection by one pixel, choose Select | Modify | Contract. The Contract Selection dialog box opens. Enter **1** in the Pixel field. After you click OK, the selection will decrease one pixel inward.

Photoshop 5   In Action

To create this luminous image, Dallas photographer JW Burkey, started by photographing a background that consisted of two backdrops, one with a painted checkerboard paper floor and the other with a marbleized background. JW also photographed a lightbulb glued to a rod so that it appeared floating in space. The lightbulb was soldered with electrical wires so that JW could shoot it illuminated.

After digitizing the Photograph into Photoshop, he created the glow around the bulb by first selecting it and then saving the selection into a new channel. He then created a new layer, loaded the lightbulb and used Select | Modify | Expand command to expand the selection. He saved this selection to another alpha channel. In the alpha channel, JW applied the Gaussian Blur filter using a large pixel radius. He loaded the alpha channel as a selection (now changed by blurring the alpha channel), then he filled it with an orange/yellow color. All in all, JW used three layers: one for the background, one for the glow, and another one for the lightbulb.

Artist: JW Burkey   **Client: Image Bank**

To complete the image, JW used Photoshop's Image | Adjust commands to color correct the bulb and its glow.

TIP: *Both Expand and Contract can be especially helpful when removing extraneous pixels that get selected or aren't selected because of anti-aliasing. For instance, you might use Select | Modify | Contract to remove extra pixels when selecting with the Magic Wand tool. Select | Modify | Expand can be useful to slightly selection created by COMMAND (Windows users: CTRL) clicking in a layer in the Layers palette to select the nontransparent areas of the layer.*

4

Using Select | Modify | Border and Smooth

The Border command is another Select | Modify menu option that changes a selection. Select | Modify | Border replaces a selection with a border selection surrounding the area of the original selection. The size of the border is specified in the Border dialog box. If you wish to see the Border command in action, create any selection, then choose Select | Modify | Border. In the Border dialog box, enter a pixel width for the border, then click OK. Fill the new selection with a color. You'll see that the border around the selection is filled, not the original selection.

The Smooth command also alters selections by adding to or deleting from the original selection. Like Expand, Contract, and Border, Smooth allows you to type in a pixel value to control the effect. The Smooth command, however, uses the pixel value as a radius. For instance, when you type in a pixel value of 8, Photoshop radiates out from a central location, evaluating 8 pixels in each direction. Thus, the actual distance examined for smoothing is 16 pixels. The Smooth command evaluates whether most of the pixels in the radius area are selected; if they are, it selects the unselected pixels. If most of the pixels in the radius area are not selected, it deselects the selected pixels.

The Smooth command can be helpful when you are trying to combine selections, blend a selection into its surroundings, or smooth the sharp edges of a selection.

To try out the Smooth command, create a star-shaped selection with the Lasso tool or the Polygon Lasso tool. Connect the points of the star by clicking and moving the mouse. Once you've created the star, execute Select | Modify | Smooth. Enter **5** pixels in the dialog box, then click OK. The edges of your star will be smoothed.

For a more dramatic look at the Smooth command, create a rectangular selection. Press SHIFT and create two other rectangular selections directly above the first, about a quarter of an inch apart. Execute the Smooth command with a high pixel value. The Smooth command will join all three selections into one selection.

In the next section, you may need to add to or subtract from a selection when you use the Magic Wand to create the background landscape in the truck collage.

Finishing the Truck Collage

Now that you've been introduced to the Lasso and the Magic Wand and you know how to add to and subtract from selections, you can create a landscape for the background of the truck collage. You'll use both the Lasso and the Magic Wand to select areas in a scanned image and fill them with colors to convert the photograph of a landscape to colored line art.

Creating the Landscape for the Truck

In order to create the landscape, open any suitable image that provides shapes and colors that you can select. For this example, a scanned image of the Rocky Mountains was used. Once the image is on screen, you'll want to zoom in to your work area. This will make it easier to select intricate areas when you use the Lasso tool. Press COMMAND-+ (Windows users: CTRL-+) to magnify your work area.

 REMEMBER: *You can use the Navigator palette to zoom in and out.*

Once you've selected an area, fill it with a color. Try experimenting with different selection tools and filling the areas with different colors. Our completed landscape is shown in Figure 4-21.

Creating the Highway

Before you paste the truck created earlier in this chapter into its setting, create a highway for it. The easiest way to create the highway is to use the Single Row Marquee tool, which creates a 1-pixel-wide selection the entire width of the document window. (Single Column creates a 1-pixel-wide selection the entire height of the document window.) You'll stroke the selection with gray to pave this roadway with color.

1. In the Toolbox, select the Single Row Marquee tool from the Style pop-up menu.

2. Create a selection by positioning the crosshair just above the bottom of the document window and clicking the mouse. A 1-pixel-wide horizontal selection appears.

3. Next, select a black or gray foreground color.

FIGURE 4-21 The completed landscape

4. Stroke the selection by choosing Stroke from the Edit menu. In the Width field box, type **4**, choose the Center option in the Location group, keep Opacity at 100%, and leave Mode set to Normal. Make sure the Preserve Transparency option is not selected. Click OK, and then save your work.

Once you've created the highway, you're finished with the landscape portion of the collage. Now it's time to tie it all together by pasting the truck into the landscape.

Placing the Truck in the Landscape

Before you can add the truck to the landscape, you need to reopen both the Truck and Landscape files. If you had created the truck on a white background, you'd now be faced with a problem: How do you select the truck so it can be copied into the file containing the landscape? Luckily, since you created the truck on a transparent background, you can easily use the Move tool to drag and drop it into the Landscape file without selecting.

Before doing this, consider how you would have solved the problem of selecting the truck if it had been on a white background: Using the Magic Wand, you would first select the white area that surrounds the truck. Next, you would execute the Select | Inverse command. This would change the selection so that everything except the white area would be selected. On screen, only the truck would be surrounded by the blinking marquee. Then, you could copy and paste it into the Landscape file. Once in the Landscape file, you might need to remove extraneous white pixels with the Layer | Matting | Defringe command.

Here are the steps for dragging and dropping the truck into the Landscape file.

1. Open the Truck file.

2. Open the Landscape file.

3. When both files are on screen, make sure that you can see them. Either position them side by side or so that they overlap with the Truck file on top of the Landscape file.

 TIP: *You can also select all nontransparent areas of a layer by pressing COMMAND (Windows users: CTRL) and clicking on the layer name in the Layers palette.*

4. Instead of copying and pasting the truck, use a shortcut: Drag the truck and drop it over the Landscape file. Select the Move tool and position the mouse pointer over the truck. Click and hold the mouse button. Next, drag the truck over the Landscape file. The pointer will change to a tiny grabbing hand. When you see a black border surrounding the Landscape file, release the mouse. The truck is now in the Landscape file. Notice that you can now see through the transparent window of the truck.

   To understand exactly what happened when you moved the truck, examine the Layers palette. If the Layers palette isn't open, open it by choosing Show Layers from the Window menu. Notice that Photoshop created a new layer in the Landscape file. The Background of the file is the landscape, and Layer 1 is the truck. Also notice that the area surrounding Layer 1 is gray or colored. This means that this is the selected, or target, layer. The target layer is the layer being edited. There is no gray area surrounding the Background section of the Layers palette, meaning that if you make any changes to the file now, only the Truck layer will be affected. The paintbrush icon next to the truck also means that it is the only layer that can currently be edited. The eye icons next to the truck and the background mean that both Layer 1 and the Background are visible.

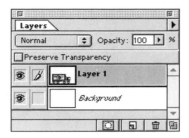

5. Because the truck is still in a layer, you can reposition it with the Move tool. Use the Move tool now to position the truck as shown in Figure 4-16.

Before you save your file, notice that the memory indicator in the lower-left corner of the screen shows two different numbers. The number on the right indicates that the memory size of the file has grown because of the new layer. When you save the file, you can flatten it to conserve memory. This will not change the image in the file, but it will merge all the layers into the Background.

6. To flatten the file when you save it, choose Save a Copy from the File menu. Select the Flatten Layers check box, then name the file **Truck Collage**. If you wish to save the file with the Layer, you must save it in Photoshop format. You can use the standard File | Save As command to save the file under a new name so that the Landscape file remains intact, or you can use File | Save a Copy without flattening the file.

That's it. You have successfully created a truck and a landscape and placed the two together in a collage.

 NOTE: *When creating collages, you may wish to create all objects in separate layers so that you can view them together, yet move and edit each layer independently. Be aware that each layer you create will increase the file size. If you wish to learn more about layers, see Chapters 15 and 16.*

Creating the Gondola Flyer and the Kids Collage

The gondola flyer collage shown in Figure 4-22(a) was assembled primarily by using the Lasso selection tool. To create the image in Figure 4-22(a), we scanned a

(a)   (b)

FIGURE 4-22   (a) Gondola flyer; (b) the gondola image used to create the flyer in
Figure 4-21 (a)

photograph of two gondolas [Figure 4-22(b)]. Next, we selected the gondolas with
the Lasso Polygon tool (the selection is seen in Figure 4-23), copied them, and
pasted them into a new document (after filling the new document with yellow and
applying the Noise filter to it to give the background some texture). Note that
Photoshop automatically placed the gondolas into a new layer in the new
document. To complete the flyer, we used the Type tool to add text.

The Kids collage shown in Figure 4-24(a) was assembled primarily by using
the Magic Wand selection tool. To create the image in Figure 4-24(a), we scanned
a photograph of a statue of some kids [Figure 4-24(b)] and another one of a
building with a window [Figure 4-24(c)] at the same resolution. Next, we selected
the kids with the Magic Wand tool (the selection is seen in Figure 4-25). In order
to get both kids selected, we needed to adjust the Tolerance value in the Magic

4

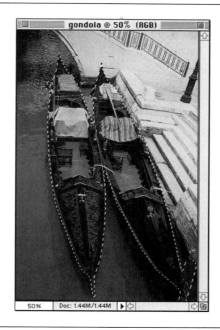

FIGURE 4-23   The Lasso tool was used to create the selection

Wand Options palette a few times until we got the right value. We also needed to add to and subtract from the selection to get the right selection.

After we had the selection we wanted, we copied the kids and pasted them into the selection of the window (which we created with the Magic Wand tool) in the building document. Note that Photoshop automatically placed the kids image into a new layer with a transparent background in the building document.

Feathering the Edges of a Selection

The last selection tool exercise shows you how to create a vignette using the Feather option, which is available for the Marquee and Lasso tools.

To take a look at how the Feather option works, start by creating a new file, 5 by 5 inches, to use as a practice document. Click on the Default Colors icon to reset the foreground and background colors.

(a)

(b)

(c)

FIGURE 4-24 (a) The kids collage; (b) the kids image used to create the collage in (a); (c) the window image used to create the collage in (a)

FIGURE 4-25   The Magic Wand tool was used to create the selection

Let's start with the Marquee Tool's Feather option with the Shape pop-up menu set to Rectangular; this will allow you to soften the edges of a rectangle. The value that you type in the Feather field determines the width of the feather edge. This value defaults to 0 pixels; the maximum value allowed is 250. Since the feather edge extends both inside and outside the selection, the actual feather will be twice the pixel value.

Activate the Rectangular Marquee tool, and open the tool's Options palette and set the Style pop-up menu to Normal. In the Feather field, type **15**. This value will give you a Feather edge of 30 pixels. Now, click and drag to make a rectangle. Press OPTION-DELETE (Windows users: ALT-BACKSPACE) to fill the rectangle with the foreground color. The feathered rectangle will look like this:

Photoshop 5 · In Action

Artist: Josh Gosfield　　　**A Time Warner Annual Report**

Josh first created the background of the image by scanning a photo he took of a television screen with interference. Once the photo was scanned, different areas were selected with the Magic Wand tool and then painted with the Edit/Fill command.

After the background was completed, Josh scanned various images and selected them using the Lasso tool with different Feather settings. This created a soft-edged effect when he pasted them into the final image.

Notice what has happened: The edges in the object have been softened across 30 pixels; the feathering begins 15 pixels within the selection and extends 15 pixels beyond the selection. The outer edges of the black rectangle have a gradient effect—they start out black and then turn gray, until they blend into the white background. This effect, called a *vignette*, is also sometimes called a *halo* or *glow*.

Creating a Vignette

The Feather option for the Elliptical Marquee tool was used to create the vignette shown in Figure 4-26. If you wish to try creating this type of special effect, start by opening an image on your screen.

First select the Elliptical Marquee tool in the Toolbox palette. Press ENTER to open the Marquee Options palette. In the palette leave the Style set to Normal, and set the Feather field to 10.

 NOTE: *Depending upon the resolution and dimensions of your image, you may wish to experiment with different Feather values.*

FIGURE 4-26   Creating a vignette

1. Click and drag to create an ellipse surrounding the area where you want to add the vignette effect. (The vignette will not appear until after you copy and paste the selection.)

2. From the Edit menu, choose Copy.

3. Create a new file in which you will paste your selection. From the File menu, choose New, and change the Width and Height settings to make them larger, if desired. Click OK.

4. From the Edit menu, choose Paste. The image is pasted into a new layer with the feathering effect that creates the vignette.

The vignette exercise is the last of the selection tool design projects in this chapter. However, we've included one more simple exercise that illustrates how selections can be used to create special effects. This exercise uses the Select | Modify | Border command, which changes the blinking marquee so that it borders the original selection. Also used in this exercise is the Select | Feather command, which feathers, or blurs, the edge of a selection. Select | Feather works just like the Feather option in the Lasso Options palette and the Marquee Options palette.

Creating Glowing Text

In this exercise, you will learn how to create a glowing, or backlit, effect for text by copying, pasting, and using the Select menu's Modify | Border and Feather commands. The Border and Feather commands control the width and intensity of the glow.

Although this example creates a glowing background for text, you can produce the same effect on any kind of selection. Here are the steps:

1. Create a new file, 6 inches by 4 inches, in RGB mode at 72 ppi. Set the background Contents to either Transparent or White.

2. You're going to create yellow text with a red glow, and you'll create the text first. Change the foreground color to yellow and the background color to white.

3. Activate the Type Mask tool.

4. Click on the center of your document. When the Type Tool dialog box appears, type **GLOW** in the text box. Set the font to Helvetica (Windows users: Arial). Enter **120** in the Size field. Then select the text and type **-10** in the Tracking field (tracking increases or decreases the spacing between letters). In the Style group, choose Bold and turn on the Anti-Aliased option. Click OK to place the text in your document.

5. Once the text selection is on screen, move it into the center of the document window by clicking inside the text selection and dragging it (using the Type Mask tool). Do not deselect.

6. Fill the text selection with the Foreground color by pressing OPTION-DELETE (Windows users: ALT-BACKSPACE).

7. Next, you will place the text into the Clipboard so that it can be copied back into the image after you have bordered, feathered, and filled it. From the Edit menu, choose Copy, and keep the text selected.

8. Now place a border selection around each letter of the text. From the Select menu choose Modify | Border, type **20** in the Width field, and click OK.

9. To soften the edges of the newly created border, choose Feather from the Select menu. Type **6** and click OK. The 20-pixel border now has a 6-pixel feather beyond its edges. (The Feather command feathers 6 pixels within the selection and six pixels beyond the selection.)

10. Now fill the selection on screen with the foreground color (red) to start creating the glow effect. Change the Foreground color to red, then choose Fill from the Edit menu. In the Fill dialog box, make sure Foreground Color is set in the Use pop-up menu, the Opacity is 100%, and Mode is Normal. Click OK. You will see the soft edges of the feathered border.

11. To make the text sharper and more readable, paste the text from the Clipboard back onto the soft-edged glow. To do this, select Paste from the Edit menu. When you paste, the yellow text in the Clipboard returns to the screen. Notice that a new layer was created when you executed the paste command.

 NOTE: *The Layer | Effects submenu includes commands for creating Inner and Outer Glow effects. Layer| Effects commands are covered in Chapter 17.*

If you'd like, you can use one or more of Photoshop's filters to create a more dramatic effect. Here we applied the Spherize filter after flattening the file. (For more information about filters, see Chapters 10 and 11.)

Conclusion

If you have read through and completed all the exercises in this chapter, you are now prepared to move on to more advanced topics, particularly those involving the use of color in your Photoshop work. The next chapter lays the groundwork for painting and image editing by covering the fundamentals of color theory. It also provides a thorough discussion of how to use the colors in the Color and Swatches palettes and explains the differences between RGB and CMYK colors.

CHAPTER 5

Understanding Color Theory

Color evokes a mood; it creates contrast and enhances the beauty in an image. It can make a dull scene vibrant and a tired image suddenly sparkle with life. The right colors can turn a lackluster Web site into a sparkling port of call.

To the graphic designer, painter, artist, or video producer, creating the perfect color is essential. When the colors aren't correct, the concept isn't complete; the image may fail to convey its information and the artistic experience may be lost. If the rich green that should radiate from a forest setting is too yellow and sickly, the magnificence of nature is not portrayed, and the "healthy" feeling of the great outdoors is lost. If the forest's reds that should glow with fire and vibrancy turn dull, a sense of decay and rust is conveyed, rather than excitement.

Producing the perfect color is no easy task. A painter must mix and re-mix paint, blending to get the perfect shades to match images seen or imagined. Photographers and filmmakers must spend hours testing, re-focusing, and adding lights until the proper scene is created. In many respects, working with color on the computer is no different. The computer creates its own set of special complications and technical difficulties. How can you ensure that the colors you see on your screen match the colors of nature or your artistic vision? And then how do you get the same colors you see on screen to appear in your printed image?

Producing the right colors in Photoshop requires a knowledge of color theory. Once you understand the basics of color theory, you'll begin to recognize the color terminology used throughout Photoshop's dialog boxes, menus, and palettes. You'll also understand the process of adding and subtracting colors when you're doing color correcting. With a knowledge of color theory, you'll know how to paint the sky a richer, fuller blue. You'll be able to pick colors so that the same luscious emerald green you create in Photoshop appears in the forest on your printed page.

To be successful in choosing the right colors in Photoshop, you must first understand color models. Color models were created to provide a way of translating colors into numerical data so that they can be described consistently in various media. For instance, referring to a color as "greenish-blue" leaves it open to interpretation based largely on personal human perception. On the other hand, assigning that color specific values in a color model—in the CMYK model it would be 100% cyan, 3% magenta, 30% yellow, and 15% black—makes it possible to reproduce that color the same way, again and again.

As you use Photoshop's color features, you'll work with several different color models: RGB, CMYK, HSB, and Lab. The RGB and CMYK color models are a constant reminder that the colors of nature, the colors on your monitor, and colors on the printed page are created in completely different ways. Your monitor creates colors by emitting red, green, and blue beams of light; it uses the RGB (red/green/blue) color model. To reproduce the continuous-tone effect of color photographs, printing technology uses a combination of cyan, magenta, yellow, and black inks that reflect and absorb various wavelengths of light. Colors created by overprinting these four colors are part of the CMYK (cyan/magenta/yellow/black) color model. The HSB (hue/saturation/brightness) color model provides an intuitive way to translate the colors of nature to the colors your computer creates, because it is based on the way humans perceive colors. The Lab color model provides a means for creating "device-independent" color, meaning that no matter whether the color is output to a monitor or printer or created on a scanner, the colors should be consistent.

5

What Is Color?

Color exists because of three entities: light, the object being viewed, and the viewer. Physicists have proven that white light is composed of wavelengths of red, green, and blue. The human eye perceives color as various wavelengths of red, green, and blue that are absorbed or reflected by objects. For example, assume you are at a picnic on a sunny day, ready to reach for a red apple. Sunlight shines on the apple, and the red wavelength of light is reflected off the apple back to your eyes. The wavelengths of blue and green are absorbed into the apple, as shown in Figure 5-1. Sensors in your eye react to the reflected light, sending a message that is interpreted by your brain as the color red.

Your perception of the red color depends on the apple, the light, and you. One apple will absorb more green and blue than another, and thus its color will appear redder. If clouds cover the sun, the apple's red will appear darker. Your interpretation of the apple will also be affected by your own physiology, by your experience as an apple eater, or by the fact that you haven't eaten all day.

The red, green, and blue wavelengths that allow you to see the apple are the basis for all colors in nature. That is why red, green, and blue are often called the primary colors of light. All colors of the spectrum are created by different intensities of these wavelengths of light. Figure 5-2 (reproduced on the "Color Theory" page in the color insert in this book) is a simple example of how different colors can be created with the primary red, green, and blue wavelengths. When the three primary

FIGURE 5-1 The apple absorbs the green and blue wavelengths; the red wavelength is reflected back to the eye

colors overlap, they create the secondary colors: cyan, magenta, and yellow. The primary and secondary colors are complements of one another. Complementary colors are colors that are most unlike each other. In Figure 5-2 you can see that

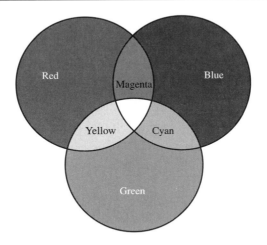

FIGURE 5-2 The primary (additive) colors and their complements. When all three primary colors are mixed together, they create white

yellow is made up of red and green. Blue is the missing primary color; therefore, blue and yellow are complements. The complement of green is magenta, and the complement of red is cyan. This explains why you see other colors besides red, green, and blue. In a sunflower, you see yellow because red and green wavelengths of light are reflected back to you, while the blue is absorbed by the plant.

Figure 5-2 also shows that all primary colors combine to create white. You might think that adding these colors together would produce a darker color, but remember that you are adding light. When light wavelengths are added together, you get lighter colors. This is why the primary colors are often called "additive colors." By adding all of the colors of light together, you obtain the lightest light: white light. Thus, when you see a white piece of paper, all of the red, green, and blue wavelengths of light are being reflected back to you. When you see black, all of the red, green, and blue wavelengths of light are being completely absorbed by the object; thus, no light is reflected back to you.

The RGB Color Model

The system of creating colors on your monitor is based on the same fundamental properties of light that occur in nature: that colors can be created from red, green, and blue. This is the basis of the RGB color model.

Your color monitor creates colors by emitting three light beams at different intensities, lighting up red, green, and blue phosphorescent material overlaying the inside of your monitor's screen. When you see red in Photoshop, your monitor has turned on its red beam, which excites red phosphors, lighting up a red pixel on your screen. Thus, seeing a scanned image of an apple on screen is different from seeing the apple that sits on top of your computer, waiting to be eaten. If you turn off the lights in your room, you won't see your red snack; but you'll still see the scanned apple, because light is being emitted from your monitor.

When you use Photoshop's RGB color picker, pixel colors can be changed by combining various values of red, green, and blue. Each of these three primary colors has a range of values from 0 to 255. When you combine the 256 possible values of red, 256 values of green, and 256 values of blue, the total number of possible colors is approximately 16.7 million ($256 \times 256 \times 256$). This may seem like a lot of colors, but remember that these are only a portion of the visible colors in nature. Nevertheless, 16.7 million colors is sufficient to reproduce crystal-clear digitized images on a monitor connected to a computer equipped with 24-bit color.

NOTE: *Before you get started it's important to remember that different monitors display colors differently. Therefore, if you haven't already done so, run the Adobe Gamma utility to calibrate your monitor. Calibrating your monitor helps insure that colors on your monitor match printed colors, as well as colors displayed on other monitors. As discussed in Chapter 1, the Adobe Gamma utility helps adjust brightness and contrast and color balance. After calibrating your monitor, you may wish to review the color space settings in the RGB Setup dialog box. (File | Color Settings | RGB Setup). By default, Photoshop selects an RGB color space called sRGB (standard RGB). You might wish to choose an RGB color space that encompasses a wider gamut (range) of colors. See Chapter 1 for more details. After you pick an RGB color space, choose Display Using Monitor Compensation in the RGB Setup dialog box. This helps ensure that colors are displayed more accurately.*

Using RGB Colors in the Color and Swatches Palettes

In this section, you'll experiment with RGB color in the Color and Swatches palettes. You'll see how colors are created from RGB color values, and learn how to set RGB color values to mix colors. If the Color and Swatches palettes aren't open, open the Color/Swatches group now by choosing either Show Color or Show Swatches from the Window menu. Since you will need to have both palettes open at the same time when working through this section, separate the Color palette from the Color/Swatches group by clicking on the Color palette tab and dragging it away from the palette group. If the Swatches palette isn't in the palette group with the Color palette, choose Show Swatches from the Window menu.

By default, the Color palette displays the RGB color model palette, unless it was changed in a previous session. You should see three bars, called color sliders, labeled R, G, and B. If you do not see the letters R, G, and B, you are in another color model's palette. To change to the RGB palette, click on the Color palette pop-up menu arrow. A list of Photoshop's color models will appear. Select RGB Sliders from the list, and the palette with the three RGB sliders will load. Beneath each slider is a triangular-shaped slider control, as shown in the following illustration. Using the mouse, you can click and drag on the slider controls to change the values of red, green, and blue in the foreground or background color. The foreground and background colors are indicated in the selection boxes (the overlapping squares in the upper-left corner of the Color palette).

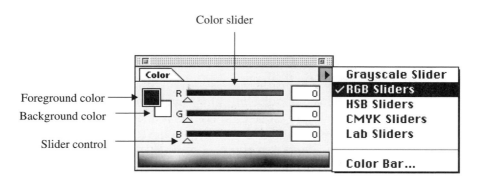

Notice that the Color palette also displays a horizontal color bar along the bottom of the palette. By default, the bar displays the spectrum, or gamut, of RGB colors. Check to see that the bar is set to the RGB spectrum by clicking on the palette's pop-up menu arrow and choosing Color Bar. The Color Bar dialog box appears.

The Style pop-up menu in the dialog box allows you to choose between RGB and CMYK color spectrum bars. You can also make the color bar display gray shades from black to white or a gradient from the foreground to background color. If the Style menu is not set to RGB Spectrum, reset it now by choosing RGB Spectrum from the list of choices.

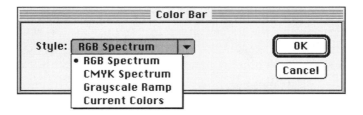

The color bar can be used to quickly pick a foreground or background color. All you have to do is click on the bar. Try clicking on it. After you click, the foreground color switches to the color you clicked on, if the Foreground selection box is selected in the Color palette. If the Background selection box is selected in the Color palette, the background color changes to the color you clicked on in the color bar. In the next section, you'll pick colors more precisely by using the Swatches palette.

TIP: *You can change background colors by pressing OPTION (Windows users: ALT) and clicking on the color bar in the Color palette.*

Using Swatches to Pick Colors

Start by clicking on the red, green, and blue color squares, or swatches, in the Swatches palette, and examine the color values of the primary colors. This will demonstrate the full range of each color component in the RGB color model. When you click on a swatch, Photoshop displays the swatch color in either the Foreground or Background selection box, as well as displaying its R, G, and B values to the right of the sliders, in the Color palette.

NOTE: *By default, Photoshop displays a range of colors in each slider in the Color palette. These colors appear because Photoshop's Dynamic Color Sliders option is activated. The Dynamic Color Sliders option allows each slider to show the range of colors available as you click and drag the slider control left or right. If the Dynamic Color Sliders option is not enabled, each slider will only show color values for red, green, or blue color components. If you need to enable the sliders, select File | Preferences | General. In the dialog box, select the Dynamic Color Sliders check box.*

In this exercise, you will only work with Photoshop's foreground color. Before you begin, make sure that the Foreground selection box (the top overlapping square to the right of the sliders in the upper left of the Color palette) is activated. If the border is not surrounding the Foreground selection box, click on that box to activate the foreground color.

To see the RGB values of the primary color red, position the mouse pointer over the red color swatch in the upper-left corner of the color swatches, in the first row. When the pointer turns into an eyedropper, click on the red swatch.

In the Color palette, notice that the R slider control jumps to the far right. The number to the right of the slider indicates the red value of the color swatch you just clicked. (If you clicked the correct shade of red, the value will be 255.) The active color in Photoshop (the foreground color) has now changed to this value of red. Take a look at the sliders for green and blue; they are both at 0, because the shade of red you clicked contains no green or blue.

To see the RGB values of the primary color green, click on the green swatch (the third from the left in the first row in the Swatches palette). The G value in the

Color palette jumps to 255, and the values of blue and red drop to 0. To see the values of the primary color blue, click on the fifth swatch from the left in the first row in the Swatches palette. Pure blue's value is 255, with no red and no green.

You can see from the foregoing color swatch tests that each primary color has a range of values from 0 to 255, to produce 256 separate color values.

 TIP: *You can change background colors by pressing OPTION (Windows users: ALT) and clicking on a swatch in the Swatches palette.*

Using Sliders to Create RGB Colors

Now that you've seen the color values of pure red, green, and blue, take a look at some colors created from the primaries. Click on any swatch in the Swatches palette, and you'll see its combination of RGB color values. Try the yellowish color, the one four rows down and four rows across. Notice the different combination of values. Click on a few of the other color swatches, and notice the combinations of the three primary colors.

The palette swatches obviously can't contain all 16.7 million colors, but by adjusting the slider controls with the mouse or by typing in values in the entry fields to the right of each slider, you can create every one of the 16.7 million colors Photoshop can display.

All three sliders work the same way. When you click and drag a slider control to the right, you are adding more color. When you drag left, you are subtracting color. With any color swatch selected, try dragging the G slider control from left to right. Notice that as you drag to the right, the green values increase, and the foreground color you are creating in the Color palette grows brighter. Now drag left; as you do, the color values decrease and the green darkens.

To create black, drag all of the slider controls to the left, setting them to 0. Watch as the foreground color in the Color palette grows darker. When all of the values reach 0, the foreground color displays black. If red, green, and blue are equal in value but are not 0 or 255, a shade of gray is created. To create white, move the slider controls in the opposite direction. By doing this you are adding light. Set each slider to its full value of 255, and you'll create white.

Using the Sliders to Display RGB Complements

If Photoshop's Dynamic Sliders option is activated in the General Preferences dialog box, you'll see a range of colors displayed in each slider when all of the

RGB sliders are set to 255 (white). The R slider displays white turning to cyan; the G slider displays white changing to magenta; and the B slider displays white changing to yellow.

Why do the sliders change colors? The designers of Photoshop are shrewdly reminding you about color theory. In each slider, you see the opposite of each primary color (its complement). The color toward the left end of each slider is showing you what happens if you subtract a primary color from white (by dragging the slider control all the way to the left). Remember the discussion earlier in the chapter of why you see yellow when you look at a sunflower? The sunflower absorbs (subtracts) the blue wavelength of light. When red and green are reflected back to you, you see yellow.

You can easily demonstrate this with the sliders. To create yellow, which is the complement of blue, drag the B slider control back to 0, and leave the R and G sliders set to 255. Thus yellow is created by subtracting blue from white. To create cyan, which is red's complement, first set all the sliders back to 255, and then drag the R slider control to 0. By subtracting the red value from the primary colors, you have created cyan. To create magenta, the complement of green, drag the R slider control back to 255 and the G slider control to 0. Magenta is created by subtracting green from the primary colors. This concept of subtracting colors is the foundation of the CMYK color model, described next.

 CAUTION: *If you save an image, close it, then change settings in the RGB Color Setup dialog box (File | Color Settings | RGB Setup) and reopen the same image; you may see that the color values in your image change on screen because you have changed RGB color spaces.*

The CMYK Color Model

The CMYK color model is based not on adding light, but on subtracting it. In the RGB model, colors are created by adding light; the monitor (or a television) is a light source that can create colors. But a printed page doesn't emit light; it absorbs and reflects light. So when you want to translate the monitor's colors to paper, another color model, CMYK, must be used. The CMYK color model is the basis for four-color process printing, which is used primarily to print continuous-tone images (such as digitized photographs) on a printing press. In four-color process printing, colors are reproduced on a printing press by using four different printing plates: C (cyan), M (magenta), Y (yellow), and K (black—black is represented by the letter K because B might also stand for blue).

Because the printed page cannot emit light, a press cannot use RGB colors to print; instead, it uses inks that can absorb specific wavelengths of light and reflect other wavelengths. By combining inks of cyan, magenta, and yellow, a commercial printer can reproduce a significant portion of the visible spectrum of colors. In theory, 100% cyan, 100% magenta, and 100% yellow should combine to produce black. However, because of the impurity of inks, the cyan, magenta, and yellow colors produce a muddy brown rather than black. Therefore, printers often add black to cyan, magenta, and yellow to produce the darker and gray portions of images. Figure 5-3 (reproduced on the "Color Theory" page in the color insert in this book) shows the secondary, or subtractive, colors overlapping to create a muddy brown. Notice that each pair of subtractive colors creates a primary color.

Using CMYK Colors in the Color Palette

To introduce you to the CMYK color model, start by switching to the CMYK color spectrum. To do this, click on the Color palette's pop-up menu arrow, and then choose Color Bar from the pop-up list. When the Color Bar dialog box opens, choose CMYK Spectrum from the Style pop-up menu. You'll probably notice that the CMYK colors are a bit duller than the RGB colors.

Now try your hand at changing colors using the CMYK sliders in the Color palette. First you'll need to switch to the CMYK color sliders by clicking on the

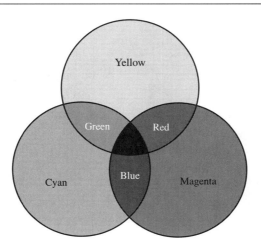

FIGURE 5-3   The secondary (subtractive) colors and their complements. When all three secondary colors are mixed together, they create a muddy brown

Color palette's pop-up menu arrow. Mac users can drag to the CMYK Sliders choice (Windows users: click on CMYK Sliders).

In the Color palette you'll also see some differences between the RGB and CMYK palettes. First, CMYK utilizes four sliders, not three. There is a slider for each subtractive color: C for cyan, M for magenta, Y for yellow, and K for black. Also, the colors are measured in percentages. The percentages provide a standard way of conveying various ink values from the design studio to the printing press.

Using CMYK percentages can be confusing, but it helps to understand that you can produce the primary colors using CMYK percentages. When you know how to produce red, green, and blue from CMYK values, you'll be better able to orient yourself when mixing or correcting colors in this color model. To aid you in creating these colors, it's helpful to have a color wheel at hand. The color wheel shown in Figure 5-4 (reproduced on the "Color Theory" page in the color insert in this book) is a simplified version of the color wheels professional color correctors use to help them add and subtract colors.

Using a Color Wheel

In a color wheel, colors are arranged in a circle to show the relationship between each color. The primary colors are positioned around the circle equidistant from one another. Each secondary color is situated between two primary colors. In this

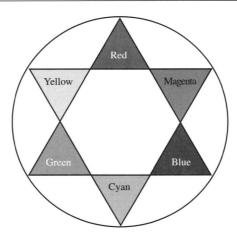

FIGURE 5-4   The color wheel

arrangement, each color is directly opposite its complement, and each color on the wheel is situated between the two colors that are used to create it.

By studying the wheel, you can see that adding yellow and magenta creates red. If you subtract both yellow and magenta, you remove red. Thus, if you want to subtract red from an image, you decrease the percentages of yellow and magenta. Another point to realize about the color wheel is that when you are adding color to an image, you are subtracting its complement. For instance, when you are making an image redder, you are decreasing the percentage of cyan (which is red's complement, directly opposite it in the color wheel).

 NOTE: *A color wheel can also be helpful when designing Web sites and interactive media. If you want to create contrast, choose complementary colors—colors at the opposite end of the color wheel. If you want to use colors similar to one another, choose adjacent colors on the color wheel. For more information about using colors on the Web and in multimedia projects, see Chapters 12 and 20.*

Using Sliders to Create CMYK Colors

Now you'll practice using both the color wheel and the CMYK sliders to create red, green, and blue. This simple exercise demonstrates how CMYK inks absorb different light waves and reflect others to produce colors, as shown in Figure 5-5.

To create red, drag magenta and yellow to 100%, and leave cyan and black at 0%. Notice that red is between yellow and magenta on the color wheel. When you see red in an image printed using four-color process printing, yellow and magenta inks have combined to absorb the blue and green wavelengths of light. The result is the color red.

To create green, drag yellow and cyan to 100%, and put magenta and black at 0%. Green is between yellow and cyan on the color wheel. When you see green in an image printed using four-color process printing, yellow and cyan inks have combined to absorb the blue and red wavelengths of light.

To create blue, drag cyan and magenta to 100%, and yellow and black to 0%. Blue is between cyan and magenta on the color wheel. When you see blue in an image printed using four-color process printing, cyan and magenta inks have combined to absorb red and green wavelengths of light.

Now try experimenting with the sliders to create additional CMYK colors. If you have a swatch book displaying CMYK percentages and the colors they

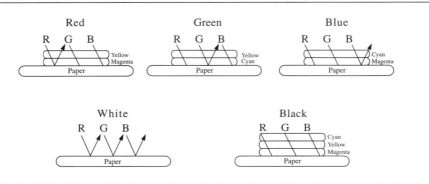

FIGURE 5-5   Wavelengths of light, absorbed and reflected

produce, use the sliders (or edit the percentages to the right of the sliders) to re-create a few of these colors, and see how close the screen color comes to the real thing.

NOTE: *If you will be creating and printing four-color separations, your file mode must be CMYK Color. See Chapter 12 for information about converting files to CMYK Color mode, and see Chapter 19 for more information about outputting CMYK files. Also note that Chapter 12 discusses how to view a CMYK preview while in RGB Color mode (View | Preview | CMYK).*

CAUTION: *Even though Photoshop allows you to choose colors using CMYK sliders while in an RGB file, be aware that these color values may change if you convert to a CMYK Color file. During the conversion, Photoshop changes color values based upon the settings in the RGB and CMYK Setup dialog boxes.*

The Out-of-Gamut Alert

Before you leave the CMYK color model and move on to the next section, it's important to realize that the color spectrums of the RGB and CMYK color models are different. The professional term for the visible color range of a color model is *gamut*. The gamut of the RGB color model is larger than that of CMYK, as shown in Figure 5-6. Therefore, if you only work with RGB color on your computer, be aware that you may be designing and editing with onscreen colors that cannot be printed.

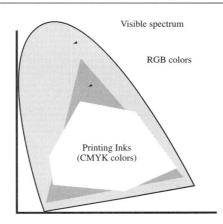

FIGURE 5-6   Visible color spectrums (gamuts) for the RGB and CMYK color models

 Fortunately, Photoshop provides a warning when you overstep the bounds of printable colors. You may have already noticed this warning: It's a small Alert symbol—a triangle with an exclamation mark inside—that appears in the Color palette.

For example, if you're working in the RGB color model (or the HSB color model) and create a color that can't be printed, the Alert triangle immediately appears. If you click on the Alert, Photoshop selects the nearest printable color. Despite this handy feature, it's important to remember that even though Photoshop is showing you that the color is printable, it is only displaying an RGB monitor's simulation of the color. Never assume that the color you see on screen is an exact representation of the printed color.

 TIP: *If you move the eyedropper over a color that is out of gamut, exclamation marks appear next to the CMYK color readouts in the Info palette.*

 TIP: *Photoshop determines exactly which colors are printable based on the settings in the RGB and CMYK Setup dialog boxes (File | Color Settings). See Chapter 12 for more information about converting from RGB Color mode to CMYK Color mode.*

The Info palette can display RGB and CMYK colors simultaneously. However, the CMYK color settings shown in the Info palette generally display the CMYK colors as they would appear after the file is converted from RGB Color mode to CMYK Color mode.

 NOTE: *If you are outputting your work to slides or video, you needn't worry about the out-of-gamut Alert, because slides and video use RGB colors. The Alert indicates that the color cannot be created by commercial printers' inks.*

The HSB Color Model

Although both RGB and CMYK are essential color models for computer graphics and printing, many designers and graphic artists find it unnecessarily complicated to try to mix colors using values or percentages of other colors. Using a color wheel helps, but neither RGB nor CMYK is very intuitive. The human mind doesn't divide colors into models of red/green/blue or cyan/magenta/yellow/black. To make such choices easier, a third color model—HSB (hue/saturation/brightness)—was created.

HSB is based on human perception of colors, rather than the computer values of RGB or printers' percentages of CMYK. The human eye sees colors as components of hue, saturation, and brightness.

Think of hues as the colors you can see on a color wheel. In technical terms, *hue* is based on the wavelength of light reflected from an object, or transmitted through it. *Saturation*, often called *chroma*, is the amount of gray in a color. The higher the saturation, the lower the gray content and the more intense the color. *Brightness* is a measure of the intensity of light in a color.

Using HSB Sliders in the Color Palette

Let's take a look at how to choose colors using the HSB color model. In the Color palette, click on the pop-up menu arrow and choose HSB Sliders. You'll see three sliders: H for changing hue values, measured in degrees; S for saturation, and B for brightness, both measured in percentages:

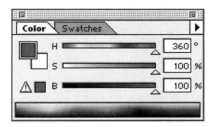

As with the sliders in the other two color models, you can change values by clicking and dragging the slider controls, or by editing the values in the entry fields to the right of each slider. The following table gives you the hue settings for different colors.

Color	Hue Setting
Red	0 or 360°
Yellow	60°
Green	120°
Cyan	180°
Blue	240°
Magenta	300°

Now try experimenting by changing saturation and brightness to other percentages and see how they affect the color red.

 TIP: *The Hue slider is the electronic equivalent of a color wheel—colors that are 180 degrees apart are complements. Use a color's complement when you want to provide contrast. Colors near each other on the color wheel provide little contrast.*

Changing Saturation and Brightness

To follow along with this exercise using the HSB color model, select the red color swatch in the first row of the color swatches in the Swatches palette. Start by taking a look at the effects of changing the saturation percentage for the red color. Move the S slider control. The intensity of the red diminishes as you decrease saturation by dragging the slider control to the left. Try it, and you'll move from red to light red to pink. When you reach 0%, the red will have changed to white.

 NOTE: *You cannot create white and black with the H slider. To create white, the S slider control must be set to 0% and the B slider control to 100%. To create black, set the B slider control to 0%.*

Before you test the B slider, click and drag the S slider back to 100% to give you a reference point for observing the effects of changing brightness. Dragging the B slider to the left will decrease the percentage of color brightness; dragging it to the right will increase the brightness.

Try it now: Drag the B slider control to the left, and you'll see that red gradually darkens. When you reach 0%, the red will have turned to black. To bring brightness back to the red, drag the control back toward 100%.

If you wish, continue to experiment with the HSB color sliders by picking a hue and then adjusting its saturation and brightness. It probably won't take long before you agree that HSB is the easiest of the color models to use, because it's the most intuitive. There's less guesswork involved in color creation when you don't have to worry about mixing other colors together. You may even decide to do all of your work in the HSB model—particularly if you're going to use Photoshop as a painting program and will not be creating output for four-color printing.

The Lab Color Model

One more color model remains to be explored. Though it's not used as frequently in Photoshop as the RGB, CMYK, and HSB color models, the Lab color model is worth investigating, particularly because it may prove helpful in certain color-editing situations. When you learn about changing modes in Chapter 9, you'll see that Lab color can be used when editing Photo CD images and when outputting to PostScript Level-2 printers.

Although you may never need to use Lab color, this color model is vital to Photoshop. Lab is the internal color model that Photoshop uses to convert from one color mode to another. In Chapter 9, you'll learn how to change modes from RGB to CMYK so that you can produce a four-color separation. When Photoshop converts from RGB to CMYK, it first converts to Lab color, then from Lab to CMYK. One reason it uses Lab is because the Lab color gamut encompasses both color gamuts of RGB and CMYK.

The Lab color model is based on the work of the Commission Internationale de l'Eclairage that was formed in the early 1900s to try to standardize color measurement. The commission designed a color model based on how the eye perceives color. In 1976, the original color model was refined and called CIE Lab. It was created to provide consistent colors, no matter what monitor or printer is being used; this is called *device-independent color*. Device-independent color isn't affected by the characteristics or idiosyncrasies of any piece of hardware.

Using Lab Sliders in the Color Palette

You might wonder why you should know anything about the Lab color model if Photoshop uses it internally. The reason is that Lab divides colors using an approach different from that of RGB, CMYK, and HSB, and gives you another perspective to editing colors: The Lab model comprises a lightness, or luminance, factor and two color axes.

Take a look at Lab color in the Color palette. Click on the pop-up menu arrow and switch to Lab Sliders. You'll see three sliders, labeled L, a, and b, as shown here:

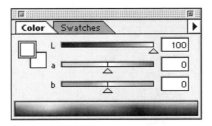

The L slider allows you to change a color's lightness, in values from 0 to 100. The a slider represents an axis of colors ranging from green to magenta; and the b slider is an axis of colors ranging from blue to yellow. The values accessible from both axes are −120 to 120. You create white by setting L at 100, a at 0, and b at 0.

Lab is useful if all you wish to do is change the lightness of a color. Also, if you need to change only the red and green components of a color, or the blue and yellow components, you can click and drag on the Lab slider controls to do this.

To see how the Lab sliders affect color, start with the L slider control set all the way to the right at 100. This provides the brightest levels for the colors you will be creating.

To see how a slider changes colors from green to magenta, set the b slider to 0. Then, click and drag on the a slider control, moving first to the right, then to the left. As you drag the a slider control to the left, the color turns to green. Now drag the a slider control to the right to see the color change to magenta. When you are done, leave the control in the middle of the a slider (set to 0). This will best enable you to see the effects of changing the b slider.

Now observe how the b slider changes colors from blue to yellow by clicking and dragging the slider control. First drag it to the right, and the color will turn to yellow. Drag to the left to see the color change to blue. If you wish to keep experimenting, try clicking and dragging on the L slider control to see how lowering the L value darkens colors.

The Color Picker Dialog Box

Now that you've examined each of the color models in the Color palette, take a look at Photoshop's Color Picker dialog box. The Color Picker provides another tool for picking foreground and background colors. The chief differences between the Color Picker dialog box and the Color palette are that the Color Picker allows you to see the values of all four color models (RGB, CMYK, HSB, and Lab) at the same time. The Color Picker also lets you access color-matching systems such as PANTONE and TRUMATCH.

To access the Color Picker, click on the Foreground Color or Background Color icon in the Toolbox. You may also open the Color Picker from the Color palette, by clicking on either the Foreground or Background selection box. If the Foreground selection box is activated, changing settings in the Color Picker affects the foreground color. If the Background selection box is selected, your settings change the background color.

Take a look at the Color Picker in action. Start by accessing the Color Picker dialog box from the Color palette to change the foreground color. Here's how: Make sure the Color palette is set to change the foreground color; a black border should surround the Foreground selection box in the upper left of the palette. If the border surrounds the Background selection box instead, click the Foreground selection box to activate it. Then click it again to display the Color Picker dialog box, as shown in Figure 5-7.

New color   Original color

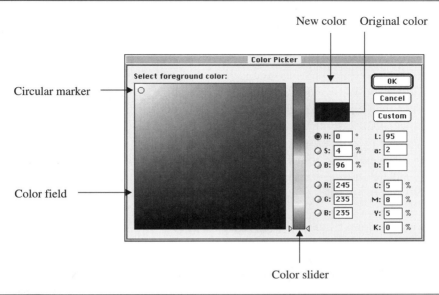

Circular marker

Color field

Color slider

5

FIGURE 5-7   The Color Picker dialog box

 NOTE: *The Color Picker will not appear if you have switched to either the Apple or Windows color picker in the General Preferences dialog box. To switch back to Photoshop's Color Picker, select File | Preferences | General. In the Color Picker pop-up menu, choose Photoshop.*

Exploring the Color Picker

Notice that all of the color models—RGB, CMYK, HSB, and Lab—are included in the Color Picker dialog box, with entry fields where you can type values for the various color components.

 TIP: *Before you start experimenting with the settings in the Color Picker dialog box, notice the color in the bottom half of the small box next to the top of the color slider. This box displays your original color. As you work, the top part of the box changes to show you the new color currently being edited (see Figure 5-7). The bottom portion of the square always remains the same. If you wish to return to the original color, you can click on the bottom of the square. This is a very handy "undo" feature.*

As you create your colors, you can pick the color model that best suits your needs. For instance, suppose you need to add more green to an image that must be output in CMYK for process printing. If you were working with the CMYK sliders in the Color palette, you might need to refer to a color wheel or try to figure out how to adjust the sliders to add green. With the Color Picker, however, you can add green by simply entering a higher value into the G field of the RGB values.

Though the Color Picker doesn't provide sliders for all color models, it does offer one vertical slider that can be used for any of the RGB or HSB color components. You convert the slider's role by clicking on one of the radio buttons that appear to the left of the HSB and RGB value fields. For instance, if you click on the R radio button, the vertical slider lets you move through red values in the RGB color model. Click on the H radio button, and you can move through hue values.

The large colored square that occupies the entire left half of the Color Picker dialog box is called the *color field*. A small circular marker in the color field allows you to change color components by clicking on it and dragging the mouse. For instance, if you click on the H radio button, the vertical slider changes hue values; now clicking and dragging on the marker in the color field changes saturation and brightness. (Dragging the circle horizontally changes saturation; dragging vertically changes brightness.)

If you don't click and drag the circle, but instead click anywhere in the color field, the circular marker will jump to the new position. The values in the dialog box and the foreground or background color displayed will change accordingly.

If the Color Picker is confusing to you at first, imagine yourself in a three-dimensional version of the color model you are using. This is often called a color model's color space. Figure 5-8 (reproduced on the "Color Theory" page in the color insert in this book) illustrates a three-dimensional view of the HSB color model. As you are swimming in this three-dimensional pool of HSB colors, the hue levels change around the perimeter of the pool. The saturation levels change as you swim out to the middle of the pool. The brightness levels change as you dive deeper into the pool.

As you move along the edges of the pool, you pass through various hues. This is the equivalent of clicking and dragging on the vertical slider control with the Hue radio button selected, while viewing saturation and brightness in the color field. As you look across the water of the pool, you see the saturation and brightness values of each hue you pass through.

If you dive straight down along the edge of the pool, you pass through various levels of brightness. From your vantage point, you see the saturation and hue

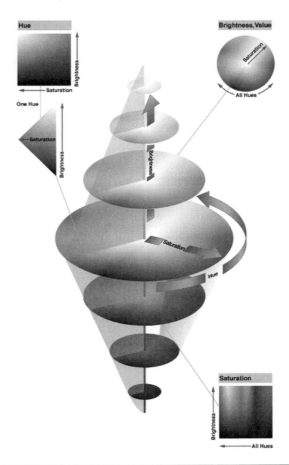

FIGURE 5-8   The HSB color model, in 3-D (courtesy of Agfa Corporation)

values of the colors according to your brightness depth. This is equivalent to clicking on the Brightness radio button while viewing saturation and hue in the color field.

Now imagine that you're swimming out to the middle of the pool, moving through the saturation levels of colors. Dive deeper and view the colors around you. The colors you see are similar to those in the color field when you clicked on the Saturation radio button.

Changing Colors Using the Color Picker

Try the Color Picker to see how you can use the combination of radio buttons, vertical sliders, and value fields to change colors. Assume that you wish to edit a color by adding more green to it. First, set the vertical slider to change green RGB values, by clicking on the G radio button.

When you drag the control for the vertical slider, notice that it functions much the same way as the horizontal sliders do in the RGB model. Dragging the slider control upward raises the green value, and dragging downward lowers it. Try this now: Click on the control and drag toward the top of the slider. As you drag higher, the green color value grows. Drag up to 255, and then back down. The highest value that appears in the G entry field is 255, and the lowest is 0.

When you clicked on the G radio button, the circular marker in the color field is set to change the R and B values of the RGB model. (If you had clicked on the R radio button instead, the color field marker would change the G and B values of RGB; clicking on the B button makes the marker control the G and R values.) When the G radio button is selected, dragging the marker upward adds red to the color you are creating, and dragging to the right adds blue.

Experiment with the marker to see how the color field controls the R and B values. Click and drag the circular marker up. As you drag, notice that the value in the R field increases. As you drag down, it decreases. Now drag to the right; this causes blue levels to increase. Drag left, and the levels decrease. You can probably guess what happens if you drag diagonally—you can change both R and B values at the same time.

Now that you have oriented yourself in the Color Picker, can you guess how to create pure green? Drag the slider control all the way up to 255, and then drag the color field marker to the lower-left corner of the color field. When your color changes to green, you'll see the same Alert sign that you saw in the Color palette, again warning you that you are viewing an unprintable color. If you click on the Alert, Photoshop chooses the closest printable color for you.

If you'd like, you can continue to experiment with the Color Picker dialog box. As you grow accustomed to it, you may even find yourself beginning to prefer it to the Color palette.

Accessing Custom Colors from the Color Picker

The Color Picker dialog box includes an important option that allows you to choose color using a color-matching system such as PANTONE or TRUMATCH. These systems can help make screen colors more predictable when they are printed.

As you've worked through this chapter, you've become aware that it is often difficult to precisely translate colors displayed on your computer screen to the printed page. The problem is compounded by the fact that not all monitors are the same, not all inks are the same, and a printed page cannot completely reproduce the color sensation of the video monitor. Video colors often look brighter than their counterparts on the printed page.

One way to obtain a better idea of how the colors on your screen will print, or at least to better predict color output, is to pick colors not by how they look on the computer screen but by their appearance in a color swatch book—a book of many color samples printed on paper, used to label or classify colors.

Suppose you wish to print a blue border around an image. You could pick a blue from a swatch book and then choose that same blue color from Photoshop's Custom Colors dialog box. During the printing process, your commercial printer will be able to match the swatch's custom color when producing your image.

 NOTE: *To accurately match colors, make sure that the colors in your swatch book have not faded.*

In deciding which swatch book to use, consider the following:

☐ Are you printing on newsprint, coated paper, or uncoated paper? Inks spread differently depending on the type of paper being used. For more information on how paper stock affects printing, see Chapter 14.

☐ Are you using spot color (explained below) or four-color process colors?

The most commonly used color-matching system was created by PANTONE. It's important to understand that PANTONE has traditionally been used for spot-color printing, not four-color separation work. Spot color is similar to printing an overlay, separate from any other color; this is quite different from four-color separation, in which cyan, magenta, yellow, and black combine to create a color. In spot color, the printer mixes inks to create a matching color and prints that one color on an individual plate. This is fine for one or two colors but would be very expensive for multiple colors.

Spot colors can be used as *fifth colors*; this is a term used when a job is printed with the standard four-color process and needs a fifth color picked for a specific match of a certain color. Fifth colors are used to create silvers, coppers, golds, deep blues, and certain greens, because they can't be created with four-color inks.

 NOTE: *To learn how to create spot colors in Photoshop, see Chapter 14.*

Using Color-Matching Systems

If the Color Picker isn't open, click on the Foreground Color icon in the Toolbox. If the Color Picker dialog box doesn't open (because the Background Color selection box was activated), click on the Foreground Color icon once again. In the Color Picker dialog box, click on the Custom button to open the Custom Colors dialog box.

 TIP: *Photoshop can search for a custom color that matches a color you have created with sliders or the Color Picker. First, create the color. Then, access the Book pop-up menu from the Custom Colors dialog box and select the swatch book (for example, PANTONE or TRUMATCH) you want the match to come from. The Custom Colors dialog box then displays the custom color that most closely matches the color you created.*

Selecting a Color-Matching System and a Color

To access a custom color, you first must access the Book pop-up menu and choose an ink-matching system, as shown in Figure 5-9. Here are brief descriptions of your choices:

☐ *ANPA Color*   These colors are used for printing to newsprint.

□ *FOCOLTONE*   This system, popular in England, includes 763 CMYK colors.

□ *PANTONE Coated, PANTONE Process, PANTONE ProSim, or PANTONE Uncoated*   Even though PANTONE is known primarily for its spot-color swatches, it also produces a process-color swatch set, PANTONE Process, with 3,006 CMYK combinations. PANTONE ProSim is a process-color simulation of spot (solid) colors. PANTONE Coated consists of spot (solid) colors printed on coated paper, and PANTONE Uncoated consists of spot (solid) colors printed on uncoated paper; uncoated colors are more muted than the coated colors.

 NOTE: *PANTONE Color Systems Cross Reference is a stand-alone software utility that matches a chosen color from one PANTONE Color System to another. Pick a color, and Cross Reference finds the best match for spot-color and four-color process printing, as well as plastics and textiles. The software even shows whether a PANTONE by Letraset Color Marker and/or PANTONE by Letraset Color Paper can match the color you've selected.*

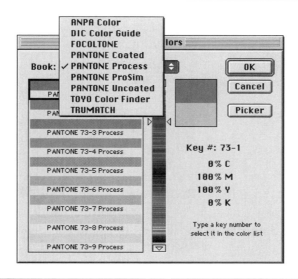

FIGURE 5-9   The Custom Colors dialog box with list of Book options open

☐ *TOYO Color Finder*   This system from the Toyo Ink Manufacturing Co., Ltd, Tokyo, Japan, provides 1,050 colors.

☐ *TRUMATCH*   The TRUMATCH system uses strictly CMYK process colors. It has approximately 2,000 process colors, arranged according to hue, saturation, and brightness.

☐ *DIC Color Guide*   This is a Japanese printing system from Dainippon Ink and Chemicals, Inc., Tokyo, Japan.

Once you've selected the color-matching system you want to use (for this exercise, choose PANTONE Process), you can choose a color. To find a color, you can either click the up or down arrow in the vertical slider of colors, or click anywhere within the slider, or type in a number on your keyboard. In Figure 5-9 we chose a reddish PANTONE color, number 73-1, by typing **73** on our keyboard. Do this on your own computer, and then click on PANTONE Process color 73-1, which will be selected on screen in the list of custom colors and in the swatch box. The vertical slider on screen will also be set to the custom color. (You can, however, select any color you want.)

Click OK to close the Custom Colors dialog box. Notice that your foreground color has changed to the PANTONE color (or the custom color) you selected. If you position the mouse pointer over the Foreground selection box in the Color palette (without clicking), the title bar of the Color palette tab displays the name of the PANTONE (or custom) color you picked.

 NOTE: *If you intend to export your Photoshop file to any program that uses short PANTONE names, make sure the Short PANTONE Names option in the General Preferences dialog box is selected before choosing PANTONE colors. To access the General Preferences dialog box, choose File | Preferences | General.*

Saving Custom Colors in the Swatches Palette

If you want to keep a custom color handy, you can add it to the swatches that appear in the Swatches palette. To add a custom color, or any color, to the Swatches palette, position the mouse pointer in the white area to the right of the last color swatch in the Swatches palette. When the pointer turns into a paint bucket, as shown here, click to create a swatch of your active color.

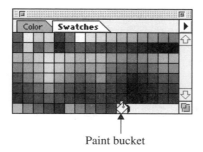

Paint bucket

5

To insert the custom color between two existing swatches, press and hold down SHIFT-OPTION (Windows users: SHIFT-ALT) while you click on a swatch or between two swatches to insert the active custom color. To replace an existing swatch with the current foreground color, press SHIFT, and then click on the swatch. Note that if the Background Color selection box is active, you will add a swatch of your background color to the Swatches palette.

 NOTE: *If you move the eyedropper over the PANTONE color in the Swatches palette, the palette tab displays the PANTONE color name.*

To delete a swatch, position the mouse pointer over a swatch and press COMMAND (Windows users: CTRL). When the pointer turns into scissors, click and the swatch will be deleted.

Saving Customized Palettes

You can continue to add your own custom colors to the Swatches palette and then save the palette so that you can access it at a later time. Just click on the pop-up menu arrow in the Swatches palette and choose Save Colors to open the Save dialog box.

It might be a good idea to save your custom palette in Photoshop's Color Palettes folder (Windows users: palettes) found in the Goodies folders, so that all of your palettes are in the same place. For the filename, type **MyColors**, and then click Save (Windows users: OK). You are now working in the Swatches palette called MyColors.

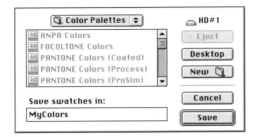

 TIP: *If you'd like, you can create your own color swatch book. Open a new file, and using the Rectangular Marquee tool, create a small rectangular selection. Fill the rectangle with a swatch color by using the Fill command in the Edit menu. With the Type tool, label the selection by typing in the name of the swatch color. Continue to create and label rectangles until you have applied all the color swatches from your palette to the new file. Save the file and print it to whatever output device you will be using with this collection of swatches. Then use the printout of the color swatches as a guide for what the swatch color will look like when printed from your output device.*

Loading and Appending Swatches Palettes

If you want to add a Swatches palette saved on disk to the palette on screen, click on the pop-up menu arrow in the Swatches palette and choose Load Swatches. Click on the Swatches palette you wish to load from the Color Palettes folder in the Goodies folder, and then click Open (Windows users: OK). After you load the color palette, Photoshop appends the palette you loaded to the palette on screen. If you wish to replace the swatches in the palette with a palette that you've saved, choose Replace Swatches instead of Load Swatches.

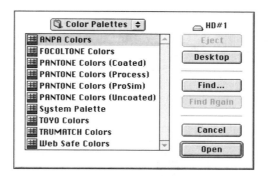

 NOTE: *To return the default swatches to the Swatches palette, choose Reset Swatches from the palette's pop-up menu.*

Conclusion

Now that you've explored the basics of creating colors in Photoshop, you're ready to move ahead and start using colors creatively with Photoshop's painting tools. You'll begin using them in the next chapter.

CHAPTER 6

Introduction to Painting Techniques

Even if you're not an artist, the scope, power, and rich diversity of Photoshop's painting capabilities are certain to inspire the creativity within you. You'll marvel at the realistic and electronic effects within your grasp. At times, you might even expect to see paint dripping down your screen from your electronic brushes. In this chapter, you'll try your hand at painting using electronic versions of a paintbrush, pencil, eraser, paint bucket, and airbrush. These tools, along with the Line, Gradient, and Eyedropper tools and Photoshop's Brushes, Color, Swatches, and Options palettes, will open a world of infinite artistic possibilities for you.

If you are not interested in Photoshop's painting features and are using the program more for its image-editing and photo-retouching capabilities, do not skip this chapter. You'll need to know the tools and techniques covered here because they are a fundamental part of electronic composition, especially when retouching. As you continue to read this book, you will see the need for these tools and techniques arise again and again.

This chapter is primarily divided into groups of short introductory exercises and projects. Although the focal point is primarily the Toolbox's painting tools, you will also use the Brushes palette to learn how to change brushes and to create, save, and load custom brushes and the Options palette to change the opacity of colors. At the conclusion of the chapter you will explore Photoshop's blending modes, accessed through the Options palette, which can change an image based on the color being applied, the color over which it is painted, and the mode that is chosen.

 TIP: *Photoshop 5's Fade command is accessible after you paint with any of its painting tools. After using any painting tool you can lower the opacity of your last stroke by choosing Filter | Fade. In the Fade dialog box, drag the Opacity slider to the left to fade the stroke. In the dialog box you can also choose a blending mode as well.*

Introduction to the Line, Paint Bucket, and Eraser Tools

The best way to learn how to use the painting tools is to start with the easiest ones—the Line, Paint Bucket, and Eraser tools. Creating artistic effects with these tools requires only a click or a click-and-drag of the mouse and knowledge of how to use the Options and Brushes palettes.

Getting Started

When working with the Line tool (and all other painting tools), you'll make extensive use of the Swatches palette to change colors. In the exercises in this chapter, you will be also using the HSB color model because it's the most intuitive one. Switch to the HSB color model by selecting the pop-up menu in the Color palette and choosing HSB Sliders.

In preparation for the introductory exercises in this section, make sure that the Options palette is visible on your screen. If necessary, open it now by choosing Show Options from the Window menu. The name and appearance of the palette changes depending on which tool is currently selected in the Toolbox.

Now take a look at the Pencil/Line Toolbox location. If the Line tool is visible in the Toolbox, click on it to select it. If the Line tool is not visible click on the Pencil tool, and hold down the mouse. When you see the Line tool appear, click and drag to select it. Once the Line tool is selected, the Options palette switches to show the Line Options palette which controls the opacity and blending mode of the lines you create. The Options palette also controls the opacities and blending modes of the Pencil, Paint Bucket, Paintbrush, Gradient, and Rubber Stamp tools. After you set the opacity and blending mode of a tool, they stay set for that tool until you change them.

 NOTE: *The element controlled by the pop-up slider in the Options palette depends on which tool you are using. When you are using the Line, Pencil, Paint Bucket, Paintbrush, Gradient, and Rubber Stamp tools, the slider sets opacity. For the Airbrush, Smudge, and Blur/Sharpen tools, the slider sets pressure. For the Dodge/Burn/Sponge tool, the slider sets exposure. (You will be introduced to the Rubber Stamp, Smudge, Blur/Sharpen, and Dodge/Burn/Sponge tools in Chapter 7.)*

If you examine the settings in the Line Options palette, you'll see that the painting blending mode and Opacity settings are either the default settings or the last settings used for that tool.

If Opacity is set to less than 100%, you will not be painting with an opaque color but rather with a tint—a transparent version of a color. Painting with a tint can create a transparent effect and different shades of colors. When you lower the opacity percentage, you make a color more translucent; when you raise it, you make the color more opaque.

Later in this section, you will lower the opacity to create tinted lines. For now, though, start with opaque lines. If Opacity is not 100%, reset it by clicking and dragging the Opacity slider control all the way to the right.

Before continuing, look at the painting blending mode pop-up menu in the Line Tool Options palette to see which blending mode is in effect. You will see one of the following words: Normal, Dissolve, Multiply, Screen, Overlay, Soft Light, Hard Light, Color Dodge, Color Burn, Darken, Lighten, Difference, Exclusion, Hue, Saturation, Color, or Luminosity. If you are working in a layer other than the Background, you will also be able to use the Behind and Clear modes. (For more information about layers, see Chapters 15 and 16.)

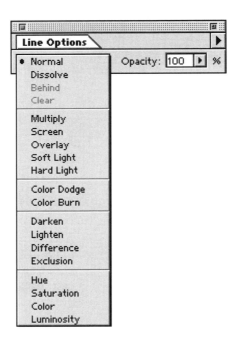

For now, you will work in Normal blending mode (the default). When you paint in Normal mode, you paint all the underlying pixels with the foreground or background color that is set in the Color palette or Color Picker dialog box. If the blending mode is not Normal, change it now by clicking on the pop-up menu and selecting Normal from the list that appears.

 TIP: *You can set the blending mode to Normal by pressing OPTION-SHIFT-N.*

Now that the options are set in the Line Options palette, you can create a new file to begin working with the Line tool. Choose New from the File menu. Set both Width and Height to 5 inches. Set Resolution to 72 ppi, use RGB Color for Mode, and set the background Contents by clicking on the White radio button in the Contents group. These settings will create a practice file that does not consume too much memory. Click OK. Once the new file appears, display the rulers and open the Info palette by selecting Show Rulers from the View menu and selecting Show Info from the Window menu. You will use the Rulers and the Info palette as measuring guides in the Line tool exercise.

Using the Line Tool to *Create Lines and Arrows*

As you've probably guessed, the Line tool is used to create lines. You can create vertical or horizontal lines or slanted lines drawn on a diagonal in increments of 45 degrees. The Line Options palette allows you to control the thickness of a line, as well as create arrowheads at the beginning and end of a line. In this section, you will use the Line tool to create lines at various thicknesses, angles, and shades, with and without arrowheads, as shown in Figure 6-1.

Let's start by examining the Line Options palette. In the palette, the Line Weight field allows you to change the pixel width of the lines you create; the default width is 1. In the Arrowheads section you can choose to have arrowheads at the start and/or end of a line by clicking on the appropriate checkbox. You can specify the size of arrowheads at either or both ends of a line by clicking on the Shape button and typing in values in the Arrowhead Shape dialog box that appears.

Use the Line tool now to create a wide, red line. In the Line Options palette, type **16** in the line Weight field. Make sure the Anti-aliased option is selected. This helps ensure that line edges appear smooth. Before creating the line, use the Color palette to change the color in the Foreground selection box. Move the H (hue) slider control so that it is set to red (either 0 or 360 degrees). The S (saturation) and B (brightness) sliders should be set to 100%.

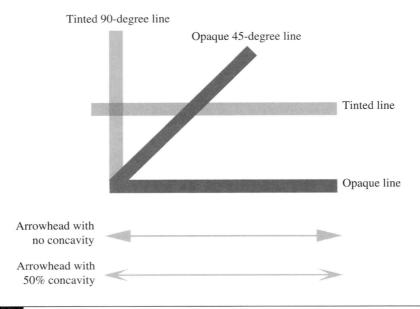

FIGURE 6-1 Examples using the Line tool

 NOTE: *Don't worry about setting the background color in the Color palette, because the Line tool only paints with the foreground color.*

Creating a Line

Drawing a line is simple. Once you have set your Line tool options, move the mouse pointer toward the middle of your document. As you move the mouse, the mouse pointer becomes a small crosshair. To create a line, all you need to do is click and drag.

When using the Line tool, it's often handy to keep the Info palette in view because it provides readouts of line length and location. Since the Info palette is grouped with the Options palette, it's generally more convenient to work with the Info palette by removing it from its palette group. To remove the Info palette from its palette group, simply click and drag on its tab (on the word Info) until it is separated from the rest of the palettes.

TIP: *You can change measurement units by clicking on the +(cross hair) icon in the X Y section of the Info palette.*

 NOTE: *If a selection exists on screen, you will only be able to use a painting tool in the selected area. To remove a selection from the screen, press COMMAND-D (Windows users: CTRL-D)—the keyboard equivalent of choosing Deselect from the Select menu.*

1. Position the crosshair about 1 inch from the left side of the screen and 2.5 inches from the top of the screen; then click and drag to the right. As you drag, Photoshop creates an outline of the line that will appear on screen.

Notice that as you drag the mouse, the values in the Info palette change. In addition to the X and Y coordinates that appear next to the crosshair icon, look at those adjacent to the icon of the tiny square with arrows (in the upper left of the palette; only visible when clicking and dragging the mouse). These X and Y coordinates, which have a small delta (triangle) in front of them, indicate the distance moved horizontally or vertically from one position to another. Next to the angle icon are A and D coordinates— the A coordinate shows the angle at which you are dragging the mouse, and the D coordinate indicates the distance you have dragged it.

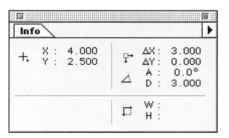

2. When you get near the right edge of the document window, release the mouse button. Not until you release the mouse button will Photoshop use the foreground color to fill the linear outline it has drawn on screen.

 NOTE: *Look carefully at the line you just created, and notice that it has a soft edge. This is because you created the line with the Anti-aliased option set.*

6

Drawing Lines to Create Angles

The Line tool allows you to draw lines in increments of 45 degrees; to do this, press SHIFT as you draw a line. You will use this constraining technique in the File Manager with File Cabinet project later in the chapter, so practice it now by drawing a line at a 45-degree angle from the left endpoint of the line already on your screen.

1. Move the crosshair to the left edge of the existing line. Press and hold SHIFT and click and drag diagonally up and to the right.

   You'll see that your movement is constrained to a 45-degree angle. When you have dragged about 3 inches, release the mouse, and Photoshop creates a diagonal line at a 45-degree angle to the original one.

   Next, you'll press the SHIFT key while clicking and dragging to draw a 90-degree angle, but this time you'll change the Opacity setting in the Line Options palette to create a tinted line.

2. In the Line Options palette, click and drag the pop-up slider control to the left, decreasing the Opacity percentage. (You can also use the keyboard to change the Opacity value in For instance, type **3** and Opacity will jump to 30%, type 31 and Opacity changes to 31%.) Before you draw the next line, use the keyboard now to set Opacity to 50% by typing **5**.

   The next line you paint, at a 90-degree angle to the first, will illustrate the effect of placing a translucent color over an opaque color. Once again, you'll start painting the line at the left endpoint of the first line you drew.

3. Position the crosshair on the left endpoint of the horizontal red line, press and hold SHIFT, and click and drag up to constrain the line to a straight vertical line.

When you release the mouse, you'll see that the new line is 50% red. Notice that even though you drew the 50% red line on top of the opaque line, the opaque line's color has not changed to the tinted shade. It's as if the intensity of the 100% red burns through the translucent version of the same color.

For an example of painting a translucent color over another translucent color, click and drag to create a horizontal line that intersects both the 90-degree red-tinted line and the 45-degree opaque red line, as shown in Figure 6-1. Where the two translucent colors intersect, a square appears with a more intense red. But once again, when the red with the 50% opacity is painted over the opaque red, only the opaque version of the color shows.

 TIP: *You can use Photoshop 5's new Measure tool as an onscreen ruler. When you click and drag with the Measure tool, a temporary line appears on screen. The length and position of the line appear in the Info palette. When you switch to another tool, the temporary line disappears. When you re-select the Measure tool, the line reappears. The length and position of the line reappear in the Info palette.*
To constrain the measure tool to 45 decree increments, press SHIFT while you click and drag. To use the Measure Tool as an electronic protractor, press OPTION (Windows users: ALT) while you click and drag to move an endpoint of the temporary line.

 TIP: *Here's a handy measuring technique for Photoshop users who haven't yet updated to Photoshop 5. If you set the weight for the Line tool to zero pixels, you can use the tool as a screen-measuring device and to tell whether an image is straight or not. When you click and drag, Photoshop creates an electronic tape measure, a thin line on screen that you can use to drag over items that you wish to measure. The linear dimensions and angle of the object will appear in the Info palette. When you release the mouse, the measuring line will disappear.*

Creating Lines with Arrowheads

Next, try the Arrowheads options. This time, you'll create a thinner line so that the effects of the arrowhead settings will be clearly visible.

1. In the Line Options palette, type **2** in the Line Weight field.

2. In the Arrowheads section, click on the Start and End check boxes. When these options are selected, the Line tool will create arrowheads at both ends of the next line you create.

   You can also control the width and the length of the arrowhead by using the Width and Length fields in the Arrowhead Shape dialog box. To open the dialog box, click on the Shape button. The Width field accepts values between 10 and 1000%. The Length field accepts values between 10 and 5000%.

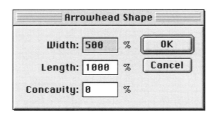

a. To create an arrowhead that is twice as long as it is wide, you can use the default settings. If they have been changed, type **500** in the Width field and **1000** in the Length field. The Width of the arrowhead will be 5 times larger than the Line width. The Length of the arrowhead will be 10 times larger than the Line width.

If you wish, you can also change the shape of the arrowhead by setting its concavity. Concavity determines the curve on the back of the arrowhead, as shown in Figure 6-1.

b. Set Concavity to 0 if it is not already set to 0, so that you can see how an arrowhead looks without concavity.

3. Click OK to accept the Arrowhead Shape settings.

4. To see the arrowheads, draw a line from left to right below the other lines on your screen. This time, the line features arrowheads at both ends.

Take a look at how concavity changes the arrowhead. First, you'll need to reopen the Arrowhead Shape dialog box, change the concavity of the arrow to 50% (values can be between –50% and 50%), and click OK; then click and drag to draw another line below the last one you created. Your screen will now look like Figure 6-1. Notice that the back of the 50% concavity arrowhead has a very distinctive curve.

If you wish to continue experimenting with the Line tool, try creating one more line below the others with Concavity set to a negative number. This will create a line with an arrowhead that looks like a diamond.

After you have finished testing the Line tool, you can proceed to the next section, where you'll learn how to paint and fill using the Paint Bucket.

Using the Paint Bucket Tool to Paint and Fill

 The Paint Bucket tool lets you quickly fill areas of an image with the foreground color or a pattern. The area painted by the tool is determined by how similar in color the adjacent pixels are to the pixel that you click on.

 NOTE: *You can alter the way the Paint Bucket paints by changing the blending mode from Normal. For instance, if you are working in a layer, you can work with the Paintbucket in Clear mode—which erases image areas rather than painting them. You can also change the effect of the Paintbucket by choosing Use All Layers in the tool's Options palette. When Use All Layers is selected, the Paint Bucket paints based on the pixels in all visible layers.*

6

The Magic Wand (covered in Chapter 4) and the Paint Bucket work in a similar way, by first analyzing the color of the pixel that is clicked on and then using the Tolerance settings in the tool's Options palette to determine the range of pixels affected. As with the Magic Wand, the greater the Tolerance, the larger the pixel range affected; the lower the Tolerance, the smaller the pixel range affected.

There is a clear difference between the two tools, however, that you need to understand: The Magic Wand selects according to the Tolerance setting, but the Paint Bucket paints over image areas according to that setting. The Magic Wand selects; the Paint Bucket paints. (To review the properties of the Magic Wand tool, see "Using the Magic Wand" in Chapter 4.)

In this section, you'll observe how various Tolerance settings determine how the Paint Bucket fills the four adjoining red lines created in the previous section. Double-click on the Paint Bucket tool to open the Paint Bucket Options palette. Start by examining the Tolerance setting—by default, it is set to 32. Like the Magic Wand, the Paint Bucket's Tolerance range is 0 to 255. If you type a low number in the Tolerance field, Photoshop applies the foreground color to contiguous areas that are very similar in color to the pixel you click on. If you enter a large number in the Tolerance field, Photoshop applies the foreground color over contiguous areas that vary greatly from the pixel you click on.

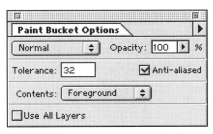

Click on the Contents pop-up menu. You'll see that the Paint Bucket tool paints with either the foreground color or with a pattern. (You will be creating and using patterns in Chapter 7.) The Anti-aliased option ensures that the paint applied with the Paint Bucket tool appears smooth, without jagged edges. The Use All Layers option applies the Tolerance setting to the layer you are in, based on a sample of the colors in all visible layers. Because you are not working in a file with layers, this option will have no effect now.

Start by testing the effects of a low Tolerance setting.

NOTE: *If you don't have the lines from the previous section on screen, create several intersecting lines using the Line tool. Use different colors and opacities for each line.*

1. Change the value in the Tolerance field to 0.

2. In order to see the Paint Bucket tool in action, you'll need to change the foreground color. Do this by picking a swatch from the Swatches palette or by moving the HSB slider controls in the Color palette. There are two ways to pick a bright blue color: In the Swatches palette, click on the first blue square in the first row of swatches; in the Color palette, you can set H to 180° and S and B to 100%. To fill with an opaque blue, make sure that Opacity is set to 100% and that Mode is set to Normal in the Paint Bucket Options palette.

3. Now move the mouse pointer to the first red, horizontal line that you drew in the previous section. As you move into the document window, the mouse pointer changes to a paint bucket. Position the tip of the paint bucket directly over any part of the line and click.

NOTE: *If you want to use a crosshair instead of the paint bucket, either turn on CAPS LOCK before you use the Paint Bucket tool or choose Precise in the Cursors group in the Preferences dialog box. To access the dialog box, choose File | Preferences | Display & Cursors.*

With a zero Tolerance setting, the Paint Bucket tool fills only the two opaque red lines with blue. When you clicked the paint bucket (or crosshair) on the horizontal opaque red line, Photoshop hunted down only the adjacent opaque red pixels and filled them with the blue color, but not the pixels painted at a lower opacity (the 50% tinted lines, or the pixels created from anti-aliasing).

To force the Paint Bucket tool to spread its paint over all the red lines—opaque *and* tinted—you will need to increase the Tolerance setting.

4. Before testing this, choose Undo from the Edit menu to reset the line's color back to red. Then change Tolerance to 200 in the Paint Bucket Options palette.

5. Once again, move the paint bucket (or crosshair) over the horizontal opaque line and click. This time the Paint Bucket tool paints all of the adjoining lines, including the tinted ones. The higher Tolerance level causes the Paint Bucket tool to paint over pixels that have a color range broader than just opaque red.

CAUTION: *If you click on one of the tinted lines instead of the opaque red lines, the Paint Bucket tool paints the entire screen blue, because the white background is within the 200 Tolerance range when applied to the 50% red tint. If this occurs, choose Undo from the Edit menu.*

6. Before continuing, save your work and name it **Bucket**.

You'll be using the Paint Bucket tool throughout this chapter, primarily to paint over areas that have been outlined with either the Paintbrush or Pencil tool or that have been previously painted. If you like, open a digitized photograph and click on different areas with the Paint Bucket. Make sure to change the Tolerance setting as you experiment, and observe the different effects.

TIP: *The Paint Bucket tool can also be used to fill a selection. When a selected area exists on screen, the Paint Bucket, like all painting tools, only paints within the selection.*

TIP: *You can press SHIFT while you click with the Paintbucket in the area surrounding the work canvas to change this part of the document window to the foreground color.*

Next, you will work with the Eraser tool, which you learned about in Chapter 3, and try out the tool's Erase to History option, which allows you to return an image to a specific state set in the History palette.

Using the Eraser Tool and the Erase to History Option

As your work with Photoshop's painting tools, you might want to erase part of your work or you might wish to erase areas to add special effects. Photoshop's Eraser tool allows you to click and drag to erase different image areas. If you paint on the Background layer, the Eraser tool simulates erasing by simply painting with the current background color. When you erase in a layer, the Eraser tool washes away the painted area (painting back in transparency), allowing you to see the layer beneath it.

NOTE: *If the Preserve Transparency option is selected in the Layers palette, the Eraser tool paints with the background color when erasing in a layer.*

NOTE: *To try out the Eraser tool, you should either open a digitized photograph or create a new file and, paint in it.*

Before you begin to use the Eraser tool, examine the different choices available in the Eraser Options palette. Open the Eraser Options palette by clicking on the Eraser tool in the Toolbox. (If the Options palette isn't displayed on screen, double-click on the Eraser tool.) In the palette, you'll see a pop-up menu, which allows you to control how the Eraser tool erases.

Click on the pop-up menu in the Eraser Options palette to examine the choices: Paintbrush, Airbrush, Pencil, and Block. By selecting one of the first three, you can erase as if you were using the Paintbrush, Airbrush, or Pencil tool. As discussed in Chapter 3, the Block option allows you to erase pixels as if it were an electronic version of a rubber eraser. When using the Pencil, Paintbrush, or Airbrush option, you can change the Opacity and use the Fade and Stylus Pressure features. When using the Paintbrush option, an additional choice—Wet Edges—is available. With all three of these options, the size of the erased stroke is determined by the selected brush size in the Brushes palette. You will learn how to use these features when the Pencil, Paintbrush, and Airbrush tools are covered later in this chapter.

TIP: *To quickly switch from one Eraser tool to another, press OPTION (Windows users: ALT) while clicking on the Eraser tool in the Toolbox; or you can press SHIFT will pressing E on the keyboard.*

To try out the Eraser tool, simply click and drag in your image. As you click and drag, the eraser erases. As mentioned earlier, if you are erasing in the background or in a layer with the Preserve Transparency option selected, the Eraser tool paints with the background color. Try setting the Eraser tool's mode to

Block and erasing several areas of the image on screen. After you've erased, you can return your image to its original state by clicking on the snapshot of the image in the History palette, or by clicking on a previous state in the History palette. You can also paint back a state set in the History palette by choosing the Erase to History feature (which works much like the History Brush). As you click and drag, the Eraser tool reverts your image to the currently set state in the History palette (to learn more about the History palette, see Chapter 9).

To try out the Erase to History feature, first select the Erase to History option in the Eraser Options palette, then open the History palette. If you've made a few changes to your image with the Eraser tool, you'll see a list of the past steps you took in the History palette. Or if you just opened an image on screen, you'll see a thumbnail of the original file on screen in the snapshot area of the palette. Click in the History Brush column to set the step that you wish to erase to. Next choose one of options in the Eraser Options palette's pop-up menu, then click and drag over your image. If you choose the Block choice in the Eraser Options palette, the Eraser icon looks like this: (⊡). As you work, you'll gradually see the previous version of your image painted back on screen.

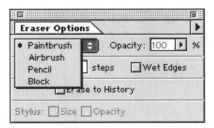

TIP: *You can activate the Erase to History option by pressing OPTION (Windows users: ALT) while clicking and dragging over previously saved image areas with the Eraser tool.*

When you are ready to proceed to the next section, close the file on screen. You don't need to save the changes because you won't use this file anymore.

Introduction to the Pencil, Paintbrush, and Eyedropper Tools

In this section you will be introduced to the painting tools—the Pencil, Paintbrush, and Eyedropper. If you wish to create the File Manager with File Cabinet project later in this chapter, these are the tools you will use. The Pencil and Paintbrush tools let you paint with brushes from the Brushes palette. The Eyedropper tool aids you in changing foreground and background colors.

Photoshop 5   In Action

Artist: Albert H. Lewis   **Promotional Material**

Albert, a New York artist, started creating these illustrations by first making detailed pencil drawings of the characters which he digitized with a scanner. After the images were scanned, Albert adjusted the brightness and contrast. Next, he used the Airbrush tool to apply broad areas of colors with a wide brush width. To add details, he used the Airbrush tool with a narrower brush. Later he used the Paintbrush and Pencil tools at varying opacities. To maintain consistency in the color of the images, Albert used the Eyedropper tool to change the foreground colors so they matched other colors in the image.

Setting Brush Cursor Preferences

Because you will be using different sized brushes in the following exercises, you may wish to switch preference settings so that the painting tool pointer is the same size as the brush with which you are painting. This can help give you a preview before painting of how a brush stroke will affect an image. To set the painting tool pointer to reflect your brush size, choose File | Preferences | Display & Cursors. In the Preferences dialog box, click on the Brush Size radio button in the Painting Cursors group. If you choose the Precise option, the tool pointer appears as a crosshair, which allows more precise alignment while working with the painting tools or other tools. The Standard option keeps the painting tool pointer set to the default settings. If you'd like, pick a setting, then click OK; otherwise, click Cancel.

6

Using the Pencil Tool to Draw and Erase

In the following exercise, you will create a file with a transparent background in which you will paint the word "ART" using the Pencil tool's Auto Erase feature. By working in a file with a transparent background, you'll be able to drag and drop the word "ART" into another file without needing to select the letters. Also, when "ART" is dropped into another file, the ART file's transparent background will allow color from the destination file to show around the letters.

Start by creating a new file large enough for the next few practice exercises. Set both Width and Height to 5 inches, resolution to 72 ppi, and Mode to RGB Color. To make the background transparent, click on the Transparent radio button in the Contents group. When you are ready to begin, click OK to display a new, untitled document. When the new document appears, notice that the document title bar displays the words "Layer 1." If the Layers palette is not open on screen, choose Show Layers from the Window menu. In the Layers palette, you'll also see the words "Layer 1" listed. When you create a new file with the Contents set to Transparent, Photoshop automatically creates a new layer, with a transparent background as the base layer. For more information about working with layers, see Chapters 15 and 16.

Getting Started with the Pencil Tool

Photoshop's electronic Pencil tool is unlike any pencil you've ever used before. It not only emulates a real pencil but can also draw lines between mouse clicks and erase by painting with the background color. It also allows you to pick different "lead" sizes from the Brushes palette.

You may be surprised to learn that the Pencil tool's "lead," or stroke, is controlled by a brush chosen in the Brushes palette. This gives the Pencil tool tremendous versatility. When you use the Pencil tool, the stroke can be thick or thin, round or square. The tool's smallest stroke is one pixel wide, which is handy for retouching images one pixel at a time.

Apart from retouching individual pixels, the Pencil tool can be used for freehand sketching. When you click and drag on screen with the Pencil tool, it paints with the foreground color, using a stroke set in the Brushes palette and opacity and blending mode set in the Pencil Options palette. No matter what the brush size or shape, the Pencil tool will always paint with a hard edge—unlike the Paintbrush and Airbrush tools, which can paint with soft edges. To see this in action, activate the Pencil tool by clicking on it in the toolbox. If the Pencil is not visible in the Pencil/Line tool Toolbox location, click on the Line tool and hold down the mouse. When the Pencil tool appears click and drag to select it.

Once the Pencil tool is activated, create a pencil stroke by clicking and dragging on screen. The stroke is created with the foreground color and is the width of the currently active brush (set in the Brushes palette).

Now take a look at the features in the Pencil Options palette. If the Options palette is not open, press ENTER to view the Pencil options. Notice the Fade, Stylus Pressure, and Auto Erase options. (Fade and Stylus Pressure also appear in the dialog boxes for the Paintbrush and Airbrush tools.) The Fade options work similarly for the Pencil, Paintbrush, and Airbrush tools and are covered later in this chapter, where you will learn how to use the Paintbrush and Airbrush tools.

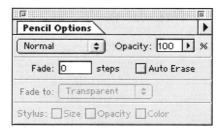

The Stylus Options

The Stylus options can only be activated if you have a stylus and graphics tablet connected to your computer. If you do have a stylus, these options are invaluable: You can control the size, color, and opacity of your painting by applying different amounts of pressure to the stylus.

Following are brief explanations of the Stylus Pressure options available for the Pencil, Paintbrush, and Airbrush tools.

SIZE   When this check box is selected, you can control the size of your brush strokes by applying different pressure with the stylus. Light pressure creates a small brush stroke; heavy pressure creates a large brush stroke. (The Stylus Pressure options for the Airbrush tool do not include size.)

COLOR   When this check box is selected, you can apply either the foreground color, the background color, or an intermediate color—a blend of the foreground and background colors. Use heavy pressure to apply the foreground color, light pressure to apply the background color, and a medium amount of pressure to apply an intermediate color.

OPACITY   When this check box is selected, you can use stylus pressure to control how opaque or transparent your brush strokes will be. The heavier the pressure, the more opaque the color; the lighter the pressure, the more translucent the color.

The figures in the following illustration, which show the various Stylus Pressure options, were created with a Wacom stylus with the Pencil tool activated.

The Auto Erase Option

The Auto Erase option in the Pencil Options palette allows the Pencil tool to work as an eraser. Remember, "erasing" in Photoshop means painting with the background color. Turning on the Auto Erase option triggers the Pencil tool to automatically switch to the background color when you paint over the foreground color.

Take a look at the Auto Erase feature in action.

    NOTE: *Before you proceed to step 1, you should have a new file on screen, with both Width and Height set to 5 inches, the resolution to 72 ppi, and Mode to RGB Color. Also, you should have a transparent background. (To make the background transparent, click on the Transparent radio button in the Contents group in the New dialog box.)*

1. If the Auto Erase option isn't selected, click on the check box in the Pencil Options palette.

   Next, select a vivid color for the foreground color and its complement for the background color from the Color palette. For instance, try blue as the foreground color and yellow as the background color.

2. If the Foreground selection box is not active in the Color palette, click on it. To choose a blue foreground color, you can either click on the first blue swatch in the first row of the Swatches palette or move the hue (H) slider control to 180 degrees, with saturation (S) and brightness (B) set to 100%.

3. Click on the Background selection box in the Color palette. To choose a yellow color, click on the yellow swatch in the first row of the Swatches palette or move the H slider control to 60 degrees, with the S and B sliders set to 100%.

   After you have chosen your colors, the next step is to select a brush from the Brushes palette to set the brush stroke the Pencil tool will use.

4. Start with a large brush size so that the Pencil tool's stroke will be dramatic. Click on the largest brush in the first row of the Brushes palette. After you click, the brush will be outlined, indicating it is the active brush for the Pencil tool.

 NOTE: *Brushes that are too large to be depicted by icons in the Brushes palette are represented by a brush with a number below it, representing the pixel width of the brush's diameter.*

   Now, with the Pencil tool's Auto Erase option enabled, create the word "ART," using capital letters.

5. Begin by clicking and dragging to start creating the left, slanted side of the capital letter "A." As you drag, the Pencil tool paints with the foreground color. When you finish the stroke, release the mouse button. To begin creating the right side of the letter "A," position the mouse at the top of the stroke you just produced. Then click and drag diagonally to the right. Notice that as soon as the mouse detects the foreground color, the Auto Erase option causes the Pencil tool to paint with the background color. Now, connect the two slanted lines by drawing the crossbar of the "A." If you start the bar by touching the left side, your bar will be yellow. If you start painting by touching the right side, the crossbar will be blue.

TIP: *If you wish, you can choose, View | Show Grid to display the grid and make it easier to follow a straight line. To change the gridline increments, choose File | Preferences | Guides & Grid.*

6. When you have completed the letter "A," start drawing the letter "R." Immediately, the Pencil tool returns to the foreground color. As you draw the "R," the Auto Erase feature causes the Pencil tool to switch to the background color whenever a stroke begins on the foreground color.

7. To create the letter "T," try a different painting technique as a special effect: Instead of dragging with the mouse, create the "T" with mouse clicks. Begin by clicking once to create a foreground-colored spot, then move the mouse halfway into the colored spot and click again. This creates a background-colored spot. Keep using overlapping mouse clicks to gradually create the letter. When you have finished, the letter will be entirely created from Pencil marks that alternate between the foreground and background colors.

For an added effect, you can add a drop shadow to your letters, by choosing Layer | Effects | Drop Shadow. You can also choose from the other commands in the Layer | Effects commands, such as Bevel and Emboss.

 NOTE: *If you are using a tablet, make sure that the Size, Color, and Opacity tablet settings are off; otherwise you will not obtain the results described above.*

Dragging and Dropping the ART Layer into Another File

After you have finished creating the word "ART" (from the previous section), you are ready to drag and drop the image over another file. Open a file in which you wish to place the word "ART." When the file is open, place the two images either side by side or so that they overlap. Next, activate the Move tool.

One of the most efficient ways of dragging and dropping one file into another, is to click and drag a layer from one file to another. Start by positioning the mouse pointer over the Art layer in the Layers palette. Click the mouse. With the mouse button still pressed, drag "ART" over the image you just opened. As you drag you'll see a tiny grabbing hand icon ( ) appear. After you've dragged the layer to the other file, release the mouse. The word "ART" will drop onto the file. Because "ART" was created in a file with a transparent background, you can see through the holes in the letters "R" and "A" as if they had been created on a clear acetate over the background file. In the Layers palette, notice that Photoshop automatically created a new layer for the "ART" image. The two eye icons in the Layers palette next to the Background and Layer 1 layers indicate that both layers are being viewed. The paintbrush icon and the highlight color surrounding Layer 1 indicate that you are currently working in this layer. Because you are working in a layer, you can reposition the entire layer without having to use a selection tool to select it, and you can move it without affecting the Background. Try using the Move tool to move "ART" into another position on screen.

If you wish to save the file with its new layer, you must save it in Photoshop format. Use the Save As command to save it under a new name so that you do not replace the original file. If you don't need to preserve the layer, use the File | Save a Copy command. When you do, the Flatten Image check box is selected automatically. This indicates that all layers in the file will be merged into a Background layer. Another way of removing layers from an image is to choose the Flatten Image or Merge Layers command from the Layers palette pop-up menu. To learn about merging and flattening layers, see Chapters 15 and 16.

 NOTE: *Most page layout programs can not read a Photoshop file. Before you export a file to a program like QuarkXPress, you will need to flatten layers and save it in a file format such as Tiff, EPS or DCS. See Appendix A for more information about saving Photoshop files in other formats.*

SHIFT-Clicking with the Pencil Tool

Now that you have completed your penmanship exercise, turn off the Pencil tool's Auto Erase option and experiment with the SHIFT key and the Pencil tool. Before you begin, create a new file to practice in. Make the file a 5-by-5-inch RGB color file with the background Contents set to Transparent.

Once the file opens, click on screen with the Pencil tool; then move the mouse to another area, press and hold SHIFT, and click again. The Pencil tool connects your mouse clicks.

 NOTE: *If you use the Pencil tool with SHIFT pressed, the Pencil paints in 90-degree increments.*

If you wish, keep experimenting with SHIFT and the Pencil tool. When you're ready to move on to the next section and explore the Paintbrush tool, you'll need to clear your screen. The easiest way to do this is to simply click on the first snapshot (entitled New) at the top of the History palette.

 REMEMBER: *If you are working on an image that does not have a transparent background, the Eraser tool paints with the background color. When working in a layer other than the Background, the Eraser tool clears pixels as if wiping colors off a clear acetate, leaving a transparent background.*

Using the Paintbrush Tool

 The Paintbrush tool is Photoshop's electronic version of an artist's paintbrush. The Paintbrush tool paints with the foreground color, using your choice of brush strokes. Using the tool's Fade options, you can also create colors that fade, or dissolve, as you paint.

Like the Pencil tool, the Paintbrush tool allows you to connect painted brush strokes by pressing SHIFT while clicking the mouse. Unlike the Pencil tool, though, the Paintbrush tool offers soft brush strokes that simulate paint applied with a paintbrush. When you activate the Paintbrush, take a moment to examine the Brushes palette; it includes a row of soft-edged brushes that were not available when you were using the Pencil tool.

Double-click on the Paintbrush tool to open the Paintbrush Options palette. You'll notice that the Paintbrush's options are almost identical to those of the Pencil tool, except that the Paintbrush does not have an Auto Erase feature. Instead, it has a Wet Edges option. The Wet Edges option produces the effect of painting with watercolors or markers rather than acrylic or oil paint. The colors created have a fully saturated appearance at stroke edges but not in the center of the stroke. If you paint an image using wet edges in a layer, underlying layers show through the brush strokes. Both the Paintbrush and the Pencil tools feature the same Stylus Pressure controls, and both include a Fade option. The choices in the Fade option allow you to create effects that cause the stroke you are painting to gradually disappear (Fade to Transparent) or gradually turns into the background color (Fade to Background). In the Fade field, you specify how many pixels (1 to 9999) the Paintbrush tool will paint before the fade-out begins. In the pop-up menu, you choose whether to Fade to Transparent or to the Background color.

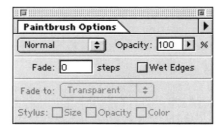

 TIP: *The effect of the brush you use changes depending on your image's resolution because the brushes in the Brushes palette are calculated based on pixels per inch. This means that a medium-sized brush will be fat when painting in an image with a resolution of 72 ppi, but thin when painting in an image at 300 ppi.*

Creating a Painter's Palette

As you work through the next few sections, you'll be performing the steps of an exercise to create a painter's palette similar to the one shown in Figure 6-2. Your experimentation with the Paintbrush tool's Fade options will be the start of the exercise. Because you will begin by painting without a Fade option chosen, check to see if there is a value other than 0 in the Fade field. If there is, change it to 0, now

Before you start painting, open a new 5-by-5-inch RGB color file on screen. Set the background Contents to White.

1. Set the foreground color to a dark gray or any dark color. In the Brushes palette, choose a medium-sized, hard-edged brush from the first row of brushes. In the Paintbrush Options palette, click and drag the Opacity pop-up slider control to 100% or press **0** on your keyboard.

2. Position the Paintbrush tool about .5 inch from the top of your screen and click and drag to create a kidney shape, representing the palette. Refer to Figure 6-2 as a guide. To paint the handle hole in the middle of the palette, click and drag again in a circular motion with the Paintbrush.

 TIP: *You can use the Pen tool to create a path of the painter's palette. Then select the path, fill it with white and stroke it.*

To create the paint dabs in the palette, use the Paintbrush's Fade to Transparent feature.

3. Double-click on the Paintbrush to activate the Paintbrush Options palette. Type **75** in the Fade field. If Transparent is not selected, choose it by clicking on the Fade to pop-up menu. These settings will cause the painting color to fade out over 75 pixels.

4. Create a couple of circular paint dabs in the painter's palette. Pick a foreground color and choose a medium-sized, soft-edged brush in the Brushes palette. Again using Figure 6-2 as your guide, click and drag with the Paintbrush tool in a circular motion in the palette. As you click and drag, the paint will gradually fade out. Do this one more time with another color to create another paint dab.

6

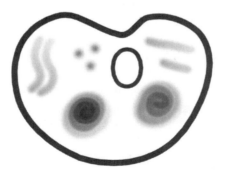

FIGURE 6-2   The Painter's Palette exercise

In order to paint the small, wavy lines in the upper-left part of the palette, you'll need to reset the Fade field so that the paint fades before you finish creating the lines.

5. In the Paintbrush Options palette, type **35** in the Fade field. Set the foreground color and then click and drag to create the two wavy lines. You'll notice that the fade-out occurs as you draw these lines.

6. Click three times to apply three soft-edged dots adjacent to the handle hole. To finish up, draw two more short, straight lines at the top-right side of the palette. Your painter's palette should look similar to Figure 6-2.

Now, assume that you want to add a few more artistic touches to the palette, with the same colors that you used to paint the lines and circles. For this, you need to use the Eyedropper tool.

Using the Eyedropper Tool

The Eyedropper tool doesn't paint, but it is an invaluable tool in the painting process; it is used to sample, or read, an image's color so that it can be used as the foreground or background color. With one quick click of the Eyedropper tool, the foreground or background color can be changed to the color of the pixel you clicked on with the tool. For example, it would be a lot of work to mix colors in the Color palette to obtain a particular flesh tone that appears in a scanned image. With the Eyedropper tool, on the other hand, you need only click on that colored portion of the image, and Photoshop's foreground color instantly changes to the flesh tone you need. This technique is a tremendous time-saver when you are color correcting and retouching scanned color images.

Before trying out the Eyedropper tool, first select it in the Toolbox. If you see the Color Sampler tool in the Toolbox, instead of the Eyedropper, click on the Color Sampler tool and hold down the mouse. When you see the Eyedropper appear, click and drag to select it. Next take a look at the Eyedropper Options palette. If the palette isn't open, press ENTER.

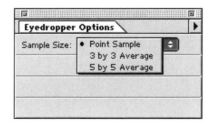

Using the Eyedropper's Sampling Options

All the Eyedropper options reside in the Sample Size pop-up menu. The default Sample Size setting is Point Sample, which narrows the Eyedropper's sample to the color value of the pixel on which you click. The 3 by 3 Average option reads the average color value of a 3-pixel-by-3-pixel area, and the 5 by 5 Average option operates similarly. To test the Eyedropper tool at its default setting, make sure the Sample Size option is set to Point Sample. (You can also reset the Eyedropper by choosing Reset Tool from the Eyedropper Options pop-up menu.)

Changing the Foreground and Background Colors with the Eyedropper

Before you begin using the Eyedropper tool, you should have the painter's palette from the previous section open on screen. If you didn't create the painter's palette from the previous section, open any digitized image. Next, move the mouse pointer toward the first paint dab you created in the painter's palette or over any color in the digitized image you have on screen. As you move the mouse into the document window, notice that the pointer changes to an eyedropper. (If CAPS LOCK is on or if the Other Tools Cursors group in the General Preferences dialog box is set to Precise, the pointer will be a crosshair, but it will still function as the Eyedropper tool.) Position the pointer over the first paint dab you created (or over any color in the digitized image you have on screen), but don't click the mouse yet. First, examine the color value readings in the Info palette.

The Info palette displays the color values of the pixels underlying the Eyedropper tool, using various color models. You can display one or two color model values at a time. If you will be sending your file to a printing press, it can be helpful to view CMYK colors at the same time that RGB or HSB colors are displayed. When CMYK colors are displayed in the Info palette, an exclamation point appears next to CMYK percentages that are out of gamut. If you are color correcting, it's very helpful to have both RGB and CMYK colors on screen because you will have a readout of the primary colors and their complements.

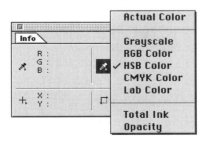

You can change to RGB, CMYK, HSB, Lab, or Grayscale by clicking on either of the eyedropper icons in the Info palette. When you click, the pop-up menu appears, as shown above. The pop-up menu allows you to choose the color model of your choice or to display opacity or the percentage of ink coverage when working with CMYK or Duotone images. Ink coverage is discussed in Chapter 12.

With the Eyedropper tool pointer positioned over the first paint dab that you created, click the mouse. Notice that the foreground color immediately changes to match the color you clicked on. To further test the Eyedropper's sampling power, move it to the outer edge of the paint dab circle (or over a light color in the digitized image you have on screen) and click the mouse. The foreground color changes to a lighter shade, reflecting the color created by the Fade to Transparent option you used with the Paintbrush tool to make the paint dab.

 TIP: *You can also click and drag over colors with the Eyedropper tool activated. As you drag, watch the foreground color change from color to color; stop when you see the color you need.*

OPTION-Clicking (Windows Users: ALT-Clicking) with the Eyedropper

From time to time, you may wish to use the Eyedropper tool to change the background color when the Foreground selection box is activated in the Color palette, or to change the foreground color when the Background selection box is activated. If the Foreground selection box is activated, you can change the background color by pressing OPTION (Windows users: ALT) while clicking on a color in the image with the Eyedropper tool. If the Background selection box is activated, you can change the foreground color by pressing OPTION (Windows users: ALT) while clicking on a color in the image with the Eyedropper tool.

Try this: Change the background color by pressing OPTION (Windows users: ALT) and clicking with the Eyedropper tool on any colored element in the painter's palette you created.

 TIP: *The designers of Photoshop recognized the tremendous value of the Eyedropper tool and made it readily available for changing the foreground color. Press OPTION (Windows users: ALT) while using the Pencil, Line, Paintbrush, Paint Bucket, Airbrush, or Gradient tools, and that tool changes to the Eyedropper tool.*

NOTE: *Using the Color Sampler tool: Sharing the Toolbox with the Eyedropper is the Color Sampler tool which samples up to four different colors on screen and provides readouts in the Info palette. When you click with the Color Sampler tool, Photoshop leaves a marker on screen at the area you clicked. In the Info palette the color values of the sample appear. The Color Sampler is most useful when adjusting or correcting colors. For instance, you can place sampler marks at the lightest, darkest, and midtone areas of your image. As you make adjustments to the image, the Info palette shows you how the adjustments affect different areas on screen. If you wish to move the samples on screen, you can click on one of the samples and drag it to another area on screen. To delete a sample on screen, press and hold OPTION (Windows users: ALT) and click on the sample on screen. Using the Color Sampler tool is discussed in Chapter 18.*

6

Using the Paintbrush's Wet Edges Option

In this section you will use the Paintbrush's Wet Edges option to create a flower like the one shown in Figure 6-3. In order to help you create the flower, you will add a new layer over an existing flower image, then use the underlying flower image as a kind of tracing guide. Before beginning this exercise, make sure that the Layers palette is open on screen. If it isn't, choose Show Layers from the Window menu.

1. Start by scanning a flower, or scan the flower image in Figure 6-3. If a scanner is not available, load any image to paint over.

2. In order to use the flower as a tracing guide, you'll need to create a new layer to use like an acetate. To create the layer, choose New from the Layer menu. In the New pop-up menu choose Layer. The options in the New Layer pop-up menu are discussed in detail in Chapters 15 and 16. For the time being, make sure that Opacity is set to 100%, blending mode is set to Normal, and Group With Previous Layer is not selected. In the Name field type **Painted Flower**, then click OK to create the layer.

   Notice that the name of the layer you just created now appears in both the title bar and the Layers palette. The two eye icons in the Layers palette next to the Background layer and the Painted Flower layer indicate that both layers are being viewed. The paintbrush icon and highlight color

FIGURE 6-3 Flower created using the Wet Edges option

surrounding the word Painted Flower in the Layers palette indicates that it is the target layer. This is the layer in which you will be painting.

3. Next, activate the Paintbrush tool and select the Wet Edges option in the Paintbrush tool's Options palette.

4. Choose a foreground color, a brush size, and, if you'd like, a Fade option If you created the Painter's palette in the previous exercise, Paintbrush tool's Fade option is set to 35. Start painting over the flower. Notice that as you paint, the colors look as if they are slightly diluted with water, with the edges less diluted. Try painting one color over another. If you release the mouse and then reapply paint over areas you've already colored, the paint grows darker.

Try painting with different brushes, both soft and hard, at different opacities.

5. Finish the flower by adding a stem and a few leaves around the stem.

6. After you have finished painting, place the flower into another image with an interesting background.

7. Open a file over which you wish to place the flower you just painted. Because you created the flower in a layer, you can drag and drop or copy and paste the flower into another file without having to use the selection tools to select it.

8. Place the two files on screen side by side or so that they overlap. Then use the Move tool to drag the Painted Flower layer into the newly opened file.

When the Painted Flower layer is in the newly opened file, you'll see that there is a new layer called Painted Flower in the Layers palette. Also, notice that you can see through the translucent areas of the flower. Move the flower into position using the Move tool. Because you are in a layer, the flower moves above the Background layer. If you wish to save your file with the Painted Flower layer, use the File | Save As command and save your file in Photoshop format. Save the file under a new name so that you do not replace the original image. If you wish to save your file but do not wish to preserve the layer, use the File | Save a Copy command to flatten the image and save it.

6

The File Manager with File Cabinet Project

Before proceeding to learn about more painting tools, you may wish to practice using the painting tools that have been covered so far. Using the Line, Paintbrush, Pencil, and Paint Bucket tools, you can create the image shown in Figure 6-4. You'll start by creating the file cabinet, then create the file manager character in another file, which will then be pasted into the file cabinet file. Although the steps are detailed as follows, feel free to improvise and experiment as you work.

Creating the File Cabinet

1. Create a new file, 7 inches wide and 5 inches high. (This size will accommodate both the file cabinet and the file manager character.) Set the resolution to 72 ppi and Mode to RGB Color. Because you want the images you will be creating to be white, set the Contents radio button to

FIGURE 6-4   The File Manager with File Cabinet project

White. When your file opens, set the Foreground color to black (press D on the keyboard).

NOTE: *If you wish to use this or any of the other images in this chapter as the basis for a project that will be printed professionally, you'll probably want to use a resolution higher than 72 ppi. Make sure that you have enough memory to handle the file size—a 5-by-7-inch RGB file at 300 ppi consumes 9MB, as compared with 532K at 72 ppi.*

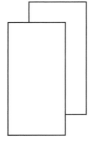

2. Your first step is to use the Rectangular Marquee tool and the Edit | Stroke command to create a rectangle. In the Stroke dialog box, set Width to 2 pixels and Location to Inside. After the first rectangle is stroked, do not deselect. Duplicate the rectangle by pressing COMMAND-OPTION (Windows users: CTRL-ALT) while you click and drag on a selection edge. Drag downward and to the left so that your image looks like the illustration shown at the left. When the rectangle is in the desired location, deselect it by clicking away from the selected area.

3. Use the Line tool with a 2-pixel width to connect the two offset rectangles at both upper corners and the bottom-right corners in order to create a

three-dimensional effect. Next, use the Paint Bucket tool to fill the side of the file cabinet. Make sure that no gaps appear in the outline of the area you are filling; otherwise the Paint Bucket tool will spread paint over the entire image. Clean up the image by removing any unwanted lines with the Eraser tool.

4. Once you have the basic structure of the cabinet created, use the Marquee tool and the Edit | Stroke command to create two rectangles for the file cabinet drawers. Duplicate the top drawer rectangle and offset it as you did with the rectangles that form the file cabinet.

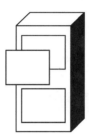

5. Use the Line tool to create a three-dimensional effect for the top drawer, and fill with the Paint Bucket tool to create a shadow along the side. Again, use the Eraser tool to remove any unwanted lines. Experiment with the different Modes and Opacities in the Eraser Options palette. Also, use different brush sizes. Then use the Line tool with a 75% opacity to create the drawer handles. To create the file folders in the cabinet, draw lines with a 50% opacity setting. Your image should look similar to this:

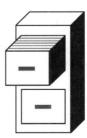

6. When you've completed the filing cabinet, save the file and name it **Cabinet**.

Creating the File Manager Character

Follow these steps to create the file manager character shown in Figure 6-4.

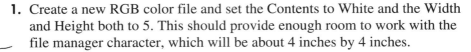

1. Create a new RGB color file and set the Contents to White and the Width and Height both to 5. This should provide enough room to work with the file manager character, which will be about 4 inches by 4 inches.

2. Use the Marquee tool and the Edit | Stroke command to create simple shapes, as shown here, to use as a rough guide for the file manager. Use the Pencil tool with a small brush to sketch a rough outline for the arms.

3. After creating the foundation for the character, use the Paintbrush tool to paint in details. Use the Eraser tool to erase any unwanted foundation lines that remain. When erasing, you may wish to experiment with the different modes and opacities in the Eraser Options palette. If you use any mode other than Block, don't forget to check the brush size you're using in the Brushes palette. Choose the color you want for the mouth, nose, eyes, ears, and hair.

4. Use the Pencil tool to create details in the shirt—the buttons, cuffs, and cuff links. Then, use the Pencil tool with your choice of colors to add the pocket, pencil, and bow tie.

5. Use the Paintbrush tool to paint in the hands. Create the disk with the Pencil tool, then continue using the Pencil tool to outline the character's pants.

6. Fill in the pants with the Paint Bucket tool. Again, before you fill them in, make sure that no gaps appear in the outline of the area you are filling; otherwise the Paint Bucket will spread paint over the entire image.

When you are satisfied with the file manager's appearance, save your work. Name the file **Manager**. Now you are ready to copy the file manager character into the file cabinet document.

Pasting the File Manager into the File Cabinet File

In this section, you will use the Magic Wand tool to select the white background of the file manager character and then *invert* the selection so that you can copy the image.

1. With the file manager character on screen, double-click on the Magic Wand tool. To ensure that you only select the white background, type **0** in the Tolerance field in the Magic Wand Options palette. De-select the Anti-aliased option, so you don't create a soft-edged selection. Next, click on the white background; only the background should be selected. Choose Inverse from the Select menu to select everything but the current selection; now only the file manager character should be selected.

2. From the Edit menu, select Copy. Close the Manager file and open the Cabinet file.

3. Select Paste from the Edit menu, and the file manager character will appear in the Cabinet document in a new layer.

 NOTE: *You can also use the Move tool to drag and drop a selection from one file to another rather than copy and paste.*

4. Next, use the Move tool to click and drag the character to a suitable position, as shown in Figure 6-4.

5. To save your work, use the Save As command and name your file **FileManager** so that you can keep the original Cabinet file intact.

You now have three files on your disk: the original Cabinet file, the original Manager file, and the final project file, FileManager. By keeping the original Cabinet and Manager files, you can always edit them and then re-create the final project.

Now that you have mastered Photoshop's basic painting tools, you are ready to progress to more advanced painting tools and techniques.

Introduction to the Airbrush Tool

 The Airbrush tool is an electronic version of the mechanical airbrush that artists use to create three-dimensional shading effects. The tool is also used to soften images with a hint of color. In retouching and painting work, the Airbrush tool is often the best tool for adding highlights and shadows.

The Airbrush tool paints in much the same manner as the Paintbrush tool, except that the Airbrush colors with a softer edge. Like the Pencil and Paintbrush, the Airbrush allows you to choose from a variety of brushes from the Brushes

Photoshop 5 In Action

Artist: Page Wood   **Commissioned Art**

Page Wood, an ex-New York artist now living in California, was comissioned to design a piece of art to screen a construction site in midtown Manhattan. This would be viewed from blocks away, as you drove by it, and close up from the sidewalk.

Page started this image by first working with markers on tracing paper. He scanned the line art in grayscale at 600 dpi, then used Painter (great for mimicking markers) to adjust and clean up the black lines. Back in Photoshop, he used the Spatter filter (Filter | Brush Strokes | Spatter) to remove digital edges here and there, or to make a line crumble nicely as it trails off. He then saved the line work as a separate layer.

Next, he made a 300 dpi RGB copy of the art and began masking all the colored areas using Photoshop's selection tools. As he painted in the different selected areas, Page tried to make contrasts between milky-smooth and highly-textured areas by using the Airbrush tool in Dissolve mode as well as the Gaussian Blur and Add Noise filters. The grainy areas got chunkier when he blew it back up 200%. Adding back the saved line layer, he colored it, painted some more, and worked on detail where needed.

palette. Unlike the other tools, however, the Airbrush Options palette does not have an Opacity slider; instead, it has a Pressure slider. The greater the pressure setting, the more paint is sprayed when you click and hold the mouse button.

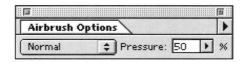

In this section and the next, you will experiment with the Airbrush tool and its Fade options. In order to perform the exercises, create a new file 6 inches wide by 4 inches high. Set the background Contents to Transparent. When you click OK, you will be in a new layer. All nonpainted areas in the layer are transparent. This is the size you will need to accommodate the Summer Sale Postcard project (shown in Figure 6-5) after the introductory exercises.

Click on the Airbrush tool to activate it. For the foreground color, choose any color swatch in the Swatches palette or create a color using the slider controls in the Color palette. From the Brushes palette, pick a large, soft-edged brush. In the Airbrush Options palette, examine the Pressure slider; if it is not set to 100%, click on the slider control and drag all the way to the right. Make sure the blending mode is set to Normal.

FIGURE 6-5   The Summer Sale Postcard project

Now, move the mouse pointer toward the document area. As you move, the pointer changes to an airbrush. (If CAPS LOCK is on or if the Painting Cursors group is set to Precise or Brush Size, your pointer will be a crosshair, but the tool will still work as the Airbrush.)

Move the Airbrush pointer anywhere in the document. Click the mouse and keep it pressed for a second or two. Notice that paint keeps spilling out. Now click and drag slowly for a few inches to see the soft, diffused spray created by the tool.

To observe the effects of painting with a lower pressure, click and drag the Pressure slider control in the Airbrush Options palette to 50%. Move the Airbrush pointer back into the document and click and hold the mouse button. This time, less paint is sprayed onto the screen by the brush.

Continue experimenting with the Airbrush tool, choosing various brush sizes and pressure settings. When you're ready, continue to the next section and explore the Airbrush's Fade options.

The Airbrush Fade Options

To open the Airbrush Options palette, double-click on the Airbrush tool or, if the Options palette is open on screen, click once on the tool. Notice that the palette options here are very similar to those for the Paintbrush and Pencil tools. The Fade options for the Airbrush work exactly as they do with the Paintbrush and Pencil. You'll remember them—they are Transparent and Background. When one of these options is selected, painting starts with the foreground color and fades out either to completely transparent or to the background color. The Fade field controls how much paint appears before the fade occurs. For both Fade options, the brush size you choose in the Brushes palette controls the width of the fade.

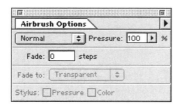
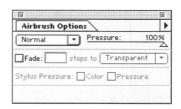

To try out the Fade options, type **100** in the Fade field of the Airbrush Options palette. Click on the pop-up menu and choose Transparent if it is not already set to this option. Set the Pressure to 100%. In the Brushes palette, choose a medium-sized, soft-edged brush. Change the foreground color, if you wish. To see the fade, click and drag in a spiral motion. As you drag, you'll see a soft-edged brush stroke that gradually fades out after 100 pixels of paint have been applied.

Next, try the Background Fade option. This time, choose Background from the pop-up menu in the Airbrush Options palette. Leave the Fade field set to 100; this will make it easier to compare the difference between the Transparent and Background fade options.

Before you begin to paint, set the foreground color to green and the background color to yellow. These two colors are near each other on the color wheel, so there won't be a great contrast as one switches to the other and the fade effect will be smoother and more realistic. Keep Brightness and Saturation set high to ensure that the colors will be bright. Now click and drag to create another spiral on screen. This time, the green, soft-edged brush stroke will gradually dissolve into the yellow you picked as the background color.

If you wish to keep experimenting, use a few other color pairs. Try working with colors that are near each other on the Hue slider, and then compare the effects to what you get when you pick a color and its complement, such as blue and yellow.

Before you continue to the next section, clear the screen by clicking on the New snapshot in the History palette.

The Summer Sale Postcard Project

If you would like to practice using the Airbrush tool, try your hand at creating the Summer Sale postcard shown in Figure 6-5. This project was designed to convey a feeling of lightness and delicacy to match the type of clothes people buy in the summer. In order to create this mood, a very soft brush stroke was needed, one that would taper off. The Airbrush tool is perfect for the job.

 NOTE: *Before you begin the Summer Sale Postcard project, you should create a new file 6 inches wide by 4 inches high, with the background Contents set to Transparent.*

Creating the Sun

The first step in this project is to create the sun. You'll use the Airbrush tool with both the Fade to Background and the Fade to Transparent options. Using both Fade options adds variety and realism, as they are perfect for giving a soft edge to the sun and for blending its color from yellow to orange.

1. Double-click on the Airbrush tool. In the Airbrush Options palette, then type **200** in the Fade field. Choose the Background option in the Fade to pop-up menu.

2. In the Brushes palette, pick any small, soft-edged brush.

3. In the Color palette, choose an orange foreground color and a yellow background color.

4. Now create the spiral that is the center of the sun by clicking and dragging in a spiral motion.

5. In the Airbrush Options palette, switch to the Fade to Transparent option to create the rays of the sun. Type **10** in the Fade field.

6. In the Brushes palette, pick a medium-sized, soft-edged brush.

 TIP: *If you want the mouse pointer size to be the same size as the currently selected brush, choose File | Preferences | Display & Cursors and select Brush size from the Painting Cursors group.*

7. Position the mouse at the edge of the sun's spiral and click and drag outward to create several rays, as shown in Figure 6-5.

8. Save your work and name the file **Summer**.

Creating the Butterfly

In this section, you will continue using the Airbrush to create the butterfly on the Summer Sale postcard.

1. Because you will be painting a sketch of a butterfly, make sure that the Fade option is no longer active in the Airbrush Options palette. If it is, enter **0** in the Fade field. In the palette, set Pressure to 25%.

2. Click on the Default Colors icon to reset the foreground to black and the background to white. In the Brushes palette, choose a small brush.

 3. Use the Airbrush to sketch an outline of a short ellipse and a long ellipse for the butterfly's body. Then create the outline of the wings.

4. Once you have sketched the outline of the butterfly, paint the wings using various shades of blue. Use different Pressure settings and different Fade options in the Airbrush Options palette.

5. When you have finished coloring the wings, you are ready to fill in the body of the butterfly. Use the Fade to Transparent option with Pressure set to 30%. Set the Fade field to a number from 2 to 30. Change the foreground color to black and choose a medium-sized, soft-edged brush.

6. Now apply the finishing touches. Create the black strokes for texture in the butterfly's body, wings, eyes, and antennae by airbrushing with a small, hard-edged brush and Pressure set to 90%.

Feel free to continue to experiment with different colors and effects on the butterfly. If you try something and don't like the results, use the Undo command. Also, don't forget that you can activate the Eraser tool's Erase to History option to revert a portion of your document to the state set in the History palette.

Creating the Text and Clothing Items

The next step in the postcard project is using the Type tool to add the words "SUMMER SALE." Remember: When you use the Type tool, Photoshop creates the Type in a new layer, and creates the type using the current foreground color, which can be changed in the Type tool dialog box.

1. Activate the Type tool and click on the upper-left side of your document window.

2. In the Type Tool dialog box, choose Times (or another typeface, if you prefer) in the Font pop-up menu. Type **40** in the Size field. Make sure the Anti-aliased check box is selected. In the text field, type **SUMMER SALE**. Click OK.

   Notice that when you use the Type tool to create text (instead of the Type Mask tool), your text is created in a new layer.

 NOTE: *If you had used the Type Mask tool instead of the Type tool, painting and filling only affects the selected text area on screen.*

3. Next, use the Move tool to move the type into position. (Note that you could have moved the type with the Type Tool dialog box open, if the Preview option had been selected.)

4. Next, render the type so you can paint over it. To render the type choose Layer | Type | Render Layer.

5. Try creating a special effect in the text by changing the foreground color and using the Airbrush tool to apply another color. When you paint over text, Photoshop applies the color to the text only, not to the entire layer, because the Preserve Transparency option in the Layers palette is automatically selected when you create text with the Type tool. With the Airbrush tool, dab a bright color over the "SUMMER SALE" letters to create highlights.

6. To finish off the project, create the clothes and the hangers. Draw the hangers with the Pencil tool and then paint the clothes over them; use the Airbrush and Paintbrush tools with whatever colors you like. If you wish, add more items. For a more painterly effect you can apply the Filter | Artistic | Dry Brush and/or Filter | Artistic | Paint Daubs.

Photoshop 5 ▸ In Action

The flaring light effect was created by applying the Lens Flare filter in the Filter | Render submenu.

The Airbrush tool was used to create the glow effects in the planet and in the arm.

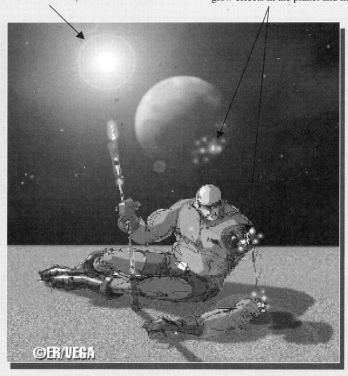

©ER/VEGA

Artist: Enrique Rivera-Vega   **Promotional Material**

Enrique began this image by creating two rectangular selections. He filled the bottom selection with color, then applied the Add Noise filter to create a gravelly texture in the foreground. He filled the top selection with black, then used the Airbrush tool to create the lighter areas in the dark background. Next, Enrique created a circular selection for the planet, then used the Airbrush tool again to create the different lighting effects within it.

The robot was first sketched with the Pencil tool, then filled using the Paintbrush and Airbrush tools. All of the glow effects were created with the Airbrush tool.

When you are satisfied with your work on the Summer Sale postcard project, save and close the file.

Creating Gradients

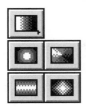

The Gradient tools allow you to fill the screen or a selection with a blend that gradually changes from one color to another or from a color to transparency. Gradients are often used to produce shading and lighting effects, as well as to quickly create visually pleasing backgrounds. By changing opacity and/or blending mode settings, you can create interesting effects by applying gradients over images and over other gradients.

The Gradient tools provides five gradient styles in their Toolbox location: Linear, Radial, Angular, Reflected, and Diamond. To access any of the different styles, click on the Gradient tool in the Toolbox. With the mouse button pressed, drag to the gradient style desired. The tiny thumbnails of the tool provide a miniature picture of how each gradient style appears. Here's a brief description:

- **Linear Gradient**   Creates gradient along a straight line. Often used to create background patterns.

- **Radial Gradient**   Creates gradient out from the center of a circular shape. Use the Radial Gradient tool to create glowing planet effects.

- **Angular Gradient**   Creates gradient around a starting point. The angular gradient colors change around the circumference (as opposed to the radial gradient where the colors radiate out from the middle).

- **Reflected Gradient**   Creates Gradient On Both Sides Of The Starting Point. A Short Click And Drag Can Create A Soft-Pipelike Effect.

- **Diamond Gradient**   Creates a gradient in a diamond shape. The diamond is created outwards from the starting point where you click and drag. The point where you release the mouse defines one tip of the diamond.

Gradients are created, controlled, and edited through the Gradient Options palettes. To access the palette, double-click on the Gradient tool icon in the Toolbox.

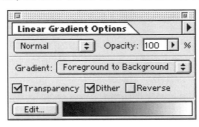

CAUTIOIN: *Be aware that various factors can affect the way a gradient prints. The blend's printed output will depend on the colors you use, the length of the blend, the file mode you are in, and the resolution at which you are printing.*

 TIP: *If you keep the Dither check box selected when creating a gradient, Photoshop smoothes the foreground and background using a process called dithering. This should help prevent banding when outputting a gradient. When banding occurs, steps or breaks are seen in the blend.*

The Gradient Tool Options

The Gradient options in the Gradient Options palette determine how colors are used in the blend. The options in the palette include the Gradient pop-up menu, which easily allows you to choose the colors that are used when the gradient is created. If Foreground to Background is selected, Photoshop creates a smooth transition between the foreground and background colors. The next option, Foreground to Transparent creates a blend from the foreground color to a transparent background. Other options create a gradation using specific colors. The last option, Transparent Stripes, creates a set of stripes that alternates between a stripe of the foreground color and a transparent stripe. Note that when you pick an option, you can see a preview of it in the bottom of the Gradient Options palette. The Gradient options may vary in how they look when applied to your document if you change the blending mode from Normal to another mode or if you adjust the Opacity slider.

When the Transparency option is selected, areas of the gradient can be made transparent, allowing image areas below the gradient to show through. The opacity of the transparency can be controlled using options in the Gradient Editor dialog box. If Transparency is not selected, color is used instead of the transparency.

When the Dither option is selected, Photoshop smoothes the foreground and background using a process called *dithering*. This should help prevent banding when outputting a blend. When banding occurs, steps or breaks are seen in the blend.

If you wish to reverse the color placement of the gradient, click the Reverse button.

 TIP: *Another technique for eliminating banding is to add a bit of noise with Photoshop's Add Noise filter, although this can affect white areas. See Chapter 10 for more details.*

When you click on the Edit button in the Gradient Options palette, the Gradient Editor dialog box is displayed. In this dialog box you can edit a gradient or create a new gradient. You'll learn more about the Gradient Editor dialog box later in this chapter.

Applying a Gradient

When you apply a gradient to your document, you can specify where you want the blend to occur by selecting an area on screen beforehand with one of the selection tools. You can even apply a blend inside text by clicking and dragging with the Gradient tool over a text selection created with the Type Mask tool.

 NOTE: *If you use the Type tool to create text, type is created in a layer. After you render the layer (Layer | Type | Render Layer), make sure the Preserve Transparency option in the Layers palette is selected before you apply a gradient. If it is not, the whole layer is filled with the gradient, not just the text.*

To apply a blend to your document, select the Gradient tool and then adjust the settings in the Gradient Options palette. Next, click and drag in the direction you want the blend to "move" toward. You can also adjust how the blend is applied by how far you drag with the Gradient tool.

Applying a Linear Gradient

The Linear Gradient tool creates a blend along a straight line. The blend is created from the point where you click and start dragging the mouse and ends where you release the mouse.

Try applying a blend that simulates a change in lighting. To produce a blend for a lighting effect, you don't want to pick colors that contrast too much. Choose a yellow foreground color (the first yellow color swatch in the Swatches palette). For the background color, lower the Hue slider about 20 degrees. This will produce an orange color. Before you begin the steps, create a new document with the Background set to White.

1. You'll create the blend in a rectangular selection, so activate the Rectangular Marquee tool and click and drag to create a rectangle about 2.5 inches wide by 2 inches high.

2. In the Toolbox, select the Linear Gradient tool.

3. Make sure that the Gradient pop-up menu in the Linear Gradient Options palette is set to Foreground to Background.

4. Now create a gradient that starts on the left with the foreground color and blends to the right into the background color. Position the crosshair about .5 inch inside the left edge of the selection. Click and drag to the right—the direction in which you want the blend to go. As you drag, Photoshop will create a line on screen, indicating where the blend will be created. To produce the blend, release the mouse about .5 inch away from the right side of the selection.

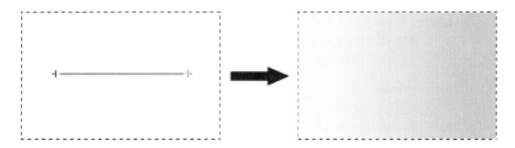

Notice that the blend appears between the two endpoints of your mouse selection. Photoshop fills the area directly before the blend with the solid foreground color and the area after the blend with solid background color. To get a sense of how Photoshop fills in the intermediate colors, open the Info palette (if it isn't already open), slowly move the mouse pointer over the blend from left to right without clicking, and watch the color values gradually change.

If you would like to experiment with a few more linear blends, clear your screen first; then try some angled blends. This is easily done by clicking and dragging at an angle with the Gradient tool. You can even hold down the constraining SHIFT key to create blends at a 45-degree angle. After you have created a few more blends, continue on to the next section to create a radial gradient. If you'd like, try experimenting with different Gradient options.

 TIP: *You can choose View | Hide Edges to temporarily hide a selection marquee. Note that this keeps the area selected.*

 NOTE: *You can edit a gradient before applying it, using the Gradient Editor dialog box, which is discussed later in the chapter.*

Applying a Radial Gradient

In this exercise, you'll see the effects of creating a radial blend when you use the Foreground to Transparent option.

Try creating a radial blend in a circular selection:

1. Create a new RGB color file, 3 inches by 3 inches. Set the background Contents to Transparent.

2. Set the foreground color to yellow.

3. In the Toolbox, select the Radial Gradient tool.

4. To create the circular selection, click and drag with the Elliptical Marquee tool.

5. In the Radial Gradient Options palette, set the Gradient pop-up menu to Foreground to Transparent.

6. To create the blend, position the mouse in the center of your elliptical selection. Click and drag in any direction toward the edge of the elliptical selection. This time, Photoshop creates the blend radiating out from the center, instead of in a straight line.

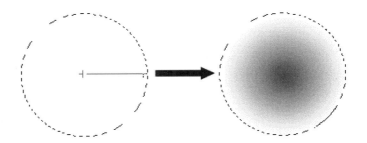

   Notice that you can see right through the lightest area of the blend. This is because you used the Foreground to Transparent option.

7. Before opening the file that you will place the blend into, deselect.

8. Open any other image. Activate the Move tool and drag the gradient over the file you just loaded on screen. You'll see that the image shows through the transparent part of the blend. The same effect could also have been produced by creating a new layer and then creating the Transparent to Foreground blend in it.

At this point you'll probably want to do some experimenting with radial blends. If you wish, you can undo your gradient and redo it. This time, when you create your gradient, click and drag in a different direction and drag for either a shorter or longer length. The distance you drag controls the distance from the start of the blend, where the foreground color is displayed as a solid color, to the end of the blend.

 TIP: *If you create a gradient with an opacity of less than 100% over an image, the underlying object will appear through the translucent blend.*

Creating a Glowing Planet Effect

Here's how you can use the Radial Gradient tool with the Elliptical Marquee's Feather Radius option to create a glowing planet effect.

1. Start by choosing a reddish foreground color and a reddish-yellow background color.

2. In the Toolbox, choose the Radial Gradient tool.

3. In the Radial Gradient Options palettes the Gradient pop-up menu to Foreground to Background.

4. Activate the Elliptical Marquee Tool palette and open its Options palette by double-clicking on the tool. Click on the Constrained Aspect Ratio radio button, and set Width to 1 and Height to 1. Set the Feather field to 15.

5. Now click and drag on screen with the Elliptical Marquee tool to create the circular selection.

 NOTE: *Before continuing, reset the Elliptical Marquee tool to Normal and change the Feather field to 0.*

6. Activate the Radial Gradient tool and position the crosshair in the center of the selection. Click and drag toward the edge of the circular selection. When you release the mouse, the blend will be created with a central red area. How much red mass is in the circle will depend on how much or how little you drag. Experiment with adjusting the red mass in the circle. Note that the Feather setting applied in step 4 creates the soft edge of the blend.

 TIP: *You can choose View | Hide Edges to temporarily hide a selection marquee. Note that this keeps the area selected.*

The Gradient Editor Dialog Box

Photoshop allows you to edit pre-existing gradients or create your own custom gradients and save them. To edit, create, or save a gradient, you need to use the Gradient Editor dialog box. To access the Gradient Editor dialog box, click on the Edit button in the lower-left corner of the Gradient Options palette.

In the Gradient Editor, pick a gradient from the scrolling list and then edit it. When you edit the gradient, you are changing the original. We advise you to pick a gradient from the scrolling list, then click on the Duplicate button, and then edit the duplicate. This way you won't lose the original gradient.

After you duplicate a gradient, you can click on the Rename button to rename the gradient. Note that you can also click on the New button to create a new gradient. There is also a Remove button, which allows you to remove a gradient if you decide you don't like it. The Save and Load buttons allow you to save and load different libraries of gradients as you need them. That way you don't have a huge scrolling list.

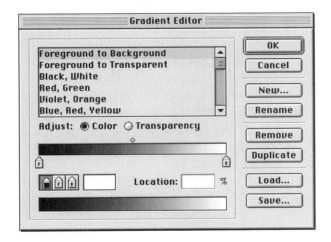

The options below the scrolling list of gradients determine how a gradient looks.

To choose or edit a starting color, click on the small pentagon shape on the left side, beneath the gradient bar. The tip of the pentagon becomes black. This indicates that you can now choose a color for the starting point. To choose a color, simply click on the rectangular swatch. After you click, the Color Picker dialog box opens, allowing you to choose a color by clicking the mouse, by entering a value, or by clicking on the Custom color icon. To choose an ending color for your blend, click on the pentagon shape on the right side of the blend, then click on the colored swatch to open the Color Picker dialog box.

 TIP: *You can also pick a color by clicking the eyedropper over any color in your document or the foreground or background color in the Toolbox.*

If you wish to use the current foreground or background color, first click on one of the pentagon icons, then click on either the F or B icons in the lower left of the Gradient Editor dialog box.

To pick a color from your image, click on the pentagon icon to the left of the F and B icons (in the lower left of the dialog box), then click in your image. You can also click in the gradient bar in the middle of the dialog box.

If you'd like, you can change the location of the starting, ending, or midpoint. To change locations, you can click on the starting, ending, or midpoint icons and drag them on the gradient bar. You can also adjust the color by entering a value into the Location field. Higher values move the color to the right, lower values move the color to the left. Note that the midpoint slider determines where the blend begins to change from the foreground to background color, or to or from Transparency. If you move the slider to the right, the blend will be produced with more foreground color than background color. Move the slider to the left, and the blend will be created with less foreground color and more background color.

To further edit the gradient, you can create intermediate points on the gradient bar. To create an intermediate point, click below the gradient bar where you want the intermediate point to appear. Then choose a color in the steps described above.

If you wish to remove an intermediate color, click on the pentagon icon and drag down.

To add the gradient to the gradient list or complete the editing process of a pre-existing gradient, click OK.

 TIP: *If you wish to reset the Gradient Editor dialog box, press OPTION (Windows users: ALT); this changes the Cancel button to a Reset button. Click the Reset button.*

Changing Gradient Transparency

One of the most intriguing features provided by the Gradient Editor is its ability to create transparent blending effects. You can create blends that start at one color and blend to 100 percent transparency or create effects that blend from one percentage of transparency to another.

To change or create a transparency, first make sure that the Transparency option is selected in the Gradient Options palette, then click on the Edit button. In the Gradient Editor dialog box, first click on the Transparency radio button in the Adjust section. Click on one of the pentagons icon below the gradient bar, then enter a percentage in the Opacity field. At the bottom of the palette, you'll see a preview of the transparency effect.

Creating and Using Custom Brushes

Thus far in this chapter, you have been using the default brushes that appear automatically in Photoshop's Brushes palette, but it's likely that you will want to create your own custom brushes (by specifying their size, shape, and other characteristics) to add more variety and style to your work, and this section tells you how. You'll also learn how to save a palette of custom brushes and load it from your hard disk.

Examining the New Brush Dialog Box

You'll start by creating a new brush based on one of the brushes already in the Brushes palette. You will use a large brush as the model because its diameter, hardness, and roundness attributes will be more noticeable than those of a smaller one. Click once on the largest hard-edged brush in the first row of the Brushes palette.

Your next step in creating a new brush is to choose the New Brush command in the palette's menu of the Brushes palette (click on the small triangle in the upper-right side of the palette). The New Brush dialog box appears, displaying the settings for the brush that was selected in the Brushes palette. In the dialog box you'll see sliders for controlling Diameter, Hardness, and Spacing and boxes for entering Angle degrees and Roundness percentages.

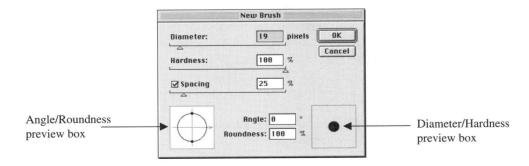

Angle/Roundness preview box

Diameter/Hardness preview box

Photoshop 5 In Action

The light beams were created with linear blends.

The lighting effects under the plane were created with blends.

The Airbrush tool was used to create the movie marquee lights.

Artist: Leslie Carbaga   Art Director: Ron Kellum   Client: Vision Cable of South Carolina

Leslie created this image for a pay-per-view advertisement. The outline for the image was sketched in Adobe Illustrator, then placed in Photoshop.

Using the Pen tool, Leslie created paths to outline each part of the image, then converted each path into a selection. Most of the lighting effects were created using the Gradient tool to produce blends in the different selections.

Leslie then touched up the image by using the Airbrush tool to paint the lights in the movie marquee and to fill the area under the marquee.

NOTE: *The Brush options from the Brushes palette pop-up menu allow you to adjust the selected brush.*

Diameter

Start by exploring the Diameter setting, which determines the size of the brush. To change this, click and drag the slider control or type a value (in pixels) into the Diameter field. Try clicking and dragging the slider control to the right. As you drag, watch the preview box in the lower-right corner of the dialog box. It may take a moment or two, but eventually a preview of the new brush size will appear. As you drag the slider to the right, the brush's diameter grows. Change the diameter to 27. If you make the brush any larger than 27 pixels, the brush is represented by a small brush icon with the size below it.

 REMEMBER: *File resolution affects the stroke of a brush. A brush that paints thickly at 72 ppi produces a thinner stroke at 300 ppi.*

Hardness

Now test the Hardness slider, which controls whether the brush paints with a soft or hard edge. This value is a percentage of the center of the brush. The best way to visualize this is to gradually drag the Hardness slider to the left and stop at every 25% interval to watch the changes in the preview box. As you drag, you'll see a light shade surrounding the brush gradually grow. This shading indicates the soft area of the brush. Drag all the way to 0% to see the preview of the softest setting. In the Hardness field, 0% produces the softest brush, 100% the hardest.

Spacing

Next, test the Spacing option, which controls the distance the brush paints as you make a stroke. The Spacing option is turned off or on with a check box.

- ☐ When the Spacing option is on, the distance you set with the slider (or typed in the Spacing field) is a percentage of the brush's diameter. Thus, when Spacing is set to 100%, the brush will leave dabs of paint spaced the same distance apart as the brush's diameter. The largest value you can enter is 999%.

- ☐ When the Spacing option is off, the brush's stroke is controlled by your mouse or stylus dragging speed. Drag slowly, and more pixels on screen "absorb" paint; drag quickly, and the brush skips over pixels.

Turn the New Brush Spacing option on and set the value to 300%, a change that will be easily seen when you start painting with your custom brush.

Angle and Roundness

The next two options in the Brushes palette, Angle and Roundness, work together. The Angle setting changes the brush shape only if Roundness is not set to 100%. (A Roundness setting of 100% produces a circular brush.) Therefore, start by changing the brush shape from a circle to an ellipse.

You can change the roundness by either typing a value in the Roundness field or by clicking and dragging either of the two dots in the preview box in the lower-left corner of the dialog box. So, to create an elliptical brush, you would click and drag one of the two dots toward the other one. As you drag, you will decrease the percentage of roundness. The lower the percentage of roundness, the more elliptical your brush will be.

Once you have created the elliptical brush, you can change the Angle setting; you either type in a value between −180 and 180° or click and drag on the arrowed axis line in the preview box.

Now try this out: Change the Angle value to create a brush that will be dramatically different from the original one. Set the Angle to 45° and the Roundness to 40%. Notice that both preview boxes reflect the changes. Before closing the New Brush dialog box, examine all the settings of your custom brush. Diameter should be 27 pixels, Hardness 0%, Spacing 300%, Angle 45%, and Roundness 40%. Click OK to accept the settings.

Your new brush appears in the bottom row of the Brushes palette.

Experiment with your custom brush using the Paintbrush tool. Click on the tool and then activate the custom brush in the Brushes palette. Click and drag on screen to test it. You'll see that the brush paints a stroke at an angle of 45 degrees and creates a dotted effect, as shown here, because of the Spacing setting in the New Brush dialog box. This brush stroke was created with the following settings: Hardness 0%, Spacing 300%, Angle 45°, and Roundness 40%.

Now return to your new brush's settings and change the Spacing and Hardness options. To do this, double-click in the Brushes palette on the brush you just created. Change Spacing to 25% and set Hardness to 100%. To accept the new settings, click OK. To see the change, try painting once again with your custom brush. As you paint, you'll see the brush now has a hard-edged stroke, and the white spaces between the brush strokes have disappeared. This brush stroke was created from these settings: Hardness 100%, Spacing 25%, Angle 45°, and Roundness 40%.

If you wish to continue experimenting, try turning off the Spacing option by deselecting the Spacing check box in the New Brush dialog box. Try a few quick brush strokes and then a very slow brush stroke. You'll see that when you paint slowly, more paint is "absorbed" by the pixels on screen. When you paint faster, fewer pixels are filled in.

Defining a Custom Brush

With Photoshop, you can design unusual custom brushes—something only an electronic painting program could produce. In this next example, you'll create a brush using the Type Mask tool. Instead of using the New Brush command in the Brushes palette pop-up menu, you will use the Define Brush command, which turns a selection or floating text into a brush. To demonstrate this, try creating a custom brush out of the dollar sign character on the keyboard. This will allow you to paint dollar signs on screen with the painting tools.

1. To begin, activate the Type Mask tool and click anywhere in your document. In the Type Tool dialog box, choose any font from the pop-up menu; then type **24** in the Size field and type **$** in the text box. Click OK to make the text selection appear on screen.

2. Next, fill the dollar sign selection on screen with black using the Edit | Fill dialog box.

3. With the dollar sign filled and selected, choose Define Brush from the pop-up menu in the Brushes palette. A $ (dollar sign) should appear in the Brushes palette.

4. Double-click on this brush in the Brushes palette. Notice that your options for altering the brush have been changed: Spacing and Anti-aliased are now the only choices available. (The Anti-aliased option is only available for small brush sizes.) Before you close the Brush Options dialog box, feel free to change the settings if you wish.

5. To use your new brush, activate either the Paintbrush or Airbrush tool and then select the $ (dollar sign) brush. All you need to do now is click on the screen, and the dollar sign will appear in the current foreground color.

 NOTE: *If you defined a brush that was created with black, it will paint opaquely when you use it. If you defined a brush that was created with gray or a color, it will paint translucently when you use it. Each time you click the mouse over the previous color, the opacity of the color will increase.*

You can purchase different typefaces that are symbols and/or ornaments and use them to create different custom brushes. (Examples of these typefaces include Dingbats, Carta, Sonata, Wood, and Wingdings.) For example, if you are using the Dingbat font, you can create star (★), snowflake (❄), sun (☼), flower (✿), and heart (♥) brushes. To create stars, press SHIFT-H or SHIFT-P. Press the letter F to create a snowflake Dingbat. Press the letter B to create a sun. To create a flower, press SHIFT-MINUS. To create a heart, press OPTION-2 (Windows users: press ALT and type **0164** on the numeric keypad).

 TIP: *In addition to using the Type Mask tool to create custom brushes, you can create custom brushes from any selected object on screen. It doesn't matter what tool you use to create the object or whether the image was created from scratch or digitized—just remember that the object must be selected before you can apply the Define Brush command.*

Continue experimenting with creating various custom brushes using the techniques described in this section. If you want to delete a brush, move the pointer over the brush that you want to delete and press and hold COMMAND (Windows users: CTRL); when the Scissors icon appears, click. You can also use the Delete Brush command in the Brushes pop-up menu to delete the currently selected brush. When you are done, proceed to the next section to learn how to save your custom brushes.

Saving and Loading Custom Brushes

If you like the custom brushes you have created and wish to use them again, you can save the entire Brushes palette to disk. When you need it again, you can load the palette from the disk.

To save your Brushes palette, including all the custom brushes you have designed, select Save Brushes from the Brushes palette pop-up menu. To keep all of your custom brushes together, it might be a good idea to save them in the Brushes folder. When you install Photoshop, the Brushes folder is automatically installed. Once you have located the folder, name your brush palette **MyBrush** and click Save.

 NOTE: *If you wish to add custom brushes that already exist in a saved brushes file to the current Brushes palette on screen, choose Load Brushes from the Brushes palette pop-up menu. After you load the brushes from your hard disk, they will be appended to the current brushes. If you wish to replace the brushes in the palette with a set of brushes saved on disk, choose the Replace Brushes command in the menu.*

Incidentally, you may have noticed that within Photoshop's Brushes folder are three different brush files: Assorted Brushes, Drop Shadow Brushes, and Square Brushes.

If you wish to load any of these or other custom brushes, just select Append or Replace Brushes from the Brushes palette pop-up menu. Try this now by choosing Replace Brushes from the Brushes palette pop-up menu. Open the Brushes folder, click on the Assorted Brushes file, and open it. The brushes in the

Brushes palette have now changed. Your Brushes palette should now look like this:

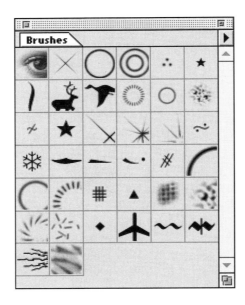

Take a few moments to experiment with the various brushes.

 NOTE: *Whenever you wish to return the default Brushes palette to the screen, choose Reset Brushes from the Brushes palette pop-up menu. When a dialog box appears, click OK.*

This concludes the exercises and projects for the painting tools and techniques. In the next section, you will learn about changing blending modes.

Blending Modes

In the Options palette of most tools, you can choose from a wide range of blending modes, sometimes called painting modes. These modes are generally used to change colors and create special effects when painting or when pasting or blending previously colored areas. How those areas are affected depends on the blending mode, the color being applied, and the range of pixels that are painted or pasted over. For instance, if you apply a red color to an image in Darken mode, only the underlying pixels in the image that are lighter than red will be darkened with the red color. If you paint in Lighten mode, only pixels darker than red will be lightened by the red color.

In addition to appearing in the Options palette, blending modes can also be set in the Layers palette and in several dialog boxes such as those for Fill, Stroke, Fill Path, Apply Image, Calculations, and New Layer.

This section describes the fundamental purpose of each mode. As you work through this book, you'll gain experience with all the modes and see how they can produce effects ranging from simple to startling. At the conclusion of this section, you will have a chance to create some special effects using the Lighten and Darken modes.

 TIP: *You can cycle forward and backwards through the blending modes of a tool by pressing SHIFT - and SHIFT +.*

Following are basic descriptions of the blending modes:

Normal   This blending mode modifies every underlying pixel with the color being applied. In Normal mode, with Opacity set to 100%, underlying pixels will be completely replaced with the color being applied. If Opacity is less than 100%, the color of underlying pixels will show through the color being applied.

 NOTE: *Normal changes to Threshold when you are editing a Bitmap or Indexed Color file.*

Dissolve   When colors are applied in Dissolve mode, the painting color randomly replaces underlying pixels. The resulting color is a mixture of the painting color and the color of the original underlying pixels. Results depend on the opacity of the painting color and the opacity of the underlying colors. This can produce anything from a speckled paint to a sandpaper effect. For more dramatic results, use Dissolve mode with a large brush and experiment with different opacities.

Behind   This mode is only available when working in a layer other than the Background. Behind mode simulates the effect of painting behind an image on screen. Painting over nontransparent (colored) areas has no effect, but the paint applied appears over the transparent areas. When working in Behind mode, think of it as painting on the back of a clear plastic acetate rather than on a painter's canvas.

Clear   This mode is also only available when working in a layer other than the Background. It appears in the Line and Paint Bucket Options palettes' mode pop-up menu, in the Edit | Fill Mode pop-up menu, and in the Mode pop-up menu of the Fill Path or Fill Subpath dialog box. Editing in this mode is similar to using the Eraser tool while working in the layer. Clear mode wipes away color, making pixels transparent.

Multiply   This mode multiplies color values, causing underlying pixels to darken. Each time a color is applied, pixels receive more of the painting color's values. Painting with black in Multiply mode produces black. Painting with white has no effect. Painting in Multiply mode can be similar to applying colored markers over an image.

Screen   This mode whitens underlying pixels, leaving them in a tint of the color being applied. If you repeatedly apply color in Screen mode, pixels grow lighter and lighter. The Screen mode is the opposite of the Multiply mode. Thus, painting with white in Screen mode produces white; painting with black has no effect.

 NOTE: *The mathematical formulas for Multiply and Screen modes are provided in the "Apply Image" sections of Chapter 14.*

Overlay   When painting in Overlay mode, underlying pixels are either screened or multiplied to blend with the painting color. When you paint, darker underlying colors cause the painting color to be multiplied; lighter underlying colors cause the painting color to be screened. When painting over images, highlights and shadows are maintained. Overlay produces no effect when painting over white or black pixels.

Soft Light   This mode produces the effect of pointing a soft spotlight on an image. If your painting color is lighter than underlying pixels, the image is lightened. If your painting color is darker than underlying pixels, the image is darkened. The effect is one of diffuse, not harsh, light being applied.

Hard Light   This mode produces the effect of pointing a harsh spotlight on an image. If your painting color is lighter than underlying pixels, the image is lightened. If your painting color is darker than underlying pixels, the image is darkened. Painting with black in Hard Light mode produces black; painting with white produces white.

    TIP: *To quickly see the difference between Soft and Hard light modes, open an image on screen. Set the foreground color to yellow or yellow orange. Select the entire screen by choosing Select | All. Use the Edit | Fill command to fill using Soft Light mode and then undo and use the Edit | Fill command to fill in Hard Light mode.*

Color Dodge   This mode lightens image areas, functioning similarly to the Dodge tool. If you are using this mode with a painting tool or in the layers palette, you can control the effect by adjusting the Opacity slider. Painting with Color Dodge has no effect if the painting color is black.

Color Burn   This mode darkens image areas, functioning similarly to the Burn tool. If you are using this mode with a painting tool or in the layers palette, you can control the effect by adjusting the Opacity slider. Painting with Color Burn has no effect if the painting color is white.

Darken   This mode only affects colors lighter than the color you are applying, causing them to be darkened by the painting color. When you use Darken, Photoshop compares the color values of the painting color with the color value of the underlying color and then creates a blend color using the darkest pixel values. (If R100, G50, B25 is painted over R25, G100, B75 in Darken mode, the resulting color will be R25, G50, B25.)

Lighten   This mode is the opposite of Darken mode. Only pixels darker than the color you are applying are modified. The darker colors are lightened by the painting color. When you use Lighten, Photoshop compares the color values of the painting color with the color value of the underlying color, then creates a blend color using the lightest pixel values. (If R100, G50, B25 is painted over R25, G100, B75 in Lighten mode, the resulting color will be R100, G100, B75.)

Difference   This mode subtracts the color values of the painting color from the color values of the underlying pixels. For instance, if R100, G50, B25 is painted over R25, G100, B75 in Difference mode, the resulting color will be R75, G50, B50. When using Difference it's helpful to remember that the pixel value of black is 0 and the brightness value of white is 255. Painting with black in Difference mode has no effect on underlying pixels. Painting over black in Difference mode produces the color you are painting with (because you are subtracting a color value from zero). Thus, if you had a black stripe against a green background and filled the entire image using Difference mode with green, the result would be a green stripe with a black background. Painting over white in Difference mode produces the inverse of the color you are painting with. Painting with white produces the inverse of the color you are painting over.

Exclusion   This mode is very similar to Difference, except the resulting color is softer than one obtained with Difference. However, painting with white or black produces the same effect as Difference: Painting with black produces no effect. Painting over white in Difference mode produces the inverse of the color you are painting with. Painting with white produces the inverse of the color you are painting over.

Hue   When you paint or edit in Hue mode, you paint with only the hue of the painting color. Thus, only the Hue value of the affected pixels is modified by the painting color, not their Saturation and Luminosity values. Applying colors to black or white pixels in Hue mode has no effect.

Saturation   When you edit or apply color in Saturation mode, you paint with the Saturation value of the painting color. Thus, only the Saturation values of underlying pixels will change. Applying colors to black or white pixels in Saturation mode will have no effect.

Color   In this mode, you paint with the Hue and Saturation of a painting color. Thus, the Hue and Saturation values of underlying pixels change, but not Luminosity. The Color mode is often used to colorize gray or monochrome images because underlying shadows and contours will show through the color that is being applied. The effect is similar to colorizing old black-and-white movies. This technique is demonstrated in Chapter 12.

 NOTE: *If you wish to colorize a Grayscale file, you must convert the file to a Color mode such as RGB Color, using the Image | Mode command. For more information about changing modes, see Chapter 12.*

Luminosity   Luminosity measures a color's brightness. When you paint in Luminosity mode, you paint with only the luminance value of a color. In Luminosity mode, the lightness and darkness values of an underlying color's pixels will change, but the color values will not. Luminosity mode is the opposite of the Color mode.

Photoshop's internal formula for computing a pixel's luminosity is

30% of Red value + 59% of Green value + 11% of Blue value

This formula always produces a number between 0 and 255. The closer a number is to 255, the closer the luminosity is to white; the lower the number, the closer the luminosity is to black. When you apply color in Luminosity mode over black or white, all RGB color values will switch to the luminosity value produced by the formula, which will apply a gray shade to your image.

NOTE: *The Hue, Saturation, Color, and Luminosity modes are based on a Hue/Saturation/Luminosity (HSL) color model. This color model is slightly different from the Hue/Saturation/Brightness (HSB) color model. Thus, if you try to evaluate the effects of painting in these modes using the HSB readouts in the Info palette, it may seem that the modes do not work exactly as specified. For instance, when you paint over a color using Hue mode, the HSB readout in the Info palette may show that the color's saturation, as well as its hue, has changed.*

Threshold   This mode only appears when working in Bitmap mode files. It indicates that you will be painting with black if the foreground color is set to 50% black or greater; otherwise you will be painting with white.

Blending Mode Exercises

In this section, you will try using the Darken, Lighten, and Behind modes with the Type and Gradient tools to see how these modes completely change how a blend is applied. First, you'll create a radial blend behind some text; then you'll create a linear blend within the letters of the text.

1. Begin by opening a new file, 5 inches by 5 inches. Set the mode to RGB and the resolution to 72 ppi. In the New dialog box, set the Contents radio button to White.

2. Select the Type Mask tool and click on screen. When the Type Tool dialog box appears, click on the Font pop-up menu and choose a font. In the Size field box, type **100**. In the Style group, check to see that Anti-aliased is selected. In the Text field, type **BLEND**. When you are finished, click OK.

3. Choose Edit | Fill. In the Fill dialog box set the Use pop-up menu to Black and click OK. Then deselect the text by choosing Select | Deselect.

4. Next, create the blend. Select the Radial Gradient tool in the Toolbox, and press Enter to open its Radial Gradient Options palette. Select the Spectrum option from the Gradient pop-up menu. Click on the mode pop-up menu and choose the Darken mode. Set Opacity to 100%.

5. Now create the radial blend. With the Gradient tool activated, click and drag diagonally from the top-left corner of your document to the bottom-right corner. The blend appears with the text over it. Because you used the Darken mode, only the areas lighter than the painting color were affected, not the darker areas. Thus, even though you created the blend over the entire screen, only the white pixels were affected, not the black text.

   Next, you'll work with the Lighten mode—the opposite of Darken.

6. In the Edit menu, select Undo to remove the effects of the blend that was created in Darken mode.

7. Before creating another blend, switch to the Linear Gradient tool in the Toolbox. In the Linear Gradient Options palette, make sure the Gradient pop-up menu is set to Spectrum. Click on the mode pop-up menu and change the mode to Lighten. To create the blend, position the mouse to the left of the word "BLEND" and click and drag to the far right side of the screen. When you release the mouse, you'll see that the blend is created inside the text, without affecting the white background. (The background is white because you chose Edit | Undo in step 6). The Lighten mode only lightens areas darker than the painting color. Thus, the black text was lightened by the blend, and the background white area was not affected. By switching to Lighten mode, you were able to change the text without first selecting it.

Next, try an exercise that demonstrates how the Behind mode simulates painting behind your image:

1. As you did in the previous exercise, create a new 72 ppi RGB file, 5 inches by 5 inches. This time, set the background Contents to Transparent before clicking OK.

2. Set the foreground color to purple.

3. With the Type tool selected, click on the middle of your document. In the Type Tool dialog box, pick a font, type **100** in the Size field, make sure the Anti-aliased option i is selected, and type the word **Paint**. Click OK, and your type will appear in your document.

4. Render the type by choosing Layer | Type | Render Layer

5. Select the Linear Gradient tool in the Toolbox. In the Linear Gradient Options palette set the Gradient pop-up menu to either Copper or Chrome, and set the mode to Behind. Now, use the Gradient tool to click and drag from left to right over the entire image.

The resulting image will appear as if you had painted behind the word on screen. The transparent background is filled with the gradient; the word is not affected.

Next, try the Hue mode:

1. Create a new 72 ppi RGB file, 5 inches by 5 inches. Set the background Contents to White before clicking OK.

2. Set the foreground color to purple.

3. With the Type Mask tool selected, click on the middle of your document. In the Type Tool dialog box, pick a font, type **100** in the Size field, make sure the Anti-aliased option selected, and type the word **Paint**. Click OK for your type to appear in your document.

4. Choose Edit | Fill. In the Fill dialog box set the Use pop-up menu to the Foreground Color option. Then click OK.

5. Deselect the selection by choosing Select | None.

6. Select the Linear Gradient Tool in the Toolbox. In the Linear Gradient Options palette, set the Gradient pop-up menu to either the Red, Green option or the Violet, Green, Orange option, and set the blending mode to Hue. Now, use the Gradient tool to click and drag from left to right over the entire image.

Note that when you use the Hue option, the color of the gradient is applied to the text and not to the white area of the document. The Hue option replaces one color with another.

You have just seen several very clear examples of how powerful Photoshop's blending modes are. You now have new options at your disposal to edit pixels not according to whether they are selected but according to their color values.

Conclusion

All the exercises in this chapter have offered but a taste of the features and special effects that await you in Photoshop. In Chapter 7, the electronic magic continues as you learn the basics of image editing.

CHAPTER 7

Introduction to Image Editing

Image editing is where the magic of Photoshop truly comes alive. With Photoshop's image-editing tools at your command, objects once hidden in darkness will suddenly emerge from the shadows. Images almost lost in the distance will gradually sharpen into focus. Images that are bland, barren, or unbalanced can be populated with just the right objects in exactly the right place. In short, Photoshop's image-editing tools allow you to produce or improve images that will look the way you want them to look.

The goal of this chapter, though, is not to concentrate on the fantastic and amazing, but rather to provide you with an introduction to the basics of image editing. We'll begin here by performing a little image-editing magic with the Blur/Sharpen/Smudge, Dodge/Burn/Sponge, and Rubber Stamp. As you did in Chapter 6, you'll use these tools from the Toolbox in conjunction with the Brushes and Options palettes.

You'll begin the exercises in this chapter by opening a digitized image. With this image on screen, you will use the Dodge and Burn tools to lighten overexposed and darken underexposed areas. You'll use the Sponge tool to saturate (intensify) and desaturate (weaken) the colors in your image. Once you've improved the image's exposure levels, you'll use the Blur and Sharpen tools to soften and clarify certain areas. With the Smudge tool, you'll blend small parts of the image to create watercolor and finger-painting effects. You'll also use the powerful Rubber Stamp tool to clone areas of the image. Finally, you'll have a chance to create patterns with the Pattern Stamp tool and revert to snapshot versions of your file using the History Brush tool.

When you are ready to begin, open any digitized image as your practice document. The examples in this chapter use a scanned image of an oriental fan. Figure 7-1 shows the original scanned image of the oriental fan with its imperfections. You can see that light areas needed to be darkened, and shadowed areas needed to be lightened. The flowers needed to be sharpened and their colors intensified so that they would stand out. The edges of the fan also needed to be softened, so that the fan would blend into a background photograph. Figure 7-2 shows the corrected fan as part of a completed project. Notice that the fan now has more flowers than in the original image—these flowers were cloned, or copied, to make the fan look more interesting. The translucent effect of the type was created by using the Type tool to add the text, then setting Opacity to 50% in the Layers palette.

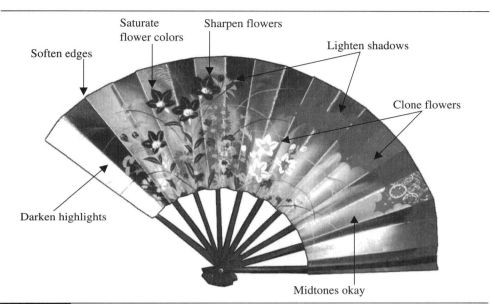

FIGURE 7-1   Corrections needed for the oriental fan image

FIGURE 7-2   Oriental fan added to background image

The Dodge and Burn Tools

The Dodge and Burn tools have begun enticing photographers out of the darkroom and into the Photoshop studio. These tools are simulations of traditional darkroom techniques. Photographers can often improve even their best work by using Dodge and Burn to block out light from or add light to a negative in order to enhance image definition. In photography, dodging is usually employed to lighten shadowed areas (the darkest portions of an image), and burning is employed to darken highlights (the brightest parts of an image). Both techniques increase the detail in a photograph. Photoshop's Dodge and Burn tools produce the same effects in a digitized image.

As discussed in "The Editing Tools" section in Chapter 2, the Dodge, Burn, and Sponge tools share one location in the Toolbox, with only one icon visible at a time (Dodge is the default tool). You can switch among the Dodge, Burn, and Sponge tools by pressing SHIFT-O.

When either Dodge or Burn is activated, the slider in the Options palette measures exposure. In photography, an overexposed image is one that is too light; an underexposed image is too dark. By clicking and dragging on the slider control, you can set the exposure level from 1% to 100%. By typing a number on your keyboard, you can step through exposure settings in intervals of 10% (typing **0** sets exposure to 100%). Increasing the exposure while using the Dodge tool intensifies the Dodge tool's lightening effect. Increasing the exposure while using the Burn tool intensifies the Burn tool's darkening effect.

 TIP: *You can change exposures by typing a number on the keyboard when the Dodge or Burn tool is selected. Typing 1 sets the exposure to 10%, typing 2 sets exposure to 20%; typing 25 sets exposure to 25%.*

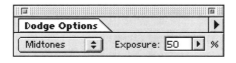

When you use the Dodge or Burn tool, the pop-up menu in the Dodge/Burn Options palette displays the following options: Shadows, Midtones, and Highlights (shown in the following illustration). *Highlights* are the brightest components of an image; *midtones* are halfway between the highlights and shadows; *shadows* are the darkest components of an image. By selecting one of these options, you can apply the Dodge or Burn tool to correct either shadows, midtones, or highlights. For instance, if you select Highlights, only highlighted areas will be affected.

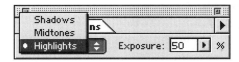

The width of the area you edit is determined by the size of the brush you pick in the Brushes palette and whether it is hard-edged or soft-edged. By allowing you to choose a brush size, an exposure level, and an image's highlights, midtones, and shadows, Photoshop provides tremendous control over brightness and darkness levels. Using a soft-edged brush with a low exposure creates a subtle effect; a hard-edged brush with a high exposure rate produces a more dramatic effect.

As you saw in Figure 7-1, the light areas on the left side of the fan are too light, almost white. The dark areas on the top of the fan are almost the same color as the flowers, causing the flowers to fade into the background and appear less visible. In the image that you have on your screen, look for areas that are too bright or too dark. These are the areas to focus on when you use the Dodge and Burn tools. Before you begin, however, use the File | Save As command to save your file under a new name so that you don't alter the original image.

 NOTE: *Dodge and Burn effects can be applied using the Color Dodge and Color Burn modes in the Layers palette pop-up menu, as well as the Mode pop-up menu in the Edit | Fill dialog box.*

Using the Dodge Tool to Lighten Image Areas

 Start by using the Dodge tool to lighten shadows, so that more detail is visible in the dark areas of your image. If the Dodge tool is not shown as the active tool in the Toolbox, position the mouse pointer over the Toolbox location, and press the mouse button. When the Dodge tool appears, select it with the mouse. Now use the Dodge tool to lighten shadow areas that are too dark.

1. In the Brushes palette, pick a soft-edged brush to make subtle changes. In the Toning Tools Options palette, set Exposure to 20%, and click on the pop-up menu and select Shadows.

2. Move the mouse pointer over a dark area of your image. (The mouse pointer changes to the Dodge tool when it enters the document window, unless CAPS LOCK is depressed or you have Precise or Brush Size selected in the Display & Cursors Preferences dialog box.) Click and drag with a few short mouse movements. As you do, you'll see that the darkest areas that you are clicking and dragging over become lighter. In Figure 7-3, you can see that the Dodge tool has lightened shadows to add tonal balance to the fan.

3. Continue using the Dodge tool to lighten all of the unwanted dark areas in your image. You might need to change the brush size, exposure, and mode to produce the desired effect.

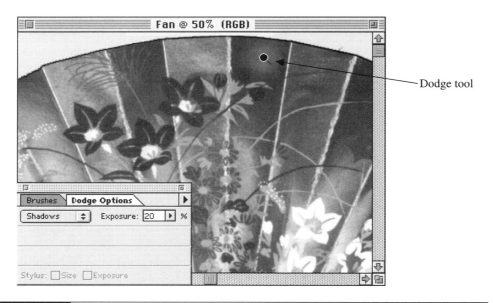

FIGURE 7-3   Lightening shadows with the Dodge tool

NOTE: *Using a stylus and digitizing tablet provides even more control when editing images with the Dodge/Burn/Sponge tool. If you turn on the Size and/or Exposure check boxes in the Stylus Pressure section of the Options palette, you can change the exposure and size of the area you are editing by applying more or less pressure to the stylus pen.*

Using the Burn Tool to Darken Image Areas

 To switch to the Burn tool, press SHIFT-O on the keyboard.

1. With the Burn tool active, change the settings in the Brushes palette. To create a subtle effect, use a soft-edged brush. In the Options palette, set Exposure to 20%. Since you want to darken only the brightest areas of the image, choose Highlights in the Mode pop-up menu.

2. In your image, look for a bright portion to start working on, and then position the Burn tool pointer over this area. (As you move the mouse pointer over the document area of the screen, the pointer changes to the Burn tool.)

 TIP: *If you wish to zoom in, use this keyboard shortcut: Hold down COMMAND-SPACEBAR (Windows users: CTRL-SPACEBAR) and click over the area that you wish to zoom in to. To zoom out, click the mouse while pressing OPTION-SPACEBAR (Windows users: ALT-SPACEBAR).*

3. When you are ready to begin, click and drag several times over the area using short strokes. As you drag, the lightest part of the image turns slightly darker. Now you can see how the rate of the darkening reflects the brush size and exposure setting you are using. Because the exposure setting is low and you are using a soft-edged brush, the darkening progresses slowly.

Figure 7-4 shows an example in which the Burn tool is adding tone to an overexposed area of the fan.

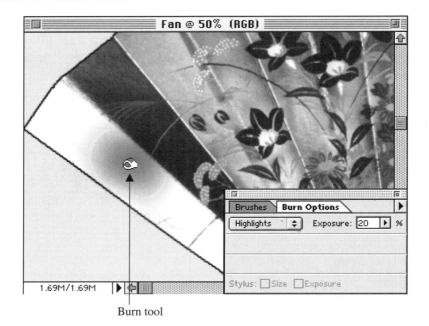

Burn tool

FIGURE 7-4 Darkening highlights with the Burn tool

TIP: *If an image area requires you to lighten or darken in a straight line (90-degree increments)—for example, if you're lightening or darkening the edges or corners of a book—press SHIFT while clicking and dragging with either the Dodge or Burn tool activated.*

If you wish to darken shadow or midtone areas that are too light, you will need to change mode settings in the Toning Tools Options palette first. Continue editing by changing to Shadows or Midtones and using various brush sizes and exposure percentages. When you've finished darkening the light areas of your image, move on to the next section, where you will use the Sponge tool.

CAUTION: *Use Dodge and Burn tools carefully. Dodging and Burning can create destructive effects. Always keep a backup of your original, or make sure you always have a snapshot of the original in the History palette.*

Photoshop 5 > In Action

**Artwork by: Mark Jenkins /   Client: Self promotion
Rucker Design Group**

To create "Presidio Horse," Mark used Photoshop to combine photographs with 3-D images created using MetaCreations RayDream Studio. The horse, cannonballs, and ground were created using RayDream. Mark created texture maps for the 3-D images in Photoshop from photographs and saved them as PICT files. (RayDream allows you to map PICT files onto the surface of 3-D elements as well as to apply PICT files as bump maps which react to the lighting in the scene.) As you can see from the intricate textures in the image, the texture maps help add a sense of realism to the 3-D models.

In Raydream, Mark rendered the 3-D items with an "automatic" alpha channel, so he didn't need to use the Pen tool in Photoshop to create masks; he simply loaded the alpha channel then pasted the selection onto a layer. The shadows cast on the ground by the horse and the cannonballs were generated in RayDream, but Mark softened them using the Blur tool in Photoshop.

The background wall and door are scanned photographs of old military installations in the San Francisco Presidio. Mark scanned the photographs into Photoshop and composited them by copying and pasting. He used the Rubber Stamp tool to erase seams where he had joined different photos. He also used the Rubber Stamp tool remove dead foliage from the base of the door.

Mark used the Dodge and Burn tools with a large brush to highlight and darken specific areas of the picture (for example the bottom edge of the wall where it meets the 3-D rendered ground). He also softened the edges of the 3-D elements to make them less perfect and more photographic. Once he was happy with the overall look, Mark flattened the layers and added four pixels of noise to help meld the 3-D and the photographic elements together.

The Sponge Tool

 As mentioned earlier, the Sponge tool shares a Toolbox location with the Dodge and Burn tools. When you choose the Sponge tool, the slider in the Sponge Options palette displays Pressure rather than Exposure, and you can choose either Desaturate or Saturate from the pop-up menu.

The Sponge tool is used to increase or decrease the saturation or intensity of a color. When saturation is added to a color, the gray level of a color diminishes; thus it becomes less neutral. The Sponge tool's Desaturate option can be quite useful when an RGB color image displays CMYK out-of-gamut colors. By rubbing the Sponge tool over these out-of-gamut colors, you can gradually dilute them so that they drop into the CMYK spectrum of printable colors.

 NOTE: *For more information about using the Sponge tool to correct out-of-gamut colors, see Chapter 12.*

Using the Sponge Tool to Saturate and Desaturate Image Areas

Start by using the Sponge tool to intensify colors in your image. To help you prevent oversaturating the colors, open the Info palette. If you make your colors too intense, the Info palette's CMYK out-of-gamut alarm appears.

1. Open the Info palette by choosing Show Info from the Window | Palettes submenu. The out-of-gamut alarm appears only when the CMYK readouts are displayed in the Info palette. If you don't see the CMYK readouts in the Info palette, click on one of the eyedroppers in the palette and choose CMYK Color.

2. Move the Sponge tool to an area of your image where the colors look dull. Before you begin to saturate the area, notice the CMYK Color readouts in the Info palette.

3. In the Toning Tools Options palette, pick Saturate from the Mode pop-up menu and set the pressure to 30%. This will produce a slow and gradual saturation. If pressure were set to 100%, the colors would saturate very quickly. In the Brushes palette, pick a medium-sized, soft-edged brush. Start saturating by clicking and dragging the Sponge tool over the dull-colored areas in your image.

TIP: _You could also use the Color Sampler tool to sample four different areas in the image, then observe how the Sponge tool changes the color values of the four different areas._

4. After you've saturated the colors in an image area, look at the CMYK Color readouts in the Info palette. If there is an exclamation point after the CMYK Color readouts, you've overstepped the CMYK color gamut, which means the colors on screen cannot be printed on a commercial printing press. If you are outputting to slides or video, you do not have to worry about out-of-gamut CMYK colors.

5. If you've oversaturated and want to desaturate, choose Desaturate from the Mode pop-up menu in the Options palette. Use the Sponge tool to lower the intensity of the colors so that they are not out of gamut. Don't desaturate too much; if you do, your colors will turn gray. When you are finished using the Sponge tool, proceed to the next section to learn about using the Blur and Sharpen image-editing tools.

 NOTE: _If you wish to completely desaturate an image or selection, use Photoshop's Image | Adjust | Desaturate command. This will change all colors to shades of gray._

The Blur and Sharpen Tools

The Blur tool softens parts of an image by, as you probably guessed, blurring them. Its counterpart, the Sharpen tool, makes image areas sharper and more distinct. Photoshop's Blur tool works by decreasing the contrast among the pixels you drag over; the Sharpen tool works by heightening contrast in neighboring pixels.

Like the Dodge and Burn tool combination, Blur and Sharpen are often used to enhance the quality of digitized images. You may wonder, though, why anyone would want to make an image more blurry. It's because scanners sometimes accentuate edges too much, causing images to look too harsh. These edges can be softened with the Blur tool. The Blur tool can be used to help soften the jagged edges of an image that is pasted into a document, so that it blends more smoothly into its surroundings. It can also be used to create subtle shadow effects.

The Blur and Sharpen tools share one location in the Toolbox with the Smudge tool. By default, when Photoshop is first loaded, only the Blur tool appears in the

Toolbox. As with Dodge/Burn/Sponge, you can switch among the Blur, Sharpen, and Smudge tools by clicking and dragging the mouse in the Toolbox. You can also press the OPTION key (Windows users: ALT) and click on the active tool in the Toolbox or press SHIFT-R on your keyboard to toggle among tools.

Now take a look at the Blur/Sharpen Options palette. If the Options palette is already open, click once on the Blur/Sharpen tool. If it isn't open, double-click on the tool to display the palette. Click on the pop-up menu to view the different modes. When the Blur or Sharpen tool is activated, the modes available to you in the palette are Normal, Darken, Lighten, Hue, Saturation, Color, and Luminosity. Also, notice that the slider in the palette now controls Pressure. (See Chapter 6 for a discussion of the different blending modes.)

The Pressure slider controls the amount of sharpening and blurring that these tools produce. The greater the Pressure percentage, the greater the effect of the sharpening or blurring. As usual, the size of the area that changes is determined by the brush size you are using—smaller brushes affect smaller areas, larger brushes affect larger areas.

 NOTE: *If you have a stylus and digitizing tablet, you can also take advantage of the two Stylus Pressure options for the Blur and Sharpen tools: Size and Pressure.*

When using Blur/Sharpen, the Rubber Stamp, and the Smudge tools, the Use All Layers check box option is available. When this option is not selected, Photoshop analyzes pixel values only in the layer in which you are currently working. If this option is selected, Photoshop samples and edits using pixel values from all visible layers, when the tool is used. Since you are working in only one layer, selecting the Use All Layers check box will have no effect when image editing. See Chapters 15 and 16 for more information about layers.

Using the Sharpen Tool to Increase Contrast

 Because it's easier to recognize the need for sharpening image areas than the need for blurring them, start by experimenting with the Sharpen tool first. If the Sharpen tool is not active, switch to it. Before you begin sharpening your own image, pick a brush size in the Brushes palette and a Pressure value in the Sharpen Options palette. Leave the pop-up menu set to Normal. By switching modes, you can control which image areas will be affected; for instance, if you choose Darken, only lighter pixels will be changed. If you use a medium-sized, soft-edged brush and a low Pressure value, the sharpening effect will be barely noticeable. A large, hard-edged brush with a high Pressure value will produce a more intense effect.

Beware of sharpening too much. If you overdo it, the colors break up and become pixelated, as shown in Figure 7-5. Here the Sharpen tool is being used to heighten the contrast in the fan's flowers. To avoid oversharpening, use the Zoom tool to zoom in and keep a close eye on the pixels being affected.

Now decide which area you want to work on, move the Sharpen tool over that area, and click and drag the mouse to begin increasing contrast. Try moving to other areas in the image to see the results of sharpening with different Pressure settings.

 REMEMBER: *Oversharpening will cause pixelation.*

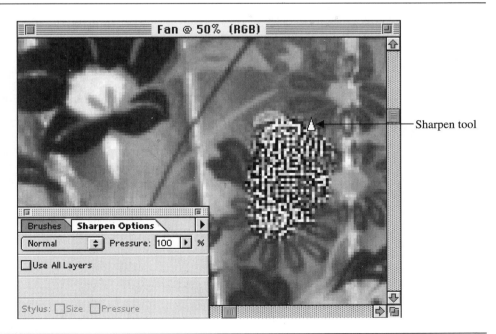

FIGURE 7-5   Pixelation occurs if you oversharpen

Using the Blur Tool to Soften Hard Edges

You can use the Blur tool to soften hard edges produced by oversharpening an image when digitizing. You can also use the Blur tool to soften overly bright highlights, or reflections that appear digitized. To switch to the Blur tool, press and hold OPTION (Windows users: ALT) while clicking on the Sharpen tool. You can also press and hold the mouse down while you select the Blur tool, or press SHIFT-R on the keyboard. Look for areas in your image that are too sharp or that have hard edges that need to be softened. Work these edges first with a low Pressure setting in the Focus Tools Options palette, so you don't blur your image too much.

Figure 7-6 shows the Blur tool being used to help soften the pixelation that occurred when the fan's flowers were being sharpened (in Figure 7-5). The Blur tool was also used to soften all of the hard edges of the fan, including the ridged perimeter after it was pasted into the final photograph.

 NOTE: *In addition to using the Blur and Sharpen tools, you can apply filters to make entire images more or less distinct. Filters are discussed in Chapters 10 and 11.*

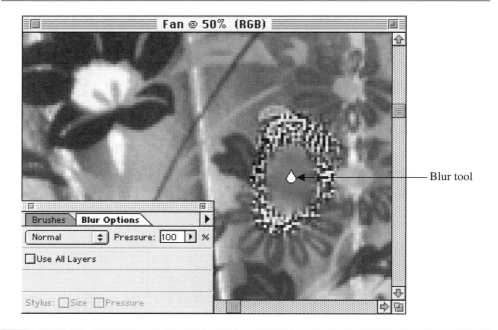

FIGURE 7-6 Using the Blur tool to soften an image

If you wish, continue to experiment with the Blur and Sharpen tools. When you're done, save your work and close the practice file. Then proceed to the next section to try your hand at more image-editing techniques with the Smudge tool, which can make your image look as though it is hand painted.

 TIP: *You can bring an oversharpened or overblurred image back to a previous state by clicking on a previous step in the History palette. Blurring an oversharpened area does not bring a digital image back to its previous state.*

The Smudge Tool

 The Smudge tool lets you blend colors as if you had smudged them together with your finger. When you use the Smudge tool, Photoshop starts with the color you clicked on and mixes it with the colors you drag over. Besides blending colors and mixing paint, the Smudge tool can be used to produce a watercolor effect in your image.

 NOTE: *The Smudge tool cannot be used on Indexed Color or Bitmap images.*

In this section, you'll have a chance to experiment with the Smudge tool by transforming a digitized image into one resembling a watercolor painting. You'll also learn how to add colors to an image by activating the Smudge tool's Finger Painting option.

1. Before proceeding, open any scanned image file, or reopen the file you started with at the beginning of this chapter. Use Save As to create another copy of your file. Name your file Water Painting. By using Save As, you will keep your original file from being affected by the changes you are going to make in the following exercises.

 NOTE: *Creating different snapshot versions of your file enables you to experiment with various designs and return to them as you are working on a project. Snapshots are discussed later in this chapter and in Chapter 9.*

 NOTE: *You can use the Image | Duplicate command to duplicate a file.*

2. Activate the Smudge tool, by clicking on the Blur/Sharpen/Smudge Toolbox location, and selecting the Smudge tool. If the Smudge Tool Options palette isn't open, press RETURN (Windows users: ENTER) or double-click on the Smudge tool. You'll begin by using the Smudge tool without the Finger Painting option. If necessary, deselect this option by clicking on the check box.

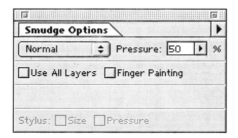

To control how the colors are smudged together, pick a brush size and a mode in the Brushes palette, and a Pressure value in the Smudge Tool Options palette. If you use a large brush with a high Pressure value, you will create a large smudge that will completely distort your image. A lower Pressure value with a small- or medium-sized brush will decrease the size of the smudge and create a less dramatic effect.

 NOTE: *The Smudge tool can be used to soften unwanted wrinkles and blemishes in fleshtones. This technique is discussed in Chapter 18.*

The blending modes that are available in the Smudge Tool Options palette are the standard choices (as discussed in Chapter 6). These can provide further control of your smudge. For example, if you use Hue mode, only the hue values will be smudged (not the saturation or the luminosity values). Similarly, use Saturation mode to change only the saturation values, and Luminosity mode to smudge only the luminosity values. If you have more than one layer on screen, you can also choose to smudge using sampled pixel values from all visible layers. To do this, click on the Use All Layers check box.

3. Pick a medium-sized, soft-edged brush from the Brushes palette. In the Smudge Tool Options palette, set the Pressure to 50% and the pop-up

menu to Normal. Move the smudge pointer anywhere in your document, and click and drag the mouse in one direction. You'll see that a small smudge of colors appears on screen. Zoom in to see a close-up view of the smudge. If you create a few more smudges, your image will start looking more like a watercolor painting, as in Figure 7-7. Experiment with various brush sizes. Also, try switching modes a few times before smudging different parts of your image.

The Smudge Tool's Finger Painting Option

You have created a watercolor effect by smudging the colors of your image together. What if you want to create a watercolor effect and add new color to your image at the same time? You can do this by activating the Smudge tool's Finger

7

Smudge tool

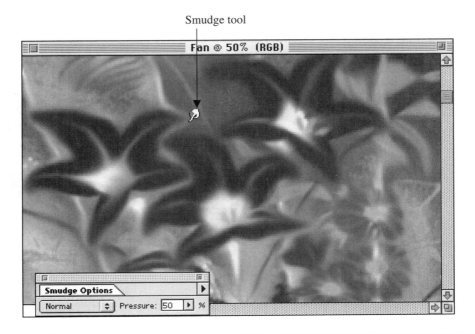

FIGURE 7-7 Creating a watercolor effect using the Smudge tool

Painting option, which smudges using the foreground color at the beginning of each click and drag of the mouse.

1. Double-click on the Smudge tool, and select the Finger Painting check box in the Smudge Tool Options palette. Leave Pressure set to 50%.

2. For this exercise, set the foreground color to a bright color so you can easily view the Finger Painting effects.

3. In the Brushes palette, continue to use a medium-sized, soft-edged brush.

4. Click and drag over an area on your document, and notice how the Smudge tool smudges with the selected foreground color each time you click and drag. Continue to experiment using other foreground colors. When you're finished, close the file and save it, if you wish.

 TIP: *To automatically activate the Smudge tool's Finger Painting option, press and hold OPTION (Windows users: ALT) as you work with the tool.*

In the next section, you'll learn about one of Photoshop's most versatile tools, the Rubber Stamp.

The Rubber Stamp Tool

 The Rubber Stamp is a cloning tool. Cloning allows you to choose different parts of an image and duplicate them to areas in the same file or in another file. This is quite different from copying and pasting. During the cloning procedure, Photoshop samples, or reads, a source area and clones it to a target area. As you click and drag in the target area in the file, a clone of the sampled area gradually appears. This process can produce an undetectable blend of old pixels and new. When executed properly, the cloning effect is often seamless and—even to the experienced Photoshop user—frequently amazing.

 TIP: *When using the Rubber Stamp tool you can also create fascinating blends between image areas by cloning one image area over another at a low opacity.*

 NOTE: *In Photoshop 5, the Rubber Stamp tool always clones based upon how the image appeared before the last stroke with the Rubber Stamp tool. This prevents you from recloning the area that you just cloned. In Photoshop 4, the Rubber Stamp tool cloned the current state of the image—which could create a streaked pattern-like effect which cloning near your clone source.*

To see the Rubber Stamp tool's options, double-click on the tool in the Toolbox, or select the tool and press RETURN (Windows users: ENTER).

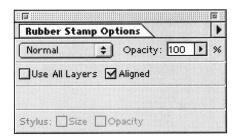

 NOTE: *The Rubber Stamp tool also has two Stylus Pressure options—Size and Opacity.*

In the next sections, the oriental fan image is used to demonstrate the basics of the Rubber Stamp tool. To follow along, open the file you used at the beginning of this chapter or load any digitized image.

Using the Clone Options to Duplicate Image Areas

Cloning can be tremendously helpful when you edit an image or retouch a photo. For example, one of the authors of this book retouched a cover for a proposed Reader's Digest travel guide. The picture that the book's art director wished to use was a photograph of a small New England town. Everything in the photo was beautiful—except for the telephone wires crisscrossing through the scene. Using the Rubber Stamp tool, parts of the trees that surrounded the wires were easily cloned over the wires to make them disappear. You'll see this example in Chapter 18, where advanced retouching techniques are introduced.

The Rubber Stamp's Aligned option allows you to clone different parts of an image to different areas of the same file or another file. When you clone using the Aligned option, Photoshop retains the same distance and angular relationship between the source area that you are sampling and the target area where the clone appears. Say, for instance, you wish to clone an image two inches directly above the original sample. After you finish cloning, if you move the mouse to another area of the file and then click and drag, Photoshop will clone whatever is two inches directly above the mouse pointer.

If the Aligned option is turned off in the Rubber Stamp Options palette, the Rubber Stamp automatically keeps sampling the original source area, so you can clone the same sample in many places after you release the mouse. For the completed fan image in Figure 7-2, the Rubber Stamp's Aligned option was used to duplicate different flowers in various areas of the fan. Had the designer wanted to clone the same flower in many parts of the fan, she would have cloned with the Aligned option off.

 NOTE: *If you are cloning in a file that has layers, you may wish to select the Use All Layers check box in the Rubber Stamp Options palette. This allows you to clone from all visible layers, rather than just the layer in which you are working.*

1. To start this exercise, select the Aligned check box in the Rubber Stamp Options palette.

2. Pick a large brush in the Brushes palette and a high Opacity setting in the Rubber Stamp Options palette. With a large brush and a high Opacity setting, the cloning will happen faster and its effect will be more obvious.

3. To clone part of your image, move the Rubber Stamp pointer so that it's over the area you wish to duplicate. Press and hold the OPTION key (Windows users: ALT) and then click the mouse to sample the area. Notice that the small black triangle at the base of the Rubber Stamp ( ) turns white ( ), and moves up a pixel. This indicates that an area has been sampled. Once you've sampled an area, release the OPTION key (Windows users: ALT) and move the rubber stamp pointer to the area where you wish the clone to appear.

4. To begin cloning, click and drag the mouse, moving the Rubber Stamp pointer over the target area. As you move the mouse, the clone will begin to appear in that area. Notice that a crosshair in the source area follows the movements of your Rubber Stamp pointer in the target area. The crosshair always remains the same distance and the same angle from the Rubber Stamp pointer, as shown in Figure 7-8. Continue clicking and dragging the mouse. The greater the area that you click and drag over, the greater the area that is cloned.

Rubber Stamp pointer
(clone/target area)

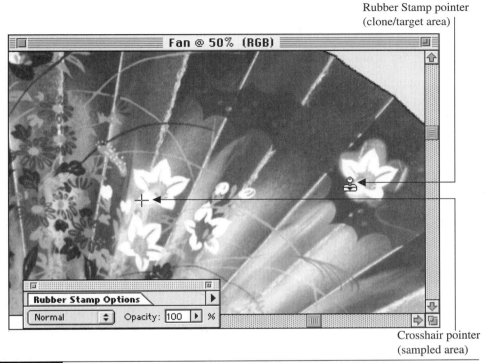

Crosshair pointer
(sampled area)

FIGURE 7-8   Using the Rubber Stamp tool's Aligned option to clone a flower

 NOTE: *As you click and drag, the Rubber Stamp tool always clones from the original source; it will not clone an area that was already cloned. This prevents a "hall of mirrors" effect—cloning the cloned area of a clone area.*

When you use the Aligned option, it's important to remember that the distance and the angle between the sampled area and the area where the clone is placed are always the same. To verify this, release the mouse button and then move the Rubber Stamp pointer to another area on the screen. Click and drag—Photoshop resamples and starts cloning again. Notice that when you clone the new area, the distance and angle between the crosshair and the Rubber Stamp pointer are the same as in the previous sample/clone pair. If you want to reset the distance between the source area and the target area, move the Rubber Stamp pointer to another area that you wish to sample, then press OPTION (Windows users: ALT) and click the mouse. Now you can move the Rubber Stamp tool to the area where you wish to clone the new sample. Subsequent sample/clone pairs will then be separated by this new distance and angle. The cloning will begin as soon as you click and drag.

If you wish to clone the same sample to different areas in your image, de-select the Aligned option. Try this now. After you deselect the Aligned check box, once again press OPTION (Windows users: ALT) and click the mouse to sample. Move the Rubber Stamp tool to the area where you want to apply the clone, then click and drag. After you've created the clone of the image, release the mouse button. Move to another area of the screen where you wish to duplicate the sample, and click and drag again. As you click and drag, another clone of the first sampled area will be created.

TIP: *You can press the* CAPS LOCK *key to turn the Rubber Stamp pointer into a crosshair (or choose Precise from the Cursors group in the Display & Cursors Preferences dialog box—File | Preferences | Display & Cursors). It's easier to use the middle of the crosshair than the Rubber Stamp pointer as a guide to judge the specific area that you are cloning. When you use this technique, you'll have two crosshairs on screen—one indicating the sample area and the other indicating the target area where the clone appears. (You can distinguish between the two crosshairs because the one indicating the sample target area has a dot in it.)*

As you work, you'll want to make the cloned image look as natural as possible. You don't want the clone to stand out from its surroundings. To make your clone blend in, experiment using the Rubber Stamp tool with different brushes, opacities, and modes. In the fan example, a soft-edged brush was used. This helped blend the new flower at the top of the fan to look as though it has always been there.

TIP: *You can also clone an image from one file to another. To do this, open the two files side by side on screen. Press OPTION (Windows users: ALT) and click over the area you wish to sample; then activate the target file. Position the Rubber Stamp pointer over the area where you wish to place the clone; then click and drag. If you are working with layers, you can sample in one layer and create the clone in another layer.*

When you've finished cloning, save your file and proceed to the next section, where you'll experiment with the History palette's Snapsnot option.

Reverting Using the History Brush

One of most unnerving aspects of image editing is the prospect of making too many changes that cannot be undone. Fortunately, Photoshop's History Brush allows you to paint back a previous version of your work. Thus, in many respects the History Brush is a cloning brush. It clones into an image a previous version of the image.

When you paint with the History Brush, you can use the Brushes palette to choose a brush type, and the History Brush Options palette to set the opacity percentage and the blending mode. These options—for example, using a soft-edged brush or lowering the opacity—can prove valuable for blending the reverted part of a file into the image on screen.

 NOTE: *The History Brush and History palette are discussed in detail in Chapter 9.*

Painting Back an Original

When you paint with the History Brush, you paint in a previous version of your image. When an image is first loaded the History Brush is automatically set to paint in the original version of the file. In the following exercise, you'll alter a file by coloring the entire screen with the background color. Afterwards, you'll use the History Brush to return part of the file to its original state. (Later in this chapter, you'll use the History Brush to paint in a *snapshot* version of the file).

1. Open any digitized image.

2. If the History palette isn't opened, open it by choosing Window | Show History. Notice that an icon representing the History Brush appears next to a thumbnail of the original image in the palette. This indicates that painting with the History Brush will return your image to its original state.

3. Choose Select | All. Then press DELETE (Windows users: BACKSPACE) to fill the screen with the background color.

7

4. Double-click on the History Brush tool. In the History Brush Options palette set Opacity to 100%. The blending mode should be Normal.

5. Before you start reverting, pick a large brush from the Brushes palette. When you start using the History Brush, the settings in the Brushes and History Brush palettes will return your file to its original form using a large brush stroke and its original opacity.

6. Now move the History Brush pointer to an area that you want to revert, and click and drag over the area. As you move the brush, you'll see parts of your image being restored; they will match the size and shape of your brush.

7. Before you finish, change Opacity to 50%, and then click and drag in the document window. Now the image is being restored with a 50% opacity. Keep this technique in mind. It might come in handy when you wish to create special effects.

 TIP: *Using the History Brush with an Opacity setting lower than 100% can produce a ghostlike effect.*

Continue experimenting. Keep Opacity set to 50% and the large, soft-edged brush selected, but switch modes from Normal to Dissolve. Dissolve, as mentioned in the "Blending Modes" section of Chapter 6, randomly dissolves the pixels in the image. The results of this effect will vary according to the image's original color. When you're done, keep your file on screen and proceed to the next section.

Blending Using a Snapshot and the History Brush

 As you're working on an image-editing project, it's reassuring to be able to return to different versions of your file. If you take a snapshot of your image as you work, you can use the History Brush to paint back in the snapshot version of your work.

To see how snapshots work, you'll blend two images together using a snapshot. In order to see the two options in action, you'll need to open two images, a source and a target image. You'll drag the source image over the target image to create a new layer, then blend the two images together. Figure 7-9 shows the effects of blending Figure 7-10 with Figure 7-11.

FIGURE 7-9   The doll and fan images blended together using the History brush

FIGURE 7-10   The doll image before blending it with the fan

FIGURE 7-11   The fan image before blending it with the doll

1. Once you have two images opened on screen, place them either side-by-side or so that they overlap.

2. Activate the source file (in Figure 7-9, it is the doll image), so that you can select it and then place it over the target file.

3. Next, you'll use the Rectangular Marquee tool to select part of the source file. Before you use the Marquee tool, you'll need to change some of the options in the Rectangular Marquee Options palette. If the Options palette is already on screen, click once on the Marquee tool; if it isn't, double-click on the Marquee tool. In the Marquee Options palette, set the Style pop-up menu to Normal, and type **5** in the Feather field. (Using the Feather option softens the edges of the source file when it is moved to the target file and therefore helps blend the two images together. Review Chapter 4 for more information about Feathering.) Using the Marquee tool, click and drag over the area you want to select in the source file.

    Once the source image is selected, activate the Move tool. Place the Move tool in the center of the selected image, and then drag and drop it over the target file. This creates a new layer in the target file.

4. Using the Move tool, position one image over the other, as desired.

5. When the source image is in position, take a snapshot of your image so that you can recall this version of your file if you need to. To take a snapshot of your image on screen, choose New Snapshot from the History Palette menu. In the New Snapshot dialog box, name the Snapshot **Combined**. To ensure that all layers are captured in the snapshot, make sure that the From pop-up menu is set to Full Document. After you click OK, a thumbnail of the current state of the image appears in the History palette.

    Now you can start blending the two images together. You'll use the original snapshot so that it blends into the target file and looks like it was always there.

6. Activate the History Brush. In the History Brush options palette set Opacity to 75%, and leave the blending mode set to Normal. In the Brushes palette, pick a medium-sized, soft-edged brush. Now you're ready to revert your image to 75% of the snapshot version.

Position the History Brush over the edges of the source image, and click and drag. As you move the mouse, you'll see the History Brush return the image to the original snapshot of the file.

7. If you take away too much of the source image and want to bring it back, you can reset the History Brush to revert using the Combined snapshot. To set the History Brush to use the Combined snapshot, click in the gray square next to the snapshot that you named "Combined." After you click, a History Brush icon appears.

 NOTE: *In Chapters 15 and 16 you'll use layers and layer masks to combine images*

8. If you wish, change the opacity, the blending mode in the History Brush Options palette, and the brush size in the Brushes palette. Next, position the History Brush pointer over the area where you want to bring back the source image, then click and drag. As you move the mouse, you'll see that the History Brush gradually returns your image to the Combined snapshot version of the file.

You have now seen how Photoshop gives you the ability to blend two files together using snapshots. If you wish, continue experimenting using different opacities, modes, and brushes. When you're finished, use the Save As command in the File menu to save your file on screen, then close the file.

 NOTE: *Using Edit | Fill, you can revert an image or selection to a step or snapshot designated by the History Brush in the History palette. To revert to a History version, first click on a snapshot or History stage in the History palette, then choose Edit | Fill. In the Fill dialog box choose History from the Use pop-up menu.*

Your next stop is the Rubber Stamp tool's Impressionist feature.

Using the History Brush Impressionist Option

Another of the History Brush's many specialties is its ability to take a scanned photograph and transform it into an impressionist painting. The Impressionist option takes the pixels from a snapshot version and blends them into the pixels of the current version of the file.

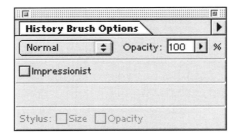

The Impressionist effect varies depending upon the brush, opacity, and blending mode used. If you use either a large, hard-edged brush or a small, soft-edged brush with a low Spacing value, you produce a very spotted effect, making it difficult to decipher what the image is supposed to be. If you wish to produce a more realistic, less impressionistic effect, use a small brush with a high Spacing value. (See "Creating and Using Custom Brushes" in Chapter 6 for a discussion on brush attributes.)

1. Start with a fresh file. Open any digitized image. Notice that the active snapshot designated by the History in the History palette is the original version of the file.

2. For this first experiment, set Opacity to 100% and the blending mode to Normal in the History Brush Options palette. To use the Impressionist option, click on the Impressionist check box in the History Brush Options palette.

3. To set the Spacing value of a brush, click on any brush in the Brushes palette. Then click on the pop-up menu arrow in the Brushes palette and choose New Brush from the list that appears. In the New Brush dialog box, set the Spacing to 300%, Hardness to 50%, and Diameter to 19 pixels. If you want your strokes to be round, keep Roundness at 100%. For strokes that look more elliptical than round, set Angle to 50 degrees and Roundness to 40%. Click OK to accept the changes.

 TIP: *You can also create a new brush by clicking on any empty brush location. This opens the New Brush dialog box.*

4. Click and drag over any area of your file. As you drag, you'll see the pixels appear to smear together, as shown in Figure 7-12, almost as if Seurat had taken control of the painting. If you'd like the effect to resemble Renoir's work, change the spacing to 25.

Additional effects can be created by using the blending modes: Normal, Dissolve, Behind, Multiply, Screen, Overlay, Soft Light, Hard Light, Color Dodge, Color Burn, Darken, Lighten, Difference, Exclusion, Hue, Saturation, Color, and Luminosity. The Behind option is only active if you are working in a file on a layer other than the Background layer. (See Chapters 15 and 16 for more information about layers.) Continue experimenting with various modes and opacities. When you are done, make sure to use either the Save or the Save As command if you wish to save your file. Before proceeding to the next section, close the file.

7

FIGURE 7-12   An effect created with the History Brush's Impressionist option

Using the Pattern Stamp Tool

 The Pattern Stamp tool allows you to paint with a pattern. To experiment with it, you need to create and define a pattern. Patterns can be used to create special effects, background textures, and fabric or wallpaper designs. In this section you'll learn how to create a pattern and then use the Pattern Stamp tool to apply it.

Using Adobe Photoshop's Patterns

When you install Photoshop, a Patterns folder is created. This folder contains PostScript patterns that were created in Adobe Illustrator for you to use in Photoshop.

To access one of Adobe's patterns, choose Open from the File menu. In the Open dialog box, locate and open the Patterns folder (inside the Goodies folder; Mac users must open the Postscript Patterns folder in the Patterns folder). You will see a long list of files. Select the Mali Primitive file (Windows users: mali.ai) and open it. In a few moments, Photoshop's Rasterize Generic EPS Format dialog box will appear. Since the pattern was created in Illustrator, which is a vector program, Photoshop needs to convert it to Photoshop's native format, bitmap. You do not need to change any of the dialog box settings if you have the default settings activated (Width: 1.25 inches; Height: 0.625 inches; Resolution: 72; Mode: CMYK Color; and Anti-aliased and Constrain Proportions selected). Just click OK. (The rasterizer options are discussed in Appendix A.)

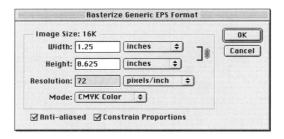

When the file appears, you are ready to define it as a pattern. In order to define any image or part of an image as a pattern, it must first be selected. In this example, you'll select the entire image.

1. Choose All from the Select menu. To define the pattern, choose Define Pattern from the Edit menu. The pattern has now been defined, and you can

proceed to use the Rubber Stamp or Paint Bucket tool or the Fill command to apply it to your file.

2. With the pattern defined and in memory, you no longer need the pattern file (Mali Primitive) open, so close it without saving.

3. Create a new 5-by-5-inch RGB file, which you'll use to see the effects of painting with a pattern using the Pattern Stamp tool.

4. When you have a new file on screen, select the Pattern Stamp tool. If the Pattern Stamp Options palette isn't open, press RETURN (Windows users: ENTER) on your keyboard. Select the Aligned option, set Opacity to 100%, and set the blending mode to Normal. The Aligned option allows you to apply a continuous pattern, no matter how many times you stop and start. If you de-select the Aligned, the pattern restarts every time you release the mouse button and click and drag again in your image.

5. In the Brushes palette, choose a large brush size.

6. Click and drag with the Pattern Stamp tool to start painting. As you paint, the Pattern Stamp tool applies the selected pattern. If you wish, try other brush sizes and opacity settings.

   As you work, you might decide that the pattern would look better with a little color, perhaps some green. One easy way of doing this is to paint the entire screen green and then use a blending mode to help paint the pattern back into the picture.

7. Change the background color to green, or to any color that you want to add to your pattern (other than black or white). Choose Edit | Fill. In the Fill dialog box, choose Background color from the Use pop-up menu, then click OK.

8. Once the background color appears over your image, activate the Pattern Stamp tool. Set Opacity to 100% and pick a large brush from the Brushes palette.

9. Establish a reference point on screen by painting a few brush strokes with the blending mode set to Normal, and then switch to the Lighten mode. This will lighten only areas that are darker than the pattern with which you are painting. Thus, when you paint the pattern with the Pattern Stamp tool in Lighten mode, the white part of the pattern will paint over the green colors on the screen. The black part of the pattern is not painted because it

is darker than the green color on screen. Try painting several brush strokes on the screen to see the effect.

If you wish to reverse the colors in the previous example, choose the Darken mode. Now, only the black part of the pattern is applied because black is darker than the underlying green color. Figure 7-13 shows the Mali Primitive pattern applied with the Normal, Lighten, and Darken modes.

 NOTE: *You can add colors to one of Photoshop's pattern files. Choose RGB or CMYK from the Mode pop-up menu when you open the file. Or open the file, then choose RGB Color or CMYK Color from the Image | Mode menu.*

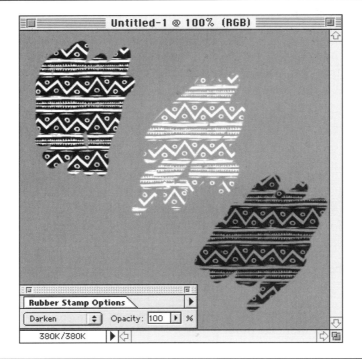

FIGURE 7-13 Applying a pattern with the Pattern Stamp tool using Normal, Lighten, and Darken modes

Creating, Defining, and Applying Custom Patterns

Now that you know how to apply one of Adobe Photoshop's patterns, you're ready to learn how to create one of your own. Although you can create a pattern in any file, it's probably best to make one in a new file. If you create each pattern in a separate file that you name and save, you'll have an easier time accessing your patterns when you wish to use them again. Since these files will be used solely to hold the design of your pattern, they don't need to be very large.

To create a pattern, follow these steps:

1. Open a new file, 2 inches by 2 inches. If you will be applying your pattern over an image, you may wish to choose Transparent from the contents group in the New dialog box. This will allow you to see the underlying image through the noncolored areas of your pattern.

2. Use any of Photoshop's tools to create a pattern.

 TIP: *You can also select a portion of a digitized image to use as a pattern.*

3. Use the Rectangular Marquee tool to select the area you wish to include in your pattern file, as shown in the following illustration. If the background of your pattern file is white and you select any white background area with your pattern, that white area will be included when you paint with the pattern.

4. While the pattern is selected, choose Define Pattern from the Edit menu.

NOTE: *If you select an area with the Feather value greater than 0, the Define Pattern command will be dimmed. The area you select cannot have a feathered edge if you want to use the Define Pattern command.*

5. Save your file and close it.

 NOTE: *Photoshop, unfortunately, can remember only one pattern at a time. The defined pattern is stored in memory until you either define another pattern or quit the program. Thus, if you want to use a pattern again, you must save the file in which the pattern was created.*

6. To apply your pattern, create a new file, 5 inches by 5 inches, or open a file to which you wish to apply the pattern.

7. When the file appears, you can use either the Pattern Stamp or Paint Bucket tool or the Fill command to apply the pattern. For this exercise, use the Pattern Stamp tool. Double-click on the Pattern Stamp tool; from the Pattern Stamp Options palette select the Aligned option.

8. Click and drag in the document to paint with the pattern using the Pattern Stamp Tool.

Try experimenting by applying your pattern with the Pattern Stamp tool, with the Paint Bucket tool, or with the Edit | Fill command. To make your pattern more interesting, you may wish to create a custom brush and apply it to different areas in the image. The music notes shown in this illustration were created with a custom brush from the Sonata typeface. (See Chapter 6 for more details on creating a custom brush.)

Renovating a Kitchen

Here's a tip for architects, interior designers, or anyone who might be involved in a renovation project. This project demonstrates how to take a scanned image of an old, dusty kitchen and transform it into a clean, modern one.

Certainly, one of the major advantages of a computer is that you can experiment with various interior and scenic designs without paying anyone to lift a hammer or a paintbrush. If you wish to use Photoshop for this type of project, you will need to scan (or have a service bureau scan) photographs of the rooms that you wish to renovate. (You'll learn more about digitizing your images in Chapter 8.) If you are thinking of using different wallpaper or colors, take photographs that include the wallpaper samples. This way, you can easily create a pattern in Photoshop from the wallpaper, and it will be at the proper proportions. Of course, you can also create your own patterns for wallpaper and floor tile designs.

Once you have digitized an image of a room, with its wallpaper and floor patterns, load your file. Figure 7-14 is a digitized image of a photograph of a kitchen before image editing in Photoshop. Notice the wallpaper samples hanging

FIGURE 7-14 The kitchen before image editing

on the wall. Figure 7-15 displays the same digitized image after the electronic renovation. In this example, the Rubber Stamp tool's cloning powers were used to remove unwanted items such as the dishes, bottles, old-fashioned light fixture, paper towel holder, and pots and pans. The Edit | Fill command was used to fill a pattern created from a wallpaper sample taped to the wall. The Burn tool dissipated the highlights, and the Sharpen tool made certain areas of the image more distinct.

This example should give you an idea of how you can save money and avoid mistakes by first visualizing (via computer) various wallpaper designs, floor coverings, and cabinet treatments.

Conclusion

From the examples and exercises in this chapter, you can see that Photoshop provides numerous possibilities when editing an image. Now that you've seen the potential of image editing, you'll probably want to learn more about digitizing images so they can be edited with Photoshop. That's the subject of the next chapter.

FIGURE 7-15   The kitchen after image editing

Photoshop 5   In Action

New sky was created with the painting and editing tools.

The Rubber Stamp tool was used to help blend the characters into the mountain.

The characters were combined with a scan of Mount Rushmore.

Artwork by: R/GA Print   **Client: Acclaim Entertainment**

R/GA Print gave artist David Mattingly photographs of the characters that would appear in this final image. David then created a painting of the characters to make it look as if they were created from stone.

Karen Sideman at R/GA Print scanned an image of Mount Rushmore, then scanned Dave's painting and combined the two together. To blend the images together, she cloned using the Rubber Stamp tool. To create a brilliant blue sky in the background, Karen used Photoshop's painting and editing tools. Mount Rushmore will never be the same.

7

Photoshop 5 In Action

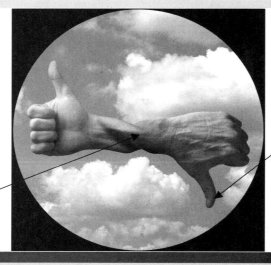

The Curves command and the Rubber Stamp tool were used to convert clay into skin.

Three separate layers were used to create this image. One for each hand and one for the twist area.

Artist: JW Burkey   **Client: Portfolio piece**

To create this image, Dallas photographer JW Burkey photographed a sky, two hands, and a clay twist. He colorized the clay twist using the Image | Adjust | Curves command. He added the skin texture by sampling skin texture from a hand with the Rubber Stamp tool, and cloning it onto the clay so that the twist area looked like skin rather than clay.

JW used three layers to create this image. He placed one hand on one layer and the other hand in another. He loaded the clay twist into the third layer. By using three separate layers, JW could make changes to the separate layers without affecting the images in the other layers.

CHAPTER 8

Digitizing, Manipulating, and Changing Image Size

Digitized images are at the core of most Photoshop design projects. When you digitize a visual image, you are translating it into digital signals so that it can be broken down into pixels and loaded into the computer. Ensuring that images are digitized correctly is crucial to the success of your work. If the digitization process is not conducted properly, image quality will likely be unacceptable and colors may be flawed. Images that are digitized at too low a resolution may look jagged or blurred, and too high a resolution may cause the file size to increase to the point where the file cannot even be edited on your computer.

Since scanning is the most widely used digitizing process, this chapter focuses on using a scanner to digitize an image directly through Photoshop. In addition, you'll experiment with some simple commands that are generally used right after scanning, including those that allow you to manipulate, correct, resize, and create special effects. You'll put your skills to work on a design project, as well as learn about other digitizing alternatives rapidly gaining popularity, such as Photo CD.

Before you can begin digitizing any image, you must first decide what equipment is necessary to properly digitize an image. For digitizing flat art, slides, or photographic prints, you will undoubtedly use a scanner. If your images are on film, you can have them digitized through Kodak's Photo CD process and then view the results in Photoshop with the aid of a CD-ROM player. If you don't already have photographs or slides to work with, you may want to use a digital or video camera to digitize your images at the time you are shooting them. You can also digitize a still frame from videotape by using a video capture card (in your computer) connected to a video recorder.

Scanning

The most important point to remember about scanners is that different scanners provide output of different quality, just as different types of cameras produce photographs of various quality. An expensive camera with a sophisticated optical system will produce sharp images with a full range of accurate colors. Images produced from a cheaper camera will, of course, be of lower quality.

Using a low-end scanner is much like shooting a picture with an inexpensive camera. A low-end desktop scanner may well suit your needs for newspaper work and other low-resolution printing. Low-end desktop scans can also be placed in documents to test layout and design concepts; this is often called *FPO* ("for position only"). After the design has been finalized, the FPO image is replaced with a high-end scan before the project starts its journey to the printing press.

High-end digitizing is the domain of the service bureau. A service bureau will scan your image on expensive prepress equipment, such as Scitex's flatbed scanner, or a rotary drum scanner manufactured by DuPont Crosfield, Linotype-Hell, or Optronics. All of these scanners employ sophisticated optical and color-correcting systems to make your images sharp. Most will also digitize an image directly as a CMYK color file.

 CAUTION: *Be aware that any image editing you do in Photoshop to FPO images cannot automatically be converted to a high-resolution scan. The work will need to be re-created on the higher-quality image. Most service bureaus and prepress houses will do this work for you if your own computer system cannot handle the file size of the high-resolution scans.*

You may be able to avoid the expense of high-end equipment by using a midrange scanner. Such scanners produce highly acceptable images, because they can process more color information than low-end scanners and they are more sensitive to the color range of an image. See Chapter 1 for more information on scanning hardware.

Before you begin scanning, you should know the dimensions of your final image and calculate the correct scanning resolution. Like monitor resolution, scanning resolution is measured in pixels per inch. More pixels in an image means it contains more information. Thus, in general, the more pixels you can pack into an image, the sharper it will be. If you scan at too low a resolution, your image may be blurry or you may see the individual jagged pixel elements in the image.

Notwithstanding the value of high-resolution images, it is generally unnecessary to scan at the highest possible resolution, because eventually a point of diminishing returns is reached. Printing presses can only produce images at a limited number of lines per inch, so the extra resolution will be wasted and may even result in images that look flat. The same holds true if your scans will be output on the Web. Since most users are viewing images on monitors that output at a minimum resolution of 640 by 480 pixels (72 ppi), it is usually unnecessary to scan images at any resolution greater than 72 ppi. If you are outputting to video, you shouldn't need to scan images at higher resolutions either, since the television standard closely translates to 72 ppi.

Why not scan everything at a high resolution, just to be safe? Consider that file size is directly related to an image's resolution. Images that are scanned at higher resolution produce larger file sizes than images scanned at lower resolution. For instance, if you take a 72-ppi image and rescan it at twice the resolution (144 ppi), the new file will be approximately four times as large as that of the original 72-ppi

8

image. Thus, if you scan at too high a resolution, the image's file may become so large that it overwhelms your computer's memory capacity.

 REMEMBER: *File size is directly related to an image's resolution. The higher the resolution, the larger the file size. It is advisable to have at least three to five times your image's file size available in RAM or on your hard disk.*

 TIP: *Some users of low-end scanners find that they get better results by scanning at high resolution and then reducing the resolution. For instance, you may find that scanning text for the Web at 300 ppi and then reducing the size to 72 ppi provides better results than simply scanning at 72 ppi.*

Calculating Resolution and Image Size

If you are producing output for a printing press, calculate the image's resolution based on the printing resolution. The resolution of a printing press is measured in lines per inch (lpi), often called *line screen, halftone screen*, or *screen frequency*. Your scanning resolution (measured in ppi) is directly related to the screen frequency. In the electronic printing process, screen frequency is determined by rows of cells composed of halftones. These halftones are built from the tiniest dots that can be produced by printers—from lasers to imagesetters. (Imagesetter dots are sometimes called "rels," or "raster elements;" laser printer dots are frequently called "pixels.") The following illustration shows how a halftone is built from a grid of pixels. Different-sized halftones combine to produce the illusion of continuous tones of grays and colors in photographs. Halftones are discussed in greater detail in Chapter 19.

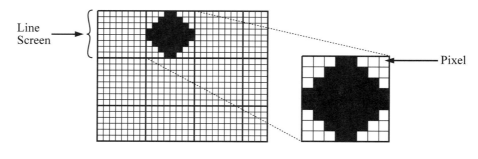

Halftone

When scanning, use this as a general rule: two image pixels are needed for every halftone to produce high-quality output for images that will be printed on a printing press (often one and one-half pixels is all you need). Thus, the process of calculating the correct scanning resolution can often be reduced to the simple formula of doubling the screen frequency:

scanning resolution = 2 × screen frequency (lpi)

For instance, if your commercial printer requires 133 lpi, you can scan images at 266 ppi.

 NOTE: *When an image is printed, a file scanned at two times the line frequency actually has four times as much information than the same file scanned at the line frequency. The number of pixels is quadrupled because pixels are added for each horizontal and vertical line screen.*

If you don't know what screen frequency will be used to print your work, ask your printer. When discussing printing resolution with your printer, you should also know what type of paper will be used. Generally, newspapers are printed at 85 lpi. Most magazines are printed on an offset press using 133 or 150 lpi. Some art books printed on coated paper use 200 lpi. Once you know what lpi you'll be using, you can calculate the resolution, or how many pixels per inch (ppi), you will need when you scan.

If you'd like, Photoshop can calculate the scanning resolution for you, as explained next. When Photoshop calculates the resolution, it also reveals the file size of the image that you will be scanning.

Letting Photoshop Calculate Image Size and Resolution

In this section, you'll have Photoshop calculate both the file size and the resolution for a grayscale or color image. Later in the chapter you'll read about calculating resolution for black-and-white line art and for images that will be enlarged.

Start by creating a new file by choosing File | New. In the New dialog box enter the dimensions of the image you will be scanning. For the example here, use 3.5 inches for the Width and 5 inches for the Height. For now, leave the resolution set to 72 ppi. (Eventually Photoshop will change this value.) If you are scanning a color image, leave the mode set to RGB Color because most desktop scanners produce colors from red, green, and blue values. If you are scanning a grayscale image, switch to Grayscale mode.

 NOTE: *If you are scanning in Grayscale mode, your file size will be smaller than in RGB Color mode because Photoshop will not need to store as much information. Most scanners use a minimum of 24 bits per pixel of information to create colors, and a minimum 8 bits per pixel for grayscale. Photoshop, however, can load 16-bit-per-pixel grayscale images and 48-bit-per-pixel RGB color images.*

At this point, notice that Photoshop has already calculated a file size. At 3.5 by 5 inches and with Mode set to RGB Color, the dialog box displays 266K as the file size. Before continuing, make sure that the Contents radio button is set to White, and then click OK.

After the new file appears, select Image | Image Size. Notice that the Image Size dialog box, shown in Figure 8-1, contains all of the information you entered in the New dialog box: Width and Height are set to the size of your image, Resolution is set to 72 ppi, and the file size is the same as it was in the New dialog box. You'll also see the Constrain Proportions and Resample Image check boxes; these options are discussed later.

Now you're ready to have Photoshop calculate your scanning resolution. In the Image Size dialog box, click the Auto button to display the Auto Resolution dialog box.

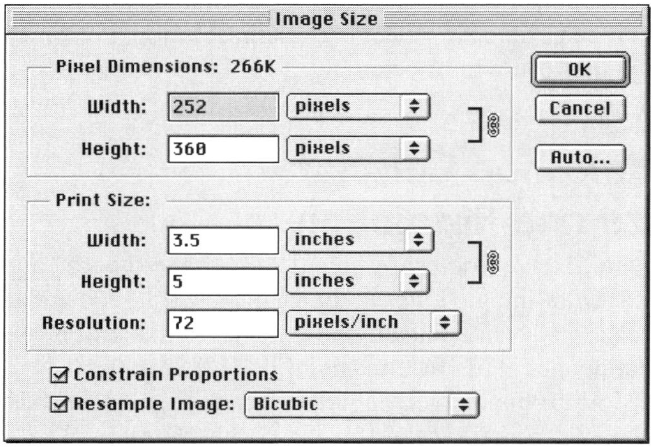

FIGURE 8-1   The Image Size dialog box allows you to change dimensions and resolution

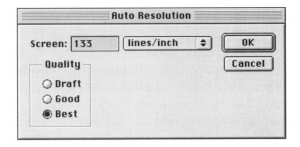

In the Screen field, type in the screen frequency that you'll be using. (If you don't know this, type **133**.) Then click on one of the three Quality radio buttons to designate how you want Photoshop to calculate image resolution. If you click Best, Photoshop will multiply the screen frequency by 2 to compute the resolution; for Good, Photoshop will multiply the screen frequency by 1.5. If you pick Draft and your screen frequency is not less than 72, Photoshop will enter 72. If you enter a screen frequency less than 72 in the Screen field, Photoshop will use that number as your scanning resolution. Click OK, and Photoshop will calculate your resolution and return you to the Image Size dialog box.

When the Image Size dialog box reappears, notice that the New Size and Resolution values have changed. Resolution now displays the desired resolution, according to your screen frequency. (If you used a screen frequency of 150, your new resolution will be 300 ppi.) New Size displays the size of the file you will be working with. Now you can compare the anticipated file size with your computer's memory capacity.

Changing Image Size

If the new file size is too large for your system to handle, you can reduce the file size by decreasing the dimensions of the image in the Image Size dialog box.

 NOTE: *If the Image Size dialog box is not on screen, open it by choosing Image | Image Size. In order to see all of the dialog box options, make sure the Resample Image check box is selected.*

Before you start making changes in the Image Size dialog box shown in Figure 8-1, note whether the Constrain Proportions check box is selected. If it is, the width-to-height ratio remains constant no matter what values you enter. (That is, altering the Width fields will cause a proportional change in the Height fields.) The chain-link icon next to the fields indicates that the values are linked.

If you know the percentage of enlargement or reduction for the file to be digitized, you can change the measurement units in the Pixel Dimensions or Print Size sections from inches to percent. To do this, click on the pop-up menu to the right of one of the Width or Height fields and choose percent. (You'll also see a columns measurement unit in the Print Size section's Width field that can be used if you will be exporting your file into a desktop publishing program that has multicolumn page-layout capability. The columns measurement uses the units specified in the Unit Preferences dialog box, discussed in the "Unit Preferences" section of Chapter 2. In this dialog box you can set the column width and the gutter size as well.)

 NOTE: *You cannot change Pixel Dimensions in the Image Size dialog box if the Resample Image check box is deselected. Resampling is discussed in the next section.*

If you don't want a proportional change, deselect the Constrain Proportions check box. Be aware, however, that if you turn off the Constrain Proportions option and then change the dimensions of an image, you will distort it.

Before you begin to resize your image, you must understand a digital imaging concept known as "resampling."

Resampling Options

When you increase or decrease an image's file size, Photoshop can add or subtract pixels in your image. Adding or subtracting pixels is called *resampling.* (By default, the Resample Image check box in the Image Size dialog box is set to on.) It's important to realize that when you resample, Photoshop must make some sacrifices in image quality. If you decrease the dimensions of your image size, Photoshop must subtract pixels; if you increase your image size, Photoshop must add pixels. When Photoshop adds pixels, it interpolates. During *interpolation,* Photoshop attempts to smooth the difference between the original pixels and the ones it adds. This can result in a somewhat blurred image.

By default, Photoshop uses the best possible method of resampling. This method is called *Bicubic.* To see the other choices, click on the pop-up menu to the right of the Resample Image check box. Nearest Neighbor is the fastest but least exact interpolation method. If you use this method, your image will probably look jagged after rotating or using other manipulation commands. With Bicubic, Photoshop attempts to improve contrast while interpolating. Although it's the best, it's also the slowest. Bilinear is the middle ground between Nearest Neighbor and Bicubic.

NOTE: *If you resample down (that is, decrease file size) and then later resample back up, the final image will not be as sharp as the original. This is because Photoshop must remove pixels, and when you resample back up Photoshop interpolates and cannot add the original pixels that were subtracted earlier.*

Here are a few important notes to remember about changing values in the Image Size dialog box when the Resample Image option is selected.

- If you decrease the print size width or height, the image file size decreases. The number of pixels in the image decreases. The Resolution setting (pixels per inch) does not change.

- If you increase the print size width or height, the file size grows. The number of pixels in the image increases. The Resolution setting does not change.

- If you decrease the Resolution setting, the file size decreases. The print size width and height do not change, but the number of pixels in the image decreases.

- If you increase the Resolution setting, the file size grows. The width and height do not change, but the number of pixels in the image increases.

Try typing a smaller number into the Print Size Width or Height field. Notice that the file size value decreases and the width and height values in pixels decrease. Although the number of pixels in the image changes, the number of pixels per inch remains the same.

Changing Image Dimensions Without Resampling

At this point, you may be wondering how you can change an image's size or resolution without resampling (adding or subtracting pixels). You can—by deselecting the Resample Image check box. If this option is *not* selected, Photoshop will not change the file size of your image when you modify its Print Size or resolution. In order to keep the file size constant, though, Photoshop must compensate by changing the resolution when you change Print Size dimensions, or changing Print Size dimensions when you change the resolution. To avoid adding or subtracting pixels, Photoshop decreases the resolution if you increase the print

8

size dimensions of your image. If you decrease the Print Size dimensions of your image, Photoshop increases the resolution.

Take a moment and try this out—it's important to understand how file size, image dimension, and resolution are related because they all affect your work. Make sure that the Resample Image check box is deselected. Notice that the chain-link icon now shows that the image dimensions and resolution are linked. In the Print Size section, enter a larger value for either Width or Height, and you'll see that Resolution drops. This makes sense: If you want to make an image larger but you don't add any information to it, the resolution decreases.

The inverse is true when you change the Resolution setting. Increase it, and Photoshop decreases the image dimensions; decrease Resolution, and Photoshop increases the image dimensions. Try entering a higher value into the Resolution field, and watch the file's dimensions drop. If you want more pixels per inch and you don't want the file size to change, the image dimensions will have to decrease.

If this concept seems confusing, here's an analogy: Assume that you have a balloon with a painted image on it, consisting of many tiny dots of paint. If you stretch the balloon out to make the image size greater, the space between each dot grows, and you have fewer dots per square inch. This is the same as decreasing resolution when file dimensions are increased. Let air out of the balloon to make the image smaller, and the dots get closer together. Similarly, an image's resolution increases when the file dimensions are decreased. In both cases, whether you stretched or shrank the balloon, the actual mass of rubber or the number of dots did not change. Likewise, with the Constrain File Size check box selected, the file size and number of pixels in your image always remain the same even if you change its dimensions or resolution.

The following chart summarizes how the Resample Image option affects your image.

	Increase Print Size	Decrease Print Size	Increase Resolution	Decrease Resolution
Resample Image check box on	Increases file size; resolution doesn't change	Decreases file size; resolution doesn't change	Increases file size; print size doesn't change	Decreases file size; print size doesn't change
Resample Image check box off	Decreases resolution; file size is unchanged	Increases resolution; file size is unchanged	Decreases print size; file size is unchanged	Increases print size; file size is unchanged

At this point, you should have a good idea about how you can control Photoshop image dimensions, file sizes, and resolution. You can even test how fast Photoshop will operate on your computer at different image sizes and resolutions. If you'd like to "test drive" your computer at your digitized image's size and resolution, return the settings in the Image Size dialog box to those needed by your image. (In our example, width is 3.5 inches, height is 5 inches, and resolution is 300 ppi.) Click OK to continue.

 TIP: *If you wish to reset the dialog box options to its original settings, press and hold OPTION (Windows users: ALT). This causes the Cancel button to change to a Reset button.*

After you click OK in the Image Size dialog box, you'll probably see your document window enlarge, because you have increased the file's resolution over its previous setting of 72 ppi. The new window size reflects the fact that more pixels are consuming each inch of the image. Remember, if you are working on any file that has a resolution higher than your monitor's (often 72 ppi), your image will be displayed larger than actual size. (For more information, see "Creating a New File" in Chapter 2.)

Now you can test to see how fast your computer will work with the anticipated file size of your soon-to-be-scanned image. Try painting with a couple of different tools to see how Photoshop responds. You don't need an image in the file to do this. Remember, even though the file has no image, pixels are pixels; it doesn't matter whether they're white, black, or colored.

 NOTE: *If you resize without resampling, the size of your image on screen will not change because you have not added or subtracted pixels. If Photoshop's rulers are displayed, they will indicate any change in image dimensions.*

 REMEMBER: *Photoshop displays your image at your monitor's screen resolution (72 ppi or 96 ppi, in most cases). The image quality on screen does not change if you raise the resolution of the image beyond your screen's resolution. You'll only see a difference when the image is printed.*

Calculating Resolution for Images You Are Enlarging

Now that you have calculated your scanning resolution and image size, you are just about ready to scan your image. But there are two more issues you might need to consider—whether the image will be enlarged during scanning or in Photoshop, and whether black-and-white line art will be scanned.

If you are going to enlarge the scanned image dimensions (likely if you are scanning slides, for instance), you'll need to increase the scanning resolution before you scan. Increasing the number of pixels in the image ensures that the quality is maintained when the image is enlarged. If you don't boost the resolution, image clarity will suffer, and the image may become pixelated. (The individual pixels in the image become evident when the image dimensions are enlarged.)

To calculate the correct scanning resolution for an image that will be enlarged for printing, use the following formula:

$$\text{Scanning resolution} = \begin{array}{c}\text{longest} \\ \text{dimension} \\ \text{in final} \\ \text{image}\end{array} \times \begin{array}{c}\text{screen} \\ \text{frequency} \\ \text{(lpi)}\end{array} \times \begin{array}{c}\text{pixel-} \\ \text{to-line screen} \\ \text{ratio}\end{array} \div \begin{array}{c}\text{longest dimension} \\ \text{of original image}\end{array}$$

As an example, assume you scan an image of 2 inches by 3 inches and want to enlarge it to 4 inches by 6 inches. (Also assume your screen frequency is 150 lpi.) Here's a step-by-step explanation of how to apply the formula:

1. Multiply the longest dimension (height or width) of the final image by the screen frequency (lpi). This produces the minimum number of pixels necessary to produce the longest dimension of the image. In our example, $6 \times 150 = 900$ pixels.

2. As discussed earlier in the chapter, to produce a high-quality image 2 pixels are needed for every line-screen inch (or every halftone dot); thus, 2 is the pixel-to-line screen ratio. In our example, $2 \times 900 = 1,800$, the minimum number of pixels necessary to produce the longest dimension of the image.

3. To obtain the scanning resolution, divide the minimum number of pixels needed to produce the longest dimension by the longest dimension of the original image. In our example, $1,800 \div 3 = 600$ ppi, the final scanning resolution.

After you've calculated the correct resolution and scanned your image at that resolution, you would then use the Image Size dialog box with the Resample Image check box deselected (no interpolation) to enlarge your image. After you enlarge, the resolution drops to 300 ppi—twice the screen frequency.

NOTE: *The preceding formula can also be written as follows:*

Scanning   largest   largest   screen
resolution = size in ÷ size original × 2 × frequency
                 final   image
                 image

NOTE: *If you are uncertain about what screen frequency or pixel-to-line
screen ratio you should use, check with your service bureau or
commercial printer.*

As previously mentioned, the foregoing calculation is extremely important
when you are scanning slides. For example, let's say you are enlarging the longest
dimension of a slide to 5 inches. Since the longest dimension of a 35mm slide is
1.375 inches, you would use the following calculation (if your screen frequency is
150): 5 × 150 × 2 ÷ 1.375. This calculation results in a scanning resolution that
would be a little less than 1,100 ppi.

Choosing a Resolution for Black-and-White Line Art

Black-and-white images, such as line art, logos, and text, are frequently referred to
as bitmap images. This term is used because only 1 bit is necessary to make each
pixel of the image black or white. As discussed in "Video Display Cards" in
Chapter 1, a bit can be either off or on. If the bit is on, the pixel is black; if it
is off, the pixel is white.

If you are scanning bitmap images, you may be surprised to learn that the
resolution must sometimes be set higher than when working with color. In color
and grayscale images, gradations of colors and grays can hide edges and make an
image blend into its background. In black-and-white images, on the other hand,
the stark contrast between black and white draws the eye's attention to outlines.

Many printing professionals suggest scanning at a resolution as high as that
of your output device. As mentioned in "Output Devices" in Chapter 1, resolution
for both printers and imagesetters is measured in dots per inch (dpi). If you are
producing output for an imagesetter with a resolution of 1,200 dpi, you should
scan at 1,200 ppi. If you are printing to a laser printer that outputs 300 dpi, you
may as well scan at 300 ppi. Even if you scan at 1,000 ppi, your 300-dpi printer
cannot add any more resolution to the image (although many printers can smooth
raster images when they output them).

8

Calculating Resolution for the Web and Multimedia

If you are scanning an image that will be output to the Web or to a multimedia program and you will be enlarging the image, calculate scanning resolution by multiplying the scaling factor by the monitor's resolution. You can use the following formula:

Scanning resolution = (longest dimension of final image ÷ longest dimension

of original image) × monitor resolution

Thus, if you are scanning an image 1 inch long and need to enlarge it to 3 inches, you would scan at 216 pixels per inch $[(3 \div 1) \times 72 = 216]$. When you enlarge the image with the Resample Image check box deselected, the resolution will drop to 72 ppi.

If you scan an image for printing at a high resolution and later need to reduce the image for output to the Web or a multimedia program, open the Image Size dialog box, turn on the Resample Image check box, enter the new resolution (72 ppi) and the new width and height, and click OK. The image resolution and size will be changed.

Using the Resize Image Assistant

The previous sections provided the theory and mathematics for resizing images. Although many Photoshop users may find the calculations required to be simple, others may wish to turn to Photoshop's Resize Image Assistant to help ease the mathematical anguish. The Image Assistant automatically calculates resolution, then resizes a copy of your image. It also warns you if your image needs to be rescanned at a higher resolution. To try out the Image Assistant, load a sample image, then choose Resize Image from the Help menu. This opens the Image Assistant. All you need to do is complete the information on screen, then click the Next button as shown in Figure 8-2. The Image Assistant asks you to enter the final size of the image that you will be creating, the halftone screen frequency, the quality you desire, and whether you want the image sharpened. If you don't like math, using the Image Assistant is the best way to insure that the images you resize maintain their quality.

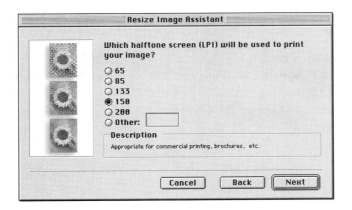

FIGURE 8-2   The Resize Image Assistant

Using File Import to Scan an Image

After you've decided which scanner to use and have calculated your scanning resolution, you are ready to start scanning. This section takes you step by step from previewing your image to scanning it from within Photoshop.

In order to scan, you will need to install the plug-in (driver) that is provided by your scanner's manufacturer, which allows you to operate the scanner from within Photoshop. To install the plug-in, copy it into the Import/Export folder within the Plug-ins folder. If you are using a scanner that supports the TWAIN standard—such as the Hewlett-Packard Scanjet—you will need to install the TWAIN software that comes with your scanner. Windows users might need to update scanning software that was released earlier than the Windows version of Photoshop. If you install the plug-in while you have Photoshop open, you'll need to Quit and restart Photoshop before you continue.

Twain_32.8BA

> **NOTE:**   *If your scanner did not come with a Photoshop plug-in, you may need to scan using the software that came with your scanner.*

Once your scanner plug-in is installed, and before you begin digitizing an image, read the instructions that came with your scanner. In particular, find out whether your scanner allows you to set the white point (sometimes called "highlight point") and the black point (sometimes called the "shadow point"). From these two endpoints, your software may be able to create a tone curve to ensure that the scanner captures the widest density range, or dynamic range.

NOTE: *Some scanning software, such as Flamingo Bay ScanPrep, may provide features not found in your scanning software.*

The explanations in this section are based on the Agfa Arcus II scanner, a midrange scanner available for both Mac and Windows users, using the Agfa FotoLook PS 3.03 plug-in. The steps described here are similar to those you'll perform for most desktop scanners.

FotoLook PS 3.03

When you're ready, turn on the scanner (if it isn't already on). Place the image face down on the scanner's glass plate. Try to get the image placed as straight as possible; otherwise, the scanned image will appear crooked or possibly cropped when it appears in Photoshop.

 NOTE: *If you rotate an image to correct crooked placement in a scanner, Photoshop needs to resample the image, which impairs image quality.*

If you are using a slide scanner, place the slide in the slide holder. The Arcus II scanner scans reflective objects, such as photographs and line art, as well as transparencies, such as slides. In this procedure, we will use the reflective option.

To begin the scanning process within Photoshop, select File | Import. If your scanner has a plug-in, you will see it in the Import submenu. Select your scanner driver from the Import submenu.

> **Agfa FotoLook PS 3.03...**
> **Anti-aliased PICT...**
> **PICT Resource...**
> **Twain Acquire...**
> **Twain Select...**

If you have a TWAIN-compatible scanner, the first time you use your scanner you must select it as the scanning source. In the File Import submenu, choose Select TWAIN 32_Source, and then select your scanner in the dialog box that appears. To start the scanning process, choose File | Import again, and choose TWAIN_32 Acquire.

NOTE: *PC users: Photoshop 5 supports the TWAIN_32 standard. It does not support TWAIN drivers created for Windows 3.1.*

Your next step is to preview the scanned image and choose a specific area of the image to scan. If you don't do this, the final image will be as large as the scanner's entire scanning area and you will wind up with a very large file size. Another reason for previewing is to make sure you haven't put the image in the scanner upside down. To begin the preview, click on the Preview button. In a minute or so the preview will appear on screen.

After the miniature image appears, select the specific area to scan, as shown in Figure 8-3. Most scanner selection controls work similarly; typically, you only need to click and drag over the specific part of the previewed image that you wish to scan. Don't worry about selecting too precisely. Once the image has been scanned, you can crop out extraneous portions in Photoshop. Notice that, as shown in Figure 8-3, the Agfa FotoLook scanner dialog box produces a handy readout of image size.

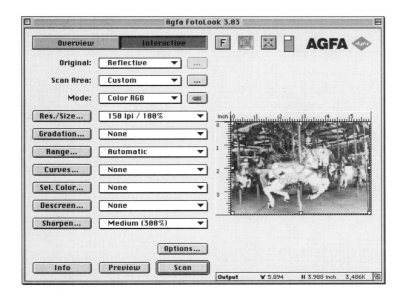

FIGURE 8-3   The Agfa scanner FotoLook plug-in previews an image and its file size and provides options for correcting images

Next, after selecting the area to be scanned, you're ready to choose a mode and scanning resolution for the digitized image. Click on the Mode pop-up menu and choose either Color, RGB, Gray-Scale, or Lineart (sometimes called Bitmap), and then choose a resolution. In this example, the Input pop-up menu was used to change the resolution to 150 lpi ppi.

Before scanning, examine the controls in your own scanning window. If you don't know the purpose of each option, consult your scanner's manual. Notice that the Agfa FotoLook scanning window includes a Range setting. When Range is set to Automatic, the scanner will automatically set its density range, or dynamic range. A scanner's *dynamic range* is the range of colors it can identify, from the brightest to the darkest. With Range set to Automatic, the scanner prescans the image to measure the brightest highlight and the darkest shadow. This helps the scanner capture the broadest dynamic range possible.

The Agfa FotoLook plug-in also features commands to eliminate color casts (shifts in color toward red, green, or blue). If an image displays too much of any of these colors, the cast can be eliminated by choosing Color from the Preferences pop-up menu. This opens the Color Preferences dialog box, where you can adjust the sliders for red, green, and blue values. Notice that the Agfa FotoLook scanning plug-in also provides a Sharpen setting, which can be used to enhance image edges. The Descreen option can help eliminate moiré patterns when you are scanning images that have been printed using screens.

Many scanners allow you to change exposure settings before you scan. If you wish, you can experiment with these settings, or make adjustments to your image later in Photoshop.

When you're ready to scan the image, click the Scan button. In a few minutes, the scan will be completed and the image will appear in a Photoshop window.

 CAUTION: *When working with digitized images, make sure you secure all reproduction rights before using them.*

The Rotate Canvas Commands

When the scanned image appears in Photoshop, you may see that despite your best efforts, the image is tilted or upside down. The Rotate Canvas commands in Photoshop's Image menu help you fix this. These commands can also be used to rotate an image that had to be scanned sideways so that it would fit on the scanner flatbed, or to turn over an image that was inadvertently scanned upside down.

Rotating a Scanned Image

To rotate an image, choose Image | Rotate Canvas. The Rotate Canvas submenu provides you with several choices, as shown here. Each option rotates your image according to the angle indicated (CW means clockwise and CCW means counterclockwise). The Arbitrary option allows you to specify a particular degree of rotation. Since this command is more flexible than the others, it's a good place to start, so select Arbitrary.

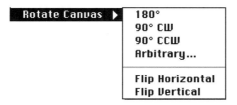

 NOTE: *If you want to follow along with these steps but you don't want to rotate or change your scanned image on screen, you can load any image or one of the images from Adobe's Samples folder.*

In the dialog box that appears, you will enter the degrees of rotation that you wish to use and specify clockwise or counterclockwise rotation. In the Angle field you can enter values from –359.99 to 359.99 degrees. So that you can easily see the results of this test, enter **45**. Click the CW radio button to rotate clockwise. Click OK.

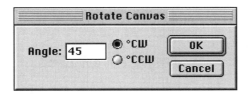

 NOTE: *Rotate Canvas rotates the entire image, regardless of whether there is a selection on screen. If you need to rotate a selection path or layer, you must use the Edit | Transform command, discussed later in this chapter.*

 NOTE: *If you rotate your image by any angle other than 90 or 180 degrees, Photoshop must interpolate to complete the rotation, possibly degrading image quality.*

You'll see that the entire screen image rotates 45 degrees clockwise. To return the screen to its original position, rotate the image again, this time 45 degrees counterclockwise.

 TIP: *After rotating an image, you can check whether it is crooked or not by aligning the edges of the image with a guide or with the edges of a palette.*

How Crooked Is It?

Occasionally you need to rotate an image but have no idea exactly what angle you need to rotate the image. How do you measure an angle on screen? Use Photoshop 5's new Measure tool. Position the tool at the base of the image area that is tilted, then click and drag from the base of the image area along its edge. The distance and angle appear in the Info palette.

Flipping an Image

The Flip commands in the Rotate Canvas submenu let you flip an image to face it in a different direction. The Flip command is applied to the entire electronic Canvas; it cannot be applied to a selection.

 NOTE: *If you wish to flip a selection or layer or path, choose Edit | Transform | Flip Horizontal or Edit | Transform | Flip Vertical.*

To flip your image horizontally, choose Flip Horizontal from the Image | Rotate Canvas submenu. Your image will flip along a vertical plane and face in a new direction. Return to the Rotate Canvas submenu and choose Flip Vertical to see the image flip along a horizontal plane, turning it upside down. Flip your image again to make it right-side up.

Now that you've rotated your image so that it's straight and flipped it to face in the direction you want, you might wish to crop it, as explained next.

Using the Cropping Tool

Cropping is very similar to taking a pair of scissors and cutting an image so that only a portion of the original is visible. You can also crop to remove unwanted border areas left over from a scan. Removing unwanted border areas is also a good way to keep the size of your file under control. You can crop by clicking and dragging the mouse or by entering dialog box options.

Before you begin to crop, select the Cropping tool in the Toolbox by clicking on the Marquee Toolbox location and keeping the mouse button pressed. When you see the Cropping tool, drag over to the tool to select it, and then release the mouse. If the Options palette isn't opened on screen, double-click on the Cropping tool to display the Crop Options palette.

The Crop Options palette contains dimension settings that are by now familiar to you. In order to activate the dimension settings, the Fixed Target Size option must be selected. If it isn't, click on it to select it. (If you want to ensure that the dimension settings match the dimensions of the image on screen, click the Front Image button in the palette.) You can specify Width and Height measurement units in inches, centimeters, points, pixels, or columns. You can also change the resolution of the cropped area. If you change the width and height measurements and you want to maintain your image's current resolution, it's important to type that resolution into the Resolution field. If you don't, Photoshop changes the resolution to compensate for the change in width or height when you eventually execute the crop.

The Cropping tool also works somewhat like the Image Size dialog box. If you have the Fixed Target Size option selected, and don't enter a resolution, it's the same as telling Photoshop to readjust the file dimensions without changing the number of pixels in the image. So if you reduce the width or height, Photoshop increases the resolution proportionally.

Conversely, if you enter a resolution without changing the height or width, Photoshop changes the image dimensions proportionally. If you increase the resolution, Photoshop decreases the image size; decrease the resolution, and Photoshop increases the image size.

If you don't set any values in the Crop Options palette, you can crop freely with the mouse, and the resolution of the image remains unchanged. You can also

8

crop freely by deselecting the Fixed Target Size option. For this experiment, deselect the Fixed Target Size option.

 TIP: *If CAPS LOCK is on or if the Tool Cursors for Other Tools in the Preferences dialog box (choose File | Preferences | Display & Cursors) is set to Precise, the pointer will be a crosshair instead of the Cropping tool icon. The crosshair pointer is more precise, because you can set the starting point of the cropping area to be exactly at the intersection of the crosshair.*

With the Cropping tool selected, click and drag over the image area that you want to retain. The area outside the selection is the portion that will be cropped out of the image. When you are satisfied with the selection, release the mouse button. Notice that the selected area on screen now includes one handle at each corner and a handle in the middle of each side. If you need to make any adjustments to the crop, click and drag any of the handles to resize the selected area. To move the entire selection marquee, simply click and drag in the middle of the selection area.

Once you're satisfied that the selected region surrounds the area that you want to keep on screen, press RETURN (Windows users: ENTER). After you press RETURN or double-click, the image is cropped. To cancel the crop and remove the bounding box from the screen, press COMMAND-. (Windows users: ESC).

 TIP: *You can also use the Cropping tool to rotate the cropping bounding box. To do this, position the mouse pointer beyond the outside edge of the cropping selection area (but not on a handle). When you see a curved pointer on screen, click and drag to rotate. After you press RETURN or double-click, the rotated section within the bounding box is cropped.*

 TIP: *To crop an image, you can also use the Rectangular Marquee to select an area and then choose Image | Crop.*

Now that you have the image cropped exactly the way you want it, you may want to make some simple adjustments to your image's brightness and contrast.

Adjusting Brightness and Contrast

Contrast is the difference between the lightest and darkest parts of an image. Brightness is the degree of light that is reflected from an image or transmitted through it.

Some scanners have a tendency to darken images, causing them to lose contrast. Images frame-grabbed from videotape also have a tendency to darken when loaded into Photoshop. When you need to make simple adjustments to the brightness and contrast levels of your image, you'll find that the Brightness/Contrast command in the Image | Adjust submenu may solve the problem. (If your image needs more extensive color correction and retouching, refer to Chapter 18.)

To use the Brightness/Contrast controls, first select an area to be adjusted, or don't select in order to adjust the entire image. Choose Image | Adjust | Brightness/Contrast. The Brightness/Contrast dialog box is a simple one: It contains a Preview check box and sliders for adjusting Brightness and Contrast.

First, make sure the Preview check box is selected so you can watch the results of your adjustments, and then begin by testing the Brightness slider. Drag the slider control to the right to brighten your image, or to the left to darken your image. Take a few moments now to adjust brightness to the best level for your image. Be careful not to overexpose or underexpose the image.

When you are satisfied with the brightness level, try adjusting the contrast. Moving the slider control to the right adds more detail; this increases the difference between the lightest and darkest portions of the image. If you drag the slider control to the left, the lightness and darkness levels will begin to merge.

If the image doesn't look as good as it did when you started, you can either drag both sliders back to their zero points or click Cancel. You can also press OPTION (Windows users: ALT) to make the Cancel button change to a Reset button. Once you are satisfied with the new brightness and contrast levels, click OK.

 TIP: *The Brightness/Contrast command can be applied in an Adjustment Layer (discussed in Chapter 16). Adjustment Layers allow you to see editing changes through a layer mask without changing the actual pixels of the image. Adjustment Layers also allow you to paint to add and subtract effects.*

Resizing an Image

You may need to increase or decrease the size of a digitized image so that it fits in a specific area when you print it or output it to the Web or a multimedia program. To resize an image, use the Image Size command in the Image menu, which is fully explained earlier in this chapter.

To change the dimensions of the image, enter a new value in either the Width or the Height field (in the Print Size section) in the Image Size dialog box. If the Constrain Proportions check box is selected, Photoshop automatically changes the other value. If the Resample Image check box is off, image resolution changes but the file size in bytes remains the same (as does the number of pixels in the image).

Remember, if you change image dimensions with the Resample Image check box selected, Photoshop must interpolate. By default, Photoshop uses its best possible interpolation method (Bicubic). Nevertheless, as discussed earlier in this chapter, you should not resize images with the Resample Image check box on, especially when you are enlarging images.

Later in this chapter, in the "Edit | Transform Design Project" section, you will work through a design project in which the example image is reduced by one-half inch. Go ahead and lower the width and height dimensions of your own image now, if you wish. But before you click OK, remember that when you decrease the size of your image (with the Resample Image check box selected), Photoshop removes pixels from it. Thus, if you later try to resample up, the image will not look as sharp as the original. Once Photoshop removes the pixels, they're gone for good; Photoshop cannot re-create them. When Photoshop resamples up, it resamples on the basis of the contents of the current file. When you are ready to have Photoshop resize your image, click OK.

Increasing the Canvas Size

Now that you have the image the size you want, you may wish to increase your work area on screen. You can do this by changing the canvas size of your image. When you increase the canvas size, you extend the perimeter of your document. This puts a useable border around the image. Later in this chapter, you'll see how you can utilize this border as an area for adding text and extra images to a document.

When a border is added, Photoshop uses the current background color as the canvas color. Before you change the canvas size, pick a background color that you like. If you want the canvas color to match one of the colors in your image, you can use the Eyedropper tool and OPTION key (Windows users: ALT) to switch background colors (as long as the Foreground selection box is activated in the Color palette). Activate the Eyedropper by clicking on it, press OPTION (Windows users: ALT), move the eyedropper pointer over the color you wish to use as your background color, and click.

To change the canvas size, choose Image | Canvas Size. In the Canvas Size dialog box (shown in Figure 8-5), notice that your image's current dimensions appear in the Width and Height fields. At this point, they are the same as those for the canvas. If you increase these values in the Width and Height fields for New Size, the perimeter, or surrounding canvas, will grow. This will produce a border around the image in the current background color.

 NOTE: *If you have layers in your document, the background color only affects the Background layer. If you have no Background layer, the border is filled with the transparency grid color for all layers.*

 TIP: *Images can be moved so that they extend beyond the Canvas. However, the Select | All command only selects to the borders of the Canvas.*

The Canvas Size dialog box also allows you to indicate the placement of your image in the canvas. At the bottom of the dialog box is the Anchor area, a grid of nine boxes. By clicking on a box, you specify the position of your image in relation to the canvas. If you select the center box, Photoshop centers your image in the Canvas. If you click on the lower-middle box, Photoshop drops your image to the bottom-middle part of the canvas. This is the placement chosen for the design project, shown in Figure 8-8, presented later in this chapter. Also, 1 inch was added to both the Width and the Height, as shown in Figure 8-5. The result is a half-inch border on the left and right sides of the image, and a 1-inch canvas area on top.

To create a canvas background for your image now, increase the Width and Height settings in the New Size area of the Canvas Size dialog box. Try adding 1 inch to both. If you wish your image to appear as shown in the design project, choose the bottom-middle placement box. Click OK to see the results.

At this point you have learned how to rotate, flip, crop, resize, and border your digitized image and change its brightness and contrast. Now proceed to the next section to take a look at some special effects that can add variety to your image. Later, you will use these techniques to create a sample design project.

FIGURE 8-4   Area within bounding box to be cropped by Cropping tool

Canvas Size

Current Size: 1.79M
Width: 2.502 inches
Height: 2.787 inches

OK
Cancel

New Size: 3.4M

Width: 3.5   inches ⬍
Height: 3.787   inches ⬍
Anchor:

FIGURE 8-5   1 inch added to the width and height to increase the canvas

Working with the Transform Commands

The commands available in Photoshop's Image | Rotate Canvas submenu allow you to manipulate the canvas. Often you'll need to manipulate a selection on screen instead. The commands that allow you to do these operations are the Transform commands that are found in the Edit | Transform submenu. The Rotate and Flip commands in the Edit | Transform submenu work exactly the same as the Rotate and Flip commands in the Image menu, except that in the Transform menu they allow you to rotate and flip a selection, a layer, or a group of layers.

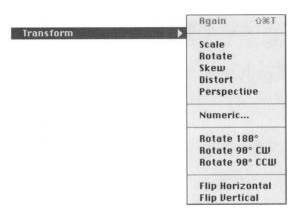

Transform ▶

Again   ⇧⌘T

Scale
Rotate
Skew
Distort
Perspective

Numeric...

Rotate 180°
Rotate 90° CW
Rotate 90° CCW

Flip Horizontal
Flip Vertical

Photoshop 5   In Action

The sphinx was scanned and then selected with the Lasso tool. It was pasted into the monitor, then shrunk with the Edit | Transform | Scale command.

The monitor was selected and then stretched using the Edit | Transform | Scale command.

Artist: Marc Yankus   **Client: Computer World**

Marc started by scanning black-and-white images of various pyramids. These were selected with the selection tools and filled with color using the Edit | Fill command. In the Fill dialog box, Marc set the mode to Darken, so that only the light areas would be painted and not the dark areas. Then he scanned a picture of a computer. Once the computer was scanned, he selected it with the Lasso tool and pasted it into the final image.

Use the Scale command to resize part of an image, Skew to slant an image, Distort to stretch an image in different directions, and Perspective to create the appearance of depth in an image.

To try any of these commands, first create a selection and then choose either Scale, Skew, Perspective, Rotate, Flip, or Distort from the Edit | Transform submenu. After you choose an Edit | Transform command, Photoshop creates a bounding box around the area that will be affected by the transformation. With the mouse, click and drag on the handles to preview the effect. When you want to apply the effect to your image, press the RETURN or ENTER key. To cancel before pressing ENTER, press COMMAND-. (Windows users: ESC).

 CAUTION: *Be aware that when you use many of the commands in the Edit | Transform submenu, Photoshop must interpolate. Image quality depends on the interpolation method set in the Preferences dialog box (File | Preferences | General) and on how many times the image is transformed.*

8

Take a few minutes to try out each Edit | Transform command. If you don't wish to apply the commands to your current image, open a new file and create some text that you can experiment with. Remember, these commands can only be applied to selections or non-transparent image areas in layers, paths and masks in Quick Mask mode. Here are some guidelines for using the Edit | Transform commands:

☐ To scale an object in proportion, press the SHIFT key while using the Scale command.

☐ When you use the Perspective command, try dragging one handle up and the opposite one down or diagonally in and out. As you drag one handle, another one will move in the opposite direction, to create a depth effect. Figure 8-6 illustrates the effect of the Perspective command applied to a text selection. Here, clicking and dragging downward on the lower-right handle caused the top-right handle to move upward. Note that before applying the Perspective command, we rendered the text layer by choosing Layer | Type | Render Layer.

☐ When you skew a selection, click and drag on any handle. All handles always move along a horizontal plane as the object is slanted.

☐ You can distort a selection by clicking and dragging on any handle in any direction. With the Distort command you can create effects that look like

FIGURE 8-6   With the Edit | Transform | Perspective command, dragging a handle distorts the image and creates depth

those created with Perspective and Skew, except that you have more control over the selected area.

After you've finished experimenting, you may want to use the Revert command to retrieve the last saved version of your file before you continue to the next section, where you'll see the image effects demonstrated in a design project. Alternatively, you can click on the first snapshot in the History palette to return to the original version of your file.

Using Free Transform

If you wish to apply several effects at once, you can use Free Transform. Using this command, you can move, scale, rotate, or skew a selection or create perspective using keyboard commands and clicking and dragging the mouse.

Here's how to use Free Transform:

1. Use a selection tool to select an area on screen that you wish to transform. If you wish to transform an entire layer, you do not need to select anything—as long you are in any layer other than the Background.

2. Choose Edit | Free Transform. A bounding box appears indicating the area that will be transformed.

3. If needed, move the bounding box into position by clicking and dragging within it. If you are not working with a selection, you can use the Move tool to move the entire layer.

   ❑ To scale the image, click and drag on a handle. To scale proportionally, press SHIFT as you click and drag. As you drag, keep an eye on the Info palette, which displays the percentage change in width and height as well as the size in width and height.

   ❑ To rotate, move the mouse pointer just beyond the bounding box area. When you see a curved double arrow, click and drag in the direction in which you wish to rotate the image.

 TIP: *While rotating, pressing SHIFT constrains the rotation to 15-degree increments.*

   ❑ To distort, press COMMAND (Windows users: CTRL), and while you click and drag on a handle. To distort symmetrically, press OPTION (Windows users: ALT), instead of COMMAND.

   ❑ To skew, press COMMAND-SHIFT (Windows users: CTRL-SHIFT) while clicking and dragging over a side (not corner) handle. The pointer turns into a white arrow with double arrows nearby.

   ❑ To create perspective, press COMMAND-OPTION-SHIFT (Windows users: CTRL-ALT-SHIFT) while clicking and dragging over a corner handle. When you see a gray arrow, click and drag the handle.

   ❑ To apply the transformation, press ENTER. (Mac users can press ENTER or RETURN). If you wish to cancel before you press ENTER, press ESC. (Mac users can also press ESC or COMMAND-.)

Using Numeric Transform

If you need to make precise transformations, you may not wish to create them by clicking and dragging the mouse. Instead, you can use the Numeric Transform

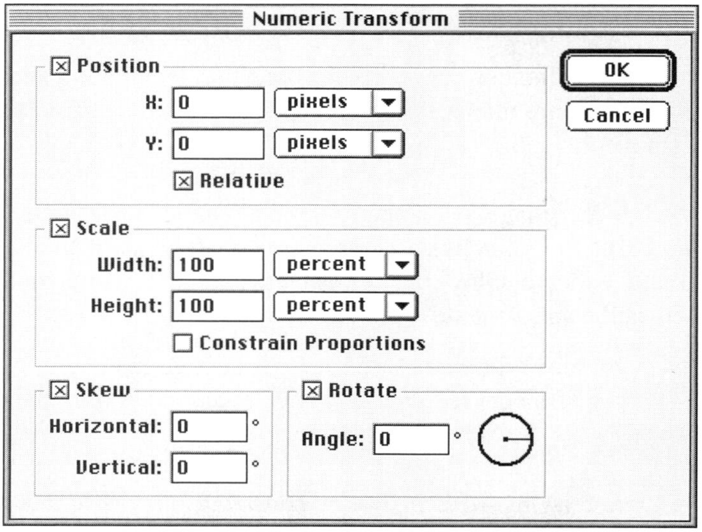

FIGURE 8-7 Numeric Transform dialog box

dialog box, shown in Figure 8-7. To open the dialog box, choose Numeric Transform from the Edit | Transform submenu. In the dialog box, you can choose which type of transformation you wish to execute by clicking on the appropriate check box: Position, Scale, Skew, and Rotate. To use the dialog box, simply enter the value you wish to move or scale by or the number of degrees you wish to rotate. You can change measurement units in the Position and Scale pop-up menus. If you wish to move a selection consisting of the nontransparent portion of a layer relative to its last position, keep the relative check box selected. Otherwise, the movement will take place based upon a zero point in the upper-left corner of your image. If you click on the Constrain Proportions check box, changing either Width or Height produces a proportional change in the other field.

Edit Transform Design Project

If you wish to complete a project like the one shown in Figure 8-8, load any digitized image or the image you used in the "Increasing the Canvas Size" section earlier in the chapter (and skip step 1).

FIGURE 8-8   A design project created using the Edit | Transform command

1. Choose a background color and then use the Image | Canvas Size command to add 1 inch to both the Width and the Height of your image. Set Placement in the Canvas Size dialog box so that the bottom-middle box is selected. This creates a .5-inch canvas border area on the left and right of your image, and a 1-inch canvas border area above your image.

2. To fill the half-inch border on the right and left sides with a duplicated portion of your image (see Figure 8-8 as an example), use the Rectangular Marquee tool to create a rectangular selection. It doesn't matter whether the selection is bigger than the half-inch canvas border because you can scale it to fit.

3. With the image area selected, duplicate it by pressing COMMAND-OPTION (Windows users: CTRL-ALT) while you click and drag the selection toward the upper-left canvas border area. *Don't deselect.*

4. Choose Edit | Transform | Scale. Scale the image by clicking on one of the four corners. If you wish, press SHIFT to constrain the dimensions proportionally.

5. When you are satisfied with the scaling, press ENTER. You can see the effects of the scaling in Figure 8-9.

6. Keep the scaled image selected so that you can reproduce it several times in order to cover the entire left and right borders. While pressing OPTION

FIGURE 8-9 The Edit | Transform | Scale command was used to shrink a selection that was created by duplicating part of the image

(Windows users: ALT), click and drag with the Move tool to duplicate the image. Do this as many times as needed to cover the borders.

Once you've assembled the border, you are ready to start creating the distorted text. Before you begin, make sure that the foreground color is set to the color you wish to use for the text (we used white).

7. Select the Type tool and click on the top canvas area. When the Type Tool dialog box appears, pick an appropriate font and size. So that the text does not appear jagged, make sure that the Anti-Aliased option is selected.

8. Type the heading you want to appear in your image. In our example, we used BANGKOK. In the Type Tool dialog box, click on the swatch to open the Color Picker. In the Color Picker dialog box, choose a color, then click OK. Next close the Type Tool dialog box by clicking OK.

9. Since you will be distorting the type, you'll need to render the type layer. To render the layer choose Layer | Type | Render Layer.

10. Your next step is to distort the type. Choose Distort from the Edit | Transform submenu. (If you prefer, you can create a different effect by choosing Perspective or Skew.) When the handles appear, click and drag on them to create the look you want. In this example, all four handles were dragged to create the distortion, as shown in Figure 8-10.

11. Move the distorted text into position. If you'd like, duplicate the text, fill it with another color (we used black), and offset it; this effect can be seen in Figure 8-8.

If you wish to execute any more image effects, feel free to experiment. In the next section, you'll learn how to create other image effects with commands from the Edit | Transform submenu.

Working with Invert, Equalize, Threshold, and Posterize

The Invert, Equalize, Threshold, and Posterize commands in the Image menu are used to remap, or reassign, pixel values in a selection or in an entire image. These commands quickly let you alter your digitized images to evenly distribute tone and color, or they can be used to create special effects that drastically change

FIGURE 8-10 The Edit | Transform | Distort command used to edit the type

brightness values. For instance, you can transform a color or grayscale image into a high-contrast black-and-white image or invert all of the color values in an image to produce a negative of the original.

TIP: *The Invert, Threshold, and Posterize commands can be applied in an Adjustment Layer. Adjustment Layers allow you to see editing changes through a layer mask without changing the actual pixels of the image. Adjustment Layers also allow you to paint to add and subtract these effects. Adjustment Layers are discussed in detail in Chapter 16.*

Creating a Negative Using Invert

The Image | Map | Invert command reverses your image, turning it into a negative of the original: All black values become white, all white values turn black, and all colors are converted to their complements. Pixel values are inverted on a scale from 0 to 255. A pixel with a value of 0 will be inverted to 255, a pixel with the value of 10 will change to 245, and so on. You may invert a selection or an entire image; if no area is selected, the entire image is inverted.

In the example in Figure 8-11, black text was entered on screen first, and then the bottom half was selected using the Rectangular Marquee. When the Image | Map | Invert command was applied to the rectangular selection, the black text within the selection turned white, and the white area between the letters turned black.

Expanding Tonal Range with Equalize

The Equalize command distributes light and dark values evenly and can be used to adjust dark scans and make them lighter. When the Equalize command is executed, Photoshop remaps light and dark values over the full tonal range from black to white. The darkest areas in the images are darkened as much as possible, and the lightest are lightened as much as possible. All other values are distributed according to the new tonal range. Images will often look brighter, exhibiting more balance and contrast.

FIGURE 8-11   The Image | Map | Invert command can be used to create a reverse (negative) effect

If an image area is selected and you execute Image | Adjust | Equalize, the Equalize dialog box will appear. Choose the Equalize selected area only radio button to Equalize only the selection. If you choose Equalize entire image based on selected area, Photoshop equalizes the entire image based upon the lightness and darkness values of the selected area.

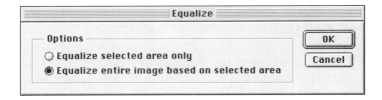

Figure 8-12(a) shows the original scanned picture of Venice. Figure 8-12(b) displays the results after the Equalize command was applied.

Converting an Image to Black and White Using Threshold

The Image | Adjust | Threshold command converts a color or grayscale image into a high-contrast black-and-white image. The Threshold dialog box allows you to pick a Threshold Level—a dividing line between black and white pixels. All pixels lighter than or equal to the Threshold Level value become white; all pixels darker than the Threshold Level are converted to black.

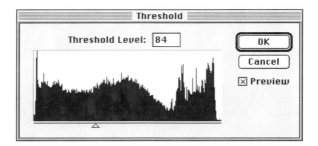

In the dialog box, you see a *histogram,* which graphically presents the brightness, or luminance, values of the pixels in the current image or selection. The histogram plots the number of pixels at each tonal level of the image. Darker values are plotted on the left side of the histogram, lighter values on the right side.

(a)

(b)

FIGURE 8-12   Scanned image(a) before and (b) after the Image | Adjust | Equalize
command is applied

You'll read more about using histograms when retouching and color correcting in Chapter 18.

Clicking and dragging on the Threshold dialog box slider control changes the Threshold Level (dragging right raises the value; dragging left lowers it). Or you can enter a value between 1 and 255 in the Threshold Level field (the default is 128). If the Threshold command is executed at the default settings, all pixels with values greater than or equal to 128 will turn white, and all pixels with values less than 128 will turn black. If the Preview check box is selected, Photoshop will show you the results of the Threshold command.

Figure 8-13 shows the picture of Venice after the Threshold command was applied.

Creating Special Effects Using Threshold and the Layers Palette

The following exercise shows you how to create an interesting artistic effect by decreasing the number of colors in an image.

FIGURE 8-13   The results of applying the Image | Adjust | Threshold command to the image in Figure 8-12(a)

1. Open any color image. If you don't have one to use, load a file from Photoshop's Samples folder.

2. Select the entire image by pressing COMMAND-A (Windows users: CTRL-A).

3. Choose Edit | Copy. (Choose Copy Merged to copy all visible layers.)

4. Paste the image over itself by choosing Edit | Paste. As soon as you paste, Photoshop automatically creates a new layer with the pasted image in it. If the palette isn't on screen, choose Window | Show Layers to view the layer.

5. To convert the new layer to black and white, choose Image | Adjust | Threshold.

   In the Threshold dialog box, make sure the Preview check box is selected, and then drag the slider control to choose a level that creates an attractive black-and-white image. When you like what you see, click OK. Don't deselect.

6. In order to create the decreased colors effect, you'll need to blend the pixels of the image in the layer with the underlying background.

7. To add the image's original color back into the dark areas of the image, choose Lighten from the mode pop-up menu in the Layers palette.

The result will be a composite image with color in what was once the darker areas and white in the lighter areas.

If you wish, continue to experiment with different opacities and modes, such as Screen and Overlay. When you are ready to continue to the next section, save your file, if desired, and close it.

Reducing Gray Levels Using Posterize

In this next exercise you will reduce the gray levels in an image using the Posterize command. This command can create some unusual special effects, because the gray contours in an image disappear and are replaced by large flat-color or gray areas.

Load any color image on screen, and then select Image | Adjust | Posterize to open the Posterize dialog box. In the Levels field, enter the number of gray levels you wish to appear in the image or selected area. Acceptable values range from 2 to 255. The lower the number, the fewer the gray levels. When the Preview check box is selected, Photoshop will preview the results of applying the Posterize command.

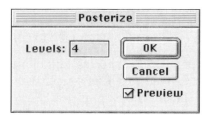

For a dramatic effect, enter **4** in the Levels field. Then raise the number of gray levels a few increments at a time to see the different effects. Figure 8-14(a) shows a scanned image of South America's Iguaçu Falls; Figure 8-14(b) shows the results after applying the Posterize command with Levels set to 4.

The remaining sections of this chapter discuss some alternative digitizing methods for use with Photoshop; these options require hardware other than scanners.

 TIP: *You can use the Filter | Fade command to fade the effect of Invert, Equalize and Posterize.*

Using Photo CD Images

If you need to have your images photographed first before digitizing them, you might be able to avoid scanning altogether. Eastman Kodak's Photo CD process transforms a roll of film into a CD-ROM disc filled with digitized images. Each disc stored in Kodak's standard Master format can hold up to 100 35mm images. The images are stored at five different sizes, from 128 by 192 pixels to 2,048 by 3,072 pixels. Low-resolution color images are about 72K in size; high-resolution images are around 18MB. Table 8-1 shows the Photo CD image dimensions in pixels and file sizes.

When you load the file, using the File | Open command, you can choose not only which image but also which version of the image you wish to load.

 NOTE: *You may find that the quality of Photo CD images differs depending on the service bureau that outputs your images.*

Choosing Resolution for Photos CD images

How do you choose which Photo CD resolution is the right one for your project? How do you determine if the number of pixels in the image is adequate for your

(a)

(b)

FIGURE 8-14   Iguaçu Falls (a) before and (b) after applying Image I Adjust I Posterize with Levels set to 4

outputting requirements? First, you must know the size of the image you need and the number of pixels per inch required for output. Assume you need to place a 4-inch image on your Web page. Since Web graphics do not need to be larger than the resolution of a standard monitor, your image resolution should be 72 ppi. If you look at Table 8-1, you'll see your best bet is probably going to be the 512 × 768. We created this table by simply typing the different pixel dimensions of Photo CD images into Photoshop's dialog box with the Resample Image check box selected.

Dimensions in Pixels	Dimensions in Inches (at 72 ppi)	Size
126 × 192	1.75 × 2.0	72K
256 × 384	3.5 × 5.33	288K
512 × 768	7.1 × 10.6	1.12K
1,024 × 1,536	14.2 × 21.3	4.5K
2,048 × 3,072	28.4 × 42.7	18MB
4,096 × 61,444	56.9 × 85.3	72MB

TABLE 8-1 Kodak's Photo CD Image Sizes in Pixels and File Sizes (Pro Photo CD only)

 NOTE: *When you load a Photo CD image into Photoshop, the Resolution field is automatically set to 72 ppi.*

Now assume you need to print a 4-inch-wide image in a publication requiring 225-ppi resolution. Since you need the pixels per inch setting to increase when you reduce the image, you need to deselect the Resample Image check box. Next you enter the 225 into the resolution field. Immediately, the Width and Height fields will tell you the maximum image size you can use at 225 ppi. You can then follow the instructions provided earlier in this chapter to resize the image using the Image Size dialog box.

Digital and Video Cameras

Digital and still-video cameras provide even more versatile alternatives to scanning. With these cameras, you don't have to purchase film, wait for it to be developed, and then scan or convert to Photo CD. By digitizing with a still-video or digital camera, you can quickly see the results by shooting in a studio with the camera connected to a computer. If the image doesn't please you, you can usually change your lighting setup and reshoot.

Still-video cameras are video cameras primarily used for taking still pictures. Many cameras require that a video capture board be installed in the computer so that images can be stored on a hard drive. Digital cameras immediately digitize an image, which can usually be downloaded directly as a digital file to the computer through a serial or SCSI connection.

Still-video and digital photography are growing in popularity—particularly in catalog work and newspaper work, in which many images of products need to be digitized quickly. Many digital cameras provide Photoshop plug-ins, so you can use the File | Import command to load the image directly into Photoshop. Many also feature on-board disks, memory cards, or hard disks. To download files to a computer, some cameras require an interface card to be installed in the computer; others, such as Kodak's DCS 460, can be plugged into a computer via a SCSI port.

Analyzing Digital Camera Features

For many photographers, the easiest way to begin evaluating the features of a digital camera is to study the camera's optical system. Since many digital cameras are really converted still cameras, you can start by shopping for a digital camera as you would for a still camera. Nonetheless, you should be familiar with digital terms, such as bit depth and resolution.

Understanding Digital Camera Bit Depth

A digital camera's dynamic range—the range of tones captured from lightest to darkest elements—is primarily determined by *bit depth*. As with scanners, the higher the bit depth, the better the image quality. Low-cost cameras, such as Apple's QuickTake, Kodak's DC 120, Kodak 210, Olympus D-320L and D-500L cameras and D-600L models capture 24 bits of color (8 bits for each RGB color). Higher-end cameras, such as Kodak's DCS 460, capture 36 bits, resulting in a more detailed picture with less noise. High-end studio equipment, like the Leaf Digital back, can capture 14 bits per RGB color.

Using Photoshop to Compute Resolution for Digital Camera Images

The Resolution of a digital camera is based upon the total number of pixels the camera can produce in an image. If you study the specifications for digital cameras, you'll quickly notice that the high-priced cameras provide better image resolution than lower-priced ones. For instance, Kodak's DCS 460, which retails for about $30,000, features a resolution of 3,060 by 2,060 pixels. Models below $500 from Apple, Kodak, Epson, and Olympus capture 640 by 480 pixels. Understanding how these resolution figures translate to image quality is extremely important, particularly if your image will eventually be printed by a commercial printer.

8

As discussed earlier, to achieve the best quality for print output, the image resolution in Photoshop should be approximately twice the screen frequency used for printing. Assume you are using Kodak's 460 camera and need to send a 6-by-6-inch, 300-ppi image to a magazine. How can you determine whether the camera can produce an image at the quality you need? Simple—let Photoshop do it for you. Here's how:

1. Start by creating a new file in Photoshop (File | New).

2. In the new dialog box, set the measurement units to pixels. Enter the pixel dimension used by your digital camera into the Width and Height fields. For the Kodak DCS 460, you would enter 3,020 and 2,020. If you were using a lower-priced camera, you might enter 640 and 480. Set the Resolution to 72 ppi. Click OK to create the new image.

3. Choose Image | Image Size.

4. In the Image Size dialog box, deselect the Resample Image check box. This turns on the link between image dimensions and resolution. Change the resolution field to the resolution needed to output your image—in this case, 300 ppi.

5. Change the measurement Units for the Print Size Width and Height to inches.

Immediately, the Width and Height fields change to display the largest image you can create at 300 ppi. For the DCS 460, the largest image size is 10 by 6.7. If you executed the same procedure using the resolution of a low-priced 640-by-480 camera, you would find that the largest image size for an image at 300 ppi is only 2 by 1.6 inches. Obviously, this camera wouldn't provide the quality you need to output a 6-by-6 image at 300 ppi.

 TIP: *If your computer isn't handy, you can calculate the maximum image size for a specific resolution by dividing the camera's horizontal and vertical dimensions (in pixels) by the pixels per inch you need for an image. For instance, 3,000 ÷ 300 = 10 and 2,000 ÷ 300 = 6.7.*

Using Digital Cameras

Once you understand how a digital camera's bit depth and resolution affect image quality, you'll be better able to judge whether one will suit your needs. Before you invest in one, however, be aware that not all models produce perfect color fidelity.

Also, note that the lenses in many low-end cameras are not designed to shoot flat art—use a scanner instead. Even if you are using an expensive digital camera, you will probably need to do some tweaking in Photoshop. Depending on the lighting conditions, you may need to sharpen your image (see Chapter 10 to learn how to use Photoshop's sharpening filters) and you may need to correct colors (covered in Chapter 18). The following sections provide brief reviews of several well-known digital cameras.

Kodak's DCS 420 and 460 Digital Cameras

Combining high resolution and excellent optics, Kodak's DCS cameras are becoming favorites with professional photographers for both news and catalog work. The DCS 420 and 460 consist of an electronic back connected to a Nikon N90 camera. The cameras accept all F-mounted lenses manufactured for the N90 and include nearly all of the standard SLR (single-lens reflex) features, including automatic exposure, flash, and self-timing.

Both DCS cameras store up to 300 images in memory per battery charge. You can also install hard disk cards for additional storage. A 170MB card can store 100 images in the 420 and 30 images in the 460.

Both cameras capture images using 36-bit color (12 bits for each RGB color). The DCS 420, which retails for under $10,000, captures 1,524 by 1,012 pixels, while the DCS 460, retailing for less than $30,000, features a 3,020-by-2,020 resolution.

Kodak digital cameras come with a plug-in that is accessed using the File | Import command. The File Import dialog box provides a preview of the image. Using the mouse, you can click on a white area of the preview to set the image's white point—the lightest part of the image. Once the white point is captured, the image can be opened into Photoshop at the proper dynamic range.

 NOTE: *Kodak's latest addition to the DCS line is the DCS 520 which captures 1728 by 1152 pixels and features a Canon EOS camera body. The DCS 520 is more compact than the 420 and 460 and costs less than $1500.00*

Video Capture

Photoshop's plug-in capabilities allow still frames to be captured from videotape. To capture video, a card must be installed in your computer to convert the television signals (NTSC) to RGB so the images can be input to Photoshop. The plug-in and video card combination also allows the RGB signals to be converted to NTSC television signals for output back to videotape. One of the best-known manufacturers of video cards for both PCs and Macs is TrueVision. TrueVision makes the Targa board for the Mac. If you are using a Mac or a PC, you might want to investigate AV computer models, which have video input and output capabilities built in.

To obtain frame-accurate control over the input and recording of the video signal, most multimedia systems require a video card that controls a videotape recorder.

Microcomputer Publishing Center (a video and prepress service bureau) in New York City digitized a variety of Effie-award-winning television commercials for *Brandweek* magazine. The images appeared as part of a special color insert featuring freeze frames from the commercials. All images were digitized and enhanced in Photoshop. A few of the images are reprinted in the following figures (with permission of *Brandweek* and Microcomputer Publishing Center). Figure 8-15 shows images from a commercial for Andersen Consulting (with permission from the company), Figure 8-16 is from a commercial for Rhone-Poulenc's Buctril Corn Herbicide (with permission from the company and Rhea & Kaiser Advertising), and Figure 8-17 is from a commercial for Little Caesars Pizza (with permission from the company and Cliff Freeman & Partners).

FIGURE 8-15   Digitized video frames a commercial advertising Andersen consulting

FIGURE 8-16   Digitized image from a commercial for Buctril Corn Herbicide

FIGURE 8-17   Digitized video frame from a commercial advertising Little Caesars Pizza

Digitized Stock Photos

If your image needs are not specific and you don't need to scan or photograph images, numerous sources of stock digital images are available. Several stock photo collections are now sold on CD-ROM discs for both the PC and the Mac. Many collections allow unlimited usage, and some contain images that are scanned on high-end drum scanners in 24-bit color. Before purchasing stock photos, check to see that the resolution and size of the images meet your needs. Also, find out whether the images are compressed, and if they are, whether a lossy or lossless compression method was used. *Lossless compression* means that no loss of picture quality occurs during compression.

Here are the names of companies that provide digitized images: Adobe, ColorBytes, American Databankers Corp., COREL, PhotoDisc, Gazelle Technologies, Image Club Publishing, Aztech New Media Corp., Dana Publishing, and Digital Stock. These companies provide digitized backgrounds: Pixar (One Twenty Eight), Xaos (Artist Residence), ArtBeats (Marble & Granite, Marbled Paper Textures, and Wood and Paper), and D'Pix. Many digital stock houses allow you to preview images on their Web sites. Here are a few Web addresses to check out: www.imageclub.com, www.photodisc.com, www.digitalstock.com, and www.vividdetails.com.

Another option for obtaining images is downloading them over the telephone with a modem. Kodak's Picture Exchange allows you online access to a variety of major image collections. The Picture Exchange software allows you to search for the type of image you want, browse through contact sheets, and download design proofs. When you wish to use the original image, you order through an onscreen order form. Fees are charged for online time and for picture use by the image provider.

Conclusion

Now that you've learned the basics of digitizing images you may want to explore techniques to speed up your day-to-day production. In the next chapter, you'll see how Photoshop's Actions palette can record your mouse clicks and make your Photoshop work more efficient.

Photoshop 5   In Action

The background is a piece of textured paper that was moved as it was being scanned.

This picture of a child was scanned, resized, and then rotated using the commands in the Edit | Transform submenu.

© Pamela Hobbs

Artist: Pamela Hobbs   **Client: Children's TV/Pentagram Design**

Pamela created the image above for the Children's TV magazine, *Sesame Street*. All of the images were scanned. First, the background was scanned. It was a piece of textured paper that was moved as it was being scanned to give the appearance of motion. To soften the transition of the move affect, the Motion Blur filter was applied. After the background was created, the pictures of children were scanned.

Each child was scanned separately and then placed into the final document. Later some of the images of the children were scaled and rotated using the commands in the Edit | Transform submenu.

8

CHAPTER 9

Using the Actions and History Palettes

In your day-to-day Photoshop work you'll probably discover that some production tasks require more perspiration than inspiration. If you're working on a multimedia or Web project, you may find that some days you spend hours just converting images from one file format to another. If you work in publishing, you may discover that you often need to apply the same curve adjustments (Image | Adjust | Curves) to every image you scan. You may also find that after you've developed a complicated technique for creating drop shadows, vignettes, or 3-D effects, you'd like to record your steps so you or someone else in your studio can repeat the steps again and again on different images. When these situations arise, you need to turn to Photoshop's Actions palette.

As you'll soon see, the Actions palette can record many of your mouse clicks and menu choices. When you need to execute these commands again, all you need to do is play the recorded action. As you work, however, you may wish to back up and undo previous steps without recording your action from scratch. When this happens, you need to use Photoshop's History palette. Although the Actions and History palettes are separate, unrelated palettes, both are production time-savers. If you know how to use both palettes, you'll be working at optimum efficiency in Photoshop, and you'll be able to spend more time at inspiration than with perspiration.

Exploring the Actions Palette

The Actions palette, shown in Figure 9-1, provides numerous features that can help speed tedious production tasks. Using the Actions palette, you can record selections, tool and color choices, as well as dialog box settings and menu commands. When you're done recording, you can play back your actions, applying them to selections or images on screen, or to multiple images in a folder.

 NOTE: *The Actions palette can't record all of your mouse movements. For instance, it can't record painting with the Paintbrush, Airbrush, or Toning tools. However, Actions do record typing with the Type tool, drawing with the Line tool, and filling with the Paint Bucket.*

When you record your keystrokes, Photoshop lets you assign them to a name in the Actions palette. Each "action" listed in the palette is composed of a series of Photoshop commands. However, you'll soon see that the Actions palette does more than just play back and record. The palette allows you to edit different commands in an action, store sets of actions on disk, and apply an action to all the

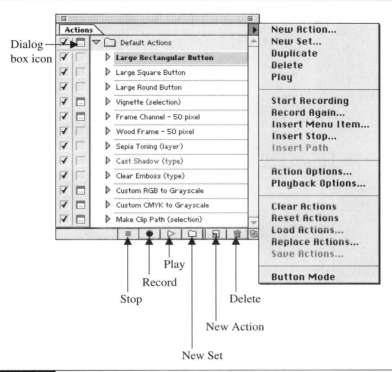

Dialog box icon

Play

Record

Stop

Delete

New Action

New Set

| FIGURE 9-1 | The Actions palette and Actions palette menu |

files in a folder. Before you begin creating and playing back your actions, you should become familiar with the features of the Actions palette.

List Mode and Button Mode

The Actions palette appears on screen in either List mode or Button mode. In List mode (Figure 9-1 is in List mode), all palette commands are available. You can record new actions, play back and stop actions, create a new set (or folder) for your actions, and delete actions by clicking on buttons at the bottom of the palette. You can also choose commands in the Actions palette menu, which is accessible by clicking on the arrow in the upper-right corner of the palette. In List mode, you see not only the different actions in the palette, but also the Photoshop commands that will run when the action is played, as shown in Figure 9-2. To see these commands, you can click on the triangle just to the left of the action's name.

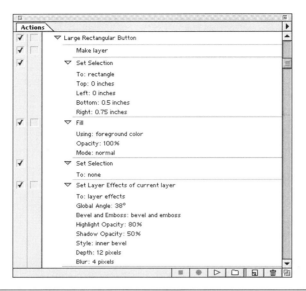

FIGURE 9-2   The commands in an action seen in List mode

In Button mode, shown below, actions can only be played back. To play back an action, you simply click on any button in the palette. To toggle the palette into Button mode, click on the Button Mode option in the Actions palette menu. After you click, a check mark appears next to the menu command. To turn off Button mode, click once again on the Button Mode option; the check mark is removed and the palette returns to List mode.

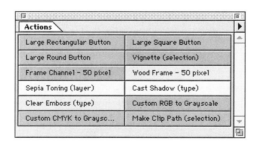

Creating a New Action and a New Set

Any Photoshop task that you must perform again and again is a candidate for recording as an action. When you create a new action, Photoshop records virtually every step you take: making a selection, clicking on a tool, and changing dialog box settings. However, be aware that Photoshop won't record everything. Some menu commands aren't recorded. For instance, if you try to create an action using File | Page Setup, the step won't be recorded. Fortunately, you can add this step by using the Actions palette menu's Insert Menu Item command (described in "Inserting Commands into Recorded Actions," later in this chapter). Furthermore, the Actions palette does not record the step-by-step creation of a path. However, you can insert a path into an action using the Actions palette's Insert Path command.

Here are the steps for creating a new action, naming it, and recording it:

1. If the Actions palette isn't on screen, open it by choosing Window | Show Actions.

   In order to create an action, the Actions palette must be in List mode. If the palette isn't in List mode, you won't see the Record and Play buttons at the bottom of the palette. To switch the palette to List mode, open the Actions palette menu by clicking on the arrow in the upper-right corner of the palette. In the Actions palette menu, click on Button Mode to deselect it.

   If you wish to store your action into a separate folder in the Actions palette, click New Set in the Actions palette menu. In the New Set dialog box, give your set a name. The name appears as a folder in the Actions palette. Later, you can save your actions into the folder to help keep the palette better organized.

2. To create a new action, click on the New Action button (the page icon) in the Actions palette, or select New Action from the Actions palette menu.

3. In the New Action dialog box, shown here, enter a name for the action.

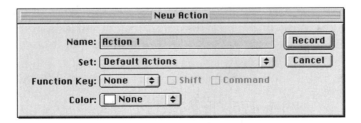

   If desired, use the pop-up menu to assign the action to the default set (folder) or a set that you created. You can also click on the Shift or Command (Mac) /CTRL (Windows) check box to have the function executed by pressing SHIFT and/or COMMAND (Windows users: CTRL) and a function key. To assign a color to an action, select a color in the Color pop-up menu. Next click on the Record button. When recording starts, the Record icon in the palette turns red.

4. Execute the Photoshop commands that you want recorded.

 NOTE: *When recording actions, most dialog box actions are recorded if you click OK. They won't be recorded if you click Cancel in a dialog box.*

5. To stop recording, click on the Stop icon in the palette or choose Stop Recording from the Actions palette menu.

 TIP: *If you wish to rename an action or assign it to a different function key after you've recorded it, first select the action, and then choose Action Options in the Actions palette menu. Alternatively, you can double-click on the name of the action in the palette.*

 NOTE: *Photoshop includes several sets of actions that are found in the Goodies folder. The sets are named: Buttons, Commands, Default Actions, Frames, Image Effects, Production, Text Effects, and Textures. To load a set, choose Load Actions from the Actions palette menu. After you load a set, click on the right arrow next to the set name to see the list of actions in the set.*

Viewing Recorded Actions

After recording an action, you should view the list of commands recorded to see if all the steps you executed were actually recorded. As you record your actions, a list of the steps appears beneath the actions. After you've viewed the steps, you can click the down arrow that appears next to the actions to hide the steps. When you click, the down arrow changes to a right arrow. To see the list of recorded commands, simply click the arrow again. To view the actual settings of dialog box commands used when you recorded your actions, click the right arrow next to the steps in your actions.

Adding Dialog Box Break Points

When a dialog box command is recorded, Photoshop records the dialog box settings as well. Often you will want the user to enter his or her own choices in the dialog box. For instance, you may record a Save command, but when the action is played, you want the user to be able to enter a new filename for the file. Using the Actions palette, you can make an action pause so the user can change dialog box settings. You can do this for all commands in an action or for individual commands.

Actions that include dialog box commands can be identified by the tiny Dialog Box icon to the left of the command (visible in Figure 9-1). If you want to make your action pause for user input in a dialog box, click on the Dialog Box icon. After you click, the dialog box turns black on screen.

An empty embossed square next to your action (an empty Dialog Box icon) indicates that Photoshop won't pause. If you wish to create a pause at every dialog box in an action, activate the Dialog Box icon next to the action's name by clicking on the icon. Note that a red Dialog Box icon next to the action's name indicates that at least one, but not all, of the dialog boxes in the action is selected. If all of the dialog boxes are selected, the dialog box adjacent to the action name is black.

Inserting Commands into Recorded Actions

As discussed earlier, the Actions palette cannot record every Photoshop menu command. For example, the Page Setup menu command cannot be recorded. However, you can insert most menu commands into an action by using the Insert Menu Item command. Here's how to insert a menu item after a specific command in an action:

1. Click on a command in the action list.

2. In the Actions palette menu, choose Insert Menu Item. After the Insert Menu Item dialog box appears, click on the menu item that you wish to add. Alternatively, you can start typing the first few letters of the command, and then click the Find button.

The new command is added after the command you originally selected in step 1.

 NOTE: *You can execute the Insert Menu Item command at the beginning of an action: Simply select the action, then click on the Actions palette's Insert Menu Item command after you create the action when you first begin recording. You can also choose Insert Menu Item while you are recording.*

TIP: *If you wish to insert the creation of a path into an action while you are recording, you must choose the Insert Path command. While recording, the easiest way to use this feature is to choose Insert Path from the Actions palette menu immediately after you create the path. If you wish to insert the path into a pre-existing action, first select the path in the Paths palette, then choose Insert Path from the Actions palette menu.*

Inserting "Stops" into Actions

The Actions palette's Stop command also allows you to add a Stop alert message on screen. When the Stop alert appears, you can add a Continue button. This can be helpful if you want the user to stop to observe the results of an action on screen and continue if the image looks the way it should. Here's how to insert a Stop alert after a command in an action:

1. Click on a command in the Actions palette. If you don't see the command, click on the right arrow next to the action's name.

2. Choose Insert Stop in the Actions palette menu.

3. In the Record Stop dialog box, shown here, enter a message in the Message field. Then click OK.

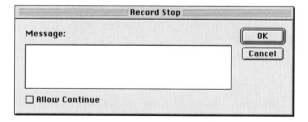

 NOTE: *You can also choose Insert Stop while recording an action.*

If you wish to allow the user to continue after stopping the action, click the Allow Continue check box. You might want to relate your message to the Allow Continue check box. For instance, you might add this to the Message field: "If the image looks great, click Continue."

Editing Actions and Re-Recording Actions

If you make a mistake when you record your action, you probably won't need to start from scratch and record it again—you may be able to edit the action by rearranging action commands or by adding commands to the action. You can also use the Record Again command to re-record specified choices within a dialog box. Here are options for editing actions:

◻ To change the order of commands in an action, simply click on the command in the Actions palette and drag it to a new position.

◻ To add commands after a command in an action, select the command in the Actions palette. Next, click on the Record button in the Actions palette, or choose Start Recording from the Actions palette menu. Now execute the command that you wish to add to your action. To stop recording, click the Stop button or choose Stop Recording from the Actions palette menu.

◻ If you want to edit only the options in dialog boxes, select the action, and then choose Record Again in the Actions palette menu. Photoshop then plays back the commands. When dialog boxes appear, enter new values in the dialog boxes. If you click OK, the new values will replace those that were originally entered when you first recorded the action.

◻ You may be able to re-record a dialog box setting in an action by double-clicking on the command in the action. This opens the dialog box that was recorded. Change the settings, then click OK to stop recording.

 TIP: *If you wish to create an action similar to another one, you don't need to record it again; simply select the action, then choose the Duplicate command in the Actions palette menu. Once the duplicate is created, you can edit the action.*

 TIP: *To integrate one action into another, you can play a previously recorded action when recording a new action.*

Deleting Commands and Actions

If you wish to delete an action from the Actions palette, select the action and click on the Trash icon. Alternatively, you can choose Delete from the

Actions palette. To delete all actions, choose Clear Actions from the Actions palette menu.

Playing Actions

Playing actions puts Photoshop on autopilot. When you play back an action, Photoshop plays each command in an action step by step. If a stop exists, the action stops. If a dialog break point exists, Photoshop allows you to change values in a dialog box. Here are the options for playing back commands in List mode:

☐ To play back an action, select the action and click the Play button. You can also choose Play from the Actions palette menu. If you are in Button mode, simply click on the action.

☐ If you want to start the action from a specific command in the action, select the appropriate command and click on the Play button in the palette, or choose Play From in the Actions palette menu.

☐ To play back only one command, press OPTION (Windows users: ALT) and double-click on the command, or select the command and choose the Play Only command in the Actions palette menu.

☐ To skip a command when an action is played, click on the check mark next to the command in the palette. After you click, the check mark disappears, indicating that the command will not be executed. To turn the command back on, click next to the command name in the check mark column. When you turn off a step in an action, the check mark next to the action name turns red.

Applying an Action to Multiple Files

If you need to apply Photoshop commands to multiple files, the Batch command is the solution. For instance you may wish to convert many files that will appear in a multimedia production to the same color palette or convert images that will appear on a Web page to a Web-safe palette.

The Batch command applies an action to every file in a folder. When you run the Batch command (found in the File | Automate submenu, not the Actions palette), you can specify whether you want the edited files to be placed in their original folder or another folder. Here's how to execute a batch action:

1. Use the Actions palette to record the action that you wish to apply to the files.

2. Move all files that you wish to apply the action to into a single folder.

3. Choose File | Automate | Batch.

4. In the Batch dialog box, shown here, specify the set and the action that you wish to run in the Play section. (If you just recorded the action, or if it is selected in the Actions palette, it will automatically appear in the Source and Set pop-up menus).

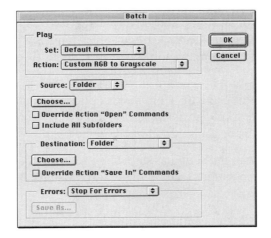

5. In the Source pop-up menu, make sure that Folder is selected.

   Click the Choose button to select the folder that contains the files you wish to apply the action to. After you click Choose, a dialog box appears allowing you to select the source folder. Click on the folder, and then click Select. If you recorded a File | Open command in your action, you will probably want to choose the Override Action "Open" Commands option. The Batch command automatically opens every file in a folder.

 NOTE: *You can also import or digitize images in a batch and apply actions to each image. If you wish to import images in a batch, choose Import in the Source pop-up menu on the Batch dialog box. After you select Import, the Choose button changes to a From pop-up menu. The pop-up menu allows you to choose from anti-aliased Pict, PICT Resource, Twain Acquire, and Twain Select (for Twain-compatible scanners). If you have a plug-in for your scanner installed, its name should appear here as well. Choose the type of image you want in the From menu. When the action runs, an Open dialog box appears, allowing you to load the type of image from disk.*

6. Click in the Destination pop-up menu to have the actions placed in a specific folder, or to have the files saved and closed, or to specify no destination (None). If you choose a folder, Photoshop runs the action, then copies the altered files to a specified folder. This is a good way to prevent your original files from changing.

7. If you wish to have Photoshop skip an action's Save commands, choose the Override Action "Save In" Commands option. If you are saving images into a destination folder, this option will prevent Photoshop from saving all of the images using the same filename.

8. If you don't want the action to stop when an error occurs, set the Errors pop-up menu so that it creates a log in a file specified when you click on the Save As button.

9. Click OK to start the operation.

Using Photoshop's Pre-Recorded Automate Commands

Photoshop's Automate command includes a set of plug-in actions. These actions are similar to those found in the Actions palette, except that they are created using a programming language such as C++, rather than from recording steps in Photoshop. Undoubtedly, in the near future you'll soon see software developers selling plug-ins that will appear in the File | Automate submenu.

Here is a description of the actions in the Automate submenu:

- **Conditional Mode Change** Allows you to change different images to one mode. For instance, you could place grayscale and RGB files in a folder and convert all of them to CMYK.

- **Contact Sheet** Creates an image of thumbnails of files in a folder.

- **Fit Image** Resizes images to the values specified in the dialog box without changing the aspect ratio. You only need to enter one value in the dialog box. When Photoshop runs Fit Image, it *resamples* (changes the number of pixels in the image).

- **Multi-Page PDF to PSD** Converts pages in a PDF File (Adobe Acrobat) to separate Photoshop files.

Storing Action Sets

If you create different actions, you can save sets of actions to disk, then load the sets as you need them. For instance, you may wish to have one set of actions for special effects, another for color correcting, and another for file conversion. Here are the steps for saving, appending, and replacing actions:

- To save a set of actions, choose Save Actions from the Actions palette menu. Name the actions in the dialog box that appears. Change destination folders, if desired.

- To append actions into the Actions palette, choose Load Actions from the palette menu. In the dialog box that appears, select the actions that you want to load and click OK. The set of actions you load is then appended to those already in the Actions palette.

- To reset the Actions palette to the original actions, choose Reset Actions in the Actions palette menu.

- To replace the actions in the palette with a set of actions saved on disk, choose Replace Actions in the Actions palette menu.

- To remove all actions from the Actions palette, choose Clear Actions from the Actions palette menu.

Rewriting Digital History

The History palette is Photoshop's answer to multiple undoes. Just by clicking on a line in the History palette, you can miraculously return to a previous state of your work—even if you didn't save it. Knowing that you have the History palette as a safety net certainly takes some of the stress out of digital creativity. It also means you can meander off on a digital diversion. If you take a wrong turn, you can always backtrack to a previous fork in the road. If you accidentally destroy a few pixels, you can remove that step from your journey.

Using the History Palette

As you've discovered from previous sections of this book, the History palette provides more than just a history of steps that you can easily undo. Using the History palette, you can create snapshots—multiple versions of your image as you work. You can also use the History Brush to paint in previous versions of your work and create special effects at the same time.

If you haven't been using the History palette, open it by choosing Window | Show History. As you work, the palette, shown in Figure 9-3, lists the editing stages of your images. Each step is described by a listing in the palette. If you want to return to a previous step, you simply click on the step, or click and drag

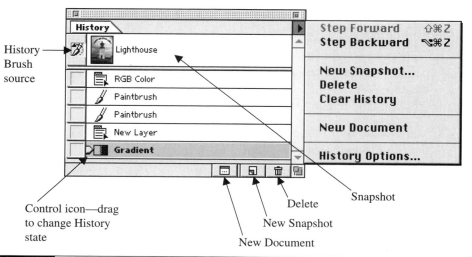

FIGURE 9-3 History palette and palette menu

the small control icon in the palette (shown next to the gradient step in Figure 9-3) to the state you wish to return to. As soon as you click, your image returns to a previous version. If you decide that you undid too much, you can click forward in the History palette to return to a later state.

 TIP: *To quickly return to a previous state in the History palette, press ALT-COMMAND-Z (Windows users: ALT-CTRL-Z). To move to the next state, press SHIFT-COMMAND-Z (Windows users: SHIFT-CTRL-Z).*

History Palette Options

Before you begin using the History palette to rewrite digital history, you'll find it helpful to explore the History palette's Options settings which control how the palette records history. To view the options in the History palette, open its menu by clicking on the tiny arrow in the upper-right corner of the palette. In the palette's menu, choose History Options.

The History Options dialog box, shown in Figure 9-4, determines several important aspects of how the History palette records your work. The Maximum History States field determines how many steps the History palette can handle. If you go beyond the number of steps listed in the palette, the History palette simply stops recording. It's not advisable to keep the number large because the History palette uses memory as it works. Thus, you could get a "Scratch Disk Full" error message if you increase the maximum states and are working with a high-resolution image.

By default the History palette automatically creates a snapshot of the opening state of your work. The snapshot appears as a tiny thumbnail image at the top of the palette. The snapshot makes it easy to revert to the opening image, without choosing the File | Revert command. To revert to the snapshot, simply click on it

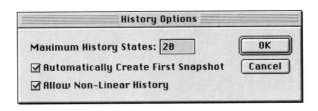

FIGURE 9-4   The History Options dialog box

in the palette. If you want to conserve some memory, you may wish to deselect the Automatically Create First Snapshot check box.

The final option in the dialog box allows you to specify whether you wish to allow non-linear history. When this option is off, the History palette keeps a continuous record of how the current image is created. For instance, if you have ten steps in the History palette, and return to step 5, then continue editing, Photoshop deletes steps 6 through 10. It replaces the old step 6 with the current change you make to your image. If non-linear history is selected, steps 6 through 10 won't be deleted. This can create a confusing history, but it also allows you to return to different steps that you might want to remain in the palette.

 TIP: *If you inadvertently return to a previous state in the History palette and delete subsequent states, you can return the deleted states to the History palette by choosing Edit | Undo.*

To further understand the difference between linear history and non-linear history, turn off the non-linear history option, then execute these steps:

1. Create a new image on screen.

2. Paint on screen with the Paintbrush.

3. Convert the image to grayscale, by choosing Image | Mode | Grayscale.

4. Return to the RGB version of the image by clicking on the Paintbrush state in the History palette. Now, paint on screen with the Airbrush tool. As soon as you use the Airbrush tool, the grayscale state is removed from the palette and replaced with the Airbrush state.

If you try the same steps with the non-linear history option selected, the grayscale state will not be deleted from the palette. You will have a color image on screen with a grayscale state in the History palette. This means the History palette doesn't reflect the image on screen; however, if desired, you could always return to the grayscale state in the palette.

Clearing History States

Photoshop provides several techniques for clearing history. You can remove a state by clicking on it and choosing Delete from the History palette pop-up menu.

Alternatively, you can click on the state and drag it to the Trash icon at the bottom of the palette. If you want to clear the History palette without altering your image (which saves memory), choose Clear History from the History palette pop-up menu.

To clear the History palette for all open documents, choose Edit | Purge | Histories.

 CAUTION: *If you close your document, the History palette is cleared even if you save the document.*

Using the History Brush

If you want to add special effects to your image, you can use one of the History states as a source for the History Brush, a technique described in Chapter 7. As you paint, the state selected in the History palette is painted back on screen. (By default, the History Brush is set to paint back the first snapshot in the palette).If you're puzzled by the History Brush, think of it as a cloning brush that clones an entire image back on screen. The image it clones is one of the states in the History palette.

To use the History Brush, you first must select the History Brush in the toolbox, then click in the History Brush column in the History palette, adjacent to the state that you want to return to. After you click, a History Brush icon (shown in Figure 9-3) appears next to that state in the History palette.

 TIP: *You can use "Photoshop's Magic Eraser" to erase to the state set in the History palette by the History Brush. To erase with the Magic Eraser, select the Erase to History check box in the Eraser Options palette before using the Eraser tool. You can also press OPTION (Windows users: ALT) while you click and drag on the Eraser tool.*

To experiment with the History Brush, load an image on screen. Then apply the Clouds filter to your image by choosing Filter | Render | Clouds. The Clouds filter completely fills the screen with cloud formations created from the current foreground and background colors. After you apply the Clouds filter, no trace of the original is left. However, using the History Brush you can paint back in the original and add blending effects as you do it.

Before you can paint with the History Brush, you must select it in the Toolbox. If desired, you can change the Opacity and Blending modes in the History Brush Options palette to create special effects. Next, move the mouse pointer to the

History Brush palette and click in the embossed square to the left of the state that you want to paint back into your image. If you applied the Clouds filter, click on the state in the History palette just before the Clouds filter state. Paint over your image. As you paint, your image gradually returns to view. When you paint, the History Brush uses the state in the History palette as a type of cloning source.

Try lowering opacity to create a blend between the History Brush state and later states. Then try choosing a Blending mode such as Dissolve or Overlay to see how the History Brush state can be blended together with other image stages. You can even choose Impressionist in the History Brush Options palette to blend the History step in as if it were an Impressionist painting. (To see the Impressionist option, double-click on the History Brush tool in the Toolbox.)

 TIP: *You can fill using the state designated by the History Brush in the History palette. Choose Edit | Fill. In the Using pop-up menu, choose History.*

Using Snapshots and Creating a New Document

Just as a snapshot in photography can freeze a moment in time, Photoshop's digital snapshots freeze a moment of digital history. As you work, you can create different snapshot versions and later return to any version you wish. To create a snapshot, you simply click on the New Snapshot icon in the History palette, or choose New Snapshot from the palette's menu. After you create a snapshot, it appears in the top section of the History palette. Any time you wish to return to the snapshot version, you simply click on it.

Snapshots also allow you to delete History states without altering your image. For example, if you create a snapshot and delete the History steps leading up to your image, the image remains unchanged. If you want to experiment, you can also use a snapshot as the source for the History Brush. This allows you to use the History Brush to gradually paint in the snapshot version. To set a snapshot as the source for the History brush, click in the History brush column next to the snapshot. After you click, the History brush appears next to the snapshot in the History palette. (When you first load an image, the History brush is set to the snapshot of your original image, as shown in Figure 9-5.)

After creating a snapshot, you may want to open the snapshot version into a new document. This is easily accomplished by clicking on the snapshot and choosing New Document from the History palette's pop-up menu or by clicking on the New Document icon at the bottom of the palette.

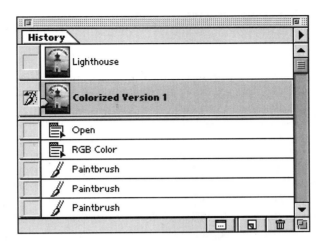

FIGURE 9-5   History Brush set to snapshot version of file

If you haven't created a snapshot in one of the previous chapters, execute these simple steps to see how they work.

1. Load an image, then use the Type tool to type some text over the image.

2. Try adding a drop shadow by choosing Layer I Effects I Drop shadow. Click OK and apply the default settings.

3. Create a snapshot by choosing New Snapshot in the History palette pop-up menu. This opens the New Snapshot dialog box, where you can enter a Snapshot name in the Name field.

 TIP: *To rename a snapshot, double click on the snapshot in the History palette. This opens the Rename Snapshot dialog box where you can enter a new name for the snapshot.*

4. Continue working on your image—add more type or create a transparent gradient over it.

5. Now assume you want to return to the snapshot version of your image. Simply click on the snapshot version of your file.

6. Try deleting History palette states that you created before making the snapshot. To delete a History state, drag it into the Trash icon at the bottom of the palette. Even though you delete the state, the image on screen remains unchanged.

7. Once you have a snapshot, you can actually delete the individual history states and save memory. Even if you delete the states leading up to the snapshot, the snapshot remains—you can always return to the snapshot version.

8. If you wish to continue experimenting without altering your original file, Photoshop easily allows you to place the snapshot version in another document. To create a new document out of your snapshot version, click on the New Document icon at the bottom of the History palette, or click New Document from the History palette menu. Photoshop immediately opens a copy of the document on screen. You can now use the new document and continue image editing.

 TIP: *You can create a new document from any state in the History palette. Click on the state, then click on the New Document icon at the bottom of the palette. When the new document is created, it opens with a new History palette.*

Conclusion

Now that you know how to record and play back actions and change history, think about all the ways you can use these handy features. You can not only use the History and Actions palettes to make your production work more efficient, but you can use the Actions palette to keep a record of your dialog box settings as you experiment and create special effects.

CHAPTER 10

Filters

Photoshop's magical filters are designed to do what most digitizing devices can't do: enhance an image and disguise its defects. A filter can turn soft, blurred contours into sharp, crisp edges, or it can soften an image that has jagged or harsh edges. Filters can also remove dust and scratches in digitized images and help eliminate color banding (abrupt changes in color values) and noise (randomly colored pixels that can appear in scanned images).

Although many filters are designed to subtly improve scanned images, others create such dramatic alterations as twisting, bending or spinning an image into motion. Some filters can grab a continuous-tone or painted image and make it appear to be made of three-dimensional blocks or pyramid shapes. Many filters create unusual, eerie, or humorous effects. Digitized images, as well as original images created in Photoshop, can be spherized, zigzagged, or twirled into a digital "soup."

The complex digital effects produced by Photoshop's filters have their roots in photography. Photographic filters are used to filter out light, to enhance images, and to create special effects. But the photographic filter can't match Photoshop's digital filters in effects or versatility. In Photoshop, filters can be applied again and again, one after another, until just the right effect is achieved for the entire image or within selections in the image. For instance, one filter might be applied to enhance the edges of an image and another to give it an embossed effect. The possibilities are endless.

How a Filter Works

Each of Photoshop's filters produces a different effect. Some filters work by analyzing every pixel in an image or selection and transforming it by applying mathematical algorithms to create random or predefined shapes such as tiles, three-dimensional blocks, or pyramids. Many filters, though, achieve their effects by first sampling individual pixels or groups of pixels to define areas that display the greatest difference in color or brightness. Once one of these filters zeroes in on such a transitional area, the filter starts changing color values—sometimes replacing one pixel's color with that of an adjacent pixel, sometimes substituting pixel colors with the average color value of neighboring pixels. The result, depending on the filter, can be a sharpening of the image, a softening of harsh edges, or a complete transformation.

Many filters invite you to be an active participant in determining the outcome of the filter's effects. Before these filters begin their work, a dialog box is presented to you in which you can control the magnitude of the filter's effects and often specify the radius (range) in which changes will occur.

How to Apply a Filter

Despite the differences among Photoshop's numerous filters, the process of

Filter	
Last Filter	⌘F
Fade...	⇧⌘F
Artistic	▶
Blur	▶
Brush Strokes	▶
Distort	▶
Noise	▶
Pixelate	▶
Render	▶
Sharpen	▶
Sketch	▶
Stylize	▶
Texture	▶
Video	▶
Other	▶
Digimarc	▶

applying each one is virtually the same. Start by opening or activating the image you wish to edit. If you wish to apply the filter to only a portion of the image, select that area with one of the selection tools; otherwise, Photoshop will apply the filter to the entire image. If you are working in a layer, Photoshop only applies the filter to colored, not transparent, areas of the layer. It will not apply a filter to more than one layer at a time.

From the Filter menu, choose one of the filter groups: Artistic, Blur, Brush Strokes, Distort, Noise, Pixelate, Render, Sharpen, Sketch, Stylize, Texture, Video, or Other. From the submenu that appears, select the filter that you wish to apply. Several of the filters are applied immediately when you select them. For others, you must set dialog box options to control the filter's results.

 NOTE: *The Digimarc filters which appear at the bottom of the Filter menu are discussed in Chapter 21.*

 NOTE: *Filters cannot be applied to Bitmap Indexed Color images or 16-bit images. Also note that some filters can only be applied to RGB Color files. Changing color modes is discussed in Chapter 12.*

Sometimes the effect of a filter on an image will be so subtle that you won't notice it, and you may wish to apply the filter again to enhance the results. To facilitate the process of reapplying filters, Photoshop copies the name of the last filter used from a submenu and installs it at the top of the Filter menu. To reapply the filter with its previous settings, just click on the first menu item in the Filter menu or press COMMAND-F (Windows users: CTRL-F). If the filter requires dialog box settings that you know you want to change from the last time it was used, you can press OPTION-COMMAND-F (Windows users: ALT-CTRL-F) to open the dialog box before reapplying the filter.

Many of the filter dialog boxes provide invaluable image previews that allow you to see the filter effect on the image before it is applied. The previews appear in a preview box as shown in the illustration following the next two paragraphs.

By clicking on the + or – icon, you can enlarge or reduce the image in the preview box by specific ratios. For instance, clicking on the + icon to change the image ratio to 200% would double the image size in the preview box; clicking on the – icon to change it to 50% would make it half the size.

If the preview box does not show the specific area you wish to view, you can adjust the view by clicking and dragging on the miniature image in the preview box. When you move the mouse over the preview box a tiny hand icon appears, alerting that you can click and drag to move the image. If you want the preview box to display an image area that is far outside the range of the preview box, you can click outside the dialog box (the mouse pointer changes to a see-through rectangle) on the image area you wish to see in the preview box.

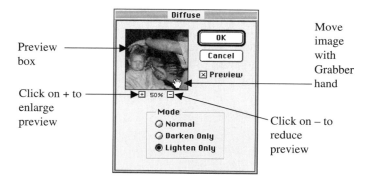

Because many Photoshop filters are sophisticated and require extensive computer processing, they may take some time to execute, particularly in a large image or selection. If you apply a filter and want to stop it before it has finished processing, you can usually press COMMAND-. (period) (Windows users: ESC) to cancel.

If you would like to try out the filters as you work through the discussions in this chapter, open the scanned image you used in Chapter 8 or choose one of the files available in the Adobe Samples folder or any other image.

 NOTE: *Some filters do not use your scratch disk while executing, so you must have sufficient RAM to complete the entire filter operation. If you do not, you may still be able to apply the filter to the image one channel at a time. See Chapters 12 and 14 for more information.*

Fading an Image Back In

After you apply a filter, you may wish to vary the effect or bring part of the image back to its original form. Photoshop's Fade command allows you to alter filter effects by gradually fading out the effects of the filter, using a blending mode. As you gradually fade out the filter's effects, the previous version of the file begins to appear in the blending mode specified in the Fade dialog box.

In order to use the Fade command, you must first run a filter. After the filter has been applied, the Fade command becomes activated in the Filter menu. To open the Fade dialog box, choose Filter | Fade (the Fade command in the menu now includes the name of the previously run filter).

To see the effects of the Fade, first make sure that the Preview check box is selected; then gradually drag the Opacity slider to the left. As you drag, the filter's effects fade from the image. Choosing a blending mode in the Fade dialog box applies the mode to the original image and the filtered image at the specified opacity.

 TIP: *The Fade command can also be used on Image | Adjust commands, such as Curves and Levels.*

Other Tips for Special Effects

As you work with filters, you can also enhance and alter filter effects by trying the following tips:

- Apply filters to one layer at a time. This technique allows you to gradually see the effect on different layers. Remember that you can only apply filters to a layer that is selected and visible.

- Apply filters to one channel at a time. This technique can also help you apply filters if you do not have a lot of RAM. You might find that you can create interesting special effects by applying different filters at different settings to different channels. Also, try applying a sharpening or blurring filter to the Lightness channel of a Lab color image or to the Black channel of a CMYK channel to experiment with different sharpening and blurring options.

- For filters that include the Repeat Edge Pixels option, enlarge the canvas area so that the image is in the middle, then run the filter. By doing this you can prevent the filter from laying the colors along the edge of the image. After you run the filter, crop the image as needed.

- Use the Actions palette to record your work. By recording your steps you'll always be able to replicate effects and dialog box settings.

- Use the History palette to create snapshots as you work. After you create the snapshot, you can experiment with the snapshot version of your image by turning it into a New Document. To do this, select the snapshot, then click on the New Document Icon in the History palette. See Chapter 9 to learn more about using the History palette and creating Actions.

The Blur Filters

The five Blur filters are often used to smooth areas where edges are too sharp and contrast is too high. They soften image edges by removing contrast. Blur filters can also be used to blur the background of an image, so that the foreground stands out, or to create a soft shadow effect.

BLUR   The Blur filter creates a light blurring effect that can be used to decrease contrast and eliminate noise in color transitions.

BLUR MORE   The Blur More filter blurs about three to four times as much as the Blur filter.

GAUSSIAN BLUR   The Gaussian Blur allows you to control the blurring effect, creating anything from a slight softening of image edges to a thick haze that blurs the image beyond recognition. This filter is named because it maps pixel color values according to a Gaussian bell-shaped curve.

In the Gaussian Blur dialog box, you specify a value from .1 to 250 in the Radius field to control the range of the blur from transitional areas. The higher the number, the greater the blur.

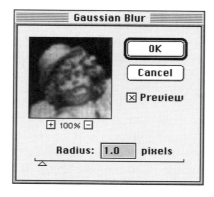

By experimenting with different Radius values, you can often eliminate moiré patterns in scanned images. A *moiré pattern* is an unwanted mottled effect that sometimes appears during the scanning of printed photographs or when an image is printed at an incorrect screen angle. Figure 10-1(a) shows a photograph, scanned from a Pratt Manhattan Art School's course catalog, of Puck standing on top of New York City's Puck building. Notice the moiré pattern over the entire image. Figure 10-1(b) shows the same image after the Gaussian Blur filter was applied. As you can see, after applying the filter the pattern is hardly noticeable.

To learn how to use the Gaussian blur to create drop shadows, see Chapter 15. Gaussian Blur is also often used to help create three-dimensional effects, as described later in this chapter in the section "Lighting Effects."

MOTION BLUR The Motion Blur filter creates the illusion of motion. It simulates the effect of photographing a moving object using a timed exposure.

The Motion Blur dialog box allows you to control the direction and strength of the blur. To set direction, type a degree value from -90 to 90 in the Angle box or

10

(a)

(b)

FIGURE 10-1   (a) Image showing a moiré pattern and (b) the same image after applying Gaussian Blur (courtesy of Pratt Manhattan and photographer Federico Savini)

use the mouse to click and drag on the radius line in the circle. To control intensity, enter a pixel value from 1 to 999 in the Distance field.

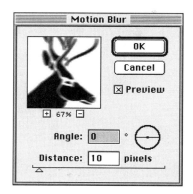

If you experiment with Motion Blur, zoom in on the pixels after blurring, and you will easily see how the filter works. It copies the image using the number in the Distance field as a guide, then offsets (shifts) the duplicate according to the Angle value, and overlays the copy of the image over the original as it lowers the opacity of the duplicate.

 The next illustration (to the left of this paragraph) shows the results of Motion Blur. In order to prevent the deer image itself from appearing blurred, the original image was selected with the Magic Wand and copied into the Clipboard before the blur was applied. In the Motion Blur dialog box, Distance was set to 60 pixels and Angle was set to 45° to match the deer's jumping angle. Then the copy of the deer from the Clipboard was pasted over the blurred image. While the copied image was floating, the original was offset about a quarter of an inch away from it.

 TIP: *If you want some parts of an image to be blurred and some not, duplicate your image in a layer. Apply the blur to the layer and create a layer mask. In the layer mask, paint with white to gradually unblur and reveal parts of the unblurred underlying layer. To learn more about layer masks, see Chapter 17.*

RADIAL BLUR The Radial Blur creates numerous interesting effects. It can spin an image into a circular shape or make it radiate out from its center.

When you activate Radial Blur, a wireframe preview appears in the filter's dialog box, providing a skeletal view of the blur's effect. This is extremely helpful because the Radial Blur often takes a long time to execute.

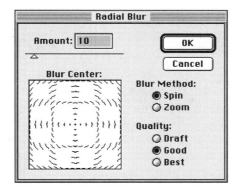

In the Radial Blur dialog box, you can select either Spin or Zoom as the blur method. If you select Spin, the blur is created in concentric circles, often making your image look as if it were spun on a potter's wheel. With Zoom, blurred image lines zoom out from the image's center point.

To control the intensity of the blur, enter a value between 1 and 100 in the Amount field or drag the Amount slider control until the blur in the preview box shows the effect you desire. The higher the value, the more intense the blur. To change the center of the blur, click and drag on the dot in the center of the Blur center box.

The Radial Blur dialog box also allows you to specify the quality of the blur. The Best option produces the smoothest blur, but it takes the longest to execute. With the Draft option, Photoshop completes the blur faster, but the results will be grainy. The Good option produces a level of quality between Best and Draft, although for large files, there may be little noticeable difference between Best and Good.

In the following illustration, the Radial Blur filter was applied to the wheel graphic at the left to produce the spinning wheel at the right. The filter was applied with an Amount setting of 30, Spin was selected as the blur method, and Quality was set to Best.

10

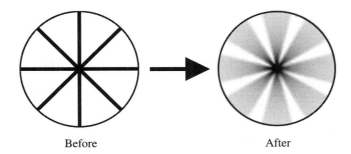

Before   After

SMART BLUR The Smart Blur allows you to create a variety of blurring effects. You can blur out the folds or wrinkles in an image or change an image so that the overlaid edges are blurred. Using the options in the dialog box, you can also turn a colored image into a black and white one, with the image's edges white.

In the Smart Blur dialog box, the Radius slider controls the distance of the blurring effect. The Threshold slider allows you to set how different the pixels must be before the blurring takes effect. If you set the Quality pop-up menu to High, the filter will be slower but the image quality will be better. The mode pop-up menu allows you to choose what part of the image to apply the blurring to. If you choose Normal, blurring affects the entire colored image. If you choose Edge Only (edges are image areas with a great deal of color variation) and raise the Threshold slider, the image edges turn white and the rest of the image turns black. If you choose Overlay Edge, the filter overlays the image edges when applying the blurring effect.

The Noise Filters

Noise, or randomly colored pixels, is occasionally introduced during the scanning process. The Noise filters blend noise with the surrounding pixels to make it less apparent. You can also use Add Noise to drown an image with so much noise that it is completely transformed into colored pixel patterns; this effect can be used to quickly create interesting and unusual textured backgrounds. Noise filters can also be used to add a grainy texture to images. Noise is handy if you are converting 24-bit images to Indexed Color for the Web or multimedia programs. The noise can help smooth transitions in the Indexed Color image.

ADD NOISE The Add Noise filter adds noise to an image, blends noise into an image, and helps diffuse color banding that can occur in blends. This filter is sometimes used to help blend images that were created with painting tools into their surroundings or to create interesting patterned backgrounds. When you use it to create background patterns, experiment with different file resolutions, because the pattern will change depending on the resolution.

Use the Add Noise dialog box to indicate the amount of noise you wish to add to an image. Enter a value from 1 to 999 in the Amount field; the greater the amount, the greater the noise effect.

Photoshop 5   In Action

The kids were photographed with the table and balloons.

Shaquille O'Neal from the Los Angeles Lakers was photographed with a tray in his hand.

With the cake selected, the Motion Blur filter was applied.

Artist: Nik Kleinberg   **Client: Sports Illustrated for Kids**

It's a bird, it's a plane, it's a birthday cake! Covers for *Sports Illustrated for Kids* are always creative, unusual, and playful. This cover began with George B. Fry III photographing the children and balloons around the table. Later, he photographed basketball star Shaquille O'Neal holding a tray beside the table while an assistant held the cake over the middle of the table at the angle seen above. For an added effect, a photograph was taken of smoke created by candles that were blown out.

After Nik scanned the photographs, he selected, then copied and pasted Shaquille into the image with the kids. Next, he selected the cake with the Rectangular Marquee tool's Feather option and then copied and pasted it into the image with the kids. After the cake was pasted and moved into position, the Motion Blur filter was applied to it. To create the streams of smoke trailing the cake, Nik pasted in the digitized photograph of the smoke. Then he pasted a portion from the original children's image over the smoke. Next, he painted the smoke back into the image with a low opacity and soft-edged brush (you can now do this with a History Brush tool). Nik also used the Airbrush tool's Fade option and a low opacity with a soft-edged brush to create more streams of smoke trailing the cake.

10

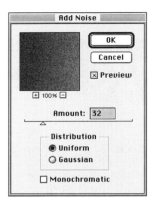

There are two Distribution options in the Add Noise dialog box. When you select Uniform, Photoshop generates noise randomly, using the Amount field value to calculate the random values. For instance, if you enter **5** in the Amount field, Photoshop will calculate random color values between −5 and 5 for each pixel's color. With the Gaussian distribution option, the noise is mapped along a bell-shaped curve. This often produces a noisier effect than that of the Uniform setting. The Gaussian option also tends to produce a greater number of light pixels. If you select the Monochromatic check box, colors will not be added to the image when noise is created. It is like adding noise to the luminance values of your image.

The following illustration shows a pattern created with the Add Noise filter. This effect was generated by first creating a dark-to-light linear blend horizontally (left to right) on the screen. Then the Add Noise filter was applied once, with the Gaussian option selected and an Amount value of 100.

DESPECKLE The Despeckle filter seeks out the areas of greatest color change in an image and blurs everything except transitional edges; thus detail is not lost. Use this filter when you need to reduce noise or to blur areas that have been pixelated because of oversharpening. The Despeckle filter can sometimes help reduce moiré patterns that can occur after scanned images are printed.

DUST & SCRATCHES   The Dust & Scratches filter hunts down small imperfections in an image or selection and blends them into the surrounding image.

Before opening the Dust & Scratches filter, select the area that includes the imperfections you want to eliminate. When you open the filter, the selected area will appear in the preview box. In the Dust & Scratches dialog box, click on the + control to zoom in to view the dust and/or scratches you want to eliminate.

In the Dust & Scratches dialog box, Photoshop uses the value entered in the Threshold field to determine which pixels to analyze when cleaning up the image. When you enter a Threshold value, the filter uses it to analyze the difference between the pixel values of the scratches and the pixel values of the surrounding pixels. If you type in **0**, the filter analyzes all pixels in an image. By typing in a number you begin to restrict the area the filter evaluates. For instance, assume you have an image area with a brightness value of 100, and in that image area you have a 1-pixel gray scratch with a brightness value of 150. If you type **49** in the Threshold field, the scratch will disappear. If you type **50** or any number over that, the scratch will not disappear.

Once the filter homes in on a scratch or an imperfection, it uses the Radius value to determine how large an area to clean up. The Radius value controls the range in the scratch or dust area that is cleaned up. If you enter too large a Radius value, your image could begin to look blurry.

Try to maintain a balance between the Threshold and Radius so that defects are removed but the sharpness of your image is maintained.

The Dust & Scratches filter, with a little help from the Rubber Stamp tool, was applied to the image in Figure 10-2(a). The result is shown in Figure 10-2(b).

MEDIAN   The Median filter also reduces noise by blending the brightness of pixels within a selection. It's called the Median filter because it replaces the center pixel in a radius area with the median brightness value of the pixels in that area. In the Median dialog box, you can enter a Radius value between 1 and 16 pixels. The Radius value is the distance the filter searches from each pixel to analyze brightness.

The Sharpen Filters

The four Sharpen filters clarify images by creating more contrast and are often used to enhance the contours of scanned images. It is often helpful to apply these filters after reducing images (Image | Image Size) or distorting images that have

(a)   (b)

FIGURE 10-2 (a) Image before applying the Dust & Scratches filter and (b) the same image after applying the Dust & Scratches filter

been edited with Edit | Transform commands. The Sharpen filters reduce the blurring that can occur after interpolation.

 CAUTION: *Be careful not to sharpen too much, otherwise distinct pixels will begin to show through, causing the image to look pixelated.*

 TIP: *If you need to sharpen small, intricate areas, particularly image highlights, it's better to work with the Sharpen tool in the Toolbox, because it is more precise. See Chapter 6.*

SHARPEN   The Sharpen filter sharpens by increasing the contrast between neighboring pixels.

SHARPEN EDGES   The Sharpen Edges filter works like the Sharpen filter, except it sharpens only the edges of an image (smooth areas are unaffected).

SHARPEN MORE   The Sharpen More filter provides a stronger sharpening effect than the Sharpen filter.

UNSHARP MASK   The Unsharp Mask filter exaggerates the sharpness of an image's edges. It is often helpful to apply this filter after converting an image from RGB to CMYK, or after any other Photoshop operation that involves interpolation. Unlike the other Sharpen filters, Unsharp Mask lets you control the amount of sharpening when you apply it.

The name of the Unsharp Mask filter is based on a traditional photographic masking technique in which a negative and a blurred positive of an image are combined to make the image stand out.

You can control the intensity of this filter's effect by entering a percentage from 1 to 500 in the Amount field of the Unsharp Mask dialog box. The greater the percentage, the greater the sharpening. A percentage of 150 to 300 usually provides good results with high-resolution images. Higher-resolution images often require a higher percentage. In the Radius field, you can specify the distance (in pixels) out from transitional edges that you want sharpened. If you enter a low Radius number, the sharpening occurs closer to image edges. The higher the Radius number, the greater the distance that sharpening will occur beyond image contours. Adobe recommends setting the Radius value between 1 and 2 for high-resolution images.

 TIP: *Instead of applying 150 percent to a high-res image, you may wish to use a percentage of 60 and apply Unsharp Mask twice.*

The Threshold field allows you to specify a comparison between neighboring pixels for sharpening. It allows you to prevent sharpening unless contrast between pixels is above the Threshold value. For instance, if the brightness values of neighboring pixels differ by 5, typing in a Threshold of **4** will cause sharpening to occur. Enter **5** or larger in Threshold, and Photoshop will ignore the pixels. Thus, the Threshold value can be used to prevent oversharpening in the entire image or a selected area. If you keep Threshold set at the default level, 0, the filter will change the most pixels possible. The higher you set Threshold, the lower the number of pixels that will be affected.

Figure 10-3 shows an image of some flowers with part of the image sharpened. The Unsharp Mask filter was applied three times, with Amount set to 50%, Radius set to 1, and Threshold set to 0. If you use too high a Radius, you may find that image contours darken.

 NOTE: *As you work, you may notice that colors in your image change after you apply the Unsharp Mask filter. Adobe recommends converting the image to Lab color mode and applying the filter to the L channel. Because the L channel is a luminosity channel, not a color channel, the sharpening will not change colors in the image. Also note that you can freely switch between Lab and RGB color modes without altering color values.*

The Render Filters

The Render filters primarily create lighting effects in your images. The filters run from the uncomplicated to the complex. For instance, the Cloud filter simply

Area sharpened

FIGURE 10-3   Unsharp Mask applied to a portion of a flower image

creates cloudlike effects on your screen. On the other end of the scale, the Lighting Effects filter allows you to point up to 16 different light sources at your image. The filter can even apply a texture to your image to make it look as if it were a lunar landscape. The 3D Transform filter allows you to take an image, such as a three-dimensional photograph and manipulate the perspective in the image.

 NOTE: *The Lighting Effects filter and the Lens Flare filter can only be applied to RGB color images.*

3D Transform

3D Transform is a new filter that allows you to manipulate a two-dimensional Photoshop image as if it were created in a 3-D program. The filter is most useful for repositioning images composed of shapes such as cubes, spheres, and cylinders. For instance, Figure 10-4a shows a multimedia button before the 3D Transform filter was used. Figure 10-4b shows the image after it was tilted slightly using the 3D Transform filter.

The 3D Transform filter is most valuable when you need to work with a digitized image that wasn't photographed at the correct angle or that needs to be adjusted so that the perspective of the entire image looks realistic.

To use the 3D Transform filter, load an image. The filter works best with images that are shaped like a cube, sphere, or cylinder. Load the filter by choosing Filter | Render | 3D Transform. In the dialog box, choose one of the modeling tools: the Cube or Sphere or Cylinder tool depending upon the type of image that

10

(a)   (b)

FIGURE 10-4   a) Image before applying 3D Transform filter and b) image tilted using 3D Transform filter

you want to transform. Next, click and drag over the preview of your image in the 3D Transform dialog box. This creates a wireframe skeleton on screen. Next, use the Direct Selection tool, (White Arrow) to drag the anchor points of the wireframe over the edges of the image area that you wish to transform.

If you wish to move the wireframe, click and drag on the edge of the wireframe with the Direct Selection tool. If needed, use the Add or Subtract Point tools to add Anchor points to the wireframe so that you can outline the image. After you add anchor points, you can use the Direct Selection tool to edit the wireframe. If you need to convert a corner point to a smooth point or convert a smooth point to a corner point, click on the point using the Convert Point tool, then drag the mouse. (Note that the Add Anchor, Subtract Anchor, and Convert Point tools work with wireframes created with the Cylinder tool.)

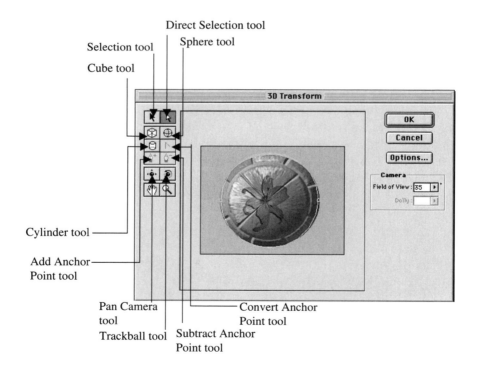

After you've outlined your image with the wireframe, use the Pan Camera and Trackball tools to manipulate the scene to the desired view. Use the Point of View and Dolly sliders on the right side of the dialog box to fine-tune the scene. To access the sliders, click on the down arrows in the Point of View and Dolly fields. As you work with the Pan Camera and Trackball tools and the Point of View and Dolly fields, the dialog box previews the results.

Before clicking OK, check the Options settings. The Resolution settings control the quality and smoothness. Choosing High Resolution and High Anti-aliasing produces high quality results, but the filter will take longer to execute. If you want to separate the wireframe selection from its background and have it appear in a layer with a transparent background, deselect Display Background. Click OK to return to the Main screen, then click OK to transform your image.

If you experiment with the 3D Transform filter, you'll find that you can't render color information over all areas that it transforms. If you transform too much you'll get a white-ribbed cylinder, cube, or sphere in part of your image area. The filter works best with slight adjustments to simple images.

 TIP: *You can activate the tools in the 3D Transform dialog box by pressing keyboard shortcuts. Here are a few:*

Selection tool	V
Direct Selection tool	A
Add Anchor Point	+
Delete Anchor Point	–
Zoom tool	Z
Hand tool	H
Toggle between the Selection and Direct Selection tool	CMD+TAB (Windows users: CTRL+TAB)

Texture Fill

Texture Fill loads a Photoshop grayscale image into an image and repeats it in order to fill a layer or alpha channel. Texture Fill is often used to load a grayscale image into an alpha channel so that it can be utilized as a texture for the Lighting Effects filter. (See the following section, "Lighting Effects," for instructions on using the Texture Fill filter as a texture map. Also, see Chapter 14 for more information on alpha channels.) You could also use Texture Fill to load a grayscale image into an alpha channel to use as a layer mask, or to create a texture effect in an image. To use Texture Fill to fill an alpha channel, first create a new alpha channel by choosing New Channel from the Channels palette. Then choose Filter | Render | Texture Fill. A dialog box prompts you to load a Photoshop grayscale file. Select the grayscale file that you want to load. After you click OK, the file is loaded and repeated so that it fills the alpha channel.

Lighting Effects

The Lighting Effects filter allows you to apply different light sources, types, and properties to an image. This helps you add depth to an image and spotlight certain areas, as well as change moods. The Lighting Effects filter can also be used to create texture maps from grayscale images. This can add a three-dimensional effect to flat images by making it appear as if light is bouncing off bumps in the texture.

 NOTE: *The Lighting Effects filter can only be applied to RGB color images.*

Choosing a Style and Light Type

In the Lighting Effects dialog box, choose a Style in the Style pop-up menu. The default style provides a medium- to full-strength spotlight with a wide focus. Later in this section, you'll learn how to name and save your settings so that they appear in the Style pop-up menu.

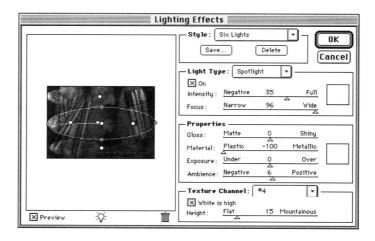

To create new lights, click on the Light Bulb icon (☼) and drag it into the image preview area in the dialog box. To duplicate a light, press OPTION (Windows users: ALT) and drag on the light. If you wish to delete a light, drag the light's circle icon into the Trash icon (🗑) in the dialog box. For each new light, you can choose a light type from the Light Type pop-up menu.

When the On check box is selected, the light is on and you can choose a light type from the Light Type pop-up menu. The following list describes the different types of lights.

- Spotlight casts the light in a long elliptical shape. To see the effects of the Spotlight, choose it from the Light Type pop-up menu. Notice that the preview box includes an ellipse and four boxes.

  In the preview box, you can move the Spotlight by clicking and dragging the center circle. You can change the angle and length of the light by dragging the handle on the end of the line to make it larger or smaller. Change the focus of the light by dragging on any of the four boxes on the ellipse. Dragging the boxes away from the center will increase the area that is lit.

TIP: *When altering the Spotlight with the mouse, you can change the size of the ellipse without affecting the angle by pressing SHIFT and dragging. Press COMMAND (Windows users: CTRL) and drag to change the angle but not the size of the ellipse.*

  If your light type is Spotlight, you can change the focus of the light, which determines the amount of light that fills the elliptical area.

- Omni casts light in all directions, as if the light were above the image. To see the effects of the Omni light, choose Omni from the Light Type pop-up menu. Notice that the preview box includes a circle and four boxes.

  To move the light, drag the center circle in the Preview box. To give the appearance that the light is closer to the image, drag one of the four boxes closer to the center. Dragging a box farther away makes it appear as though the light is farther away.

- Directional light casts light in one straight direction. To see the effects of the Directional light, choose Directional from the Light Type pop-up menu. Notice that the preview box does not include an ellipse.

10

Directional only allows you to change the direction and angle of the light. To move the light, drag on the center of the circle. To change the height, drag the square at the end of the line. The longer the line, the farther away the light will be. Decreasing the size of the line creates a more intense light.

When using Omni, Directional, or Spotlight, drag the Intensity slider to control the strength of the light. The slider ranges from 100 (brightest) to –100 (pure black). A value of 50 is considered normal intensity. A negative value produces an effect similar to a black light.

The Focus slider is only available when using the Spotlight. Dragging the slider toward Widen broadens the scope of the light within the ellipse. Dragging the slider toward Narrow produces the effect of a thinner light beam being applied to an image.

If you wish to change the color of the light, click on the rectangular swatch in the Light Type section. This will open the Color Picker dialog box, where you can pick a lighting color. (If the Apple or Windows Color Picker is selected in the General Preferences dialog box, the Apple/Windows Color Picker will appear instead.)

 NOTE: *If a style contains several light types and settings, pressing TAB will move you from one light type and its settings to another.*

Choosing a Property

All lights share a set of properties. The following is a summary of each property.

- **Gloss** determines how light reflects off an image. Use the slider to vary the surface from Matte to Shiny.

- **Material** controls whether the light or the object the light is shining on has more reflectance. The slider allows you to drag from Plastic to Metallic. Plastic reflects the light's color. Metallic reflects the color of the image on screen.

- **Exposure** either lightens or darkens the shining light.

- **Ambiance** allows you to create the effect of blending light from the light source with the room light in an image.

Before experimenting with the Ambient slider, note the swatch to the right of the Properties group. Clicking on the swatch allows you to pick a color for the Ambient light. If you drag the Ambient slider to 100 (to the right), Ambient light intensifies (adding the color from the swatch) so that it is not diffused with the light from the Light Type section. Drag the slider to the left, and the Ambient light gradually diminishes.

Saving Lighting Styles

The Lighting Effects dialog box also allows you to save your own lighting styles to disk. When you save a style, settings for all lights in the Lighting Effects dialog box are saved and the style's name appears in the Style pop-up menu. To save the settings on screen as a style, click the Save button. In the dialog box that opens, enter a name for your style and then click OK.

If you are using Texture Channels, it's important to note that the named style reads the channel's number, not its contents. This means that when you open the image, the texture you need must be loaded in the Channels palette. If you need to make the style appear in another document, you must duplicate the channel into that document. For information about duplicating a channel, see Chapter 14.

If you wish to delete a style, select it in the Style pop-up menu and click the Delete button.

Using the Texture Channel

The Texture Channel allows you to use a channel to add texture to an image. In order to use this feature, you must first choose a texture in the Texture Channel pop-up menu (the texture can be an alpha channel, one of the RGB channels from your image, or even the currently active layer). When a texture is chosen, Photoshop bounces lights off contours in the image that correspond to the texture. Use this to create terrain and embossed effects in your image, as shown in Figure 10-7. To create this effect, the flower shown in Figure 10-6 was used as a texture channel when the Lighting Effects filter was applied to Figure 10-5.

FIGURE 10-5   Image before applying the Lighting Effects filter

FIGURE 10-6   Image used as basis for Texture Fill

FIGURE 10-7   Image after applying the Lighting Effects filter with a texture channel

Figure 10-8 shows an example of applying the Lighting Effects filter to a new file. In the new file, we applied the Clouds and Add Noise filters to create a colored background. Next, we created a new channel to which we applied the Texture Fill filter with the flower image (Figure 10-6)—so that it repeatedly filled the alpha channel (the steps for doing this are described in the next section). Then we applied the Lighting Effects filter with the Texture Channel option selected. By doing this, the items in the alpha channel were applied to the document, creating a textured, embossed effect.

Any texture can be copied into or created in an alpha channel to use as a texture, then you can select the channel from the Texture Channel pop-up menu. In the list of choices you'll see the RGB channels of your image, as well as any alpha channels you have added. (See the steps that follow for adding a channel to your image.) If you are working in a layer, the Texture Channel pop-up menu allows you to select a Transparency choice for your layer. You can use this option to add a black or colored edge to the perimeter of a nontransparent area of your layer.

If you wish to create an embossed effect, select the White is high check box. This creates the appearance of light being emitted from the image surface. Turn off this option if you want light to shoot down into the depths of your texture. To

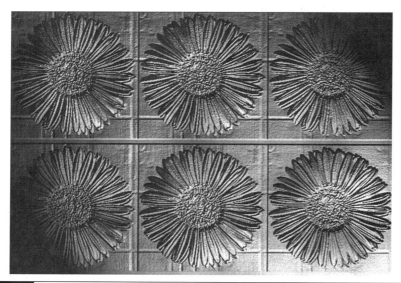

FIGURE 10-8 Image after Lighting Effects filters with a texture channel is applied to a new document

create a more bumpy texture, drag the slider toward Mountainous. A less bumpy texture will be produced if you drag the slider toward Flat.

 TIP: *The Adobe Photoshop CD ROM includes a folder of textures that can be loaded by the Lighting Effects filter. The textures include Brick, Carpeting, Caviar, Confetti, Footprints—even Dragon Scales. The textures can be found in the Textures for Lighting Effects folder in the Other Goodies folder.*

Creating a Lighting Effect with a Texture Fill

The CD-ROM that accompanies Photoshop includes a variety of textures to try out with the Lighting Effects filter. If you don't have a texture map to use, here are step-by-step instructions for converting a color image to grayscale and then using the grayscale image as a texture with the Lighting Effects filter. You can use either the Adobe Samples folder images or any other two images.

First, load the file that you wish to use as a texture and convert it to Grayscale mode.

1. Load the image that you wish to use as a texture. Use the File | Save As command to save it under another name. This ensures that you do not overwrite the original file.

2. To change the image into a grayscale file, choose Image | Mode | Grayscale. An Alert appears asking whether you wish to Discard color information. Click OK.

3. The file on screen will now be a grayscale image. Choose File | Save, then close the file.

 NOTE: *make sure you save your file as a Photoshop grayscale file. The filter will not accept images in any other format.*

4. Open the file that you wish to apply the texture to.

Next, you will create a new channel and load the grayscale image from steps 1-3 into the new channel using the Texture Fill filter.

5. Open the Channels palette by choosing Window | Show Channels.

6. Click on the Channels palette pop-up arrow. In the list of choices choose New Channel. (Another way to create a new channel is to press and hold OPTION (Windows users: ALT) and click on the dog-eared page icon in the Channels palette.) If you wish, enter a name in the dialog box to name the filter. Then click OK. Notice that the new channel (Alpha1) is selected in the Channels palette. This indicates that it is the target channel—the channel currently being edited.

7. To load the texture image into the new alpha channel, choose Filter | Render | Texture Fill. When the Open dialog box appears, choose the grayscale image (the image from steps 1-3). Notice that the pattern filling the screen is created from the grayscale image in the alpha channel.

8. To return to the RGB composite channel and the composite view of your image, click on RGB in the Channels palette.

10

9. Open the Lighting Effects dialog box by choosing Filter | Render | Lighting Effects.

10. In the Filter dialog box, load the texture by choosing Alpha1 in the Texture Channel pop-up menu. If you named your channel in step 6, select the channel name.

You should see the texture applied to the image on screen. To intensify the effect, move the Height slider to Mountainous. Before clicking OK to close the dialog box, experiment with different lighting effects.

Creating Beveling Effects with the Lighting Effects Filter

The Lighting Effects filter can be used to quickly create three-dimensional beveling effects with its texture channel. Using the Lighting Effects filter and its Texture Channel option, you can quickly bevel a shape for a special effect as shown in Figures 10-9 and 10-10. In the following example, a button shape is first created in a new alpha channel.

FIGURE 10-9   Beveled button created using the Lighting Effects filter

FIGURE 10-10   Beveled text created using the Lighting Effects filter

10

1. Create a new RGB color file, 2 inches by 2 inches. Set the resolution to 72 ppi.

2. Create a new alpha channel by clicking on the dog-eared icon at the bottom of the Channels palette or by choosing New Channel from the Channels palette pop-up menu. (The entire channel should be black. If it isn't, double-click on the channel in the Channels palette and select Color Indicates Masked Area.)

3. Set the Foreground color to white.

4. Use either the Rectangular or Elliptical Marquee tool to create a marquee selection in the new alpha channel on screen. Don't deselect.

5. Next, fill the marquee selection with white by pressing OPTION-DELETE (Windows users: ALT-DELETE) on your keyboard.

TIP: *Instead of using the Marquee tool to create a selection and then filling it to convert it into a shape, you can use Photoshop's Pen tool to create a path and then fill it. You can also import shapes you have created in Adobe Illustrator into Photoshop.*

6. Deselect the selection on screen by choosing Select | None or pressing COMMAND-D (Windows users: CTRL-D).

7. To create a soft-edged effect, apply a blur to the image by choosing Filter | Gaussian Blur. Use a setting of 1.5 to 2.0.

 NOTE: *If you are working with a high-resolution file with a large shape, you will probably have to increase the setting in the Gaussian Blur filter dialog box. When working with low-res files and small shapes, you will probably have to decrease the setting in the Gaussian Blur filter dialog box.*

 TIP: *You can alter the beveling effect by putting a border around the selection (Select | Modify | Border) and then filling and blurring the border.*

8. Select the RGB channel in the Channels palette by clicking on it.

9. Open the Lighting Effects dialog box by choosing Filter | Render | Lighting Effects. In the dialog box, set the Texture Channel option to the new alpha channel—Alpha 1. Adjust the Height slider, the White is high check box, and the lights and direction to achieve the final effect.

Clouds

The Clouds filter transforms your image into soft clouds by using random pixel values that fall between the foreground and background colors. Therefore, you need to set the foreground and background colors to the colors you want the clouds to be. If you wish to create a less diffused cloud effect, press SHIFT when you choose the Clouds command.

TIP: *You can also use the Clouds filter to create a colored background. Set the foreground and background colors to any bright colors and then apply the filter. Once you've applied the Clouds filter, you might want to try either the Filter | Noise | Add Noise, the Filter | Distort | Glass, the Filter | Distort | Ripple, or the Filter | Distort | Ocean Ripple filter to add more texture to your background.*

To try out the Clouds command, create a new 5-by-5-inch RGB color file. Set the foreground color to blue and the background color to white. Apply the Clouds filter by choosing Filter | Render | Clouds.

 TIP: *The Clouds filter also works in grayscale images.*

Difference Cloud

The Difference Clouds filter inverts your image, blending it into a cloudlike background. The effect is very much like a combination of the Clouds command and the Difference painting/editing mode. When the filter is applied, a cloudlike effect is generated from random pixel values that fall between the values of the foreground and background colors. Next, the filter subtracts the pixel values of the cloud data from the pixel values of your image. If you keep running the filter, a marbleized version of your image will result.

If you'd like to test the effect, open any file. Set the foreground color to blue and the background color to yellow and then run the Difference Cloud filter.

Lens Flare

The Lens Flare filter creates an effect similar to that of a bright light shining into the lens of a camera, as demonstrated in Figure 10-11.

The Lens Flare dialog box allows you to set the brightness of the light, the center of the light source, and the lens type. In the Brightness field, type in or use the slider control to enter a value between 10 and 300 percent. Click anywhere on the image icon to choose a center point for the light source. After you click, a

10

FIGURE 10-11   The highway image after applying the Lens Flare filter

crosshair indicates the center point. Before executing the filter, choose one of the Lens Type radio buttons.

Crosshair ———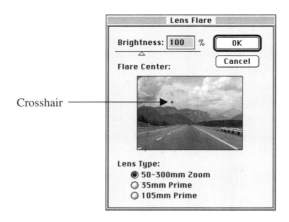

NOTE: *The Lens Flare filter only works on RGB color files. Also, the filter does not work in computers without a math coprocessor (FPU chip) unless you have a PowerPC CPU.*

The Pixelate Filters

The Pixelate filters break your image down into pieces to make them look as if they were created from large blocks and squares. Besides making your image more mosaic-like, the Pixelate filters generally flatten them as well.

COLOR HALFTONE   The Color Halftone filter makes an image appear to be created from large halftone dots. Photoshop creates this effect by dividing the image into rectangular grids and then filling each rectangular grid with pixels to simulate the halftone dots. The width and height of the grid are controlled by the Max. Radius field. The dot placement in the image is controlled by the screen angles that you choose.

CRYSTALLIZE   The Crystallize filter sharpens images by moving similarly colored pixels together into a polygonal grid of pixels. The size of the polygon is controlled by the value entered in the Cell Size field. Figure 10-12 shows the effect of the Crystallize filter when applied with a cell size of 10 pixels to the flower image from Figure 10-6.

FACET   The Facet filter gives a hand-painted look to an image by grouping and changing sampled pixels into blocks of similarly colored pixels. When this filter is applied, solid and similar colors are emphasized.

FRAGMENT   The Fragment filter creates an unfocused effect by copying an image's pixels four times, averaging them, and then offsetting them. This filter will quickly create an unfocused background over which you can paste objects to make them stand out.

MEZZOTINT   The Mezzotint filter recreates your image out of dots, lines, or strokes. In the Mezzotint dialog box, choose the desired effect from the Type pop-up menu. The Fine Dots choice often provides a mezzotint that looks closest to your original. To see the effects of the filter, load any image and then click on each choice in the Type pop-up menu to see the results. If you don't have an image to use, try applying the filter to the flower (Windows users: flower.jpg) image from the Tutorial folder.

10

FIGURE 10-12   The flower image from Figure 10-6 after applying the Crystallize filter

MOSAIC   The Mosaic filter gives your image a mosaic effect. If you are using Photoshop to create video animation, you can use the Mosaic filter to replicate a technique commonly used in television, which causes an image to appear to gradually break up into pieces and then disappear. Some artists even use the Mosaic filter to make high-resolution images look digitized. In the Mosaic dialog box enter a number between 2 and 64 pixels in the Cell Size field or click and drag on the slider. The filter creates the mosaic effect by making all pixels in a cell the same color.

POINTILLIZE   The Pointillize filter breaks up an image into random dots, producing an effect much like that of a pointillist painting. You can control the size of dots in the filtered image by entering a cell value between 3 and 300. When the Pointillize filter is applied, Photoshop uses the current Background color as the background.

The Distort Filters

The Distort filters are used to create distortions that vary from rippling an image to twirling and twisting it. How you use them is up to you. If you are creating original art with Photoshop's tools, you will find that many of the Distort filters can save you time when you are creating unusual effects.

Diffuse Glow

The Diffuse Glow filter diffuses highlights from images, creating a glowing effect. In the Diffuse dialog box, the Graininess slider adds a sandy type of grain effect. Drag the slider to the right to increase the effect. The Glow Amount slider increases the effect of a glowing light on the image (if the light is the background color).The Clear Amount slider controls how much of your background color appears over the image. The lower the value, the greater the area that the background color covers.

Displace

The Displace filter can bend, shatter, and twist an image. Unfortunately, of all the filters in Photoshop's varied collection, the Displace filter is probably the most difficult to understand and the hardest to predict. The results seem unpredictable because the filter not only obeys your dialog box directions, but also relies on a *displacement map* to displace your image. You can apply the Displace filter to any Photoshop file, other than a Bitmap mode file.

The Displace filter is run differently than other Photoshop filters: After the Displace dialog box settings are accepted, the filter doesn't immediately begin processing. Instead, an Open dialog box appears, allowing you to select a file to use as the displacement map. After the displacement map file is chosen, the Displace filter shifts image pixels according to color values in the displacement map.

Color values in the displacement map are measured on a scale from 0 to 255. Low values (darker colors) produce a displacement down and to the right in the filtered image. Midrange values (near 128) produce little displacement. High values (lighter colors) produce a displacement up and to the left.

If you wish to experiment with the Displace filter, you can use a variety of displacement maps included with the Photoshop package. They can be found in the Displacement Maps folder in the Plug-ins folder.

10

Practice with the Displace Filter

The best way to get a feel for the Displace filter is to apply the filter using one of Photoshop's textures and analyze the effects. (The Textures folder can be found in the Goodies folder.)

1. Before you begin, open the texture called Bumpy Leather to take a look at how the light and dark areas are dispersed in the image. After examining the file, it's a good idea to close it (so that you don't inadvertently apply the Displace filter to it rather than to your image).

2. Open an image on screen to which you wish to apply the filter. If you'd like, you can choose a file such as the Rockies from the Adobe Samples folder (Goodies | Samples | Rockies).

3. Choose Filter | Distort | Displace.

   In the Displace dialog box, you can enter values that control the degree of horizontal and vertical displacement. By entering a value in the Horizontal Scale field, you specify how much the filter will shift your image left or right according to the color values in the displacement map. The value in the Vertical Scale field specifies the amount the filter will shift your image up or down according to the color values in the displacement map. The highest allowed percentage, 100, displaces your image 128 pixels in areas corresponding to black or white in the displacement map.

   ```
   ┌─────────────────── Displace ───────────────────┐
   │                                                 │
   │   Horizontal Scale: [10    ] %    ┌──────────┐  │
   │                                   │    OK    │  │
   │   Vertical Scale:   [10    ] %    └──────────┘  │
   │                                   ┌──────────┐  │
   │                                   │  Cancel  │  │
   │                                   └──────────┘  │
   │   Displacement Map:     Undefined Areas:        │
   │   ● Stretch to Fit      ○ Wrap Around           │
   │   ○ Tile                ● Repeat Edge Pixels     │
   │                                                 │
   └─────────────────────────────────────────────────┘
   ```

4. For this exercise, you'll use low displacement values. (Higher values would displace your image so much that you wouldn't be able to decipher the results.) Enter **30** for the Horizontal Scale and **30** for the Vertical Scale.

   There are two choices for handling displacement maps that are not the same size as the area to which you are applying the filter. The Stretch to Fit option transforms the size of the displacement map to match the image. The Tile option uses the displacement map as a repeating pattern.

Photoshop 5 In Action

Fundamental Photoshop Technical Editor, Jeff Kryvicky (New York artist), created this image as an example of how you can create an image from start to finish primarily using Photoshop filters.

Jeff started by creating a new 5 by 5 inch document (72pp) with a white background. He set the foreground color to blue and the background color to yellow. Next, he applied the Filter | Render | Difference Clouds filter several times. After applying Difference Clouds, he ran the Displace filter with the Horizontal field set to 20 pixels and the Vertical field set to 0 pixels. When running the Displace filter, he used the Bumpy Leather texture as the Displacement Map (the Bumpy leather filter can be found in the Textures folder located in the Goodies folder).

To achieve the planet-like effect, Jeff applied the Spherize filter (set to 100), and then he applied Filter | Render | Lens Flare to add a highlight. To give the lens flare a spherical look, he applied the Spherize filter once more.

As finishing touches, Jeff cropped the sphere and added an outer glow and some lens flare for stars and suns behind the sphere.

10

You can also control the destiny of pixels that would normally be cast off screen by the displacement effect. Under Undefined Areas, the Wrap Around option will wrap the image so that it appears on the opposite side of the screen. The Repeat Edge Pixels option disperses the extra pixels over the edges of the image; this can sometimes create distinct color bands if the color of the extra pixels is different from the rest of the edge.

5. To keep your image from becoming too distorted, select the Tile and Repeat Edge Pixels options and click OK.

6. An Open dialog box appears, in which you will choose a file to use as a displacement map. Open the Bumpy Leather file from the Textures folder (Goodies | Textures | Bumpy Leather).

In a few moments, your image will be displaced according to the Bumpy Leather texture. For most images, you'll probably see an effect of the image shattering into pieces.

Now that you know how to run the filter, you can begin to analyze how the Displace filter works. Perhaps the most complicated fact about this filter is that its behavior depends on the number of channels in the displacement map. As mentioned in Chapter 2, a channel is somewhat similar to a color plate used by a printer. RGB and Lab color images consist of three channels, a CMYK file has four channels, and a grayscale image has one channel.

In one-channel displacement maps, the Displace filter displaces along the x- and y-axes. Darker values in the displacement map displace pixels downward according to the Vertical Scale value in the dialog box and to the right according to the Horizontal Scale value. White values are displaced upward according to the Vertical Scale value and to the left according to the Horizontal Scale value.

When the displacement map has more than one channel, the filter displaces according to the first two channels only: horizontally according to the first channel and vertically according to the second channel. In the first channel, darker areas cause displacement to the right and lighter areas cause displacement to the left, according to the dialog box values. In the second channel, dark areas displace the image downward and white areas displace upward, according to the dialog box values. Thus, to predict the outcome of the filter, you not only need to think in different dimensions but you must also try to figure out how the color range in the displacement maps will affect the image.

If the Displace filter seems confusing to you, try creating your own simple one-channel displacement map and analyze the results. Follow these steps:

1. Create a new grayscale file and set the width and height to about the same size as the image that you will be applying the filter to.

 TIP: *Choose Select | All, then Edit | Copy, then File | New. The dimensions in the New dialog box will be the same as the document on screen.*

2. Create a radial blend from black to white in the middle of the screen. Save the circle file in Photoshop's native format. This will be your displacement map.

3. Open the image that you want to apply the filter to. Choose Filter | Distort | Displace.

4. In the Displace dialog box, type **0** in the Horizontal Scale field and **50** in the Vertical Scale field. Choose both the Stretch to Fit and Repeat Edge Pixels options. Click OK.

5. When the Open dialog box appears, select the file that contains your radial blend.

After the filter has finished processing, you will see that the image pixels corresponding to the darkest areas of the displacement map area have moved down. Pixels corresponding to the white displacement areas have moved up.

6. Now undo the changes so that you can analyze the horizontal displacement. Select Edit | Undo. Or you can choose Filter | Fade and drag the Opacity slider to view how the image has changed.

7. Select the Displace filter again. This time, type **50** in the Horizontal Scale field and **0** in the Vertical Scale field. Click OK. Use the same displacement map that you used before.

This time, when the filter is applied, the darker areas displace your image to the right; white areas are displaced to the left.

The Displace filter was applied to the car image shown in Figure 10-13(a) using the white-to-black radial blend shown in Figure 10-13(b) as the displacement map. The white area (the foreground color) of the blend was enlarged using the Gradient Editor dialog box. When the filter was applied, 70 was the value for both Horizontal Scale and Vertical Scale in the Displace dialog box. The result is shown in Figure 10-13(c). The car was bent up and slightly to the left

10

(a)   (b)

(c)

FIGURE 10-13   (a) The original car image, (b) the displacement map, and (c) the image after applying the Displace filter

in the areas corresponding to the light areas in the displacement map and was bent down and to the right in areas corresponding to the dark portions of the displacement map.

 TIP: *You can also apply the Displace filter on text to create scratchy type effects. Try using some of the filters in the Textures folder as displacement maps.*

Glass

The Glass filter allows you to distort your image to make it look as though it were seen through glass. The filter creates rippling effects according to a texture. Four preset textures are provided with Photoshop: Blocks, Canvas, Frosted, and Tiny Lens. However, you can use any Photoshop image as a texture. The Distortion slider controls how prominent the appearance of the texture will be. The

Smoothing slider smoothes the texture, Scaling adjusts the size of the texture, and the Invert option reverses the light and dark areas in your image.

If you want to experiment with the Glass filter, try using it with the Bottles file from the Samples folder (found in the Goodies folder). If you apply the filter using the Blocks, Canvas, Frosted, and Tiny Lens options, you'll get a good idea of how versatile the filter can be. The Frosted option can often make a scanned image look as if it were painted on screen.

Ocean Ripple

The Ocean Ripple filter distorts an image to make it look as though it were seen through rippling ocean waves. The Ripple Size and Ripple Magnitude allow you to manipulate the ripple effect. Drag the Ripple Size slider to the right to increase the size of the ripples. Drag the Magnitude slider to the right to increase the distortion.

Pinch

The Pinch filter is used to "squeeze" an image inward or outward. Figure 10-14(a) shows a clock graphic before the Pinch filter was applied; Figure 10-14(b) shows it after applying an outward pinch at –100% (100% results in an inward pinch). Before the Pinch filter was applied, it was selected with the Rectangular Marquee tool. By leaving more space in the marquee selection on the right side of the clock, a slight leftward tilt in the pinch effect was produced.

10

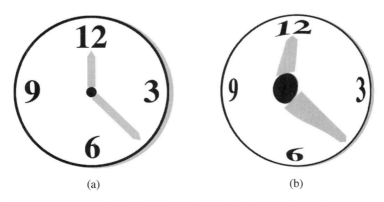

(a)   (b)

FIGURE 10-14   The clock graphic (a) before and (b) after applying the (Outward) Pinch filter

Polar Coordinates

The Polar Coordinates filter converts an image's coordinates from Rectangular to Polar or from Polar to Rectangular.

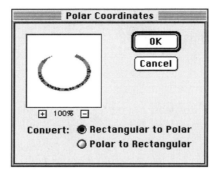

This filter can take a rectangular object and bend it into a circular shape. Figure 10-15(a) shows a pencil graphic before using the Polar Coordinates filter; in Figure 10-15(b) the pencil has been bent by the filter with Rectangular to Polar selected. When the filter was applied, no selection was made on screen. If the pencil had been selected, the filter would have made it look somewhat like a round pie with a wedge cut out of the top.

(a)   (b)

FIGURE 10-15   The pencil graphic (a) before and (b) after applying the Polar Coordinates filter with the Rectangular to Polar Option

When you select the Polar to Rectangular option in the dialog box, the Polar Coordinates filter takes a circular object and stretches it. The following illustration shows the effects of applying this filter with the Polar to Rectangular option to the clock graphic from Figure 10-14(a). The snaking line at the bottom was created because a rectangular selection was made around the clock before the filter was applied.

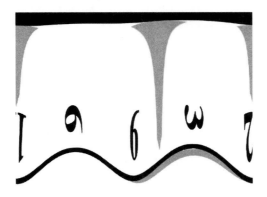

10

Ripple

The Ripple filter transforms an image by displacing its pixels to create a ripple effect. The following illustration shows what happened to the Polar Pencil from Figure 10-15(a) after the Ripple filter was applied. To create this effect, the Ripple Amount was set to 100 and the Ripple Frequency to Large.

Shear

The Shear filter bends an image according to a curve established in the Shear filter's dialog box. The effect can be used to bend and elongate an object.

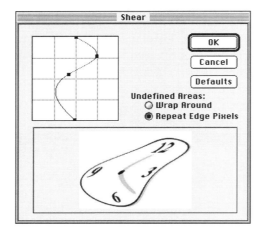

To establish the curve in the Shear dialog box, click and drag on the vertical band in the dialog box grid. Each click produces another control point that can be dragged to create the curve. If you need to reset the curve back to its starting position, press OPTION (Windows users: ALT) and click on the Reset button. When the filter is applied to an object, it will bend along the curve you have established in the dialog box.

 TIP: *If you want to bend a horizontal line, first bend a vertical line by applying the Shear filter to it. Then rotate the bent line so that it is on a horizontal plane.*

Here is the clock graphic shown in Figure 10-14(a), this time with the Shear filter applied:

Spherize

The Spherize filter transforms a selection into a spherical shape. Use it to give text or an object a three-dimensional or bloated effect. In Figure 10-16, the Spherize filter has been applied to the truck from Chapter 4 with a grid background. To

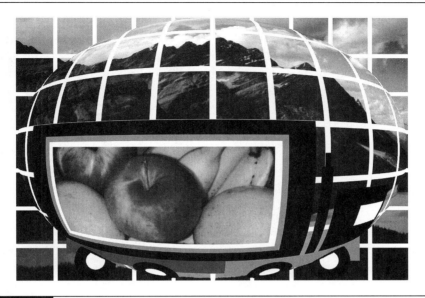

FIGURE 10-16 Truck image from Chapter 4 after applying the Spherize filter

create this effect, the Amount field in the Spherize dialog box was set to 100% and Mode was set to Normal. To view more examples of the Spherize filter in action, see the *Time* magazine (image 9) and *Boston Globe* magazine (image 13) covers in the color insert in this book.

Twirl

The Twirl filter creates swirling pinwheel effects, with the rotation focused toward the center of the object. When you apply it at maximum strength, the Twirl filter makes your image look as if it were whipped in a blender. Here once again is the clock graphic, showing the Twirl filter's effect when set to 150 degrees:

Wave

The Wave filter helps you create many different undulating effects by providing various wavelength options to distort an image. In the filter's dialog box, values can be entered by clicking and dragging on slider controls or by typing numbers into fields.

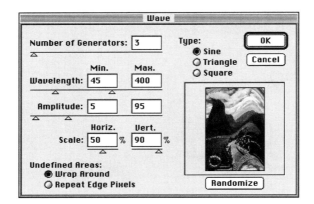

In the Number of Generators field you can control the number of waves generated, from 1 to 999. The more waves you generate, the more distorted the effect, because the peaks and dips of the wavelengths begin to intersect, causing more and more havoc in your image. Creating multiple waves is somewhat analogous to one ocean wave crashing into others: The more waves that crash together, the greater the turbulence.

You can specify the distance between wave crests by entering a minimum and maximum Wavelength value. The height of each wave is controlled by the value specified for the minimum and maximum Amplitude values. Wavelength and Amplitude values can range from 1 to 999.9.

You can select a wave Type of Sine (curved), Triangle, or Square. The Scale percentages determine the degree of the distortions horizontally and vertically; values can range from 0% to 100%.

 CAUTION: *If you wish to replicate your wave results on other images, do not click the Randomize button, because it creates a random starting point for the wave effect.*

When the Wave filter is applied to it, an image can sometimes blend and twist off the screen. The Undefined Areas options allow you to control the destiny of these outcast pixels. If you select Wrap Around, images will wrap to the opposite side of the screen. The Repeat Edge Pixels option disperses the extra pixels over the edge of the image; this can sometimes create distinct color bands if the color of the extra pixels is different from the rest of the edge.

 TIP: *You can also apply the Wave filter to a border selection of an image. When you do this, you convert the straight edges to curved edges.*

Figure 10-17(b) shows the image in Figure 10-17(a) after the Wave filter was applied to create a tidal wave effect.

(a)   (b)

FIGURE 10-17   A dock in New Zealand (a) before and (b) after applying the Wave filter

Zigzag

This filter can be used to create ripples-in-a-pond and twirling effects. The effect is controlled by the values entered in the Amount and Ridges field and whether you choose the Pond Ripples, Out from Center, or Around Center options in the Zigzag dialog box. Figure 10-18 demonstrates how the Zigzag filter's Pond Ripples option can be used to create the illusion of pond ripples out of almost anything. In this case, the ripples were created in the flower image shown in Figure 10-3.

The Stylize Filters

The Stylize filters are used to create the look of impressionist paintings and other painterly effects. Many of these effects are so dramatic that you may hardly recognize your original.

FIGURE 10-18 The flower image (Figure 10-3) after applying the Zigzag filter with the Pond Ripples option

Diffuse

The Diffuse filter creates an unfocused effect that breaks up an image as though it were being seen through frosted glass. The effect is created by shifting pixels at random (Normal option), by replacing light pixels with darker ones (Darken Only option), or by replacing dark pixels with lighter ones (Lighten Only option).

Emboss

The Emboss filter creates a raised effect by outlining the edges in a selection and lowering surrounding color values. This filter is often used for designing raised type or creating a relief effect.

In the Emboss dialog box, the direction of the embossing is controlled by the Angle field. Values can range from –180 to 180 degrees. You can type in the value or click and drag the angle indicator in the circle; dragging clockwise increases the angle, and dragging counterclockwise decreases the angle.

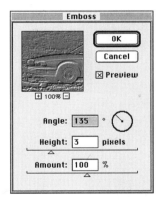

The height of the embossing is controlled by the value in the Height field, which can range from 1 to 10 pixels. To raise or lower the color values in the embossed image, enter a value from 1% to 500% in the Amount field. The lower the percentage, the lower the amount of color; the higher the percentage, the more color is applied to edges.

Figure 10-19 shows the effects of the Emboss filter applied to the car image from Figure 10-13(a). In the Emboss dialog box, the Angle was set to 135°, the Height was set to 10 pixels, and the Amount was set to 200%. Before the filter was

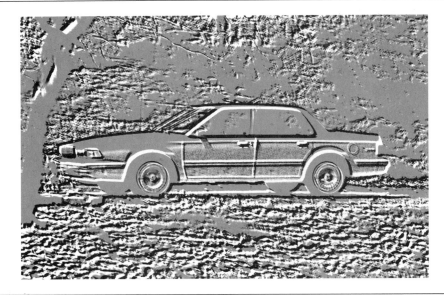

FIGURE 10-19   The car image from Figure 10-13(a) after applying the Emboss filter

applied, the contrast of the image was increased with the Brightness/Contrast command in the Image I Adjust submenu. This emphasized the edges in the image, thereby enhancing the effect of the Emboss filter.

Extrude

The Extrude filter transforms an image into a series of three-dimensional blocks or pyramids, depending on the option set in the dialog box. Use it to distort images or to create unusual 3-D backgrounds. Figure 10-20 shows the effect when the Extrude filter's Pyramids option is applied to a radial blend from a dark color to a lighter one.

In the Extrude filter dialog box, you can set the size of the base of the blocks or pyramids by typing a value from 2 to 255 in the Size field. Enter a value from 1 to 255 in the Depth field to control how far the objects extrude from the screen. Choose the Random radio button if you want the depth of each extruding object to be set to a random value.

FIGURE 10-20   The effects of the Extrude filter applied to a radial blend

10

If you want brighter parts of the image to protrude more than darker parts, select the Level-Based radio button. This option links the pyramid or block depth to color values. If you choose the Solid Front Faces check box, the face of the block is filled with the average color of the object, rather than that of the surrounding image. To ensure that no extruding object extends past the filtered selection, choose the Mask Incomplete Blocks check box.

Find Edges

The Find Edges filter searches for image areas that exhibit major color changes and then enhances transitional pixels. It can make an image look as though it were outlined with a pencil. In Figure 10-21, the Find Edges filter has been applied to the car image of Figure 10-13(a). First, though, the contrast of the image was increased with the Brightness/Contrast command in the Image I Adjust submenu. This enhanced the effect of the filter by adding more edges for the filter to outline.

FIGURE 10-21   The car image after applying the Find Edges filter

Glowing Edges

The Glowing Edges filter accentuates image edges similarly to the effect provided by the Find Edges filter. Unlike Find Edge, Glowing Edges allows you to control edge width (from 1 to 15 pixels), the Edge Brightness, and Smoothness. The filter also fills in dark areas to enhance the glowing effect.

Solarize

The Solarize filter creates the effect of a positive and negative of an image blended together. In photography, you accomplish similar results by adding light during the developing process. See Chapter 13 to learn how to create a solarized effect with the Image | Adjust | Curves command.

Photoshop 5 ▶ In Action

The Centurion character was lightened so that the message would be readable.

The text was embossed using various filters and alpha channels.

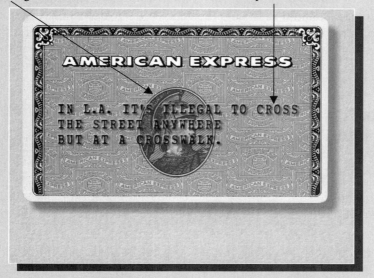

Artist: Russel Cook, Ogilvy and Mather Advertising   **Client: American Express**

Russell Cook, an artist at Ogilvy and Mather Advertising, created the above image as a public service sign for American Express. Variations of the sign have appeared in many airports around the world.

Russell used the Rubber Stamp tool to clean up the scan of an American Express card. Then the type was imported from Adobe Illustrator. Once the type was in Photoshop, an alpha channel was created for it. The alpha channel was duplicated and inverted so that one alpha channel could be used for the highlights and the other for the shadows. Russell then used the Image I Adjust I Threshold command to isolate highlights and shadow areas. The Gaussian Blur and Motion Blur filters were applied to the shadowed text's alpha channel.

Once the card was perfected, it was laid over a textured background, where a shadow was added. When the card was complete, it was imported into QuarkXPress, where the following text was added: "Welcome to Los Angeles. We're here to help."

10

Tiles

The Tiles filter divides an image into tiles according to values specified in the filter's dialog box. Figure 10-22 shows the effect of the Tiles filter when it is applied with the default settings to the flower image of Figure 10-3. In the Number of Tiles field, enter the minimum number of tiles you want to appear in each row and column of tiles. In the Maximum Offset field, enter the maximum distance (as a percentage) that you want the tiles offset from their original positions. If you want the area between the tiles filled with color, choose the Background Color or Foreground Color radio buttons in the Fill Empty Area With section. Choosing the Inverse Image radio button causes a reverse color image of your original image to appear through the tile cracks. Choosing the Unaltered Image radio button makes the tiles appear over the original image.

Trace Contour

The effect of the Trace Contour filter is similar to that of the Find Edges filter, except that Trace Contour draws thinner lines around edges and allows you to

FIGURE 10-22   The flower image after applying the Tiles filter

specify a tonal level for transition areas. In the Trace Contour dialog box, you can enter a value between 0 and 255 in the Level field. Darker pixels correspond to lower numbers; lighter pixels to higher numbers. The Upper and Lower options allow you to choose whether you want contours traced above or below the Level value.

Wind

The Wind filter creates a windblown effect by adding small horizontal lines. The Wind filter dialog box allows you to choose how strong the wind effect is and in what direction you wish the wind to blow. In the Wind dialog box, select the Wind radio button to create a wind effect. To create a stronger wind effect, choose Blast. If you choose the Stagger option, the wind lines will be offset from one another. In the Directions group, choose From the Left or From the Right to set the wind direction. In Figure 10-23, the Wind filter was applied to the car image from Figure 10-13(a), first with the filter's Blast option selected, and then with the Wind option selected. The Direction was set to From the Left, which is the default direction.

10

FIGURE 10-23   The car image after applying the Wind filter

The Painterly Effects Filters

The filters in the Artistic, Brush Strokes, Sketch, and Texture submenus are designed to add painting and sketchlike qualities to your images. Some of the filters can make a scanned photograph look as though it were painted by the hand of a skilled painter.

Most of the filters that provide painterly effects are quite easy to use. The dialog commands are self-explanatory, and the previews provide an excellent rendition of what the final image will look like. The Artistic filters include Colored Pencil, Cutout, Dry Brush, Film Grain, Fresco, Neon Glow, Paint Daubs, Palette Knife, Plastic Wrap, Poster Edges, Rough Pastels, Smudge Stick, Sponge, Underpainting, and Watercolor.

The Artistic filters allow you to give your photographs painterly effects. Figure 10-24 shows the effect of applying the Cutout filter. Another interesting filter in the Artistic group is the Underpainting filter, which provides a variety of options for changing the texture and lighting in an image. By using Underpainting, you

(a)   (b)

FIGURE 10-24   (a) Before and (b) after applying the Cutout filter

can create 3-D textures, giving an image a Brick, Burlap, Sandstone, or Canvas texture. You can even load a Photoshop image and use it as the basis of a texture.

The Brush group filters allow you to control the digital brush strokes in an image. The brush filters include Accented Edges, Angled Strokes, Crosshatch, Dark Strokes, Ink Outlines, Spatter, Sprayed Strokes, and Sumi-e. Spatter makes your image look as if it were created with spattered paint. Crosshatch not only creates brush strokes but also blurred lighting effects. Sumi-e can make your image look as if it were created from broad charcoal brush strokes, as seen in Figure 10-25.

In general, the Sketch filters attempt to make your images look as though they were sketched by hand. They include Bas Relief, Chalk & Charcoal, Charcoal, Chrome, Conté Crayon, Graphic Pen, Halftone Pattern, Note Paper, Photocopy, Plaster, Reticulation, Stamp, Torn Edges, and Water Paper. Most filters, such as Chalk & Charcoal, Charcoal, and Graphic Pen, come close to a hand-sketched look. Figure 10-26 shows the effects of applying the Graphic Pen filter.

Some Sketch filters provide unusual effects. For instance, Chrome can make your image look like a silvery mess. Reticulation can make your image look as though it were created from tiny pieces of colored sand or tiny insects.

10

FIGURE 10-25   Image after applying the Sum-e filter

FIGURE 10-26 Venice image after applying the Graphic Pen filter

Perhaps the most startling of the Painterly filters are in the Texture group. The Texture filters include Craquelure, Grain, Mosaic Tiles, Patchwork, Stained Glass, and Texturizer. One of the most startling is Craquelure, which makes your image look as it if contained small, three-dimensional cracks—almost like a textured tile with cracks in it. If you want lots of cracks, decrease the crack spacing in the Craquelure dialog box.

FIGURE 10-27   Image after applying the Mosaic Tiles filter

10

 NOTE: *To see how the Craquelure filter can be used to add texture to a 3-D figure created in Fractal Poser, see Chapter 17.*

The Grain filter's Sprinkles option can make your image look as though it were created from colored sprinkles from an ice cream parlor. The Stained Glass filter makes the image look like stained glass. Patchwork creates a patchwork quilt type of effect (which resembles a soft mosaic). The Mosaic Tiles filter, illustrated in Figure 10-27, provides a 3-D tile effect more interesting than the tiles produced in the Pixelate/Mosaic filter.

Video Filters

Photoshop's Video filters were designed for images that will be input from video or output to videotape.

NTSC COLORS   These filters reduce the color gamut of the image to acceptable levels for television.

 TIP: *Photoshop users who will be outputting to video should consider using RGB Color spaces designed for video such as SMPTE-C and PAL/SECAM. For more information about changing RGB color space settings, see Chapter 1.*

DEINTERLACE   This filter smoothes video images by removing odd or even interlaced lines. This filter is needed when a video frame is captured between an odd and even field and a blurred scan line becomes visible. The filter's dialog box gives you a choice of substituting the line by duplication or interpolation.

The Other Filters

The filters in this menu are a diverse group that don't fit into any other major category. Perhaps the most interesting is the Custom filter choice, which allows you to create your own filter.

Custom

If you would like to try your hand at creating your own filter, select Custom from the Other submenu. You won't be able to create filters as sophisticated as Photoshop's filters, but you can design your own sharpening, blurring, and embossing effects.

In the Custom dialog box, you can control the brightness values for all pixels that will be filtered. Each pixel evaluated is represented by the text field that is in the center of the matrix of text fields in the dialog box. The value entered in this box is the number by which Photoshop multiplies the current pixel's brightness. You can enter between –999 and 999.

By typing numbers in the surrounding text fields, you can control the brightness of adjacent pixels in relation to the pixel represented in the center box. Photoshop multiplies the brightness value of adjacent pixels by this number. In other words, with the Custom dialog box's default settings, the brightness value of the pixel to the left of the central pixel will be multiplied by –1.

In the Scale field, you can enter a value that will be used to divide the sum of the brightness values. In the Offset field, you can enter a value that you want to have added to the Scale's calculation results.

When the filter is applied, Photoshop recalculates the brightness of each pixel in the image or selected area, summing up the multiplied values used in the dialog box matrix. It then divides this result by the Scale value and adds the Offset value, if there is one.

- To create a sharpening filter, you'll need to increase the contrast between neighboring pixels. If you balance a set of negative numbers around the central matrix pixel, you will sharpen your image.

- To create a blur filter, surround the central matrix pixel with positive numbers. The positive numbers reduce the contrast between pixels as the matrix formula passes over the images.

- To create an embossing filter, balance positive and negative values around the central matrix area.

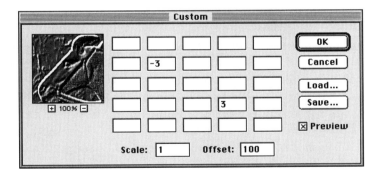

Figure 10-28 shows an image before and after increasing contrast and applying a custom emboss filter.

Try your hand at creating a filter or two, using the foregoing suggestions and examples as a guide. You can save and reload your custom filters by using the Save and Load buttons in the Custom dialog box.

(a)   (b)

FIGURE 10-28 Image (a) before and (b) after applying a custom emboss filter

High Pass

The High Pass filter suppresses areas that contain gradual increases in brightness and preserves portions of the image that exhibit the sharpest transitions in color. When you apply this filter, it removes shading and accentuates highlights. In the High Pass filter dialog box, you can control the size of the transition edge by typing a pixel value from 0.1 to 250 in the Radius field. A large value leaves more of the image's pixels near transitional points. A lower value preserves only the edges of the transition areas. When the filter is applied, it analyzes each pixel from the starting pixel to a specified Radius distance.

HSL&HSB

This filter can be found in the Optional Plug-ins folder (in the Other Goodies folder) on the Macintosh version of the Adobe Photoshop CD-ROM. The HSL&HSB filter is included in order to allow users of previous versions of Photoshop to work in the HSL (Hue/Saturation/Lightness) and HSB

(Hue/Saturation/Brightness) modes. (In Photoshop 2.5, HSL and HSB were removed from the Modes menu and Lab color was added. These changes were made before a Windows version of Photoshop was released. Thus, there is no HLS&HSB filter on the Windows CD ROM version of Photoshop.)

When the HSL&HSB filter is applied, a dialog box appears, allowing conversion from RGB to HSL or to HSB. You can also return from HSL or HSB to RGB. When this filter is applied, the RGB components of an image are converted to HSL and HSB components and vice versa.

When you convert an RGB file to either HSB or HSL, RGB's red channel becomes the hue channel, the green channel becomes the saturation channel, and the blue channel becomes the brightness or lightness channel. Once the filter is applied, you can make changes to each separate channel and then use the filter to convert the image back to RGB.

 NOTE: *See Chapter 12 for information about viewing images in separate channels; see Chapter 14 for information about editing images in channels.*

Maximum

The Maximum filter expands light areas and diminishes dark areas. When the Maximum filter is applied, the current pixel's brightness value is replaced by the maximum brightness of surrounding pixels. The distance of the surrounding pixels can be specified by entering a value from 1 to 10 in the Radius field.

The filter can be used in an alpha channel to increase the light area in the channel. (Alpha channels can be used for masking out parts of an image so that they can be edited in isolation, as discussed in Chapter 14.)

Minimum

This filter is the opposite of the Maximum filter: It expands dark areas and diminishes light areas. The Minimum filter can be used in an alpha channel to increase the dark areas. When the Minimum filter is applied, the current pixel's brightness value is replaced with the minimum brightness values of surrounding pixels. The distance of the surrounding pixels can be specified by entering a value from 1 to 10 in the Radius field.

10

Offset

The Offset filter moves the filtered image according to values entered in the Offset dialog box. In past versions of Photoshop, this filter was often used to create shadowed effects. In version 5.0, you can accomplish very much the same result by choosing the Edit | Numeric Transform command, and you can use the Layer | Effects | Drop Shadow command to create drop shadows.

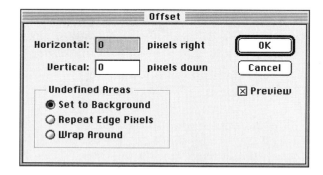

In the Offset filter dialog box, specify whether you wish the image to move horizontally and/or vertically. In the Vertical and Horizontal fields, you can enter values between –30,000 and 30,000. Positive values offset right and up; negative values offset left and down. If you wish to have the background of the image filled with the current background color, select the Set to Background radio button.

The Offset filter also includes options for handling pixels that would be offset out of the screen area. The Wrap Around option wraps these pixels so that they appear on the opposite side of the screen. The Repeat Edge Pixels option disperses the extra pixels along the edges of the image.

Using Filter Factory

If you'd like to try your hand at creating filters that are quite a bit more fancy than those allowed by Photoshop's Custom filter, you should investigate Filter Factory, which is included in the Optional Plug-ins folder (in the Other Goodies folder on the Adobe Photoshop Application CD-ROM). When you create a filter with Filter Factory, a plug-in filter is produced that contains an image preview and slider controls, if desired. When the plug-in is moved into Photoshop's Plug-ins folder, Photoshop treats it as it does plug-ins created by third-party software companies.

The plug-in appears in the Filter menu, and its name and copyright information appear in the About Plug-ins dialog box.

Included in this section are step-by-step instructions for creating a simple filter with Filter Factory. If you'd like to delve deeper into creating filters, print out the instructions that accompany Filter Factory from the Adobe Photoshop Application CD-ROM. Although you don't have to be a computer programmer to create filters with Filter Factory, the instructions will probably be easier to understand if you've had some programming experience or have written formulas with applications such as Microsoft Excel or Lotus 1-2-3.

In order to use Filter Factory, copy the Filter Factory plug-in into your Plug-ins folder. In order to load Filter Factory, you must restart Photoshop. Once you reload Photoshop, open any RGB color image on screen.

To use Filter Factory, first click on the Filter menu. In the menu you'll see a new menu choice called Synthetic. Choose Synthetic | Filter Factory. The Filter Factory dialog box then opens.

In the dialog box, you'll see a preview box, sliders, and an area for creating an expression, or formula, for the Red, Green, and Blue channels of your image. As you can probably guess, this means that Filter Factory only affects RGB color images. The formula that you enter into the R text field changes color values for pixels in the Red channel; Green and Blue channels are changed by expressions entered in the G and B text fields.

Before you create a filter in Filter Factory, you should have some idea about what you want your filter to do. Then, you need to figure out the expression that must be typed into the R, G, and B fields to achieve the desired effect. When you write your expression, you must remember that all R, G, and B pixels can have a value from 0 to 255. Dark pixels have lower pixel values; light pixels have higher pixel values.

If you start delving into Filter Factory, you'll learn that Filter Factory also addresses pixels in terms of a two-dimensional grid system. For instance, the second pixel in the fifth row of your image in the channel would be addressed as (2,5). Filter Factory also has its own set of functions that can return the values of slider controls, return the color value of any pixel on screen, and generate random values. The example in this section's illustration can add a solarized and/or negative look to your image. It was chosen to demonstrate how easy it is to create a simple filter and to show you how to integrate slider controls into a filter.

The filter you are going to create will subtract the value that the user sets with three sliders from the color values in each Red, Green, and Blue channel.

10

Type the following in the R field: **ctl(0)-r**. The purpose of the ctl function is to return to Filter Factory the number generated by clicking and dragging on a slider. The 0 in the ctl function represents the first slider in the dialog box. Thus, the expression in the R field tells Filter Factory to subtract the slider value from the color value in the Red channel. Note that all expressions must be typed in lowercase. Also, if you make a mistake, a yellow Alert sign appears below the field label. To find the error in the expression, click on the yellow Alert sign. (Ignore the yellow Alert until you are done typing.)

In the G channel, type **ctl(1)-g**. In the B field, type **ctl(2)-b**.

At this point you can try out your filter by dragging the first three sliders in the Filter Factory dialog box as shown here:

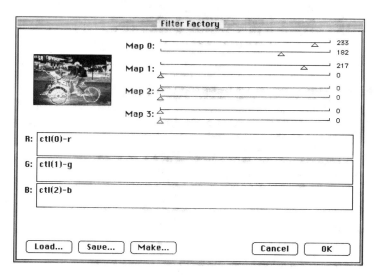

If you're happy with the results, you can save the text expression in the R, G, and B fields by clicking on the Save button. The expression can later be reloaded into Photoshop using the Filter Factory Load button, or it can be loaded into a word processing program as a text file.

To save your filter as a plug-in, click the Make button. In the Make dialog box, text entered into the Category field will appear in Photoshop's Filter menu as a choice alongside Blur, Sharpen, Pixelate, and so on. Text entered into the Name field appears as a choice when the Category word in the Filter menu is selected. If you name several filters using the same Category name, the names will appear as choices in your category's submenu.

Photoshop 5 In Action

After one of the TVs was copied and pasted several times at different opacities and offset, the Motion Blur filter was applied to give the appearance of motion.

The linear blend in the background was created using the Gradient tool. After the blend was created, the Add Noise filter was applied to reduce the chance of banding when the image was printed.

The shadow was created by applying the Gaussian Blur filter to the alpha channel with the selection in the alpha channel was loaded, it was darkened using the Image/Adjust/Levels command.

Designer: John Brown   Electronic Retouching: Jaime Ordoñez   Client: HBO TV

This image was created as a promotion for HBO. The concept began with a sketch created by designer John Brown. Then Jaime Ordoñez recreated the image in Photoshop. Jaime started by creating the background from a blue-to-white linear blend using the Gradient tool. After he created the blend, he applied the Add Noise filter to reduce the chance of banding when the image was printed.

Photographer Craig Blankenhorn shot various images of model Tony Melovia with the TVs so that Jaime could select the best shots and paste them into the final image. After the photographs were digitized, Jaime silhouetted Tony and the televisions, using selection tools and the Pen tool. He copied Tony's head from one image, his stomach, hands, legs, and shoes from other images. The shadow was created by selecting Tony with the TV. Jaime then offset the selection of Tony and the TVs in an alpha channel. Next, he applied the Edit | Transform | Skew and Perspective commands to the alpha channel. Jaime blurred the alpha channel using the Gaussian Blur filter, then loaded the blurred selection and darkened the selection using the Image | Adjust | Levels command. (For more information about using alpha channels, see Chapter 14.)

The HBO logo in the TVs was first created in Illustrator, then placed into an alpha channel in Photoshop. After the alpha channel was loaded as a selection, it was feathered and then colorized with the Image | Adjust | Color Balance command. This created the glow around the logo. The selection in the alpha channel was loaded again and filled with black to create the logo. To give the appearance of motion to the falling TV, one of the TVs was copied, then pasted several times at different opacities and offset. Afterward, the Motion Blur filter was applied.

10

Enter the data for the text fields, as shown next. Type the appropriate information into the Copyright and Author fields.

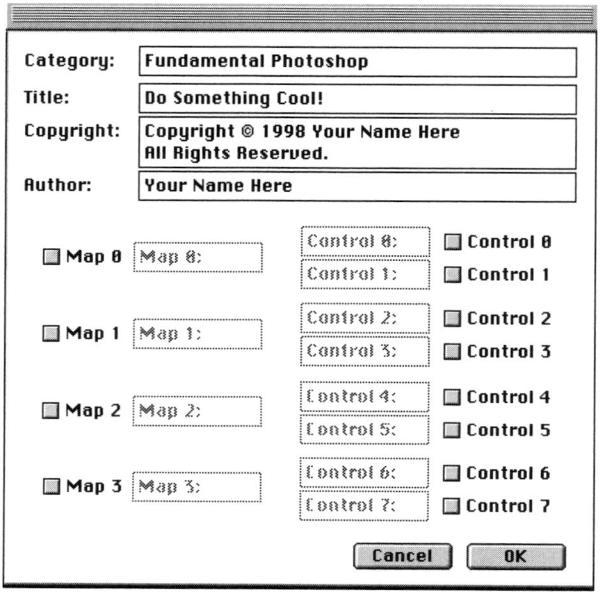

Category:	Fundamental Photoshop
Title:	Do Something Cool!
Copyright:	Copyright © 1998 Your Name Here All Rights Reserved.
Author:	Your Name Here

☐ Map 0 Map 0:
☐ Map 1 Map 1:
☐ Map 2 Map 2:
☐ Map 3 Map 3:

Control 0: ☐ Control 0
Control 1: ☐ Control 1
Control 2: ☐ Control 2
Control 3: ☐ Control 3
Control 4: ☐ Control 4
Control 5: ☐ Control 5
Control 6: ☐ Control 6
Control 7: ☐ Control 7

[Cancel] [OK]

After you've entered data in the text fields, name your sliders. Click on the check boxes adjacent to Control 0, Control 1, and Control 2. Clicking on the check boxes generates three sliders in your filter. Text entered into the Control text boxes will appear adjacent to the sliders. Type Red, Green, and Blue into the appropriate fields. You do not need to change the Map check boxes. These can be used if you wish to set up your sliders in groups of two. To save your filter plug-in, click OK. In the dialog box that appears, set the target directory so that you save your filter into the Plug-ins folder or the Filter folder.

Before you try out your filter, you must restart Photoshop. After Photoshop reloads, run your filter by first clicking on the Filter menu. In the Filter menu, you should see the Fundamental Photoshop submenu. Click on Fundamental Photoshop, and the Do Something Cool filter choice will appear.

Fundamental Photoshop ▶ **Do Something Cool...**

Select Do Something Cool to open the Filter dialog box. In it, you will see a preview box with three sliders labeled Red, Blue, and Green. Now test the filter. If you find that the slider controls are somewhat sticky, just click on the slider bar rather than trying to drag the slider triangles.

As you can see, it's not too difficult to create a custom filter with Filter Factory. If you'd like to try creating another custom filter, here's a more sophisticated expression primarily designed to give you an idea of how different Filter Factory functions work. The expression averages each pixel with the pixel two columns to its left and two columns to its right. It then adds a random value based on the slider settings to the average of the three pixels. The result is a noise filter in which color values can be controlled by sliders.

If you'd like to create the filter, enter the following expressions into the R, G, and B text fields in the Filter Factory dialog box:

In the R text box: **src(x-2,y,0)+src(x,y,0)+src(x+2,y,0)/3+rnd(-ctl(0),ctl(0))**

In the G text box: **src(x-2,y,1)+src(x,y,1)+src(x+2,y,1)/3+rnd(-ctl(0),ctl(0))**

In the B text box: **src(x-2,y,2)+src(x,y,2)+src(x+2,y,2)/3+rnd(-ctl(0),ctl(0))**

Here's a brief explanation of the expressions. The src function returns pixel values from separate channels according to specified coordinates. For instance, src(5,6,0) returns the value of the fifth pixel in the sixth row of the Red channel. Channel 0 is red, Channel 1 is the Green channel, and Channel 2 is the Blue channel. The code rnd(-ctl(0),ctl(0)) instructs Filter Factory to generate a random number between plus or minus the value returned by the first slider in the dialog box. Thus, if the slider were set to 150, random numbers could be between –150 and 150, inclusive.

For a complete list of Filter Factory functions and more details about how to use them, see the documentation provided on the Adobe Photoshop CD-ROM. Who knows? With Filter Factory, you may be the next Kai Krause.

10

Conclusion

In exercises in later chapters of *Fundamental Photoshop*, you will often need to apply filters, particularly sharpening and blurring filters. As you work, remember not to overdo the effects of filters. Often, the subtlest changes are the best. If you are fascinated with the powerful effects of filters, proceed to Chapter 11 to learn how third-party filters can add more dazzling effects to your Photoshop images.

CHAPTER 11

Filters from Third-Party Manufacturers

In Chapter 10, you explored the tremendous power and versatility of Photoshop's plug-in filters. Yet some Photoshop users just never seem to get enough of a good thing. If you're looking for some Photoshop stocking stuffers to help you quickly create special effects, you'll be happy to know that Photoshop's open architecture has spawned an entire industry of third-party filter manufacturers. Some filters, such as Kai's Power Tools, invite you to explore a world of endless digital textures and effects; others, such as Alien Skin Eye Candy, save you hours of time by creating shadows, bevels, and glows. You won't even need to open the Channels or Layers palette.

This chapter covers just a few of the third-party filters currently on the market. Many third-party filters are priced at about $100 and are well worth the cost if they can save you time. In order to use a third-party filter, you must install it in Photoshop's Filter folder. When you load Photoshop, most third-party filters appear at the bottom of the Filter menu (below Photoshop's Other Filter submenu).

 REMEMBER: *As you work with third-party filters, you may also want to use layers, blending modes, adjustment layers, and layer masks to add to the filters' effects.*

 NOTE: *For information about stand-alone software that allows you to morph or create interesting 3-D objects, turn to Chapter 17.*

MetaCreations' Kai's Power Tools

MetaCreations Kai's Power Tools is undoubtedly the most popular and well-known third-party filter. It allows you to create an endless variety of textures and other effects such as page curls, twirls, kaleidoscope effects, 3-D spheres, parquet and perspective tiling, and animate textures. When some Photoshop users look at the choices provided by KPT, they are overwhelmed; others, however, feel like little kids in a candy shop—there's so much to choose from that they want to try out everything.

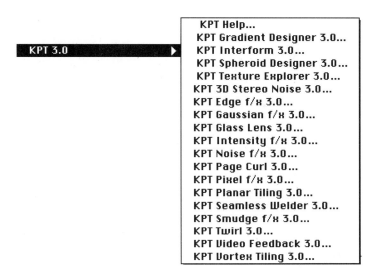

To begin creating a texture from a blank Photoshop file, you may want to use the KPT Texture Explorer filter, because it has the most available options.

When you choose the KPT Texture Explorer filter, the KPT Explorer dialog box, shown in Figure 11-1, appears. There you can start by picking a preset texture from the Presets pop-up menu in the lower-left corner of the dialog box. The texture you create appears in the large rectangle surrounded by smaller rectangles in the right half of the dialog box. If you wish, you can click on one of the smaller rectangles to alter the effects of the texture in the center rectangle (the one you're creating). You can also click on the 3-D balls on the left side of the dialog box to produce variations of your texture. In order to fine-tune your texture, you may want to adjust the direction, opacity, glue (similar to Photoshop's blending modes), hue, saturation, brightness, contrast, blur, squeeze, or cycle of a texture.

Another filter, which allows you to easily create a texture from scratch, is the KPT Gradient Designer. Not only can you use this filter to create a texture from a blank Photoshop file, but you can also use it to add depth to a texture created with the KPT Texture Explorer filter. Figure 11-2 shows the Gradient Designer dialog box, which we used to apply a translucent gradient to a texture created with KPT Texture Explorer.

After you begin creating a texture, you can proceed to use more KPT filters to alter your texture. For example, in Figure 11-3 we used the KPT Texture Explorer filter and the KPT Gradient Designer filter to create a texture. Next, we used the KPT Glass Lens filter to add 3-D spheres; first, we created an elliptical selection, and then we applied the filter until the desired 3-D effect had been achieved.

11

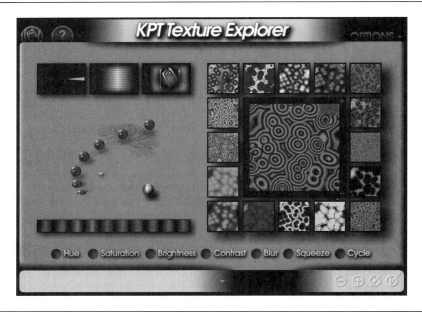

FIGURE 11-1 The KPT Texture Explorer dialog box allows you to create an endless number of textures

FIGURE 11-2 The KPT Gradient Designer dialog box allows you to create an unlimited variety of gradients

FIGURE 11-3   A texture created with the KPT Texture Explorer, KPT Gradient Designer, and KPT Glass Lens filters

11

Some of the other enticing KPT filters include the KPT Vortex Tiling filter, which allows you to either apply a normal vortex or a pinch vortex; the KPT Video Feedback filter, with which you can apply either a video feedback or a telescope feedback effect; the KPT Twirl filter, which allows you to apply either a twirl or a kaleidoscope effect; and the KPT Planar Tiling filter, with which you can apply either a parquet tiling or a perspective tiling effect. Figure 11-4 shows the dialog boxes for these filters and some of the effects created in them.

   NOTE: *KPT was used to create the background textures in image 25 of the color insert.*

   NOTE: *To learn more about Kai's Power Tools, check out MetaCreations Web site at www.metacreations.com.*

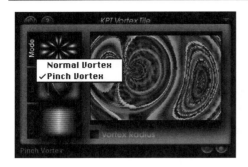

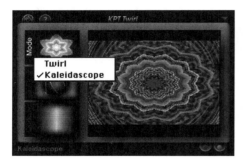

FIGURE 11-4   Four of the many KPT filters and their dialog boxes

Using Vertigo Dizzy to Create 3D Effects

If you want to be able to manipulate, light, and render 3-D models in Photoshop, Vertigo Dizzy maybe what you're looking for. Vertigo is a software company primarily involved in 3-D graphics for the Silicon Graphics platform. Their Dizzy plug-in allows you import 3-D models created in 3DMF file format into Photoshop.

 NOTE: *3DMF is a file format created by Apple computer as a cross-platform file format. Many newer Mac and cross-platform 3-D programs, such as those created by Meta Creations and Strata, support it.*

Using Vertigo Dizzy, you can import a 3-D model, manipulate it in Photoshop, change lighting, and render it. If you don't have access to 3-D programs, you can use Vertigo's free library of over 300 3-D models. (3-D models can also be purchased and downloaded from the Web.)

After you load a 3-D model you can add lights to the screen by clicking and dragging. You can use tools to manipulate your model in 3-D space, twisting or turning it. As you work you can choose to have your image rendered in dot view, wireframe, or shaded mode.

 NOTE: *To find out more about Vertigo, see Vertigo's Web site: www.vertigo3d.com.*

Xaos Tools' Filters

Xaos Tools publishes three extremely versatile filters: Paint Alchemy, Terrazzo, and TypeCaster. Paint Alchemy allows you to add numerous painterly effects to enhance textures or digitized images, as shown in Figure 11-5. Figure 11-5(a) shows a digitized image before applying the Paint Alchemy filter, and Figure 11-5(b) shows the final image after applying the filter. Figure 11-5(c) shows the Paint Alchemy dialog box settings used to create the image in Figure 11-5(b). The dialog box controls allow you to change the angle, size, and transparency of brush strokes. You can make the transparency of your brush strokes vary from 10 to 85 percent, depending upon image saturation. The program also allows you to alter the effects of filters by creating brushes from digital files.

Xaos Tool's Terrazzo filter allows you to create kaleidoscope patterns or tiles from digitized images of textures. You can create a selection and then apply the filter, or you can apply the filter with no selection having been created. When the dialog box appears, as seen in Figure 11-6, you can create a kaleidoscope pattern by moving or resizing the wireframe triangle over the image. After creating a kaleidoscope, you can directly apply it to the Photoshop image or texture, or you can choose to save the kaleidoscope as a tile to your hard disk. This tile can then later be applied to any Photoshop image or selection by using the Edit | Define Pattern command. See Chapter 7 for more information about using the Define Pattern command.

If you need to create 3-D effects, Xaos Tools' newest filter, TypeCaster, may be just what you are looking for. When you choose the TypeCaster filter, a dialog box (shown in Figure 11-7) appears, allowing you to control the 3-D effect. First, you pick a font from the Font pop-up menu; then you type your text in the Text field. Next, you customize your 3-D effect with the tools along the left side of the preview window with the Face, Bevel, Extrude, and Lights windows.

11

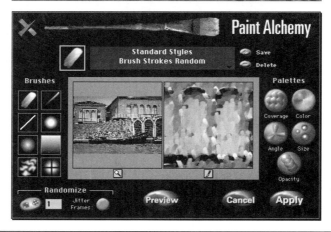

FIGURE 11-5 Digitized image (a) before and (b) after applying the Paint Alchemy filter; (c) the Paint Alchemy dialog box settings used to create the effect shown in Figure 11-5(b)

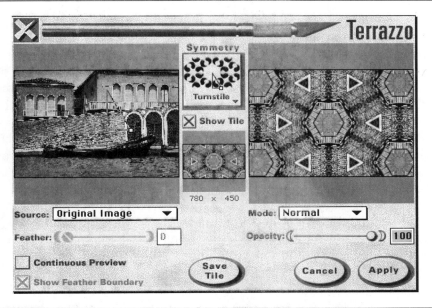

FIGURE 11-6 The Terrazzo filter dialog box allows you to create kaleidoscope patterns or tiles

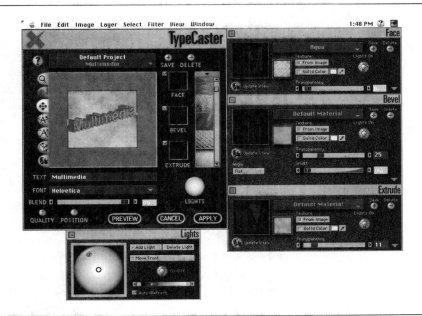

FIGURE 11-7 The TypeCaster filter dialog box allows you to create 3-D effects

NOTE: *Visit Xaos' Web site at: www.xaostools.com.*

Alien Skin Eye Candy

Alien Skin's Eye Candy filters allow you to quickly create numerous eye-catching effects that would normally involve time-consuming manipulation of channels, selections, and layers. We've found several of Alien Skin's filters helpful when we needed to add various effects to our multimedia productions. (One of these screens appears on our Web site: www2.infohouse.com/~addesign.) All the filters provide previews and sliders that allow you to easily fine-tune your results.

The latest version of the product includes 20 special effects filters. You can use them to create many effects, including carved images, chrome, cutouts, drop shadows, fire, fur, glass, glow, noise, inner bevels, motion trails, outer bevels, smoke, stars, swirls, water drops, and weaves. Figure 11-8 shows some of the filter's dialog boxes. Notice that each one allows you to customize the effect by moving sliders. Note that you can save your settings so that they can be stored for future use. Additionally, each filter provides a preview in which you can zoom in and out.

 NOTE: *Visit Alien Skin on the Web at www.alienskin.com.*

DataStream Imaging Systems' WildRiverSSK

WildRiverSSK is a new arrival on the plug-in scene. This suite of seven sophisticated special effects filters includes Chameleon, a color manipulation tool; MagicCurtain, to create textures and billowing drape effects; TileMaker, for creating posterized and mosaic-like effects; Magic Frame, for creating borders and multicolor frames; and TV snow for creating static and rainlike effects. All of these filters create attractive and unusual effects, but Photoshop users will probably find themselves using the DekoBoko and MagicMask filters most often.

DekoBoko (Japanese for "concave" and "convex") allows you to bevel buttons, text, and images instantly, as seen in Figure 11-9. It not only creates the beveled edge, it also allows you to choose how much of a bevel you want, the color, and how the color is applied.

The centerpiece of WildRiverSSK is MagicMask, shown in Figure 11-10. With this filter you can create satin, woodblock, quilting, drop shadow, metallic, and even license plate-like effects. Using this elaborate filter, you can combine effects

The Photoshop Portfolio

Artist: Robert Bowen and Ryszard Horowitz
Client: Horowitz+Bowen Studio

© Ryszard Horowitz and Robert Bowen 1994

1 This fantastic image was created as an experiment to explore digital design possibilities. The idea for the image came from the collaborative efforts of both Ryszard and Bob, who carefully plan and execute each image they create so it cohesively reflects a uniform idea. Before starting in Photoshop, several pencil sketches were first created by Ryszard and Bob.

The image is composed of various digitized images from photographs taken by both artists. The fish, mountains, moon, and baby were all photographed separately. The eagle is a digitized image of a live eagle taken in a studio. The splash is an image taken of water being pumped into an aquarium. A photograph of a Plexiglas tray pouring water is the basis of the cuboidal block pouring water into the lake.

To create the final image, Bob worked in Photoshop on a Silicon Graphics Indy and an Apple Macintosh computer. He used Alias' Power Maker on the Indy to map the mountains and the lake to the cuboidal block. With Ryszard's collaboration, Bob created several low-res versions until they decided on the final image. Next, Bob enlarged the low-res image. He carefully used the Info palette with the Line tool as a measurement instrument to measure angles and distances in the low-res image so he could replicate them in the high-res version.

When creating the image, Bob used the Pen tool to outline the eagle. To blend images together, Bob often used the Border command to place a selection border around an image. Then he would blend the selection into its surroundings with the Gaussian Blur filter and Photoshop's Lighten or Darken modes.

Refer to Appendix D for detailed descriptions of how the rest of these images were created.

2

2
Artist: Ryszard Horowitz-R/GA Print
Client: R/GA Print
(promotional materials)

3
Artist: J.W. Burkey
Personal Experience

4
Artist: Larry Hamill
Stock Image

3

4

5

6

7

5
Artist: Kenneth Gore
Self promotion

6
Artist: Nik Kleinberg
Photographer: George B. Fry III
Client: Sports Illustrated for Kids

7
Artist: Christopher Evans
Client: Pathways Productions

The Photoshop Portfolio

The Photoshop Portfolio

8

Artist: John Stephens
Client: Electronic Photo-Imaging

9

Artist: Christopher Ching
Client: MacHome Journal

10

Artist: Marcos Sorensen
Client: Juice Magazine

11

12

13

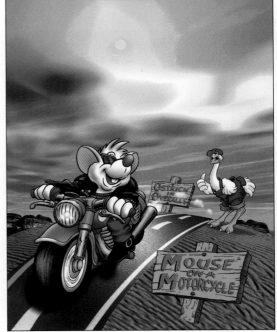

11
Artist: John Ennis
Client: Harper Collins

12
Artist: Rico Lins and Mauricio Nacif
Client: Washington Post Magazine

13
Artist: Peter Jivkov
Client: Waldman Publishing

The Photoshop Portfolio

14

 The Photoshop Portfolio

14
Artist: Sanjay Kothari
Client: Houghton Mifflin Co.

15
Artist: Sanjay Kothari
Client: Adobe Systems Incorporated

15

The Photoshop Portfolio

16

Artist: Adam Cohen
Client: Community Development
Block Grant Association

17

Photographer: Howard Berman
Digital Imaging: R/GA Print
Client: Computer Associates

18

Artist: Eric Kunzendorf
Portfolio Piece

17

18

19
Artist: John Stephens
Client: Electronic Photo-Imaging

20
Artist: John Ennis
Client: Dorchester Publishing

21
Artist: John Ennis
Client: Dorchester Publishing

21

20

22

Artist: Henk Dawson
Client: Motorola

23

Artists: Page Wood, Myra Wood for Imagic, Inc.
Massey Rafani, Joel Wayne-Creative Directors
Massey Rafani, Jon Sparrman, Mykal Aubry-Art Directors
Herb Ritts, Michael Smith-Photographers
The Idea Place-Agency
Client: Warner Bros. Pictures

24

Artist: Henk Dawson
Client: Graphic Artists Guild

The Photoshop Portfolio

The Photoshop Portfolio

25

Artist: Adele Droblas Greenberg
Client: AD. Design & Consulting

26

Artist: Pamela Hobbs
Client: PC Magazine

27

Artist: Wendy Grossman
Stock Image

28

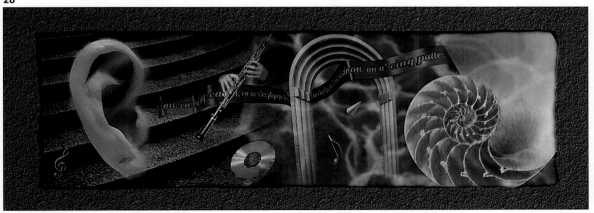

28
Artist: J.W. Burkey
Client: Image Bank (Stock Image)

29
Artist: Larry Hamill
Self Promotion

30
Artist: Adam Cohen
Client: PC Computing Magazine

30

29

31

32

The Photoshop Portfolio

33

34

35

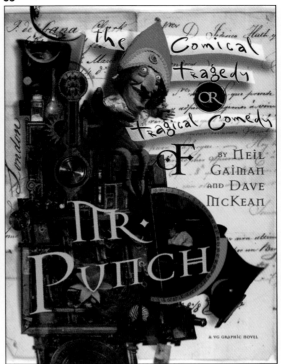

© 1994 Neil Gaiman and Dave McKean

36

 The Photoshop Portfolio

34

Artist: John Craig
Client: Stanford University

35

Artist: Dave McKean
Client: Victor Gollancz

36

Artist: John Craig
Client: Informix Corp.

37

The Photoshop Portfolio

37

Artist: Marcio Pereira
Client: The Saint Nightclub

38

Artist: James Dowlen
Client: Vanstar Corp.

39

Artist: James Dowlen
Client: Vanstar Corp.

39

38

40

41

42

43

40

Image before retouching
and color-correcting
Photograph courtesy of Gene Ahrens

41

Image after retouching
and color-correcting
Artist: Adele Droblas Greenberg
Client: Reader's Digest General Books

42

Image before retouching
Photograph courtesy of Library of Congress

43

Image after retouching
Artist: Adele Droblas Greenberg
Client: Reader's Digest General Books

The Photoshop Portfolio

FIG 5-2

The primary (additive) colors and their components. When all three primary colors are mixed together, they create white.

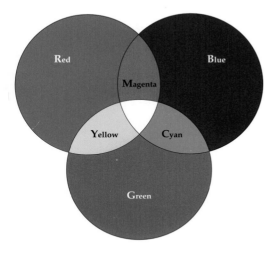

FIG 5-3

The secondary (subtractive) colors and their complements. When all three secondary colors are mixed together, they create a muddy brown.

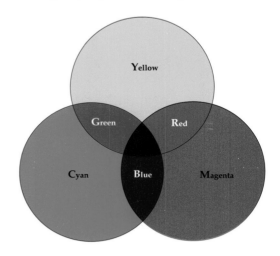

FIG 5-4

Each color in the color wheel is opposite its complement and between the two colors that create it.

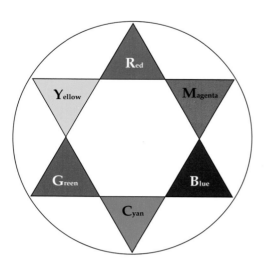

FIG 5-8

The Hue, Saturation, and Brightness color model. (Courtesy of Agfa Corporation)

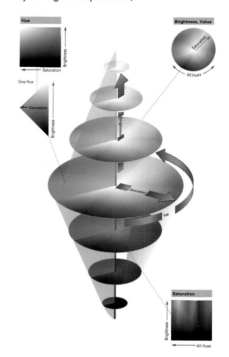

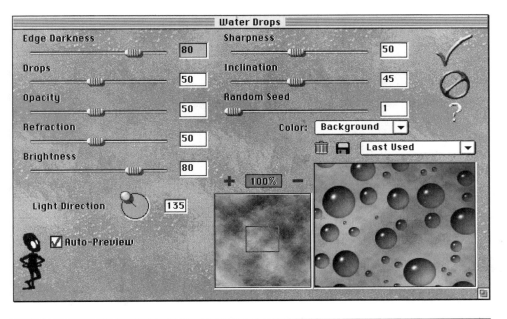

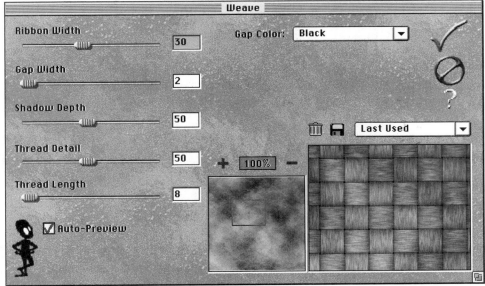

FIGURE 11-8 Alien Skin Eye Candy filter dialog boxes

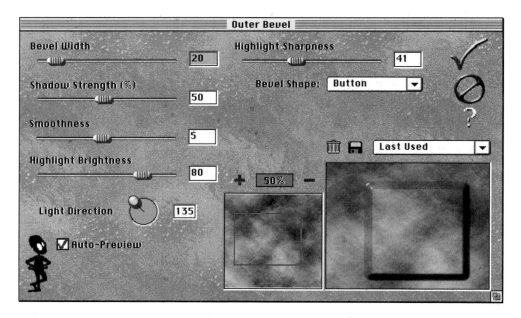

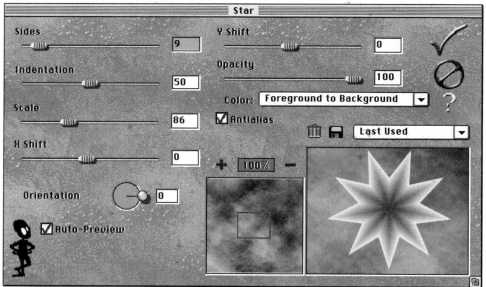

FIGURE 11-8   Alien Skin Eye Candy filter dialog boxes (*continued*)

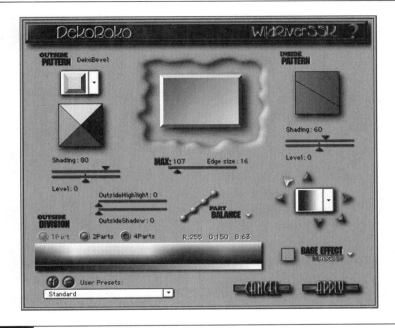

FIGURE 11-9 The DekoBoko filter allows you to easily create multimedia buttons

to create unusual images such as fiery metallic type. If you purchase these filters, make sure you read through the manual and tutorials; they show you how to get the most from the filters by saving selections and reapplying the filters with different effects.

 NOTE: *Visit DataStream's Web site at www.datastrem.com.*

Arrivo Select MaskGrower

Although Photoshop 5 includes new selecting tools such as the Magnetic Lasso tool, users are always looking for faster and more powerful selecting tools. Several third-party filter manufacturers have released plug-ins that extend Photoshop's selection capabilities. One of the easiest to use of these plug-ins is Arrivo Select's MaskGrower.

11

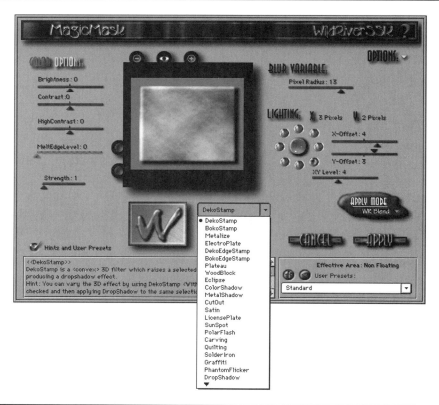

FIGURE 11-10   The MagicMask filter allows you to create a wide variety of interesting effects

This plug-in is based on a planting analogy. First you plant Foreground Seeds within the image area that you want selected; you can also plant Background Seeds outside of the area that you want selected. When you are ready to create your mask, you simply click the Grow button. After the selection is created, you can use the Add Seed and Delete Seed tools to modify the selection, or use the plug-in's Photoshop-like Lasso tools. Other utilities in MaskGrower allow you to fill holes in your selection or spots outside selected areas.

 NOTE: *Arrivo's Web site is www.arrivo.com.*

 NOTE: *To learn about Photoshop's advanced masking features, see Chapters 13 and 14.*

Extensis Plug-in and Software

Extensis Corporation has become the king of Photoshop plug-ins with a variety of tools that speed and enhance digital imaging. The following sections provide a brief review of Extensis products that add to the power of Photoshop.

Extensis Mask Pro

Extensis Mask Pro will certainly prove to be one of Extensis' most valuable plug-ins. It allows you to create intricate masks quickly and efficiently.

When you mask you can quickly switch between a Brush tool or a Pen tool that works much like Photoshop's tools. As you paint with the brush, you mask away the area that you don't want included. In many respects, working with Mask Pro's Paintbrush is like erasing an image with the Eraser tool set to Paintbrush mode. However, as you paint, you can soften or harden the edge of your brush and/or increase or decrease brush size by using the slider controls. Many users find that this is a more efficient way to create intricate masks than using a Paint tool in Photoshop. While creating a mask, you can paint back in image areas that you inadvertently masked out. Figure 11-11 shows a carousel horse in the process of being masked with the Paintbrush tool. For fine-tuning the image edge of the mask, we zoomed in to see the individual pixels in the image.

For particularly intricate masks, you can set "Keep" colors and "Drop" colors in the Keep and Drop palettes. Once these colors have been set, you can paint a mask using the Magic Paintbrush, which keeps colors in the Keep palette and paints over colors in the Drop palette. Using the Magic Paintbrush, you can tackle some of the toughest masking subjects, such as masking an image of something as intricate as frizzy hair.

Mask Pro also includes a *clipping path* feature that is different from Photoshop's. In Photoshop, clipping paths are created from Pen tool curves. (Clipping paths allow you to silhouette an image so that a white background does not appear around the image when it is exported into a drawing or page layout program. See Chapter 13 to learn how to create clipping paths with Photoshop's Pen tool). Extensis Mask Pro creates a clipping path from vector information which speeds the print production process and often leads to more reliable printing.

11

Extensis PhotoFrame

If you need to create intricate and artistic borders around images, you should definitely investigate Extensis PhotoFrame. The package includes preset frames as

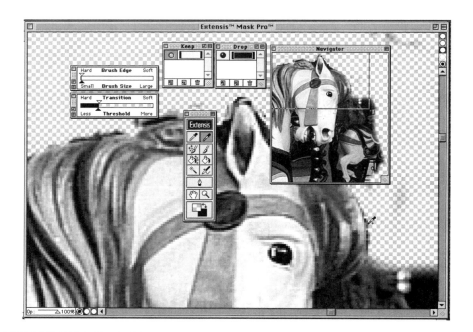

FIGURE 11-11   Mask being created with Extensis Mask Pro

well as commands that allow you to create your own artistic frames. The commands are quite simple to use, and you can quickly create an image edge in seconds. Figure 11-12 provides an example of the type of border you can create and some of the commands that allow you use to edit the border.

Extensis PhotoTools

Extensis PhotoTools provides a helpful grab bag of digital effects, all listed as separate plug-in utilities found in a PhotoTools menu that appears in Photoshop. The plug-ins include

- **PhotoBar**   allows you to create custom toolbars that run Photoshop commands at the click of a button

- **PhotoBevel**   creates an assortment of different beveling effects

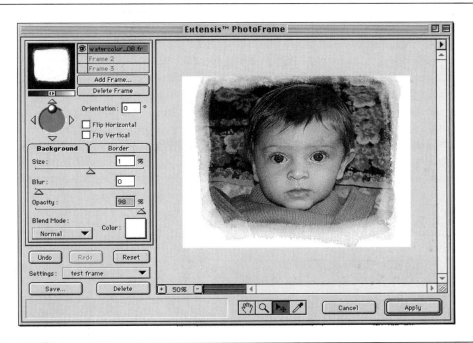

FIGURE 11-12 Image border created with Extensis PhotoFrame

☐ **PhotoButton** a utility for creating Web and multimedia buttons

☐ **PhotoEmboss** not only embosses but also creates shadow and blurring effects

☐ **PhotoGlow** creates glow effects

☐ **PhotoCast** not only creates drop shadows but also allows you to create shadows that can be blurred and easily transformed to simulate perspective

☐ **PhotoText** allows you to set type directly into your image

Web and multimedia designers will particularly like PhotoBevel and PhotoButton, both of which provide more extensive beveling than Photoshop's Layer Effects commands. Using PhotoBevel, you can create flat, round, sloped or double bevels. You can apply the bevels to the inside or outside edge of a selected area. PhotoButton, shown in Figure 11-13, is particularly handy for quickly creating 3-D buttons. The plug-in allows you to create inner and outer bevels, change colors, and use and edit a small library of pre-built shapes. Figure 11-13 shows a beveled star created in PhotoButton. After we created the button, we clicked and dragged on different points to edit the new shape.

Many Photoshop artists who haven't upgraded to Photoshop 5 will find PhotoTools' PhotoText to be particularly helpful. PhotoText can be used as a substitute for Photoshop's Type dialog box. When you open PhotoText, your image appears in the PhotoText window, enabling you to set type directly in your image. PhotoText works very much like a text tool you might find in a page layout program such as QuarkXPress, Adobe PageMaker, or Corel Ventura. You simply click on screen to establish a text block. You can immediately see if you are creating type that is too large or too small. You can control leading, tracking, and

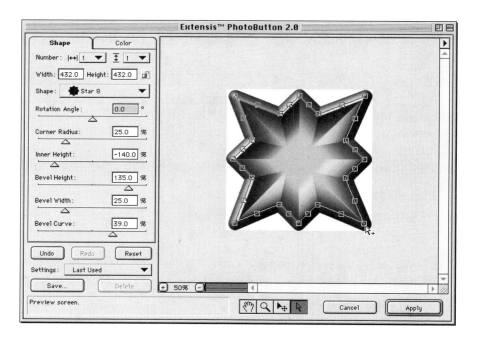

FIGURE 11-13   Multimedia button created with PhotoButton

kerning and even change character width. You can also change the size and style of any letter independently of all other letters in the text block. The filter includes a set of menus and a tool palette that allow you to move text and change the color of text, as well as quickly change the foreground and background colors.

Extensis Intellihance

If you need to quickly color correct and sharpen images, but don't want to spend the time tweaking different Photoshop image adjustment commands, you should investigate Extensis Intellihance. Intellihance features a one-click image enhancement button that can eliminate up to 12 steps in Photoshop. If you don't want to use the one-click enhancement feature, Intellihance includes specific commands for eliminating color casts, removing undesirable moiré and other patterns in scanned images, enhancing saturation, and changing brightness and contrast. Since most of these commands can be activated from one dialog box, you can quickly enhance an image with just a few quick mouse clicks.

Extensis Portfolio

If you're having a hard time keeping track of images or need to search for them again and again, then you should investigate Extensis Portfolio—a stand-alone image management application (not a Photoshop plug-in). Using Extensis Portfolio (originally called Fetch), you can view, organize, manage, and select images, digital movies, and sounds. You can even allow different users to access the same portfolio of images over a network.

When you add images to a catalog in Portfolio, you're essentially creating a custom image database. The images conveniently appear as thumbnails, shown in Figure 11-14, but can be viewed larger if you double-click. When you need to find images, you can search by name or keyword. You can enter a description for each image and create custom entry fields to help you further organize and describe your images.

 NOTE: *To learn more about PhotoTools and other Extensis products, check out the company's Web page at www.extensis.com.*

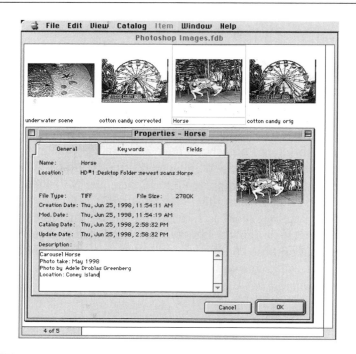

FIGURE 11-14   Thumbnails and an enlarged image view in Extensis Portfolio

Conclusion

In this chapter, we've covered only a small sampling of the third-party filters currently available. If you seek more in the way of startling and unusual effects, investigate Human Software Squizz, Andromeda Software Inc.'s Filter Series 4, which allows you to convert 2-D images into 3-D shapes. An example of one Andromeda filter is shown in image 18 of this book's color insert. If you use a program that renders 3-D models, you might also want to check out Knoll Software's CyberMesh, distributed by Puffin designs (www.puffindesigns.com), which allows you to create 3-D models from grayscale images. CyberMesh was designed by John Knoll, one of the original creators of Photoshop.

If you're interested in exploring the world of plug-ins further, there's an extensive list at Adobe's Web site: www.Adobe.com. The fastest way to get there (if you have an Internet connection) is to simply click on Photoshop's Eye icon at the top of the Toolbox.

CHAPTER 12

Converting Modes for Printing, Multimedia, and the Web

Thoughout this book you have been working primarily in RGB Color mode, Photoshop's default image mode. Although RGB Color allows you to access the full range of Photoshop image-editing menus and commands, many Photoshop projects require that you convert images from RGB Color to another mode. For instance,

- ☐ To output a file for four-color process printing, you must convert to CMYK Color mode.

- ☐ When you need to work with a display of 256 (or fewer) colors for Web or multimedia output, you can switch to Indexed Color mode.

- ☐ For other projects, you may need to remove all color from an image. In this case, you can convert from any color mode to Grayscale mode. From Grayscale you can convert to Bitmap (black and white) mode.

- ☐ To add color to a grayscale image, you need to convert from Grayscale mode to one of Photoshop's color modes (RGB Color, Indexed Color, CMYK Color, or Lab Color).

Switching modes also allows you to create special printing effects such as duotones and mezzotints. A *duotone* is a grayscale image in which two inks, usually black and another color, are printed over each other. The resulting extra color can add interest and depth to a grayscale image. A *mezzotint* is a bitmap image created from randomly shaped dots.

In this chapter, you'll have a chance to explore Photoshop's eight modes: Bitmap, Grayscale, Duotone, Indexed Color, RGB Color, CMYK Color, Lab Color, and Multichannel. You'll learn how to switch between one mode and another and, most importantly, from RGB Color to CMYK Color.

 NOTE: *If you change modes in an image that has layers, Photoshop allows you to choose whether or not to "flatten" the image before the mode change. If you flatten the image, its file size will be reduced and all layers will be merged into the Background layer. When converting from RGB Color to CMYK Color it is generally advisable to flatten the image before converting it. This will help ensure that layer-blending modes effects (such as Overlay, Hard Light, etc.) appear as desired.*

RGB Color Mode

RGB Color is Photoshop's native color mode. As discussed in Chapter 5, in RGB Color mode, all colors are created by combining different values of red, green, and blue. In Photoshop's RGB Color mode, over 16.7 million colors are available to you. You can view and edit each of the red, green, and blue color components, called *channels*, individually. Viewing an image's channels can help you better understand the difference between one mode and another.

In order to see the RGB channels that make up an RGB Color image, open any RGB Color file on your screen. (If you don't have an RGB image, load an image from Photoshop's Samples folder.) With your file displayed, open the Channels palette by choosing Show Channels from the Window menu.

 NOTE: *In order to ensure that you are viewing colors properly in RGB Color mode, it is extremely important that you run the Adobe Gamma utility to calibrate your monitor, then review the settings in the RGB Setup dialog box (File | Color Settings | RGB Setup). For more information, see Chapter 1.*

Using the Channels Palette

When the Channels palette opens, you'll see the three RGB channels listed. There's also a composite channel, where all channels combine to produce one color image. The eye icon (👁) indicates that the components of a particular channel are being viewed. The dark or colored area to the right of the eye icon means that the channel is selected and its contents will be affected if the image is edited. When a channel is selected, it is often referred to as the *target channel*. The thumbnail image in the channel is a miniature version of the image on screen. You can change the size of the palette's thumbnail by choosing the Palette Options command in the Channels palette's pop-up menu.

12

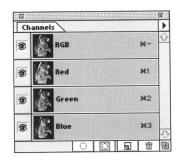

You'll have a better sense of how RGB colors combine to create an image if you take a look at each channel. To do this, click on the name of the channel in the Channels palette. For instance, to view only the Red channel, move the mouse over the word "Red" in the Channels palette. When the hand icon ( ) appears, click on Red, or use the keyboard shortcut COMMAND-1 (Windows users: CTRL-1). In the image on your screen, you will only see the Red channel.

 NOTE: *You'll probably see the channel as a grayscale image; Photoshop does not display the individual channels in color unless you change one of the default Preferences settings. To see the channels in color, select File | Preferences | Display & Cursors. In the Preferences dialog box, select the Color Channels in Color check box. Click OK.*

Take a look at each one individually. Press COMMAND-2 (Windows users: CTRL-2) to view the Green channel and then COMMAND-3 (Windows users: CTRL-3) to view the Blue channel. Notice that the eye icon next to the Blue channel in the Channels palette is visible and that the Blue Channel section in the Channels palette is selected. This means that the Blue channel is the only channel in view and the only channel that can be edited. If you'd like, you can view and edit two channels together, independently of the third. While viewing the Blue channel, press and hold SHIFT while you click on Green in the Channels palette. You will see both Blue and Green channels together on screen. Now you can begin to see how the colors combine to create the image. If you wish to deactivate and hide a channel, you can SHIFT-click on the channel name in the palette. To return to the composite view, click on the RGB composite channel, or press COMMAND-~ (Windows users: CTRL-~).

In addition to viewing the RGB channels, you can also edit within them to create special effects. For example, you could click on a channel name so that it will be the only channel that can be viewed and edited and then apply a filter to it. You can also apply paint to each channel separately. If you paint with white in a channel, you will be painting with that channel's color (red, green, or blue); if you paint with black, you add that channel's complementary color to the image.

Switching from RGB to Other Modes

The three RGB channels and the millions of colors that can be produced in RGB images provide you with the proper colors for output to slides and video or for printing to an RGB color printer. However, as you work with Photoshop, your design goals or the output requirements of a project may necessitate switching modes. The following chart lists the modes to which you can convert from RGB Color, with a brief explanation of each one.

 NOTE: *From RGB Color (or any other color mode), you cannot convert directly to Bitmap (black and white) or Duotone; you must convert from RGB Color to Grayscale mode first.*

Mode	Description
Grayscale	256 shades of gray. From Grayscale you can switch to Bitmap to work in black and white, or to Duotone.
Indexed Color	Reduces number of colors to 256 or fewer. Commonly used before outputting images to the Web or multimedia programs.
CMYK Color	Used for four-color process printing. Allows you to produce color separations.
Lab Color	Encompasses both RGB and CMYK color gamuts. Used by Photo CDs and PostScript Level 2 printers.
Multichannel	No composite channel is created. Channels are viewed separately. When you delete a channel from RGB, Lab, or CMYK modes, Photoshop automatically switches to Multichannel. In Multichannel mode, you can rearrange the channels in the Channels palette which may be helpful when printing images with Spot Color channels.

 NOTE: *You can also convert a 48-bit RGB or 64-bit CMYK color image to an 8-bit RGB or CMYK color image. By default, Photoshop uses 8 bits per color channel (256 color values) for RGB images. Many mid-range and high-end scanners can scan using 16 bits per color channel. 16-bit-per-channel images provide more precise color information. However, if you load a 16-bit-per-channel image into Photoshop, you cannot use every tool and editing command. For instance, you cannot apply filters to 16-bit-per-channel images. Therefore, you may wish to convert a 16-bit-per-channel image into an 8-bit-per-channel image. To convert a 16-bit-per-pixel image to an 8-bit-per-pixel image, choose Image | Mode | 8 bit/Channel.*

When you convert from RGB Color to another mode (except Multichannel), Photoshop changes the color data in the image's file; if you save the file after converting, you will not be able to return to the original color mode unless you are converting between RGB and Lab Color. Thus, before converting from RGB Color to another mode, it's wise to use the File | Save As command to create a second copy of your file. That way, you can always return to your original RGB file, if necessary.

In the next section, you will convert your RGB color image to a CMYK color image. Before proceeding, use the Save As command to save a copy of your image, and rename the new file ModeTest.

CMYK Color Mode

CMYK Color mode is used for viewing and editing images for output by a commercial printer. If you are working with an RGB color file and need to produce four-color separations, you should convert the image from RGB Color mode to CMYK Color mode. CMYK color images are divided into four channels, one for each of the process colors used to create four-color separations: Cyan, Magenta, Yellow, and Black. From the four channels, a prepress house produces the four pieces of film needed by a print shop to create the cyan, magenta, yellow, and black printing plates. When the image is printed, the tiny colored ink dots from each plate combine to create countless varieties of color.

If your images are digitized on a high-end scanner, they will probably be saved as CMYK files. These scanners can convert from RGB to CMYK "on the fly"— during the process of digitizing the image. When the scanned image is loaded into Photoshop, it will open as a CMYK image in CMYK Color mode. Photo CD "profiles," available from Kodak, can convert Photo CD files directly to CMYK Color mode when the images are opened.

 NOTE: *If you are working with a CMYK Color file, it is not advisable to convert it to RGB Color and then back to CMYK Color. When you convert back to RGB Color, you lose color data that will not be restored when you convert it back to CMYK Color.*

Converting from RGB Color to CMYK Color

Before you convert a file from RGB Color to CMYK Color, bear in mind that CMYK color files are larger than RGB color files, due to the addition of the fourth channel. Thus, working in RGB Color mode is generally quicker, particularly if your computer is not fast. It's often advisable not to convert a file to CMYK Color until all image editing is complete. If, however, you are color correcting an image that you will be printing on a printing press, you may want to convert to CMYK Color before you complete a project. This will allow you to edit using the same colors that will be used when the image is printed. When you edit in CMYK Color mode, you'll be able to color correct and edit the four individual channels.

Although converting an RGB color file to CMYK Color is a simple process, it's vital to understand the steps Photoshop goes through to complete the conversion. If you don't, you may not be happy with the color quality of the printed image. To begin the conversion process, you simply select CMYK Color from the Image | Mode submenu. The conversion process can take several minutes. When it's done, the RGB colors will be converted to CMYK equivalents, and you will have a larger file because of the fourth channel.

 TIP: *After a conversion to CMYK, it is often advisable to run the Unsharp Mask filter to sharpen image details. See Chapter 10 for more information.*

When the conversion begins, Photoshop internally converts from RGB Color to Lab Color, then to CMYK color. When Photoshop makes the conversion it analyzes the settings in the RGB Setup and the CMYK Setup dialog boxes, both accessed via the File | Color Settings command. Using the information in these dialog boxes, Photoshop creates the CMYK Color file. Thus, it's important to understand the settings of both the RGB Setup and CMYK Setup dialog boxes.

 CAUTION: *Photoshop selects sRGB as its default RGB color space in the RGB Setup dialog box (File | Color Settings | RGB Setup). If you will be converting RGB Color images to CMYK Color, you should switch to an RGB color space that encompasses more printable colors, such as SMPTE-240M. See Chapter 1 for more details.*

The CMYK Setup Dialog box

One of the primary purposes of the CMYK Setup dialog box is to provide Photoshop with information about the ink and paper your commercial printer will be using. Photoshop uses this information to fine-tune the conversion so that the CMYK colors are the most appropriate for your particular print job.

NOTE: *If you are editing a CMYK color image, changing the settings in the CMYK Setup dialog dialog box only changes the display of the image. It doesn't affect the display of RGB Color images.*

To access the CMYK Setup dialog box, choose Color Settings from the File menu and select CMYK Setup from the submenu.

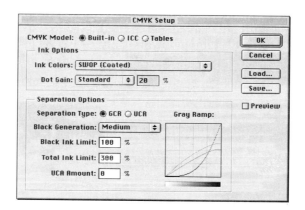

By default the Built-in option in the CMYK Model section is selected. If Built-in isn't selected, select it now to view the Ink Options which allow you to choose from various printing inks with different paper options.

Click on the Ink Colors pop-up menu to view the choices available. The default setting is SWOP (Coated) for coated paper. The SWOP (Specifications Web Offset Proofing) organization has published specifications for web offset printing. Choosing one of the SWOP settings means you are choosing inks and papers according to these specifications. Among the other choices are: SWOP (Uncoated) and SWOP (Newsprint).

When you make a choice in the Ink Colors pop-up menu, the value in the Dot Gain field, explained next, is updated automatically.

 NOTE: *If you click the Preview check box in the CMYK Setup dialog box, the screen display previews the changes in your image only if it is a CMYK color image.*

UNDERSTANDING DOT GAIN   The Dot Gain field indicates the percentage of dot gain expected on a printing press. Dot gain is the bleed, or spreading, of the ink that occurs on paper when an image is printed on a printing press. Dot gain is caused by halftone dots that print larger or smaller than their actual size on film or on the printing plate. This unavoidable phenomenon is most noticeable in midtones and shadow areas of printed images, where the halftone dots are the largest. The degree of dot gain is primarily determined by the printing paper. When Photoshop converts to CMYK Color, it adjusts CMYK percentages in the converted image to compensate for dot gain. In general, higher dot gain percentages result in a lighter final separated image.

At first glance, the number in the Dot Gain field may seem quite large, but it's really not as bad as it seems. The percentage is measured in terms of the ink increase beyond the size of midtone halftone dots in the film output from the imagesetter. Photoshop then takes the dot gain value and creates a "power" curve that it uses to calculate dot gain in other areas beside midtones.

 NOTE: *If you wish to see a visual representation of how much dot gain compensation is applied to different image areas, choose Curves in the Dot Gain pop-up menu. Editing the curve is discussed in Chapter 19.*

Because the dot gain value is entered automatically when you change the Ink Colors selection, there's generally no need to enter a number in the Dot Gain field. As long as you know the printing process you will be using, you generally won't need to change the value in the Dot Gain field.

You may, however, wish to change the Dot Gain setting when you calibrate your system to a proof (or sample printout). This subject is covered in Chapter 19. You may also wish to change the Dot Gain settings based upon advice from your commercial printer.

 CAUTION: *Dot gain settings used in the previous version of Photoshop will produce different results in Photoshop 5. For instance, a 20% dot gain setting in Photoshop 5 provides more dot gain compensation than a 20% dot gain setting in Photoshop 4.*

The CMYK Color Setup dialog box also includes Save and Load buttons, which allow you to save your settings and reload them to use again in another file.

If you are working with an image on screen and you are certain of the correct CMYK Setup settings for your project, go ahead and select the appropriate choice in the Ink Colors pop-up menu and click OK. Otherwise, if you made changes to the CMYK Color Setup dialog box while working through this section, click Cancel now so that the default settings remain intact. Next, take a look at the Separation Options section, which is also used during CMYK conversion.

Separation Options

The Separation Options section of the CMYK Setup dialog box controls how the black plate is created during the separation process. In most cases, the default dialog box settings should provide good results. The Save and Load buttons allow you to save and reload the settings you make here; this is helpful when you need to return to a particular set of print settings or wish to reload the Black Generation custom curve (explained next).

 CAUTION: *If you experiment with the CMYK Setup dialog box settings as you work through this section, be sure to change them back to the defaults. These settings should only be changed on the advice of your commercial printer or prepress house.*

As discussed in Chapter 5, cyan, magenta, and yellow can theoretically produce all of the colors needed for commercial printing. Unfortunately, however, when the three colors overprint, ink impurities produce a muddy brown color instead of pure black. To remedy this, a black plate is added to increase contrast and produce blacker blacks. When black is added, levels of cyan, magenta, and yellow can be reduced to enhance printing quality. The two primary techniques used to substitute black for CMY colors are UCR (Under Color Removal) and GCR (Gray Component Replacement).

The decision to use either GCR or UCR in Photoshop is often determined by paper stock and printing requirements. GCR is generally used for coated stock and UCR for uncoated stock.

In UCR separation, levels of cyan, magenta, and yellow are subtracted from gray and shadow areas and replaced with an appropriate amount of black. In GCR separation (Photoshop's default), levels of cyan, magenta, and yellow are subtracted from both gray and colored areas. To compensate for the removal of one or all three of the colors when GCR is chosen, an appropriate amount of black is added. The degree of black replacement can be specified in the Black Generation pop-up menu of the Separation Options section.

You probably won't need to delve deeply into the inner workings of GCR; the basic theory is that one of the three process inks (CMY) often is the gray component of a color. The gray component is the ink that lightens or darkens; the other two inks provide most of the color. When GCR is applied, the gray component ink is reduced and black is added. For instance, consider a digitized image of green grass that is primarily composed of cyan and yellow, with a small percentage of magenta darkening the image. During the separation process, if the GCR option is selected, a portion of the magenta is reduced and replaced with black. Theoretically, GCR can result in better gray balance and better reproduction of saturated colors; however, it may also remove some details from darker areas.

 NOTE: *Despite what you read or are told about the advantages of GCR over UCR (or vice versa), don't make any choices without contacting your print shop.*

In the Separation Options section of the CMYK Setup dialog box you'll also see a grid with a slope portraying the gray ramp is displayed. The Gray Ramp grid provides a visual representation of how the process inks produce neutral or gray colors based on the settings in the dialog box. The x-axis charts the color value from 0% to 100%. The gray bar depicts the actual shade of gray from white to black. The y-axis charts the ink that will be used to produce the gray value.

GCR AND THE GRAY RAMP   The best way to understand how the Gray Ramp works is to see what happens when you turn off the black plate while the GCR option is enabled. To turn off the black plate, select None in the Black Generation pop-up menu. This menu controls the amount of black substituted in the image when the GCR option is used.

As soon as you click None, the Gray Ramp changes, showing you that the grays will be produced with approximately equal amounts of cyan, magenta, and yellow, but no black. If you use None as the setting and convert from RGB to CMYK, no black plate is generated.

Now, click on Medium in the Black Generation pop-up menu. The Gray Ramp shows that CMY levels are reduced, with black used to help produce grays starting in areas just lighter than the image's midtones. Switch among the choices in the Black Generation menu, and you'll see that as more black is added, the CMY inks are reduced. If you choose Maximum and convert from RGB to CMYK, black and grays are created from the black plate. This setting is commonly used when outputting images that contain large amounts of black.

The Custom selection in the Black Generation pop-up menu lets you manually control the generation of the black plate. When you choose Custom, a Black Generation dialog box appears, in which you can customize black generation by clicking and dragging on a curve. After you adjust the curve and click OK, the cyan, magenta, and yellow levels are changed according to the black curve.

When you choose the GCR separation option, the UCA (Undercolor Addition) Amount field at the bottom of the Separation Options section allows you to add cyan, magenta, and yellow back into the areas that contain the highest percentage

12

of black in an image. When you add cyan, magenta, and yellow, black is not subtracted. This results in more intense blacks, which can help prevent shadow areas from appearing too flat. Values between 0 and 100% are accepted in the UCA Amount field. Once again, if you change settings, you will see the results in the Gray Ramp. And remember: Any value entered in this field should also be approved by your commercial printer or prepress house.

Before continuing, if you have changed the Black Generation menu selection, return it now to the default setting, Medium. In most situations, Medium provides good results when you convert from RGB to CMYK.

UCR AND THE GRAY RAMP   To see how the UCR option affects the Gray Ramp, click on the UCR radio button in the Separation Options section. Notice that the black ink increases in the dark shadow areas, whereas the appropriate CMY colors are decreased in these areas.

Setting Ink Limits

The Black Ink Limit field in the CMYK Setup dialog box allows you to tell Photoshop the maximum ink density that your commercial printer's press can support; the default value is 100%. This means that the darkest black (K) value in your converted CMYK color image can be 100%. The default setting for the Total Ink Limit is 300%. This means that the total percentage of your CMY inks together will not be over 200% (300% – 100% = 200%, 100% being the Black Ink Limit). If you lower the values in these fields, you'll see that the maximum values for the CMYK inks drop in the Gray Ramp. Again, the same warning applies here: Do not change any values without consulting your print shop.

 NOTE: *To view the total percentage of CMYK inks in the Info palette, set one of the Eyedropper readouts to Total Ink.*

Separation Tables

If you are going to be printing Photoshop files with a variety of inks or printing systems, the settings you choose in the CMYK Setup dialog box (with the Built-in option selected) can be saved as a separation table. If you save a separation table, you do not need to save the individual settings in these dialog boxes. Saving the table essentially saves the settings in the CMYK Setup dialog box on disk.

When you want to convert an image that needs a particular group of settings, you just load the settings from the CMYK Setup dialog box instead of having to re-enter the settings. Using a separation table often results in a speedier completion of the RGB-to-CMYK conversion, because the separation table Photoshop uses in that conversion has already been created.

Once you have established the settings in the CMYK Setup dialog box, you can have Photoshop build a separation table. To do this, click the Tables radio button in the CMYK Setup dialog box, then click the Save button and wait for Photoshop to build a separation table. Next, when a dialog box appears, name your table and save it on your disk. After you name and save your separation table, you can later load it by clicking on the Load button (after clicking the Tables radio button) and choosing the table file from the list of files in the dialog box.

When a separation table is loaded, the Separation Tables dialog box displays the name of the table in the To CMYK Table section. This is the table that Photoshop uses when it makes the CMYK conversion.

Using ICC Profiles

Photoshop 5.0 allows you to convert to CMYK using ICC (International Color Consortium) profiles for specific output devices. As discussed in Chapter 1, an ICC profile is essentially a description of a color space. You would only use profiles if your image workflow includes ICC-aware applications (such as Adobe Illustrator and Adobe PageMaker 6.5). The color profiles are handled by Apple ColorSync Manager and Adobe's built-in color management system. Both color management systems attempt to steer the gamut of colors in your image to the range of printable colors that can be output by your printer.

If you choose to build a separation table with an ICC profile, the settings in Photoshop's Ink and Separation Options sections are ignored. Instead, the color management system takes the information from the ICC profile to create the separation table.

12

NOTE: *Mac users: In order for the Build Tables Using Apple ColorSync option to be available, Apple ColorSync must be installed. ColorSync is a control panel that can be installed when you install Photoshop.*

To use an ICC profile, click the ICC radio button in the CMYK Setup dialog box, then choose a profile. If you are using Apple's ColorSync color management system, choose ColorSync; to use Photoshop's built-in color management system, choose Built-in (this will generally provide better results than ColorSync). The Intent pop-up menu is somewhat confusing. Here is a brief description of each of its options:

☐ **Perceptual**   Choose Perceptual to maintain color relationships among the colors even if the colors change during the separation process. This is the most common choice because it generally provides the most attractive color. Perceptual is often used for Photographic images.

☐ **Saturation**   Choose Saturation to maintain the saturation relationship among the colors. Use this if you are printing color charts and graphs.

☐ **Relative Colorimetric**   Choose Relative Colorimetric to prevent the colors that are within the profile gamut from changing. Choose this option if you are printing logos or other items where the color values should be precise. Note that this choice may result in the clipping of colors that cannot be printed. The Absolute Colorimetric choice is not often used because the "white" point of the image is not matched when colors are converted.

In the dialog box choose Black Point compensation to convert the darkest neutral color in the image of the source color space to the darkest neutral color of the destination color space. Otherwise, black will be used.

 NOTE: *If your printer is not listed in the profile list, you may be able to obtain a profile from your printer's manufacturer.*

CMYK Preview

Now that you have an understanding of what goes on behind the scenes, you're almost ready to convert your image from RGB Color mode to CMYK Color mode.

Gamut Warning and CMYK Preview

Before converting from RGB Color to CMYK Color, you can have Photoshop check to see if any RGB colors are beyond the CMYK color gamut. You can also have Photoshop create a preview of the CMYK colors.

 NOTE: *For more information about the CMYK color gamut, see Chapter 5.*

To see if any of your colors lies beyond the CMYK gamut, choose Gamut Warning from the View menu. In a few moments, Photoshop turns any out-of-gamut colors in your image to a deep gray tone. If you wish, you can change the opacity or color of the Out of Gamut warning by choosing Transparency & Gamut from the Preferences dialog box (select File | Preferences). In the Preferences dialog box, enter a new opacity or click on the swatch labeled Color in the Gamut Warning section to open the Color Picker.

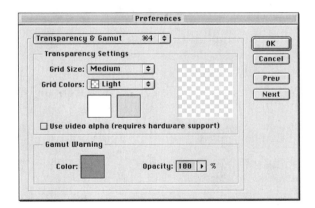

If you wish to select the out-of-gamut colors so that you can edit only within them, choose Color Range from the Select menu. In the Color Range dialog box, choose Out of Gamut from the Select pop-up menu. To ensure that you can see your entire image, leave the Selection Preview pop-up menu set to None. After you click OK in the Color Range dialog box, only the out-of-gamut colors are selected.

12

NOTE: *For more information about using the Color Range command, see Chapter 18.*

The easiest way to correct your out-of-gamut colors is to use the Sponge tool. In the Sponge Options palette, set the pop-up menu to Desaturate. Now you can click and drag over the out-of-gamut areas displayed on your screen. As the Sponge tool desaturates, the gray Out of Gamut warning color will gradually disappear; colors will return to your image, but these colors will be within the CMYK color gamut. As you continue to work, be careful not to desaturate too much; this can cause your colors to turn gray. You may also wish to use a color process swatch book as a reference guide (as described in Chapter 5) in conjunction with the Info palette readouts.

 TIP: *As you desaturate, you might find it helpful to view your image with and without the out-of-gamut gray warning colors. This will make it easier to check your progress as you remove the out-of-gamut colors. To do this, open a duplicate window on screen by choosing New View from the View menu. Turn the Gamut Warning on in one window, and leave the menu command deselected in the other.*

To see a CMYK preview, select CMYK Preview from the View menu. When Photoshop previews the colors, it does not convert the image to CMYK Color mode but attempts to display the RGB colors in their CMYK equivalents.

 TIP: *You can view the RGB colors of an image and their CMYK equivalents simultaneously in two windows. To do this, choose New View from the View menu in your RGB color file. This creates a duplicate window of your RGB file. In the duplicate window, select CMYK Preview from the View menu. In Photoshop 5, you can preview each of the CMYK colors as well as CMY without the Black channel.*

To turn off the CMYK Preview, choose CMYK Preview again in the View menu (this also removes the check mark from the CMYK Preview menu command). Now you're ready to start the conversion from RGB Color mode to CMYK Color mode.

Completing the CMYK Conversion

Once you are satisfied that all out-of-gamut colors have been removed from your RGB color image, you're ready to convert to CMYK Color mode. First, if you haven't already backed up your file, use the Save As command to create another version of your image. Then, to begin the conversion, choose CMYK Color from the Image | Mode submenu. (If you have Layers, you will be asked to flatten your image. See Chapter 15 for more information about Layers.) When the conversion is complete, the mode displayed in the title bar changes from RGB to CMYK. After converting, it is often advisable to run the Unsharp Mask filter, as explained in Chapter 10, to sharpen the image.

After the file has been converted, open the Channels palette and notice that it now displays four channels. If you look at the File Size indicator (toward the bottom left-hand corner of your screen), you'll see that the extra channel has increased the size of the image file. Take a moment to click on each of the channels to see how the image is created from the four process colors, cyan, magenta, yellow, and black.

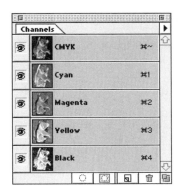

One of the advantages of working in a CMYK color file is that Photoshop will not allow you to paint with out-of-gamut colors. Also, you can edit in the four individual channels or in any combination of the four channels. This is helpful when you want to color correct in the individual channels or when you are creating interesting special effects.

Here's a design tip for adding color to a black-and-white (bitmap) image without affecting the underlying black color. This technique is possible because you can turn off editing in the black channel while you paint in the CMY channels. First, convert the black-and-white line art to CMYK Color. (If you have a bitmapped image, you need to use the Image | Mode submenu to convert from Bitmap to

12

Grayscale, then from Grayscale to CMYK Color.) Once the image is in CMYK Color mode, deactivate the Black channel so that the black plate will not be affected. In order to do this, position the pointer over the Black channel in the Channels palette. Press and hold SHIFT as you click the mouse. Now turn on the eye icon so that the contents of the Black channel are visible. Do this by clicking in the eye column to the left of the Black channel. Now you can see the Black channel, but any editing changes you make will not affect it. Now, use Photoshop's painting tools to add color to your image. When you are done painting, click on CMYK in the Channels palette to see the Composite image.

After converting to CMYK, you will probably want to save the file so that it can be output for proofing purposes. This often means saving the file in EPS, TIFF, or Scitex CT format before sending it to a service bureau or prepress house. Before you send the file to a service bureau, you may need to export your EPS or TIFF file to a page-layout program such as QuarkXPress. For more information about saving Photoshop files in EPS, TIFF, and Scitex CT formats, see Appendix A.

Indexed Color Mode

Converting a file to Indexed Color mode is a step commonly taken before outputting an image to the Web or to a multimedia program. Indexed Color mode is used because it reduces the number of colors in an image to 256 or fewer colors. The GIF file format used by many Web designers requires images to contain 256 or fewer colors. Multimedia producers commonly use Indexed Color images to keep file sizes as small as possible. Indexed Color is also used by multimedia producers to ensure that their productions can be viewed on computer systems that can't display over 256 colors.

 NOTE: *To learn how to convert Indexed Color images to GIF89a format for Web output, see Chapter 20.*

When you convert a file to Indexed Color, Photoshop reduces the channels in the image to one and creates a color table that is essentially a palette of colors tied to the document. This table is called a color lookup table (CLUT), and it acts as a type of index for the colors in the image.

You can convert to Indexed Color from RGB Color, Grayscale, or Duotone mode. This section covers how to convert an RGB color file to Indexed Color and edit the related color table. If your RGB color file contains more than 256 colors, you will lose color information when you convert to Indexed Color. Although you can convert from Indexed Color back to RGB Color, Photoshop will not return the original colors to the file. Thus, you should always keep a backup copy of your original color file before converting.

 NOTE: *Once you convert to Indexed Color mode, Photoshop's filters will not be available. You must execute these before converting to Indexed Color.*

Converting from RGB Color to Indexed Color

If you wish to experiment with Indexed Color, choose Revert from the File menu to return to the RGB Color version of the ModeTest file that you created at the beginning of this chapter. If you wish to use another file, you can load any RGB Color file. Make sure that you use the Save As command first to rename the file so that you will later be able to return to the original version.

The Indexed Color Dialog Box

To convert an RGB color file to Indexed Color, choose Indexed Color from the Image | Mode submenu. In the Indexed Color dialog box, you can choose the desired number of colors, a color palette, and, if you wish, a dithering pattern. When you work in the dialog box, turn on the Preview check box to preview how your image will look after the conversion.

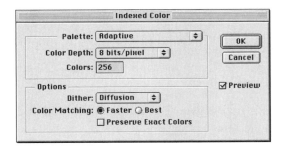

12

Use the Color Depth pop-up menu to specify the number of colors for the Indexed Color file.

 NOTE: *You can only lower the Color Depth in the pop-up menu when Uniform or Adaptive is chosen in the Palette pop-up menu.*

The Palette options provide a variety of color choices for the Indexed Color file. Read the following descriptions; then, if you wish to take a look at the results of using each palette option, click on a radio button and make sure that the Preview checkbox is selected.

☐ **Exact**   This option is only available if the image contains 256 or fewer colors. When Exact is chosen, Photoshop builds a table using the same colors that appear in the original RGB color image. When this option is selected, the number of colors in the image is changed according to the resolution setting. No dithering is necessary, because no new colors need to be simulated.

☐ **System**   This option uses the Mac or Windows default system palette.

 TIP: *If you are working on a multimedia project (not for the Web) that that doesn't use scanned images, the System palette choice often produces very suitable results.*

☐ **Web**   This option, which provides 216 "Web-safe" colors, matches the palette most often used in Web browsers. It uses six different RGB colors to create the 216 colors (6×6×6=216). See Chapter 20 for more information about choosing Web-safe colors.

☐ **Uniform**   This option creates a palette from a sample of colors from the color spectrum. If you choose this option and choose 8-bit as the Color Depth, note that Photoshop creates a palette of 216 colors. It takes six color levels of red, six color levels of green, and six color levels of blue to create the 216-color palette. Using the Uniform option, you can create palettes of 27, 64, 125, or 216 colors.

☐ **Adaptive**   This option generates a color table from the most commonly used colors in the image being converted. If you wish to have more control over the Adaptive palette conversion process, first select an area of the image that includes the colors you wish to retain. In the conversion to Indexed Color, Photoshop chooses colors based more on the colors in the selection than on all the colors in the image. When this option is chosen, you can specify how many colors you want in the color palette by choosing a bit depth in the Color Depth pop-up menu or by entering the number of colors in the Colors field.

- **Custom** This option allows you to create your own custom color table for the file. When you select this option, the Color Table dialog box appears, in which you can edit, save, and load color tables. You can also choose from several predefined color tables. When you choose a predefined table or edit a table, the colors of the image on screen will change to those in the color table when it is applied to your image. The colors are applied to the image when you click OK in the Color Table dialog box. For a description of each predefined table, see the next section, "Viewing the Predefined Colors."

- **Previous** This option uses the palette from the previous conversion, which is useful when you are converting several images at a time. This choice can be very handy when you use an Action to convert many images to the same palette for multimedia productions. The "Photoshop in Action" section in Chapter 20 provides an example of using this technique.

Below the Palette options is the Dither pop-up menu. Dithering combines different-colored pixels to give the appearance of colors that are not actually in the image. Choosing a dithering option may be advisable, because the color table that is created may not contain all of the colors in your image. Dithering is often used when converting images that include gradients. Following are descriptions of the Dither options:

- **None** Choose None if you do not wish dithering to occur. When this option is chosen, Photoshop picks the closest match it can find in the color table to replace a missing color in the converted image. This usually results in sharp color transitions.

 TIP: *None is a good choice if you are creating areas with flat, constant colors; you generally don't want to see dots in flat colors.*

- **Pattern** This option uses a pattern of random dots to simulate a missing color. This option is only available if the System palette option is selected.

- **Diffusion** When you choose Diffusion, Photoshop diffuses the color inaccuracies to surrounding pixels in an image.

 TIP: *Diffusion is a good choice for scanned photos and images that contain gradients. Also, applying a Noise filter to an image can also create a dithering pattern.*

NOTE: *Eight-bit color systems can only display one 256-color palette at a time. This means that all buttons and elements on a multimedia page designed for an 8-bit system should be converted to Indexed Color using the same color palette. If you need to convert many files to the same color palette, create an Action (see Chapter 9) to batch-process your images. You might also wish to create a "superpalette" by loading several images into one file, then creating a palette from this file. After the palette is created, apply it to other images that will appear on the page using the Previous palette choice.*

 TIP: *When working on a multimedia project, try to use as few palettes as possible; switching palettes can cause flashes on screen.*

Viewing the Predefined Colors

There are two ways to access the Color Table dialog box in order to choose a predefined color table. If you have already converted to Indexed Color, you can choose Color Table from the Image | Mode submenu. If you haven't yet converted, first choose Indexed Color from the Image | Mode submenu, and then select Custom in the Palette pop-up menu.

In the Color Table dialog box, the predefined tables are accessed by clicking on the Table pop-up menu. Here's a brief description of these tables—you may want to try selecting each one to view the colors produced.

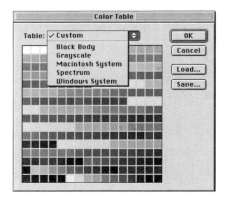

☐ **Black Body**   This option transforms the color table based on the colors produced when a black body radiator is heated. You'll see a range of colors from black to red, as well as orange, yellow, and white. This table can be used for scientific applications or to produce a hot, glowing effect.

- **Grayscale**   This table produces transitional colors through 256 shades from black to white.

- **Spectrum**   This table produces the colors in the color spectrum.

- **Macintosh System or Windows System**   This table is the standard Mac or Windows color palette.

Editing the Indexed Color Table

If you would like, you can open the color table that is being used by your image and edit the colors. To do this, your image should first be converted to Indexed Color.

Once you have an Indexed Color file on screen, select Color Table from the Image | Mode submenu; the color table for your file will be displayed. Now you can edit any color in the table by clicking on the color. After you click, Photoshop's Color Picker appears, allowing you to change the colors. Use the dialog box options to pick a color that is not already in the color table, then click OK. After Photoshop returns to your document, notice that each pixel that contained the color you clicked in the Color Table dialog box is converted to the new color.

Photoshop's Indexed Color also allows you to change a range of colors in the table at one time. This can be helpful if you want to prevent the color changes in your image from being too dramatic. To change a range of colors, select Color Table from the Image | Mode submenu. In the Color Table dialog box, click and drag through a row of colors. When you release the mouse, the Color Picker appears with the message "Select first color." Choose a color and click OK. The Color Picker reopens with the message "Select last color." When you click OK, a gradient of colors—from the first color you specified to the last color—appears in the color table. Click OK in the dialog box to see the effects in your image.

 TIP: *When the Color Picker opens, you can also click Custom to choose PANTONE colors.*

 TIP: *The preceding technique can be used as a quick way to colorize a grayscale image. First load the grayscale image, then convert it to Indexed Color. Next, choose Image | Mode | Color Table. Select the entire table. When the "Select first color" message appears, choose a starting color, click OK, and then choose an ending color. After you close the color table, your image will be colorized. This technique can be also handy for changing the colors of GIF images that will be used on the Web.*

12

Saving and Loading Indexed Color Tables

If you wish to create a custom color table to use with other documents, you can return to the Color Table dialog box and click the Save button to name the table and save it on disk. When you wish to apply it to a document, click the Load button to load it. After the table is loaded, click OK in the Color Table dialog box to have the colors from the table appear in the document on screen.

 TIP: *Saved tables can be used when exporting RGB color images to GIF89a format. See Chapter 20 for more details.*

 TIP: *You can load a saved Indexed Color table into the Swatches palette and paint with those colors. To load the table, choose Load Swatches from the Swatches palette pop-up menu. (Windows users: Click on the File of type pop-up menu to see the Color Table palette files with the .ACT file extension.) You can also load a Swatches palette into a Color Table by clicking on the Load button in the Indexed Table dialog box. (Windows users: Click on the File of type pop-up menu to see the Swatch palette files with the .ACT file extension.)*

Grayscale Mode and the Grayscale Setup Dialog box

Grayscale files are 8-bit images that can be composed of up to 256 shades of gray. When a color file is converted to grayscale, all color information is removed from the file. Although the Image | Mode submenu allows you to convert a grayscale file to a color mode file, you will not be able to return the original colors to a file that has been converted to grayscale. Thus, before converting a color image to grayscale, it's advisable to use the Save As command to create a copy of your color file so that you have a backup.

If you are working on grayscale images for print, make sure that the Grayscale Setup dialog box (File | Color Settings | Grayscale Setup) is set to Black Ink. As discussed in Chapter 1, when you choose the Black Ink option in the dialog box, Photoshop uses the dot gain setting in the CMYK Setup dialog box to compensate for dot gain when it converts to Grayscale mode. Since Dot Gain darkens an image on press, the larger the dot gain percentage in the CMYK Setup dialog box, the lighter the gray tones will be in the final grayscale image.

If your grayscale images will appear on the Web or in a Mutimedia project, choose the RGB option in the Grayscale Setup dialog box, instead of Black Ink. You can click the Preview button in the dialog box to preview the image for either option.

Converting from a Color Mode to Grayscale

If you need to convert your digitized color image to grayscale or black and white, you will first need to convert your file to Grayscale mode. From Grayscale, you can convert to a Duotone or Bitmap file. (Duotones and bitmapped images are discussed later in this chapter.)

If you don't have a color file on screen, load one now so that you can convert it to grayscale (try the ModeTest file that's been used throughout this chapter). Then select Grayscale from the Image | Mode submenu. An Alert will appear, warning that you will be discarding the color information in the file. (If you have layers in your image, an Alert will ask you if you wish to flatten your image but won't ask you to discard the color information.) After you click OK, your file will be converted to a grayscale image and the Channels palette will display only one channel, Black.

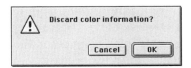

When working with a grayscale image, the Color palette displays only one grayscale slider, labeled K (Black). You can change the percentage of gray by clicking and dragging on the slider control. The lower the percentage, the lighter the shade of gray is; the higher the percentage, the darker the shade of gray.

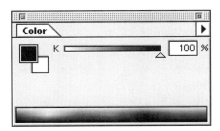

When Photoshop converts to grayscale, it uses a formula to convert the color information to gray values. Notwithstanding the formula's accuracy, you still may decide that the grayscale version needs some tonal corrections. If this is the case, you can make simple tonal adjustments using the Brightness/Contrast command in the Image | Adjust submenu. To learn more advanced techniques for making tonal adjustments to grayscale images, see Chapter 18.

 TIP: *You can remove the color from an RGB image and create a variety of different grayscale style images using Photoshop 5's Channel Mixer (Image | Adjust | Channel Mixer). The Channel Mixer is discussed in Chapter 18.*

Converting from Grayscale to a Color Mode

While working with an image in Grayscale mode, you cannot add color to it. If you wish to add color to a grayscale image, convert the image to one of the color modes (RGB Color, CMYK Color, Lab Color, or Indexed Color) by selecting that mode from the Image | Mode submenu. After you convert it, you can colorize the image.

Colorizing Grayscale Images

Using the computer to colorize a grayscale image is similar to the process of adding color to old black-and-white movies. Like the process of creating colorized movies, transforming a grayscale image into color allows the image's shadows, contours, and definition beneath the color to show through.

To start colorizing, you will need to load a grayscale image. (As usual, to ensure that you will be able to return to the original grayscale image, it's always advisable to use the Save As command and rename the file.) Then open the Colors palette by choosing Show Color in the Window menu. Select Image | Mode, and convert your file from Grayscale to RGB Color or CMYK Color. This will allow you to add colors to your image.

Set the foreground color and choose the Paintbrush tool in the Toolbox. If the Brushes palette isn't open, choose Show Brushes in the Window menu. In the Brushes palette, select a medium-sized, soft-edged brush.

You'll start painting the image with the Paintbrush tool, but before you do, double-click on the Paintbrush to open the Paintbrush Options palette. In the palette, set Opacity to 100%, and in the Mode pop-up menu, select Color as the painting mode. Notice the result: The portion you paint changes color, but you can still see the underlying shadows and textures. This is because you are painting in Color mode. When you paint using Color mode, Photoshop paints with only the hue and saturation of a color. This allows the underlying brightness values to show through your painting color. If you were painting in Normal mode at 100% Opacity, the opaque color would completely cover the image.

If there are large areas that you wish to color in your image, use the Pen tool or a selection tool to create a selection. Then choose Fill from the Edit menu and set the Mode pop-up menu to Color. After you click OK, color will be applied to your image, but again, the underlying lightness and darkness levels will show through the color.

You may wish to experiment with the Darken, Lighten, Multiply, Overlay, Soft Light, and Screen painting modes. Lighten and Darken, in particular, can be used to add various color tones to areas already colorized. (For a review of Darken, Lighten, Multiply, Overlay, Soft Light, and Screen, see "Blending Modes" in Chapter 6.) Also, you may wish to activate the Blur or Smudge tools to blend colors together. You can use the Sharpen tool to enhance detail by increasing contrast as well.

Using the Colorize Option in the Hue/Saturation Dialog Box

Photoshop also allows you to adjust colors from a variety of dialog boxes that can be accessed from the Image | Adjust submenu. You'll be using these commands extensively when retouching and color correcting (in Chapter 18). Only the Hue/Saturation command is discussed here, because it includes an option specifically designed to colorize.

Before experimenting with the Hue/Saturation command, select an area in your image that you wish to colorize. Choose Hue/Saturation from the Image | Adjust submenu. In the dialog box, make sure that the Preview check box is selected. The preview lets you see the changes in your image as you colorize. Then select the Colorize check box, and the selection you have just made will change to the Hue of the foreground color (unless it is black). The Saturation value will be 25 with a lightness of 0.

12

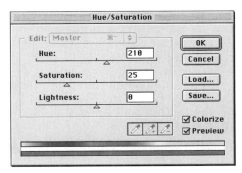

Photoshop 5 In Action

The white areas of the image were colored.

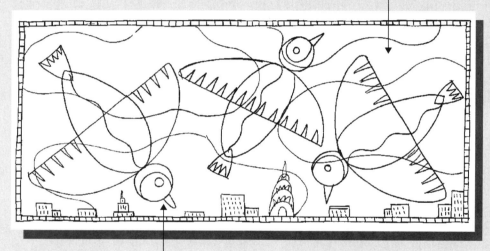

Artist: José Ortega

Black-and-white line art drawing

The black marker lines of the image were colored.

José began this project for New York's Metropolitan Transit Authority (MTA) by first using a marker to make this line drawing. He then scanned the image as black-and-white line art. Once the image was digitized, he removed any dust spots with the Eraser tool and closed white gaps in the marker lines with the Pencil tool.

Photoshop 5 ▶ In Action

The white areas no longer exist. They were filled using the Darken blending mode.

Artist: José Ortega　　　　　　　**Client: Metropolitan Transit Authority**

The black marker lines no longer exist. They were colored by using the Lighten blending mode.

After the black and white line art drawing was digitized, José converted it to a color image by choosing RGB Color from the Image | Mode submenu. He colored the white areas of the image by using the Paint Bucket tool with different Tolerance settings and the Darken blending mode. By using the Darken blending mode, José prevented the black marker lines from being affected. After filling the white areas, he colored the black marker lines by using the Lighten blending mode.

To complete the project, he selected the entire image with the Rectangular Marquee tool and created a black frame around it using the Edit | Stroke command.

12

Adjusting the Hue slider will change the color of the image. Adjusting the Saturation slider will change the amount of gray in a color. When you are colorizing a grayscale image, the more saturation you add, the stronger the colors will be and the less gray they will contain. Adjusting the Lightness slider allows you to control how light or dark the color will be.

Now, try working with the Hue/Saturation sliders. To move through the color spectrum, drag the Hue slider control right or left. Drag it all the way to the left, to 0, and you'll see the color gradually change to red. Drag to the right to 360 degrees, and you'll see the colors return to red. If you find it confusing that you returned to red, think of the slider as the linear equivalent of a color wheel. When you move along the wheel, you eventually return to the color with which you began. Figure 12-1 shows how the Hue slider values and their corresponding colors would appear if arranged on a color wheel.

If you wish, you can change the Saturation setting. If you drag the Saturation slider control to the right, saturation increases; dragging left decreases saturation. Moving the Lightness slider control to the right toward 100 lightens your color; sliding it to the left toward 0 darkens it. With Lightness set to 100, the color changes to white; −100 changes it to black. By adjusting the Lightness slider control, you can even add color to pure white and pure black image areas.

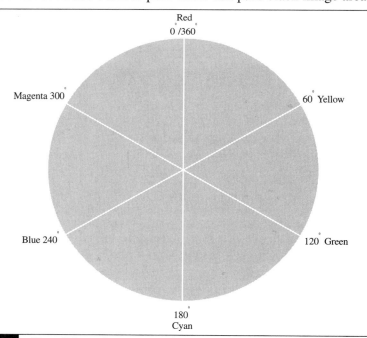

FIGURE 12-1   Hue slider values arranged on a color wheel

After you decide what combination of Hue, Saturation, and Lightness you want to apply to an image area, you can save your settings so that they can be applied to other files. Click the Save button, and a dialog box appears, allowing you to enter a name for the settings. After naming your settings, click Save (Windows users: OK) to return to the Hue/Saturation dialog box. When you wish to use these color settings again, select another area of the image or open another image; then return to the Hue/Saturation dialog box and load your color settings by clicking the Load button and opening your Hue/Saturation settings file. If you wish to exit the Hue/Saturation dialog box and apply the settings now, click OK; otherwise, click Cancel.

 TIP: *After you have finished colorizing, you may want to create special effects by applying any of Photoshop's filters from the Filter menu. See Chapter 10 for more information on filters.*

Converting from Grayscale to a Duotone

Printing a grayscale image with an extra gray or colored ink can add depth and dimension, making the image look more interesting and dramatic. These enhanced grayscale images are called duotones. In Photoshop's Duotone mode you can create monotones, duotones, tritones, and quadtones—grayscale images to which you add one, two, three, or four colors. This printing technique lets you create interesting images less expensively than by printing four-color images.

In order to create a monotone, duotone, tritone, or quadtone image, you must start with a grayscale image or convert a color image to a grayscale image. Only while in Grayscale mode can you access the Duotone mode.

In this section, you will create a duotone from a grayscale image. Start by loading any color file and converting it to Grayscale mode. If you wish, use the ModeTest file that was converted to Grayscale earlier in the chapter.

1. Select Duotone from the Image | Mode | Duotone menu. In the Duotone Options dialog box, Type is set to Monotone by default (or however you last set it). When the Monotone option is selected, notice that Ink 1 is active. Next to Ink 1 are two squares. The square with the diagonal line represents the Duotone curve—a visual representation of how the duotone ink distribution. The second square is the color swatch box. This represents the color that you are applying to your image. To activate another Type

12

option, click on the Type pop-up menu and make your selection. Select the Duotone option, because that is the option most commonly used.

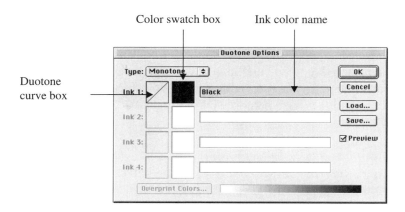

Color swatch box   Ink color name

Duotone curve box

When you choose Duotone from the Type pop-up menu, Ink 1 and Ink 2 are active, but Ink 3 and Ink 4 are not. This is because duotones are composed of only two colors. The number of inks that appear depends on the option you select in the Type pop-up menu.

NOTE: *When Photoshop prints a duotone, it prints the inks in ascending order. Thus, the darkest ink is usually the first ink and the lightest ink is the last ink in the Duotone Options dialog box.*

2. Notice that for the Duotone option, you need to pick a second ink color. Click once on the white color swatch box to the right of Ink 2. The Custom Colors dialog box appears.

   In the Custom Colors dialog box, you can either pick a custom color or click on the Picker button to access the Color Picker dialog box and then enter CMYK percentages for a process color.

3. To pick a PANTONE Coated color in the Custom Colors dialog box, click on the Book pop-up menu and choose PANTONE Coated if it is not already displayed. To choose a color, type 2645. Notice that PANTONE 2645 CV becomes the active color (or PANTONE 2645 CVC if the Short PANTONE Names option in the General Preferences dialog box isn't selected—if you are printing separations from QuarkXPress or PageMaker

you need to use short names). Click OK to confirm the change and to return to the Duotone Options dialog box.

 NOTE: *If Photoshop does not find the correct color, try quickly retyping the Custom Color number on your numeric keypad.*

To see the effects of your changes, make sure that the Preview check box is selected in the Duotone Options dialog box. When the Preview option is on, you will see that your image is displayed with black and PANTONE 2645 CV.

Controlling Duotone Ink

After you have selected the second ink color for a duotone, you may want to control ink density in shadow, midtone, and highlight areas. You do this by adjusting that ink's curve. In duotone images, black is usually applied to the shadow areas and gray or another color is applied to the midtone and highlight areas.

 NOTE: *Before and after you make adjustments in the Duotone Curve dialog box, you may want to open the Color palette to see the different shades of Ink 1 and Ink 2.*

To change the way an ink is applied to an image, follow these steps:

1. Return to the Duotone Options dialog box by choosing Duotone from the Image | Mode submenu. In the Duotone Options dialog box, click on the box with the diagonal line in it for Ink 1 or Ink 2. The Duotone Curve dialog box appears, containing a graph depicting the ink coverage over different image areas.

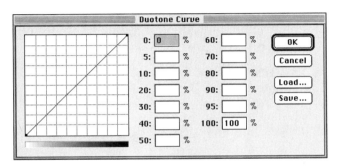

In the Duotone Curve dialog box, observe the graph on the left and the percentages on the right. In the graph, the x-axis represents the tonal range in the original image, from highlights to shadows. The y-axis represents the ink density values. The default settings of the graph are always represented by a diagonal line. The diagonal indicates that the printing ink percentage matches the black percentage value of every pixel in the image. This means if the image contains black values of 100%, they will print at 100 percent density (a 100 percent dot of the specified ink color) for the specified ink. A 50% midtone pixel will be printed at a 50 percent density (a 50 percent dot of the specified ink). The diagonal line can be adjusted by clicking and dragging it or by typing percentage values in the entry fields on the right. The numbers entered into the fields set ink density. The 0% field represents highlights (the lightest portions of the image), the 50% field represents the midtones, and the 100% field represents shadows (the darkest portions of the image). Thus, if you enter **80** in the 100% box, it means an 80 percent dot of the specified ink will be used to print the darkest shadow areas.

2. Click on the middle of the diagonal line and drag downward. When you click, a small dot (control point) is added to the curve, and a value is entered into the 50% field. (If you did not click exactly on the middle of the curve, Photoshop enters a value in the field corresponding to the point where you clicked.) The value entered is the percentage of ink density for midtone areas.

3. Try making some adjustments in the curve by clicking and dragging and by typing percentages into the fields. When you drag the curve upward, you add more of the ink to the image; drag the curve downward, and you use less ink. If you type a percentage into the field, a corresponding control point appears on the curve.

 NOTE: *You can save a Duotone Curve and load it into the Curves dialog box (Image | Adjust | Curves). You can also load a curve that was created in the Curves dialog box into the Duotone Curve dialog box.*

4. When you have finished experimenting with adjustments to the curve, click OK to return to the Duotone Options dialog box. Click OK again to see the adjusted curve's effects on your image.

Viewing the Duotone's Readouts in the Info Palette

Once you have examined your duotone image on screen, you may decide to make adjustments to the curve or to change the color of the inks. Before you do, it's often a good idea to analyze the true colors in your image by viewing the Eyedropper's readouts in the Info palette. Viewing these readouts of ink percentages ensures that you don't rely totally on how the image looks on your monitor.

If the Info palette is not open, select Show Info from the Window menu. If the Info palette readout does not display two inks, click on the Info palette's pop-up menu arrow. In the Info Options dialog box, in First Color Readout, choose Actual Color from the Mode pop-up menu. Because all duotone colors are displayed in the first readout, you can hide the second readout by also setting it to Actual Color. Click OK to confirm the settings. The image's actual color values in percentages for both inks appear in the Info palette.

 TIP: *Consult your printer to find out what a good total ink coverage would be for your job. Then set the Info palette's Second Color Readout to display Total Ink so that you can monitor the ink percentages.*

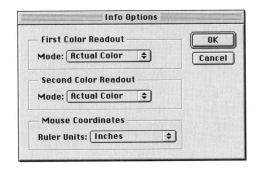

 TIP: *For a shortcut to changing the First and/or Second Color Readout settings in the Info Options dialog box, click on the first and/or second Eyedropper in the Info palette.*

Now move the mouse pointer over different areas of your image. Notice that the Info palette displays the percentage of each individual duotone ink. This can help you judge the degree of change if you edit the curve in the Duotone Curve dialog box, as well as give you a sense of how the image will print, regardless of the brightness settings on your monitor.

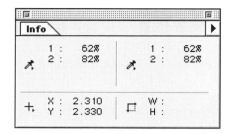

 TIP: *Use the Color Sampler tool to set sample points in your image before converting to Duotone mode. In Duotone mode, you can then adjust the curves while you view the readouts and preview on screen.*

Saving and Loading Duotone Settings

Use the Save and Load buttons in the Duotone Options dialog box to save duotone curves, ink settings, ink colors, and overprint colors (colors printed on top of each other). To save your settings, reopen the Duotone Options dialog box (select Duotone in the Image | Mode submenu), then click on the Save button. In the dialog box, name the file and click on Save (Windows users: OK). Once you have saved a setting, it can be loaded and applied to other grayscale images that you wish to convert to duotones.

 NOTE: *Clicking the Overprint Colors button allows you to adjust the screen display of overprint colors (two colors) so that you can visualize how colors will look when ink combinations are output. After you click the Overprint Colors button, you can click on the color swatch in the Overprint Colors dialog box to adjust the colors. When adjusting the overprint colors, it's best to use a printed sample of the overprint colors as a guide. Also note that the adjustment in the Overprint Colors dialog box only affects screen display.*

PHOTOSHOP'S PRESET DUOTONE CURVES If you are hesitant about picking your own colors for creating duotones, you can use Photoshop's preset inks and curves for duotones, tritones, and quadtones. These ink and curve samples are loaded on your hard disk during Photoshop installation. You can find them in the Duotone Presets folder.

To access the sample set, click the Load button in the Duotone Options dialog box. In the Open dialog box, use the mouse to move to the Duotone Presets folder and open it. Inside it you will see three folders: Duotones, Quadtones, and Tritones. Inside each of these folders are other folders for Gray, PANTONE, and Process (CMYK Color) files. Select and open a Gray, PANTONE, or Process file from within its folder. After you open a file, you will be returned to the Duotone Options dialog box. Click OK to apply the settings to your image.

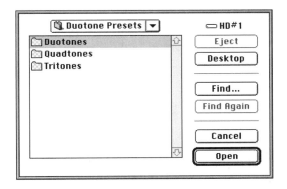

CREATING A SEPIA   In the Process Tritones folder, accessed by opening the Tritones folder (Windows users: Tritone) found in the Duotone Presets folder, Photoshop has included four different sepia settings for you to use. A *sepia* is a light reddish-brown tone applied to a photograph to give it an aged effect. Try creating a sepia, using the same file you used in the preceding section.

1. Open the Duotone Options dialog box by choosing Duotone from the Mode menu.

2. To load one of Photoshop's Sepia settings, click on the Load button in the Duotone Options dialog box. Then open the Duotone Presets folder, and from there select the Tritones folder (Windows users: Tritone).

3. From within the Tritones folder, open the Process Tritones folder.

12

4. In the list of files, notice BMY Sepia 1, BMY Sepia 2, BMY Sepia 3, and BMY Sepia 4. Select and open any one of these Sepia files. Instantly, the settings appear in the Duotone Options dialog box.

5. To preview the changes to your image, click OK in the Duotones Options dialog box.

After you have previewed the settings, you may want to try another sepia setting; just repeat the above steps to do so.

After you have created a sepia image, you may wish to add to your document other objects or images that contain more colors than the ones in your tritone file. In order to do this, you must convert the tritone file to Indexed Color, RGB Color, Lab Color, or CMYK Color. However, if you convert back to grayscale, your original grayscale image returns, not the curve-adjusted image.

Converting Duotones to Spot Colors

Although a Duotone is a one-channel image, you can convert it to a Multichannel mode image which converts the duotone colors to separate spot colors. The Spot colors appear as printing plates in the Channels palette. Once the image is converted, you can reorder the position of the colors by clicking and dragging the color in the Channels palette. You can also create a selection in a channel and remove color from a portion of the channel. (See Chapter 14 to learn more about using Spot Colors in Photoshop.)

To convert a Duotone mode image to a Multichannel mode image choose Image | Mode Multichannel.

Printing a Duotone

Before you print your duotone (or tritone or quadtone) image, you need to specify settings for halftone screen angles, printing resolution, and screen frequency. For more information about these printing options, see Chapter 19.

To print the file, choose Print from the File menu. If you wish to print a composite image, click OK; otherwise, select Separations in the Space pop-up menu and then click OK.

To print a duotone from QuarkXPress or Adobe Illustrator, save the Photoshop file in EPS format, as explained in Appendix A. If you are using PANTONE or any spot colors in your image, you need to have the same PANTONE names in QuarkXPress and Adobe Illustrator as you do in Photoshop. Because QuarkXPress

Photoshop 5 In Action

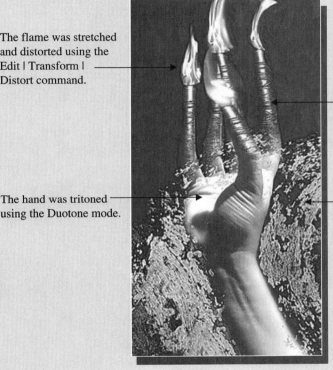

The flame was stretched and distorted using the Edit | Transform | Distort command.

The hand was composited with the metal end of a paintbrush.

The hand was tritoned using the Duotone mode.

The background texture is a digitized image of a burned saucepan.

© 1994DC Comics Inc.

12

Artist: Dave McKean   Client: Vertigo/DC Comics

This version of the "Five of Wands" tarot card is one image from a completely digital 78-card Tarot deck, all created by the artist.

Dave began by scanning a photograph of his wife's hands. He composited the hand with digitized images of the metal end of a paint brush and of flames. Using the commands in the Edit | Transform submenu, Dave twirled and stretched the flames to enhance the fire effect. He then created a Tritone out of the hand by converting it to Duotone mode and then selecting three inks to create a tritone. The tritone effect changed the color of the hand to better match the color of the metal paintbrush handle.

The unusual background texture was created in an unorthodox manner—by scanning the bottom of a burned saucepan.

and Illustrator use "short" PANTONE names, the Short PANTONE Names option must be selected in Photoshop's General Preferences dialog box. (Select Preferences from the File menu and then choose General.) If the Short PANTONE Names option was not activated when you chose your PANTONE colors, you must return to the Duotone Options dialog box and choose them again, or you can type in the correct names.

If you will not be outputting your duotone (or tritone or quadtone) files yourself, consult with your prepress house or print shop to ensure that the images will be output properly.

Converting from Grayscale to Bitmap

In order to convert an image to black and white, the image must be converted to Bitmap. In Bitmap mode, many of Photoshop's editing options are not available; thus it is often preferable to edit in Grayscale mode and then convert to Bitmap. In this section, you'll learn the different options available when you convert to Bitmap, as well as how to create a mezzotint.

Only grayscale and multichannel images can be converted to Bitmap mode. When you convert from Grayscale mode to Bitmap mode, a dialog box appears, in which you set the output resolution of the file and the conversion method. After you make your choices, click OK to apply them to your image. Following are descriptions of the five conversion methods.

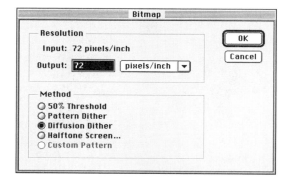

50% Threshold

This conversion method creates high-contrast black-and-white images. When the conversion is executed, Photoshop sets the threshold level at 128 pixels. All pixel values in the grayscale image below 128 are converted to black; all pixel values of 128 and greater are converted to white.

 TIP: *To obtain better results, you may wish to choose Image | Adjust | Threshold to better control the image's appearance before converting to Bitmap.*

Pattern Dither

In this conversion, the gray levels are changed into geometric patterns composed of black and white dots.

Diffusion Dither

This conversion method uses a diffusion process to change a pixel to black and white. This diffuses the error between the original grayscale pixels and the black and white pixels. The result is a grainy effect.

Halftone Screen

This conversion method makes the image appear as if it is a grayscale image printed using a halftone screen. Halftone Screen is typically used to print images on non-PostScript printers.

In the Halftone Screen dialog box, choose a Frequency, Angle, and Shape for the halftone pattern.

- Acceptable values for the screen frequency (often called *line screen*) range from 1.000 to 999.999 for lines per inch and from .400 to 400 for lines per centimeter. Decimal values are acceptable. Newspapers often use a screen frequency of 85; magazines, 150. If you do not know the correct screen frequency, check with your print shop.

- Screen angles from –180 to 180 may be entered.

- Shape choices are Round, Diamond, Ellipse, Line, Square, and Cross.

Halftone Screen settings may be saved and loaded by using the Save and Load buttons in the dialog box.

12

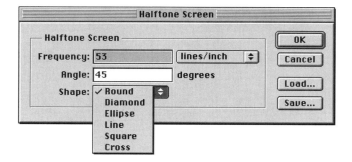

Custom Pattern

This conversion method allows you to apply a custom pattern to a bitmapped image. This option will be dimmed unless a custom pattern is defined. To define the pattern, select an area with the marquee and choose Edit | Define Pattern before converting to Bitmap.

Creating a Mezzotint

A mezzotint is a black-and-white image that appears to consist of randomly shaped dots. Mezzotints are used to create special effects in black-and-white images. Traditionally, mezzotints were created with halftone screens designed to produce random or unusual dot effects. In Photoshop, creating a mezzotint is fairly easy and can be accomplished in just a few steps.

 NOTE: *You can also use Photoshop's Mezzotint filter to create mezzotints. For more information, see Chapter 10.*

Before you can create a mezzotint, you must first define a pattern. After you convert from Grayscale mode to Bitmap mode, you apply the pattern to the bitmapped image to create the mezzotint. For this exercise, load a Pattern from the Patterns folder which is in the Goodies folder.

1. Select File | Open. Open the PostScript Patterns folder located in the Patterns folder, and open the Mezzotint-shape file.

2. After you have opened the mezzotint pattern file, the EPS Rasterizer dialog box appears, containing settings for the Width, Height, Resolution, and Mode of the pattern. Click OK to accept the default settings, and the pattern will appear.

3. Choose Select | All to select the entire pattern. Then choose Define Pattern from the Edit menu and close the file.

 TIP: *Before defining the pattern, you may wish to use the Blur or Blur More command from the Filter | Blur submenu to blur the pattern you will be using in the conversion process, so that the edges of the pattern blend together.*

4. Load the file to which you want to apply the mezzotint. (If the file is not a grayscale image, you'll need to convert it by choosing Grayscale from the Image | Mode submenu. If you wish, you can use the Skull file in the Samples folder.)

5. Convert the Grayscale mode image to Bitmap mode by choosing Bitmap from the Image | Mode submenu.

 TIP: *Before you convert your grayscale image to a bitmap image, there are a few steps you can take to enhance or alter the effect of the mezzotint. Use the Brightness/Contrast command in the Image | Adjust submenu so that the converted bitmap image will display more contrast. This will produce fewer dots and more solid blacks and whites.*

6. When the Bitmap dialog box appears, select the Custom Pattern option. (It will no longer be dimmed because you defined a pattern in steps 2 and 3.) Enter an Output Resolution (the higher the Output Resolution, the better the image pattern quality). The Input Resolution is the resolution of the original file. Click OK.

You should now have a mezzotint on screen. Figure 12-2 shows an image before a mezzotint was applied, and Figure 12-3 demonstrates the mezzotint effect.

After you have created a mezzotint, you may wish to add color to enhance the image, or create some special effects. To add color to a bitmapped image, you must first convert to Grayscale and then to a color mode.

12

FIGURE 12-2 Before creating a mezzotint

FIGURE 12-3 Bitmap mezzotint effect applied to photograph shown in Figure 12-2

Converting from Bitmap to Grayscale

When you convert from Bitmap mode to Grayscale mode, the Grayscale dialog box appears, allowing you to enter a Size Ratio from 1 to 16. The Size Ratio is the multiple by which you wish to decrease an image's size. For instance, if you enter **2**, the final image will be one-half its original size. Enter **3**, and the image will decrease to one-third its original size.

Using Several Modes to Create a Colored Mezzotint Effect

Here's a design tip that utilizes a combination of mode changes to create a colored mezzotint effect. To produce the effect, start with a color file; then select your entire image and choose Copy from the Edit menu. Next, create a mezzotint by first defining a pattern, then converting the color image to Grayscale mode, and then from Grayscale to Bitmap mode using the Custom Pattern method. After the mezzotint is created, convert from Bitmap to Grayscale and then to a color mode.

After you have converted from Bitmap to a color mode, paste the copied colored image. Use the Lighten mode in the Layers palette to blend the black-and-white mezzotint image with the colored image.

Lab Color Mode

As mentioned earlier in the book, Lab Color is the internal format Photoshop uses while making mode conversions. For instance, when Photoshop converts from RGB Color to CMYK Color, it first converts the RGB colors to Lab Color and then converts from Lab Color to CMYK Color.

Lab Color mode images have three channels: a Lightness (or luminance) channel and two color channels designated as channel a (green to magenta) and

12

Photoshop 5 ▶ In Action

Design Director: Michael Grossman   **Art Director: Mark Michaelson**

Before converting to Bitmap mode, the Brightness/Contrast command in the Image | Adjust submenu was used to increase contrast in the image.

After the image was converted from Bitmap mode to CMYK Color, it was filled with color (yellow) using the Paint Bucket tool.

When converting to Bitmap mode, the Diffusion Dither option was chosen to create the black-and-white dot patterns.

Production: Carlos Lema   **Client: Entertainment Weekly**

When Entertainment Weekly decided to publish an article on the movie "JFK," design director Michael Grossman and art director Mark Michaelson decided to include an image of John F. Kennedy on the magazine's cover. Michael and Carlos Lema worked with a grayscale photo of Kennedy. To make the grayscale image more interesting, they slightly distorted it using the Skew command in the Edit | Transform submenu. From Bitmap mode, the image was converted back to Grayscale and then to CMYK Color, so that color could be added and separations could be created from the image.

channel b (blue to yellow). Use Lab Color mode if you wish to edit an image's lightness independently of its color values. To do this, click to activate the Lightness channel in the Channels palette. In the Lightness channel, you can edit the Lightness values of an image or even select the entire image and paste it into a new file. The copied image in the new file will be a grayscale version of your original because you copied and pasted only the Lightness component of the image.

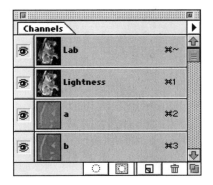

As discussed in Chapter 4, Lab Color is a device-independent color model that helps provide consistent color on various output devices. Thus, Lab Color is also the model used for transferring files between different color systems. For instance, Kodak's Photo CD uses YCC for its images. YCC is Kodak's own version of the Lab Color model; Y is the lightness, or luminance, value, and the two C channels are similar to Photoshop's channels a and b. Thus, when you load a Photo CD image into Photoshop, there should be little or no loss of color data. Because PostScript Level 2 takes advantage of Lab's device-independent color model, Lab Color is the recommended mode for printing to PostScript Level 2 printers.

12

Conclusion

As you have read in this chapter, the color modes in Photoshop are vital to producing CMYK separations, duotones, and mezzotints. In upcoming chapters, you'll add alpha channels to an image in order to create masks and special effects. You'll also learn how various dialog boxes allow you to adjust colors in individual channels.

CHAPTER 13

Creating Paths and Masks with the Pen Tool

When you create objects with Photoshop's Pen tool, it's almost like being in two programs at once: a painting program and a drawing program. Unlike Photoshop's painting tools, which paint directly onto the electronic canvas, the Pen tool creates wireframe shapes that exist *above underlying pixels*. This allows the Pen tool in Photoshop to create Bézier curves and intricate objects in much the same way as pen tools in programs such as Adobe Illustrator and Freehand. As in Illustrator and Freehand, objects created by the Pen tool are called *paths*. However, unlike drawing programs, Photoshop paths are not primarily used for drawing; instead they're most commonly used for tracing over image areas to create masks (which can be turned into selections) to aid in image editing.

Creating Paths and Masks with the Pen Tool

A path can be a point, a line, or a curve, but usually it's a series of line segments or curve segments connected by their end points. Because they don't lock down onto the background pixels on screen, paths can easily be reshaped, reselected, and moved. They can also be saved and exported to other programs. Thus, paths are unlike any object created with Photoshop's painting tools and unlike any selection created by Photoshop selection tools.

The most common way of creating a path is to use Photoshop's Pen, Freeform Pen, or Magnetic Pen tool. The Pen tools and the path-editing tools are all located in the one Toolbox location. As you'll see throughout this chapter, the Pen tools work in conjunction with the Paths palette.

The commands accessed through the Paths palette allow paths to be filled, stroked, and turned into selections. Without these commands, the intricate and precise shapes you create with Photoshop's Pen tools would be useless, because most of Photoshop's menu commands and tools have no effect on paths. However, in Photoshop 5, the Edit | Transform commands can all be applied to paths.

 NOTE: *Several images in the color insert, particularly image 30, provide excellent examples of how paths are used by professional Photoshop artists.*

Before you can begin to turn paths into artwork and into Photoshop selections, you need to learn some fundamentals. Since most paths created with the Pen tools consist of lines and/or curves, this chapter begins with an explanation of how to create straight and curved path segments and how to join them together. You'll learn how to change a smooth corner into an angled corner and how to change a path into a selection (and vice versa).

Then you'll be introduced to the Fill Path, Stroke Path, Make Selection, and Save Path commands in the Paths palette. Once you learn how to save paths,

Photoshop 5 > In Action

New York City artist, Wendy Grossman created this image for Electronic Musician Magazine. Wendy generally starts her images by creating a pencil sketch. After scanning the sketch into the computer, she e-mails it to the client for approval. Once she receives approval from the client she begins creating the image.

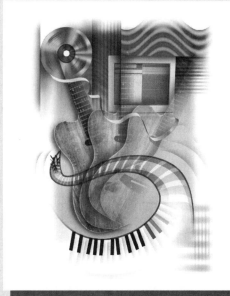

To create the two focal points in this image—the bottom part of the guitar and the keyboard—Wendy primarily used the Pen tool. She created a path for the keyboard, turned the paths into selections and filled them with black. To fade out the keyboard, Wendy created a Layer Mask, then airbrushed away areas she wanted to fade out.

To create the bottom of the guitar, Wendy converted the path into a selection and filled it with white. To produce the texture for the guitar, Wendy used a scanned wood texture, then applied the Image | Adjust | Levels command to fine-tune

Artist: Wendy Grossman   Client: Electronic Musician Magazine

the color and saturation. To create the guitar neck, Wendy scanned a photo of a guitar, selected it and copied the neck on top of the bottom of the guitar. She created the other guitars by selecting the first one, duplicating it and rotating the duplicates in different layers. Each guitar was set at a different opacity in the layer it was in.

To create the movie reel, Wendy used her scanned pencil sketches as a guide to create an oval selection, then subtracted the middle from the selection. She applied MetaCreations KPTGradient Designer filter to the oval selection. Wendy let part of the pencil sketch show through to make the black film more believable. To create the film strip, she created a path in Photoshop, exported it as an Illustrator path, and imported it into Adobe Dimensions where she extruded it into a 3D object. Later, she imported the 3-D filmstrip into Photoshop.

13

you'll be able to reload and hide different paths. If need be, you can convert the paths to selections so that the selections can be used as *masks*. A mask allows you to protect an area on screen so that you can edit, paint, or apply a filter within it—without affecting surrounding portions of the image.

At the end of the chapter, you'll learn how to create another type of mask, called a *clipping path*. Clipping paths are typically used to silhouette an area and mask out the background image areas so that only the area within the clipping path will appear when the file is placed into other programs, such as Illustrator, PageMaker, and QuarkXPress.

Pen and Path Palette Fundamentals

To access the Pen and path editing tools, you can press P on your keyboard, or click on the Pen tool's Toolbox location with the mouse. If you keep the mouse button pressed, you'll not only see the Pen tools, but the path editing tools as well.

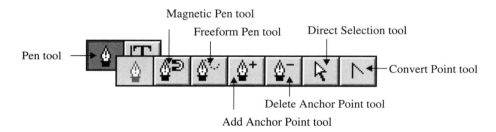

At first glance, you may find the Pen tool a little confusing because it seems as though there are five Pen tools. Here is a brief summary of what all the tools do.

 TIP: *You can select each of the Pen tools, one at a time by pressing SHIFT-P.*

- ☐ The *Pen tool* is the most precise of all of the Pen tools. Use it when you need to create smooth and intricate paths. Using the Pen tool is covered in detail in this chapter.

- ☐ The *Magnetic Pen tool* creates a path by automatically tracing over image edges, as you click and move the mouse or click and drag.

- ☐ The *Freeform Pen tool* works like a real pen tool. It allows you to create paths as you click and drag to create shapes.

- ☐ The *Add Anchor Point tool* (the pen with the plus sign) is used to add points to a path that has already been created.

- The *Subtract Anchor Point tool* (the pen with the minus sign) is used for subtracting points from a path.

- The *Direct Selection (Arrow) tool* is used to select and deselect paths and points on paths.

- The *Convert Point tool* lets you convert a smooth corner of a path into a sharp corner, and vice versa.

As mentioned earlier, once you create a path, it appears in the Paths palette. If you add segments and shapes to the path, they are considered subpaths of the path that appears in the Paths palette. When you create a new path by clicking on the New Path icon in the Paths palette, Photoshop hides all other paths. To view a hidden path, you simply click on its name in the Paths palette.

The icons at the bottom of the Paths palette are shortcuts for commands that appear in the palette's pop-up menu. These icons let you quickly fill a path with color, stroke a path with a foreground color, load a path as a selection, make a path from a selection, create a new path, and delete a path.

Take a moment to click on the pop-up menu arrow now, and examine the choices offered. Notice the commands Fill Path and Stroke Path (Fill and Stroke Subpath, if you have a subpath selected). When you wish to fill or stroke a path, you must access these commands from the Paths palette, *not* from the Edit menu's Fill and Stroke choices.

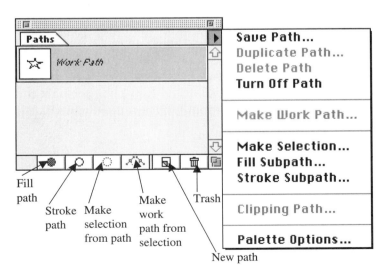

13

Another important point to remember is that Photoshop's tools and many of its menu commands do not affect a path unless you convert a path to a selection first.

Before you begin to use the Pen tool, click on the Paths pop-up menu and choose Palette Options. When the Paths Palette Options dialog box appears, make sure that the second radio button next to the second starfish (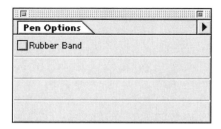) is selected. This allows you to see a small thumbnail of your path in the Paths palette (using a large thumbnail might slow down screen display). If you choose None, the thumbnail preview is turned off. Click OK to close the dialog box. Next, take a look at the Pen Options palette. Open it by double-clicking on the Pen tool (the first pen icon in the Tool palette).

The sole option in the palette is the Rubber Band check box.

When this option is selected, a path segment trails the Pen tool after an anchor point is created. As you move the Pen tool on screen, the segment is displayed from your last mouse click to the current pen position, as if you were stretching a rubber band. If you don't turn the Rubber Band option on, each path segment appears only after you click the mouse to connect anchor points, rather than as you move the mouse.

Select the Rubber Band option now to turn it on; then click on the palette's Close box (Windows 95/NT users: click on the X in the upper-right corner) to close the palette. In the next sections, you'll see how the Rubber Band previews path segments as you create them.

Creating Paths

There are several ways to create paths:

☐ The quickest is to simply start by clicking on screen with one of the Pen tools. When you create a path this way, Photoshop displays it in the Paths palette and names it Work Path. Later you can save the path to give it a specific name.

 You can click on the New Path icon in the Paths palette. After you click, Photoshop creates a new path and automatically names it Path 1 in the Paths palette. Subsequent paths are named Path 2, Path 3, Path 4, etc.

 You can choose New Path from the Paths palette's menu. This opens the New Path dialog box, where you can enter a name for the path. After you click OK, the name of the path appears in the Paths palette. As a shortcut, you can press OPTION (Windows users: ALT) and click on the New Path icon. (If a Work Path—a path without a name—is selected in the Paths palette, the New Path command is replaced by the Save Path command.)

REMEMBER: *When you create a new path, Photoshop hides all other paths from the screen. To view a hidden path, click on the path's name in the Paths palette.*

Drawing with the Freeform Pen Tool

 The Freeform Pen tool is the easiest of Photoshop's tools to use. All you need to do to create a path with the Freeform Pen tool is to click and drag. When you use the Freeform Pen tool you draw pretty much the same you would draw if you had a real pen in your hand. Use the Freeform Pen tool to create a quick outline on screen. Once you create a path, you can always fine-tune it by adjusting it with either the Direct Selection tool or one of the other editing tools discussed later in this chapter.

In this section, you'll see how you can create a simple path with the Freeform Pen tool and turn it into a selection. Start by loading an image that includes an object that you want to select. For instance load the CMYK balloons file in the Samples folder (located in the Goodies folder), and try to trace over a balloon. Before you start using the Freeform Pen tool, select it in the Tool palette, then double-click on the tool to view the tool's Options in the Freeform Pen Options palette. The Curve Fit option in the palette controls how many anchor points the Freeform Pen tool creates. The higher the number, the fewer the anchor points, and thus the simpler the curve. In general, simpler curves are easier to edit and produce smooth curves. Unless you are creating a very complicated path, leave the Curve Fit field ast the default setting of 2 pixels. You can enter a value from- .5 to 10 in the field.

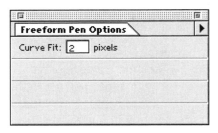

NOTE: *The Curve Fit option in the Freeform Pen Options palette controls the number of anchor points created. It is described in detail in the next section.*

Now start creating a path by moving the Freeform Pen tool over an area on screen, then click and drag to outline the object. As you click and drag, the Freeform Pen tool creates the path. To stop creating the path, simply release the mouse button. If you wish to continue the path from where you stopped, click on the last anchor point, then continue clicking and dragging. If you wish to finish the path to create a closed path, click and drag to where you started the point. When you return to the path's starting point, a tiny circle appears on screen. Release the mouse when you see the circle.

Now that you have a path on screen, you can turn it into a selection, fill it, or stroke it. These subjects are covered in more detail later in this chapter. However, if you wish to quickly turn the path into a selection, simply click on the Make Selection icon in the Paths palette. Once the selection is created, you activate any Photoshop command that affects selections. You can copy and paste, run a filter, correct the colors in the image, and so on.

Tracing with the Magnetic Pen Tool

Creating complicated paths can take some time to master with the Pen tool. If you don't have the time, you may want to try your hand at the Magnetic Pen tool. This tool helps you create intricate paths by automatically snapping to image edges that you trace over. Before you try out the tool, load an image that includes an area that you wish to mask. Then activate the Magnetic Pen tool in the Tool palette by clicking and dragging to it, or by pressing OPTION (Windows users: ALT) and pressing P until the Magnetic Pen tool is selected.

After you select the Magnetic Pen tool, double-click on it in the palette to open the options in the Magnetic Pen Options palette. Here are the options in the palette:

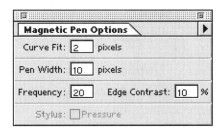

- **Curve Fit** controls how many anchor points the tool creates. The higher the number, the fewer the anchor points, and thus the simpler the curve. You can enter a value from 0.5 to 10 in the field.

- **Pen Width** controls image edge detection. The Magnetic Pen tool uses the value in the Pen Width field to determine how far from the Pen pointer to look for image edges. When the value is set to 10 pixels (the default setting), the Magnetic Pen tool detects image edges up to 10 pixels away. If you are trying to trace over an image that includes twists and turns, you'll probably want to lower the value. Acceptable values are from 1 to 40 pixels.

 NOTE: *Stylus users: Click the Stylus Pressure option in the dialog box. Adding pressure to the stylus increases Pen Width.*

 TIP: *You can increase the magnetic Pen Width one pixel at a time by pressing]; to decrease one Pen width one pixel at a time press[.*

- **Frequency** controls how fast the Magnetic Pen tool adds anchor points. Higher values drop anchor points faster. Enter values between 5% and 40%.

- **Edge Contrast** controls how the Magnetic Pen tool reacts to different contrast values along image edges. Enter higher values to have the Magnetic Pen tool recognize edges that contain more contrast. Enter lower percentage values to detect lower contrast. As a general rule, when tracing over images with high contrast edges, you can set the Edge Contrast percentage and Pen Width high. On images with less contrast set the Edge Contrast and Pen Width low.

To trace an image with the Magnetic Pen tool, start by clicking to establish a magnetic point, then move the Magnetic Pen along the edge of the object (you

13

don't need to keep the mouse button clicked). The Magnetic Pen starts creating a path based upon the image's edge contrast and the Magnetic Pen option settings. If the path of the Magnetic Pen jumps off the edge you are tracing, simply click the mouse to add a magnetic point, then continue to move the mouse along the object.

Here are three ways you can end the path:

- ☐ To end the path and close it, double-click.

- ☐ To end the path and close it with a straight line segment, press OPTION (Windows users: ALT) and double-click.

- ☐ To end the path and leave it as an open path, press ENTER (Mac users can press ENTER or RETURN).

 TIP: *To temporarily draw in freehand mode, press OPTION (Windows users: ALT) as you click and drag the mouse.*

 TIP: *To create a straight path segment as your work, press OPTION (Windows users: ALT) and click the mouse.*

We created Figure 13-1 using the Magnetic Pen tool. We wanted to add a shell to the original image (Figure 13-2), so we traced a shell from another image (Figure 13-3) with the Magnetic Pen tool. As we worked, we found that occasionally we needed to stop and click along image edges to ensure that the Magnetic Pen captured the edge precisely. Once we created the path, we converted it into a selection by clicking on the Make Selection icon at the bottom of the Paths palette. To complete the image, we added type. We used Photoshop's Layer | Effects | Drop Shadow and Layer | Effects | Bevel and Emboss commands to add depth to the type. To bend the type, we used the Filter | Distort | Shear command. If you want to practice with the Magnetic Pen tool, try tracing over an image in one file, convert it into a selection, then copy and paste it into another file. If the Samples folder is installed on your hard disk, try using these techniques to mask a balloon from the CMYK Balloons file, and paste it into the Big sky file.

FIGURE 13-1   Final shell composition

FIGURE 13-2   Original image

13

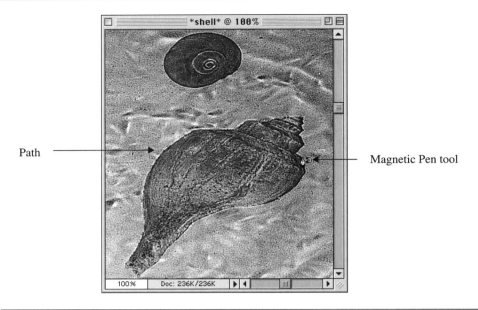

Path ⟶

Magnetic Pen tool ⟵

FIGURE 13-3   Magnetic Pen tool masking seashell

Drawing Straight Paths

When you use the Pen tool to create a straight path, you first click to establish a starting point, then move the mouse to another position and click again to establish the end point. Each time you click the mouse to establish a starting or ending point, you create an *anchor point*.

In this section, you will learn how to create straight paths by connecting anchor points. To begin, create a new file, 5 inches by 5 inches. To make it easier to execute the following steps, select Show Rulers from the View menu.

1. If the Pen tool isn't activated, click on it and move it into your document about 2 inches from the top and 1 inch from the left, then click. A small gray or black square appears on screen; this is the first anchor point. In the Paths palette, notice that a work path is created. Work Path is the default name Photoshop assigns to all new paths.

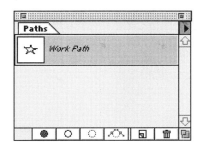

 NOTE: *If a path already exists on screen, creating a new path adds the new path to the existing work path. If you wish to create a new path, click the New Path icon in the Paths palette, or choose New Path from the Paths palette menu.*

 NOTE: *If CAPS LOCK is on or if the Other Cursors Precise option is selected in the Preferences Display & Cursors dialog box, the pen pointer changes into a crosshair. The effects of using the Pen tool are the same whether you work with the pen pointer or the crosshair.*

2. Move the Pen tool to the right, about 1.5 inches away from the first anchor point, and click. This creates a second anchor point, connected to the first anchor point with a straight path segment. Notice that the second anchor point is gray or black and the first one is now hollow. The gray or black anchor point is the one that is currently selected; the hollow anchor point is no longer selected. Also notice that the Work Path thumbnail in the Paths palette updates as you make changes to the Work Path on screen.

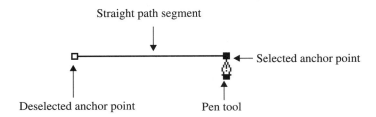

 CAUTION: *When drawing straight paths, don't click and drag the mouse when you click to create an anchor point or you will create a curve rather than a line.*

3. Press and hold SHIFT while you create a third anchor point anywhere on your screen.

 NOTE: *If you press and hold SHIFT, this will constrain the Pen tool so that the path segments are drawn to the nearest 45-degree angle.*

The path you have just created is called an *open path.* An open path has two end points, a beginning and an end. As long as you have an open path and the Pen tool is activated, the Rubber Band will keep stretching from your last anchor point to the Pen tool's current position. Thus every time you click the mouse, you will be extending the open path. To stop Photoshop from extending an open path every time the Pen tool is clicked, you can save a path or close a path. You can also click again on the Pen tool in the Toolbox or switch to the Direct Selection tool and deselect. You'll learn how to save, close, and deselect paths later in this chapter.

If you make a mistake while creating your first path, press DELETE (Windows users can also press BACKSPACE) once to erase the last path segment. Be careful not to press DELETE twice; if you do, you will erase the entire Work Path. If you press DELETE three times, all paths on the screen will be erased.

If you wish to continue experimenting with the Pen tool, move on to the next section, where you will learn how to deactivate the Pen tool in order to move a segment of a path or the entire path.

Selecting, Manipulating, Copying, Joining, and Deselecting Paths

After you have created a path, you might want to adjust it by moving an anchor point or the entire path. Or you may need to duplicate the path so you can use it elsewhere in the document.

To complete the following exercise, you will need to have a path created on screen. Either use the path from the previous exercise or create a new path. After you have a path on screen, you'll select an anchor point by first deactivating the Pen tool and then activating the Direct Selection tool in the Paths palette.

 1. Click on the Pen tool, then keep the mouse button pressed to activate the Direct Selection tool so you can select an anchor point. You can also access the Direct Selection tool by pressing P on your keyboard until the Direct Selection tool is displayed in the Toolbox.

2. Position the Direct Selection tool over the anchor point you wish to adjust, and click to select it. The selected anchor point turns black.

   If you don't see anchor points on your path, click anywhere on the path to display the anchor points. If all anchor points on your path are selected, you first need to deselect the path by clicking away from the path. Then click on the path again.

3. Drag the selected anchor point to a new location. When you click and drag, the path's angle and size are adjusted according to the angle at which you drag the anchor point and how far you move it. Notice that the path moves as if it were floating on another layer above the background pixels. Also notice that the Work Path in the Paths palette is updated.

4. Anchor points can also be moved using the directional arrow keys on your keyboard. Try this: Press the UP, DOWN, LEFT, and RIGHT arrow keys a few times. The selected anchor point moves in the direction of the keys you press in 1-pixel increments. If you press and hold SHIFT while you press one of the directional arrow keys, the selected anchor point moves in 10-pixel increments.

   To move the entire path as a single entity, every anchor point in the path must be selected. One technique for selecting additional anchor points is to SHIFT-click on each unselected anchor point. If the path you need to select is large, press OPTION (Windows users: ALT) and click on any segment or anchor point to select the entire path. You can also select an entire path by clicking and dragging over the entire path with the Direct Selection tool pointer.

5. Select the entire path on your screen by pressing OPTION (Windows users: ALT) and clicking on any segment or anchor point of the path. All the anchor points turn black or gray when the path is selected. Then click on any segment of the path and drag the path to a new location. Once a path is selected, you can copy it.

 TIP: *You can select different path segments by clicking and dragging over them with the Direct Selection tool. You can add to a path selection by pressing SHIFT and clicking anchor points or path segments.*

6. To copy the path, press OPTION (Windows users: ALT) while you click and drag the path with the Direct Selection tool to a new location (you'll see a

13

small black arrow as you click and drag). A duplicate of the path will appear. After the duplicate appears, release OPTION (Windows users: ALT) and the mouse button.

 TIP: *Here are several other ways to copy paths: (1) Select a path in the Paths palette, then choose Duplicate Path in the Paths palette menu. (2) Drag the path in the Paths palette to the New Path icon. (3) If you press OPTION (Windows users: ALT) and drag to the New Path icon, the Duplicate Path dialog box opens, allowing you to name the path before copying it.*

When you copy a path or create new path segments, Photoshop considers the segments to be subpaths. On screen, you now have two subpaths. To Photoshop, you still have one path on the screen, but the path is composed of the two subpaths. This distinction becomes important later in this chapter when you begin to use the Paths palette pop-up menu commands, such as Save Path, Fill Path, and Duplicate Path.

7. Now try joining the two subpaths on screen. First, reactivate the Pen tool. Click on the end point of one subpath, then click on the end point of the second subpath. The two subpaths become one path.

To deselect the path, activate the Direct Selection tool and then click away from the path. All of the anchor points disappear. Note that the anchor points will reappear when the path is reselected. After you deselect, you can create another subpath if you'd like.

Now that you understand the basics of drawing and adjusting straight paths, you are ready to learn about working with smooth curves, one of the features for which the Pen tool is best known. Before continuing, delete the path currently on your screen by pressing DELETE once if no anchor points on the path are selected. Press DELETE twice if any anchor point is selected. If you have more than one path on screen, press DELETE three times.

Drawing and Adjusting Curves with the Pen Tool

The Pen tool's ability to draw smooth curves with precision makes it an invaluable aid when you need to create any curved shape or selection. Drawing a curve with the Pen tool does, however, take some getting used to. You can't just draw a curve on screen as you would with the Lasso tool or one of the painting tools. As you'll see in the next exercise, drawing curves that slope in different directions with the Pen tool requires a moving, "seesaw" motion with the mouse.

If you do not have a document open, create a new one now; make it a 72-ppi file, 5 inches by 5 inches, with a white background. If the rulers and Info palette are not already displayed, select Show Rulers from the View menu and Show Info from the Window menu to turn these features on. If you are already in a document that has a path in it, click the New Path icon at the bottom of the Paths palette before beginning the exercise.

1. With the Pen tool selected, move the Pen's tip about 1 inch from the left side of your screen and about 2 inches down from the top. Click (an anchor point will be created) and drag down about 1.5 inches to begin the process of creating a curve that faces down. As you drag, the Pen pointer changes to an arrowhead, indicating that you are specifying a direction for the curve.

   As you drag, a *direction line* extends in opposite directions from the anchor point, as shown in Figure 13-4. Later, you'll see that the size and angle of the direction line determine the length and slope of the curve. The two end points of the direction lines are called *direction points*. By clicking and dragging on either of the direction line's direction points, you can move the direction line, and thus change the shape of the curve. Once the curve is created and deselected, the direction lines and points disappear.

 TIP: *Pressing SHIFT constrains direction lines in 45-degree increments.*

13

2. Now create the second anchor point for the curve. Move the Pen tool horizontally to the right about 1 inch from the first anchor point. To create a curve, click and drag straight up, as shown in Figure 13-5. Notice that the curve ends at the new anchor point. As you drag, the curve takes shape and a new direction line appears. Release the mouse after dragging up about 1.5 inches.

   Don't worry if you are feeling a little overwhelmed by all of the lines, points, and other items on your screen. At this stage, the most important concept to remember is that *the curve slopes in the direction in which you drag the mouse.* The first part of the curve you drew slopes downward (the

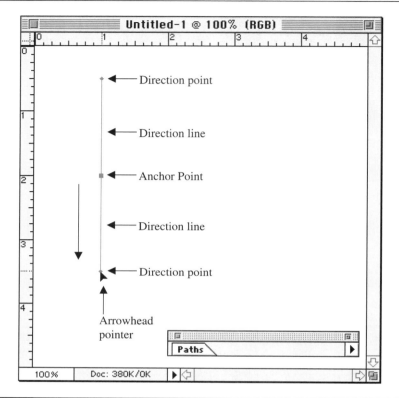

FIGURE 13-4 Clicking and dragging downward starts the process of creating the lower part of the curve

direction in which you originally dragged the mouse). The second part of the curve slopes upward, the direction in which you dragged in step 2.

 NOTE: *The curve you see on the screen is called a Bézier curve, named after the French mathematician Pierre Bézier, who defined the shape of a curve in mathematical terms with four direction points. By adjusting the direction points, you have complete control of the size and shape of the curve.*

3. To adjust the curve, you need to switch from the Pen tool to the Direct Selection tool. In the Paths palette, click on the Direct Selection tool. Then click on the bottom-left direction point of the curve and drag to the right.

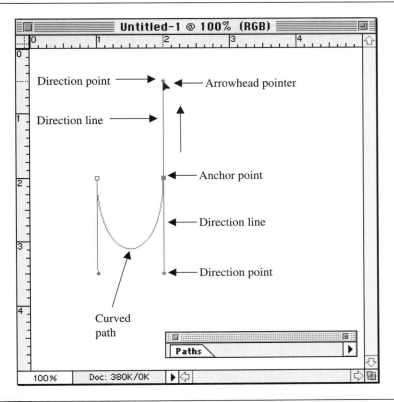

FIGURE 13-5   Clicking and dragging upward creates the upper part of the curve

Now click on the bottom-right direction point of the curve and drag to the left. Notice that the curve gets more pointed. If you wish to flatten the curve, drag both bottom direction points in opposite directions.

Another way to adjust the shape of a curve is to click on the curve segment itself with the Direct Selection tool, and then click and drag. When you do this, both direction lines will adjust themselves according to how you move the curve. You can also change the height and depth of the curve by clicking and dragging on the direction points to make the direction line larger or smaller. Try these techniques now in the next step.

4. Click and drag on the bottom-left, then bottom-right direction points to make both direction lines smaller and thus reduce the size of the curve.

After you have experimented with changing the direction lines, click and drag on the direction points to return the direction lines to their original length of about 1.5 inches from the anchor point.

5. Select the Pen tool again and click on the last anchor point you created so that you can create another curve segment.

6. To begin creating the next curve, move the Pen tool 1 inch directly to the right of the last anchor point you created. Then click and drag straight down approximately 1.5 inches, as shown in Figure 13-6.

Notice the smooth transition between the two continuous curves that you have created. The point between the two curves is called a *smooth point*. When the direction line that intersects a smooth anchor point is adjusted, the curves on either side of the smooth point change.

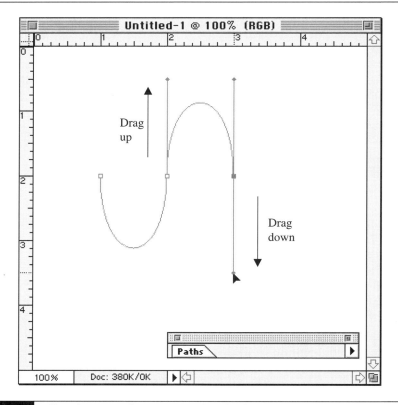

FIGURE 13-6 Creating a continuous curved path with the Pen tool

Besides changing the slope of a curve, you can also change its width by moving either one of its anchor points. Try this next.

7. Before changing the width of a curve, you must activate the Direct Selection tool. Here's a shortcut: With the Pen tool selected, press and hold COMMAND (Windows users: CTRL) to change the pen pointer (or crosshair) to the Direct Selection tool.

 TIP: *When the Pen tool is activated, you can temporarily activate the Direct Selection tool by pressing and holding COMMAND (Windows users: CTRL).*

8. Change the width of the curve you just drew by clicking on the last anchor point with the Direct Selection tool and then dragging to the left about .5 inch. Release the mouse to return to the Pen tool.

9. Continue creating curves, alternating between clicking and dragging up, then down. To practice some more, you may want to first press DELETE twice and delete the path currently on screen; then you can start all over again. If you create your first anchor point by dragging up, the first curve will slope upward.

 NOTE: *To make the direction lines of a curve segment reappear after a path is deselected, click on that curve segment with the Direct Selection tool.*

10. When you are done practicing, clear the screen by pressing DELETE twice. If you have more than one subpath on screen, press DELETE three times.

 TIP: *When creating curves, try to create the fewest anchor points possible—as far away from each other as you can. Also, don't create anchor points in the middle of the bulge of paths.*

Drawing Scalloped Curves

You can also draw curves so that they all point in the same direction. These scalloped curves can be used to create curved border effects around images. Scalloped curves cannot be drawn like the continuous curves you just created. When you create scalloped curves, you create a corner point in order to change the

13

direction in which the curve is drawn. As you'll see in the following exercise, the direction lines that stem from corner points do not work the same as direction lines that bisect smooth points: A corner point's direction line controls only one side of one curve.

1. To create the first curve, begin by positioning the Pen tool about .5 inch from the left side of your document window and about 2 inches from the top. The first curve you create will point upward, so start by clicking and dragging straight up about 1 inch.

2. Move the mouse horizontally to the right about 1.5 inches from the last anchor point. Click and drag straight down about 1 inch.

 TIP: *You can press SHIFT to constrain the anchor points, then press SHIFT again to constrain the direction line.*

The next curve you create will point in the same direction as the first curve. To accomplish this, you need to create a corner point between the curves.

3. To create a corner point, press OPTION (Windows users: ALT) while you click on the anchor point that you created in step 2. Notice that one of the direction lines disappears. Continue to keep OPTION (Windows users: ALT) pressed while you drag diagonally up to the right about 1 inch from the anchor point, to create a new direction line. Release OPTION (Windows users: ALT). This direction line will allow you to draw the next curve in the same direction as the line you just created.

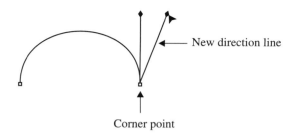

New direction line

Corner point

4. To create the second curve, move the Pen tool directly to the right about 1.5 inches away from the last anchor point. This will be the end point of the curve that you are about to create. Click and drag straight down about 1 inch, and a curve will appear.

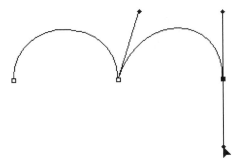

5. To create the third scalloped curve, repeat the technique used in steps 3 and 4. Position the mouse over the last anchor point you created, press OPTION (Windows users: ALT), and click and drag diagonally up to create a new direction line. Move the mouse about 1.5 inches to the right of the anchor point, and then click and drag down about 1 inch to create the curve.

6. When you are ready, delete the path currently on screen by pressing DELETE twice.

Creating a corner point to control the direction of a curve also enables you to create paths in which straight segments are joined to curves, as explained next.

Connecting Curves and Straight Paths

When you are using the Pen tool and working with paths, you'll often need to connect a line to a curve or a curve to a line. Shapes made of both curves and lines are all around you: vases, bottles, paddles, and so on. When you want to trace any of these shapes with the Pen tool or create them from scratch, you'll need to master the Pen tool techniques described in the following exercise.

Start by creating a curve and connecting a line segment to it.

1. If the Pen tool is not activated, select it. Position the Pen tool about 1 inch from the left side of the screen and about 2 inches from the top. To begin, click and drag straight up about 1 inch.

2. To create the curve, move the mouse 1 inch to the right from the first anchor point; then click and drag downward about 1 inch.

13

3. Next, create the corner point that will allow you to connect this curve to a line. Press OPTION (Windows users: ALT) and click once on the last anchor point you created. Notice that the bottom direction line disappears. Release the mouse and OPTION (Windows users: ALT).

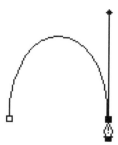

4. To create a line that connects to the curve, move the Pen tool to the right horizontally about 1 inch from the curve's second anchor point and click. Remember, if you want to create a line at an angle of 45 degrees (or increments thereof), you can press and hold SHIFT while you click. The curve is now connected to a line.

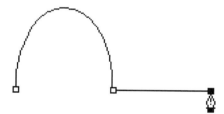

5. Now clear your screen by pressing DELETE twice, and try creating a line that connects it to a curve.

6. Create a line segment about 1 inch long by connecting two anchor points. If you need to review the steps to create line segments, refer to the earlier section "Drawing Straight Paths."

7. Use the OPTION (Windows users: ALT) key to create a corner point so the line can be connected to a curve. Press and hold OPTION (Windows users: ALT) while you click on the last anchor point you created and then drag diagonally upward to the right about 1 inch. When the direction line is

created, release the OPTION (Windows users: ALT) key and the mouse
button.

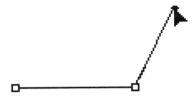

8. Now, to create a curve that connects to the line, move the Pen tool
   horizontally about 1 inch to the right of the corner point. Then click and
   drag straight down about 1 inch. If you need to adjust the curve, use the
   Direct Selection tool.

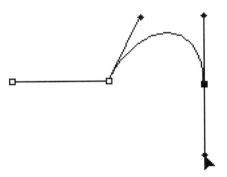

9. When you are finished practicing, clear the screen by pressing DELETE
   twice. If you have more than one path on screen, press three times.

Creating a Closed Path

The next technique you will learn is how to close a path. A closed path is a path
that ends at its starting point. Once a path is closed, you can move the pen pointer
away from it and create other paths. In this next exercise, you will create a closed
path in the shape of a triangle by connecting three anchor points.

   If you don't have a document open on screen, create a new one, 5 inches by 5
inches, with a white background. Make sure that the rulers and Info palette
are displayed.

1. Activate the Pen tool and move it up toward the top-middle part of the document. Using the ruler and Info palette as guides, position the Pen tool about 2.5 inches from the left side of the document window and about .5 inch down from the top. Click the mouse to create the first anchor point of the triangle.

2. To create a second anchor point, move the Pen tool diagonally down and left about 2 inches (in the Info palette, the x-axis is approximately 1.00 and the y-axis is approximately 2.5) and then click. This creates a line segment from the first anchor point to the second anchor point.

3. To create a third anchor point, move the Pen tool horizontally to the right of the second anchor point about 3 inches (at the 4-inch mark on the ruler) and click. This creates a line segment from the second anchor point to the third anchor point.

4. To close the path, you must return to the starting point of the triangle. Move the Pen tool to the first anchor point. You will see a small loop at the bottom-right side of the Pen tool; this indicates that you have returned to your starting point. Click the mouse and the path will be closed. When you click on the last anchor point, notice that the Info palette displays angle and distance readouts.

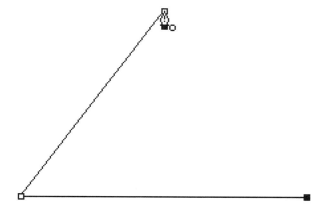

Leave the triangle displayed on your screen and proceed to the next section, which explains how adding, subtracting, and editing points on a path can change its shape.

Adding/Subtracting Points and Switching Between a Smooth Point and a Corner Point

You've learned how to adjust a path by moving anchor and direction points. Paths can also be reshaped by adding or subtracting anchor points, and by converting smooth points to corner points and vice versa. By combining these techniques with your drawing skills, you will be able to edit the shape of most any path.

In this next exercise, you will transform the triangular path you created in the previous section into a diamond shape and then back to a triangle. If you do not have the triangle from the previous section on screen, create one in the middle of your document window now. You'll start creating your diamond by activating the Add Anchor Point, or Pen+, tool.

1. With the triangular path displayed, activate the Add Anchor Point tool from the Toolbox.

2. To transform the triangle into a diamond, you need to add an anchor point to the base of the triangle. Position the Add Anchor Point tool in the middle of the base of the triangle. Click the mouse, and a new anchor point is added to the path at the point where you clicked.

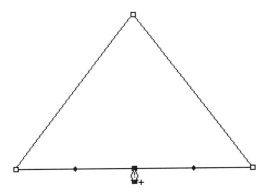

3. To move the new anchor point down to begin creating the diamond shape, you need to switch from the Add Anchor pointer to the Direct Selection tool. Fortunately, Photoshop does this for you automatically.

4. Once the Add Anchor Point tool switches to the Direct Selection tool, click on the new anchor point you created in step 2 and drag it downward about 2 inches, so that the triangle begins to look like a diamond.

5. Notice that the new point is a smooth point. You can turn the round edge into a corner point by using the Convert Point tool in the Toolbox. Select the Convert Point tool, and then click on the smooth point, as shown in Figure 13-7(a). The smooth corner point changes to a sharply angled corner point, as shown in Figure 13-7(b).

Your diamond is now finished. Suppose, though, that you've changed your mind and want the diamond switched back into a triangle. To do this, you will need to subtract the last anchor point you created.

6. To delete the last anchor point you created, click on the Subtract Anchor Point, or Pen–, tool. Then click on the anchor point you used to create the diamond. The corner point disappears, and the diamond shape immediately snaps back into a triangle.

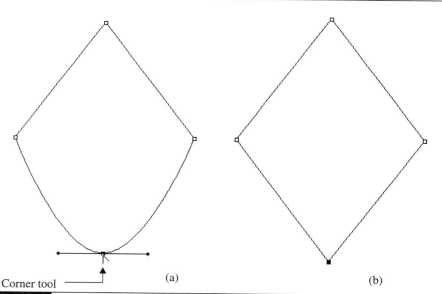

Corner tool ———

(a)   (b)

FIGURE 13-7   (a) Use the Convert Point tool to convert a smooth point to a corner point; (b) the path after the smooth point is converted to a corner point

The ability to convert from smooth points to corner points and corner points to smooth points allows you to quickly edit paths and change their shapes. For example, you can outline a curved object by first connecting straight segments, and then generate the necessary curves by changing corner points into smooth points.

The following exercise demonstrates how you can transform a sharply cornered wedge into a heart shape by changing corner points to smooth points. Before proceeding, delete the triangle you now have on screen by pressing DELETE twice.

1. Using the Pen tool, create and connect four anchor points to create a wedge shape. To make the wedge, start by creating an anchor point in the upper-left corner of your screen. Create the next anchor point at the bottom of your screen, then create another one in the upper-right corner. Continue creating the closed path so that it looks like this one:

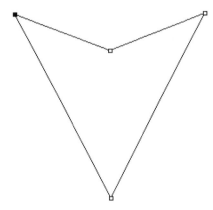

2. Now transform the two top corner points of the wedge to smooth corner points. Start by activating the Corner tool in the Paths palette.

3. Position the Corner tool on the top-left corner point, and click and drag downward to the left until a curve is created. Notice that as you drag, the Corner tool changes to an arrowhead pointer because a direction line for the curve is being created.

13

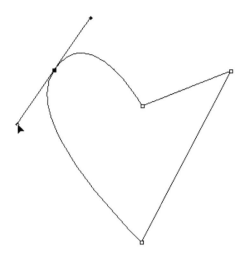

4. To create a curve out of the top-right corner point, click and drag upward to the left on this corner point with the Corner tool. Stop when a curve is created.

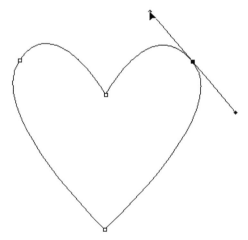

5. If you wish to make adjustments to the curves of the heart, click and drag on the curves' direction points using the Direct Selection tool.

6. At this point, you may wish to fill, stroke, or save the heart path that you just created. If so, turn to the section "Filling and Stroking Paths and

Subpaths" or to the section "Saving, Hiding, Loading, and Deleting Paths" later in this chapter.

Rotating, Scaling, Skewing, and Distorting Paths

Since most of Photoshop's menu commands have no effect on paths, many old-time users of Photoshop never venture beyond the Paths and Toolbox palettes when using the Pen tool. Photoshop 5 is certain to change old habits because the Edit | Transform commands are all activated when a path is selected. Try selecting a path or even an anchor point of a path, then click on the Edit menu—you'll see Free Transform Points and the Transform Points commands available. Click on the Transform path submenu, and a whole new world of path manipulation is open to you.

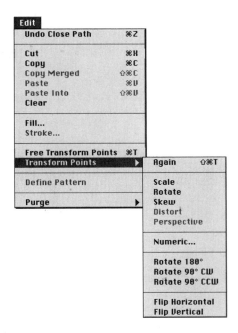

Since the Transform commands are discussed in Chapter 8, we won't repeat instructions for each Transform submenu command. However, here is a list of keyboard shortcuts for using the Free Transform command. Before executing Free Transform, select a path or path segment, then choose Edit | Free Transform. A bounding box with handles will appear around the selected path.

▢ To move, click and drag within the bounding box border.

- To rotate, drag outside the bounding box border in an arc-like movement. Figure 13-8 shows a path being rotated.

- To scale, click and drag on a handle (press and hold SHIFT to scale proportionally).

- To skew, press SHIFT-COMMAND (Windows users: SHIFT-CTRL) and click and drag on a handle.

- To symmetrically distort a path, press OPTION (Windows users: ALT), then click and drag.

- To distort freely, press COMMAND (Windows users: CTRL).

- To create perspective, press SHIFT-ALT-COMMAND (Windows users: SHIFT-ALT-CTRL) while clicking and dragging.

- To move the center point on a path before executing the Transform command, click and drag on the center point.

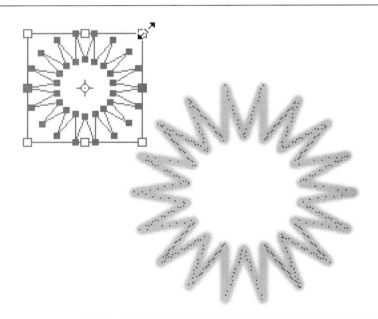

FIGURE 13-8   Path being scaled with Edit | Transform

☐ To transform a duplicate of a selected path, press OPTION-COMMAND-T (Windows users: OPTION-CTRL-T). You can now edit the duplicate without altering the original. (Make sure you select the entire path, before executing this command.)

TIP: *You can duplicate the path or create another path and apply the same transformation to the new path by choosing Edit | Transform Points Again. To duplicate a path and apply the previous transformation, press SHIFT-OPTION-COMMAND-T (Windows users: SHIFT-OPTION-CTRL-T).*

☐ To apply the transformation, press ENTER (Mac users can press RETURN or ENTER).

☐ To cancel a transformation, press ESC (Mac users can also press COMMAND-).

Converting a Path into a Selection

As you work with paths, you'll often need to convert them to selections. Once a selection border is created from the path, you'll be able to use all of Photoshop's commands that affect selections. For instance, you can color correct the area within the selection or apply a filter to it.

NOTE: *Color insert Image 25 shows an example of how selections created from paths can be used.*

In this exercise you'll learn how to turn a path into a selection and to merge both a path and a selection into one selection. To start, if you don't have a blank document on screen, create a new file, 5 inches by 5 inches.

1. Start by using the Pen tool to create a rectangular *path,* approximately 2.5 inches by 2 inches.

2. Use the Elliptical Marquee tool to create a circular *selection* that overlaps the rectangular path. This is illustrated at the top of page 35.

13

Photoshop 5   In Action

New York City artist, Adam Cohen, created this image for the cover of Golf Shop Operation (GSO) Buyers Guide. To create the image, he used a variety of layers. He also used paths as often as he could in order to keep sharp, clean edges and create reuseable masks that wouldn't make the file size larger.

Adam begins his files by creating a rough sketch, which he shows to his client for approval. After the client approves the sketch Adam scans it into Photoshop. With the scanned sketch in Photoshop, he scales it into position. Adam copies the sketch into a separate layer to use it as a guide. Adam, hides and displays the sketch as he needs.

As Adam works he copies a small portion of the sketch into a new layer and begins working on that portion. Usually that entails crating various paths with the Pen tool, which he turns into selections and then paints with the Airbrush. By using various paths for one object, he can isolate different areas and fill one area with a lighter color for the highlights and another area for the shadows. In the case of the wood texture for the golf club, he filled the area with a pattern and used the Image | Adjust | Hue/Saturation command to change the lighting in different areas. To fade areas in layers, Adam often paints with the Airbrush tool to edit a layer mask. Also, by placing items in different layers, he could set the layers to different opacities so that one layer is visible through another.

Artist: Adam Cohen   Client: Golf Shop Operation (GSO) 1998 Buyers Guide

When creating an image, Adam usually places all of the shadows in one layer. To create the shadows in layers, Adam usually creates a large selection with the Lasso tool. He then holds down Command (Windows users:CTRL) and presses the ARROW key once, which makes the Photoshop automatically select the object. Pressing the ARROW key once in the opposite direction moves the object back to its original position. To store the selection, Adam saves the selection to an alpha channel by choosing Select | Save Selection. Then he deselects the selection. Next, he loads the selection from the alpha channel and moves the selection to the place he wants the drop shadow to fall. Then he subtracts the alpha channel from this selection. Adam now has the top shadow selection. He then moves to the background layer and copies and pastes the background which creates a new Layer. Using the Brightness/Contrast command Adam darkens the background shape. Finally, Adam merges this layer with the shadows in one shadow layer.

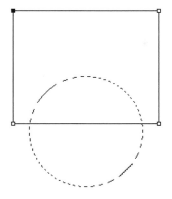

3. Open the pop-up menu in the Paths palette, and choose Make Selection. This opens the Make Selection dialog box, where you specify the type of selection you want to create from any paths or selections on screen. You can also open the Make Selection dialog box by pressing OPTION (Windows users: ALT) and clicking on the Make Selection icon (⬚) in the Paths palette.

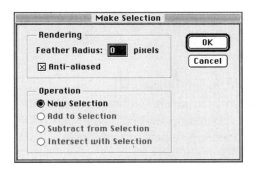

In the Make Selection dialog box, the Feather Radius and Anti-aliased options function exactly as they do with Photoshop's selection tools. Use the Operation options to specify how you want the selection to be created. The Operations options are as follows:

☐ *New Selection*   Creates a selection from the path only. In the example here, only the rectangular path would be turned into a selection.

☐ *Add to Selection*   Adds the area specified by the path to the current selection on screen. In the example here, a selection would be created from both the rectangle and circle together.

☐ *Subtract from Selection*   Removes a path from a selection. In the example here, the rectangular area that overlaps the circle would be removed from the circular selection border.

☐ *Intersect with Selection*   Creates a selection from the area where the path and selection overlap. In the example here, the selection would be transformed into one selection, including only the overlapping areas of the rectangle and circle.

Try each of these options with the example on your screen. First select the New Selection radio button and then click OK. Photoshop creates a selection from the rectangle only. Choose Edit | Undo to remove the selection. Now return to the Make Selection dialog box to try out any of the other options.

 NOTE: *You can also convert a path into a selection by clicking on the Make Selection icon in the Paths palette or by clicking and dragging the path name over the Make Selection icon. When the Make Selection icon changes color, release the mouse button. Mac and Windows users can press ENTER on the numeric keypad to quickly create a selection out of a path. When you create a selection this way, Feather and Anti-aliasing options retain their last settings.*

Path Keyboard Commands

Photoshop 5 users updating from a previous version might be surprised to find that some of their favorite Path-editing keyboard commands no longer work. To help old and new Pen users, here's a review of Pen tool keyboard shortcuts, both old and new:

Select Direct Selection tool when using any Pen tool	COMMAND/CTRL
Switch between Pen + and Pen – (with pointer over anchor point)	OPTION/ALT
Switch from Pen tool to Convert Point tool	OPTION/ALT
Switch from Direct Selection to Convert Point tool when over anchor point	OPTION-COMMAND/ALT-CTRL
Select another anchor point with Direct Selection tool activated	SHIFT-click
Select entire path with Direct Selection tool activated	OPTION/ALT-click

Duplicate path with Direct Selection tool selected	OPTION/ALT-click and drag
Duplicate path with Pen tool selected	OPTION-COMMAND/ALT-CTRL-click and drag
Convert path to selection	ENTER
Add to a selection	Select path and press SHIFT-ENTER
Subtract from a selection	Select path and press OPTION/ALT-ENTER
Intersect with a selection	COMMAND-OPTION/ALT-CTRL-SHIFT-ENTER

Converting a Selection into a Path

Now that you've seen how Photoshop creates a selection out of a path, let's take a look at how to transform a selection into a path. Occasionally, it's easier to create a path from a selection, rather than constructing it from scratch with the Pen tool. For example, you might wish to create a path from an intricate Magic Wand selection that would take too much time to create using the Pen tool. You could also COMMAND-click (Windows users: CTRL-click) on a layer (other than the Background) in the Layers palette to create a selection from the nontransparent areas of a layer, then turn the selection into a path. You could also create an intricate selection by pressing OPTION-COMMAND-1, 2, or 3 (Windows users: ALT-CTRL-1, 2, or 3), which creates a mask from the channel values of an RGB or Lab Color image (press 1, 2, 3, or 4 in a CMYK image), then turn this selection into a path.

To convert a selection into a path, you use the Make Work Path command in the Paths palette, or click on the Make Work Path icon in the Paths palette.

 CAUTION: *If you have a work path on screen (a path that isn't named or saved), and then create a path from a selection, the new path replaces your original path. So, save your work paths if you want to keep using them.*

The following exercise demonstrates how Photoshop creates anchor points when converting a selection border into a path. You can change any selection into a path, but in this exercise you'll work with a figure-eight because the path will require numerous anchor points. Begin by clearing the screen of all selections by choosing None from the Select menu. Then remove all paths by pressing DELETE three times.

   1. Activate the Lasso tool; then click and drag to create a figure eight.

13

Photoshop 5 > In Action

Pattern shapes created with the Pen tool

Drop shadow shape created by subtracting selections

Artist: Adam Cohen Client: Working Woman Magazine

Adam used two abstract backgrounds to create this illustration for *Working Woman* magazine. In the center of each of the abstract backgrounds, Adam began to create rays using the Path tool. In each newly created ray, he changed the color by adjusting the hue and saturation controls. Next, he cut out a dollar sign shape from one of the backgrounds and pasted it into the other. Adam added a drop shadow and airbrushed a highlight around the edge of the dollar sign.

To help create the drop shadow, Adam created a selection out of the dollar sign paths and saved the selection into a channel. He moved the dollar sign figure, then created another selection and saved the new placement as a selection in another channel. Later, he subtracted one channel from the other channel to create a sliver selection, which he darkened to use as the drop shadow.

2. To turn the figure-eight selection border into a path, select Make Work Path from the pop-up menu in the Paths palette.

The Make Work Path dialog box contains a field for setting the Tolerance value, which determines the number of anchor points the path will include. The default Tolerance value is 2 pixels; you can specify from .5 to 10 pixels. If you enter a high Tolerance value, fewer anchor points will be used and the resulting path will be smoother. Select a low Tolerance value and more anchor points will be used, resulting in a bumpier path.

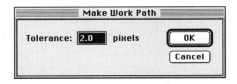

3. In the Make Path dialog box, type **1** in the Tolerance field and click OK. When the path appears, click on it with the Direct Selection tool so you can examine the number of anchor points that were created. Count the number of anchor points.

4. Now try a higher Tolerance setting and observe the results. First, return to a selection on screen by clicking on the Make Selection icon in the Paths palette. Then reopen the Make Path dialog box. Enter **10** as the Tolerance setting and click OK. When the path appears, click on it with the Direct Selection tool and count the number of anchor points. Observe that the higher Tolerance value results in fewer anchor points.

13

 CAUTION: *Converting selections to paths sometimes creates paths that are too complicated for printers to print. In this situation, your best bet is to delete some anchor points with the Anchor Point tool or re-create the path using a higher Tolerance setting. Also note that paths created from selections may not look exactly like your original selection.*

You've now learned the fundamental techniques required to work with the Paths palette, the Pen tools, and the Direct Selection tool. In the next section, you'll learn how to fill or stroke a path with a color or pattern.

Filling and Stroking Paths and Subpaths

Photoshop allows you to fill a path with the foreground color or with a pattern or from a state in the History palette. You can also fill and stroke a path using many of the same blending modes that appear in the Painting tools and Layers palette. When you stroke or fill a path, Photoshop strokes or fills the entire path, including all subpaths—noncontiguous joined segments. When you stroke a path, the stroke width is determined by the current brush size of the stroking tool.

To fill or stroke a path or subpath, use the Fill Path/Subpath or Stroke Path/Subpath command from the Paths palette's pop-up menu. Paths cannot be filled or stroked by Photoshop's Edit | Fill or Edit | Stroke commands.

When you fill or stroke a path, Photoshop fills or strokes underlying pixels *beneath* the path and leaves the path as a separate independent object. This means that you can move the path and execute Fill Path or Stroke Path again, or edit the path—without affecting the filled or stroked images on screen.

 CAUTION: *You cannot fill or stroke a path when a marquee selection is on screen, unless the marquee is over the path.*

How Photoshop Fills a Path

When you choose the Fill Path command from the Paths palette pop-up menu the entire path will be filled—if there are no intersecting or overlapping segments. The following illustrations show how Photoshop fills a path with overlapping or intersecting segments.

When filling paths (including clipping paths, explained later in this chapter) Photoshop uses a Postscript rule called the Even-Odd Winding rule. It's not essential that you understand this rule. But if you are going to create complicated paths, you might wish to read the following explanation.

To understand how the Even-Odd Winding rule works, first pick a point in your image that is within the path, but not on the path. Then draw an imaginary line through any path segments out to the edge of the document window. Now count the number of times a path crosses the imaginary line. If the number is even, the point where the imaginary line starts will not be filled. If the number is odd, the area will be filled.

Filling a Path Composed of Subpaths

When filling a path, it's important to remember that Photoshop considers all path segments and subpaths on screen to be one path. Before you fill a path you must deselect, so that no segments are selected. If you select any part of a path, the Fill Path command changes to Fill Subpath in the Paths palette pop-up menu.

To see how Photoshop fills and strokes paths composed of subpaths, you must have at least two separate path segments displayed. If you deleted the figure-eight path created in the previous exercise, create another closed path now, before beginning the next exercise.

1. Use the Pen tool to create a square subpath to the right of the figure-eight (or any other subpath). To ensure that all subpaths will be filled, deselect any path that is currently activated or selected. To deselect, activate the Direct Selection tool in the Paths palette and click away from the path segments.

2. To fill all paths on screen, click on the pop-up menu and select Fill Path. The Fill Path dialog box appears. The Fill Path dialog box will also be displayed if you press OPTION (Windows users: ALT) and click on the Fill Path icon (⬚) at the bottom of the Paths palette.

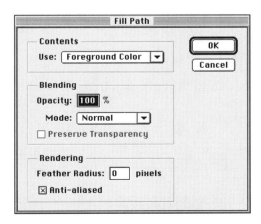

3. In the Fill Path dialog box:

a. The Use pop-up menu should be set to Foreground Color (make sure your foreground color is darker than your background canvas color). The Use pop-up menu also offers options for filling the path with the Background Color, a pattern, the selected state in the History palette, Black, 50% Gray, or White.

b. As in the standard Fill dialog box, you can choose an Opacity setting and a painting Mode for blending. Type **50** in the Opacity field and make sure the Mode is set to Normal. The Preserve Transparency check box will be active if you are working in a layer that has a transparent background. If you check this option, transparent areas will not be affected by the Fill.

 TIP: *If you are working in a layer, you can select the Clear blending mode to erase the interior of the path and show the layer beneath it.*

c. As in the Lasso tool's dialog boxes, the Feather Radius and Anti-aliased options are used to soften edges. Feather Radius values can be from 0 to 250 pixels.

4. Click OK. Both the figure-eight and the square subpaths are filled according to your specifications.

 TIP: *You can fill a path by clicking on the Fill Path icon or clicking and dragging the path name over the Fill Path icon. This will fill with the current settings in the Fill Path dialog box.*

Stroking a Path

If you don't have the two subpaths on screen from the previous section, create two subpaths now, then deselect.

Now try stroking the path.

1. Change the foreground color to a color that will allow you to see the effects of the stroke.

2. To stroke a path, click on the pop-up menu in the Paths palette, and select Stroke Path, or press OPTION (Windows users: ALT) and click on the Stroke Path icon ([○]) at the bottom of the Paths palette.

3. When the Stroke Path dialog box appears, open the Tool pop-up menu. You'll get a list of the painting and editing tools that use the Brushes palette.

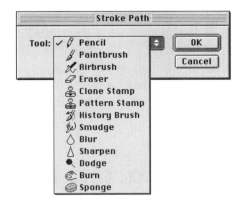

4. Apply an Airbrush stroke to your path. Select Airbrush from the Tool pop-up menu in the Stroke Path dialog box and click OK.

The path is stroked using the current brush size in the Brushes palette and opacity settings for the Airbrush tool. To better control how the stroke is applied to the path, you may wish to first select the tool with which you will stroke the path and choose the specific settings you want in the Options and Brushes palette for that tool. Then click on the Stroke Path icon at the bottom of the Paths palette. Instead of opening the Stroke Path dialog box, Photoshop will automatically stroke with the activated tool in the Toolbox, using its Brushes palette settings.

 TIP: *You can stroke a path by clicking on the Stroke Path icon in the Paths palette or by clicking and dragging the path name over the Stroke Path icon.*

 TIP: *You can have one path with multiple strokes. First apply a thick stroke, then a medium stroke in a different color, and finally a smaller stroke in another color.*

Filling or Stroking a Subpath

As stated earlier, if you don't wish to fill or stroke an entire path, Photoshop allows you to fill or stroke a subpath. When you click on a path segment, or SHIFT-click to activate more than one segment, Photoshop considers that segment to be a subpath.

To see the effects of stroking a subpath, change the foreground color and make sure a selection tool in the Toolbox is selected. Then choose the subpath you wish to stroke by clicking on it with the Direct Selection tool. This activates the subpath. You do not need to select every anchor point in the path. Next, click on the pop-up menu in the Paths palette. Notice that the Stroke Path command has changed to Stroke Subpath. In the Stroke Subpath dialog box, select a tool, then click OK. Only the subpath you clicked on is stroked.

Saving, Hiding, Loading, and Deleting Paths

After you create a path, you may wish to save it; by saving a path you can give it a name and create a clipping path out of it.

When a path is saved, Photoshop saves all path segments as one path on screen, whether they are selected or not. If you edit the path after saving it, or if you add a subpath, the changes to the path will be saved automatically. After you save a path, you can hide it and create more paths. This ability to hide an object is somewhat similar to that of drawing programs that allow you to work in layers. But, unlike drawing programs, or Photoshop's own Layers palette, if you save multiple paths in Photoshop, you cannot view the multiple saved paths simultaneously.

 NOTE: *It's important to understand that a saved path does not receive an assigned disk filename. Rather, you provide a name for the path that will appear in a list in the Paths palette. The path names that appear in this list are only available in the document in which they were created and saved. If you wish to copy a path from one document into another document, you can use the Edit | Copy and Edit | Paste commands. You can also drag a path name from the Paths palette into another open document or drag the path itself into another open document with the Pen's Direct Selection tool. The path name, as well as the path itself, will be available in the other document.*

In the next exercise, you'll learn how to save a path, hide a path, and then reload the path. Before you begin, make sure that you have one path displayed on screen.

1. After you've created a path, you may want to save it, especially if you are using the Pen tool to isolate an area of a digitized image. Later, you can

Photoshop 5   In Action

The background was created by scanning a rough-textured paper.

The different pieces on the face were scanned in separately and then placed in the final image.

The mortarboard was created using the Pen tool.

The diploma, hand, and jacket were created using the Pen tool.

13

**Artist: Rico Lins   Client: The Boston Globe Magazine
Art Director: Lucy Bartholomay**

Lucy had Rico create this humorous image for the cover of the *Boston Globe* magazine issue featuring an article on whether a college degree is worth the price.

Rico started the image by scanning a rough-textured paper that was used as the background. He used the Pen tool to create the mortarboard, jacket, diploma, and hand. Once these shapes were created, they were filled using the Fill Path command in the Paths palette.

All the pieces in the face were scanned in separately, selected, and then pasted into the final file.

convert the path into a selection to use as a mask. To save a path, click on the pop-up menu in the Paths palette and select Save Path. You don't have to select a path before you select the Save Path command. When you apply the command, all path segments on screen are automatically saved.

 TIP: *You can also save a path by dragging the words "Work Path" over the New Path icon at the bottom of the Paths palette or by double-clicking on the Work Path in the Paths palette. Note that a work path is saved with a document even if you don't give the path a name.*

2. In the Save Path dialog box, you can name the path, if you wish, by typing the name in the Name field. Click OK. Notice that the name of the path now appears in the Paths palette.

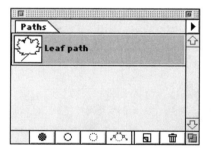

If you wish to rename the saved path, double-click on the name of the path in the Paths palette. The Rename Path dialog box will appear, allowing you to rename the path.

3. Now hide the path you just created, so that you can name and save another path. Click below the name you assigned the path in the Paths palette, or choose Turn Off Path in the Paths palette pop-up menu. The path on the screen will disappear, but the Path name remains in the Paths palette.

4. Create another path.

5. Choose Save Path from the pop-up menu in the Paths palette. In the Save Path dialog box, Path 2 appears in the Name field; give the path another name if you wish, and click OK to save the path. The name of the path now appears in the Paths palette.

6. With two paths now saved, you will be able to see how you can view them independently. To return to the first path, click on the name of the path in the Paths palette. This path now appears on screen. To view the second path, click on the name of the second path in the Paths palette. The area around the path name turns gray.

   Continue to experiment, and adjust your saved paths, if you wish. Remember, once a path is saved you can edit it without resaving.

 TIP: *If you wish to quickly hide all paths on screen so you can create a new path, click directly below the last path name in the Paths palette; make sure you don't click on an icon. (You may need to enlarge the Paths palette.)*

7. Before proceeding to the next section, delete the second path you created. First, activate the path by clicking on the name you assigned to the second path in the Paths palette. Then select Delete Path from the pop-up menu in the Paths palette. You can also delete a path by clicking on the path name and dragging it over the Trash icon (🗑) at the bottom-right corner of the Paths palette. When the Trash icon changes colors, release the mouse.

 CAUTION: *Even though a path is saved, it can be deleted by pressing* DELETE *when any Pen tool or the Direct Selection tool is activated in the Paths palette.*

 NOTE: *Photoshop Paths are saved when you save in TIFF, JPEG, or PICT file formats.*

Duplicating Paths

Now that you know how to save a path, you can create a duplicate of it using the Paths palette.

13

To duplicate the current path on screen, simply choose Duplicate from the Paths palette's pop-up menu. Alternatively, click and drag the Path name from the Paths palette over the New Path icon (⬓) in the palette. When the Duplicate Path dialog box opens, enter a name for the new path. After you click OK, the duplicate as well as the original path will appear in the Paths palette.

Exporting a Path from Adobe Illustrator to Photoshop

Since Adobe Illustrator's path capabilities are greater than Adobe Photoshop's, you may want to export a path from Illustrator to Photoshop. You can do this by loading both programs. Next, open the file with the Illustrator path in it and a new file in Photoshop (into which you will import the path). In Illustrator select the path with the Select tool and press and hold the COMMAND (Windows users: CTRL) key while you drag and drop the path from Illustrator to Photoshop. Another way you can do this is by copying and pasting:

1. Choose Edit | Copy in Illustrator, activate (or load) Photoshop, then choose Edit | Paste.

2. A dialog box appears asking whether you wish to Paste as Pixels or Paste as Paths. Select the Paste as Paths option. After you paste, all paths are included in the work path. If you want each path to appear as a separate path in the Paths palette, paste each path individually, then save each one by choosing Save Path in the Paths palette menu.

Exporting a Path to Adobe Illustrator

Exporting a path from Photoshop to Illustrator can be valuable, especially after you've created a path in Photoshop by tracing over a digitized image, and want to use it in Illustrator.

To export the path so that you can integrate it into a design in Illustrator, choose Export in the Photoshop File menu. From the Export submenu, choose Paths to Illustrator. Choose the path name from the Write pop-up menu. Name the file and click Save (Windows users: OK). The file can then be loaded directly into Illustrator. To do this in Illustrator, just execute the File | Open command, locate the file, and open it. To activate and select the path in Illustrator, choose Select All in the Edit menu.

If you don't need to save your path, but you do want to export it into an existing Illustrator file, select the entire path and then use Edit I Copy in Photoshop, then Edit I Paste in Illustrator to drop the path into the Illustrator file. To do this, you must have either Illustrator 5.0 or later for the Mac, or Illustrator 4.0 or later for Windows.

If you wish to create a silhouette mask out of a Photoshop image and place only the masked portion in another application (such as Illustrator or a page layout program), you must create a clipping path, as described next.

Creating and Saving Clipping Paths

One of the most useful features in the Paths palette is the Clipping Path command. A *clipping path* silhouettes an area, masking an image so that only the portion of the image within the clipping path will appear when the Photoshop file is placed in another application.

Figure 13-9(a) shows an Alaskan brown bear image before the Pen tool was used to create a clipping path. Figure 13-9(b) shows the results after the Bear file with the clipping path was placed in Adobe Illustrator. Only the bear was included in the clipping path, so that it could be placed on top of a new background in Adobe Illustrator. Note that the edges of the bear against the background are not

(a)   (b)

FIGURE 13-9 (a) The original Alaskan brown bear image, before the clipping path was created; (b) only the image area within the clipping path appears in Adobe Illustrator

13

(a)

(b)

FIGURE 13-10 (a) Image of leaves with a path around one; (b) a close-up of the leaf with a path;

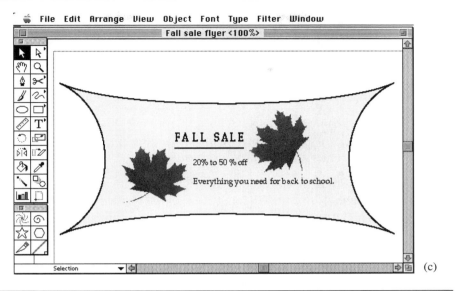

FIGURE 13-10   (c) only the image area within the clipping path appears in Adobe Illustrator

soft. If you're going to be using clipping paths, it's important to realize that clipping paths allow no feathering. Thus, it can be rather difficult to create soft transitions between the object in your clipping path and its background in an illustration or page layout program.

Figure 13-10 is another example of using a clipping path. Figure 13-10(a) shows an image of leaves. Notice that the leaf at the top-left-hand corner has a path around it. Figure 13-10(b) shows a close-up of the leaf with the path, which was used to create a clipping path. Figure 13-10(c) shows the results after the leaf image with the clipping path was placed in Adobe Illustrator. Only the leaf with the path was included in the clipping path, so that it could be placed on top of a new background in Adobe Illustrator. In Figure 13-10(c), the leaf image was also duplicated and rotated.

The following exercise guides you through the procedures required to turn a path into a clipping path and to save the file in EPS format so it can be imported into another program.

13

1. Open a file that contains an image that you wish to silhouette and export to Illustrator or a page layout program. If you don't have a suitable image, use one from the Photoshop Samples folder.

2. Create a path around the portion of the image that you wish to include in the clipping path. You may want to review the sections on "Drawing and Adjusting Curves" and "Connecting Curves and Straight Paths."

3. Once you've created the path, choose Save Path from the pop-up menu or double-click on the work path name in the Paths palette. In the Save Path dialog box, enter a name for your path.

4. After the path is saved, choose Clipping Path from the pop-up menu in the Paths palette. When the Clipping Path dialog box appears, click on the Path pop-up menu and select the name of your saved path.

 NOTE: *Only one path can be saved as a clipping path.*

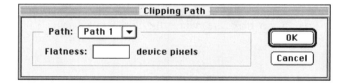

In the Clipping Path dialog box, you can adjust the Flatness value to *flatten,* or simplify, paths that may be too complicated to print. You can leave this field empty unless you receive a PostScript "limitcheck" error when printing the clipping path image in another application. If you do receive this error, you can try entering a number into the Flatness field. A higher Flatness value will reduce the number of straight lines that will be needed to define the curve, thus simplifying the curve. If you flatten the curve too much, however, you will alter the shape of the entire path. Acceptable Flatness values are from .2 to 100 pixels. Try entering a value from 1 to 3 in the Flatness field for low-resolution printers and 8 to 10 for high-resolution printers.

 TIP: *If you're interested in experimenting with different flatness values, try printing out simple paths set to different flatness values, then print them on your laser printer. As flatness gets higher, you'll see circular shapes printed like polygons.*

Photoshop 5 In Action

The background scene was photographed in Florida, then scanned.

Chicago Bulls star Scottie Pippen was photographed sitting on foam stairs. After the photograph was scanned, the Pen tool was used to outline Pippen. This image was later copied and pasted over the bull.

The stuffed bull was shot in California, and then scanned. Once it was scanned, the Pen tool was used to outline it. The bull was later copied and pasted into the final image.

Artist: Nik Kleinberg   Client: Sports Illustrated for Kids

Nik created this "unbelieva-BULL" image for a *Sports Illustrated for Kids* cover using photographs taken by George B. Fry III.

After all the shots were taken, they were scanned separately. First the background was scanned, then the bull, and then Pippen. After the bull and Pippen were scanned, the Pen tool was used to silhouette (outline) each image. The paths were saved and then turned into selections with the Paths palette's Make Selection command. The selections were copied and then pasted into the final image to make it appear that Pippen was having the ride of his life.

13

5. To save the path as a clipping path, click OK. Notice that the name of the path will become outlined in the Paths palette. The image on screen will not change. You will see the effects of creating a clipping path only when the file containing the clipping path is placed in another program.

In order to use the clipping path in another program, you must save the Photoshop file in EPS format. To save your clipping path, choose Save As or Save a Copy from the File menu. When the dialog box appears, name your file, choose Photoshop EPS from the Format (Window users: Save As) pop-up menu, and click OK. The EPS Options dialog box appears.

 NOTE: *If your document contains alpha channels, choose File | Save a Copy so you can save in EPS format without the alpha channels. For more information about alpha channels, see Chapter 14.*

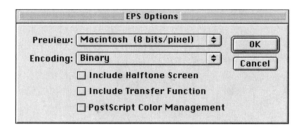

 TIP: *If you choose Macintosh preview in the EPS dialog box, you can view the clipping path transparency in most Mac drawing and page layout programs; the Windows preview choice (TIFF) does not allow you to see the transparency effect of the clipping path in other applications. Nevertheless, the clipping path effects appear when the document is printed.*

For more information about saving in EPS format, see Appendix A.

When the Photoshop document is placed in Illustrator or a page layout program, only the portion of the image within the clipping path appears. (If you used the Windows preview option (TIFF) in the EPS dialog box, you won't see the effects of the clipping path on screen; however the document should print properly.)

NOTE: *CMYK color images with clipping paths can also be saved in DCS file format. Saving in DCS file format is discussed in Appendix A.*

Conclusion

If you've followed the exercises in this chapter from beginning to end, you've progressed to a more sophisticated level of expertise with the Paths palette and the Pen tools. Now that you're familiar with the scope of the Paths palette commands, you'll want to keep the palette handy. As you become proficient at using the Pen tools, very few shapes or objects will be beyond your grasp.

In the next chapter you'll learn how to create and save masks using the Quick Mask mode.

13

CHAPTER 14

Advanced Masking Techniques, Channels, and Spot Colors

B efore computers came along, the traditional method of isolating parts of an image for color correcting, image editing, and retouching was to create a mask. A *mask* is a type of stencil, often translucent, that is laid over an image to protect certain areas and allow others to be edited. Cutouts in the mask make selected portions of the image accessible for painting and editing, while the remainder of the image is protected by the stencil. Although the process of creating a mask can be time consuming, it allows work on the image to be performed precisely.

In many ways, the selections you create with Photoshop's selection tools are masks. When a selection is on screen, all the painting and editing work you do affects only the area within the blinking selection marquee. Unlike a traditional mask, however, a selection is temporary. When a new selection is created, the previous one disappears. As discussed in Chapter 13, one method of retaining a selection is to create a path with the Pen tool. Unfortunately, the Pen tool can be difficult to master, and creating intricate paths takes time. To meet the need for maintaining multiple reusable selections that are easy to edit, the designers of Photoshop developed an electronic masking capability that surpasses both the Pen tool and the traditional mask. This electronic capability allows you to save a selection as a mask in an extra channel, called an *alpha channel*, attached to your image.

Once an alpha channel is created, you access it through the Channels palette. The mask in the alpha channel can be loaded on screen to serve as a selection. Using alpha channels, you can reload complicated selections, and easily switch back and forth among selections while working on a document. As you'll see in this chapter, you can even paint on screen to create an intricate mask that can be used as a selection or to create transparency effects.

If the relationship between a mask, an alpha channel, and a selection sounds complicated, don't worry. The examples in this chapter lead you gradually from creating simple masks and working with alpha channels to sophisticated commands that let you superimpose channels and files to create exquisite effects.

As you work through the exercises, you'll see a new and powerful facet of Photoshop open up for you. You'll never have to worry about intricate selections disappearing into the digital stratosphere if you inadvertently click on the screen or close your file. Once you learn how to use masks, you'll be able to save, load, and easily edit any selection, no matter how complex. Not only will this be helpful in your day-to-day Photoshop work, but you will also gain the skill to create sophisticated three-dimensional effects that require precise control over light sources and shadows.

Working with Quick Masks

Perhaps the easiest way to understand the relationship between masks and channels is to start by using Photoshop's Quick Mask mode, which creates a temporary mask and a temporary alpha channel. A Quick Mask is similar to a *rubylith*, the red-colored translucent film that is used as an overlay to protect parts of an image in print production.

Like a rubylith, a Quick Mask allows you to view your work through a translucent "overlay." The areas on screen covered by the overlay are protected from image editing; the cutout areas not covered by the overlay are not protected. (If desired, you can change the Quick Mask settings so that the reverse is true.) In Quick Mask mode, the shapes of the cutout areas (the unprotected areas) are easily edited with Photoshop's painting and editing tools. In Photoshop 5, you can even edit the mask with the Edit | Transform commands. When you exit Quick Mask mode, the unprotected areas are transformed into selections (or one selection).

 Take a look at the Quick Mask mode icon in Photoshop's Toolbox: The default setting is a shaded square with a clear circle cut out of it. The shaded area represents the translucent mask; the circle cutout is the unprotected area. The Standard mode icon (beside the Quick Mask icon) depicts what you will see when you exit Quick Mask mode: The overlay is gone, but a blinking selection marquee remains on screen.

Creating a Quick Mask

In this section you'll create a Quick Mask and use it to edit a selection. If you wish to follow along, load a file on screen in which you wish to create an intricate selection. (Our example uses an image of a pork chop on a dinner plate.) We created the Quick Mask along the edge of the plate so that we could later add variety to it and make it look more interesting.

Begin by creating a small elliptical selection with the Elliptical Marquee tool in your image, as shown in Figure 14-1. Don't deselect.

 REMEMBER: *Here are a few points to remember about selection:*

- *If you inadvertently deselect, you can reselect the last selection by choosing Select | Reselect*

- *After you create a selection, you can choose Select | Transform Selection, then move it, rotate it or scale it.*

- *You can also move a selection with the Move tool.*

14

Clicking once on the Quick Mask mode icon puts you in Quick Mask mode; double-clicking on the icon activates Quick Mask mode and opens the Quick Mask Options dialog box as well. To view the dialog box options, double-click on the icon. Once the Quick Mask Options dialog box appears, as shown in Figure 14-2, you'll see that a red overlay also appears on screen. If the default settings are in use, the red overlay area represents the protected area. The unprotected area (the area not covered by red) is the area you originally selected.

 NOTE: *If you can't see the unprotected area on screen because the Quick Mask Options dialog box opened in front of it, move the dialog box by clicking and dragging in its title bar (on the words "Quick Mask Options").*

Selected area

FIGURE 14-1 Image before entering Quick Mask mode (photograph courtesy of Stacy Kollar Photography)

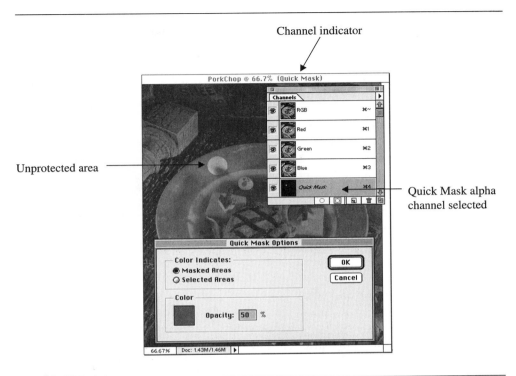

Channel indicator

Unprotected area

Quick Mask alpha channel selected

FIGURE 14-2   Image in Quick Mask mode with translucent color overlay (compare with Figure 14-1)

14

In the Quick Mask Options dialog box you can designate whether you want the color overlay to indicate the masked (protected) areas or the selected (unprotected) areas. By default, the Masked Areas radio button in the Color Indicates section is selected. The default color setting for the overlay is red with a 50% opacity. With the Masked Areas radio button selected, the specified color and opacity are applied to all areas in the image except those that were selected before you entered the Quick Mask mode. When the Selected Areas radio button is selected, the translucent colored overlay appears within your selection, rather than around it. (If this is the case now, click on the Masked Areas radio button.)

TIP: *The Quick Mask Mode icon in the Toolbox indicates whether the red overlay covers the selected or non-selected areas. If you choose Masked Areas in the Quick Mask Options dialog box, the icon is a gray rectangle with a white circle. If you choose Selected Areas, the icon is a white rectangle with a gray circle.*

 TIP: *You can switch between the Masked Areas and the Selected Areas options without opening the Quick Mask Options dialog box by pressing OPTION (Windows users: ALT) and clicking on the Quick Mask icon. The Quick Mask icon will change to reflect the option you have chosen.*

You can change the overlay color by clicking on the swatch in the Color section of the Quick Mask Options dialog box; this opens Photoshop's Color Picker. If you change the percentage in the Opacity field beside the color swatch, the translucency of the overlay is adjusted accordingly. For the following exercise, leave the default Mask Options settings selected (Color Indicates Masked Areas, and the overlay color at 50% red). Click OK to continue.

You are now in the Quick Mask channel overlay. Before continuing, take a moment to look at Figure 14-2 to see how your surroundings have changed. First, examine the document's title bar. You should see Quick Mask rather than RGB.

The Channels palette should now be open; if it isn't, open it by choosing Show Channels in the Window menu. In the Channels palette, notice that a new channel called Quick Mask has been added (this is an alpha channel). Next to the Quick Mask channel, the eye icon (👁) means the channel is visible, and the highlighted area surrounding the words "Quick Mask" indicates the channel is selected and can be edited. The selected channel is often called the *target channel*. Notice that there are eye icons next to each of the RGB channels also, but that none of the RGB channels is a selected area. Thus, even though you can see your image on screen, any editing changes you make now will not affect it, but only the mask.

Editing a Mask in Quick Mask Mode

One of the great advantages of using masks is that you can resize and fine-tune them with painting tools. By altering the brush size of the Paintbrush, Airbrush, and Pencil tools in particular and carefully painting in Quick Mask mode, you can create extremely intricate masks.

When you paint in a mask, you change the unprotected and protected areas (which changes the selection marquee on screen after you exit Quick Mask mode).

When you paint to edit the mask, you can use only black, white, or shades of gray. Your Color palette is now restricted to 256 shades of gray. If the Color palette isn't on screen, open it, and notice that you can paint only with black, white, or shades of gray.

When you paint with white in Quick Mask mode, you add to the unprotected area (the selected area). When you paint with black, you subtract from the unprotected area (and add to the protected area). Painting with gray shades creates a type of "partial" selection when you exit Quick Mask mode. When this selection is filled with an opaque color, the result is a translucent color.

The following table summarizes the effects of painting with white, black, or gray when the Color Indicates Masked Areas radio button is selected in the Quick Mask Options dialog box:

Painting Color	Effect in Quick Mask Mode	Effect in Standard Mode
White	Subtracts from colored overlay (protected area); adds to unprotected area	Adds to selection marquee
Black	Adds to colored overlay (protected area); subtracts from unprotected area	Subtracts from selection marquee
Gray	Creates transparency effects	Creates a partially transparent selection

To see how painting in white edits the mask and changes the selection, set the foreground color to white. Select any painting tool and click on a medium, soft-edged brush in the Brushes palette. (A soft-edged brush will produce a selection with feathered edges; a hard-edged brush will create a sharper selection.) Make sure Opacity is set to 100% in the tool's palette.

Use the Paintbrush tool to paint around the entire rim of the plate. As you paint with white, the translucent overlay melts away. As you remove the overlay, you increase the size of the selection that will appear when you exit Quick Mask mode.

 TIP: *You might want to zoom in and use a smaller brush so that you can carefully select the rim and nothing else. If you make a mistake, just paint with black to add to the overlay.*

Before leaving Quick Mask mode, take a moment to view the Quick Mask channel without the composite image displayed. This will give you an idea of exactly what happened in the channel when you painted with white. To turn off the RGB composite display, click on the eye icon to the left of the RGB channel in the

Channels palette. The RGB composite image disappears, and you will see the black mask and the white, unprotected area. When you painted with white, you subtracted black from the mask. Only when the RGB composite image and mask appear on the screen together is the mask displayed in a translucent color. Restore the RGB image by clicking on the eye icon next to the RGB channel in the Channels palette.

Using Edit Transform with Quick Mask Mode

Before exiting Quick Mask mode, take a look at a little known feature available in Photoshop 5. Assume you need to move the masked area on screen. There's no way you can do this with a painting tool. However, when you are in Quick Mask mode, Photoshop 5's Edit | Free Transform and Edit | Transform commands are available. This means that you can move, scale, rotate, flip, distort, even use Apply the Perspective command to the Quick Mask.

Try resizing your quick mask by choosing Edit | Free Transform. Then click and drag on one of the bounding box handles to resize the mask. Press ENTER (Mac users can also press RETURN) to finish the transformation; or press ESC to cancel.

Now that you have isolated an area of your image, you are ready to return to Standard mode, where you can use the selection that the mask creates.

Exiting Quick Mask Mode

To exit Quick Mask mode, click on the Standard mode icon in the Toolbox or type Q on the keyboard to toggle back and forth. The selection marquee now appears around the entire plate, as shown in Figure 14-3. In other words, the work you did with the Paintbrush tool in Quick Mask mode is now transformed into a selection. Notice that Quick Mask no longer appears in the window's title bar. In addition, if you examine the Channels palette, you'll see that the Quick Mask channel is no longer listed. Thus, your selection remains, but the alpha channel containing the mask has disappeared.

 NOTE: *If you painted with white in several different areas in the Quick Mask channel, several selection marquees appear on screen when you exit Quick Mask mode.*

FIGURE 14-3   The selection reflects the area that was painted with white in the Quick Mask channel

Now you can edit or color correct the area with the selection. Try using the Brightness/Contrast controls in the Image | Adjust submenu to increase the contrast. As you adjust brightness and contrast, only the selected area of the plate changes. When you're finished, don't deselect.

As mentioned earlier, our task was to make the rim of the plate more interesting. Suppose you'd like to apply a pattern to enhance your selection. This creates a problem: You need to create a selection to define the pattern, but if you do this, you will lose the selection around the rim of the plate. The solution is to save the selection. Keep your selection on screen and proceed to the next section.

Saving and Loading a Selection

Any Photoshop selection can be saved, whether or not it was created in Quick Mask mode. When a selection is saved, Photoshop creates a mask from the selection and places it in an alpha channel.

To try this out, make sure you have a selection on screen, then choose Save Selection from the Select menu. The Save Selection dialog box opens. This dialog box allows you to save a selection into a new channel to any open document, or to a new document. In the next section, you'll have a chance to explore the dialog box options. For now, notice that the Destination Document pop-up menu shows the name of your current document. The Destination Channel pop-up menu is set to New. Click OK to create the new channel.

 TIP: *To automatically save a selection to an alpha channel, click on the Save Selection icon ( ) in the Channels palette.*

Notice that the Channels palette now contains a new channel, Alpha 1. The selection around the rim of the plate, created in the previous section, is now stored in Alpha 1 so it can be recalled after you define a pattern.

Click on the eye icon column next to Alpha 1 to see the mask that is stored in the Channels palette. An overlay similar to the Quick Mask overlay appears over your image. Click on the eye icon next to the RGB channel to turn it off. Without the underlying image, the mask now appears in black and white. Return to your composite image by clicking on the RGB eye icon again, and the overlay returns. To hide the overlay from view, click on the eye icon next to Alpha 1.

 TIP: *You can toggle back and forth between the alpha channel and the RGB composite channel by pressing COMMAND-4 (Windows users: CTRL-4) to access alpha channel #4 and COMMAND-~ (Windows users: CTRL-~) to access the RGB composite.*

With your selection stored, you can safely select another area on screen and define it as a pattern. Using the Rectangular Marquee tool, select a small area on screen that you would like to use as a pattern. Next choose Define Pattern from the Edit menu.

Now recall the original selection by choosing Load Selection from the Select menu. When the Load Selection dialog box appears, notice that Alpha 1 automatically appears in the Source Channel pop-up menu and that the Source Document pop-up menu shows the name of your current document. Other options in the dialog box will be covered in the next section. Click OK to load the selection.

The mask from Alpha 1 is placed on the screen as a selection.

TIP: *Here are three ways to make selections from channels:*

- *To automatically load a selection from an image's channel or alpha channel,* COMMAND-*click (Windows users:* CTRL-click) *on the name or number of the channel in the Channels palette*

- *Press* COMMAND-OPTION *(Windows users:* CTRL-ALT) *and the channel number. For instance, to make a selection from the color information in a file, press* COMMAND-OPTION-*1, 2, or 3 (Windows users* CTRL-ALT-*1, 2, or 3) for* RGB *or Lab files.*

- *Drag the channel over the Make Selection icon at the bottom of the Channels palette.*

Once the selection appears, apply the pattern using the Edit I Fill command. In the Fill dialog box, select Pattern from the Use pop-up menu. Enter **20** in the Opacity field and set Mode to Normal; then click OK. Figure 14-4 displays the results of applying a pattern (created from the feather shown in the image) with a 20% Opacity to the rim selection.

FIGURE 14-4   The plate after the pattern was applied to the selection

14

TIP: *You can create a selection from the non-transparent areas of a layer by pressing COMMAND (Windows users: CTRL) and clicking on the layer in the Layers palette. Then save it into an alpha channel by clicking on the Save Selection icon in the Channels palette.*

 NOTE: *Alpha channels represent a standard method of conveying transparency from one application to another. Many 3-D modeling programs and digital video programs use alpha channels to indicate masked areas. If you create an alpha channel in a 3-D program, and load the image into Photoshop, you will see the mask in the Channels palette. You can then choose Select | Load Selection to load the mask into Photoshop.*

Changing Settings in the Save and Load Selection Dialog Boxes

As you've seen from the previous example, the Save Selection dialog box allows you to save selections. The Load Selection dialog box allows you to load a selection from an alpha channel.

In this section you'll explore the options in the Save Selection and Load Selection dialog boxes that allow you to add to, subtract from, and intersect selections stored in alpha channels. To follow the discussion in this section, you should have the file from the previous section on screen with its alpha channel. If you don't have the file on screen, load any image and create a selection. Next, save the selection by using the Select | Save Selection command, then deselect.

To accurately view the effects of the options in the Save Selection dialog box, the colored overlay mask with the cutout area should be displayed on screen. To see the overlay, you should have the alpha channel you just created or any other alpha channel you will be editing in view and editable. Also, the other Channels (RGB, R, G, and B) in the Channels palette should be in view. Thus, the eye icon should appear next to the name or number of the alpha channel and all the other channels in the Channels palette. The alpha channel you will be editing should be selected. If the alpha channel is not set up this way, click on the alpha channel in the Channels palette to select it. To display the eye icons of the other channels, click on the eye icon column of that channel.

Before exploring the Save Selection operation options, you must create a new selection on screen. Create this selection so it slightly overlays the cutout area of the colored overlay on screen. Use any selection tool to create the selection, then open the Save Selection dialog box by choosing Select I Save Selection.

As you saw in the previous example, the New option in the Destination Channel pop-up menu allows you to save a selection in a new alpha channel. By choosing a channel in the Destination Channel pop-up menu, you can alter the selection stored in a pre-existing alpha channel. If you are in a layer (other than the Background), the Channel pop-up menu will also allow you to create a layer mask in a new channel from your selection. Layer masks are discussed at the end of this chapter and in Chapter 15. When you select a pre-existing channel in the Destination Channel pop-up menu, the dimmed options in the Operations group become active. To see these options in action, choose Alpha 1 in the Destination Channel pop-up menu. Try out each option by choosing the radio button, then clicking OK. After you see the effects on screen, choose Edit I Undo, then try another option. Before you begin, make sure that the Destination Document pop-up menu is set to the name of your document and not to New. This way, the effects will take place in the document you have open on screen and not in the new document.

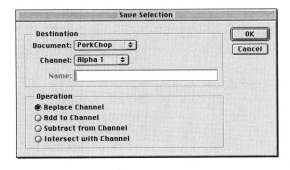

- ☐ **Replace Channel**   This option creates a new selection, completely replacing the selection in the channel chosen in the Channel pop-up menu.

- ☐ **Add to Channel**   This option creates another selection in the channel or adds to the selection in the channel.

- ☐ **Subtract from Channel**   If the selection on screen overlaps with the selection saved in the channel, the overlapping area is subtracted from the selection in the channel. If the areas do not overlap, the selection in the channel is not affected.

- ☐ **Intersect with Channel**   If the selection on screen overlaps with the selection saved in the channel, the overlapping area becomes the selection in the channel. If no areas overlap, the selection in the channel disappears.

14

After you're done experimenting with the Save Selection dialog box, change the settings in the Channels palette so you'll be able to see selection marquees on screen. First, turn off Alpha 1 in the Channels palette by clicking on RGB. When the highlighted area disappears from Alpha 1, it means that editing work will not affect this channel. Turn off the eye icon next to Alpha 1 in the Channels palette. This removes the overlay from the screen. Now you can take a look at the options in the Load Selection dialog box.

The Load Selection dialog box loads selections stored in an alpha channel onto the screen. Before exploring the different options available in the dialog box, create a selection on screen, then choose Load Selection from the Select menu. In the Load Selection dialog box, the Source Document pop-up menu allows a selection to be loaded into any open document. Make sure that the pop-up menu is set to the name of your document. The Source Channel pop-up menu allows you to choose a channel from any open document on screen.

If you are working in a layer, the Source Channel pop-up menu provides a transparency option. This allows you to load the nontransparent areas of the layer as a selection.

```
┌─────────────────────────────────────────────┐
│              Load Selection                  │
│ ┌─ Source ──────────────────┐   ┌─────────┐  │
│ │ Document: │PorkChop  ⬍│    │   │   OK    │  │
│ │                           │   └─────────┘  │
│ │  Channel: │Alpha 1   ⬍│    │   ┌─────────┐  │
│ │           ☐ Invert        │   │ Cancel  │  │
│ └───────────────────────────┘   └─────────┘  │
│ ┌─ Operation ─────────────────────────────┐  │
│ │ ◉ New Selection                         │  │
│ │ ○ Add to Selection                      │  │
│ │ ○ Subtract from Selection               │  │
│ │ ○ Intersect with Selection              │  │
│ └─────────────────────────────────────────┘  │
└─────────────────────────────────────────────┘
```

At this point, you can choose how you want the selection stored in the alpha channel to affect the selection on screen. Feel free to try any of the choices.

The four Operation options in the Load Selection are summarized as follows:

☐ **New Selection**   This option creates a new selection, replacing any previous selection on screen.

☐ **Add to Selection**   This option adds to the selection on screen or creates an additional selection on screen.

☐ **Subtract from Selection**   If the selection in the channel would overlap with the selected area on screen, the selection area from the channel is subtracted from the selection on screen. If the selections do not overlap, the selection on screen is unchanged.

■ **Intersect with Selection**   If the selection in the channel would overlap with the selection on screen, the overlapping area becomes the selection. If no area overlaps, nothing is selected on screen.

    TIP: *To add, subtract, or intersect an alpha channel to, from, or with a selection in the composite channel (such as RGB or CMYK), use these shortcuts:*

□ *To add, press* COMMAND-SHIFT *(Windows users:* CTRL-SHIFT*), then click on the channel.*

□ *To subtract, select the channel, then press* COMMAND-OPTION *(Windows users:* CTRL-OPTION*), then click on the channel.*

□ *To intersect, press* COMMAND-OPTION-SHIFT *(Windows users:* CTRL-ALT-SHIFT*), then click on the channel.*

Now that you've created and altered selections stored in alpha channels, you may want to copy your alpha channel into another file so it can be used with other documents.

Duplicating an Alpha Channel

The Duplicate Channel command in the Channels palette pop-up menu allows you to create an exact duplicate of a channel. The Duplicate Channel command can place a duplicate of a channel in an existing file or in a new file.

The Duplicate Channel command can be used to duplicate channels into new files so they can be deleted from their original file, helping to keep file size to a minimum. By duplicating the channel into a new file, the channel can always be loaded back into the original file with the Duplicate Channel command. It can also be loaded as a blinking selection marquee with the Select I Load Selection command. Some Photoshop users also use the Duplicate Channel command to help get a mask started in an alpha channel. To use this technique, first convert your image to Lab color mode and duplicate the L channel, or duplicate one of the RGB channels (duplicate the one that exhibits the most contrast). After you duplicate the channel, use the mask-editing techniques described in this chapter to fine-tune the mask.

14

To duplicate an existing channel, click on the channel that you want to duplicate in the Channels palette, then choose Duplicate Channel from the Channels palette pop-up menu.

In the Duplicate Channel dialog box, rename the channel, if desired, in the As field. Use the Document pop-up menu to choose the Destination file for the channel. If you wish to place the existing channel into a new channel in a new document, choose New from the Document pop-up menu. Name the new file in the Name field, if desired.

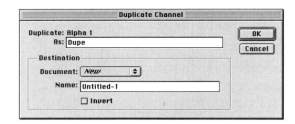

The Invert option for the Destination is similar to choosing Invert from the Image | Adjust | Invert submenu. This option changes light pixels to dark pixels and dark pixels to light, producing a negative of your image.

 TIP: *To quickly duplicate a channel from one file into another file, click and drag the name or number of the channel from the Channels palette into the other document. You can create a duplicate of a channel in the same file by clicking and dragging the name or number of the alpha channel over the New Channel icon ( ) in the Channels palette.*

 REMEMBER: *You can also use the Select | Load Selection command to load a selection from any open file.*

Deleting a Channel

Once you've duplicated a channel into another file or if you're done working with a channel, you may wish to delete the channel from the document it is in. If you still have the rim selection stored in an alpha channel from a previous exercise, delete it to keep your file size as small as possible. If you have any other channels that you don't need, delete them now.

To delete a channel, first select it, then choose Delete Channel from the Channels palette pop-up menu.

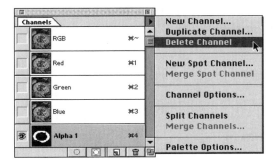

As a shortcut, you can click on the channel you want to delete, then click on the Trash icon in the Channels palette. You can also position the mouse pointer over the channel you wish to delete in the Channels palette. The pointer will change to a pointing hand icon. Click and hold down the mouse button, then drag the channel toward the Trash icon (🗑). As you drag, the pointer will change into a grabbing hand icon. Drag the tiny hand icon over the Trash. When the Trash changes colors, release the mouse and the channel will be deleted.

 TIP: *Pressing CONTROL and clicking on a channel (Windows users: right button click) displays a menu allowing you to delete the channel or duplicate it.*

Creating and Editing an Alpha Channel

The New Channel command in the Channels palette's pop-up menu allows you to create a new alpha channel. You can then work in the channel and create a mask from scratch using a painting, editing, or selection tool. To utilize the mask as a selection, you can execute the Select | Load Selection command.

In this section, load a new file on screen as you learn how to create and edit a channel using the New Channel command. Start with no selection on screen.

To create a new alpha channel, click on the pop-up menu in the Channels palette, and choose New Channel. As a shortcut, you can create a new channel by pressing OPTION (Windows users: ALT) and clicking on the New Channel icon (🖫) in the Channels palette. A new alpha channel appears in the Channels palette, and the New Channel dialog box opens. We named our channel Plate. Enter a descriptive name in the Name field. In the Color Indicates section, choose the Selected Areas radio button. This way, when you paint with black, you will be creating a selection; when you paint with white, you will be subtracting from the

14

selection. Note that this is the opposite of the settings you had when you created the Quick Mask earlier in this chapter. Leave the color swatch set to red and Opacity set to 50%. Click OK.

 NOTE: *At any time, you can edit the Channel Options settings for an alpha channel by double-clicking on the channel in the Channels palette, or by clicking on the channel in the palette, and then choosing Channel Options in the Channels palette's pop-up menu.*

Your screen will now be white because you are in a new, empty channel, and you are viewing only the channel, not the image. Notice in the Channels palette that the eye icon appears beside the new channel (Plate) and that the channel is selected, indicating that it is displayed and that you can edit it. At this point, none of the other channels can be viewed or edited.

 TIP: *You can create a new channel by clicking on the New Channel icon (⬚) at the bottom of the Channels palette. If you want to open the New Channels dialog box, press and hold OPTION (Windows users: ALT) while you click on the New Channel icon.*

Now you are ready to create a mask. But you'll want to see the mask in relation to the image on screen. To view the RGB image, click in the Eye column next to the RGB composite channel. After you click, all of the channels will be visible, but only the Plate alpha channel will be editable (it's the only one with highlight color surrounding its name in the Channels palette).

Creating and Editing a Mask in an Alpha Channel

After you create an alpha channel, and turn on the eye icons for the RGB image as well as the alpha channel, mask editing is displayed over your image with a translucent red overlay. The red overlay is a representation of the grayscale mask created in the channel. The overlay is used so that you can see your image and the mask at the same time.

Before you begin creating a mask in the channel, click on the Default Colors icon to set foreground to black and background to white. Use the Paintbrush to paint over an area on screen that you would like to have selected. You will be painting with the same type of translucent overlay you worked with in Quick Mask mode. If you make a mistake, you can erase the overlay by simply clicking and dragging with the Eraser. (This works because the Eraser paints with the background color, white; you could also use the Paintbrush to paint with white.)

The following table summarizes the effects of painting in an alpha channel when the Color Indicates Selected Areas radio button is selected in the Mask Options dialog box. Remember, this is the setting that is opposite the one used when you created the Quick Mask earlier in this chapter.

Painting Color	Effect on Colored Mask Overlay	Effect When Selection Is Loaded
White	Subtracts from colored overlay (unprotected area); subtracts from unprotected area	Subtracts from selection marquee
Black	Adds to colored overlay (unprotected area); adds to unprotected area	Adds to selection marquee
Gray	Adds a partial overlay	Creates a partial selection

After you've painted with the colored overlay, take a look at what appears in the new channel. To view the channel as a separate image, turn off the eye icons in the other channels by clicking on the eye icon next to the RGB composite channel. This hides the display of the RGB channels and leaves the alpha channel on screen. Notice that you painted in black.

To load the alpha channel's black area on screen as a selection, first select the RGB composite by clicking on RGB in the Channels palette, or press COMMAND-~ (Windows users: CTRL-~). Note that the alpha channel is no longer the target channel. Then choose Load Selection from the Select menu. If you wish to edit the selected area, try applying the Distort/Twirl filter with a setting of 999 degrees. With the filter applied, the food turns into soup, as shown in Figure 14-5. When you've finished applying the Filter | Distort/Twirl filter, delete the Plate alpha channel using the Delete Channel command in the Channels palette's pop-up menu.

14

FIGURE 14-5   After the selection is loaded and the Distort/Twirl filter is applied, the pork chop turns into soup

As practice, try using the New Channel command to create an alpha channel to mask a different area of your file so you can safely edit in that area. After you're done, you may wish to save your file with the alpha channel. Proceed to the next section to learn how to do this.

NOTE: *You may wonder why Photoshop (as well as other applications such as MetaCreations Painter) use grayscale alpha channels to store masks. A gray mask can indicate a change in opacity, something not visible with a selection marquee.*

When you create a selection with one of Photoshop's selection tools, it functions as a mask with 100 percent opacity. Thus, if you copy and paste the selection, the selection's pixels completely replace the image area you paste over. However, if you use a mask created by painting with gray in an alpha channel, the gray represents a change in opacity. If you paint with gray in a mask, then load the mask as a selection (Select \ Load Selection) the selection does not represent a selection with 100 percent opacity. If you use the selection created from the gray mask to copy and paste, the image you copy will blend with the image you paste it over—as if you pasted an image with a lower opacity over another.

Working with Masks

Once you've learned the various ways to create and work with alpha channels, you'll often find that each image that you need to mask requires a slightly different approach. For instance, you may be able to get a mask started by simply clicking and dragging with one of the selection tools, then saving the selection. If your image is very well defined with very light and very dark areas, you may be able to duplicate one of the RGB channels or the L channel of a Lab Color image, then use the duplicated channel as the basis for a mask that you edit. We've found that one of the best ways to get started creating masks is to create a selection with Photoshop's Magnetic Lasso or create a path with the Magnetic Pen and then turn it into a selection. Once the selection is created, we save the selection (Select | Save Selection). After the selection is saved, we then edit the mask with the Paintbrush tool, viewing the image through the red overlay. We used this technique to mask the polar bear shown in Figure 14-6. After we masked the polar bear we placed it in a new background, seen in Figure 14-7. Here are the steps we used to create the mask. If you wish to follow the steps we took, try masking any image, or use the Skull or Thai boat images from the Samples folder.

1. Load the image that you wish to mask on screen.

2. Activate the Magnetic Lasso tool. If the edges of the mask need to be soft, make sure to raise the Feather value field in the Magnetic Lasso Options palette before you create the selection. Remember that the amount of feathering you use is related to the resolution of your image. If you are working with a 72-pixel-per-inch image, a feather of 4 pixels creates a larger feather than a 4-pixel feather in a 300-pixel-per-inch image. For more information about feathering, turn to Chapter 4.

 NOTE: *If you forget to set the Feather value before you select your image, you can always add a feather after you create the selection by choosing Select | Feather.*

3. Begin outlining the image that you want to mask with the Magnetic Lasso tool. Remember to click along the image edge if the Lasso moves off the image. Don't worry if your selection isn't perfect—in step 5 you'll learn how to edit the mask to fine-tune the selection. To close the Magnetic Lasso selection, you need to click where your starting and ending point

14

FIGURE 14-6   Original polar bear before creating mask

FIGURE 14-7   Masked polar bear placed in a new background

meet, as seen in Figure 14-8. For more information on using the Magnetic Lasso tool or any other selection tool, turn to Chapter 4.

4. Once you create the selection, save it by choosing Select | Save Selection. If, desired, name the Channel in the Save Selection dialog box (We named our channel Bear). After you click OK, Photoshop automatically creates an alpha channel with the mask in it. To see the alpha channel you created, open the Channels palette (Window | Show Channels).

5. To see a full-screen version of the mask, click on the words "Alpha 1" (unless you've named the channel) in the Channels palette. Figure 14-9 shows the mask we created of the polar bear in an alpha channel.

6. To view the mask as a translucent overlay (as seen when you click on the Quick Mask icon), you first must have Alpha 1 as the active channel and all the other channels viewable. To activate the Red, Green, and Blue channels, click on the eye column next to the RGB channel in the Channels palette. At this point you should still have the eye icon displayed for Alpha 1, and Alpha 1 should still be the selected channel, as shown in the

Magnetic Lasso tool

FIGURE 14-8   Magnetic Lasso tool creating a selection

14

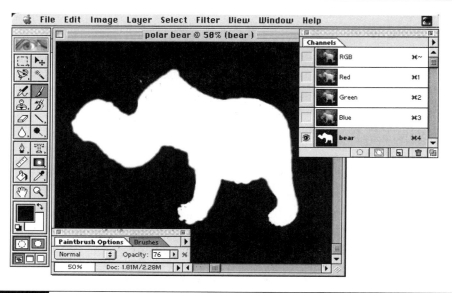

Mask in alpha channel

illustration below. The alpha channel needs to be the selected channel because you will be editing the mask in the channel, not your RGB image.

7. If you wish, you can change the color of the translucent overlay in the Channels Options palette by double-clicking on Alpha 1 in the Channels palette. We changed the overlay color from red to green, because the bucket the bear was holding was red. Otherwise, as we worked, we might have become confused as to what was the mask and what was the bucket. To edit the mask we picked a soft-edged brush and painted with black to add to the mask (add to the selection) and we painted with white to subtract from the mask (subtract from the selection). We painted with gray when we wanted a translucent mask. Note that you can also create a translucent mask by setting the Foreground color to black and lowering Opacity in the Paintbrush Options palette.

8. As we edited the mask, we switched settings in the Color Indicates Masked Areas option and the Color Indicates Selected Areas option. The Masked Areas option displays the color overlay in protected areas; the Selected Areas option displays color overlay in non-protected areas. By using this technique we could easily see whether our masking efforts needed adjustments. If we saw a gap when we switched between the two options, we knew we needed to continue fine tuning the mask.

9. Once we finished editing the mask, we loaded the new selection that we had created by choosing Select | Load Selection. Again, to test how well we created the mask, we copied the bear and pasted into a new file with a green background (paste your image into any color other than the color in the image). If we saw part of the background in the copied image, we knew we had to go back to the original file and continue editing the mask.

Saving a File with Alpha Channels

After you've created an alpha channel, you may wish to have it saved with your file so the mask can be loaded as a selection at a later time. If you save your file in Photoshop's native format or in TIFF format, all alpha channels are automatically saved with the file. If you wish to save a copy of an image in another file format without its alpha channels, choose File | Save a Copy. Choose a file format from the Format (Windows users: Save As) pop-up menu. If the format will not accept alpha channels, the Don't Include Alpha Channels check box will automatically be selected and grayed out. For more information about saving in other formats, see Appendix A.

Using the Color Range Command

Another helpful command that allows you to create masks very quickly is Photoshop's powerful Color Range command. Color Range creates a selection based upon color. In some respects, the Color Range command is like a combination of the Magic Wand tool and the Select | Similar command in that Color Range selects a color range anywhere in an image. When using Color Range, you can choose to have Photoshop select colors according to preset colors, or you can have it create a selection according to the colors sampled in your image. As you'll see in the following example, the Color Range dialog box previews the selection in a mask.

To try out the Color Range command, load an image on screen. If you don't have an image, get an image from the Adobe Samples folder. To open the Color Range dialog box, choose Color Range from the Select menu. The rectangular preview area in the middle of the dialog box displays either the mask or your onscreen image. Click on the Image radio button and you will see your image in the Preview box. Although you will probably be most interested in monitoring the mask in the Selection preview, choosing the Image radio button is helpful when you zoom into specific image areas. The Image radio button will always show you the entire image or selection, even if you have zoomed into a small area on screen.

Now click on the Selection radio button to see the mask. Notice that the mask is mostly black because the Color Range command has not begun its search for colors. Once you specify what color range you want selected, the selection will be represented by light areas in the mask.

To specify which colors you'd like selected, use the Select pop-up menu, which allows you to pick from preset colors or colors that you sample with the dialog box's Eyedropper from a gamut of colors. The Select pop-up menu also allows you to select according to shadow, midtones, and highlights. Try a quick test to see how the dialog box can select specific colors for your image.

1. From the Select pop-up menu, choose Reds.

Notice that an area of the mask gets lighter. This corresponds to the red areas on screen. It is the area that will be selected when you return to your image.

 TIP: *You can quickly toggle back and forth from the image preview to the mask preview by pressing and holding CTRL (Mac users can press CTRL or COMMAND).*

2. Try choosing Yellows from the Select menu.

Next, you'll take a look at how the Selection Preview pop-up menu can help you preview the selection. As you read through a brief explanation of the options in the Selection Preview pop-up menu, try out each one by clicking on the menu choice.

☐ **Grayscale** previews your image in grayscale. The preview on screen appears as it would if it were in an alpha channel. This mode can be helpful when the Select menu is set to Highlights, Midtones, or Shadows.

☐ **Black Matte** displays the mask of the selected areas in color. All other areas are black. This mode is especially helpful in seeing a selection that will be created in dark image areas.

☐ **White Matte** displays the selected areas in color. All other areas are white. This mode is especially helpful in seeing a selection that will be created in light image areas.

☐ **Quick Mask** displays the image using the current settings in the Quick Mask Options dialog box.

Now assume that you want to select only the flesh tones in the image, or any other color area in your image. Before continuing, set the Selection Preview pop-up menu back to None. You can specify this color range by clicking on the image with the Eyedropper that appears in the dialog box. In order to use the Eyedropper, you will need to change the Select pop-up menu. When you use this option, you can extend a selection by clicking on the Eyedropper+; you can reduce the selection by choosing the Eyedropper−.

14

To select using a sampled color:

1. In the Select pop-up menu, choose Sampled Colors.

2. Move the Eyedropper over the flesh tones in the image on screen, and select another color you wish to use. Click the mouse.

   Notice that the mask turns lighter in areas corresponding to the color you chose.

3. If you wish to soften selection edges, drag the Fuzziness slider to the right. If you drag the slider very far to the right, the selection will be extended. Drag it to the left to reduce the selection.

4. Now, extend the selection by clicking on the Eyedropper+, move it into your image on screen, and select a darker fleshtone or other dark area.

After you click, the white area of the mask is extended to include this color range. To see the actual selection in your image, click OK. When the image returns on screen, you'll see the blinking marquee surrounding the area specified in the mask. At this point, you could either begin to edit the selection using the Quick Mask mode or save the selection to an alpha channel.

 TIP: *When the Eyedropper is over your image, you can toggle to the Eyedropper+ by pressing SHIFT, or to the Eyedropper– by pressing OPTION (Windows users: ALT). Also note that if you SHIFT and click on the document with the Eyedropper tool you can set color sampler points.*

Alpha Channel Techniques

The following sections provide exercises that will broaden your understanding of alpha channels and put you on the road to creating sophisticated effects with them.

Using Alpha Channels to Create Shadowed Text

Now that you possess the power to save and load selections, creating special effects becomes easier. For instance, you can easily create shadowed text, as shown in the following illustration, by utilizing the alpha channel features already covered in this chapter. In this exercise you'll create two alpha channels: one for the shadow area of the text and the other for the text.

Photoshop 5 > In Action

The sky was created using the Gradient tool.

Using the selection tools, the architectural engraving was selected and then saved to an alpha channel using the Select | Save Selection command. Once the channel was created, it was easy to isolate the building and apply color.

The stock certificate was selected and the Perspective command was used to add depth.

A mask of the architectural engraving was created by first selecting the engraving and then executing the Select | Save Selection command.

Using Photoshop's Select | Feather command, the edges of the stock certificate were blurred.

14

Artist: Marc Yankus   **Client: General Electric**

Marc created this cover image for an annual report by scanning black-and-white architectural engravings, a page from the *Wall Street Journal*, a stock certificate, an American dollar, a Japanese yen, a German deutsche mark, and some ticker tape. After the images were scanned, they were placed into a file and different masks were created of the images. The masks were put to use by first executing the Select | Load Selection command. After the selections were loaded, they were edited and colored.

NOTE: *The following exercise presents one of the numerous ways of creating shadow effects in Photoshop. You can often create shadow effects more quickly using channels. See Chapters 3, 15, and 17 to learn how to create drop shadows using layers.*

1. Create a new RGB color file 5 inches by 5 inches and then open the Channels and Color palettes if they are not already open. Set the foreground to a light color.

2. Next use the Type Mask tool to create some text on screen. For our example we used an Adobe font called Remedy Double Extras. When the text is on screen, move it into the center of your document window. Fill the text with the foreground color. Keep the text selected.

3. While the text is still selected, choose the Select | Save Selection command to create a mask in an alpha channel (Alpha 1) of the text floating on screen. In the Save Selection dialog box, leave the default settings; the Destination Document pop-up menu is set to Untitled 1 and the Destination Channel pop-up menu is set to New. Click OK. Don't deselect the text on screen.

4. Now create a duplicate mask in an alpha channel of the text floating on screen. Choose Select | Save Selection. Again, don't change the default settings in the Save Selection dialog box, and click OK. After you have a mask of the floating text in the second alpha channel (Alpha 2), deselect the floating text.

 REMEMBER: *If you deselect a selection you can return to the last selection by choosing Select | Reselect.*

5. Click on Alpha 2 in the Channels palette to activate the alpha channel.

6. Next, you will offset the text in Alpha 2 to begin creating the shadow effect.

7. To offset the text in Alpha 2, choose Offset from the Filter | Other submenu. In the Offset dialog box, type in the amount you want to offset the text horizontally and vertically. Type a positive number less than 10 in the Horizontal and Vertical fields to offset the shadow text to the right and down (a negative number offsets to the left and up). Choose the Wrap Around radio button in the Undefined Areas group and click OK.

 TIP: *If you want to create a dramatic effect and make the type look as if it is jumping off the page, increase the Offset values in the Offset filter's dialog box.*

8. If you want your shadow to have a soft-shadowed look, apply the Gaussian Blur filter to Alpha 2. In the Gaussian Blur dialog box, type in a number between 1 and 10 depending upon how much of a blur you want. If you don't want a soft-shadowed look, skip this step and proceed to step 9.

9. Next, load the selection from Alpha 1 into Alpha 2 by choosing Select | Load Selection. When the Load Selection dialog box appears, make sure that the Channel pop-up menu is set to Alpha 1, then click OK. The selection from Alpha 1 should now appear in Alpha 2.

10. Fill the selection in Alpha 2 with black using the Edit | Fill command. The white area you see in Alpha 2 will create the drop shadow after you load the selection.

 NOTE: *If the Selected Areas option is still selected in the Channels Options palette (from the last exercise), choose Masked Areas instead. To open the Channels Options palette, double click on the Channel in the Channels palette.*

11. Click on the letters "RGB" in the Channels palette to return to the composite image.

12. Now, choose Load Selection from the Select menu. In the Load Selection dialog box, choose Alpha 2 from the Channel pop-up menu, then click OK. After the selection appears, fill it with a dark color. Deselect to see the effects.

At this point, both the text and drop shadow selections are saved in two different alpha channels. This means that at any time you can fill your entire screen with white and then reload the selection in Alpha 1 (text), fill it with a color, then reload the selection in Alpha 2 (shadow), and fill it with a different color. You can also fill either selection with a blend or apply a filter.

Even though this exercise applied a drop shadow to text, you can apply the same steps to create a drop shadow on any object. Just skip steps 1 and 2 and, before you start step 3, make sure that your object is selected before you choose Select | Save Selection.

Save your file if you wish and proceed to the next section to learn how to create three-dimensional effects using alpha channels.

Creating a Three-Dimensional, Raised-Type Effect

You can create striking three-dimensional effects by loading and filling selections from alpha channels. You can even save a sliver of a selection that has just the look you want and reload it to be used as a light source or a shadow. The exercise in this section demonstrates how to create a raised-type, or embossed, effect by filling one selection as a light source and another selection as a shadow.

Before starting, examine Figure 14-10. Notice the raised look of the text; it is created primarily from the thin slivers of light and dark along the sides of the letters. The white slivers along the left edges create the illusion of a light source, and the dark slivers along the right edges appear as shadows. Together, they create the depth needed to produce the raised-type effect.

In the exercise, you'll create a separate mask for the light source and another for the shadow. Then the selections are filled with white and black. If you keep these steps in mind as you work through the exercise, you'll have a clearer idea of why you are executing each step. The concepts presented here can be used in other situations where a raised, recessed, or beveled effect is needed.

 NOTE: *This example provides a look at how to manually create 3-D effects. Photoshop can automatically create many 3-D effects for you using the commands in the Layer | Effects menu. These commands are covered in Chapter 17.*

1. Start by opening any file to which you would like to add raised text. If you don't have a suitable image, load the Big Sky file from the Adobe Samples folder.

FIGURE 14-10   Three-dimensional, raised-type effect (photograph courtesy of Stacy Kollar Photography)

2. Activate the Type Mask tool and click on screen to open the Type Tool dialog box. Type the text to be added to your image and click OK. Once the type selection appears on screen, move it to the desired position.

3. While the text is still selected, choose Save Selection from the Select menu. In the Save Selection dialog box, make sure the Document pop-up menu is set to Big Sky and the Channel pop-up menu is set to New. Name the channel **Black Shadow**; this is the channel you will use to create the shadow for the text. Select the Masked Areas radio button for the Color Indicates option, and click OK.

4. In the Black Shadow channel, deselect the text. To lay the groundwork for creating the black shadow slivers, apply the Emboss filter to the entire channel. Choose Emboss from the Filter | Stylize submenu, and in the Emboss dialog box type **135** in the Angle field, **3** in the Height field, and **100** in the Amount field. Click OK to execute the filter.

14

5. Next, duplicate the alpha channel by clicking on it and dragging it over the New Channel icon at the bottom of the Channels palette. The second channel will provide the basis for the light source for the raised text.

6. To rename the duplicate channel, double-click on it in the Channels palette. When the Channel Options dialog box appears, name the alpha channel **White Shadow** and click OK.

 TIP: *You can copy and rename a channel at the same time by pressing OPTION (Widows users: ALT) while you drag the channel onto the New Channel icon.*

7. From the Image | Adjust | Invert submenu, choose Invert to reverse the light and dark areas on screen.

8. Next you will isolate the white area of the alpha channel. Choose Threshold from the Image | Adjust submenu. In the Threshold dialog box, set the slider control somewhere between 200 and 255 and click OK. Before continuing, compare your image with Figure 14-10. Remember that white represents the image area that will become a selection.

9. Now isolate the area that will provide the black shadow for the text. Click on the Black Shadow channel in the Channels palette; when the channel is active, choose Threshold from the Image | Map submenu. In the Threshold dialog box, set the slider control somewhere between 200 and 255 and click OK. Once again, compare your image with Figure 14-10. The white area on screen represents another selection that will be loaded into your image. This selection area will be filled with black.

10. Now you are ready to create the raised-type effect. Select the RGB composite channel by clicking on RGB in the Channels palette or by pressing COMMAND-~ (Windows users: CTRL-~).

11. To create the shadow portion of the text, load the Black Shadow selection. Choose Load Selection from the Select menu, and select Black Shadow in the Source Channel pop-up menu. Keep the Document pop-up menu set to Big Sky. Click OK. When the selection appears, fill it with black. To

examine the shadow you just created, hide the selection marquee by choosing Hide Edges from the View menu.

12. To create the light source for the text, choose Select | Load Selection again and select White Shadow in the Source Channel pop-up menu. Keep the Document pop-up menu set to Big Sky. Click OK. When the selection appears, fill it with white. Deselect.

This three-dimensional effect can be applied to any object or shape, not just to text. Also, if you'd like, you can reload the White Shadow and Black Shadow selections and fill them with other colors using various opacities. Try experimenting to create different effects. Fill the Black Shadow selection with white and the White Shadow selection with black, then try filling the white selection with yellow at a 50% opacity.

If you wish to create your own three-dimensional effects, start by analyzing shadow and light sources, and text or object areas. Use the Offset and Emboss filters to help create displacement effects. Use the Image | Adjust submenu's Threshold or Invert commands, or the Image | Adjust | Levels command to control the brightness levels. Experiment by filling the selections with the different colors.

Now that you know how to create and use alpha channels, you may wish to explore the other commands in the Channels palette's pop-up menu. But before you go any further, use the File | Save As command to save your document under a new name.

Splitting and Merging Channels

A powerful utility offered in the Channels palette allows you to split the channels in a color image into separate files. After you split the channels, you can edit an image's separate channels and then merge them back together. In the next section, you'll see how splitting and merging channels can be used to create a colored mezzotint effect.

To split the channels, choose Split Channels in the Channels palette's pop-up menu. The split documents will appear on screen as grayscale images, and the original document is closed.

14

Photoshop 5 | In Action

Two alpha channels were created for the face of the text.

Two alpha channels were created for the beveled edge.

Artwork by: Daniel Clark   **Client: Dauz Drums**

Daniel started creating this image by setting the type in Freehand, using the typeface Lubilan Graph. After the type was set, it was imported into Adobe Dimensions in order to create the beveled 3-D perspective. The Adobe Dimensions 3-D wireframe outline was brought into Adobe Photoshop. Once the text was brought into Photoshop, four alpha channels were created: two for the face of the text (for the upper and lower half), and two separate alpha channels for the beveled edge (one for the small beveled edge and another for the large extrusion—the thickness of the letters).

Once the alpha channels were created, Daniel created the chrome effect by using the Gradient tool to create various blends. The foreground color was set to black and the background color to white.

You can also combine separate channels into a composite image by using the Merge Channels command. To execute this command, all channels to be merged must be open on screen. They must be grayscale images, and their width and height in pixels must be equal. You can merge Photoshop documents together using the Merge Channels command, as long as the documents meet these conditions. In the Merge Channels dialog box, you can specify the number of channels you want to merge and to what mode (RGB color, CMYK color, and so forth).

 TIP: *If you have a DCS file that you can't load or that won't print in your desktop publishing program, you may be able to solve the problem by merging the separate files into one CMYK file. After you merge the channels, save the file in one of Photoshop's DCS formats.*

Merge Channels	
Mode: RGB Color ▼	OK
Channels: 3	Cancel

Click OK, and another dialog box appears where you specify the channels into which you want each open document on screen loaded.

Merge RGB Channels	
Specify Channels:	OK
Red: Book Cover.Red ▼	Cancel
Green: Book Cover.Green ▼	Mode
Blue: Book Cover.Blue ▼	

After you click OK, a new image consisting of the formerly split documents appears in an untitled window.

14

Using Split Channels/Merge Channels to Create a Colored Mezzotint Effect

The Split Channels and Merge Channels commands can be used to create an interesting colored mezzotint effect. First, load an RGB color or CMYK color file. Then use the Split Channels command to split the image into separate grayscale files.

Next, create a custom pattern by opening Mezzotint-shape in the Postscript Patterns folder (in the Goodies/Patterns folder). To define the pattern, choose Select | All, then Edit | Define Pattern. From the Mode menu, change each file to Bitmap, and choose the Custom Pattern option in the Bitmap dialog box. Click OK to apply the pattern. Do this to every file, and then convert each file back to grayscale.

Next, use the Merge Channels command to merge the channels back together. The color image will reappear, but with a black mezzotint pattern overlaying the colors. The final effect will depend upon the colors in the original image.

 NOTE: *Photoshop's Mezzotint filter (Filter | Pixelate | Mezzotint) can also create a variety of colored mezzotint effects. See Chapter 10 for more details.*

Creating Blending Effects with the Apply Image Command

Once you've learned the fundamentals of creating and using alpha channels, the power of Photoshop's Apply Image command opens a new world of design possibilities. Apply Image allows you to create exquisite and often striking effects by superimposing channels over other channels. Like Photoshop's Calculations command, covered later in this chapter, the Apply Image command will Add, Subtract, Multiply, and Screen the values of each pixel in a channel with the corresponding pixel values of another channel. The resulting or target image's channel is changed based upon the calculations applied to the pixel values of the source channels and the target image's channel.

 NOTE: *The Layers palette allows you to create many of the same effects provided by the Apply Image dialog box. Most users find layers easier to use. For more information about using layers, see Chapters 15 and 16.*

Before you begin to use the Apply Image command, it's important to remember the fundamentals of how a digital image is created. As discussed in Chapters 1 and 8, every Photoshop image is created from a grid of pixels. You might think of an image as being created by painting in the rows and columns of grid boxes on a sheet of graph paper. Each grid box is the equivalent of a pixel, and each pixel has a color value from 0 to 255.

When Photoshop executes the Apply Image or Calculations command, it blends channels together by applying calculations to the corresponding pixel values in each channel. For instance, when Photoshop applies the Difference command, it subtracts corresponding pixel values. This means that the value of the first pixel in the first row in one channel is subtracted from the value of the first pixel in the first row of the second channel. The second pixel's value in the first row of the first channel is subtracted from the second pixel's value in the first row of the second image, and so on.

It is important to understand that pixel values are measured on a scale of 0 to 255, with 0 representing the darkest value and 255 representing white. Therefore, when pixel values increase, the image grows lighter, and when pixel values decrease, the image grows darker.

 NOTE: *When you are working with a composite image, 0 to 255 represents brightness values of all the RGB channels. If you are a bit puzzled by the representation of brightness values in an image, think of them as a grayscale version of your image. A visual representation of an image's brightness values can be seen by choosing Histogram from the Image menu. For more information about histograms, see Chapter 18.*

Since Photoshop executes the Apply Image command on a pixel-by-pixel basis for channels, it will operate only on images that are exactly the same width and height in pixels. If you wish to use the Apply Image command on channels from two images that are different sizes, you can crop one or use the Image | Duplicate command to create a duplicate of one image. After the duplicate is created, you can copy and paste the image you need into the duplicate.

 NOTE: *The mathematical formulas for many Apply Image blending options are provided in this section. Undoubtedly, you won't want to keep your calculator accessory open on screen to compute pixel values before applying commands. The formulas are supplied here not so you have to do the math but to help you understand how the commands work and aid you in predicting their outcomes.*

Using the Apply Image Dialog Box

The Apply Image dialog box allows you to blend a source channel with a target channel. The channels can be in the same document or in different documents. The

14

easiest way to see how Apply Image works is to create a simple blend between an image and a channel with some text in it. This is how the effect in Figure 14-11(a) was created.

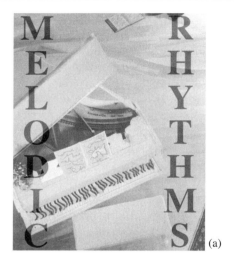

(a)

(b)

M
E
L
O
D
I
C

R
H
Y
T
H
M
S

(c)

FIGURE 14-11   (a) Image after using the Image | Apply Image command;
(b) photograph of piano (courtesy of Stacy Kollar Photography);
(c) text created in alpha channel

The Apply Image command was applied to the digitized image of the piano in Figure 14-11(b) and the alpha channel with text in Figure 14-11(c) to create the effect shown in Figure 14-11(a). The Apply Image dialog settings are shown in Figure 14-12. The dialog box settings will be discussed in detail later in this section.

To complete the following example, load any image on screen. If you don't have an image to load, use the Big Sky file from the Samples folder in Adobe Photoshop's Goodies folder. Once the image is loaded, create a new channel by clicking on the New Channel icon (the dog-eared icon in the bottom of the Channels palette). In the New Channel dialog box that appears, name your channel Text. Make sure the Color Indicates Selected Areas radio button is selected (this will place a white background in the channel) and click OK. When the channel appears, click on the eye column next to the RGB composite channel in the Channels palette to turn on the view of the RGB composite. This allows you to see the image in the Big Sky file while you work in the alpha channel.

Make sure that your foreground color is black. Use the Type Mask tool to add text to the Text channel. After the text selection appears, position it as desired with the Move tool, then fill with Black. Next deselect the text. Before executing the Apply Image command, turn off the eye next to the Text channel. Next, make the RGB channel the target channel by clicking on it in the Channels palette. If you do not select the RGB channel, you might inadvertently apply the Apply Image

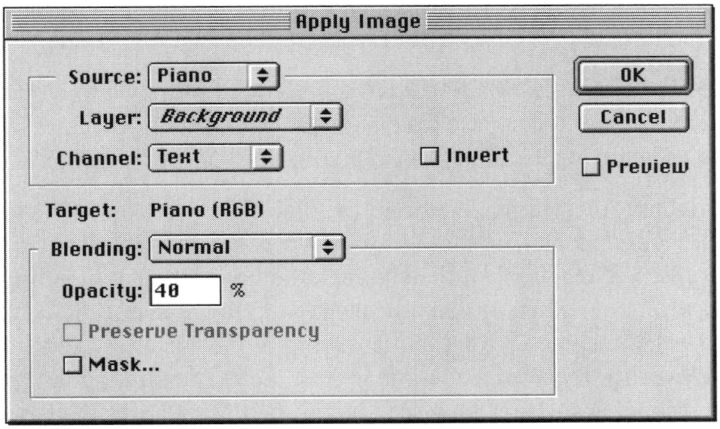

FIGURE 14-12   The Apply Image dialog box settings for the example shown in Figure 14-11

command to the Text channel rather than the composite RGB channel of the target image on screen.

At first the commands you see in the dialog box might seem a little bewildering, but once you understand their purpose, you'll find that Apply Image is actually rather easy to use. Here's a review of the dialog box options.

- The Source pop-up menu at the top of the Apply Image dialog box allows you to choose a document file that you wish to use as one of the blending files. Only documents that have the same width and height in pixels as the active document on screen appear in the Source pop-up menu.

- The Layer and Channel pop-up menus allow you to pick a layer and a channel from the source document.

- The Channel pop-up menu allows you to pick a channel from the source document to use for the blend. If you choose a layer in the Layer pop-up menu (other than the Background), the word "Transparency" appears in the Channel pop-up menu. If you use this option, a mask of the channel is used in the blend. In the mask, transparent layer areas are black, and colored areas are white.

- If your document does not have any transparent layers, the word "Background" appears in the Layer pop-up menu. If your source image has several layers, the Layer pop-up menu allows you to choose Merged. If you choose this option, the Apply Image command applies calculations to the source image as if all its layers were merged into one layer.

- The Invert check box adjacent to the Source group allows you to invert the pixel values of the source pixels. If you click Invert, black pixels will be read as white, white as black, and pixel values of colors as their complements.

- By default, the Target section in the dialog box is where the Apply Image effect will appear. The target image is always the current active document on screen. The names of the channel and layer that the blending effect will appear in are shown in parentheses next to the name of the target image. The target channel and the target layer are the currently selected channel and layer for the active document on screen. The target channel and the target layer are both surrounded by a highlight color in the Channels and Layers palette.

- The Blending pop-up menu allows you to pick from a group of blending effects. Select the Blending pop-up menu now to see the list of choices. Each choice produces a different effect by telling Photoshop to use a different set of pixel calculations when blending source and target pixels.

Notice that several of the choices in the pop-up menu are the same names that appear in the Mode menu in different palettes and dialog boxes. These perform virtually the same functions when blending channels as they do when painting.

- In the Opacity field, enter the Opacity percentage that will be used when channels are blended together. Low opacities will make the source channel more translucent. High opacities make the pixels in the source channel less translucent.

- The Mask check box allows you designate a channel in an image to use as a mask. As you'll see later in this section, the dark areas in the mask hide corresponding areas of the source image, allowing more of the target pixels to show through. Light areas in the mask reveal more source pixels and fewer of the target pixels.

- The Preserve Transparency check box becomes accessible only when your target layer is not the background. When the Preserve Transparency check box is selected, transparent areas of the target image will not be affected by the Apply Image command.

Now that you're familiar with the dialog box options, you can try creating a simple blend between the image on screen and the text channel.

1. First, set the Source group. By default the active document on screen appears in the Source pop-up menu. Since it is the only document on screen, no other files appear in the Source pop-up menu. If you are using the Big Sky file, the word "Background" appears in the Layer pop-up menu. If you are using an image that has layers, Merged will be the default. You can choose a layer from the pop-up menu or choose Merged.

2. Before you change the Channel pop-up menu to Text, notice that the target image is your active document. Since you want to blend the Text channel with the document on screen, choose Text from the Channel pop-up menu.

3. Since this is just a simple demonstration of the Apply Image dialog box, leave the Blending pop-up menu set to Normal. Change Opacity to 40%. Then click on the Preview check box. On screen you will see the channel text blended with your image.

4. To create an effect of lighter type blending against the background, click on the Invert check box, next to the Source group. This lightens the text and darkens the background.

14

Before you proceed to investigate the various Blending options Apply Image has to offer, try changing the Opacity setting. If you lower Opacity, you will see the fruit image becomes more prominent; raise opacity and the text from the channel becomes darker.

If you wish to apply the Apply Image command, click OK, then use the File | Save As command to save your document under a new name. Otherwise, click Cancel and continue to explore the blending options offered by Apply Image.

In the next examples, you will use the Preview check box to examine the different Apply Image options. After you've examined the effect, you can either Cancel or click OK to apply the effect to your target document. If you'd like the blending effect to appear in a new file, choose New Document from the Result pop-up menu, then click OK.

Remember that if you are using important files, choose File | Save As to rename your document so that you do not overwrite your original files.

Add and Subtract

The Add and Subtract Blending options add or subtract the values of corresponding pixels in the source channel and a channel in the target image. As mentioned earlier, if an image's pixel values increase, the image grows lighter; if the pixel values decrease, the image grows darker. Thus, the Add Blending option can be used to blend and create a lighter target image, and the Subtract Blending option can be used to blend and create a darker target image.

Both Blending options allow you to adjust the pixel values of the target image by entering a Scale value and an Offset value. To understand these values, let's analyze the formulas Photoshop uses to add and subtract. Here is the Add command formula:

$$\frac{\text{Source} + \text{Target}}{\text{Scale}} + \text{Offset} = \text{Result}$$

This formula adds the pixel values from the Source and Target to produce a brighter target image. The sum of the Source and Target pixels is divided by the Scale factor; thus Scale can be used to decrease the brightening effect. Scale can be any number between 1.000 and 2.000, inclusive. If Scale is 2, the calculation will yield exactly the average brightness of both images. The Offset factor can be any number between −255 and 255. Adding a positive Offset number lightens the image; adding a negative Offset number darkens the image.

The Subtract Blending option formula uses the same components as the Add formula, except that the source pixels are subtracted, as is the Offset value.

$$\frac{\text{Source} - \text{Target}}{\text{Scale}} - \text{Offset} = \text{Result}$$

Here is an exercise to try out the Add and/or Subtract Blending options using the Hands file, which can be found in the Samples folder. In this exercise, you'll blend the Hands file with another file created with the Clouds filter. Since both files need to have the same dimensions in pixels, the easiest way to create the Clouds file is to duplicate the Skull file, then create the clouds over the duplicate file.

1. Open the Skull file (or any file in which you want to Add or Subtract brightness).

2. To duplicate the file, choose Duplicate from the Image menu. In the Duplicate Image dialog box, name the new file Clouds.

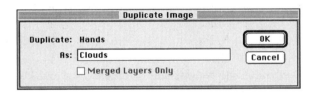

3. Before you add color, you'll need to convert the Clouds file to RGB color. To do this, choose RGB Color from the Image | Mode menu.

4. To change the duplicate image into clouds, first change the foreground color to blue and the background color to white. To create the cloud effect, choose Clouds from the Filter | Render submenu.

   Now you can blend the two images together—first with the Add command, then with Subtract.

5. Choose Apply Image from the Image menu. In the Apply Image dialog box, note that the Target file is the Clouds file because it is the active image on screen.

   a. Set the Source pop-up menu to be the Skull file (the Channel pop-up menu is black because the image is a grayscale image).

   b. Set the Blending pop-up menu to Add.

   c. In the Scale field, type **2**; in the Offset field, type **30**. Set Opacity to 100%. Make sure the Preview button is selected.

14

The result will show the Skull file lightened against the Clouds background.

d. If you wish to lighten the effect, increase the Offset value.

e. Now try the Subtract command by choosing Subtract from the Blending pop-up menu. This will produce results opposite from those of the Add Blending option. The Scale factor should be set to 1. The blended images will be darker. Raise the Offset value if you wish to lighten the image.

Difference and Exclusion

The Difference Blending option subtracts the pixel values of the target channel from a channel in the source image. The results of the Difference Blending option are fairly easy to predict because the calculation is quite simple:

$$Source - Target = Result$$

With this formula, if darker target pixels (other than black) are subtracted from lighter pixels, the blended target pixels will be darker than the source pixels and lighter than the original target pixels. Also, two very bright pixels subtracted from each other will result in a dark pixel. Subtracting from black leaves image areas unchanged. Subtracting from white inverts the color. If a negative number results from the calculation, that number is used as a positive number.

The image in Figure 14-13(b) was combined with the alpha channel containing black and white stripes shown in Figure 14-13(c) to create the effect in Figure 14-13(a). The dialog box settings for the Apply Image command are shown in Figure 14-14. The target image shows you that when black is subtracted from the source, no change is produced (because the pixel value of black is 0). When white

FIGURE 14-13   (a) Image after using the Difference Blending option in the Apply Image dialog box; (b) photograph of Aruba; (c) black-and-white strips created in alpha channels

14

(a pixel value of 255) is subtracted from the source, the result is a negative of those image areas.

If you'd like to see the Difference Blending option in action, load any color image, or use the Rockies file from the Adobe Samples folder. Once your file is on screen, select New Channel from the Channels palette's pop-up menu. In the New Channel dialog box, make sure the Masked Areas radio button is selected, then click OK. In the channel, create a series of white stripes, as shown in Figure 14-13(c). After creating the stripes, click on the RGB channel to select it as your target channel. Then execute the Apply Image command. In the Apply Image dialog box, set the Source to the Rockies file, set the Channel pop-up menu to be Alpha 1 (the new channel you just created), and set the Blending pop-up menu to Difference. Keep Opacity at 100%. Make sure the Preview check box is selected so you can see the results.

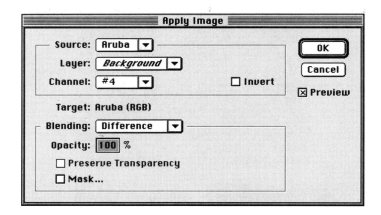

FIGURE 14-14   Apply Image dialog box settings for the example shown in Figure 14-13

If you use white and dark colors, the Exclusion blending mode produces the same results as difference. If you use the Apply Image command with two different colored source images, Photoshop provides a softer effect than that produced by Difference.

Lighter and Darker

The Lighter Blending option compares the values of every pixel in the source and target images. Any pixel that is lighter in the source channel will replace darker pixels in the target image. When grayscale images are blended, lighter pixel values replace darker pixel values. When you are blending two composite color channels, Photoshop compares the color value in each channel, then uses the lighter value (higher value in RGB images) to produce the effect. This could mean that the colors in the target/result image could be quite different from the source or original target pixels. For instance, assume a source image pixel in the RGB channel is Red 50, Blue 150, Green 200. Its corresponding pixel in the target is Red 25, Blue 100, Green 75. After Apply Image is executed, with the Lighter option chosen, the pixel values in the target file will be Red 50, Blue 150, Green 200.

The Lighter Blending option has a similar effect to that created by the Lighten blending mode (see Chapter 6). The Darker Blending option produces the opposite effect: Any pixel that is darker in the source channel replaces lighter pixels in the

FIGURE 14-15 (a) Image after using the Lighter Blending option in the Apply Image dialog box; (b) Source image; photograph of Aruba; (c) Target image; brick wall (courtesy of D'pix Inc.)

14

target image. In the previous example of pixel values, Darker would result in a pixel value of Red 25, Blue 100, Green 75. The effect of this command is similar to that created by the Darken painting/editing mode (also described in Chapter 6).

The Lighter Blending option was applied to the RGB channels of both the source (Aruba) and target (Bricks) images shown in Figures 14-15(b) and 14-15(c) to achieve the result shown in Figure 14-15(a). Notice that the lighter brick mortar pixels appear in the target (Bricks) image rather than the corresponding darker pixels from the Aruba image. Throughout much of the target image, the lighter texture of the bricks is also visible. Figure 14-16 illustrates the Apply Image dialog box settings for this example. Had the Darker option been applied instead of Lighter, the dark trees would have been more dominant in the target image.

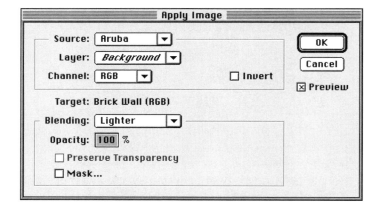

Apply Image dialog box settings for the image example shown in
Figure 14-15

If you wish to try out the Lighter and Darker Blending options, try blending the
Rockies file with an image created with the Clouds filter. First, load the Rockies
file from the Adobe Samples folder. Then use the Image | Duplicate command to
create a duplicate of the file and name it Clouds. Set the foreground color to a light
blue and the background color to dark blue. Execute the Clouds filter by choosing
Clouds from the Filter | Render submenu.

Execute the Image | Apply Image command. The target file will be the Clouds
file because it is the current active document. Set the source image to be the
Rockies file. Make sure the Channel pop-up menu is set to RGB. In the Blending
pop-up menu choose Lighter. Set Opacity to 100%.

In your target image, you will see that the darkest areas of the image are
completely replaced by the lighter pixels from the clouds, creating a misty effect.

Multiply

The Multiply Blending option produces the effect of two positive transparencies
placed over each other and viewed over a light table. The effect is similar to that
created by the Multiply blending mode described in Chapter 6.

The Multiply formula multiplies the two source values and divides the result
by the brightness value of white (255). Thus, applying the Multiply Blending
option to a dark image and a light image will produce a dark Destination image.

Here is the formula:

$$\frac{(\text{Source})(\text{Target})}{255} = \text{Result}$$

Using the Multiply Blending option, you can easily create the effect of a portrait emerging out of dark shadows. Try an exercise using the Rockies file from the Adobe Samples folder.

First, open the Rockies file. Create a new channel and name it Gradient. Make sure the Masked Areas radio button is selected and click OK. Click on the eye icon column to view the RGB composite channel, so you can see the image while you work in the channel. Make sure that your target channel is your Gradient channel.

Next, using the Gradient tool, create a white-to-black radial blend in the Gradient channel. Set the foreground color to white and background color to black, then set the Gradient style to Foreground to Background. With both the Gradient channel and the Rockies file visible, create the blend from the middle of the image by dragging with the Gradient tool from the middle to the end of the document window. Turn off editing in the Gradient channel and set the target channel to RGB by clicking on RGB in the Channels palette. Turn off the eye next to the Gradient channel by clicking on it.

Execute the Image | Apply Image command. The Source pop-up menu will be the Rockies file. Set the Channel pop-up menu to be the Gradient channel. The target image will be the Rockies file. Make sure the Preview check box is selected, then choose Multiply from the Blending pop-up menu.

Your final composite image shows darker pixels enveloping outer areas of the image. The Rockies image appears through only the very lightest areas of the blend.

Screen

The opposite of the effect created by Multiply can be achieved with the Screen Blending option: the effect of layering one film negative on top of another and printing the combined image on photographic paper. The result is similar to that of using the Screen painting/editing mode (discussed in Chapters 6 and 15).

The relatively complicated Screen formula generally ensures that the resulting target pixel values will be greater than the source pixel values; thus, the Screen Blending option produces an overall lighter target /result image.

$$255 - \frac{(255 - \text{Source})(255 - \text{Target})}{\text{Scale}} = \text{Result}$$

FIGURE 14-17 (a) Image after using the Screen option in the Apply Image dialog box; (b) photograph of a model (courtesy of Stacy Kollar Photography); (c) gradient created in an alpha channel

The Screen Blending option was used to combine the image of the model in Figure 14-17(b) with the radial blend in Figure 14-17(c) to create the final image in Figure 14-17(a). The radial blend was created in a new alpha channel in the Model file. Then the Screen Blending option in the Apply Image dialog box, shown in Figure 14-18, was used to blend the source and target images together. The resulting effect is a *vignette*; the Screen Blending option used the white pixels in the Gradient channel to overpower the dark pixels in the model image. It also took the pixels in the model image that corresponded to the dark part of the blend and lightened them.

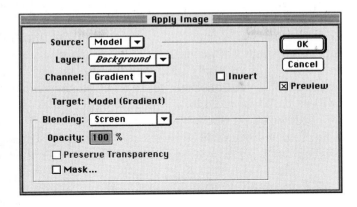

FIGURE 14-18   Apply Image dialog box settings for the example shown in Figure 14-17

You can easily create this vignette effect using the Rockies file in the Adobe Samples folder. Follow the same basic steps that you used for the Multiply Blending option in the previous section, except this time use the Gradient tool to create a black-to-white radial blend in the alpha channel, rather than a white-to-black (or use the same files with the Invert check box selected). After you execute the Apply Image command with the Screen Blending option, your final image shows that the white pixels in the blend have more influence than the darker pixels in the Rockies file. If you wish to darken the effect, set the Midpoint slider in the Gradient Editor dialog box to at least 50% before creating the radial blend. This will produce a large black area in the radial blend.

Overlay

Whether Overlay screens or multiplies depends upon the colors in the target channel. When bright source colors blend with the target channel, they are screened; when dark colors blend with the target channel, they are multiplied. The highlights and shadows of the target channel are always maintained.

To see the Overlay Blending option in action, try blending the Big Sky file with one of the other Adobe Samples files. As explained earlier, when blending two images together, they must have the same dimensions in pixels. Use the Image | Duplicate command to create a duplicate of the file, then copy the Fruit file into it.

14

Here's a brief review of the steps. After you open the Big Sky file, use the Image Duplicate command to create a duplicate of the file. Name the duplicate **MySky**. Now open another file from the Adobe Samples folder, then use the Select | All command to select the image. Then copy and paste the image into the MySky window. Choose Image | Apply Image to open the Apply Image dialog box. Set the source image as your original file, and the source channel to RGB. The target file will be the MySky file. Make sure the Opacity is set to 100%. Make sure the Preview check box is selected, then choose Overlay from the Blending pop-up menu. The preview image will show the source and target files composited together. The bright areas of the Big Sky file will be prominent in the blended image.

Soft and Hard Light

Now that you've had a chance to try out several of the blending options in the Apply Image dialog box, experiment with the Soft Light and Hard Light commands on your own. Both Soft Light and Hard Light will Screen or Multiply depending upon on the colors of the target image. In both blending modes, if the source channel pixels are lighter than the target pixels, the target pixels are lightened. If the source channel pixels are darker than the target pixels, the target pixels are darkened. Soft Light applies a soft, spread-out lighting effect, while Hard Light applies a harder, more direct lighting effect. If you don't have images to use, try creating a linear blend in one file and blending it with the Rockies file using Hard and Soft Light.

Using the Apply Image Dialog Box Mask Option

Now that you've examined the options in the Blending pop-up menu, you might wish to try some more sophisticated blending techniques by using the Mask check box in the Apply Image dialog box. The Mask check box allows you to use a channel as a mask for the target image. By default, darker image areas in the mask will allow more of the target image to show through the composite. Lighter mask areas hide target image areas. Thus, in areas that correspond to light pixels in the mask, the source image, rather than the target image, is more predominant in the final blended image.

To help you visualize how the Mask option works, suppose you are creating a patriotic image containing images of the president, the vice president, and the flag of the United States. Assume the president is the source image, the vice president is the target image, and the flag is the mask. In this case, assume the mask is a composite RGB channel. When the images are blended together, the source image is more prominent in the lighter areas of the mask, and the target image is more prominent in the darker areas of the mask. Thus, the image of the president would be more apparent in the areas corresponding to the flag's white stripes, while the vice president would be more apparent in the areas corresponding to the red stripes.

Figure 14-19 shows the results of the Apply Image command when executed with the Mask option. In this case, we used a blend in an alpha channel as a mask, though a separate file could have been used. The piano [Figure 14-11(b)] was the source image, and the model [Figure 14-17(b)] was the target image. We used the blend that was created in a channel in the model file as a mask [Figure 14-17(a)]. The Apply Image dialog box settings for this example are shown in Figure 14-20. When the Apply Image command was executed, the piano appeared in areas corresponding to the lighter areas of the mask, and the model appeared primarily in areas corresponding to the darker part of the mask.

If you wish to try out the Apply Image's Mask option, you can create a similar effect as that shown in Figure 14-19 by using two files. If you don't have two files

14

FIGURE 14-19   Image after using the Mask option in the Apply Image dialog box to combine the piano and model images

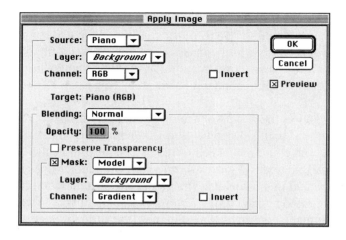

FIGURE 14-20   Apply Image dialog box settings for the example shown in Figure 14-19

to use, you can follow the steps described below using two files from the Adobe Samples folder. To ensure that both files are the same size and resolution, you'll duplicate one file, then copy a file into the duplicate.

Load the Big Sky image file on screen, and use the Save As command to create a new copy of the file. Name the file **Masker**. Then use the Image | Duplicate command to create a duplicate of it. Name that file **Bottleblend**, then click OK.

Next, open the Bottles file. Press COMMAND-A (Windows users: CTRL-A) to select the entire file. Then, copy and paste this image into the Bottleblend file. Deselect. Then flatten the image by choosing Layer | Flatten Image. To preserve memory, close the original Bottles file.

In the Masker file, create a new channel by pressing OPTION (Windows users: ALT) while clicking on the New Channel icon in the Channels palette. Name the channel **Gradient**. In the New Channel dialog box, make sure that the Color Indicates Masked Areas option is selected. Click OK.

Click on the eye icon column next to the RGB channel. This will enable you to see the image while you work in the alpha channel, but you won't affect the image.

Before creating the linear blend (we used a radial gradient in our example, but the linear gradient produces a better effect with the bottles image), make sure the foreground color is set to black and the background to white. Select the Linear

Gradient tool in the Toolbox. In the Gradient Options palette, choose Foreground to Background as the Gradient style.

To create the blend, click and drag in the Masker alpha channel from the left of the screen to the right of the screen. Now click on the RGB channel and turn off the eye icon in the Channels palette next to the Gradient channel.

Next, you will use the Apply Image command to blend the files together. When the composite is created, the gradient in the alpha channel will mask out everything but the middle of the Masker file. Areas corresponding to black in the gradient will appear in the target image; areas corresponding to white won't appear.

From the Image menu, choose Apply Image. Set the Source document to Bones and the Channel to RGB. The target file should be the Masker file. Set the Blending pop-up menu to Normal and Opacity to 100%. Click on the Mask check box. Set the Mask pop-up menu to the Masker file, since this is where the blend for the mask was created. Set the Channel pop-up menu to Gradient.

The Preview results will show the Masker image blending from its middle into the fruit image. If you wish to lighten the effect, change the Blending mode to Screen. Apply Image produces an ethereal fade-out effect in areas that correspond to the Gradient alpha channel fading from black to white. To see a completely different effect, click on the Invert check box in the Mask section. Clicking on Invert shows you how the image would look if you had created a white-to-black radial blend (rather than a black to white).

On your own, try out different blending options with the Mask option selected. After you've had a chance to experiment, continue to the next section to explore the Calculations dialog box, which also allows you to combine channels.

Using the Calculations Command

The Image menu's Calculations command provides many of the same features as the Apply Image commands. Both allow you to create blends between channels by choosing a blending option and changing opacity. Both dialog boxes require that all images used have the same width and height in pixels. The primary difference between Apply Image and Calculations is that the Calculations command does not produce its effects in a composite channel. The resulting effect can appear in a selection in any channel or alpha channel other than an image's composite channel. The Calculations command can also create the result in a new channel or a new file with a new channel in it. The result can also be a layer mask. A *layer mask* is a mask created in a new channel that allows you to hide or reveal portions of different layers. After the mask is created, it can easily be edited to reveal more or less of the layer you are in and more or less of the underlying layer.

 NOTE: *For an in-depth discussion of layer masks, see Chapter 16.*

Since the blending options in the Calculations dialog box are the same as those in the Apply Image dialog box, the individual blending options will not be discussed here. Instead, the following section provides a simple demonstration of how to create a blend between two channels with the Calculations command. In the example, the result of the calculations is placed in the original image as a selection, then the image is pasted into the selection. This is followed by step-by-step instructions for using the Calculations command to create a layer mask.

Start by loading the Big Sky file or any other image. Use the File | Save As command to rename the file **Scenery**. Create a new channel in the file by pressing OPTION (Windows users: ALT) and clicking on the New Channel icon in the channels palette. Name the channel **Text**. Make sure the Masked Areas radio button is selected.

Make sure that the foreground color is set to white, and the background color set to black. Activate the Type Mask tool and click in the left side of the channel. Select Times or any other serif typeface between 80 and 100. Enter the word **SUNLIGHT** in the text area, then click OK. Use the Type mask tool to position the word in the center of the channel, and fill with white, then deselect. Next, create another channel, and name it **Radial**. Double-click on the Line tool and set the Line Width to 25 pixels.

Next, create a white cross that extends to the edges of the channel. Use the Radial Blur filter to create a blurring effect in the channel. In the Radial Blur dialog box, set the Amount to 25, Blur Method to Spin to, and Quality to Draft. After the filter runs its course, reselect the RGB channel to make it the target channel.

Next, you will clear the scenery image from the screen. Choose Select | All. Then choose Edit | Cut to fill the entire screen with black and place the Scenery image in the Clipboard. Later you will paste the image back into a selection created by the Calculations command.

To open the Calculations dialog box, choose Calculations from the Image menu. The following illustration shows the settings for the Calculations dialog box that you'll need to complete this exercise.

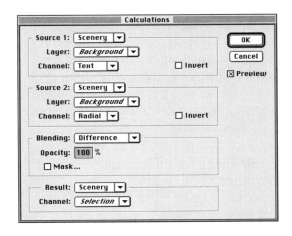

As mentioned earlier, the Calculations dialog box includes the same blending features as the Apply Image dialog box. To see the blending choices, click on the Blending pop-up menu. As in the Apply Image dialog box, Opacity can be set by entering a percentage. Unlike the Apply Image dialog box, the Calculations dialog box allows you to specify two sources. The channels in the source documents contain the data that Photoshop uses when it applies Calculations.

The Source 1 pop-up menu allows you to choose any open document on screen whose pixel dimensions in width and height match the active document's pixel dimensions. In the Layer pop-up menu, you can choose the layer from the Source 1 document that you wish to use when blending. The Channel pop-up menu allows you to choose any channel from the Source 1 document that you wish to use when blending.

The Source 2 pop-up menu works exactly the same as the Source 1 pop-up menu. Only images whose pixel dimensions are the same as the active document's will appear in the pop-up menu. The Layer and Channel pop-up menus refer to layers and channels in the Source 2 document. At this point, the name of your new document appears in the Source 1 pop-up menu. Set Channel to the text channel.

The Result pop-up menu allows you to choose where the results of the Calculations dialog box will appear. If you choose New in the Result pop-up menu, and New in the Channel pop-up menu, the results of the Calculations command will appear in a new document with one channel in it. You could then duplicate the channel to any document when needed.

In the Channel pop-up menu, you can choose the channel in the Result document where you want the blended channel to appear, or you can have the result appear in the Result document as a New Selection. If the Result document has a layer in it, you can set the Result channel to be a layer mask.

14

Before continuing, note that the Calculations dialog box includes a Mask option. If you click on the Mask check box, the dialog box expands to allow you to choose a source document for the mask, as well as the channel and layer that the mask is in. When a mask is used, dark areas of the mask allow more of the document to appear and light areas allow the Source 2 image to appear.

For each of the Source 1, Source 2, and mask channels chosen, an Invert option is available. If Invert is chosen, the channels' pixels are inverted to create a negative of the image.

As in the Apply Image dialog box, the Preview check box is an invaluable aid in predicting blending effects. When using the Calculations dialog box, the preview appears in the active document on screen. Click the Preview check box to preview the Difference effect.

If you followed the steps at the beginning of this section, you now have the Scenery image on screen. Set the Channel for the Source 1 image to be the Text channel. For the Source 2 image, set the Channel to the Radial channel since you will be using it as the second source for the effect.

To create the blend effect, use Difference Blending mode. This will subtract the pixel values of the Radial channel from the pixel values of the Text channel. To choose the blending mode, select Difference from the Blending pop-up menu.

In this example, leave the result file set to the document on screen, and set the result channel to be a Selection. Later you will paste the scenery image from the Clipboard into this selection.

Now execute the Calculations command by clicking OK. On screen you will see a selection. The selection is the result of subtracting one alpha channel from another. Now choose Edit | Paste Into to paste the original image back into the selection. On screen you'll see the image through the selection created from text and blurred lines. (Note that this automatically creates a layer mask, discussed in the next section and in Chapter 16.)

Creating a Layer Mask Using the Calculations Command

The following steps show how to use the Calculations commands to create a layer mask. A layer mask is an extremely versatile mask that allows you to reveal or hide different areas in different layers. Using the calculations command, you can create a layer mask by blending channels from different images or one image. After the mask is created, it appears in both the Channels and Layers palettes.

The following example demonstrates how to create a layer mask from two channels with textures in them.

1. Open an image on screen that contains two layers. If you don't have an image to use, copy and paste the Rockies file into the Sky file. Choose File | Save As and name the file **Final**.

2. Now create a new alpha channel by pressing and holding the OPTION key (Windows users: ALT) while you click on the New Channel icon in the Channels palette. In the New Channel dialog box, select the Color Indicates Selected Areas. Name the channel **Mosaic**.

3. In the alpha channel, use the Mosaic Tiles filter to create a texture. To execute the filter, choose Filter | Texture | Mosaic Tiles. In the Mosaic Tiles dialog box, set the Size to 45, the Grout Width to 7, and Lighten Grout to 3.

4. Now create another alpha channel. In this channel execute the Add Noise filter at a very high setting. Choose Filter | Noise | Add Noise. Now reselect the RGB channel, or press COMMAND-~ (Windows users: CTRL-~).

 CAUTION: *Do not select the Background in the Layers palette; otherwise you will not be able to create the layer mask for Layer 1.*

5. Choose Calculations from the Image menu. In the Calculations dialog box, the Source 1 and Source 2 documents are both the same document on screen. Set the Source 1 channel to be the channel with the Mosaic tiles effect. Set the Source 2 channel to be the channel with the noise effect.

6. Choose Screen as the Blending mode.

7. In the Result section, choose Layer 1 mask in the Channels pop-up menu. This tells Photoshop that you want to create a mask out of the blend between the two channels.

8. A preview of the mask will appear in the Final file on screen. When the layer mask is created, the mask you see will appear in a new channel, and in the Layers palette.

9. To create the layer mask, click OK.

14

10. The image screen will change to reveal a blend between the two layers in the image. Notice that the top layer is more prominent in areas corresponding to the dark part of the mask, and the bottom layer is more prominent in areas corresponding to the light part of the mask.

One of the most intriguing features of layer masks is that the image on screen is actually a type of preview of how the image will appear when the layer mask is applied. The appearance of the image on screen changes because you are viewing it through the layer mask. You can edit the mask without actually changing the pixels in the Result image.

Notice that the Channels palette now has a new channel named Layer Mask. If you wish to edit the mask, you could click on the words "Layer Mask." If you paint with a dark color in the mask, you will reveal more of the top layer. If you paint with a light color, you will hide more of the top layer and reveal more of the bottom layer.

If you are happy with the effect the layer mask produces, leave it on screen to edit later, or you can apply it to your image or discard it. Applying it to your image changes the pixels in the image. To apply or discard the layer mask, you drag the layer mask icon in the Channels palette into the Trash in the Channels palette. Try dragging the layer mask into the Trash now. A dialog box will appear. If you wish to apply the layer mask to your image, click Apply. If you wish to discard the layer mask, choose Discard. To cancel and leave the layer mask on screen, click Cancel.

At this point feel free to experiment with different sources, blending options, and opacities with the Layer Mask option.

 NOTE: *Many layer mask operations can be handled from the Layers palette. For more information, see Chapter 15.*

Creating Spot Colors

A spot color is a premixed color that is printed on a separate printing plate. Often spot colors are used when only one or two colors need to be printed over a portion of an image. Spot colors are often used as a fifth color (in addition to CMYK colors) to attract attention to logos or text. Typically, spot colors are first chosen from a PANTONE or TRUMATCH swatchbook as a means of matching and predicting how colors will be printed. As discussed in Chapter 5, colors created by PANTONE, TRUMATCH, and other companies can be searched for in

Photoshop 5 In Action

The recessed-type effect was created using alpha channels and the Image | Calculations and Image | Adjust | Levels commands.

The background image is a photograph of a rock that was scanned.

Artist: Daniel Clark **Client: Petersen Publishing**

Daniel started creating this calendar cover by scanning a photograph of a rock into Photoshop. Next, he traced the "4Wheel & Off-Road" logo in Freehand and filled it with black. In the digitized rock file, he created a new alpha channel and placed the logo into it.

While the logo was still floating, he copied and pasted it into two other alpha channels. In each alpha channel, he blurred and then feathered the floating logo. Next, he deselected the logo and offset it. The alpha channel that would then be used for the highlighted areas of the recessed text was offset to the right by using the Filter | Other | Offset command. (The alpha channel that would be used for the shadow areas of the recessed text was offset to the left using the same filter.) After the filter was applied, the logo in each alpha channel was inverted using the Image | Adjust | Invert command. This produced white type on a black background.

To create a mask for the highlighted area of the text, the Image | Calculations command was used with the Darker blending option selected. In the Calculations dialog box, the digitized rock file was chosen in all the Source pop-up menus. The Source 1 Channel pop-up menu was set to the very first alpha channel (containing the text that was not offset). The Source 2 and Destination Channel pop-up menus were set to the highlight channel (the second channel). To create a mask for the shadow area of the text, the Image | Calculations command was also used with the Darker blending option. The same settings were used, except that the Source 2 and Destination Channel pop-up menus were set to the shadow channel (the third channel).

Once the masks were completed, Daniel loaded each selection individually and used the Levels command to darken or lighten the selection to complete the recessed effect. For a finishing touch, he exported the file to MetaCreations Painter, where he used a textured airbrush tool to add cracks to the letters.

14

Photoshop's Custom Color palette. The palette is accessed by choosing Custom from Photoshop's Color Picker. When you create colors using Photoshop's spot color channels, Photoshop opens up the Color Picker .

Although spot colors in Photoshop will prove adequate for many digital imaging projects, designers will find projects requiring spot colors with well defined images are better handled in drawing programs like Adobe Illustrator and page layout programs such as Quark XPress and Adobe PageMaker. Photoshop's spot colors will not automatically *knockout* underlying colors. (When one color knocks out an underlying color, the underlying color is removed. This prevents one color from overprinting another color, and thus producing a third underlying color.) In Photoshop, spot colors overprint the composite image and overprint other spot colors. (A technique for manually knocking out an underlying color is discussed later in this section.)

Despite these drawbacks, creating spot colors in Photoshop is quite easy and logical.

 NOTE: *Although you can create spot colors in RGB Color and Grayscale mode files, spot colors can only be printed from CMYK Color and Multichannel mode files. If you will be exporting an image with a spot color to another program, your Photoshop file must be saved in DCS 2.0 format. CMYK Color, Multichannel, and Grayscale mode files can be saved in DCS 2.0 format. See Appendix A for details about saving in DCS format.*

 TIP: *If you wish to apply a spot color to an entire image to tint the image, create a duotone and apply the color to the duotone plate. Creating duotones is discussed in Chapter 12.*

Using a Channel to Create Spot Colors

The easiest way to get started creating spot colors is to create a selection. Here are steps for creating spot colors using a spot channel:

1. Load an image on screen to which you wish to apply a spot color.

2. Open the Channels palette by choosing Windows | Show Channels.

3. Create a selection on screen, or load a previously saved selection by choosing Select | Load Selection.

4. In the Channels palette menu, choose New Spot Channel (you can also press COMMAND (Windows users: CTRL) while you click on the New Channel icon in the Channels palette.) This opens the New Spot Channel dialog box.

5. In the New Spot Channel dialog box, click on the color swatch to open the Color Picker dialog box. Choose a PANTONE, TRUMATCH or other custom color by clicking the Custom button. In the Book pop-up menu, click on the color you wish to add to your image (you can also type the color's number on the keyboard). Click OK to return to the New Spot Channel dialog box.

6. To specify the Solidity of the color, enter a value between 0 and 100% in the Solidity field. Entering a value of 100% provides an on-screen simulation of how a printed ink completely covers any inks beneath. (The solidity value does not affect printed output.)

TIP: *A Solidity of 0% can be used to simulate a varnish. Varnishes can be used as a protective or glossy coating.*

7. To apply the spot color to your image, click OK.

8. If you need to change the settings in the New Spot Channel dialog box, double-click on the spot channel in the Channels palette; or select the channel, then choose Channel Options in the Channel pop-up menu.

TIP: *To convert an alpha channel to a spot channel, double-click on the channel. In the Channel Options dialog box, click the Spot Channel option. Click on the color swatch to choose a color. After you've chosen a color, select a solidity percentage.*

NOTE: *If you use a custom color for a spot channel, do not rename the spot color channel. If you rename the channel, the color may not be interpreted by the other publishing applications.*

14

Adding Spot Colors with Painting Tools

Once you create a spot color channel you can edit the color using Photoshop's painting and editing tools. For instance, you can use the Paintbrush tool to paint spot colors in an image. You can click and drag with the Eraser to remove spot colors.

Before you can edit with a painting or editing tool, you must first create a spot color channel by choosing New Spot Channel in the Channels palette or follow the steps described in the section above.

After you've chosen a color, and closed the New Spot Color dialog box, set the foreground color to black to paint with the spot color. To paint with a lower opacity, paint with a shade of gray. Painting with the Eraser tool or painting with white removes the spot color.

Editing Overlapping Spot Colors

If you are using more than one spot color, you may wish to prevent one spot color from overprinting underlying spot colors. To prevent overprinting of spot colors, you can delete the area in one channel where the spot channels overlap. In order to delete the colors, you select the area in the spot channel that you want printed, then delete the underlying area. Essentially, this means you can manually knock out color beneath a spot color channel. You can use this process when spot colors overlap other spot colors, or when spot colors overlap CMYK colors. Here are the steps:

1. Select the spot color channel that you do want to print. In other words, select the spot channel from which you will not be deleting overlapping color.

2. Create a selection on screen from the spot color channel by choosing Select | Load Selection. In the Load Selection dialog box, choose the correct channel in the Channel pop-up menu; then click OK. Alternatively, you can create the selection by pressing COMMAND (Windows users: CTRL) and clicking in the spot channel in the Channels palette.

3. Before continuing, make sure that the background color is set to white. Now, click on the spot channel that you want to knockout—the channel from which you want to remove color. Press DELETE (Windows users: BACKSPACE).

TIP: *After creating the selection in step 2, you can expand or contract it by choosing Select | Modify | Expand or Contract. This affects the area deleted in step 3.*

Printing Spot Colors

Since a spot color channel simulates a printing plate, you will need to use Photoshop's Separations option to print separations. As mentioned earlier, separations can only be printed in CMYK Color or Mulitchannel mode images. If you need to convert your image to CMYK color, choose Image | Mode | CMYK Color. (See Chapter 12 for details about converting from RGB to CMYK color.) To print separations, choose File | Print. In the Space pop-up menu, choose Separations. When the image is output, the name of each spot color appears when the channel is printed.

If you wish to print out your image as a composite (on one page) as a proof, you can merge the spot colors with the image's other channels by choosing Merge Spot Colors from the Channels Pop-up menu. This deletes the spot channel from the Channels palette and flattens layers in images. Note that the colors will not look exactly the same as when printed on a printing press because the colors in the composite will be created from Cyan, Magenta, Yellow, and Black.

 NOTE: *When you print, spot colors are overprinted according to their order in the Channels palette. If you wish to move a spot above one of Photoshop's CMYK channels, convert the image to Multichannel mode, then click and drag in the Channels palette to move the spot color channel.*

Conclusion

You've seen in this chapter how valuable channels can be in image editing, creating special effects, and blending images together. In Chapters 15 and 16, you'll learn how layers can be used to blend images together and create layer masks.

14

CHAPTER 15

Working with Layers

Layers open up a new world of artistic freedom and design possibilities. When you start using layers, digital art you imagined but never thought feasible will lie within your grasp. Layers set you free from many of the restraints imposed by a pixel-based program. They allow you to experiment with an infinite range of design possibilities without having to spend hours of time selecting, reselecting, or returning to earlier versions of your files.

When you work in a layer, it's as though you're editing an image on a sheet of acetate: Images below the acetate can show through the transparent areas. If you have multiple layers, you can reposition them in any order. If you erase an object on a layer, background images will show through. Move the layer and all objects on the layer move together as a group, independent of other layers.

This chapter starts with a discussion of layer fundamentals, and then proceeds to show you techniques for blending images. You will learn how to create and delete layers, move objects in layers, change target layers, and rearrange layers. Once you've mastered the technical aspects of creating layers, you can move on to explore the artistic possibilities opened up to you by the Layers palette.

Exploring the Layer Menu and Layers Palette

The Layer menu and Layers palette are your command centers for managing layers. The Layers palette allows you to create new layers, reorder layers, select a target layer to edit in, merge layers, create layer masks, and delete layers.

In the following exercises you'll learn how to use the Layer menu and Layers palette by working with a few simple shapes and some text. This will provide you with an in-depth introduction to layer fundamentals. As you work through the following exercises, you'll create a design with a rectangle, a circle, and text, as shown in Figure 15-1. Each element will be created in a separate layer. Later, you'll blend each element together by changing opacities and using the Dissolve blending mode.

In order to get under way, you'll need to open the Layers palette and create a new document on screen.

1. If the Layers palette isn't open, open it now by choosing Show Layers from the Window menu.

2. Start by creating a new RGB color file, 7 inches wide by 5 inches high at 72 ppi. Set the background Contents to white by clicking on the White radio button in the Contents group, then click OK.

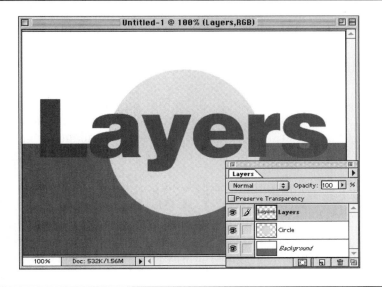

FIGURE 15-1   Three layers were used to create this image, as indicated in the Layers palette

After the file opens, notice that the word "Background" appears in the top section of the Layers palette. The base layer of any file that is created without a transparent background appears in the Layers palette designated as the Background. Also notice the eye icon (👁) that appears to the left of "Background." This indicates that the background is visible in your document. The paintbrush icon (🖌) and the highlighted or colored area surrounding the word "Background" in the Layers palette mean that the Background is the current target layer. The target layer is the layer you are editing.

15

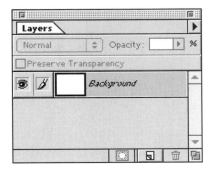

Before adding a layer to your file, create an object on the background so that you see how it affects the Layers palette.

3. Use the Marquee tool to create a rectangle that covers the entire bottom portion of your file and fill it with red, as seen in Figure 15-1. Then deselect.

In the Layers palette, notice that a red rectangle appears in a miniature thumbnail version of the layer. Before continuing, you might wish to change the size of the thumbnail in the palette.

Changing the Palette Thumbnail Size

By default, the Layers palette shows you a thumbnail of all layers in a document. The thumbnails are handy reminders of exactly what is in each layer. Keeping an eye on the thumbnails is also a helpful way to ensure that you don't edit the wrong layer. To adjust the size of the thumbnails in the Layers palette, click on the Layers palette's pop-up menu arrow and choose Palette Options from the list of choices. This will open the Palette Options dialog box. In the dialog box, click on the radio button alongside the thumbnail size you'd like on screen, then click OK. We recommend that you keep the thumbnails as small as possible so they don't consume valuable screen space. Also, if you pick a large size, you might find that the thumbnails slow down the screen display a bit.

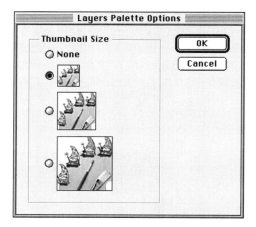

Creating New Layers

As you work through this chapter, you'll see that Photoshop provides a variety of different ways to create layers. Here's a summary of the most common methods of creating layers:

- The simplest way to create a new layer is to click on the New Layer icon (the dog-eared page) in the Layers palette. This creates a new layer and automatically assigns it a name: Layer 1, Layer 2, etc.

- Press OPTION (Windows users: ALT) and click on the New Layer icon in the Layers palette (Keyboard shortcut: Press COMMAND-SHIFT-N (Windows users: CTRL-SHIFT-N). This allows you to name the layer before it is created.

- Choose Layer | New | Layer.

- Click on the pop-up menu arrow in the Layers palette to open the Layers palette menu, then choose the New Layer command.

- A new layer can be created by dragging and dropping an image from one file to another.

- A layer can be created from a selection. After making the selection, choose Layer | New, then Layer Via Copy or Layer Via Cut. If you choose Layer Via Cut, the selection will be cut and pasted into a new layer. If you choose Layer Via Copy the selection will be copied into the new layer.

Now, assume that you wish to add a circle and text to your image. If you add them to the background, the circle and text will be locked down onto it. If you create one layer for the circle shape and one for the text, as shown in Figure 15-1, you will be able to move and edit either the circle or the text without affecting the other layers. Next, you will create a new layer and then add the circle to your image.

1. Start the process of creating a layer by pressing OPTION (Windows users: ALT) and clicking the New Layer icon ( ) at the bottom of the Layers palette. Doing this opens the New Layer dialog box. In it, you'll see

15

options for changing opacity, setting a blending mode, and grouping layers. You'll learn how to use these options later in this chapter. At this point, name the layer by typing **Circle** in the Name field, then click OK.

```
┌──────────────────── New Layer ────────────────────┐
│                                                    │
│  Name: │Circle                    │   ┌────OK────┐ │
│                                                    │
│  Opacity: │100 │ % Mode: │Normal      ▲▼│ ┌─Cancel─┐│
│                                                    │
│         ☐ Group With Previous Layer                │
│         ☐ (No neutral color exists for Normal mode.)│
│                                                    │
└────────────────────────────────────────────────────┘
```

Notice that the word "Circle" appears in the title bar of your document. This indicates that you are working in the Circle layer. It may not seem like it now, but when you have several layers on screen, it's very easy to forget what layer you're working in. So, every now and then as you're working, take a quick glance at the title bar.

```
Untitled-1 @ 100% (Circle,RGB)
```

Now examine the Layers palette. At the top of the palette is the word "Circle," which indicates that it's the top layer in the document. The layer at the top of the palette is always the top layer in the document; the layer on the bottom is the base layer of your image. In the Layers palette, you'll see an eye icon to the left of the word "Background" and an eye to the left of the Circle layer. This indicates that both the Background and Circle layers are visible. The paintbrush icon next to the Circle layer means that only the Circle layer can be edited. Notice that the colored shading appears only in the Circle layer section of the Layers palette. This confirms what the document title bar is telling you—that you are working in the Circle layer. This is your target layer. As soon as you create a new layer, Photoshop automatically designates it as the target layer. Now you are ready to create a circle in the Circle layer.

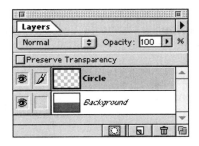

2. Switch to the Elliptical Marquee tool in the Toolbox. You can quickly toggle between the Elliptical and Rectangular Marquee by pressing OPTION (Windows users: ALT) and clicking on the Marquee tool in the Toolbox, or by pressing SHIFT-M on your keyboard. Use the Elliptical Marquee tool to create a circle about 3.75 inches in diameter in the middle of your document that overlaps the rectangle on screen, as seen in Figure 15-1. Fill this circle with yellow color, then deselect.

Now take a look at the memory indicator in the lower-left corner of the screen. In the next section you'll learn how layers increase file size.

Checking Layer Memory

As you create layers, you should know how much memory the layers are consuming. To find this out, first make sure the memory readout in the lower-left corner is set to show document memory, not scratch disk memory. Check this now by clicking on the pop-up menu arrow in the lower-left corner of your document. The pop-up menu should be set to Document Sizes. If it is not, change it.

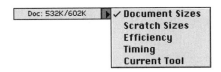

15

As mentioned in Chapter 2, the document size number on the left indicates the size of your image without any layers (this is also the size of the file sent to your printer in Photoshop format), while the number on the right indicates the file size with all layers included. When a new layer is created, colored areas in the layer add to your file's size. This is a fact of life with layers that you need to get used to. Fortunately, the transparent area of a layer does not add to document memory. Later you'll learn how to merge layers to reduce file size and flatten layers so that you can drop the file to its original size.

When working with layers, it's easy for file size to grow quickly. If you do not have extra memory or a lot of free space available on your scratch disk, you'll have to work carefully with layers, possibly merging them as you finish working on different image areas. If you need to keep doing this, though, you're taking some of the versatility out of working with Photoshop. If you want to work with many layers, your best bet is to install more RAM and/or purchase the largest hard disk you can afford to use as a scratch disk. Once you're free of memory worries, you'll be able to work comfortably with several layers in your document.

Now that you've been cautioned about the memory consumption of layers, you're ready to add another layer to your image. Be aware that when you add another layer to the file on screen, the file size could reach over 1MB. The file size will depend on the amount of information you put in the layer.

 NOTE: *Higher image cache settings (File | Preferences | Image Cache) speed layer operations but take up more hard disk space and RAM. If you are working with large files, you may wish to increase the default setting beyond 4.*

Adding a New Layer with the Type Tool

In this section, you'll create a new layer by entering text with the Type tool. When the text appears, Photoshop automatically creates a new layer.

1. Start by setting the foreground color to blue.

2. Activate the Type tool by clicking on the Toolbox, then click anywhere in the middle of the screen.

3. When the Type tool dialog box appears, pick a font (the font in Figure 15-1 is Helvetica Black with the Tracking set to -3) and set the Size to 130. Make sure the Anti-aliased option is selected, and click on the center alignment icon. Type the word **Layers** in the text box. If you have the Preview option selected in the check box, you'll see the type appear on screen as you enter it into the dialog box. If you wish, you can also, click and drag on screen (not in the dialog box) to reposition the type. After you've finished entering the type, click OK.

4. Now take a look at the Layers palette. As discussed in Chapter 3, Photoshop automatically creates a new layer when you create text with the Type tool. Notice in the Layers palette, that there is now a text layer named "Layers," (or whatever you typed in the Type dialog box).

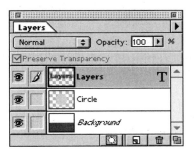

Notice that your file size has increased. Now examine the Layers palette. The new layer appears with the eye icon next to it, as does the Circle layer. But the text layer is the only layer with the paintbrush next to it and the color surrounding its name. The eye icon means that the layer is visible; the paintbrush means that the layer can be edited. Any image editing you do now affects only this layer. Even though you see the circle clearly on screen, you cannot edit it now, because it is not in the current target layer. Photoshop allows you to have only one target layer at a time. Thus, if you wish to move or edit the circle, you will need to switch target layers.

15

Moving Objects in Layers

As mentioned earlier, layers are like sheets of acetate overlaying each other. If you move a Photoshop layer, all objects in the layer move as one, as if they were all on the same acetate sheet. Being able to move layers independently of other layers gives you the freedom to quickly experiment with many design options without worrying about the pixels locking down on the underlying images.

Using the Move Tool's Auto Select Layer Option

In Photoshop you can move a layer by simply clicking and dragging on it with the Move tool. However, before using the Move tool, you should take a look at the tool's Options palette because its functionality changes based on its palette's settings. To load the tool's Options palette on screen, double-click on the Move tool.

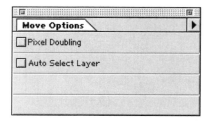

The most important choice in the palette is the Auto Select Layer option. When Auto Select Layer is *not* selected, clicking and dragging anywhere in a layer moves the entire layer—even if you click and drag over a transparent area. If Auto Select Layer is chosen, the Move tool ignores transparent areas, and only moves a layer if you click over a non-transparent area. If multiple layers exist, the move tool looks for non-transparent image areas. If you click and drag over a non-transparent image area, you will move the first layer beneath the Move tool with non-transparent image information — even if it isn't the active layer.

For instance, if you've been following the exercise so far, you have text in the active layer. Turn on the Auto Select Layer option, then click and drag over any part of the circle that is not covered by text. The Move tool activates the Circle layer and moves the circle—even though the original active layer was the text layer.

The Pixel Doubling option provides a bit of digital magic that provides you with a faster preview of the layer that you are moving. When Pixel Doubling is selected, Photoshop doubles the size of the pixels as you click and drag. When you release the mouse the pixels are restored to normal size.

Moving and Linking Layers

If you wish to move a layer in 1-pixel increments, first activate the Move tool, then press any of the directional arrow keys on the keyboard. Pressing SHIFT while pressing any of the directional arrow keys moves the layer in 10-pixel increments (a 10-pixel increment moves you one frame in a Filmstrip file created in Adobe Premiere).

Photoshop also allows you to link layers together so they can be moved as a unit. In the next exercise, you'll practice moving the Circle and text layers independently, then linking them so they move as one unit.

Before you begin, make sure you have a circle in a layer, the word "Layers" in a layer, and a red and white background, as shown in Figure 15-1.

1. Try moving the text you just created by first activating the Move tool, then clicking and dragging on the text. As you drag the text, the entire layer moves. Move the text to different locations on screen to experiment with image composition.

   If you want to move the circle in the Circle layer with the Auto Select Layer option off, you need to switch target layers. To switch target layers, simply click on the name of the layer that you wish to use as your target layer. Try activating the Circle layer.

2. To set the Circle layer as your target layer, click on the word "Circle" in the Layers palette. The Circle layer in the palette is selected and the title bar of your document now includes the layer name.

   Now that you have switched target layers, you can either edit or move the Circle layer and position it independently of the Background and the text layer named "Layers."

15

TIP: *You can move to a higher layer and make it the target layer by pressing OPTION-] (Windows users: ALT-]). To move down, press OPTION-[(Windows users: ALT-[). To move to the base layer, press SHIFT-OPTION-[(Windows users: SHIFT-ALT-[). To move to the top layer, press SHIFT-OPTION-] (Windows users: SHIFT-ALT-]).*

3. To move the yellow circle on screen, use the Move tool to click and drag on the circle and reposition it so that it is placed near the text.

You might wish to move several layers at a time. Photoshop allows you to do this, as long as the layers are linked. Layers other than the target layer can be linked to the target layer by clicking on the empty column (link column), which appears to the left of the layer name and to the right of the eye column in the Layers palette. After you click, the link icon (🔗) appears in the column. If you click on the link column, above or below the target layer, Photoshop links that layer with the target layer. Clicking in the link column next to other layers adds those layers to the layers that are already linked. Step 4 describes how to link the Circle and text layer.

4. To link the Circle and text layers, first make sure that the Circle layer is your target layer. Then, click on the link column to the left of the word "Layers" and to the right of the eye column in the Layers palette. A link icon will appear next to the text layer in the Layers palette.

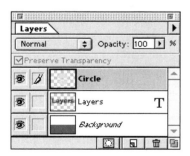

5. To move the two linked layers, activate the Move tool, then click and drag anywhere on screen. Both the circle and the text will move together.

NOTE: *Photoshop 5 does not clip parts of layers that extend beyond the canvas.*

Aligning and Distributing Linked Layers

Once you've linked layers together, you can have Photoshop automatically align a linked layer or several linked layers at the top, bottom, left, right, or middle of the active layer. For instance, you can have Photoshop automatically align the middle of the text with the middle of the circle shown in Figure 15-1. Of course, you could do this manually using the Move tool, but Photoshop's aligning options will do it for you quickly and precisely. To align linked layers with the active layer, choose Layer | Align Linked. Then choose one of the following commands in the submenu:

 TIP: *If you create a selection on screen, you can align a layer or several linked layers to the selection. After you create the selection, the Layer | Align Linked command changes to Layer | Align to Selection.*

- ☐ **Top**   Aligns the top of linked layers to the top of the active layer. If a selection exists in the active layer, the linked layer aligns to the top of the selection.

- ☐ **Vertical Center**   Moves the linked layers up or down and aligns the pixels to the vertical center of the active layer. If a selection exists in the active layer, the linked layer aligns to the vertical center of the selection. If you find the concept of "vertical center" hard to conceptualize, imagine having two layers, each with a different sized toy doll standing against a transparent background. The vertical center of each image would approximately be the navels of the two dolls. If you chose Layer | Align Linked | Vertical Center, the doll in the linked layer would move up or down so that its navel would be aligned to the navel of the doll in the active layer.

- ☐ **Bottom**   Aligns the bottom edge of the linked layer to the bottom of edge the active layer or to the bottom of a selection border. If a selection exists in the active layer, the linked layer aligns to the bottom of the selection.

15

□ **Left**   Aligns the left edge of the linked layer to the left edge of active layer. If a selection exists in the active layer, the linked layer aligns flush left to the left edge of the selection.

□ **Horizontal Center**   Moves the linked layer left or right to align to the horizontal center of the active layer or to the horizontal center of a selection. To help you conceptualize horizontal layers, think of two different sized dolls, both posed in a reclining position in two different layers. If you apply the Horizontal Center option, the doll in the linked layer would shift left or right to align to the navel of the doll in the active layer.

□ **Right**   Aligns the right edge of the linked layer flush right with the right edge of the active layer. If a selection is in the active layer, the linked layer aligns flush right to the right edge of the selection.

You can also have Photoshop distribute three or more linked layers. When you distribute linked layers, it spaces the layers equidistantly. To distribute linked layers, first link three or more layers; then choose an option in the Layer | Distribute Layers submenu, which provides the following choices: Top, Vertical Center, Bottom, Left, Horizontal Center, Right. Each choice essentially tells Photoshop where to start distributing the layers. For instance, if you choose Top, Photoshop starts the distribution process from the top pixel of each layer. If you choose Horizontal Center, Photoshop starts from the horizontal center pixel of each layer.

 CAUTION: *When aligning or distributing layers, Photoshop ignores pixel values that are less than 50% opaque. Thus, if the active layer includes a border that is less than 50% opaque, aligned linked layers would not align to the actual edges of the layer. Instead, alignment would occur where the pixels where greater than 50% opaque.*

Before continuing to the next section, try aligning the text and Circle layer at their horizontal center position by choosing Layer | Align | Horizontal Center. Then unlink the layers by clicking on the chain icon in the link column.

Viewing and Hiding Layers

If you wish to view only the images in one layer without seeing objects in other layers, you can hide the other layers. To hide a layer, you need only click on the layer's eye icon in the Layers palette. Clicking on the eye icon turns the icon off and hides the corresponding layer. Clicking again in the same place (the eye column) returns the eye icon back to the Layers palette and brings the layer into view. If you click and drag over different eyes in the eye column, you will hide all of the corresponding layers. If you click and drag in the eye column again, the layers and their corresponding eyes will return to view.

In this section you'll delete a portion of the circle, as shown in Figure 15-2, then hide the other layers to see how the Circle layer was affected. Before you begin, make sure that you are working with the elements in Figure 15-1 and that the Circle layer is your target layer.

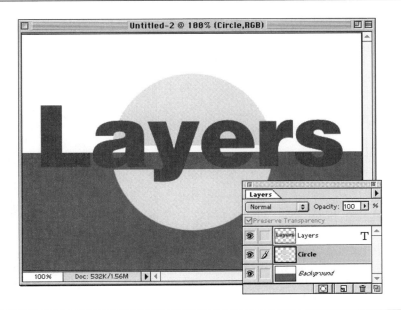

FIGURE 15-2   When a portion of the circle is deleted, the background shows through the deleted area

Start by making a rectangular selection in the middle of the circle and then deleting the area inside the selection.

1. Activate the Rectangular Marquee tool then create a rectangular selection approximately one-quarter-inch wide in the middle portion of the circle.

2. To delete this section of the circle layer, press the DELETE key. Only the yellow area of the circle is removed, as shown in Figure 15-2. Neither the text nor the background is affected because each is in other layers. When you delete, you wipe away the yellow pixels of the circle, leaving behind its transparent background. The text and background show through the transparency. You'll be able to see this by hiding both the Background and the text layer.

3. Hide the background by clicking on the eye icon next to the word "Background." After you click on the eye icon, it disappears from the Layers palette, and the white and red background disappears from the screen. The Circle and text layers remain on screen. You should now see the familiar transparent checkerboard pattern in the Circle and text layers. This indicates that the backgrounds of the text and Circle layers are transparent.

 NOTE: *If you wish to change the checkerboard pattern of a transparent layer, choose Transparency & Gamut from the File | Preferences submenu.*

4. Hide the text layer by clicking on the eye icon next to its layer name in the Layers palette. Now only the Circle layer remains on screen. In the middle of the circle you see the checkerboard pattern.

 TIP: *If you OPTION-click (Windows users: ALT-click) on the eye column, Photoshop hides all visible layers except the layer of the eye you clicked on. If you OPTION-click (Windows users: ALT-click) again in the same area of the eye column, all layers will be visible.*

To return the text and Background layers to the screen, click on the eye column to the left of the text layer and to the left of the word "Background" in the Layers palette. Before continuing, take a look at your image without the Circle layer.

5. To hide the Circle layer, click on the eye icon next to the circle. The circle vanishes. All you see are the text and Background layers. It's important to realize that the Circle layer is still your target layer. Notice that the selection color still surrounds the word "Circle" in the Layers palette and the word "Circle" still remains in your title bar. This means that editing the file now will affect only the Circle layer, even though you don't see the Circle layer on screen.

6. To make the Circle layer visible, click on the eye column next to the word "Circle." The circle reappears on screen.

 TIP: *You can copy all visible layers into the Clipboard by selecting an area on screen and then choosing Edit | Copy Merged. You can then paste the visible layers into another file, where the selection will appear flattened into one layer.*

Reordering Layers in the Layers Palette

Now assume that you would like the circle in Figure 15-2 to overlap the text, rather than the text overlapping the circle. There's no need to cut and paste between layers. All you need to do is reposition the layers' stacking order in the Layers palette by clicking and dragging with the mouse. To make the Circle layer overlap the text layer, you can drag the Circle layer above the text layer. Try it now.

To change the order of the layers in the Layers palette, position the mouse pointer over the word "Circle" in the Layers palette. The mouse pointer will change to a pointing hand icon (🖑). Click and keep the mouse button pressed, then drag up. As you drag, the pointing hand will change to a grabbing hand icon (✊), and an outline of the Circle layer will move into the Layers palette. Once the Circle layer is above the text layer, release the mouse. On screen, the circle now overlaps the text. In the Layers palette, the Circle layer is now the top layer.

15

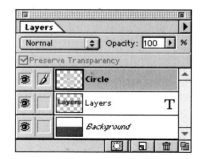

 TIP: *You can move the target layer down by pressing COMMAND-]*
(Windows users: CTRL-]); move the target layer up by pressing
COMMAND-[(Windows users: CTRL-[). You can also move the target layer
by using the Layer | Arrange command. In the Layer | Arrange submenu,
you can choose to move a layer forward, backward, to the front of all
layers, or to the back of all layers.

 TIP: *The Background layer in the Layers palette cannot be moved unless*
you change its name. The easiest way to change the name of the
Background layer is to double-click on the word "Background" in the
Layers palette. The Make Layer dialog box will appear with Background
renamed Layer 0. Click OK to activate the change.

 TIP: *If you have no Background layer and wish to create one, choose*
Layer\New\Background.

Before continuing to the next section, reorder the layers so that the text is the
top layer and the Circle layer is below it.

Changing Layer Opacity

The Layers palette provides a variety of options that allow you to blend images
and create special effects. The easiest way to blend layers is to change the Opacity
setting in the Layers palette. When you change opacity, you change it for the entire
target layer.

On screen, assume that you would like the red background in Figure 15-2 to
show through the circle that overlaps it. One way of achieving this is to lower the
opacity in the Circle layer.

1. To lower opacity in the Circle layer, first make sure that the Circle layer is the target layer. Remember, the target layer is the layer that is selected in the Layers palette. If the Circle layer is not selected in the Layers palette, click on the word "Circle."

2. To change opacity for the Circle layer, click on the small arrow next to the Opacity readout. When the slider appears, move the triangle beneath the slider to the left. Set the Opacity slider to 50%.

 TIP: *If the Move tool, a selection tool, or the Hand or Zoom tool is selected in the Toolbox, you can change the opacity for a layer by typing a number on your keyboard. Type **1** to set opacity to 10%; type **0** to set opacity to 100%. Type **25**, to change opacity to 25%.*

3. The Info palette keeps track of the opacity of a layer. To see the opacity readout for the Circle layer, open the Info palette by choosing Show Info from the Window menu. Then click on one of the eyedropper icons, and choose Opacity. Next, click on the eye icon next to the word "Background" in the Layers palette to hide the background (the Opacity readout in the Info palette will not appear if the background is visible). Now, move the mouse pointer over the circle and notice that an Op value of 50% is displayed in the Info palette.

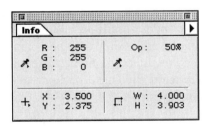

4. Move the mouse pointer over the text and notice that the Op value is 100%. If you wish, experiment by changing the text layer to the target layer and changing its opacity. You won't, however, be able to change opacity in the Background layer, unless you rename it. The Opacity slider in the Layers palette and the Op value in the Info palette are active only if you are in a

15

layer with a transparent background or if a floating selection exists on screen. After you are finished experimenting, make sure that all layers are displayed on screen.

Your next step in exploring the Layers palette is to investigate how the blending modes can create special blending effects between layers.

 REMEMBER: *If you fill a selection on screen or move a selection with the Move tool, you can change the selection's opacity by choosing the Fade command in the Filter menu. In the Fade dialog box, drag the Opacity slider to the left to lower Opacity.*

Special Effects with Blending Modes

Now that you've become familiar with layer fundamentals, you might wish to start exploring more ways to blend images using the Layers palette. One of the fastest ways to create special effects while blending layers is to use the Layers palette's mode pop-up menu. In order to access the mode pop-up menu in the Layers palette, you must be in a layer other than the Background, or have a floating selection on screen. Make either the Circle or text layer from Figure 15-2 your target layer.

Take a moment to click on the mode pop-up menu. You'll see a familiar list of choices, starting with the word "Normal" and ending with the word "Luminosity." These are the same blending modes described in Chapter 6. They work very much the same way when blending layers as they do when painting with the painting tools. When used with layers, the blending modes affect the target layer and the layer directly beneath it. Try using the Dissolve mode to break up the colors of the images in the Circle and text layers:

1. If the Circle layer from Figure 15-2 isn't your target layer, select the Circle layer as your target layer by clicking on the word "Circle" in the Layers palette. If the Circle and/or Background layers are hidden, click in the approximate area in the eye column to view them.

2. To change blending modes, click on the mode pop-up menu and choose the Dissolve mode. The Dissolve mode randomly changes the pixels, using the

colors of the target layer and the layer below it. Keep the Opacity for the Circle layer set to 50%.

3. Next, set the target layer to the text layer by clicking on the word "Layers" in the Layers palette.

4. Use the Dissolve mode once again. Set Opacity to 70%. This time, the effect will dissolve pixels from the text and Circle layers. After you change the mode to Dissolve, adjust Opacity as desired. Your image should look somewhat like Figure 15-3.

You'll have a chance to practice using different modes later in this chapter when you load different images on screen. For now, if you'd like to experiment, try the Lighten, Darken, and Difference modes.

As you experiment with blending modes, you might wish to add more colors to the layers on screen. When editing layers, one option that can prove helpful is the Preserve Transparency check box that appears at the top of the Layers palette.

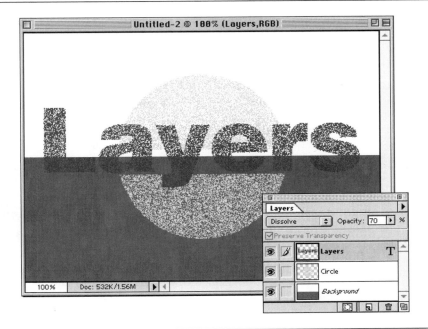

FIGURE 15-3   The Dissolve mode applied to the text and Circle layers at 70% opacity

TIP: *To quickly experiment with different blending modes, press SHIFT–+ to step forward through the blending modes on at a time; press SHIFT– to step backwards through the blending modes.*

Preserving Transparency and Rendering a Type Layer

The Preserve Transparency option locks in the transparent area of a layer so that it cannot be edited. This feature can be helpful when you are filling selections in layers or when you are painting in layers. If you wish to paint or fill a type layer, the layer must be rendered onto the background pixels. After the text is rendered, the type cannot be edited in the Type Tool dialog box. In the next exercise, you'll try out the Preserve Transparency option with the text layer from Figure 15-3. Assume that you want to change the colors of the text in the text layer but don't want to inadvertently paint over the text. Here's how to do it with the Preserve Transparency option:

1. Set the target layer to the text layer by clicking on the word "Layers."

2. To render the type layer, choose Layer | Type | Render Layer.

3. In the Layers palette, make sure that the Preserve Transparency option is selected.

4. Set the foreground color to the color of your choice.

5. Activate the Paintbrush tool and begin painting over the text with broad brush strokes.

Notice that no matter where you paint on the type, the transparency area of the layer remains transparent. If you'd like to experiment a bit more, use the Gradient tool to create a blend over the text. You'll see that only the letters will be affected by the blend.

 TIP: *On layers other than the Background, you can select non-transparent areas by pressing the COMMAND key (Windows users: ALT) and clicking on a layer name in the Layers palette.*

NOTE: *If you create elements in a transparent layer and then decide that you want to erase some of them with the Eraser tool, note that the Eraser produces slightly different effects depending on whether or not the Preserve Transparency option in the Layers palette is selected. If the Preserve Transparency option is not selected when using the Eraser, the transparent background shows through the area you erased. If you use the Eraser to erase elements in the layer with Preserve Transparency on, the Eraser applies the background color. Both options do not, however, affect the transparent areas.*

Using the Edit | Transform Commands with Layers

The Transform commands in the Edit menu allow you to embellish and tweak selections and images in layers. As discussed in Chapter 8, the Transform commands allow you to scale, rotate, skew, distort, and add perspective to selections and individual and linked layers. If you apply a transformation to a linked layer, the transformation affects all nontransparent elements of the linked layers.

All of these Transform commands work in a similar fashion. After you execute the Edit | Transform menu command, Photoshop places a bounding box around nontransparent image areas. As you manipulate the bounding box with the mouse, the effect is previewed within the box, as shown in Figure 15-4. In this figure, the Perspective transformation was applied to the linked text and Circle layers. After editing the bounding box, you can then double-click within the bounding box to apply the transformation. Note that you must first render your text in order to apply the Perspective or Distort transformation commands.

If you want to execute several transformations with the mouse, your best bet is to choose Edit | Free Transform. When the bounding box appears you can then skew, rotate, or distort using the mouse. If you'd like, try transforming the text on screen, or create text in a new layer. Then choose Edit | Free Transform. After you execute the command, the text will be enclosed by the bounding box. Here is a summary of how to use the mouse to transform the object in the bounding box:

- To scale, click and drag on a bounding box handle.

- To rotate, click and drag outside the bounding box.

15

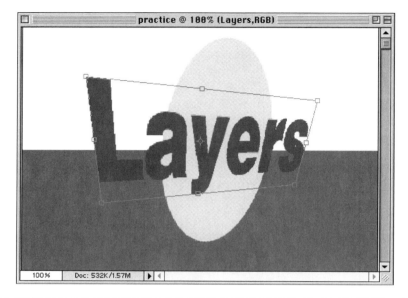

FIGURE 15-4   The Perspective transformation applied to the linked text and Circle layers

- ☐ To distort, press OPTION (Windows users: ALT), then click and drag on a bounding box handle.

- ☐ To skew, press COMMAND-SHIFT (Windows users: CTRL-SHIFT), then click and drag on a side handle of the bounding box. (You'll see the pointer change to a white arrow along with a small double arrow.)

- ☐ To create perspective, press COMMAND-OPTION-SHIFT (Windows users: CTRL-ALT-SHIFT), then click and drag on a corner handle of the bounding box. (You'll see the pointer change to a gray arrowhead.)

After you have manipulated the bounding box, double-click in the bounding box or press RETURN (Windows users: ENTER) to complete the transformation. If you don't wish to apply the effect, press ESC to cancel (Mac users can also press COMMAND-.).

Here are a few tips that may come in handy when you are transforming layers:

◻ You can duplicate a layer while transforming it with the Free Transform command by pressing COMMAND-OPTION-T (Windows users: CTRL-ALT-T). If you wish to duplicate while using one of the Edit I Transform commands, press OPTION (Windows users: ALT) while selecting the command.

◻ You can repeat a transformation with a layer other than the one you originally transformed. To repeat the transformation choose Edit I Transform I Again.

◻ You can change the center point of the transformation by clicking and dragging on the centerpoint icon, before beginning the transformation. This is most useful when rotating.

 REMEMBER: *The Edit I Transform commands also transform selections, paths and the mask in Quick Mask mode. See Chapter 14 for more information about using Quick Mask mode.*

Deleting Layers

To remove a layer from your image, you must first set it to be the target layer. Once you have set the target layer, you can remove the layer either by choosing Layer I Delete Layer or Delete Layer from the Layers palette pop-up menu or by dragging a layer into the Trash icon (🗑) in the Layers palette.

Here's how to delete the Background layer from your file: In the Layers palette, position the mouse pointer over the word "Background." The icon will change to a pointing hand. Click and drag the layer over to the Trash icon in the Layers palette. As you drag, the icon will turn into a grabbing hand icon. Move the grabbing hand icon over the Trash icon. When the Trash icon changes colors, release the mouse. The red and white background will be removed from your file and from the Layers palette.

Before you place the circle and text (Figure 15-3) into another file, your next step is to compress them into one layer by using the Merge Layers command.

15

Merging and Flattening Layers

The Merge Visible command found in the Layer menu is used to compress all visible layers into one layer. If you have a Background layer, the layers are merged into it. If you don't have a Background layer, or if the background isn't visible, the layers are merged into the target layer. Hidden layers are not affected. This command can be helpful if you have completed your design work and don't need to make changes in specific layers. By merging layers, you can also keep your file size low.

Try merging the layers in your practice document by choosing Merge Visible from the Layers palette pop-up menu.

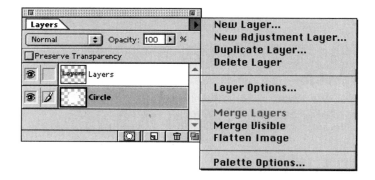

After the layers are merged, the file size is reduced. Notice that transparency of the elements is still intact, even though there is only one layer in the Layers palette.

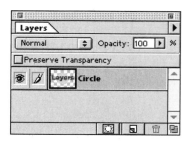

Another option that compresses visible layers and reduces file size is the Flatten Layers command. It's important to understand the difference between flattening and merging layers. Unlike merging layers, flattening layers removes all hidden layers from the file. The flattened file has no transparent background. This means that it can be saved in a variety of different file formats, not just Photoshop's. Before you save your file, proceed to the next section to learn how to duplicate a layer from one file into another.

TIP: *You can merge a layer with its underlying layer by choosing Layer | Merge Down. You can also merge all visible layers into a new layer. After you create the layer, press and hold OPTION (Window users: ALT) while you choose Layer | Merge Visible.*

TIP: *You also use the History brush to create fade effects between merged layers. After you've merged layers, set the History brush state in the History palette to the step where you created the layer that you eventually merged. When you paint on screen with the History brush, you'll be painting in the pre-merged version. See Chapter 9 to learn more about the History palette and History brush.*

Duplicating a Layer into Another File

Now that you have deleted the Background and merged the Circle and text layers in your practice file, you can place the merged layers into another file by using the Layer | Duplicate Layer command or by choosing Duplicate Layer from the Layers palette menu.

1. Open any file that you wish to use as a new Background file. If you don't have an image to use as a background, open a file from Adobe's Samples folder. After the file is loaded, activate your practice image by clicking on it.

2. To place the merged Circle layer from your practice file into the file, choose Duplicate Layer from the Layers palette pop-up menu. In the Duplicate Layer dialog box, choose the file that you want to place the layer into by clicking on the Document pop-up menu and choosing the file. To copy the layer into the Background file, click OK. Notice that the elements in the Circle layer from your practice file retain their names and transparency.

   NOTE: *You can also copy a layer from one file to another by dragging the layer name from the Layers palette into an open file's document window. In addition, you can drag individual or linked layers from one file into another. However, if you copy linked layers from one document to another, drag and drop the layer from the document window with the Move tool, not from the Layers palette. If you drag from the Layers palette only one layer will be copied.*

15

Photoshop 5 ▶ In Action

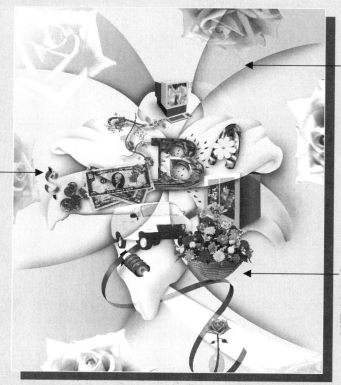

Digitized images created in RayDream Designer and Adobe Dimensions were placed in Layer 1.

All of the shading was created in Layer 2. The shadows were created using the Airbrush tool and alpha channels.

The shapes that were created in Illustrator were placed into the Background layer.

Artist: Wendy Grossman   **Client: FTD Florist**

Wendy used various programs to create the different elements in this image. After the separate elements were created, she composited them together using Photoshop's layers.

In Adobe Illustrator, Wendy sketched the background shapes, the computer and refrigerator, and then placed them into the Background layer. In Layer 1, she placed images she created in RayDream Designer (the letters, basket, flower vase, and stem), the images she created in Adobe Dimensions (the dollar sign and the ribbon), and the images she scanned (the money, truck, and flowers). Wendy added shading effects in Layer 2. To create the shadows for various elements she used the Airbrush tool and alpha channels. In this layer she also created the spotlight.

The final step was to place the scanned flowers along the edges of the image. These were pasted into the image using different opacities and modes.

The Circle layer is duplicated into the Background file, and the elements are placed in the center of the background. If your Background file is smaller than the elements in the Circle layer, Photoshop will not clip the elements in the Circle layer. This means that the portion of the layer that is not visible still exists.

Saving a File with Layers

If you wish to save your file with all its layers, use the File | Save As command to save the file in Photoshop format. If your document already has a name, enter a new name for your file so that you don't replace the original version.

As discussed in Chapter 4, if you wish to flatten layers when you save your image, choose the File | Save a Copy command and make sure the Flatten Image option is selected. Once the Flatten Image option is selected, you can click on the Format (Windows users: Save As) pop-up menu and choose a file format. For more information on using different file formats, see Appendix A.

 TIP: *When a layer is flattened using File | Save a Copy, only the visible layers appear in the flattened file. You can use Save a Copy to save layers as separate cast members for Macromedia Director. The Photoshop in Action in Chapter 20 provides an example.*

Now that you have learned the fundamentals of using layers, you're probably eager to use them to create special effects.

Creating Special Effects Using Layers

After exploring the Layers palette, you're now ready to create some special effects by using layers. In the following sections, you will use layers to create drop shadows, place images into text, and blend images using the Layers palette's blending modes.

 NOTE: *Using the Layer | Effects | Drop Shadow command is covered in Chapter 17.*

Creating Drop Shadows Using Layers

In this section you're going to create a drop shadow by duplicating a layer and then applying the Gaussian Blur filter to the duplicate layer. The blurred layer will create the shadow effect. By creating the drop shadow in a layer, you'll have complete flexibility as to where the shadow appears and how much of a three-dimensional effect you wish to create. Figure 15-5 shows a drop shadow applied to a digitized maple leaf ( ) over a background of clouds ( ).

NOTE: *Chapter 18 covers creating drop shadows using Photoshop's Layer | Effects commands.*

Before you begin producing the drop shadow, start by using the Clouds filter to create a background for your final image. If you prefer, you can skip steps 1–3 by loading a digitized background image. Start by opening the Layers palette; if it isn't open, open it by choosing Show Layers from the Window menu.

1. Create a new RGB color file, 5 inches by 5 inches, with the Contents radio button set to White. When the new file is on screen you are ready to begin creating clouds.

2. Next, set the foreground color to light blue and the background color to white. These are the colors that the Clouds filter will use.

3. Apply the Clouds filter by choosing Clouds from the Filter | Render submenu. Your file now looks like soft clouds against a blue sky.

FIGURE 15-5 Leaf with drop shadow created with layers

TIP: *To add to the clouds effect, keep reapplying the filter by pressing COMMAND-F (Windows users: CTRL-F). To diminish the clouds effect, keep pressing SHIFT-COMMAND-F (Windows users: SHIFT-CTRL-F) to gradually fade out the filter.*

4. Open the image to which you wish to apply the drop shadow. The image should be smaller in size than the Background file on screen and have the same resolution. If you don't have an image, you can use the Guitar file in the Samples folder (in Photoshop's Goodies folder) because it is silhouetted in a layer with a transparent background.

 NOTE: *Before creating a drop shadow, you may wish to silhouette the image using the Pen tool, the Select | Color Range command, and/or the selection tools. By using a silhouetted image as the image to which you apply the drop shadow, you will make the shadow look more realistic.*

Next, you'll place the image you want to apply the drop shadow to into the background image and create a layer at the same time. There are several techniques you can use. You could copy the image and paste the image into the Background file, but perhaps the easiest way is to drag and drop the guitar file into the Background file.

5. Use the Move tool to click and drag the file into your background image. As you drag out of the original file, the pointer changes to a tiny grabbing hand. When the grabbing hand icon enters your file with the background image, a black frame will surround the file. After you see the black frame, you can release the mouse. This will create a new layer over the background, with the leaf in the new layer. Notice that in the Layers palette you now have Background and Layer 1.

15

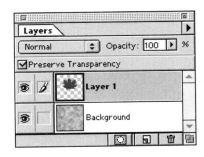

Note that your target layer is the layer that you just created. As mentioned earlier, the title bar and the colored area of the Layers palette indicate the target layer you are in.

6. Use the Move tool to position the image in the center of the file.

Now you are ready to create the drop shadow. To do this, first duplicate the layer you just created, then use the duplicate layer to create the shadow. To duplicate a layer, you can either choose the Layer | Duplicate Layer command or drag a layer in the Layers palette over the New Layer icon.

7. To duplicate the layer, position the mouse pointer over the words "Layer 1" (the layer that you wish to duplicate). The mouse pointer will change to a pointing hand. Click the mouse and drag the layer over to the New Layer icon. As you drag, the pointer changes to a tiny grabbing hand. Drag the grabbing hand icon over the New Layer icon. When the New Layer icon changes colors, release the mouse. A copy of the Leaf layer is automatically created. To change the name of the layer, double-click on the words "Layer 1 copy" in the Layers palette. This opens the Layer Options dialog box. Type in the words **Drop Shadow** in the Name field, then click OK.

 NOTE: *You can create a duplicate of a layer by first selecting the layer in the Layers palette and then choosing Layer | Duplicate Layer or Duplicate Layer from the Layers palette pop-up menu. You can name the layer in the As field of the Duplicate Layer dialog box and choose a destination for that layer in the Document pop-up menu. The destination of the duplicated layer can be any open file or a new file.*

At this point you should be viewing all layers (all eye icons are displayed in the Layers palette) and your target layer should be the Drop Shadow layer (this is the layer that is selected in the Layers palette). Also, notice that the words "Drop Shadow" now appear in the title bar of the current document.

 REMEMBER: *Although you can view more than one layer at a time, you can edit only one layer at a time.*

8. With the Drop Shadow layer as the target layer, use the Move tool to move the image in this layer so that it is slightly offset from the image in Layer 1. Offset it in any direction.

After you've moved the image in the Drop Shadow layer, your next step is to darken it to create the shadow effect. It will be easier to do this if the drop shadow layer is the only layer visible on screen.

9. To hide the image in Layer 1 and the Background layer, turn off the eye icons for both Layer 1 and the Background layer by clicking on each layer's eye. Leave the eye icon next to the Drop Shadow layer so that you are viewing only this layer on screen.

   Now that you are viewing only the leaf in the Drop Shadow layer, you can fill it with the color you want the drop shadow to be. In the next step, the Preserve Transparency check box in the Fill dialog box will be activated so that the Edit | Fill command fills only the image on screen, not the transparent area.

10. Set the foreground color to the color you want the drop shadow to be. Choose either a very dark green or black, depending on the desired effect. From the Edit menu, choose Fill. In the Fill dialog box, set the Use pop-up menu to Foreground Color, set the Mode pop-up menu to Normal, and set Opacity to between 80 and 100%, depending on the desired effect. Make sure the Preserve Transparency option is selected. Then click OK to fill the leaf.

To create the soft drop shadow effect, apply the Gaussian Blur filter to the Drop Shadow layer.

11. Choose Gaussian Blur from the Filter | Blur submenu. In the Gaussian Blur dialog box, use a number between 3 and 10 in the Radius field. The higher the number, the greater the blur effect. Click OK to activate the changes.

 REMEMBER: *If the Preserve Transparency option is selected in the Layers palette, the Gaussian blur will have no effect.*

12. To view the image in Layer 1 and see the effects, click on the eye icon next to Layer 1. Notice that the image in the Drop Shadow layer is on top of the image in Layer 1. To place the image in the Drop Shadow layer below the image in Layer 1, click on Drop Shadow in the Layers palette and drag it over Layer 1.

13. If you would like to move the shadow, make sure that the Drop Shadow is your target layer. If you need to change target layers, click on Drop Shadow in the Layers palette. Then use the Move tool to move the shadow.

15

When you are happy with the position of the shadow, activate the eye icon next to the word "Background" in the Layers palette to see the entire image.

At this point, if you wish to reposition the image and the drop shadow together, you will need to link the layers. As discussed earlier in this chapter, the Layers palette allows you to link layers so that you can move more than one layer at a time.

14. If you want to link the image in the top layer and its shadow so that they can be moved together, make sure that Drop Shadow is the active layer. To link the layers, move the mouse into the blank area to the right of the eye icons and to the left of Layer 1 in the Layers palette. Click the mouse. A chain, called the *link icon,* appears next to the Drop Shadow layer. This means that the two layers are temporarily linked and will therefore move together. With the Move tool activated, you can now move both the top layer and the Drop Shadow layer together. To unlink the layers, click on the link icon in the Layers palette.

To save your file with its layers, save using the Photoshop file format. Name your file **Shadow**. If you want to duplicate your image and drop shadow, proceed to the next section. Before you proceed, create a duplicate of your file with its layer so that you won't affect the file you just created. To create a duplicate file and close the onscreen file, choose File | Save As. In the Save As dialog box, type **Shadow2**, and make sure the format is set to Photoshop. Click Save to create a duplicate file.

Duplicating an Image with Its Drop Shadow

After you've completed all the steps in the previous exercise, you may want to create yet another image with a drop shadow. The easiest way to do this is to merge the leaf and its shadow together, then duplicate the merged layer. To do this, you need to first hide the Background layer.

1. To hide the Background layer, click on the eye icon next to the word "Background" in the Layers palette.

2. To merge the image and its shadow, choose Merge Visible or Merge Linked from the Layers palette pop-up menu. In the Layers palette, notice that the two layers (Layer 1 and Drop Shadow) are merged into the target layer.

3. After the layers have been merged, you can unhide the Background layer by clicking in the eye column next to the word "Background" in the Layers palette.

4. To duplicate the merged layers, click on Drop Shadow in the Layers palette and drag it over the New Layer icon. A new layer named "Drop Shadow copy" appears in the Layers palette and becomes the target layer. The Drop Shadow layer with the original leaf image and drop shadow is directly below the Drop Shadow copy layer (the new layer that was just created).

5. To see the two images with their drop shadows, use the Move tool to drag the image and its shadow in the Drop Shadow copy layer in any direction. As you drag, you'll see the original leaf image in the Drop Shadow layer. You may also want to move the original leaf image in the Drop Shadow layer. To do so, set the Drop Shadow layer to the target layer and then move the original leaf image with the Move tool.

At this point, feel free to embellish the image on screen. You may want to use some of the Image menu commands to scale, rotate, lighten, or color. Figure 15-6 shows two leaves with drop shadows after various Image menu commands were applied.

After you've saved your work, close your file and proceed to the next section to learn how the Layers palette can help you blend images together.

15

FIGURE 15-6   Image after Drop Shadow layer was copied, scaled, and rotated

Blending Two Images Using the Modes in the Layers Palette

Earlier in the chapter you saw how the Dissolve mode created an unusual speckled blend between layers. In this section you're going to add a layer to an image and use the Layers palette's Mode pop-up menu to experiment with different blending effects. By trying out the modes with images, rather than with the simple shapes used at the beginning of this chapter, you will gain a better understanding of the power of the Layers palette's Mode pop-up menu.

If you don't have two images that you want to blend, use the Sky file and the Bottles file in the Adobe Samples folder. You'll use the Sky file as the Background underlying layer and the Bottles file as the target layer. If the Layers palette isn't open, open it now.

1. Open both files that you want to blend and place them side by side or so they overlap. If you overlap the images, put the image you wish to use as the overlying (target layer) over the image you want for your background (underlying layer).

2. Once both files are on screen, activate the Move tool and drag the file you want to place in the target layer over the background, underlying layer. Photoshop creates a new layer.

 REMEMBER: *If you drag an image into another file, Photoshop does not clip any image areas that extend beyond the work canvas. However, if you choose Select | All, only the area within the canvas border is selected. To learn about changing canvas size, see Chapter 8.*

As discussed earlier in this chapter, you can use the Opacity slider and the Mode pop-up menu in the Layers palette to control how the pixels in one layer will blend with pixels in the underlying layer. In this situation, the modes in the Layers palette work much the same way as when a painting tool is activated. (To review the blending modes, see Chapter 6.) The difference, though, is that Photoshop applies the blending modes based on the pixels in the target layer and the underlying layer, rather than the foreground color and the color you are painting over.

 NOTE: *The modes and opacity options become active when a floating selection exists on screen. This means that you can change modes and opacity to create the blend effect between the floating selection and the underlying layer.*

Now try switching from one mode to another. Here's a brief review of how some of the more powerful modes in the Layers palette work:

☐ To create a composite where darker pixels in the target layer replace corresponding lighter pixels in the underlying layer and darker areas from the underlying layer replace lighter pixels in the target layer, choose Darken.

☐ To create a composite where lighter pixels in the target layer replace corresponding darker pixels in the underlying layer and lighter pixels from the underlying layer replace darker pixels in the target layer, choose Lighten.

☐ To blend the Hue and Saturation values of the target with the underlying layer, choose Color. The Luminosity value of the underlying image will not be affected, thus preserving the underlying layer's brightness levels.

15

NOTE: *As discussed in Chapters 8 and 18, a histogram is a visual representation of an image's brightness or gray levels. To prove to yourself that the brightness values of the image don't change when the Color mode is chosen, view the histogram (Image | Histogram) of your underlying layer with the target layer hidden. View the histogram again (in Color mode) with both layers visible. The histogram doesn't change.*

☐ To create a darker composite from the pixel values of both the target and underlying layers, choose Multiply. This can produce a result similar to overlaying colored magic markers.

☐ To create a lighter composite from both the pixel values of the target and underlying layers, choose Screen. This often creates the effect of bleaching out colors from an image.

☐ To create a random effect from the pixels in both the target and underlying layers, choose Dissolve and use the Opacity slider to adjust the results. As you lower the Opacity, the top layer gradually dissolves, revealing more of the underlying layer.

☐ To create a blend using the texture of your target layer, choose Luminosity. Photoshop creates a blend with the brightness values of the target layer and the Hue and Saturation of the underlying layer.

☐ To subtract the color values of one layer from another layer, choose Difference. Difference can darken an image and change a color to its complement in areas underlying or overlying white regions in another layer.

☐ To lighten or screen where light areas overlap and darken where dark areas overlap, and still preserve the highlights and shadows of the underlying layer, choose Overlay.

Figure 15-7(c) shows a backyard scene that was placed in a layer over the waterfall background image, shown in Figure 15-7(b), to create the composite shown in Figure 15-7(a). After the new layer for the backyard scene was created, the Darken mode was selected in the Mode pop-up menu of the Layers palette. Remember, when the Darken mode is applied, Photoshop compares the pixel values in the target layer to the pixel values in the underlying layer. It then replaces lighter pixels with corresponding darker pixels. Thus, in Figure 15-7(c), the lighter areas of the waterfall were replaced by the darker trees and fence from the backyard scene. To make more of the underlying image visible, Opacity in the Layers palette was lowered to 50%.

(a)

(b)   (c)

FIGURE 15-7   A blend between two layers created using the Darken mode and low Opacity in the Layers palette; (b) underlying layer; (c) target layer

15

Conclusion

As you've seen from this chapter, layers provide numerous ways of juxtaposing and compositing images. Changing opacities and modes provides almost limitless possibilities for different effects. In the next chapter you'll learn how Photoshop's composite controls, layer masks, and transformation layers provide you with even more power when you work with layers.

CHAPTER 16

Advanced Layer Techniques

Throughout this book, you've seen how layers provide you with almost limitless power to edit and blend images together. This chapter further illustrates the versatility of layers. As you work through this chapter, you'll explore how you can blend images together pixel by pixel. You'll also discover how to create layer masks, which enable you to paint in a mask to hide a portion of one layer as you reveal portions of the layer or layers beneath it. Layer masks, combined with layer blending modes, present you with even more ways to blend images together. At the end of this chapter, you'll learn how adjustment layers can provide you with a means of editing and correcting images through a layer. Using adjustment layers, you can even grab the Paintbrush tool and adjust images with the stroke of a brush.

Using Composite Controls to Blend Images Together

Photoshop's Composite Controls allow you to control exactly which elements from a target layer and underlying layers will appear in a composite image. The Composite Controls are the sliders that appear in the Layer Options dialog box, shown below.

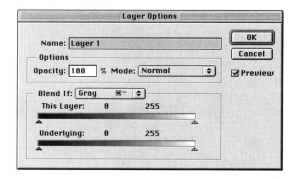

With the sliders, you can pick which pixels in the underlying layers will be replaced by the pixels in the target layer. The Composite Controls sliders can be accessed by first clicking on a layer name in the Layers palette, then choosing Layer Options from the Layer menu or Layers palette pop-up menu, or by double-clicking on the target layer in the Layers palette.

The following exercise demonstrates how to use the Layer Options dialog box sliders and its options. For the exercise, you will need two images: one image to be the underlying background image, and another to be the image that will be blended with the overlying target layer.

For example, The Layer Options dialog box sliders were used to blend two layers together to create the composite shown in Figure 16-1(a). Figure 16-1(b) shows the contents of one of the layers, a textured background. Figure 16-1(c) shows an image of a boat, the contents of the other layer. Adjusting the sliders allowed the lightest pixels from the boat layer to be eliminated so that the textured background could show through.

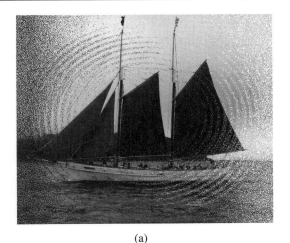

(a)

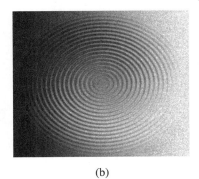

(b)

(c)

FIGURE 16-1   (a) Composite image created using Composite Controls; (b) underlying layer created with the Gradient tool and the Add Noise filters; (c) target layer

16

The background image shown in Figure 16-1(b) was created by applying the Zigzag and Add Noise filters to a Linear blend. (See Chapter 10 for a review of the filter commands and Chapter 6 for a review of creating blends.) If you wish to re-create this background for the following exercise, create a new file, 3.5 inches high by 4 inches wide. Set the background contents to white by choosing the White radio button in the Contents group.

After you create the new file, choose a dark foreground and a light background color to be the starting and ending colors for the Linear blend. To transform the image into a rippled pond, apply the Zigzag filter in the Filter | Distort submenu. Choose the Pond Ripple radio button and set Amount to 87 and Ridges to 20. Next, apply the Add Noise filter (in the Filter | Noise submenu) with the Distribution set to Uniform and the Amount set to 20, and click the Monochromatic option (to prevent more colors from being added). Apply the filter two or three times if you want to add more speckling.

Now that you have created the textured image for the underlying layer (the Background), your next step is to create a new layer. In this layer you will place the image you wish to blend with the underlying layer. Create the new layer by pasting one image on top of another, as described in the following steps:

1. Open a file that you wish to blend with the textured background you just created. If you do not have a file to use, you may want to open a file from the Samples folder.

2. Select the entire file, or an area of it, that you wish to paste into the Background file.

3. From the Edit menu, choose Copy, and then close the file.

4. Activate the textured background image. Choose Paste from the Edit menu. Open the Layers palette if it is not already open. Note that the new layer you created is the target layer—the layer that is selected in the Layers palette.

5. Choose Layer Options from the Layers palette pop-up menu or double-click on the top layer to open the Layer Options dialog box.

The options in the top of the Layer Options dialog box are already familiar to you from the New Layer dialog box. The options in the bottom of the dialog box, in the Blend If section, are called Composite Controls. The Composite Controls feature several options for controlling how pixels in an overlying layer and an underlying layer blend together. These options are examined in the paragraphs that follow.

Composite Controls Sliders

The Composite Controls sliders let you control exactly which pixels to include and exclude from the target layer (the top slider: "This Layer") and underlying layer (the bottom slider: "Underlying"). For both sliders, the black slider control affects dark areas and the white slider control affects light areas. The range of both sliders is from 0 (black) to 255 (white).

When the This Layer slider's black slider control is dragged to the right, darker pixels of the target layer are not included in the composite image. When the This Layer slider's white slider control is dragged to the left, lighter pixels of the target layer are not included in the composite image. All pixel values designated in the range between the target layer's slider controls appear in the composite image.

With a little experimentation, the effects of the two sliders will be more apparent to you, so let's continue with the exercise.

 NOTE: *Before you begin adjusting the sliders, make sure the Preview check box is selected in the Layer Options dialog box so that you can preview the results.*

Try dragging the This Layer slider's black control to the right. This will remove the darker pixels from your target layer. Drag the white control to the left, and you remove the lighter pixels in the target layer from the composite. The results will be more obvious if you drag the black control back to 0 before moving the white control.

Before you begin experimenting with the Underlying slider, reset the Composite Control sliders to their original settings. This will make it easier for you to see the effect of adjusting the Underlying slider controls. To quickly reset all options, press OPTION (Windows users: ALT). The Cancel button will change to a Reset button; click this to reset the settings and remain in the dialog box.

Now consider the Underlying slider: When you click and drag the black slider control to the right, dark areas from the underlying image will be added into the composite. As you drag, underlying pixels with values from 0 to the value set by the black slider control will appear in the composite. Clicking and dragging the white slider control to the left will add light areas from the underlying image to the composite. As you drag, underlying pixels with values ranging from that set by the

16

white slider control to 255 will appear in the composite image. Thus, values between the black and white controls are the pixel values in the underlying image that will not appear in the composite image. These pixels will be replaced by pixels from the target layer in the composite image.

Try clicking and dragging the Underlying slider's black control to the right. As you drag, you add dark pixels from the underlying layer and remove any pixels from the target layer that would have appeared over this area. Move the Underlying slider's black control back to 0 and then move the white control to the left. Notice that as you drag, you are adding light pixels from the underlying layer to the composite and removing pixels from the target layer image in the composite.

Splitting the Slider Controls

To create a smoother composite effect, you can split each individual slider control (▲) into two parts (◢ ◣). To split a slider control, press OPTION (Windows users: ALT) and then click and drag on one of the edges of the control. For each slider control that is split, you will see two values showing the range between the split controls. The pixels in the range defined by the split slider control will be only partially colored. This can help smooth the blend between the target layer and underlying pixels.

To gain familiarity with how your composite image will be affected by splitting the slider controls, experiment with all four of the controls on both the This Layer and the Underlying slider bars.

Other Composite Controls Options

The remaining options in the Layer Options dialog box allow further possibilities and refinements when creating a composite image.

The Blend If pop-up menu allows you to control the blend based upon the color values of individual color channels. When viewing an RGB image, the word "Gray" in the Blend If pop-up menu indicates that the Composite Controls affect the luminance or brightness values of the pixels in all channels. In an RGB color image, Blend If lets you work separately in the red, green, or blue channel of the image. Thus, if Red were chosen in the Blend If pop-up menu, you could control the range of red values (from 0 to 255) for both the target and underlying layers.

You'll also find the familiar Mode pop-up menu and Opacity setting in this dialog box. By entering an Opacity value less than 100%, you can make your target layer more translucent. The Mode pop-up menu offers you the same modes that are available in the Layers palette. These modes work almost exactly as they do when you use the Layers palette to blend layers together (as described in the previous chapter), but with one major difference: The effect applies only to the pixel values specified by the Composite Controls sliders.

Experiment with the modes and opacities in the Layer Options dialog box until you achieve the effects you desire. Once you are satisfied with the preview of your image, click OK to activate the changes.

Now that you've explored the Layer Options dialog box's powerful blending options, you probably feel that you've exhausted all of Photoshop's blending features. However, there are still more powerful Layers palette options to investigate that allow you to create effects that seamlessly blend images together. Save your file if you wish. Then close it and proceed to the next section to learn about how one image in a layer can mask out another image in another layer.

 REMEMBER: *You can use context-sensitive menus to activate a layer. With the Move tool selected, press CTRL and click in an image (Windows users: click the right mouse button). If the Move tool is not selected, press COMMAND-CTRL and click (Windows users: press CTRL and click the right mouse button).*

Placing Images Within Other Images Using Clipping Groups

When you are working with layers, you can create a special layer group in which the bottom layer controls the shape, transparency, and mode of the other group members above it. This type of layer group is called a *clipping group*.

In the next examples, you'll see how clipping groups can be used to place one image into the shape of another image. One image is used as the shape; the other is the background image that is placed into the shape. The image that is used for the shape creates a mask. This technique is often used to place textures or other images into text. The next few examples show you different ways of creating and using clipping groups to place one image into another image.

Using the Group with Previous Layer Option

In this example, you will place an image into a shape, as shown in Figure 16-2. To achieve the effect, you will need two images: One image will be used for the shape of the final image, and the other will be placed into the shape. In Figure 16-2, a

| FIGURE 16-2 | A clipping group used to place the sailboat image from a layer into the leaf image in another layer |

sailboat was used as the image that was placed into the leaf shape. To create the silhouetted leaf, the Pen tool was used to outline a digitized leaf. The drop shadow behind the leaf was created using the steps described in the section "Creating Drop Shadows Using Layers" in Chapter 15. When both images were placed in a clipping group, the leaf masked the sailboat image, making it appear as if the sailboat were in the leaf. Try out the following steps to create the same effect with two images. If you don't have a silhouetted image to use, load the Guitar file (from the Samples folder, in Photoshop's Goodies folder) to use as your background shape.

1. Start by opening the image that you wish to place into the shape. If you don't have an image, you may want to use one from the Samples folder. Open the Layers palette if it isn't already open.

2. Next, open or create the image you want to use as the shape. If you are going to use a digitized image, use an image that has been silhouetted. If you don't have an image to use and are using one of the images that comes with Adobe Photoshop, open the Guitar file in the Samples folder.

 NOTE: *If you wish to design your own shape, first create a new layer in your file, and then use the selection tool or the Pen tool to create the shape in the layer. Next, fill the shape with color.*

3. After you open the file with the silhouetted image, use the Move tool to drag and drop it into the file of the image that will eventually appear in the shape (the destination image). To drag and drop one image into another, place the images side by side or so that the shape image (silhouetted image) overlaps the destination image. Activate the Move tool, and then click and drag the shape image into the destination file. When the pointer touches the destination image, it will change to a grabbing hand. Position the grabbing hand in the middle of the destination image, and release the mouse. A new layer will be created in the destination image, with the shape image in a layer.

4. Rename the layer by double-clicking on the name of the new layer in the Layers palette. Name the layer "Shape."

5. If you wish, use the Edit | Transform | Scale or Edit | Free Transform command to enlarge the image in the Shape layer. This will make more of the image show in the shape. (If you wish to review the Scale command, see Chapter 8.)

   To use a clipping group to place an image into the shape on screen, the Shape layer must be underneath the bottom layer in the Layers palette. Unfortunately, Photoshop won't let you do this if your base layer is named "Background." Try moving the Shape layer underneath the Background layer. You'll see that the layers won't switch positions. Here's a trick that will allow you to switch positions: Rename the Background layer.

6. The quickest way to change the name of the Background layer is to double-click on the word "Background" in the Layers palette. When the Make Layer dialog box appears, notice that the layer is now named "Layer 0." Click OK. Now move the Shape layer below Layer 0 (or below the bottom layer in your Layers palette).

Now that you've changed the order of the layers, proceed to the next step to learn how to create a clipping group.

7. Move the mouse pointer to the dividing line in the Layers palette that separates the Shape and Layer 0. Press and hold OPTION (Windows users: ALT). When the mouse pointer changes to a grouping icon, click the mouse button to create a clipping group. After you click, the image changes on screen so that the layer above the shape is seen within the shape. Notice that the Shape layer in the Layers palette is underlined and that the line dividing the two layers has changed from a solid line to a dotted line. This

indicates that the layers are in a clipping group with the Shape layer at the base of the group. Notice also that the layers being clipped are indented in the Layers palette.

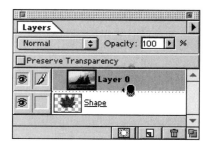

 NOTE: *To create a clipping group, you can also choose Group with Previous from the Layer menu, or COMMAND-G (Windows users: CTRL-G) To ungroup, press COMMAND-SHIFT-G (Windows users: CTRL-SHIFT-G).*

As you just saw, creating a clipping group changes the shape of all visible layers above the base layer in the group to the shape of the base layer. In the example above, you created a clipping group by OPTION-clicking (Windows users: ALT-clicking) between layers in the Layers palette.

8. At this point, you can reposition the image in the shape, or reposition the shape itself. If you'd like, you can move either of the layers independently of the other or link them so that they move together. If you wish, you can also use the Layer | Transform | Scale command to resize the image that is in the shape. If you rescale the image, sharpen it with a sharpening filter, if necessary. You can also lighten or darken the image in the shape with the Brightness/Contrast command in the Image | Adjust menu. You can experiment with various opacity settings and modes in the Layers palette. You can also apply a drop shadow to the image in the Shape layer by following the steps described in Chapter 15 in "Creating Drop Shadows Using Layers."

9. When you are satisfied with the image's appearance, you may wish to flatten the layers in the image to conserve memory.

10. If you wish to save your layers with your file, use the Photoshop format; otherwise, use the File | Save a Copy command to flatten the layers when you save.

11. After saving your work, close the file on screen and proceed to the next section.

 NOTE: *If you wish to remove a layer from a clipping group, you can choose Ungroup from the Layer menu. Or OPTION-click (Windows users: ALT-click) on the dotted line dividing the clipping group members in the Layers palette.*

 NOTE: *You can clip more than one layer—just OPTION-click (Windows users: ALT-click) again on the dividing line between the next layer above the clipping group. You can also create more than one clipping group in the Layers palette.*

 TIP: *Once you create a clipping group, you can paint, add gradients, and so on to the target layer. As you work, the clipping group is still maintained. Also note that clipping groups are often used to color correct silhouetted images with an adjustment layer (adjustment layers are discussed later in this chapter).*

Placing an Image into Text Using Edit | Paste Into

In this section you'll create a travel advertisement by using the Edit | Paste Into command to place an image into text, as shown in Figure 16-3. When you paste an image into a selection, a new layer is created and the selection creates a layer mask for the pasted image.

1. Start by opening an image of a city or landscape. If the Layers palette isn't open, open it now by choosing Show Layers from the Window menu.

2. When the image is on screen, choose Select | All, and then choose Copy from the Edit menu. When the image is copied to the Clipboard, close the file and create a new file. When you choose New from the File menu, you'll see that the settings in the New dialog box reflect the dimensions of the image stored in the Clipboard. In the New dialog box, make sure that the radio button in the Contents group is set to Transparent. Click OK to create the new file.

3. When the new file appears, activate the Type tool; then click in the middle of the image to open the Type Tool dialog box. In the text box, type **VENICE** or a word or phase you want to type in. We chose the following settings: Font: Helvetica; Size: 70; Tracking: –3; and Style, Bold. (We

16

FIGURE 16-3   The Paste Into command and layers were used to paste an image into the text

selected the text in the Type Tool dialog box, before changing Tracking.) Make sure that the Anti-aliased option is activated, and click on the center alignment icon. Click OK to have Photoshop place the text on screen. If necessary, use the Move tool to reposition the text in the middle of the screen.

 TIP: *The example in Figure 16-3 uses Helvetica Black. If you have this font, use it instead of Helvetica. Using Helvetica Black, or any heavy typeface, allows more of the image to appear through each letter.*

 NOTE: *If you type in two lines of type, you may want to enter a value in the leading field to control the line spacing. The smaller the leading, the closer together the lines appear. The larger the leading, the more space there is between the two lines. In Photoshop, leading is measured from baseline to baseline. You can enter leading values from .10 to 1,296.*

4. Use the Edit I Transform I Scale command to enlarge the type to the size of your document. This will allow more of the image to show through the letters. (If you wish to review the E | Transform | Scale command, see Chapter 15.)

 CAUTION: *If you scale too much, your text may appear fuzzy at the edges.*

5. Now turn the text into a selection by pressing COMMAND (Windows users: CTRL) and clicking on the text layer in the Layers palette.

6. With the text selection on screen, choose Paste Into from the Edit menu. Your image now appears in each letter of the text.

   As soon as you paste, notice that a new layer appears in the Layers palette. Alongside the layer icon in the palette is another icon indicating that a layer mask has been created. The layer mask creates a mask out of the text selection so that the image shows through the white area of the mask. In the next section, you'll learn how you can paint with the Paintbrush tool to create blending effects in layer masks. If you wish to experiment, click on the layer mask thumbnail icon, and try painting with different shades of gray. By painting with different shades of gray, you can reveal more of the image through the layer or hide different parts of the type. After you have finished, click on the text layer's thumbnail icon to reactivate the layer.

7. If you wish to reposition the image in the text, use the Move tool and then click and drag in your text. If you wish, you can also use the Edit | Transform | Scale command to resize the image that is in the text. If you rescale the image, sharpen it with a sharpening filter, if necessary. (Don't click on the layer mask thumbnail in the Layer palette, or you'll affect the layer mask and not the layer. If you did click on the layer mask thumbnail, click on the layer thumbnail or layer name to turn editing back on.)

8. If you wish to move the text and image together, click between the layer mask thumbnail and the layer thumbnail. A chain icon will appear. You can then drag the text and image as a group.

9. If you'd like, click on the bottom layer and either paste in more images or add a gradient.

10. When you are satisfied with the image's appearance, save your image with both layers by saving your file in Photoshop format.

When you are ready, close the file on screen and proceed to the next section.

16

Using Layer Masks to Blend Images Together

Photoshop's Layer Mask option combines the power of layers with the power of masks in alpha channels. Layer masks can be used to help create seamless composites between layers. Unlike the other options you've explored in this chapter, a layer mask allows you to use a painting tool to edit a mask between two layers. As you gradually wipe away areas in the mask, you reveal or hide image areas from different layers. This allows images from the underlying layer or layers to appear through the areas you mask in the target layer. The result can be a beautiful mix between layers or an ethereal effect in which images in one layer gradually fade into another.

When using a layer mask, you paint with shades of gray (including black and white). This is exactly like editing an alpha channel, as described in Chapter 14. By using different shades of gray or different opacities of black and white, you can control how transparent the target layer becomes, and thus how much of the underlying layer or layers appears through it. When you create a layer mask, Photoshop allows you to create the mask hiding the entire layer or revealing the entire layer. If you have a selection on screen, you can choose to create the mask hiding the selection or revealing the selection.

Figure 16-4(a) shows the results of a layer mask used to gradually blend the Koala bear image seen in Figure 16-4(c) with an image of the Sydney Opera House seen in Figure 16-4(b).

When working with a layer mask, your image changes on screen according to how you edit the layer mask. It is important to understand, however, that you are not actually editing your layer: You are editing a mask, and viewing your layers through the mask. Photoshop is providing you with a preview of how the image will appear once the layer mask in the Channels palette is applied to the layer. For this reason, working with a layer mask provides you with the ability to always undo any previous changes you have made. Once you're satisfied with the onscreen effect of the layer mask, you can decide whether you want to apply the effects to the layer.

If this sounds like an elaborate procedure, don't worry. You'll soon see that using and applying a layer mask can be quite simple. The following exercise leads you step by step through the process of creating a layer mask and using the mask to blend one layer into another.

If you don't have two images that you want to blend together, use the Big Sky and Bottles files in the Samples folder. In this exercise, you'll drag and drop one file into another—which automatically creates a new layer. Then you'll add a layer mask and edit the mask.

(a)

(b)

(c)

FIGURE 16-4   (a) Two layers blended together using a gradient in a layer mask, (b) Background layer, (c) Koala layer

16

Before you begin, make sure that both the Layers and Channels palettes are open as separate palettes on screen. If these palettes are in a palette group, separate them by clicking and dragging on the Layers or Channels palette's tab and dragging away from the palette group.

1. Open the file that you wish to use as your base layer. If you are using the Samples images, this will be the Big Sky file. Next open the file that you want to apply the layer mask to. If you are using the Samples folder

images, this will be the Bottles file. Set up the files on your screen so you can drag the Bottles file into the Big Sky file.

2. Next, activate the Move tool and drag one file over the other: the Bottle file on top of the Big Sky file (if you are using the samples file). Photoshop will create a new layer for the Bottle file. Notice that in the Layers palette you have a Background and Layer 1 (the file you just dragged over).

3. Before you create a layer mask, make sure the target layer is Layer 1 (the Bottle file, if you are using the Samples files). To create the layer mask, choose Layer | Add Layer Mask | Reveal All.

 TIP: *You can also create a layer mask by clicking on the New Layer Mask icon at the bottom of the Layers palette (the dotted circle in the shaded square).*

In our example, a layer mask was added to the Koala layer.

Notice that the title bar now includes the name of your file, the name of your layer, and the words "Layer 1 Mask."

In the Channels palette, you will see that a new channel appears called Layer 1 Mask. (If you don't see these words, you'll probably need to enlarge the size of the palette.) Notice that the Layer 1 Mask in the Channels palette is selected. This means that any changes you make on screen will now affect only the mask, not your image.

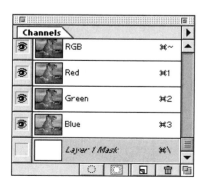

Photoshop 5 ▶ In Action

The arcing water was created using R/GA Print's own proprietary 3-D modeling software.

The moon was created by combining a photograph of a clay model of the moon and a photograph of a person.

The Squirt can is a product shot. White was added with the Airbrush tool to the area around the base to create a cloud effect.

The earth image is a NASA photograph.

Photograph by: Steve Bronstein   Digital Imaging: R/GA Print   Client: A&W Brands/Squirt

The painting tools were used to create stars over a black background. Next, a digitized image of the earth and a product shot of a Squirt can were pasted into the file. A clay moon with the contours of a face in it was sculpted by a model maker and then photographed by Steve Bronstein. Steve then took a photograph of a person whose round visage would provide a good man-in-the-moon face. Both the moon and face photographs were scanned and combined using the Edit | Paste Into command and Composite Controls. To remove color from the face but leave the gray values, the Luminosity mode was used. Then the Rubber Stamp was used to enhance the blending effect. The painting tools and painting modes were used to turn the Man in the Moon purple.

To complete the image, Steve took a photograph of water squirting out of a hose. The photo was scanned and them warped using R/GA's own proprietary 3-D modeling software. The Squirt can was then pasted into the final image.

16

Viewing and Controlling the Layer Mask in the Layer Palette

In the Layers palette, the mask (at this point, a white rectangle, because there is nothing in the mask) appears directly to the left of the layer name. Notice that the paintbrush icon that used to be in the Layers palette has disappeared and is replaced by the Layer Mask Selected icon. This icon tells you that all editing you do now affects the layer mask, not the layer.

You can click in the Layers palette to turn editing in the layer mask off or on:

- ☐ To turn off editing in the layer mask, click on the layer's name or layer thumbnail (the rectangle with a miniature of your image). After you click, the paintbrush returns, indicating that any editing you do affects the layer, not the layer mask. You'll also notice that the black border disappears from the layer mask thumbnail, and appears around the layer thumbnail.

- ☐ To turn the layer mask back on, click on the layer mask thumbnail icon, the rectangle to the right of the image thumbnail (to the left of the Layer name). After you click, the paintbrush disappears and the Layer Mask Selected icon reappears instead of the paintbrush. The black border now returns to the layer mask thumbnail.

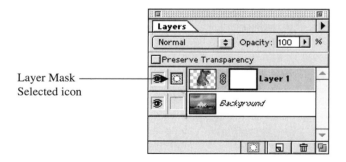

Layer Mask Selected icon

Between the layer's thumbnail and the mask thumbnail is a chain icon. The chain means that the layer and its mask are linked. If you move the layer, the mask moves with it; if you move the mask, the layer moves with it.

- ☐ If you wish to unlink the layer from its mask, simply click on the chain icon.

◻ To link the layer to its mask, click in the space between the layer thumbnail and the layer mask thumbnail icon. The link icon appears.

Next you'll have a chance to edit the layer mask by painting over it with the Paintbrush tool. Before continuing, make sure that the Layer Mask Selected icon appears next to the eye icon in the Layers palette. If it doesn't, select the mask by clicking on the layer thumbnail mask icon (to the right of the layer icon, on the left side of the layer name).

 NOTE: *If you did not create a layer mask, place an image on a layer on screen above the background or another layer. Then choose Layer | Add Layer Mask | Reveal All.*

As you complete the following steps, you won't actually be changing pixels in the target layer, even though it appears that they are changing. When the layer mask thumbnail is selected, Photoshop shows you how your image appears through the layer mask that you are editing.

 TIP: *If you wish to view or edit the layer mask as it appears in its channel, OPTION-click (Windows users: ALT-click) on the layer mask thumbnail. To return the layers into view, OPTION-click (Windows users: ALT-click) again. If you wish to view or edit the mask in Quick Mask mode, press SHIFT-OPTION (Windows users: SHIFT-ALT) and click on the layer mask thumbnail icon.*

Creating Special Effects by Editing the Layer Mask

Before you begin editing, open the Color palette on screen. Notice that your palette of painting colors has changed. In the Color palette, the color slider now indicates a range from black to white. When you edit the layer mask, you can paint only in black, white, or shades of gray. If you paint with black or darker colors, you will hide areas in the target layer (because you are adding to the mask); paint with white or lighter colors, and you reveal areas in the target layer (because you are subtracting from the mask). If you paint with gray, you create a blend between the two layers.

1. Set the foreground color to black.

16

NOTE: *Before you begin to edit the layer mask, make sure that the Layer Mask Selected icon appears next to the target layer's eye icon in the Layers palette. If you see a paintbrush icon instead, the layer mask is not selected. Select the layer mask by clicking on the layer mask thumbnail icon to the left of the layer name in the Layers palette. The paintbrush will be replaced by the Layer Mask Selected icon.*

2. Try using the Paintbrush tool with a soft-edged brush to paint over the image in the target layer. Make sure the Mode pop-up menu in the Paintbrush Options palette is set to Normal and Opacity is set to 100%. As you paint, the areas you paint over turn transparent. *Painting with black hides target layer image areas and reveals underlying layer image areas.*

REMEMBER: *When the layer mask thumbnail icon is selected, all painting and editing affects only the layer mask.*

3. Change the foreground color to white.

4. Try painting with white over the areas you just painted. Notice that the portions of the image that you wiped away gradually return (see Figure 16-5). *Painting with white in the layer mask reveals the target layer and*

FIGURE 16-5 Koala and Sydney Opera House blended together using a layer mask

hides the underlying layer. To vary the effect, try changing to different shades of gray in the Color palette and keep painting or change the opacity in the Options palette. As you paint, you'll see a blend between the target layer and the underlying layer. Painting with 50% gray blends equal parts of the target and underlying layer. Painting with darker shades of gray reveals more of the underlying layer; painting with lighter shades of gray reveals more of the target layer.

Next, try editing the layer mask by creating a gradient.

5. Now create a blending affect by applying a linear gradient. Start by choosing the Linear Gradient tool in the Toolbox. Press RETURN to open the Gradient Linear Options palette. In the palette, set the blending mode pop-up menu to Normal, Opacity to 100%, and the Gradient pop-up menu to Foreground and Background. Before you use the Gradient tool, set the foreground color to white and the background color to black. Position the mouse pointer about one inch from the left of the screen, then click and drag to the right of the screen. Now the target layer gradually appears on screen.

6. If you wish to experiment further with layer masks, try adding text to the mask by typing the text directly into the mask. Press OPTION (Windows users: ALT) while you click on the mask icon in the palette. This allows you to edit the grayscale mask directly on screen. Set the foreground color to white, and type text using a large point size on screen. After you've typed the text, press OPTION (Windows users: ALT) and click to remove the full-screen version of your mask. You'll now be able to see parts of the target layer through the type in the mask.

Creating a Blending Effect with a Filter

To create an interesting blending effect, load any image on screen. Then create a new layer. In this new layer apply the Filter | Render | Clouds command (make sure the foreground color is blue and the background color is white before you apply the filter). Next, activate the layer in which you have your image. Then add a layer mask to the image, by choosing Layer | Add Layer Mask | Reveal All. (Note that if your image is on a layer callout Background, you can't add a layer mask to it; you need to double-click on it to rename it.) Now press OPTION (Windows users: ALT) and click on the layer mask in the Layers palette to place the grayscale mask on screen. Apply a gradient, then apply the Mosaic Tiles filter

(Filter | Texture | Mosaic Tiles) to the mask (or use another texture filter). To increase the depth of the texture, apply the Filter | Stylize | Emboss filter. Next press OPTION (Windows users: ALT) and click on the layer mask again to return the RGB image to the screen. You'll now see your images through the mosaic and emboss in the mask. At this point you may want to do some color correcting to the RGB image so that you can better see the image and the effect; if so, try using one of the Image | Adjust commands. (For more information on using the Image | Adjustment commands, turn to Chapter 18.) This is how we created Figure 16-6. The building is in one layer, clouds are in another, and the layer mask was created from a gradient and the Mosaic Tiles and Emboss filters.

NOTE: *If you wish to edit the layer mask in the mask channel, open the Channels palette on screen. Click on the eye column to the left of the mask channel. The red overlay (discussed in Chapter 14) appears. You can now use the painting tools to edit the mask by adding to and subtracting from the overlay. When you're done editing, click on the eye column in the Channels palette again to make the overlay disappear.*

FIGURE 16-6   Example of Mosaic Tiles and Emboss filters applied to a layer mask

TIP: *You can temporarily hide the layer mask if you wish to view the image without the effects of the mask. To turn off the layer temporarily, choose Layer | Disable Layer mask, or press and hold SHIFT while clicking on the layer mask thumbnail icon (the thumbnail appears to the left of the layer name). To view the mask again, choose Layer | Enable Layer Mask or SHIFT-click again on the layer mask thumbnail icon.*

Applying or Removing a Layer Mask

Once you've completed editing the mask, you can decide whether to apply the layer mask, save your image with the mask, or discard the mask.

Applying the layer mask removes the mask from the Layers palette and applies the visual effects to the actual pixels in the target layer. Here are the steps:

1. Select the layer mask thumbnail in the Layers palette.

2. Choose Remove Layer Mask from the Layer menu, or click on the Trash icon in the Layers palette. You can also drag the layer mask thumbnail icon into the trash.

3. An alert appears, asking: "Apply mask to layer before removing?" The alert allows you to Apply, Discard, or Cancel. If you choose Apply, the layer mask will be applied to your image. If you choose Discard, the layer mask will not be applied to your image. If you choose Cancel, the Remove Layer Mask command will be ignored. To apply the layer mask, choose Apply. The target layer on screen is now updated to reflect the changes you made to the layer mask.

16

After you've applied the layer mask, the layer mask thumbnail disappears in the Layers palette. Any image editing you do now in the target layer only affects that layer.

Layer Mask Tips and Tricks

If you'd like to experiment more with layer masks, try dragging another image into your file and creating a layer mask for it. After the new layer appears on screen, create a selection, and then create the mask out of the selection by choosing Layer | Add Layer Mask | Reveal Selection or Hide Selection. After the mask is created, edit it with the paintbrush or airbrush.

Here are a few shortcuts for creating and using layer masks and converting layer masks to selections.

- Click on the new layer mask thumbnail icon at the bottom of the Layers palette to create a layer mask that reveals the entire target layer. Paint with black or a shade of gray to reveal the underlying layer (as well as all underlying visible layers). Paint with white to hide the underlying layer.

- If you have a selection on screen, clicking on the new layer mask icon reveals the target layer in the selection; in all other areas you'll see the underlying layer.

- OPTION-click (Windows users: ALT-click) on the new layer mask icon at the bottom of the Layers palette to create a layer mask that hides the entire target layer (revealing the underlying layer). Paint with white or a light shade of gray to reveal the hidden parts of the target layer.

- If you have a selection on screen, OPTION-clicking (Windows users: ALT-clicking) on the new layer mask icon hides the target layer in the selected area but shows the underlying layer in the selected area.

- In the Channels palette you can duplicate a layer mask by clicking and dragging the layer mask thumbnail icon over the new mask icon.

- You can load a selection created from a layer mask using the Channel pop-up menu in the Load Selection dialog box (Select | Load Selection).

- To create a selection in the target layer from your layer mask, press CTRL (Windows users: click the right mouse button) and then click on the layer mask thumbnail. A pop-up menu appears allowing you to choose whether you want to create a new selection, add to one on screen, subtract, or create an intersection between the layer mask and a selection on screen. You can also use keyboard commands: If you wish to make a selection out of the layer mask, press COMMAND (Windows users: CTRL) and click on the layer mask thumbnail icon. To add a selection made from the layer mask to a

Photoshop 5 ▷ In Action

Artist: JW Burkey   **Client: Image Bank**

This image is a stock image JW created for the Image Bank. It also appeared on the cover of the July 1998 issue of *Professional Photography Magazine*.

To create this image, JW photographed and scanned a hand. He used Strata StudioPro to create the three dimensional number 1. Next, JW used Photoshop to composite the two elements together. JW imported the number 1 into the hand file. JW used Photoshop's Layer Mask feature to seamlessly blend the two elements. With the layer mask enabled, JW used the Airbrush tool and alternated between painting in black and white to show and hide more of the finger and the number 1. He continued to do this until he achieved the desired effect.

To create the transparency effect, he painted in the layer mask at an opacity of less 100% of black.

To create the glow in the image, JW inverted the photograph of the hand he had taken.

16

pre-existing selection in the target layer, press SHIFT-COMMAND (Windows users: SHIFT-CTRL) and then click on the layer mask thumbnail; to subtract the layer mask from a selection in the target layer, press COMMAND-OPTION (Windows users: CTRL-ALT). If you wish to create a selection from the intersection of a selection in the target layer and the layer mask, press COMMAND-OPTION-SHIFT (Windows users: CTRL-ALT-SHIFT) and click on the layer mask thumbnail in the Layers palette.

- To temporarily turn off the visual effects of the layer mask, press SHIFT and click on the layer mask thumbnail icon in the Layers palette. SHIFT-click again to see the mask effects.

- To see and edit the layer mask full screen, OPTION-click (Windows users: ALT-click) on the layer mask thumbnail icon in the Layers palette. Repeat the procedure to return your image to the screen.

- You can drag and drop a layer linked to a layer mask from one file to another.

When you're done experimenting with layer masks, use the File | Save a Copy command to flatten the image to conserve memory and rename the file, or use the Save As command to save the file with its layers under a new name.

Using Adjustment Layers

Using adjustment layers, you can color-correct and make tonal adjustments to your images through a mask. If you don't like the effects or need to change them, you can "undo" them or adjust them without changing the actual pixels in your image. When you start working with adjustment layers, you'll soon find yourself saving hours of time when you need to make tonal and color corrections to images. Adjustment layers are extremely valuable; fortunately, they're also very easy to create.

Using adjustment layers, you can apply Photoshop's color-correction commands—Curves, Levels, Brightness/Contrast, Color Balance, Hue/Saturation, Selective Color, Channel Mixer and Color Range—through a mask. (Curves, Levels, Color Balance, Hue/Saturation, Channel Mixer and Color Range are discussed in detail in Chapter 18). You can also create adjustment layers for effects that remap the pixels of layers: Invert, Threshold, and Posterize. When using any of the adjustment layer options, you see the effects on screen, through the adjustment layer. If you remove the adjustment layer, your image returns to its original state.

As you work, you can create one adjustment layer over another. For instance, you might create one adjustment layer that uses the Curves command to adjust an image's tonal effects. On top of that adjustment layer you might create another adjustment layer that changes an image's color balance. On top of that adjustment layer, you could create another one to change the hue and saturation of an image. After you print a proof, you could return to make changes to any adjustment layer.

 TIP: *Changes to an adjustment layer affect all of the layers beneath it. If you wish to make an adjustment layer affect specific layers, create a clipping group out of the Adjustment layer and the layers you want in the clipping group. As discussed earlier, to create a clipping group, OPTION-click (Windows users: ALT-click) on the line separating the two layers in the Layers palette.*

Creating and Editing Adjustment Layers

Before creating an adjustment layer, open an image on screen that you wish to edit or correct. If you wish to edit or color-correct a selection, make a selection on screen.

1. To create an adjustment layer, choose New from the Layer menu. In the New submenu, choose Adjustment layer. As a shortcut, you can press and hold COMMAND (Windows users: CTRL) while you click on the New Layer icon in the Layers palette.

2. After the Adjustment Layer dialog box opens, enter a name for the adjustment layer in the Name field.

3. In the Type pop-up menu, choose the type of adjustment you wish to make.

4. In the Adjustment Layer dialog box, change the mode or opacity if desired. Click OK.

5. The next dialog box that opens allows you to edit the image. The dialog box is the same one you would see if you had simply chosen Image | Adjust | Levels, or Image | Adjust | Curves, etc. After you make adjustments in the dialog box, click OK. The Layers palette adds the

16

adjustment layer to the Layers palette. In the palette, the name of the adjustment appears.

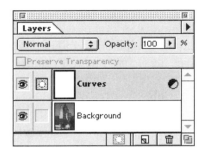

 TIP: *You can create an adjustment layer and not change any of the tonal or color commands in the dialog box: Just click OK to create a "dummy" adjustment. You can then use this layer to apply a blending mode to affect the layers below it. Multiply, Screen, Soft Light, Hard Light, Color Dodge, Color Burn, Difference, and Exclusion can alter your image. Change Opacity in the Layers palette to fine-tune the effect.*

If you want to reopen the adjustment layer to make further editing changes, double-click on the adjustment layer in the Layers palette (the layer with a partially filled circle in it). Alternatively, you can select the layer in the palette and choose Layer | Adjustment Options.

 TIP: *If you want to hide the effects of the adjustment layer in your image, simply click on the adjustment layer's eye icon in the Layers palette. To view the effects of the adjustment layer, click in the eye column again.*

Editing Adjustment Layer Masks

You can fine-tune the effects of an adjustment mask by painting in the mask layer with a painting tool. Painting in an adjustment layer edits the adjustment layer's mask, just as painting in a layer mask edits the layer mask. When you paint, only black, white, and shades of gray are available. If you paint with black, you remove the adjustment layer's effect. To reveal the full effect of the layer, paint with white. Painting with a shade of gray partially reveals or partially hides the effect.

To try out the effects of editing a layer adjustment mask, open an image on screen.

1. Create a new adjustment mask by choosing Layer | New | Adjustment Layer.

2. In the Layer dialog box, choose Hue/Saturation in the Type pop-up menu. When the pop-up menu opens, click Colorize. Adjust the Hue slider to change hues, and then click OK.

3. Now try editing the adjustment layer's mask. Open the Color palette. Note that only a grayscale slider is available because you are painting in a mask layer. Select a dark shade of gray, and then activate the Paintbrush or Airbrush tool and paint. As you paint, you gradually remove the Colorize effect. The darker the shade of gray, the more you paint away the effect. If you paint with a lighter shade of gray, you paint more of the Colorize effect into the image. As you work, take a look at the adjustment layer thumbnail icon, which shows you a miniature view of the mask you are editing.

4. Now paint the Colorize effect back on screen. Change your painting color to white, and paint the same area you painted over in step 3.

If you want to experiment more, try painting with different modes and creating a gradient in the adjustment layer.

Here are a few tips about editing and using the masks in adjustment layers:

- You can temporarily turn off the effects of an adjustment layer mask by pressing SHIFT and clicking on the adjustment layer thumbnail in the Layers palette. SHIFT-click again to return the adjustment layer effects to your image.

- You can create a selection out of the adjustment layer mask, and you can add, subtract, or intersect this selection with selections on screen. To access the selection options, CTRL-click on the adjustment layer thumbnail icon (Windows users: right-click on the adjustment layer icon).

- You can open the adjustment layer mask and edit the mask in its channel by OPTION-clicking (Windows users: ALT-clicking) on the adjustment layer thumbnail in the Layers palette. Repeat the procedure to return to your image.

☐ You can drag an adjustment layer from one file to another in order to apply the same effect to different files. Just click on the adjustment layer in the Layers palette and drag it into the other file.

☐ You can use the mask created in an adjustment layer in the Apply Image (Image | Apply Image) and Calculations (Image | Calculations) dialog boxes. Masks from adjustment layers can also be accessed in the Channels pop-up menu in the Load Selection dialog box (Select | Load Selection).

☐ If you applied an adjustment layer to a selection, you can move the adjustment layer area by clicking and dragging it with the Move tool.

 REMEMBER: *You can create one adjustment layer on top of another. And you can create clipping groups from adjustment layers and layers.*

Merging and Removing Adjustment Layers

If you're happy with the changes you made to your image with the adjustment layer, you can make the adjustments permanent by merging layers. To merge a layer with the layer below, choose Merge Down from the Layer menu, or choose Merge Down from the Layers palette. To merge the adjustment layer with all visible layers, choose Merge Visible from the Layer menu or from the Layers palette menu.

If you want to discard an adjustment layer, click on it and choose Layer | Delete Layer or click on the trash icon in the Layers palette, or drag the adjustment layer into the trash.

 NOTE: *For more information about merging and deleting layers, see Chapter 15.*

CHAPTER 17

Creating Layer Effects and Special Effects

Throughout this book you've experimented with a variety of special effects: drop shadows, mezzotints, filter effects, glowing text, images that appear through text, beveled buttons, and posterized and colorized images. This chapter takes you on a tour of a variety of special effects that you can quickly create using various Photoshop commands and techniques. You will see how layers, channels, blending modes, and filters can be combined to create striking textures and 3-D lighting effects that can be applied to both images and text. Also included is an overview of software that can help spice up your Photoshop work. Some of these products allow you to turn your images into digital goo; others, such as MetaCreations Painter 3-D, allow you to paint a Photoshop pattern or image over a 3-D object. Use this chapter to help inspire you to combine all of the features of Photoshop, and try out other digital imaging software.

Creating Layer Effects

Undoubtedly, the fastest way to generate eye-catching special effects is to use Photoshop's Layer Effects commands. Using layer effects, you can quickly create drop shadows, glows, and emboss and bevel effects. The Effects dialog box even includes a Pillow Emboss style which we used to create Figure 17-1 As you'll soon see, if you want to quickly create Web or multimedia buttons, your first stop should be Photoshop Layer Effects commands.

Applying Layer Effects Commands

Applying layer effects is quite easy: You don't need to step by step blur, emboss, duplicate, and offset layers. All you need to do is create a shape or text or image in a layer, then choose an effect from the Layer | Effects submenu. The effects include Drop Shadow, Inner Shadow, Outer Glow, Inner Glow, Bevel, and Emboss. Immediately, Photoshop opens the Effects dialog box, and previews the effect on screen (if the Preview checkbox is selected). The basis of most effects

FIGURE 17-1   Pillow emboss layer effect

are highlights and shadows applied using Photoshop's layer-blending modes. If you wish to alter or tweak an effect, you can change blending modes, opacity, and lighting colors. Some commands allow you to change lighting angles and blur options as well.

Although you might find that some 3rd party special effects filters provide more startling effects than Photoshop's layer effects, you may find that Photoshop's are easiest to edit and reapply. For instance, as soon as you create an effect, an "*f*" appears in the active layer, designating it as layer effect. If you need to edit the effect, you simply double-click on the "*f.*" After you apply an effect, you can easily add another one, by clicking the Next button in the Effects dialog box to move to another effect's dialog box. You simply click the Apply button and the next effect is added to your image.

Another great feature of layer effects: you can easily copy and paste the settings of one effect into another layer in the current document or another document. Once you paste the effect, it is applied to any object in the pasted layer, or any new object created in the layer.

Creating a Drop Shadow and Bevel

To get the most intriguing effects out of layer effects, you'll often find that two effects are better than one. The steps below show you how to apply both a drop shadow and an inner bevel to text or to an image. We used this technique to create Figure 17-2. To create the arrow, we used the Line Options palette's Arrows option (see Chapter 6 for more details about using the Line tool). To add the

FIGURE 17-2   Drop Shadow and Inner Bevel layer effects

17

speckled effect to the arrows, we applied Photoshop's Glass filter (Filter | Distort | Glass) with the Tiny Lens texture.

1. Use the Type tool to create type on screen, or create a new file with a transparent background. In the transparent layer create a shape, or use the Line tool to create an arrow.

2. To create a drop shadow, choose Layer | Effects | Drop Shadow. The Effects dialog box opens with the Preview check box selected. As long as the Preview check box is selected, a live preview of the effect appears on screen.

3. In the Effects dialog box, you can edit the drop shadow effect by changing the blending mode, opacity, and angle of the shadow. The Distance option controls how far the shadow is from the image on screen. The Intensity option controls the darkness of the shadow color. To change the color of the shadow, click on the black swatch next to the layer-blending mode. This opens the Color Picker, where you can pick a color for the shadow. Once you are satisfied with the look of the shadow, do *not* click OK.

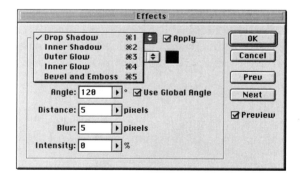

 TIP: *You can also drag the shadow on screen with the mouse to change distance and lighting angle settings.*

4. To add a bevel to the image, choose Bevel and Emboss from the Effects dialog box pop-up menu. You can also click the Next button to move to Bevel and Emboss one effect at a time.

5. In the Bevel and Emboss subdialog box, click Apply. To create the bevel effect, click the Inner Bevel option in the Style menu.

6. Adjust the Angle and Blur options to fine-tune the effect, then click OK

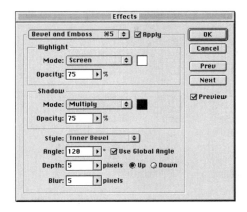

Creating Recessed Type

Creating a woodcut or recessed effect is quite easy using layer effects. To create the effect seen in Figure 17-3, we applied the Inner Shadow effect, then applied the Outer Bevel style from the Bevel and Emboss effects subdialog box.

Here are the steps we took:

1. Type text using the Type tool, or create an object in a layer.

2. Open the Inner Shadow layer effects by choosing Layer | Effects | Inner Shadow. At this point don't change the default settings, and do *not* click OK.

FIGURE 17-3   Inner Shadow and Outer Bevel effects applied

17

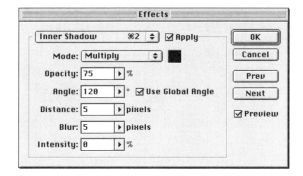

3. Choose Bevel and Emboss from the Effects pop-up menu, or click the Next button to move to the Bevel and Emboss effect.

4. In the Bevel and Emboss subdialog box, click the Apply option, then choose Outer Bevel from the Style pop-up menu. Once again, the default settings are a good way to start. Adjust any of the options to fine-tune the effect. If you wish to change the color of the shadow, click on the black swatch in the Bevel and Emboss dialog box and change colors when the Color Picker opens. Then return to the Inner Shadow dialog box, and change the shadow color there as well.

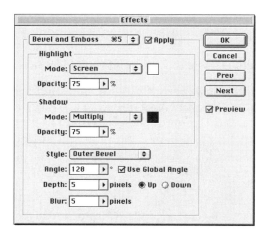

5. Click OK to execute the effect.

Setting Lighting Angles for Effects

The Drop Shadow, Inner Shadow, and Bevel and Emboss Layer Effects commands allow you to set a lighting angle. As you work, you can change the angle setting to apply a specified angle to a specified command. If you wish to apply a global angle to each command, select the Use Global Angle option in the dialog boxes. To set a new global angle, choose Layer | Effects | Global Angle. In the Set Global Angle dialog box, enter a global angle or click and drag on the slider to change the angle. If you keep the Preview check box selected, you'll see a live preview of how the angle change affects the image on screen.

Layer Effects Tips

As you work with layer effects, here are a few handy tips to remember:

- To edit a layer effect, double-click on the "*f*" in the Layers palette.

- If you need to repeat an effect, you can copy and paste the effect settings without copying and pasting the actual image. To copy a layer effect, select the layer where you created the effect. In the Layer | Effects submenu, choose Copy Effects. To paste the Effect into a layer, choose Layer | Effects | Paste Effects. To copy the effect into multiple layers, first link the layers by clicking on the paintbrush icon of an inactive layer (see Chapter 15 for more details). Choose Layer | Effects | Paste to Linked. If any previous effects existed, the pasted effects replace them.

- To remove all layer effects from a layer, choose Clear Effects from the Layer Effects submenu.

- If you apply more than one layer effect to a layer, you can remove individual effects by pressing OPTION (Windows users: ALT) and clicking on the name of the effect in the Layer | Effects submenu. (You'll see a check mark next to the effects that are being used.) Alternatively, you can open the Effects dialog box, and deselect the Apply option from the specific subdialog boxes.

- To convert a layer effect to standard Photoshop layers, select the layer containing the effect, then choose Create Layers from the Layer | Effects submenu. This breaks the effect into multiple layers where you can see

17

how the effect was created. You can then further edit the images in these layers to create more effects.

☐ You can further edit Layer effects by changing the blending mode in the Layers palette after creating a Layer effect.

When using Layer Effects dialog boxes, you can press the UP or DOWN ARROWS on the keyboard to increase or decrease percentage, degree, or pixel values after clicking in a field.

Photoshop Special Effects

In this section, you will see how you can create beveled effects, different backgrounds, and other interesting effects the old fashioned way—by manually creating multiple layers, applying filters, and using the Move tool. As you work through the examples in this chapter, don't be afraid to experiment. If you want to keep track of your experiments, record an Action. Later, you can play back the Action and edit it to perfect your effects.

Creating Embossed Type

To create the embossed effect shown in Figure 17-4, we used three different versions of the type in three different layers. We used the Type Mask tool and floated the text, then created a layer from the floating text. This process maintained the textured background within the borders of the text.

1. Start by creating a background. You can either use a digitized image or create your own background using the Clouds filter (Filter | Render | Clouds) or the Texturizer filter (Filter | Texture | Texturizer).

2. Once you have a background image on screen, create some type using the Type Mask tool. If you wish to move your type into the middle of the screen, click on your text with the Type tool and drag it into position.

 NOTE: *You can create the beveled effect on any kind of image. Instead of using the Type Mask tool, use a Selection tool to make a selection border around part of your image.*

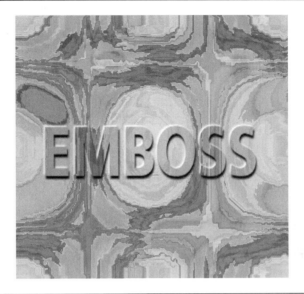

FIGURE 17-4   Embossed type effect

3. Now send the type selection into a layer by choosing Layer | New | Layer Via Copy. After the layer is created, double-click on Layer 1 and rename the layer **Type**. If desired, adjust the placement of the text with the Move tool.

4. Next, duplicate the Type layer two times by dragging the layer name (Type) in the Layers palette over the New Layer icon twice.

 NOTE: *Instead of duplicating the layer twice, you could duplicate it once and use the Emboss filter on the new layer to create a highlight and a shadow effect.*

5. Rename the two layers by double-clicking on them in the Layers palette. Name one Highlight and the other Shadow.

17

6. Move the Type layer in the Layers palette so that it is above the Highlight and Shadow layers. Then, use the Move tool to move the Highlight layer diagonally up and to the left.

7. Next, you will fill the nontransparent areas of the Highlight layer with white. First choose Edit | Fill. In the Fill dialog box, set the Fill pop-up menu to White, Opacity to 100%, and Mode to Normal. Very important: Make sure that the Preserve Transparency check box is selected. Click OK to apply the settings.

8. Using the Move tool, drag the Shadow layer diagonally down and to the right. Then fill it with black by choosing Edit | Fill. In the Fill dialog box, set the Fill pop-up menu to Black, Opacity to 100%, and Mode to Normal. Once again, make sure that the Preserve Transparency check box is selected. Click OK.

9. Using Figure 17-4 as a guide, adjust the different layers to achieve the desired effect.

10. If you want to soften the bevel effect, apply the Gaussian Blur filter to the Highlight and Shadow layers. You can also reduce the opacity of the layers. In addition, you may want to use either the Levels or Curves command on the Type layer to change the midtones, highlights, or shadows.

Creating Soft Beveled Text

The following steps create a soft beveled effect, as shown in Figure 17-5. Some of the techniques used in this example are similar to those used to create the text in image 37 of the color insert.

FIGURE 17-5   Soft beveled effect

1. Create your own background using the Clouds filter (Filter | Render | Clouds) or the Texturizer filter (Filter | Texture | Texturizer).

2. Set the foreground color to Black and the background color to White.

3. Activate the Type tool, then place some type on screen.

4. Create a selection out of the type by pressing COMMAND (Windows users: CTRL) and clicking on the type layer in the Layers palette.

5. Save the selection to an alpha channel by choosing Select | Save Selection.

6. Deselect the selection on screen, then reduce the opacity of the black type by clicking and dragging the Opacity slider in the Layers palette. Set the level to around 20%.

7. Create a new layer on screen, and fill the layer with 100% black.

8. Load the selection from the alpha channel into the black layer you just created by choosing Select | Load Selection. Choose the correct channel in the Channel pop-up menu. Fill the selection with 100% white by choosing Edit | Fill and choose White in the Use pop-up menu. Deselect the type.

9. Make sure that the Preserve Transparency check box is not selected in the Layers palette. Apply a Gaussian Blur to the type. For a low-resolution image, set the blur to 1.5. For a high-resolution image, set the blur to about 2.5.

10. Load the text selection from the alpha channel (Select | Load Selection). In the Load Selection dialog box, choose the correct channel in the Channel pop-up menu. Then use the Marquee Selection tool to offset the selection down and to the right slightly.

11. Invert the selection by choosing Select | Inverse.

12. Now subtract the inverted selection from the blurred type by pressing DELETE (Windows users: BACKSPACE). Deselect.

17

13. On screen, the type should already look soft. Apply the Emboss filter to enhance the effect (Filter | Stylize | Emboss). We used a low angle and low height in the dialog box. Experiment to get the best effect.

14. At this point you can choose to vary the effect with different blending modes. For instance, try Soft Light. Also try painting with the Airbrush using the Soft or Hard Light blending mode. You may also wish to adjust the placement of the text with the Move tool.

Creating Flying Type

This effect turns a text selection into a path so it can be distorted. After the text is distorted, filters are applied to create a blurred flying effect.

1. Create a background on screen using the Clouds or Texture filter.

2. Add type to the screen using the Type Mask tool.

3. Next, you will convert the type to a path so you can distort it. Open the Paths palette. In the Paths palette menu, choose Make Work Path (you can leave the Tolerance settings at the default number 2.0), or click on the Make Work Path icon.

4. Activate the Direct Selection tool (the arrow tool found with the Pen tools). Click and drag on anchor points to distort the type. You may wish to add anchor points (use the Pen+ tool), and drag it to enhance the distortion.

 NOTE: *You can also select path points and distort the path using Edit | Transform.*

5. After you've distorted the type, select the entire path by clicking and dragging over it with the Direct Selection tool. Next, change the path back into a selection by choosing Make Selection from the Paths palette menu, or click on the Selection button in the Paths palette. If you choose the Make Selection command, leave the Feather Radius option set to 0 pixels.

6. Save the selection to a channel by choosing Select | Save Selection. Deselect by pressing COMMAND-D (Windows users: CTRL-D).

7. Next, erase the path. Use the Direct Selection tool to click and drag over all of the letters, then press DELETE (Windows users: BACKSPACE).

8. Create a new layer by clicking on the New Layer icon in the Layers palette, then load the text selection back on screen by choosing Select | Load Selection. In the Load Selection dialog box, choose the correct channel in the Channel pop-up menu.

9. Fill the type in the new layer with a color.

10. Next deselect. Run the following filters (varying the effects creates different distortions): Filter | Blur | Gaussian Blur; Filter | Blur | Motion (set the angle to about 20 degrees); Filter | Stylize | Wind (set the direction to From the Left).

11. Create a new layer to hold another version of the text. Now you'll load another version of the text, to make the image more legible. Choose Select | Load Selection and choose the correct channel from the Channel pop-up menu. Then fill the selection with same color you chose in step 9.

 NOTE: *If you haven't created more selections, you can reselect the previous selection by choosing Select | Reselect.*

12. Choose Soft Light as the blending mode in the Layers palette. The combination of the blurred layer with the Soft Light unblurred layer allows you to see the flying effect and read your text.

Creating a Glass Effect

The following effect, shown in Figure 17-6, is a quick and simple way to simulate glass. The glass effect is caused by slightly blurred embossed text, combined with two layer blending modes: Hard Light and Difference.

1. Create a background texture on screen. We used the Clouds filter with the foreground color set to Blue and the background set to White. Then we

17

FIGURE 17-6   Glass effect

applied the Filter I Distort I Zigzag command to create the Pond ripple effect.

2. Use the Type tool to create white type on screen. Render the Type by choosing Layer I Type I Render Layer.

3. Apply the Gaussian Blur filter (Filter I Blur I Gaussian Blur) at a low setting. Next, apply the Emboss filter (Filter I Stylize I Emboss).

4. In the Layers palette, set the blending mode to Hard Light.

5. Duplicate the type layer by dragging it over the New Layer icon in the Layers palette.

6. Set the blending mode to Multiply. Then use the Move tool to offset the layer so you can fine-tune the 3-D effect.

7. If you wish to enhance the effect, lower the opacity in the Layers palette and create an Adjustment layer, then use the Hue/Saturation option to adjust the colors.

Creating Screened Type

In Figure 17-7, we combined some type with an image of a sailboat using layers. Using the Soft Light blending mode allowed the shimmering light of the background to show through the image. Here's how to duplicate the effect.

Open an image that includes reflective light. We used a sailboat image in which light reflects off the water. If you don't have an image, you might wish to use the Rockies file in the Samples folder (located in Photoshop's Goodies folder).

1. Create a new layer and fill it with white by choosing Edit | Fill. If Preserve Transparency is on in the Layers palette, turn it off. Then set the layer Opacity to 14%.

2. Set the foreground color to Black.

3. Activate the Type tool and add some type to the screen. We typed the word "sailing" and used the Vertical Type Tool dialog box to position the text vertically.

FIGURE 17-7   Effect created with layers and blending mode

17

REMEMBER: *When using the Vertical Type tool, you can use the Rotate option in the dialog box to turn the letters on their sides.*

4. Set the Layer Options blending mode to Soft Light to allow the shimmering background light to show through the text.

Creating Quick Image Blends with Selections

You can create interesting effects by making a selection out of one channel of an image. After you make the selection, simply copy and paste it into another.

If you are in an RGB file, pressing COMMAND-OPTION-1 (Windows users: CTRL-ALT-1) selects the red information, COMMAND-OPTION-2 (Windows users: CTRL-ALT-2) the green information, and COMMAND-OPTION-3 (Windows users: CTRL-ALT-3) the blue information. If you are in a Lab file, you can make a selection out of the Lightness channel by pressing COMMAND-OPTION-1 (Windows users: CTRL-ALT-1). If you are in a grayscale image, also press COMMAND-OPTION-1 (Windows users: CTRL-ALT-1). Here's how to create an interesting blend using this selection technique.

1. Open a file and convert it to Lab Color mode by selecting Image | Mode | Lab.

2. Press COMMAND-OPTION-1 (Windows users: CTRL-ALT-1) to select the Lightness channel.

3. Choose Edit | Copy (If your image contains layers, choose Edit | Copy Merged to copy all visible layers).

4. Close the image, and don't save the changes.

5. Open another file and choose Edit | Paste. The final image shows a blend between the two images. The first image will display different opacities depending upon the lightness values in the original image.

Creating Textured Backgrounds Using Filters and Layers

If you wish to create textured backgrounds, Photoshop's Filters and Layers palettes will help get you started.

Here's how to create a crumpled fabric effect:

1. With a new file on screen, pick a color for the foreground and another for the background. Next, apply the Difference Clouds filter (Filter | Render | Difference Clouds).

 NOTE: *The color on screen will be the color of your fabric. If you want to change the color, use an Adjustment layer.*

2. Now duplicate the layer you are on by dragging it over the New Layers icon in the Layers palette.

3. Apply the Filter | Sketch | Chrome filter to the duplicated layer.

4. Set the blending mode in the Layers palette to Hard Light.

 REMEMBER: *You can also use Adjustment layers, layer masks, and different blending modes and change layer opacity to create the background effect you want.*

Creating Ice Texture

Here's how to create a background texture that looks like glacial ice:

1. With a new file on screen, set the foreground color to a dark yellow and the background color to white. Next, choose the Difference Clouds filter.

2. In order to get a nice ice color, create an Adjustment layer and choose the Color Balance option. In the Color Balance dialog box, move the Cyan/Red slider to the left so that you reduce Cyan in the layer. When you are happy with the color, click OK.

3. Now duplicate the background layer by dragging it over the New Layers icon in the Layers palette.

4. Apply the Filter | Sketch | Bass Relief filter to the duplicated layer.

5. Next, set the blending mode in the Layers palette to Soft Light to blend the two layers together to create the ice effect.

17

Photoshop and 3-D Programs

If you are specifically interested in creating 3-D models and wrapping your Photoshop textures around them, or if you wish to integrate your Photoshop projects into 3-D images, check out Strata StudioPro, MetaCreations Infini-D, MetaCreations RayDream Designer, and Electric Image. You might also be interested in MetaCreations Detailer, which allows you to wrap textures around simple 3-D objects. Although Adobe Dimensions will not allow you to wrap a Photoshop texture around a 3-D object, it allows you to create 3-D objects, export them as Illustrator files, and then easily import them into Photoshop. In Figure 17-8, we imported the 3-D objects created in Dimensions into a Photoshop file and added a background created with the Clouds and Add Noise filters.

 NOTE: *If you'd like to create 3-D walkthrough effects, investigate Strata's Virtual 3D and Virtus Walkthrough.*

FIGURE 17-8 Effect created with Adobe Dimensions and Photoshop

Strata StudioPro

Using Strata StudioPro you can create 3-D models from scratch or import Adobe
Illustrator files and either extrude or revolve them to make them 3-D. After
creating a model, StudioPro allows you to apply numerous lighting and texture
effects to the 3-D objects or background. You can use Photoshop to create textures
for lights, objects, and backgrounds. (Mac users should save files in PICT format;
Windows users: BMP format). You can also use Photoshop to create transparency
effects in StudioPro, as seen in Figure 17-9. To create the image, a sphere was
created in StudioPro. Then three files were created in Photoshop: a green texture, a
file with one black dingbat character, and an inverted version of the black dingbat

FIGURE 17-9   Image created with Strata StudioPro and Photoshop textures

17

(this created a white dingbat with a black background). The black dingbat is shown below.

In StudioPro a new texture was created using the three Photoshop files.

 NOTE: *Strata StudioPro, like many other 3-D programs, also allows you to create 3-D animation.*

 TIP: *For more information on Strata StudioPro, see Strata's Web page at www.strata3d.com.*

MetaCreations Poser

If you've ever tried drawing a 3-D human figure on the computer, you'll appreciate MetaCreations Poser. Using Poser you can quickly create three-dimensional human forms and pose them. You can import the human forms into Photoshop or you can use a Photoshop texture to wrap around a Poser figure.

When you first load Poser, you're greeted by a fully modeled human figure. Using the Poser pop-up menus, you can choose poses from different libraries such as Action sets, Comic sets, and Sporting sets. Figure 17-10 shows an example of the Ideal Male Adult in the Alien Abduction pose from Poser's Sets library. Using the program's Move tool, you can spin the object in three-dimensional space. When you turn the character around, its back is fully modeled. Before you render the model into a 3-D image, you can choose a muscle texture or apply a texture created in another program.

Figure 17-11 shows an example of a Poser model with Photoshop's Craquelure texture applied to the 3-D model. After the 3-D model was rendered in Poser, it

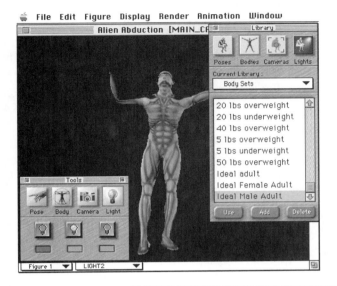

FIGURE 17-10   Poser allows you to quickly create 3-D human figures

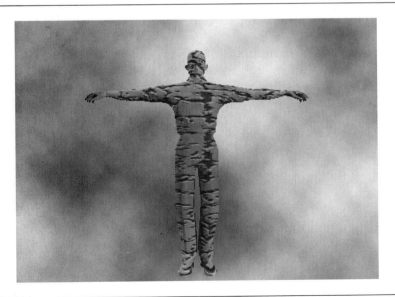

FIGURE 17-11   Photoshop's Craquelure texture applied to Poser image

17

was saved and loaded into Photoshop, where we applied the Clouds filter to the background. The procedure is so quick and simple, we've provided the steps:

1. Create a texture in Photoshop. We created a new blank file and applied two filters: Clouds (Filter | Render | Clouds) and Craquelure (Filter | Texture | Craquelure).

2. Save the file in PICT format (Windows users: BMP).

3. Open Poser. Choose a model, lighting, and pose. Apply the Photoshop file as a texture or bump map by choosing Render | Surface Material. (In the pop-up menus for Bump map and Texture, you can load PICT (for Mac users) and BMP (for Windows users) files.

4. Save the file in Poser in PICT or BMP format. When the file is saved, Poser automatically creates an alpha channel that masks the human figure from its background.

5. Open up the Poser image in Photoshop.

6. Load the selection in the alpha channel (which was created by Poser) by choosing Select | Load Selection.

7. Apply the Clouds filter. The filter is applied to the selection surrounding the human figure.

Painting Textures with MetaCreations Painter 3D

Painter 3D has garnered excellent reviews in the computer industry because it is one of the very few programs that allow you to actually paint a texture onto a 3-D model. In most 3-D programs, applying a Photoshop texture to a 3-D image can sometimes be a catch-as-catch-can process.

Painter 3D allows you to import Photoshop images and wrap them around 3-D objects or apply them to the background of a 3-D object. You can create a simple 3-D object in Painter 3D and wrap a Photoshop image around it, as seen in Figure 17-12. Painter 3D also allows you to import 3-D models created in DXF and

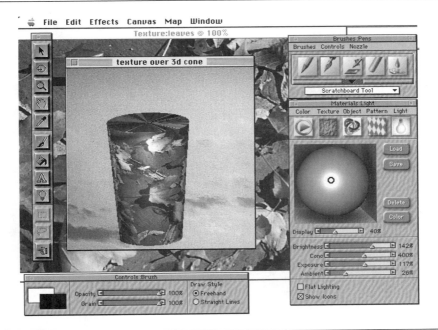

FIGURE 17-12   Photoshop texture wrapped around a 3-D object in MetaCreations
Painter 3D

3DMF formats (industry standard 3-D formats). Besides textures, Painter 3D
allows you to add surfaces such as bumps, glows, and reflections.

For Photoshop users, Painter 3D provides extra features: You can import layers
into Painter 3D. You can create textures in Painter 3D and export them into
different Photoshop layers.

Creating 3-D Terrains with MetaCreations Bryce

If you wish to quickly create striking 3-D landscapes or supernatural
extraterrestrial terrains, your best bet is to turn to MetaCreations Bryce. To see an
image created with Bryce, turn to image 20 in the color insert.

17

Using Bryce is quite easy. You can start by simply clicking on terrain, sphere, and cube objects in the Create palette. You can move and resize the terrain or any other shapes. To add atmosphere, you can click on Sky and Fog presets. To add material to your models, you can create bump maps of muddy stones, grass, or icy snow. The effects and possibilities of this program are enormous. You can even take a grayscale image from Photoshop, save it in PICT format, and turn the Photoshop image into a terrain. Figure 17-13 shows a 3-D image being created in the main document window of Bryce.

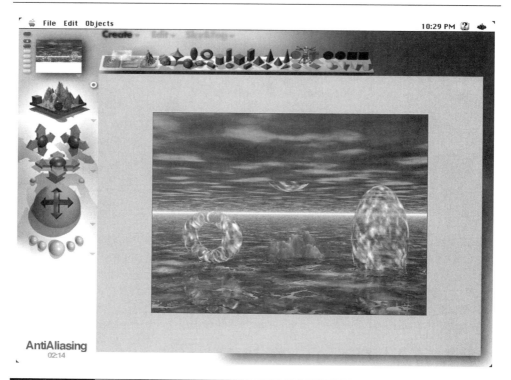

FIGURE 17-13   3-D image created in MetaCreations Bryce

Photoshop 5 In Action

Artist: Larry Hamill   **Client: Stock Image**

Artist/Photographer Larry Hamill created this monetary collage by photographing coins and bills from a variety of different countries. Larry then scanned the photos and used the Levels command to increase contrast. Then he applied the Unsharp Mask filter (Filter | Sharpen | Unsharp Mask), resized the image, and saved it in PICT format.

Next, Larry opened the PICT file in MetaCreations Bryce, where he created two planes with the currency. He also wrapped the currency texture file around a pyramid and sphere. When Larry completed his image editing work, he rendered the file in Bryce.

17

Photoshop and Morphing Programs

Several stand-alone software programs allow you to transform one image into another as if they were made of rubber. These include Morph by Gryphon Software, Digital Morph by MetaCreations, Elastic Reality by Avid Technology, and Kai's Power Goo by MetaCreations. Kai's Power Goo is one of the newest on the market.

MetaCreations Kai's Power Goo

Kai's Power Goo allows you to import one Photoshop image and distort it in various ways, as seen in Figure 17-14(a) and 17-14(b), or to import two Photoshop images and combine the two to make one image, as seen in Figure 17-15.

When you load the program, you have the option of entering either the Goo Room or the Fusion Room. If you choose to enter the Goo Room, you can distort an image by clicking on either the Grow/Shrink, Move, Smear, Nudge, Mirror Toggle, Smooth, Ungoo, Bulge, Twirl, Rotate, Stretch, Squeeze, Static, or Unwind

(a)   (b)

FIGURE 17-14   Image (a) before and (b) after gooing

FIGURE 17-15   Two images composited in MetaCreations Kai's Power Goo

buttons and dragging on your image. If you choose to enter the Fusion Room, you can combine two Photoshop images.

Once you have altered your Photoshop image, you can choose to save it as a Photoshop image. You can also save multiple versions to create an animation out a sequence of different digital goos.

Photoshop and 2-D Programs

Occasionally, you'll find that you'll need to use another 2-D program and Photoshop together to get the effect you want, as shown in Figure 17-16. For example, in Chapter 3 we used Adobe Illustrator to create type on a curve and then imported it into Photoshop and placed it over a photograph. In Chapter 7, we imported Illustrator designs and transformed them into patterns. In Chapter 13, we exported a Photoshop file with a clipping path to silhouette our image.

17

FIGURE 17-16   Image created with Adobe Illustrator and Photoshop

Other 2-D programs that are frequently used by Photoshop artists are MetaCreations Painter, MetaCreations Expression, and Macromedia Freehand.

MetaCreations Painter

If you find that Photoshop's Paint and Airbrush don't provide all of the painting tools you need, you should investigate MetaCreations Painter, one of the most powerful and versatile programs available both for Macs and Windows. If you create floaters (similar to layers) in Painter, the blending mode can be read by Photoshop.

Painter allows you to paint with charcoal, pastel, oil, watercolor brush, and many other effects. There's even a brush called the Image Hose, which allows you to paint with digital images. When you paint, numerous palettes and pop-up menus allow you to control brush size and bristle effects. Painter also lets you take your

Photoshop 5 ▶ In Action

Artist: Larry Hamill   Client: Ohio Insurance Magazine

Larry Hamill, an Ohio artist and photographer created this tiger mosaic for the cover of Ohio Insurance Magazine. To create the image, Larry started by photographing a tiger at a zoo. In Photoshop, he scanned the tiger, then used the Levels command to adjust the contrast. He also boosted the eyes by airbrushing the irises, making them bigger and sharper.

Next, Larry opened the file in MetaCreations Painter, where he created the mosaic effect. In Painter, Larry cloned the image, then chose Painter's Canvas | Make Mosaic command. He began painting the mosaic by hand using a WACOM tablet, because he feels that real mosaics have some imperfections.

After the mosaic was completed, Larry imported both the mosaic and the original file into separate Photoshop layers. Larry then used the Eraser tool to erase the mosaic around the eyes and mouth of the mosaic, so that the original eye and mouth (in a layer below) would show through.

17

paintings and turn them into digital movies. Figure 17-17 shows an image created with Painter. To create the image, we scanned a photograph of pears, then used Painter's tracing paper option and different brushes (Ink and Watercolor) to create the painting.

If you combine the power of Photoshop and Painter, you can create endless amounts of interesting effects. To see an example of a Painter image within a Photoshop project, see image 20 in the color insert.

 NOTE: *For more information about MetaCreations Painter, see MetaCreation's Web page at www.metacreations.com and our Web page at www2.infohouse.com/~addesign.*

MetaCreations Expression

MetaCreations Expression is a program that combines the features of drawing programs and paint programs into one package. When you paint in Expression, you paint with vector-based brushes. This means that your images are not resolution-dependent and that you can easily rescale your images without worrying about image resolution. Also, each image created is a separate object, so it is quite easy to move and rescale each one.

Expression opens files in Mac PICT, CorelDRAW 3, 4, 5, and 6, and Windows CGM and WMF formats. You can save in Illustrator, CGM, CorelDRAW Exchange, PICT, WMF, and EPS formats. Images can also be saved as bitmaps in Adobe Photoshop 2.5 format, which can be read by the current version of Photoshop. This means you can create drawings, save them, and load them directly in Photoshop.

FIGURE 17-17   Image created using MetaCreations Painter

Expression allows you to create brush strokes that can be stretched and manipulated. The brush strokes can be objects. As you click and drag, the object takes the shape of the brush stroke. These effects are shown in Figure 17-18. You can also create a gradient and apply hatching to the gradient. The hatching thickness follows the thickness of the gradient.

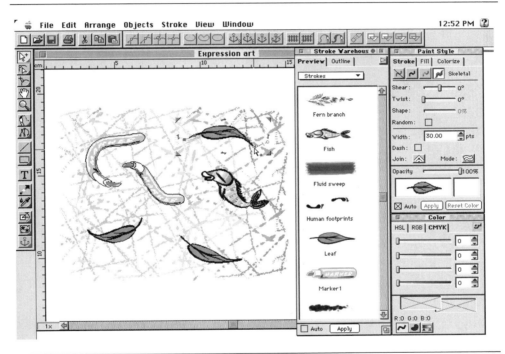

FIGURE 17-18   Objects painted with MetaCreations Expression

17

CHAPTER 18

Retouching and Color Correcting

A Photoshop image frequently undergoes numerous transformations before it is finally output to the printed page, to video, or to a transparency. No matter what the project, an essential and often unavoidable step is color correcting or retouching. These steps are critical to making the final design match the Photoshop artist's vision.

Color correcting involves changing an image's hue, saturation, shadows, midtones, and/or highlights so that the final output has the most appealing appearance possible. Color correcting is often required to compensate for loss of color quality as a result of digitization. The process of translating your Photoshop image to the printed page often makes color correction a necessity as well. For instance, paper stock, resolution, and impurity of printers' inks may force you to adjust your Photoshop image's colors to produce a suitable printed version. Color correcting is important in making sure that an image's colors conform to those of the original, and may in fact produce an improvement over the original. You may also need to *retouch* an image. In addition to removing imperfections in an image, retouching can even make it appear better than real life.

For example, nature often doesn't cooperate by providing the perfect weather, the perfect setting, or the perfect face. A photo of a beach resort taken on a damp, cloudy day will show the beach and water looking brown, the sky gray, the models pale, and the picnic food soggy and uninviting. Photoshop's color-correcting tools can turn the sky and water magnificent shades of blue, make the models tan, and turn the sand pearly white. When reality must take a back seat to your message or design goals you can summon the magic of retouching.

Retouching can remove little bits of litter and debris from the beach. It can smooth a few wrinkles or clear up a pair of bloodshot eyes in a tired face. Even the picnic food can be made to look more inviting. With the cloning option of Photoshop's Rubber Stamp, you can even toss more shrimp on the barbecue and add more strawberries to the shortcake.

Clearly, retouching and color correcting often go hand in hand. To get you started with the fundamentals of these operations, this chapter begins with a discussion of how to improve the tonal qualities of a grayscale image. After you learn how to correct a grayscale image, you'll see how to retouch faded, damaged old photographs. Next, you'll apply retouching techniques to eliminate wrinkles and blemishes in a face and learn how to improve outdoor scenes. The chapter concludes with the steps for color correcting images.

Since both retouching and color correcting require the use of many of the tools and techniques discussed throughout this book, you may wish to review some previous chapters. For color correcting, you should be familiar with the basics of color theory (Chapter 5). For advanced color-correction work, you will need to know how to select areas using the Pen tool (Chapter 13) or isolate an area in Quick Mask mode in order to save selections to channels so they can be reloaded later (Chapter 14). For retouching, you will need to know how to use the Eyedropper, Rubber Stamp, Pencil, Paintbrush, Airbrush, Smudge, Blur/Sharpen, and Dodge/Burn/Sponge tools (Chapters 6 and 7). You may also need to know how to use the Dust & Scratches filter (Chapter 10).

Both color correcting and retouching call for some artistic skills that require practice. The more experience you gain with Photoshop's color-correcting commands and retouching tools, the better your skills will be. You'll also be able to save yourself and/or your clients a substantial amount of money if you can correct images and retouch them on your desktop computer. The color examples you'll see in this chapter are from professional work created in Photoshop that in previous years would have required high-end computer workstations or dot etchers who would edit the individual halftone dots by hand on the film separation.

Before You Begin

This chapter won't just introduce you to new Photoshop commands; it will also show you how to obtain the best-quality results from your work. With this goal in mind, we must again emphasize the importance of *calibration* before you commence any color-correcting or retouching project. If your monitor is not calibrated, you may well find that your final image is quite different from the one you were working with on screen in Photoshop. Be sure to follow the steps in the section on monitor calibration and color management in Chapter 1.

Analyzing the Image

When you start with the best possible original and digitized image, you'll have less retouching and color-correcting work to do. If the original image is underexposed, overexposed, damaged, or defective in any way, the digitized version will reflect this. Thus, before digitizing, always try to obtain high-quality originals, since corrections are easier if problems are small. Of course, correcting a bad image may not be impossible, but it could involve completely re-creating parts or even most of the original image. You'll have to decide whether it's worth the time to perform major surgery.

18

After your image is digitized, look carefully for imperfections. Many digitized images may seem near perfect when viewed on screen at actual size, but flaws may become apparent when the images are magnified or printed. To properly analyze an image, zoom in to different areas and carefully check for noise or *posterization*, which is a lack of sufficient gray levels, and for whether the image is sharp and crisp or blurry and out of focus. Keep in mind that if an image looks flawed on screen, it may be best to redigitize it with better equipment or at a higher resolution before retouching and color correcting.

 NOTE: *Always view your images at 100%. If you view them at a different percentage, you may be viewing flaws that are produced by the screen.*

One of this book's authors, Adele Droblas Greenberg, worked on a project that involved correcting faded and scratched grayscale images for a Reader's Digest book. She digitized the images on a midrange scanner (Agfa Arcus) rather than on a low-end scanner. Images that had been test-scanned on a less sophisticated scanner often exhibited noise and black blotches in shadow areas. The blotches were caused by posterization. The images were eventually rescanned on the Agfa Arcus to ensure that no problems arose during the printing or tonal-correcting process.

 NOTE: *For more information on digitizing your images, review Chapter 8.*

Once you have the best possible digitized image, avoid the temptation to dive right in and start making changes. Take a few moments to identify your objectives. Decide carefully how you want to improve your image. Your goal is obviously to make the final image look as good as, or better than, the original; nevertheless, it should still look natural and believable.

After you've digitized your image, use the File | Save As or File | Save A Copy command to make a backup of your original digitized image. This is extremely important because you may find that color correcting or retouching removes details or colors that shouldn't have been replaced. If you need to start again from scratch, or to sample part of the original image so you can clone back the detail you've removed, you can always use the backup. While working with an image, try to save different snapshots in the History palette (discussed in Chapter 9). That way you'll always be able to return to a previous version. Another very powerful aid is adjustment layers (discussed in Chapter 16). Using adjustment layers, you can view tonal and color correcting without changing the actual pixels in your images.

TIP: *As you work with color correcting commands, you can use the Fade command to fade out (lower the opacity) of the last effect. After using one of the commands in the Image | Adjust submenu, choose Filter | Fade.*

Whether you are working on a color or grayscale image, start the correction process by taking readings of the image using the Info palette and the Eyedropper and Color Sampler tools. The Info palette assists you in reading gray and color values. When you move the Eyedropper or click the Color Sampler over various areas in the image, the Info palette reads out the exact color or gray values of the underlying pixels. Once you grow accustomed to reading them, you'll learn to rely on the Eyedropper readouts (rather than on your monitor) as a true guide to an image's tones and colors.

 NOTE: *Before you begin using the Eyedropper and Color Sampler tools to gauge grayscale and color adjustments, it's a good idea to set their sample size to a 3-by-3 pixel sample rather than Point sample, which evaluates only one pixel at a time. This way, one errant pixel won't unduly influence the Info palette readout. To reset the sample size, double-click on the Eyedropper in the Toolbox and choose 3-by-3 Average from the Sample Size pop-up menu in the Eyedropper Options palette. Next, select the Color Sampler tool and double-click on the tool to change the Sample Size in the Color Sampler Options palette.*

Using Adjustment Layers

As you work and color correct images, Photoshop gives you the power to return to your image and change settings again and again through adjustment layers. As discussed in Chapter 16, adjustment layers allow you to view your image corrections through a mask. You can edit the mask without affecting the underlying pixels. This means you can experiment with image corrections, print proofs, and then go back to make further adjustments until the image is as perfect as you can make it. If you need to change a previous adjustment, you make the change through the adjustment layer. Here's a brief review of the steps you need to take to create an adjustment layer.

1. If you wish to correct a selected area, create a selection on screen.

2. Choose Layer | New | Adjustment layer. Alternatively, you can COMMAND-click (Windows users: CTRL-click) on the new layer icon at the bottom of the Layers palette.

18

3. When the New Adjustment Layer dialog box opens, give the layer a name.

4. In the Type pop-up menu, choose the type of adjustment you wish to make.

5. Click OK.

6. When the adjustment dialog box appears (with Curves, Levels, etc.), change the settings to correct your image. Click OK to see the affect of the adjustment.

7. If you created a selection on screen, and need to move the area where the adjustment is applied, simply click and drag this area with the Move tool.

8. If you need to return and make further adjustments, simply double-click on the adjustment layer name in the Layers palette. When the dialog box opens, edit the adjustment layer by changing the dialog box settings.

 NOTE: *If you wish to change the name of an adjustment layer, double-click on the layer thumbnail in the Layers palette (rather than the layer name), then enter a name in the Name field.*

When using adjustment layers, remember that you can use one adjustment layer on top of another adjustment layer. When correcting images, it's often best to start with an adjustment layer that corrects the tones in your images (lightness, darkness, contrast). Then create another adjustment layer to correct color balance, and then correct adjustment layers to fine-tune specific colors in your image. It's also important to remember that you can use clipping groups to apply specific adjustments to specific layers. Finally, remember that you can use the Paintbrush and Airbrush tools to edit the mask in the adjustment layer. When you edit the mask, you can fine-tune the effects of the adjustment layer to specific image areas. For more information about editing the mask in adjustment layers, see the section entitled "Editing Adjustment Layer Masks" in Chapter 16.

Correcting a Grayscale Image

Before you start correcting a grayscale image, it's important to ensure that your settings are correct in the Photoshop Color Settings submenu. To view the Grayscale settings, choose File | Color Settings | Grayscale Setup. If you are correcting a grayscale image that will appear on the Web or in a slide or multimedia production, choose the RGB option. When you choose RGB, Photoshop does not compensate on screen for dot gain. Gamma settings from Photoshop's Gamma utility (discussed in Chapter 1) are used to fine-tune screen brightness and contrast.

If you are working on an image that will be printed, choose Black Ink in the Grayscale Settings dialog box. When you choose Black Ink, Photoshop adjusts the screen to compensate for dot gain that occurs when printing (it does not change the actual data saved in the file or how the file is output). The dot gain settings used are those specified in the CMYK Setup dialog box (File | Color Settings | CMYK Setup); these setting are discussed in Chapter 12. To see the effects of dot gain, when the dialog box is opened make sure that the Preview option in the CMYK Setup dialog box is selected.

 NOTE: *The dot gain setting in the CMYK Setup dialog box affects the conversion from RGB to Grayscale and RGB to CMYK Color. If you load a Grayscale or CMYK file, Photoshop does not use the dot gain settings to change the data saved to the file or change how the file is output, only how it is viewed on screen.*

If you wish to learn how to correct the tones of a grayscale image, open any grayscale image, or open the Skull file in Photoshop's Samples folder (in the Goodies folder).

When you make tonal corrections, you increase detail in the shadows, midtones, and highlights of an image. Figure 18-1(a) displays a digitized photograph that will be used to demonstrate the techniques involved in correcting a grayscale image. The photograph, taken in the late 1800s, is of Medora von Hoffman de Mores, a French nobleman who came to the Dakotas to raise cattle. The problems in the photograph are numerous: Details are faded, the image is too dark, and dirt and dust spots are sprinkled throughout. Ken Chaya, art editor of the Reader's Digest book *Discovering America's Past*, asked Adele Droblas Greenberg to retouch the photograph of Medora. Figure 18-1(b) shows the photograph after the gray tones were corrected and the image was retouched. The final image was converted to a sepia. (The finished retouched sepia is shown as image 4 in the color insert of this book.)

Figure 18-2 and Figure 18-3 show an image before and after retouching. The processes we used to retouch these images are virtually the same ones we used to retouch the image in Figure 18-1. Read on to learn how we retouched the image.

18

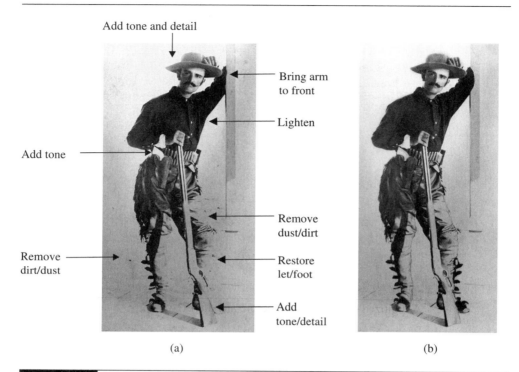

Add tone and detail

Bring arm to front

Lighten

Add tone

Remove dust/dirt

Restore let/foot

Remove dirt/dust

Add tone/detail

(a)   (b)

FIGURE 18-1 A digitized old photograph of Medora von Hoffman de Mores in the late 1800s (courtesy of the Library of Congress), before and after tonal adjustments and retouching

Using the Eyedropper and Info Palette to Take Readings

Once you have a grayscale image on screen and the Eyedropper tool is activated, open the Info palette. With the Eyedropper selected and the Info palette on screen, move the Eyedropper over different parts of your image. Notice that the K (black) value in the Info palette displays the percentage of black in the area touched by the Eyedropper. Your next step is to take readings of the darkest and lightest points in your image. It's important to do this because areas with less than 5% black tones will often print as white. Dot gain in printing may cause areas with over 95% black tones to look blotchy. If you are outputting to newsprint, dot gain increases, so try to keep the darkest shadow areas around 80% (as a general rule, 85% for uncoated paper and 0 % as your whitest white, 95% for coated paper). In Figure

FIGURE 18-2 A digitized old photograph before and after retouching

FIGURE 18-3 A digitized old photograph before and after retouching

18

18-4, you can see that the darkest shadow area reads 99% K (black). Soon you'll see how these dark areas were diminished.

 NOTE: *The paper, screen frequency, and printing press used all affect the quality of the final output. Consult your print shop if you have questions.*

Once you know the values of your darkest and lightest points, take a reading of the midtones. If the midtone areas are too light or too dark, you'll probably want to adjust these levels during the tonal-correction process.

 REMEMBER: *You can also use the Color Sampler tool to take up to 4 readings which are displayed in the Info Palette. After you click, Photoshop leaves a sample icon at the point at which you clicked. You can then move the sample by clicking and dragging it with the Color Sampler tool. To remove a sample icon from the screen, press OPTION (Windows users: ALT) and click on the sample location.*

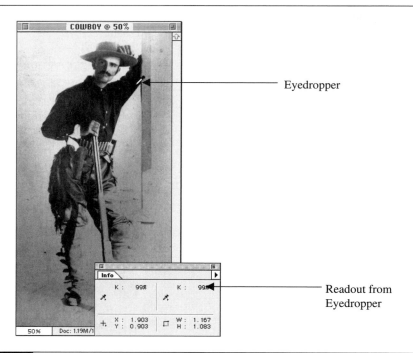

FIGURE 18-4   Reading the darkest areas of the image with the Eyedropper tool

Since it's impossible to take a reading of every pixel of your image by using the Info palette and the Eyedropper, it's often valuable to view a histogram of the image, as described next.

Using a Histogram to View the Tonal Range

When you open a grayscale image on screen, every pixel in the image can have a value between 0 (black) and 255 (white). Darker pixels have lower gray values; lighter pixels have higher values. A *histogram* plots the disbursement of the gray tones in an image and gives you a visual sense of an image's tonal range. To display a histogram of your image select Histogram from the Image menu. If part of your image is selected, the histogram charts only the selected area.

The Histogram dialog box graphs the number of pixels in relation to the tonal range of all possible gray values in an image. The horizontal (x) axis represents the possible gray values from 0 to 255. The vertical (y) axis represents the number of pixels for each tone/color. Beneath the x-axis is a gradient bar showing the actual gray levels from black to white. Dark image areas are graphed on the left of the graph, midtones in the middle, and light areas on the right. The height of each vertical line represents the number of pixels for each tone on the x-axis; the higher the line, the more pixels at that gray level are in the image.

If the histogram is weighted predominantly toward the right, your image is probably too light. This is often called a High Key image. If it is weighted toward the left, it's probably too dark. These are called Low Key images. A histogram that bulges in the middle is stuffed with too many midtone values and thus may lack contrast. In general, a well-balanced image will show pixels spread over the entire tonal range, with most in the midtone area. This is often called a Normal Key image.

The Histogram dialog box also displays the following precise statistics of your image:

- The mean value represents the average brightness.

- The Std (Standard) Deviation value represents the variance of the brightness values in the image.

- The Median value represents the middle brightness value in the image.

- The value in Pixels is the total number of pixels in the image or selection.

When you move the mouse within the graph, the pointer becomes a crosshair. When you move the crosshair over the histogram, the Level, Count, and Percentile values will change, as follows:

18

- Level represents the level of grays at the crosshair location on the graph: 0 is the darkest level (black) and 255 is the lightest level (white).

- Count represents the number of pixels at the crosshair location on the graph.

- Percentile is a percentage based on the crosshair's position on the x-axis, from 0% to 100%.

- Cache Value represents the cache value Photoshop is using when the Histogram is displayed. This value changes if the Use cache for histogram option is selected in the Image Cache section of the Preferences dialog box (File | Preferences | Image Cache). When this option is chosen in the Preferences dialog box, the Histogram is created from a sampling of pixels from the image, rather than all pixels. This results in a faster display.

  Move the crosshair from left to right over the histogram. As you do, the Level and Pixels values display brightness values and a pixel count. Next, click and drag in the middle of the histogram. A colored or black bar appears above the area over which you drag, and the Level readout displays the gray-level range.

 TIP: *As you make adjustments to your image during the correction process, you should return periodically to the histogram to get a sense of how your changes are affecting the tonal range.*

The histogram's crosshair readout in Figure 18-5 shows that at level 255 the pixel count is 0. Thus, there are no white pixels in the cowboy image, and no need to reduce the highlights in the image. Figure 18-6 shows the histogram after very dark values were eliminated to ensure better printing of shadow areas. Notice that the histogram's crosshair readout indicates that at level 0 (black), the pixel count is 0.

If you are viewing the histogram of the Skull file, notice that the image is weighted toward mid to dark pixelswith light pixels representing the skull.

When you think you are well acquainted with the tonal distribution in your image, you are ready to make tonal adjustments to that image.

 TIP: *If you wish to view a histogram when a spot color channel or alpha channel is selected in the Channels palette, press ALT (Windows users: OPTION) as you choose Image | Histogram.*

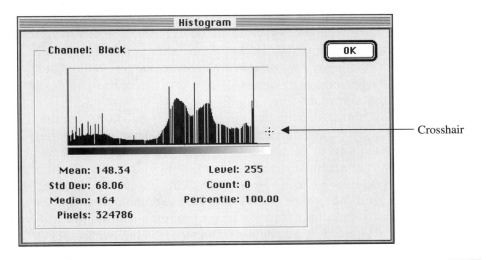

FIGURE 18-5 Histogram of cowboy image, before tonal adjustments

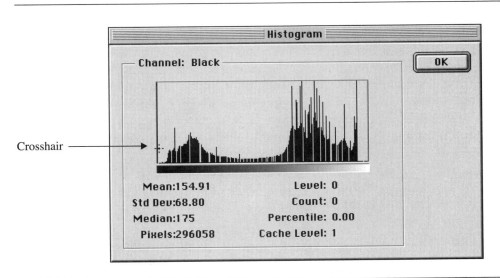

FIGURE 18-6 Histogram of cowboy image, after tonal adjustments

18

Adjusting a Grayscale Image

What do you do if the shadows in your image are over 95%, the highlights under 5%, and the midtones either too dark or too light? When you make tonal adjustments, you often must increase the brightness or contrast. Sometimes you need to expand the tonal range of an image—the range from the lightest point in the image to its darkest point.

To change the darkest, lightest, and midtone areas in an image, you can use either the Levels, Curves, and/or Variations commands in the Image | Adjust submenu. (You won't use the Image menu's Brightness/Contrast command because it has no controls for adjusting shadows, highlights, and midtones.) The command you choose for adjusting these elements in your image will often depend upon the image itself and on how comfortable you are with the available tools. Sometimes you may need more than one Image | Adjust command to complete the operation successfully. Practice using these commands before you attempt to correct images in a real project.

The next three sections tell you how to use the Image | Adjust | Variations, Levels, and Curves commands to improve tonal range by adjusting highlights, midtones, and shadows for grayscale images. All of these commands can also be used for correcting color images, as discussed later in this chapter.

Using the Variations Command

The Variations command provides a simple and quick way to visually adjust highlights, midtones, and shadows, using miniature image previews—undoubtedly the most intuitive way to adjust tones in an image. Unfortunately, this method does not provide exact adjustment for the color or grayscale values in image areas. Though you can make an image's highlights, midtones, or shadows lighter or darker by clicking on the thumbnail images, you cannot specify a precise value for lightness or darkness (as you can using the Levels or Curves commands).

 NOTE: *If the Variations command does not appear in the Image | Adjust submenu, the Variations plug-in has not been installed or was removed from the Filters folder in the Plug-ins.*

Open the Variations dialog box by selecting Variations in the Image | Adjust submenu. The original image, before adjustments, is displayed in the thumbnail labeled "Original" at the top of the dialog box. You make your adjustments to the shadows, midtones, and highlights by selecting the appropriate thumbnail. To make image areas lighter or darker, click on a thumbnail labeled "Lighter" or "Darker;" the effects are then displayed in the Current Pick thumbnail. Generally, if you darken shadows and lighten highlights, you add contrast to your image. If you lighten shadows and darken highlights, you decrease the contrast. If you want to revert to the original image, press and hold OPTION (Windows users: ALT) while you click on the Original thumbnail, or on the Reset button.

The Fine/Coarse slider allows you to specify the level of change in brightness that will occur when you click on a Shadows, Midtones, or Highlights thumbnail. When you drag the slider control to the right, toward Coarse, the difference between lighter and darker grows larger. When you drag the slider control to the left, toward Fine, the difference decreases. Each increment on the slider is double the previous incremental change.

The Show Clipping option, shown in Figure 18-7, turns grayscale image areas to a white color if making them lighter or darker pushes, or boosts, the area to pure black or pure white. (In Color images the Clipping option turns image areas a neon color.)

To try out the Variations command, move to the Shadows column and click on the Lighter thumbnail. This tells Photoshop to make the darkest parts of the image lighter. Notice how the thumbnails change to reveal the Current Pick. Try another variation: Move to the Highlights column and click on the Darker thumbnail; this will darken the lightest parts of the image. If you wish, try adjusting the Fine/Coarse slider and then examine the effects on various thumbnails.

 NOTE: *Unfortunately, when the Variations dialog box is open, you can't move the Eyedropper over your image to gauge the degree of change as you can when the Levels and Curves dialog boxes are used. Also note that if you don't see changes in your image, you probably have the Fine/Course slider set too fine.*

Be sure to cancel the adjustments you have made before exiting the dialog box if you don't want to change your image. To cancel your changes, click Cancel or press OPTION (Windows users: ALT) while you click on the Original thumbnail.

Using the Levels Command

With the Levels command, you reduce or increase shadows, midtones, and highlights by dragging sliders. It allows more precision than the Variations command because specific values can be entered in the Levels dialog box. Another

18

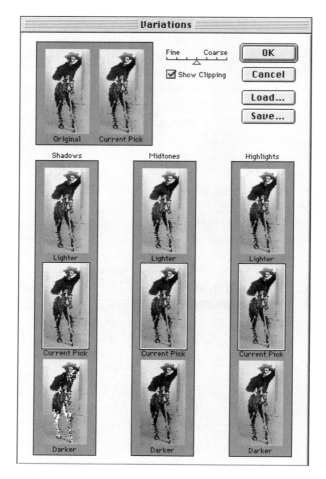

FIGURE 18-7 The Variations dialog box with the Show Clipping option enabled

advantage to using the Levels command is that it allows Eyedropper/Info palette readings to be taken while you make tonal adjustments. The Info palette displays these readings as "before" and "after" settings.

 REMEMBER: *You can use the Levels command in an adjustment Layer.*

Select Levels from the Image | Adjust submenu; the Levels dialog box displays a histogram of your image or selection. Directly beneath the histogram, along the bottom axis, is the Input Levels slider, which allows you to add contrast by adjusting shadows, midtones, and highlights. The white slider control on the right side primarily adjusts the image's highlight values. When you move the white slider control, corresponding values—0 (black) to 255 (white)—appear in the right-hand Input Levels field at the top of the dialog box.

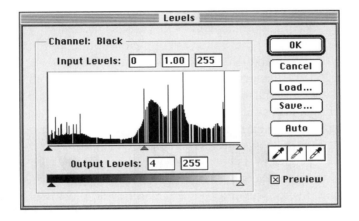

The black slider control on the left of the Input Levels slider primarily adjusts shadow values. Its corresponding values appear in the left-hand Input Levels field at the top of the dialog box. The values for shadows, like those for highlights, range from 0 (black) to 255 (white).

The middle slider control represents the midtones, or gamma, in the image or selection. The default gamma setting, which appears in the middle Input Levels field, is 1.00. Moving the middle slider control to the left raises the gamma value and primarily makes midtones lighter; moving it to the right primarily makes midtones darker. When the gamma is set at 1, it's always equidistant from the shadows and highlights.

When you change values for shadows, midtones, or highlights in the Levels dialog box, Photoshop remaps, or shuffles, the image's pixels accordingly. For instance, if you reset the white Input Levels slider control from 255 to 230, values that were 230 are remapped to 255; highlights are thus brightened, and the total number of highlight pixels is increased. The rest of the pixels in the image are reassigned to reflect the new white value. For instance, you'll also see the midtone lightened. The exact number of pixels and how they are remapped is based upon

18

how far you drag the slider control, so be aware that lightening the highlights can cause a rippling effect that partially lightens midtones and shadows.

When the preview check box in the Levels dialog box is selected, the image or selection changes according to the values in the Input Levels fields.

The Output Levels slider at the bottom of the dialog box reduces contrast by subtracting white or black from an image. Move the black slider control to the right and you will subtract shadow areas from your image, thereby lightening it. Move the white slider control to the left and you will subtract highlight areas, thus darkening your image. When the image is lightened or darkened, Photoshop remaps the pixels according to the new Output Levels values.

For instance, if you drag the white Output Levels control to the left, resetting it from 255 to 200, you remap the image so that 200 is the lightest value. Any pixels with a value of 255 are changed to have a value of 200, and all values are remapped accordingly to make the image darker. The same is true if you move the black control. If the black control is moved from 0 to 50, 50 becomes the darkest value in the image. Pixels that were 0 would now have a value of 50.

At this point, you may be somewhat confused about the difference between the Input Levels and Output Levels sliders. When you drag the left Output Levels slider control to the right, the values increase and the image lightens. But the values also increase when you drag the left Input Levels slider control to the right—yet the image darkens.

Here's the distinction between the two: Assume you change the left (black) Input Levels value to 40. This tells Photoshop to take all the shadow values between 40 and a lesser value and change them to 0 (black). Thus darker pixels are added and the image grows darker. The difference between the lightest and darkest pixels is increased; thus the contrast is increased. On the other hand, if you move the left (black) Output Levels slider control to the right to 40, you are telling Photoshop to take all pixels with values of 0 to 39 and shift them to be 40 and more. Thus darker pixels are subtracted and the image brightens, but the contrast is reduced. Also, remember that the Input Levels slider focuses on highlights, midtones, and shadows; the Output Levels slider adjusts the entire tonal range.

If the shadows in your image are too dark, try dragging the left Output Levels slider control to the right. Figure 18-8 illustrates how this was done to decrease the black areas in the cowboy image. After the blacks were decreased—with the Levels dialog box still open—the mouse pointer (which turns into an Eyedropper if CAPS LOCK is not depressed) was placed over the image to measure the degree of change. Notice that the Info palette in Figure 18-8 shows the before-and-after readouts: 99% dark areas were changed to 97%. To avoid lightening midtones and highlights, the shadow areas were not reduced any more in the Levels dialog box;

Eyedropper readouts, before and after adjustment

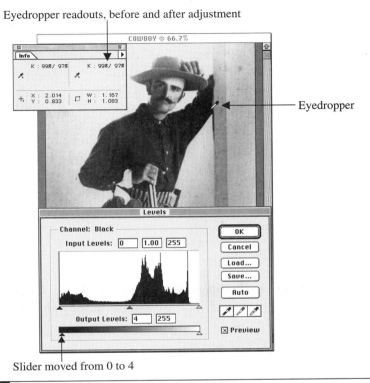

Eyedropper

Slider moved from 0 to 4

FIGURE 18-8 Using the Levels dialog box to lighten shadows

rather, for fine-tuning the shadows, the Curves dialog box was used, as you'll see in the next section. If the white areas in your image are too light, try dragging the white Output Levels control to the left.

If you've moved the sliders too much in your experimentation and you're unhappy with the results, you can reset the image by holding OPTION (Windows users: ALT) while you click on the Reset button in the Levels dialog box. (When you press OPTION or ALT, the Cancel button changes into a Reset button.)

 TIP: *If you achieve Levels settings that you think you will use frequently, you can keep them handy by clicking on the Save and Load buttons. You can even work on a low-resolution image, save the settings, and apply them to high-resolution files.*

18

You might have noticed the three Eyedropper icons and the Auto button in the Levels dialog box. The white and black Eyedroppers can be used to automatically expand an image's tonal range, which can become compressed during the digitization process. The Eyedroppers and the Auto button function similarly to the Auto Levels command in the Image | Adjust submenu. These will be discussed later in this chapter.

 TIP: *While using the Levels, Curves Hue/Saturation command, you set color Sample points by pressing SHIFT and clicking in your image. To move a sampler press SHIFT while you click and drag. To delete a sampler, press SHIFT-OPTION (Windows users: SHIFT-ALT) and click on a sampler.*

Next you will investigate Photoshop's most powerful and precise tool for adjusting colors and tones: the Curves dialog box.

Using the Curves Command

The Curves dialog box is probably the most versatile and powerful of Photoshop's tone- and color-correcting utilities. It allows the adjustment of any point on an image's tonal curve. By clicking on your image when the dialog box is open, you can also find where that portion of your image is plotted on the curve. When the cowboy image (Figure 18-1a) was corrected, the Curves dialog box was used to precisely pinpoint shadow areas that were above 95%.

 REMEMBER: *The Curves command can be used in an adjustment layer.*

Select Curves from the Image | Adjust submenu. In the Curves dialog box, you see a graph displaying a diagonal line. The x-axis (horizontal) on this graph represents an image's Input values; these are the brightness values in the image when the dialog box opens. The y-axis (vertical) represents the Output values, which will be the new values after the curve is changed. Perhaps it's easiest to think of Input values as the "before" values and Output values as the "after" values. When the dialog box first opens, since no values have been changed, all Input values equal all Output values. This produces a diagonal line because at each point on the graph, the x- and y-axis values are the same. The range of both Input and Output values is from 0% (white) to 100% (black).

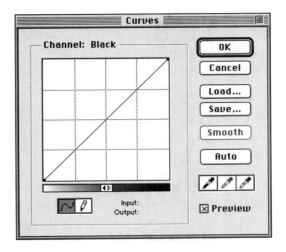

To see a readout of the points on the diagonal line, move the mouse pointer over the graph. The pointer will change to a crosshair. Move the crosshair anywhere on the diagonal line and you will see that both the Input and Output values are displayed at the bottom of the Curves dialog box. Notice that both values are the same. If the dialog box hasn't been changed from its default settings, the gradient bar (under the graph) depicting the gray values of the x-axis starts at white and gradually blends to black. If the gradient bar on your screen starts at black and blends to white, click on either one of the arrows in the middle of the bar, or click on the bar itself, to reset the curve to the default settings.

When white is the starting point on the x-axis, the bottom-left corner of the graph—with coordinates of 0%, 0%—plots the lightest possible part of an image. The upper-right corner—100%, 100%—represents the darkest possible area in an image. The slope of the line represents the tonal range, with its bottom depicting the image's shadows and its top the image's highlights. The middle of the slope represents the midtones. The coordinates between the midtones and the highlights are called the *quarter (1/4) tones.* The coordinates between the midtones and the shadows are called the *three-quarter (3/4) tones.*

Since the curve allows you to change an image's tonal range, highlights are adjusted by clicking and dragging on the bottom part of the diagonal line in the graph, shadows by clicking and dragging on the top part of the diagonal line, and midtones by clicking and dragging in the middle of the diagonal line.

If you click on the arrows in the gradient bar to reverse black and white endpoints, the tone curve is also reversed, causing shadows to be represented at the

18

bottom left of the graph and highlights at the top right. This also causes Input and Output levels to be displayed in brightness values from 0 (black) to 255 (white). You may prefer to work using percentage values, since the percentages of black correspond to the percentage values of halftone dots that make up a printed grayscale image.

The curve icon and the pencil icon at the bottom-left of the dialog box tell you what mode you are in. When the curve icon is active (the background of the icon is black) you are in curve mode; in this mode you adjust the diagonal line by setting *control points* on it and then dragging the point to move the line until it becomes a curve (you can also enter values in the Input and Output fields). When the pencil icon is active, you are in *arbitrary mode*; in this mode the pencil is used to draw new lines in the graph. The arbitrary mode is used primarily for creating special effects. The Preview check box allows you to preview changes made by the curve in the image behind the dialog box. If the Preview check box isn't selected, click on it now.

As stated earlier, the Curves dialog box is unique because it can pinpoint any area of an image along the curve's tonal range. When you position the mouse pointer over part of an image and click, a circle appears on the curve, displaying exactly where that image area is plotted. All image areas corresponding to that point on the curve are edited by adjusting the point where the white circle appears.

To see this powerful feature in action, move the mouse pointer outside the Curve dialog box and click anywhere in your image. Notice that the mouse pointer turns into the Eyedropper tool and the circle appears on the curve, representing the pixel's exact tonal location. (Note that when working with a CMYK image, this feature only works when viewing the curves of the individual color channels, not the CMYK composite.) Now click on any dark or shadow area of your image. The circle appears near the top of the curve. Examine the Input and Output values; they should reflect high numbers (75 to 100%). Now click on any highlight or bright area. The circle moves toward the bottom of the curve, and Input and Output values decrease to about 25% or less. Click on the gray or midtone areas of your image. Now the circle is in the middle of the curve, and the Input and Output values are near 50%.

 NOTE: *You can enlarge the Curve dialog box by clicking on the dialog box's Zoom box. This can make it easier to create intricate adjustments. Also note that OPTION-clicking (Windows users: ALT-clicking) in a white area of the curve makes the grid cells in the curve dialog box a quarter of their size.*

To help you better understand how to use the curve to adjust shadows, midtones, and highlights, assume you want to lighten the darkest areas of your image and darken the lightest areas. First you must determine where the darkest parts of your image lie on the curve. To do this, move the pointer to the darkest part of your image. The pointer will change to an Eyedropper. Now click the mouse. Immediately, you'll see a circle appear on the curve. Note the percentage in the Input/Output readout at the bottom of the dialog box. This is the percentage of black for the area you clicked on. Now try decreasing the percentage of black by clicking where the circle appeared and dragging down. As you drag, try to keep the Input percentage as close as possible to its original percentage, but make the Output percentage lower. As you drag, your image becomes lighter. Dragging the curve tells Photoshop to take the darkest pixels and remap them to make them lighter. This lightens the shadow areas. But because you are clicking and dragging a curve, and not just one individual point, other Input values besides the one represented by the control point now have new values. You can see this by examining the middle point of the curve; it's now lower. When you clicked and dragged on the shadow area of the curve, some of the midtone values came along for the ride. If you truly want to isolate the shadow area and keep other Input values from changing, click on the graph to establish control points to serve as anchors on the curve, as described next.

Before proceeding, note that the Input and Output fields became activated as you dragged the curve. To fine-tune your adjustments you can enter values into the Input and Output fields. For instance, you could set the input value to 98% and the Output value to 90% by typing in values rather than by clicking and dragging the mouse. This would remap pixels that were originally 98% gray to 90%.

 TIP: *Once you select the Input or Output field, you can increase or decrease a value by pressing the UP or DOWN ARROWS on your keyboard. This also works in most Photoshop dialog boxes and palettes.*

Suppose you wish to darken the highlights in your image, but you want to restrict the change from the midtones. Click on the brightest area of your image to see where this is plotted on the curve. To prevent areas other than the highlights from changing, set a control point. To set a control point in the midtone area, click about halfway along the curve. A small dot appears, indicating that a control point exists. Create another control point at the beginning of the highlight area. Now position the pointer on the bottom area of the diagonal, and then click and drag up. Notice how the curve bends as you drag the new control point while the other

18

control points serve as anchors. To prevent swaying in the middle of the curve, you can add more control points. If you need to eliminate a control point, click on the point and drag it off the curve, or COMMAND-click (Windows users: CTRL-click) on a point.

Figure 18-9 shows the Curves dialog box being used to lighten just the darkest shadows of the cowboy image. Look carefully and you'll see control points applied at each quadrant along the diagonal line, as well as one additional point in the shadow area. This point was dragged downwards to lighten the darkest

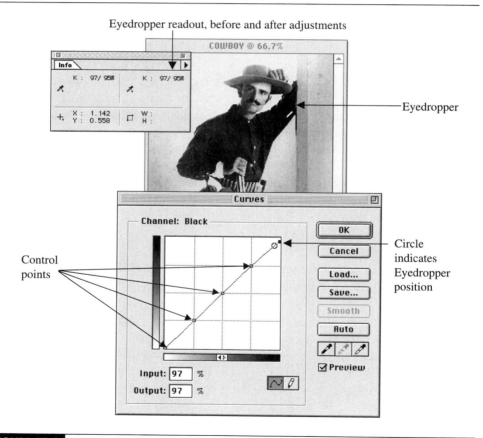

FIGURE 18-9   Using the Curves dialog box to lighten shadows

shadows. Afterward, the mouse pointer, which turns into an Eyedropper, was placed over the image to sample the change. The mouse was clicked to locate the adjusted image area on the curve, and a circle appeared in the graph to indicate the area that was clicked on. The Info palette confirmed that the image areas had been changed to the desired percentage, 95%.

Figure 18-10 illustrates how various points on the curve can be selected at one time. Multiple points were selected by pressing SHIFT, then clicking on the curve. (When you use this technique the control points turn black.) The selected points move in unison when they are dragged. In Figure 18-10, several points in the shadow area of the curve were selected, then dragged to lighten those areas. You can keep multiple control points locked in on the curve. By selecting multiple points Here are a few tips and shortcuts for using curves:

☐ To select control points, press SHIFT as you click on the curve.

☐ To de-select control points, press SHIFT and click on selected control points.

☐ Use the UP, DOWN, LEFT, RIGHT arrow keys to move selected points. To move in increments of 10, press Shift as you press the keyboard arrow keys.

To gain more of a feel for using the curves, try a few more tonal adjustments. After you adjust the curve, always examine the Info palette to see the before and after percentages. First, reset the curve by pressing OPTION (Windows users: ALT) and then clicking on the Reset button. Assume that you've already adjusted an image's highlights and shadows, yet the image is too dark. To lighten an image overall, set a control point in the middle of the curve and drag the curve downwards. If your image is too light, you can darken it by dragging in the opposite direction.

Reset the slope to the default settings again so that you can create a curve that will be used to bring out the contrast particularly in the highlight and shadow areas of images that are flat. This type of curve is called an *S curve*. To create it, drag the top part of the slope up to darken shadows; then drag the bottom of the

18

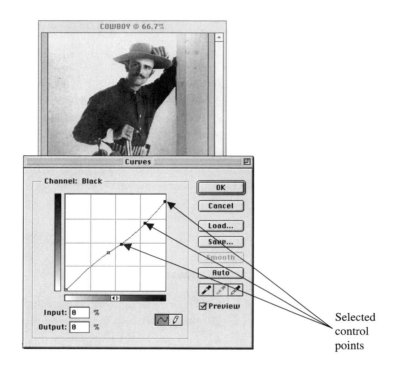

Selected
control
points

FIGURE 18-10   Selected control points moved to lighten shadows

---

slope down to lighten highlights. This creates the S-shaped curve shown in Figure 18-11.

 NOTE: *This same curve will increase contrast in a CMYK image.*

 REMEMBER: *The curve set in these examples uses percentages. Your dialog box settings may be set from 0-255 rather than 0-100%. If you are not using percentages, you should reverse the shape of the curves.*

With the S curve created, move the mouse pointer over your image and examine the Info palette. Notice the readout that shows the before-and-after brightness values.

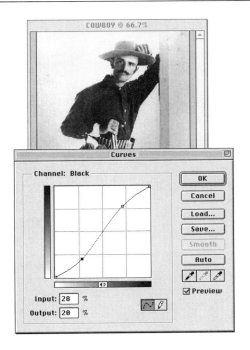

FIGURE 18-11   Creating an S curve to add contrast to an image

If you'd like, continue experimenting with the Curves dialog box, making adjustments to the highlights, midtones, and shadows in your image. Remember, if you find a setting for the curve that you will need later, save it by clicking on the Save button. A curve can be reloaded by clicking on the Load button.

  NOTE: *Saved curves can be used as Duotone curves and vice versa.*

  TIP: *You can simulate a duotone effect using adjustment layers and the Curves command. First load a grayscale image on screen. Convert the image to RGB or CMYK using the Image | Mode command. Next, create an adjustment layer, and set the type to Curves. In the Curves dialog box, choose a color channel. Then click and drag the curve to add color to the image. To alter the effect, change modes and/or opacity in the Layers palette.*

18

Using the Curves Arbitrary Mode to Create Special Effects

In both grayscale and color images, you can create special effects by clicking on the Curves dialog box's pencil icon and then dragging it over the graph to create either lines or curves. Before leaving the Curves dialog box, try using the pencil icon in the Arbitrary mode. To switch from the Curve mode to the Arbitrary mode, click on the pencil icon at the bottom of the Curves dialog box.

One effect you can create is to posterize (reduce the gray levels of) your image. Reset the curve to the default settings, then use the pencil to create some small lines cutting through the diagonal line, as shown in Figure 18-12. The more lines you create and the longer they are, the greater the posterizing effect will be.

To invert your image to create a negative, click on the top-left corner of the graph; then press and hold the SHIFT key while you click on the bottom-right corner of the graph. This produces a diagonal line from the top-left corner to the

FIGURE 18-12   Use the pencil to draw lines along the graph in the Curves dialog box to create a posterized effect

bottom-right corner, thus making all black areas white and all white areas black, as shown in Figure 18-13. Creating this slope produces the same effect as executing the Image | Adjust | Invert command, which is described in Chapter 8.

To create a *solarized* effect, which turns part of your image into a negative, use the pencil to change your graph to look like the one in Figure 18-14. To create this graph quickly, click on the top-left corner of the graph, then SHIFT-click in the center of the graph. SHIFT-click again on the top-right corner. The resulting image looks the same as if you had applied the Solarize filter from the Filter | Stylize submenu.

There are many other unusual color special effects you can create by using the pencil icon to adjust the graph in the Curves dialog box. For instance, you can use the pencil to create a few individual lines and then join them by clicking on the Smooth button.

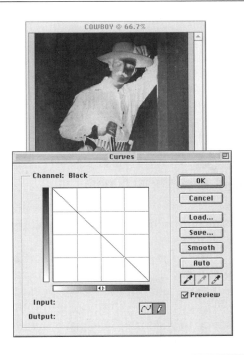

FIGURE 18-13   Reverse the slope to create a negative image

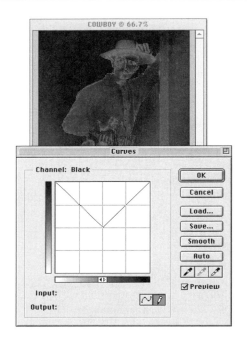

FIGURE 18-14   Use this graph to create a solarized effect

Using the Dodge and Burn Tools to Darken and Lighten Areas

If the areas in your image that need lightening or darkening are small and don't need much tonal adjustment, you might wish to use the Dodge and/or Burn tools for the task.

As discussed in Chapter 7, the Dodge and Burn tools are used to lighten and darken, respectively, portions of an image. Take a moment now, if you need to, and review the Dodge and Burn tools, which can also be used to make tonal corrections.

The Burn tool was used to add tone to the pistol in the cowboy's holster, shown in Figure 18-15. Here the Exposure value was raised to 25% to add more contrast to the lighter midtones.

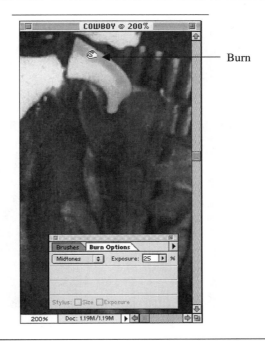

Burn

FIGURE 18-15   Using the Burn tool to darken the lighter midtones of the pistol handle

 TIP: *If you need to correct an image that doesn't have any tone in certain image areas, you may want to use the Rubber Stamp tool to clone in tone from other areas.*

 TIP: *After painting a stroke with the Dodge or Burn tool, you can lower the opacity of the last stroke in the Fade dialog box (Filter | Fade).*

Once you are happy with the shadows, midtones, and highlights of your image, you're ready to perform any retouching that might be necessary to clean up the image or make it better than the original. Before you begin retouching, you should develop a game plan. Decide which areas you will fix first, and which ones you will do last. To get started and give yourself a better feel for your image, it's often best to begin with the elements that will be easiest to fix, and then proceed to the more difficult ones. Once you have analyzed your image and decided how to proceed, you are ready to begin retouching.

18

Photoshop 5 In Action

Retouching Images

(a)

(b)

Artist: Nick Bowen

Artist, Nick Bowen, from Fleetwood, PA created this final retouched portrait from two different images.

Nick wanted the pose length and hands of figure (a) but it had some "nasty" gouges. Luckily, Nick had another negative (figure (b)) which was a slightly different pose with the face in better condition. So, Nick decided to clone the good parts of figure (b) over to figure (a).

Nick started cloning by establishing a sampling point in the corner of the left eye of figure (b) of the same location in the damaged eye of figure (b). Using a medium soft brush, he cloned all of the area within the glasses lens and some of the forehead to cover this damaged area in figure (a). The ear area of figure (b) did not match the head outline of figure (a), so he started the ear with another sampling point in figure (b) and picked the same ear area in figure (a). Now the head contour around the new ear was mismatched and his over brushing created background stucco textures from figure (b) that did not match figure (a).

Nick chose a sampling point on the wall of figure (b) and matched it to the same reference point on the wall of figure (a). Using a smaller, harder brush he cloned the wall right up to the edge of the head and smoothed out the contour of the head to make it look more natural.

Photoshop 5   In Action

(c)

To correct the exposure, Nick used the Levels commands to establish black and white point, keeping an eye mainly on the suit and face tonal scale. He lowered the midtones with an eye on the upper grays of the face. He planned to go back into the face and enhance any blacks that werr lightened too much.

At this point, he did the rest of the repair work on the gouges, scratches and dust spots. While cloning works best for larger areas of repair, he used the smudge tool set to "darken" for small white marks.

Nick has found that even a softish focused face can be made to seem sharper if the main details are enhanced. If the whole facial area is sharpened, the grain of the image gets too rough. So he goes over the eyes and other facial details with a small brush and the Dodge/Burn tool set to about 20%. He darkens under the eyelids and in the corners of the eyes, as well as inside the nostrils and ears and along the lip-line. He lightens the highlights of the lips, nose and eyelids, sometimes adding a reflection in the eye(s). The effect is of a sharper, more contrasted face, without doing these operations overall.

Finally, Nick toned down hot highlights on the surrounding wall by using a large, soft brush to Burn.

TIP: *As you work, it's often helpful to have two windows open, both containing the same image but set to different magnifications. This way you can zoom into a specific area, yet view the results of your work simultaneously at actual size. To open a duplicate window on screen, choose New Window from the View menu. Also, don't forget that when you zoom in, you can use the Toolbox's Pencil tool with the smallest, hard-edged brush to edit your image one pixel at a time.*

Now continue reading to see how the worn and faded cowboy photograph in Figure 18-1(a) was retouched.

Retouching Old Photographs

Old photographs often present significant challenges in retouching. The pictures are often marred by spots and scratches, as well as being torn and faded. For badly damaged photographs, be prepared to apply some painting and drawing skills to re-create entire sections in your digitized image.

Start by looking for any dust, dirt, scratches, or spots that appear in your image as a result of the digitizing process or due to a flawed original. Spots and scratches can usually be eliminated by using the Rubber Stamp's cloning option to clone background areas over the particles. If you do need to correct spots and scratches, experiment with different opacities and brushes until you achieve a soft and natural effect. Another method of removing dirt, dust, and scratches from an image is to use the Dust & Scratches filter. See Chapter 10 for more details.

In the cowboy image, the dirt spots in the original photograph and the dust spots introduced by the scanner were cloned away with the Rubber Stamp. After the spots were removed, the hat was the next item to be retouched, since it was the simplest part of the project. A sample from another part of the hat was duplicated over the faded area. The retouching continued from the hat down to the leg and foot—the most difficult area to correct.

Follow along with the techniques used to retouch the cowboy image, and try them in the Skull file in the Samples folder or in the image you are using. If you are working with the Skull file, you may wish to retouch the cracks on the front of the skull. If you have a scanner, you might wish to scan image 42 from the color insert to practice retouching.

To restore the cowboy's left arm, the Eyedropper, Airbrush, Paintbrush, and Rubber Stamp tools were all put to use. First the Eyedropper was activated to change the foreground color to match the gray tone of the arm. Then the Airbrush tool was selected and used to paint a light outline to serve as a boundary that would not be painted over. The boundary line helped Adele visualize the missing limb while she worked to re-create it.

The area where the limb was re-created was painted using the Rubber Stamp and the Paintbrush, with a medium-sized, soft-edged brush. Although a mask could have been used to isolate the arm, it wasn't necessary. If the area beyond the boundary line had been painted over, it could have been easily corrected by changing the foreground color to the correct color and painting with that color.

> **REMEMBER:** *If you want to be cautious, or if an area is particularly intricate, you should create a mask and then work in the unprotected (selected) area bordered by the mask. See Chapter 14.*

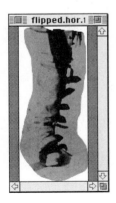

The Airbrush tool was also used to restore detail and tone to the shotgun. The edges of the shotgun's handle were restored with a small, hard-edged brush with Pressure set at 50%.

After the simpler retouching tasks were completed, all that remained was to completely restore the lower part of the left leg. This was more difficult to repair because it required that more details be created. Several steps were involved: First, the Airbrush tool was used to sketch the left leg, as shown in Figure 18-16. Again, the outline served as a boundary line to visualize the missing limb.

Once the left leg was sketched, the Lasso was used to select the lower-right leg. This selection was duplicated by pressing COMMAND-OPTION (Windows users: CTRL-ALT) and dragging on the

18

Photoshop 5 In Action

Before Retouching

Jacket was too light, lacking tone.

Notice the unnatural-looking white brush strokes.

Notice the white brush strokes and that the leg is barely noticeable.

Photograph courtesy of the Library of Congres

This picture of hobos taken in the early 1900s was needed for the Reader's Digest book *Discovering America's Past*. Years ago a retoucher began correcting the image traditionally, but stopped in the middle of the job. Notice the white brush strokes on the pants and jacket sleeve of the hobo on the right, and on the jacket sleeve of the hobo in the center. These were painted in by the retoucher. Adele was asked to finish the job so that the picture looked natural.

Photoshop 5 In Action

Tone was added
to jacket.

After Retouching

The white
brush strokes
were
removed

The white
brush strokes
are gone and
the leg is
more visibly
defined.

Retouched by: Adele Droblas Greenberg   **Client: Reader's Digest**
General Books

Before beginning to retouch the image, Adele used the Eyedropper tool to take readings of the image. Areas that were too dark (in the background) were lightened, and areas that were too light (the white brush strokes and the ground) were darkened using the Levels and Curves dialog boxes. In addition, she used both the Dodge and Burn tools to lighten and darken various areas in the image that needed to be corrected.

To add more tone to the jacket of the hobo on the left, Adele used the Rubber Stamp tool. Then she used the Airbrush tool with a soft-edged brush and varied the opacity setting and brush size to create a more natural-looking image. Before activating the Airbrush tool, Adele used the Eyedropper tool to change the foreground color to match the gray tones in the image.

To paint over the white brush strokes on the jacket sleeve and pants of the hobo on the right and on the jacket sleeve of the hobo in the center, Adele used the Airbrush and Rubber Stamp tools.

18

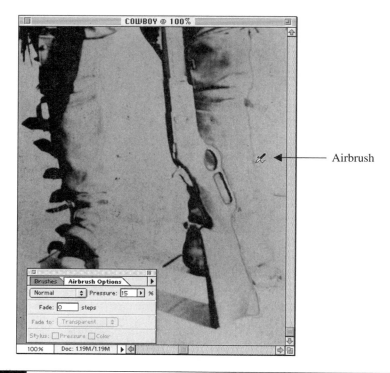

COWBOY @ 100%

Airbrush

Brushes Airbrush Options

Normal   Pressure: 15 %

Fade: 0 steps

Fade to: Transparent

Stylus: Pressure Color

100%   Doc: 1.19M/1.19M

FIGURE 18-16 Using the Airbrush to create an outline for the missing part of the left leg and foot

selection. The selection was flipped, using the Edit I Transform I Flip Horizontal command, and then the leg was cut and pasted into a new file. Remember, when you copy or cut an image and create a new file, the new file settings will be the same size as the cut or copied image.

After the right leg was duplicated, flipped, and placed in a new file, the flipped image and the original one were placed side by side so that the flipped leg could be cloned into the original file. In Figure 18-17, the crosshair indicates the sampled area; the Rubber Stamp pointer shows the target area where the cloning is being applied.

Before using the Rubber Stamp's clone option, Adele saved the file so she could revert to the last saved version if necessary. When working in Photoshop 5,

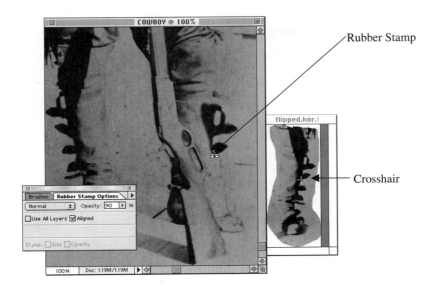

FIGURE 18-17   Retouching the lower-left leg by cloning the flipped lower-right leg

Adele often creates Snapshots in the History palette, so she can later paint in a Snapshot version of the file with the History brush, if needed.

After all the retouching was finished, the Unsharp Mask filter was applied to the image to sharpen it and bring out details. Chapter 10 describes how to use Photoshop's sharpening filters.

Removing Wrinkles or Freckles from Faces

Another common task of the retoucher is to eliminate facial wrinkles and otherwise touch up images of people—particularly for advertising projects. Using the Rubber Stamp's cloning feature and the Smudge and Airbrush tools, you can easily remove wrinkles and blemishes.

In the following illustration, the image on the left shows wrinkles surrounding a person's eye before retouching; on the right is the retouched image.

18

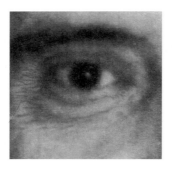

Eye with wrinkles
before retouching

Eye without wrinkles
after retouching

The trick to removing wrinkles, or any other facial blemish, is to apply a vibrant skin color over that area of the image. Dark skin crevices can easily be blended into lighter flesh tones with the help of the Smudge and Rubber Stamp tools.

Start by using the Zoom tool to magnify the target area. Next, use the Eyedropper to change the foreground color to the desired skin color. Then use the Smudge, Rubber Stamp, and Airbrush tools to blend skin tones together in the magnified area. For a gentler, softer effect, use a small-to-medium, soft-edged brush with Opacity in the Options palette set from 2% to 90%.

In our example, the smaller wrinkles were blended into the face using the Smudge tool. To remove the more pronounced lines, the Rubber Stamp's cloning option was used to clone the surrounding tones. The Airbrush tool was then applied to produce a more subtle blend.

If you want to try removing wrinkles and/or freckles from an image, Open up one of the files of people from the Stock Art folder on the Adobe Photoshop CD ROM

   TIP: *Also helpful when removing wrinkles: Try selecting with the Lasso tool, feathering the selection as needed, then using Image | Adjust | Curves to match the surrounding tones.*

Retouching Landscapes

Retouching not only restores old photographs and makes people look younger and more glamorous; it is also used to transform landscapes so that they are more attractive than their real-life originals.

For example, the art director of Reader's Digest General Books, Dave Trooper, wanted the scene for the cover of a proposed book, *Back Roads of America,* to look better than reality. The original image was a near-perfect photograph of a lovely New England scene. Figure 18-18 shows the image before retouching (also reproduced as image 1 in the color insert of this book).

Marring the beauty of the original image were the telephone poles and overhead wires running through the town. For the cover design, Dave wanted to put a map next to the photograph and to remove the road sign for Junction 14. The stop light warning sign, barely visible behind the trees, was also deemed a detraction that needed to be erased. Figure 18-19 shows the final retouched image (also reproduced as image 2 in the color insert of this book).

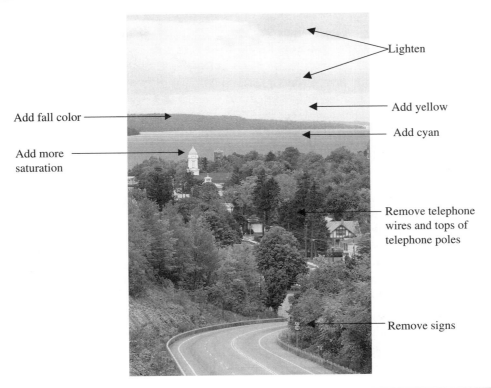

FIGURE 18-18   Digitized photograph of a New England scene (photograph courtesy of Gene Ahrens)

18

FIGURE 18-19   Proposed book cover after retouching and color correcting

The Junction 14 sign was the first item to be retouched. The Rubber Stamp's cloning option was used to remove it, with a medium, hard-edged brush rather than a soft-edged brush. A soft-edged brush would have made the cloned area look unnatural because the leaves on the trees were sharp and crisp, not soft and faded. To maintain a natural look, a variety of different leaves from several tree areas were sampled and cloned over the sign. During the cloning process, the Opacity in the Rubber Stamp Options palette was set to varying values between 65% to 85% to blend the leaves into the trees.

Crosshair

Rubber stamp

To eliminate the stop light warning sign, part of the road was cloned over the sign, and the trees were extended into the road. The Rubber Stamp's cloning feature and the Airbrush were both used to retouch the area. Some of the railing area was re-created with the Airbrush because the cloning tool couldn't create a perfect match between the old railing and the new railing.

Then the Rubber Stamp's cloning option was used again, this time to remove the unwanted wires. For a more natural effect, both a hard-edged and a medium soft-edged brush were used. Opacity was set to about 75% to blend the new leaves with the old leaves.

Rubber stamp

Crosshair

18

The next section provides an overview of how to undertake a color-correction project, and we will continue using the book cover project as an example. If you have a grayscale image on screen, close it now because you will be using a color file for the remainder of this chapter. If you wish to create another version of your file, use the File | Save As or Save a Copy command. Otherwise, close the file without saving it.

Color Correcting

Many of the same issues involved in grayscale tonal correcting also arise when you're *color* correcting. As with grayscale images, it may not be possible to transform an inferior color original or poorly scanned color picture into a perfect image. Exposure and lighting defects found in many grayscale images are also the most common problems in color images. But correcting color is much more complicated than correcting grays because every pixel has the potential of being any one of millions of possible colors, rather than just 256 levels of gray.

The number of colors in an image brings up an important display issue: If your image contains many more colors than your monitor can display, color correcting that image will be difficult. With a video card that displays only 256 colors, you won't be able to accurately judge the colors of continuous-tone images by their appearance on screen. So if you are serious about color correcting, you will want to invest in a 24-bit video card, which can display over 16 million colors.

Even if your system is calibrated and you are working in 24-bit color, you must still be wary of how colors look on your screen. As discussed in Chapter 5, differences between onscreen and printed colors are to be expected. The best way to judge colors is by using the Eyedropper tool and the Info palette. If you are working on color images that will be printed, it's crucial that CMYK colors are displayed in the Info palette. This readout will display exclamation points alongside the CMYK values of any colors that fall outside the CMYK printing gamut. Remember, the View | Gamut Warning command previews out-of-gamut colors. See Chapter 12 for more information.

Always check the Info palette when you're analyzing onscreen colors. For instance, if an apple on the screen looks rich, juicy, and crisp, but the Info palette reading lacks a high magenta percentage, this tells you that your monitor is not displaying the correct colors. For bright red, you should see CMYK values of approximately cyan 20%, magenta 100%, yellow 80%, and black 5%, or RGB values of red 161, green 0, and blue 49.

To see the Eyedropper and Info palette in action, load an RGB or CMYK file (if you don't already have a color image on screen). For an RGB file, you can load the Thai boat file from the Samples folder. For a CMYK file, load the CMYK Balloons file from the Samples folder.

If the Info palette is not displayed, open it now. If you do not see the RGB and CMYK percentages, click on the palette's pop-up menu in the Info palette. In the Info Options dialog box, make sure that the Mode pop-up menus for First Color and Second Color Readouts are set to RGB and CMYK.

You might wonder why you should keep the RGB values displayed in the Info palette if you are working on a CMYK color file. As discussed in Chapter 5, when you *add* cyan, magenta, or yellow to an image, you *subtract* its complement (red, green, or blue). When you *subtract* cyan, magenta, or yellow, you *add* the color's complement. With both color readouts showing in the Info palette, you'll be able to judge how much of a color or its complement is added or subtracted.

Take a look at the relationship between RGB and CMYK colors in your image. Move the mouse pointer over your image, and notice that any color showing a high RGB value displays a low percentage of its CMYK complement, and vice versa. For instance, a color with a high red value displays a low cyan percentage, and a color with a high cyan percentage displays a low red value. The relationship between RGB and CMYK colors is clearly depicted in a color wheel, as discussed in Chapter 5. Before you start color correcting, you may wish to get a color wheel (such as the one shown on the first page of the color insert of this book) and keep it handy. On a color wheel, each color resides between the two colors that create it. For instance, green is created by adding cyan and yellow. On the opposite side of each color is its complement; for example, opposite green on the color wheel is magenta.

Color-Correcting Tips

As you work on color-correction projects, here are a few suggestions to keep in mind:

☐ **Fashion** Work carefully with white and black fabric because it's difficult to maintain detail and definition in very dark and very light image areas. Be careful not to oversharpen, or fabric will not look real. Too high a percentage of yellow can make white look dull. Low cyan values will keep reds vibrant; low yellow values will keep blues vibrant. You might wish to obtain fabric samples so you can compare real colors and materials with screen colors.

18

☐   **People**   Strands of hair should be as sharply defined as possible. Teeth should be white rather than dull and yellow, though pure white teeth will look unreal. Consult your print shop concerning the effects of dot gain on flesh tones. Here are some CMYK and RGB values to use as starting points: (C=20%, M=45%, Y=50%, K=0%) or (R=203, G=154, B=125) should be a satisfactory reading for Caucasian flesh tones; for black flesh tones, aim for (C=40%, M=45%, Y=50%, K=30%) or (R=123, G=106, B=93).

☐   **Food**   It's often impossible to make all the food in a shot look delicious. For example, brilliant red tomatoes may look delicious, but meat that red will appear raw. Analyze or ask your client what should be the center of attention in the image. Foods that have bland, unrecognizable colors, such as cereals and soup, can be difficult to correct.

☐   **Outdoors**   Strengthen greens, blues, and reds with the Sponge tool. Use black to make greens darker, rather than magenta, which will lower saturation. Examine the grays in an image to make sure they are gray and aren't exhibiting color casts. When creating sky, the relationship between cyan and magenta will determine the shade of sky you are creating. For instance, by adding more and more magenta, you can go from bright blue to dark blue.

☐   **Snow scenes**   Snow should not be pure white because detail will be lost. Concentrate on adding detail to the highlights. Avoid losing detail in darker areas when enhancing whites.

RGB or CMYK?

A question that many Photoshop users wrestle with is whether to work in an RGB Color or a CMYK Color file. In making your decision, consider the following guidelines.

If you are outputting to slides or video, color correct in RGB because slides and video use RGB colors rather than CMYK. Note that if you are creating images for an onscreen presentation or the Web, you may be using only 256 RGB colors rather than thousands or millions of RGB colors. If this is the case, you may want to set your monitor to 256 colors instead of thousands or millions so that you actually work in the amount of colors you'll be using and can therefore color correct more accurately. Many new computers usually display either thousands or millions of colors.

For output to a commercial printing press, you may want to color correct in CMYK so you will be working with the same colors that your print shop uses for your job.

It is helpful to color correct in CMYK colors when you are adjusting blacks in your image. If need be, you can change only the blacks in a CMYK file by making adjustments to the black channel (with RGB colors, no black channel is available).

Since CMYK files are always larger than their RGB counterparts, you may wish to color correct in RGB mode, then output your image to either slide or chrome. You can give a prepress house the slide or chrome to be scanned and converted to CMYK.

 CAUTION: *If you are working with an RGB color file with the Info palette's CMYK reading displayed, be aware that the CMYK color equivalents reflect the settings in the CMYK Color Setup dialog box. For more information about this dialog box, see Chapter 12.*

If you are correcting an image that was digitized on a high-end scanner, chances are that the image was saved as a CMYK color file. If you scanned the image yourself on a low-range or midrange flatbed or slide scanner, the file will probably be digitized in RGB rather than CMYK. Digital and video cameras digitize images in RGB rather than CMYK color.

If you wish to work in CMYK mode, you can do so by converting your RGB color image to CMYK color. But do not convert to CMYK without first verifying the settings in the RGB Color and CMYK Color Setup dialog boxes. (As discussed in Chapter 1, most Photoshop users who are outputting for print, should change Photoshop's Default RGB Color space from sRGB to SMPTE-240M.) Before converting an image to CMYK, review Chapter 12. It's important to understand that if you convert to CMYK with improper calibration settings, you may be forced to return to your original RGB file. Once you have reset the calibration options to the correct settings, you'll need to reconvert to CMYK and start color correcting again from scratch.

If your system cannot handle large, high-resolution CMYK color files, another alternative is to work on a low-resolution color file and save your dialog box settings Then use the Load button in the Levels, Curves, Hue/Saturation, and Variations dialog boxes to apply the settings to the high-resolution version, and make final color adjustments as needed. Alternatively, you can create adjustment layers in the low-resolution files, and drag them from the Layers palette into the high-resolution files. Then make the final adjustments in the high-resolution files.

18

Procedures for Color Correcting

When you are ready to color correct an image, your first steps should be to correct the overall tonal range of the image, and then proceed to correct specific areas.

The New England scene in the Reader's Digest book cover, first discussed in the "Retouching Images" section of this chapter, will be used here to demonstrate the steps involved in color correcting.

The image was scanned by a prepress house on a high-end drum scanner to obtain the best digitization. In the scanning process, the image was converted to a CMYK file and saved in TIFF format. Since the file was over 30MB, it was saved on a removable hard disk cartridge so it could be delivered to the client.

After examining a Matchprint (a proof made from film separations) from the original scan, it was decided that the clouds should be lightened so that the book title would stand out as much as possible. The decision to color correct was made not because the original image or scan was flawed but because the design of the book cover required it. The art director also decided to enhance the color of the foliage in the town. Additionally, he felt that the colors of the water and church dome were a little light and that the saturation should be increased. Finally, he wanted a more autumn-like look to the hills across the bay.

Before color correcting, the colors in the Matchprint were compared to those on the CMYK color file on the monitor. After the two were analyzed, slight calibration changes were made in the CMYK Setup dialog box. (For more information on calibrating to a proof, see Chapter 19.)

Taking Readings with the Eyedropper and Info Palette

The next step in color correcting the New England image was to analyze the problem areas as well as the good areas using the Eyedropper and Info palette to carefully evaluate the colors.

Once you know the RGB values or CMYK percentages of the image areas, you can evaluate the colors that need to be added or taken out, and in what percentage. In the photograph for the proposed book cover, readings were taken of the clouds, water, hills across the bay, church dome, and foliage. The Eyedropper readings of some of the foliage showed a predominance of cyan, with little yellow and little magenta. These would obviously need to be boosted to improve the impression of autumn colors.

Using a Histogram to View the Tonal Range

After analyzing the areas that needed enhancement, the next step was to view the image's histogram. As explained earlier in this chapter, a histogram is useful for examining the tonal range of an image—from its brightest to its darkest points. In a color image, a histogram provides not only a visual impression of the brightness values of the entire image but of the separate channels as well.

The histogram of the New England image before color correcting revealed that the tonal range was fairly broad, with few shadow pixels.

To view a histogram of an RGB image, you can load the Rockies file from the Samples folder. Or you can load a CMYK file, the CMYK Balloons file from the Samples folder.

With the image file open on screen, choose Histogram from the Image menu. Click to open the Channel pop-up menu. If you are viewing a CMYK image, the Channel pop-up menu allows you to view brightness (luminosity) values of the CMYK composite and the color values of the individual Cyan, Magenta, Yellow, and Black channels. For an RGB image, you'll see a Luminosity channel for the composite brightness values and one for each of the Red, Green, and Blue channels.

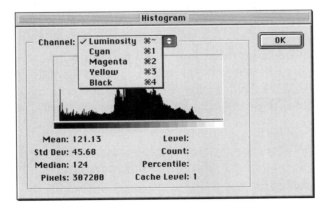

If you are viewing the Rockies file, click on the Channel pop-up menu in the Histogram dialog box and take a moment to view each channel to see the color values. You'll see that the Red and Green channels do not contain many dark or light pixels. Much of the dark and light values in the image are from pixels in the Blue channel. If you are viewing the Balloons file, you'll see that the image has no

18

100% black pixels, though it does have some pure white pixels. After you've read through the chapter, try creating an adjustment layer, and using the Curves command to make minor changes. Drag the lower-left corner of the luminosity up slightly. This will darken some of the lightest pixels and add a bit more contrast to the image.

Setting a White, Black, and Neutral Point

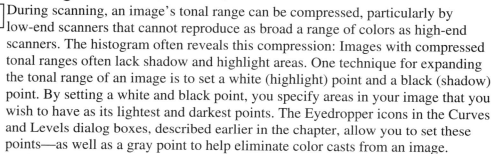During scanning, an image's tonal range can be compressed, particularly by low-end scanners that cannot reproduce as broad a range of colors as high-end scanners. The histogram often reveals this compression: Images with compressed tonal ranges often lack shadow and highlight areas. One technique for expanding the tonal range of an image is to set a white (highlight) point and a black (shadow) point. By setting a white and black point, you specify areas in your image that you wish to have as its lightest and darkest points. The Eyedropper icons in the Curves and Levels dialog boxes, described earlier in the chapter, allow you to set these points—as well as a gray point to help eliminate color casts from an image.

The tasks of eliminating color casts and setting white and black points are often handled during the digitization process. If your image was scanned on a high-end scanner and converted to CMYK (as the New England image was), you will probably not need to set a white, black, or gray point. On the other hand, when you work with RGB-digitized images or images converted from RGB to CMYK color, you should be aware of how setting these points can be helpful.

In Photoshop you can set the white and black points automatically, manually, or by setting levels in the Color Picker. Before you work through the following paragraphs describing these methods, load any color image on screen.

Setting the White and Black Points Automatically

The easiest way to set the white and black points is to have Photoshop do it automatically. If you set the white and black points automatically using Photoshop's default settings, the lightest areas in an image are remapped to white and the darkest areas to black. This often expands the tonal range, providing more contrast in images that are flat and dull.

With your color image on screen, open the Levels dialog box (choose Levels from the Image | Adjust submenu). To have Photoshop set the white and black points automatically, click on the Auto button. Immediately, you will see a change in your image, which is reflected in the histogram. In the histogram, you'll often see that the balance between shadows, midtones, and highlights is improved.

To ensure that Photoshop does not use only one tone when it sets the white and black points, a preset *clipping* percentage range is built in when Photoshop adjusts the image. This can prevent very light or very dark areas from overly influencing the tonal change when Photoshop sets the white and black points.

This clipping range can be changed in the Auto Range Options dialog box. To open the dialog box, press OPTION (Windows users: ALT) and click on the Auto button. Acceptable values for the Black Clip and White Clip fields are from 0% to 9.99%. The value entered is the percentage that Photoshop will ignore when it automatically sets the white and black points. For instance, if you enter 9% in the Black Clip field, Photoshop ignores the darkest 9% of your image when it redistributes pixel values after you click on the Auto button.

If you are unhappy with the results of Photoshop's automatic setting of the white and black points, you can return your image to its original settings. First press and hold down OPTION (Windows users: ALT); the Cancel button will change to a Reset button. Click Reset to return your image to its original settings, and then try the manual method of setting white and black points.

 NOTE: *The tonal range of an image can also be expanded by executing the Auto Levels command in the Image | Adjust submenu. This command produces the same effect as the Auto button in the Levels dialog box, and uses the clipping percentage set in the Auto Range Options dialog box.*

Manually Setting the White and Black Points with the Eyedroppers and Color Picker

If you are color correcting an RGB image that you will convert to CMYK or if you are correcting a CMYK color image, you may wish to gain more control when you set the white and black points to ensure you don't lose detail in highlight and shadow areas. From the Levels and Curves dialog boxes, you can use the Eyedroppers to access the Color Picker to set color levels for the white and black

18

points. If you choose this method, you'll first want to take color readings with the Eyedroppers to locate the lightest and darkest parts of your image. But don't click on the Eyedroppers in the dialog box yet.

First, locate the lightest and darkest parts of your image. Move the mouse pointer (which will change to an Eyedropper) over the lightest areas of your image, and examine the Info palette readouts as you go. Very light areas display high values of each RGB component. Generally, when evaluating an image to set the white point, you should search for highlight areas with detail, not pure white areas.

Next, locate the darkest part of your image and move the Eyedropper over it. Dark image areas display low values of each RGB component. When searching for the black point, look for shadow areas that are not pure black.

 NOTE: *With the Levels dialog box open, you can identify the lightest and darkest portions of an image by using the OPTION-drag (Windows users: ALT-drag) method described earlier in this chapter. Make sure that you deselect the Preview check box.*

Now that you've found the lightest and darkest points, you're ready to set a white and a black level. To set a value for the white level, double-click on the white Eyedropper in the Levels dialog box. The Color Picker dialog box opens; notice the words "Select white target color" at the top.

Let's assume you want to ensure that the lightest areas of your image are not pure white, that is, not created from the absence of ink on paper. Entering the Cyan values from 5 to 7 with Magenta and Yellow both set from 2 to 3 with Black (K) set to 0 should provide good results. Click OK to close the Color Picker.

Now move the Eyedropper tool over the lightest portion of your image that you identified earlier, and click the mouse. Photoshop automatically adjusts the tonal range in the entire image using your new white point—any pixels lighter than the white point you set become pure white.

The procedure for setting a target value for the black point is virtually identical to that for setting the white point, except you use the black Eyedropper. Double-click on the black Eyedropper. The Color Picker dialog box opens, and you'll see the words "Select black target color" at the top. Photoshop's default values are C 64%, M 54%, Y 53%, K 100%. (These values should produce good results if you are converting an RGB image to CMYK with Photoshop's default color settings.) Lowering the black value a few percentages can also produce satisfactory results. Click OK to close the Color Picker.

Now move the Eyedropper pointer over the darkest portion of your image that you identified earlier, and click the mouse. The tonal range is adjusted proportionally to your new black point—all pixel values that were darker than this value are now set to black.

If the results of setting the black and white points are not satisfactory, try setting different points in the image, or slightly adjusting the White and Black point levels in the Color Picker. Also, remember that not all images will improve when setting the white and black points, and that different images printed on different types of paper may require different black and white points.

 NOTE: *When you are setting the white and black points of a grayscale image, you may wish to set the white point at 5% in the K field (leave the CMY fields blank) and the black point at K=95% (again, leave the CMY fields blank).*

 NOTE: *If you set color levels for white and black points in the Color Picker dialog box, they will be used when you set the white and black points with the Auto button, or use the Auto Levels command in the Image | Adjust submenu.*

After setting the white and black points, you may wish to fine-tune the tonal balance in your image by lightening or darkening it. If so, you can use the Output Levels slider in the Levels dialog box to reduce the white and dark values of your image. As described earlier in this chapter, drag the right-hand Output Levels slider control to the left to reduce the brightness in image highlights, and drag the left-hand Output Levels slider control to the right to lighten shadow areas. You may also want to enhance the midtones; do this by clicking on the middle (gamma) Input Levels slider control. As discussed earlier in this chapter, dragging left lightens midtones, and dragging right darkens them.

When you're satisfied with the tonal adjustments in your image, click OK. Your next step is to eliminate any color casts that may exist.

Adjusting for Color Casts by Defining a Neutral Tone

Color casts can be the result of several factors. Photographs taken in fluorescent light often produce pink color casts. Outdoor images taken with indoor film might display a blue color cast. Indoor scenes shot with daylight film may yield a yellow color cast. Color casts can also be introduced inadvertently during the digitizing process.

Both the Curves and Levels dialog boxes include a gray Eyedropper icon that can be used to reduce color casts. Here are the steps: Click on the gray Eyedropper in the dialog box and move it over your image to the most neutral, or gray, area. Click, and any color cast should disappear or be diminished. Photoshop shifts the hue and saturation values to match neutral gray and continues to shift hue and saturation values to eliminate color casts. If you wish to specify the gray that Photoshop uses when it sets its neutral gray level, you can double-click on the gray Eyedropper. This opens the Color Picker dialog box in which you enter the desired values.

Creating Masks to Isolate Areas to be Color Corrected

After you have adjusted the basic tonal range in your image and eliminated any unwanted color casts, you can proceed to the tasks of fine-tuning problem areas in your image. To color correct specific areas of an image, you must select them first. As discussed in Chapters 13 and 14, it is often helpful to create masks of these areas in alpha channels or using the Pen tool, since you will likely need to select them again and again. (There are various ways to create and edit a mask in an alpha channel. For more information, see Chapter 14.)

NOTE: *If you wish, you can use one of the Pen tools to create a selection. First, create a path and then click on the Make Selection icon in the Paths palette. For more information about paths, see Chapter 13.*

In the New England image, five different masks were created in alpha channels: one for the church dome, one for the water, one for the hills across the bay, and two for different parts of the sky. These masks were created so that they could be reloaded in case more changes were needed. Because alpha channels increase file size, only one mask was included in the New England file at a given time. The masks that weren't being used were exported into a new file using the Select I Save Selection command. Masks of the foliage were created when needed using the Lasso tool (the Magnetic Lasso tool could also have been used) and the Quick Mask mode. The Select I Color Range command could also have been used. These masks weren't saved; they could easily be re-created, and they didn't need to be as precise as the others.

Using the Image | Adjust Commands to Color Correct

Once all of the preparation work has been accomplished, you are ready to begin selective color correction. The same Image | Adjust commands you used to correct grayscale images are also available for correcting color images—except that more options are available. For instance, the Variations command allows saturation to be added and subtracted. The Curves and Levels dialog boxes allow you to work with the individual RGB or CMYK channels.

In color correcting the New England image, a selection was generally loaded before a dialog box was opened. As mentioned earlier, Adele had previously duplicated channels into separate files in order to work more efficiently. When she needed to load the mask selection, she opened the file containing the alpha channels with the masks. Then she chose the Select | Load Selection command to copy the selection into the New England image file. She loaded the dome selection using the Select | Load Selection command and used the Variations command to color correct the dome.

Using the Variations Command

Often it's a good idea to begin correcting specific selections with the Variations command because it's the easiest and most intuitive color-correction tool to use. As described in the grayscale portion of this chapter, the Variations dialog box features thumbnails that preview how your image will be changed.

If you'd like to experiment with the Variations command, start by selecting an area of your color image, or load another selection you want to work with.

Choose Variations from the Image | Adjust submenu. When you are working with a color image, the Variations dialog box also allows you to adjust the saturation of a color, in addition to shadows, midtones, and highlights. Strong, full colors are saturated; pale colors are undersaturated; and neutral tones, such as black, white, and gray, contain no saturation. In most instances, fully colored, saturated images are preferable—but too much saturation can also make an image look unreal, gaudy, or blotchy, which can also cause printing problems.

In the New England image, the Variations command was used to add a touch of yellow to the midtones of the church dome. Figure 18-20 shows the church dome selected; in the Variations dialog box, the Midtones radio button was chosen. After the midtones were enhanced, the Saturation radio button was selected, and the More Saturation thumbnail was clicked to boost saturation. The changes transformed the dome from looking flat to looking full-bodied. The

18

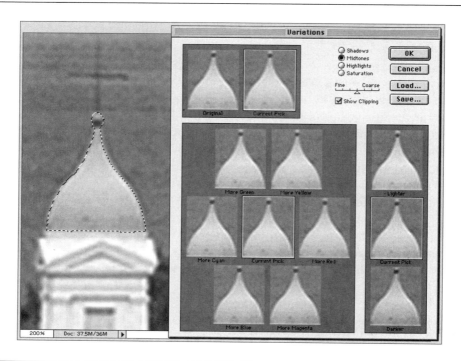

FIGURE 18-20 Using the Variations dialog box to adjust the saturation in the church's dome

Sponge tool with its Saturation option could have also been used. If you oversaturate, you can use the Sponge tool's Desaturate option.

 NOTE: *If you like how the variation command works you might wish to investigate Vivid Details Test Strip, a color correcting plug-in for Photoshop.*

Using the Color Balance Command

The next step in correcting the New England image was to add fall colors to the foliage in the town using the Color Balance command. This command allows you to mix colors together to improve the color balance in an image. If you have a sense of color theory, you will find the Color Balance dialog box to be very intuitive.

REMEMBER: *The Color Balance command can be used in an adjustment layer.*

Before the Color Balance dialog box was opened, Eyedropper/Info palette readings of various selections of the foliage were taken and written down. During the correcting process, the Lasso tool and the Quick Mask mode were used to isolate the background trees that would be corrected.

Choose Color Balance from the Image | Adjust submenu. In the Color Balance dialog box you will see radio buttons for selecting Shadows, Midtones, and Highlights, and three color sliders. The first slider ranges from Cyan (on the left) to Red (on the right). The second slider ranges from Magenta to Green, and the third ranges from Yellow to Blue. If you move a slider control to the right, you add that slider's RGB color to your image. Move the slider control to the left, and you add that slider's complement (a CMY color) to your image. By clicking and dragging the slider controls, you can move through the range of each RGB color and into the color range of its CMYK complement. RGB values go from 0 to 100, and CMYK colors are measured in negative numbers from 0 to −100.

Keeping the Preserve Luminosity check box selected helps ensure brightness values don't change while you adjust color balance.

The slider triangles turn black, gray, or white depending upon whether the Shadows, Midtones, or Highlights radio button is selected.

In the New England image, the various selections of trees were made to look more autumn-like by adjusting the Color Balance sliders and selecting the Shadows, Midtones, and Highlights radio buttons. Most selections required adding more magenta and yellow and decreasing cyan. As the colors were changed, the Eyedropper tool and Info palette were used to compare the old CMYK values to the new settings to ensure that they were the right color.

After the foliage was corrected, the hills selection was loaded to receive the same color correction. Red, magenta, and yellow were added to the shadows, midtones, and highlights. Besides providing fall color, the change also enhanced the detail in the hills. Figure 18-21 shows the selected hills and the red, magenta, and yellow values added to the midtones.

Using the Levels Command

The next step in color correcting the New England image was to add cyan to the water. To do this, the Image | Adjust | Levels command was used because it allows more precise control than the Variations command. The Levels dialog box, like the Curves dialog box, gives you access to individual color channels for color correcting.

18

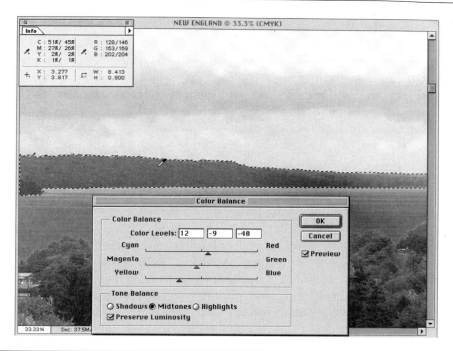

FIGURE 18-21   Using the Color Balance dialog box to add fall colors to the hills across the bay

To add more cyan to the water, the Cyan channel was selected from the Channel pop-up menu in the Levels dialog box. The right-hand Output Levels slider control was dragged to the left to 236, as shown in Figure 18-22. This took the lightest cyan value over 236 and remapped it to 236, making the cyan level darker; all values over 236 were remapped accordingly. (If the left-hand slider control had been dragged instead of the right, cyan would have been subtracted and red, cyan's complement, would have been added.) Notice that the Info palette in Figure 18-22 shows that when cyan was increased, the level of red displayed in the Info palette decreased.

If you'd like to try your hand at color correcting a CMYK file, begin by assuming you need to reduce cyan levels. Open the Levels dialog box and switch channels in the Channel pop-up menu to Cyan. Click and drag on the right Input Levels slider control to reduce cyan. Assume you need to color correct the reds of an RGB file. Select a red area on screen; then open the Levels dialog box and switch channels in the Channel pop-up menu to Red. Click and drag on the

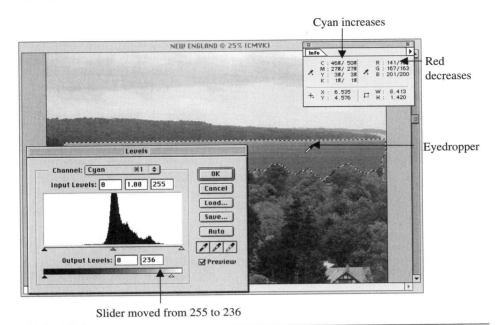

Slider moved from 255 to 236

FIGURE 18-22   Using the Levels dialog box to add more cyan to the water

left-hand Output Levels slider control. Notice that as you drag to the right, red is added. If you drag the right-hand Output Levels slider to the left, cyan is added. For each RGB and CMYK channel, the sliders move from one color to its complement. The left-hand Output Levels slider control is always an RGB color, and the right-hand Output Levels slider control is its CMYK complement. The left-hand Input Levels slider control is always a CMYK color and the right-hand Input Levels slider control is always an RGB color.

Using the Curves Command

The next step taken in the New England image was to lighten the clouds in the sky using the Image l Adjust l Curves command. As discussed earlier in this chapter, the Curves dialog box allows a specific area to be corrected precisely by pinpointing the area on the curve, and so it was the best tool to use to correct the clouds. Before the correcting process began, the cloud selections were loaded as needed with the Load Selection command.

18

Like the Levels dialog box, the Curves dialog box allows entry into channels for correcting. Unlike working in an RGB image, Photoshop, when color correcting CMYK images, only plots image points on the curve when you work in a channel other than the Composite channel. When working with a CMYK color file, if a CMYK channel is chosen in the Channel pop-up menu, dragging upwards on the curve adds the channel's color (when the gradient bar is set for light to dark); dragging downwards subtracts the color, adding its complement. If you click on the gradient bar so that it changes from dark to light, the directions for dragging the curve are reversed. When the gradient bar is set for light to dark, the Input and Output Levels are measured in CMYK percentages; otherwise, input/output is displayed in brightness values from 0 to 255. When you are working with an RGB color file, if a channel is chosen in the Channel pop-up menu (and the gradient bar is set for light to dark), dragging downwards on the curve will add the channel's color; drag up, and you add the channel's complement.

Since the easiest way to lighten the dark clouds in the New England image was to remove black from the selection, the Black channel was chosen in the Curves dialog box. Next, the Eyedropper was used to click on the middle of the dark area in the cloud selection. A circle appeared on the curve showing the precise point that represented the cloud's color. To lighten the image, the part of the curve where the circle appeared was dragged downwards and to the right. This lightened all areas in the same tonal range within the selection that corresponded to the curve value.

After the blacks were reduced in the cloud area, the Cyan channel was selected so that cyan could be reduced in the darkest parts of the light clouds. To reduce cyan and add a bit of red, the part of the curve representing only the darkest part of the cloud was dragged downwards. The Info palette in Figure 18-23 shows the change in the cyan (14% to 8%) and red (224 to 237) after the Eyedropper was clicked to resample the corrected area. When cyan was reduced, its complement, red, was added automatically. During the correction process, several points were selected, by SHIFT-clicking on the different points. After the points were selected, they could be dragged together as a group.

 TIP: *If you SHIFT-click in the Channels palette to select more than one channel at a time, the selected grouping of channels will appear in the Channel pop-up menu in both the Curves and Levels dialog boxes.*

 REMEMBER: *You can SHIFT-click in your image to set Color Sampler points.*

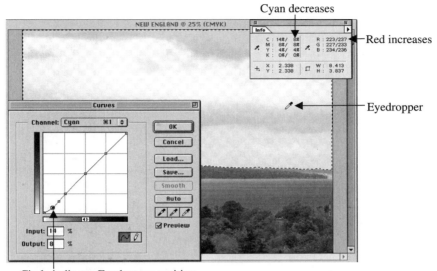

FIGURE 18-23   Using the Curves dialog box to reduce cyan and add red to the clouds

To complete the correction of the clouds, a sensation of sun and warmth was added by adjusting the Yellow channel's curve upwards.

After each of the above corrections, the Eyedropper was used to sample areas that were changed. By keeping an eye on the Info palette, it was possible to gauge the amount of each change.

Once all color correcting was done, the Unsharp Mask filter was applied to sharpen the image. (For more information on the Unsharp Mask filter, see Chapter 10.) The image was then saved on a Syquest cartridge and delivered to Reader's Digest General Books, and from there to the prepress house that had scanned the image. Using the retouched and color-corrected image file, the prepress house produced a Matchprint, which was used as a proof before printing the image. A color print of the final image is reproduced as image 41 in the color insert of this book.

If you wish to experiment with the Curves command using an RGB image, load an RGB file. In the Curves dialog box, set the Channel to Red. Then click and drag downwards to add the red to the image. If you wish to experiment further with this image, reset the image to its original state by holding down OPTION (Windows users: ALT) while clicking on the Reset button. To use the curve to increase contrast in the overall image, set the channel to RGB. Next, click on the

18

Photoshop 5   In Action

Artist: Kenneth Gore   Client: Kansas City Holiday Inn Sports Bar "Georges"

Kenneth Gore, a New York City artist, created this photomontage which can be seen in George's Sports Bar at the Kansas City Holiday Inn. The final image is 78 inches high and 180 inches wide. He created the file at 13 inches by 30 inches, a 100.4 MB file. The image was output using 3MScotchprint.

Kenneth created the background pattern by scanning logo type in Photoshop. All images of the scanned images and logos were provided by the KC CHIEFS/ROYALS. The original images are black and white, but Ken colored them using the Colorized option in the Hue/Saturation and the control sliders in the Hue/Saturation dialog box (Image | Adjust | Hue/Saturation). After scanning the images, Kenneth applied textures using the Craquelure filter (Texture | Filter | Craquelure).

Ken created the cuts and corners by erasing them with the Eraser tool and using the Airbrush to create ragged edges. Kenneth simulated tape using the Pen tool. He filled the paths and applied the Add Noise filter to keep grain very much present in the image. He created the major shadows in the image by airbrushing selections originally created as paths with the Pen tool.

To create the tacks, Ken used Strata StudioPro, a 3-D modeling and animation program. He rendered the tacks with an alpha channel and opened the images in Photoshop. He copied the tacks, then distorted and sheared them using the Edit | Transform commands, saving selections as he worked. He then feathered them and saved for fills of shadows.

middle of the curve to set a control point, then drag up on it at about the three-quarter point toward the top of the curve to create an S shape, as shown earlier in this chapter. More contrast is created because you've increased the highlights and darkened the shadows.

If you wish to work with a CMYK file, try experimenting in the Cyan channel of the image. Dragging the curve downwards subtracts cyan, adding cyan's complement; dragging upwards adds cyan. As with an RGB image, creating an S curve in this image in the composite channel adds contrast to the image.

 TIP: *Use the Curves command for individual channels to help eliminate color casts.*

Using the Hue/Saturation Command

Even though the Hue/Saturation command was not used to color correct any part of the New England image, this dialog box can be very helpful when you wish to focus on changing the hue, saturation, or lightness values of specific colors. Photoshop's Hue/Saturation dialog box features a preview option which allows you to preview exactly how a color is being changed. In the dialog box, two color bars represent colors as they appear in the color wheel (see Chapter 5 for a discussion of using the color wheel, as well as definitions of hue and saturation). The upper slider represents colors before changes have been made, and the lower bar will show you how the change affects the hues on the color wheel.

Your first step is to decide exactly what colors you wish to correct in your image. You can correct the reds, yellows, greens, cyans, blues, or magentas. Each of these choices is available in the Edit pop-up menu. If you wish to edit all of the colors, choose Master in the Edit pop-up menu.

To try out the Hue/Saturation dialog box, load an image on screen. Assume that you wish to correct the red areas of an image. Choose Reds from the Edit pop-up menu. Notice that as soon as you pick a color, the Eyedroppers on screen become activated. You can use the Eyedropper to click on a red area on screen to set the specific area that you wish to correct. Try clicking on a red area on screen with the Eyedropper (or pick another color depending upon your image). Notice that the color bars at the bottom of the dialog box register the area that will be corrected. If you want to expand the area, select the Eyedropper+, if you wish to reduce the area, click on the Eyedropper–. Then click in your image.

18

TIP: *While using the Eyedropper tool, you can activate the Eyedropper+ tool by pressing* SHIFT *and the Eyedropper– tool by pressing* OPTION *(Windows users:* ALT*).*

To make hue adjustments, simply drag on the Hue slider. Dragging to the right simulates a clockwise rotation around the color wheel; dragging to the left simulates a counter-clockwise rotation around the color wheel. As you click and drag, notice how the hues in your image change. Now locate the red area on the first color bar on the bottom of the dialog box. Note the color below it should be the color that you see on screen. As noted above, the bottom slider is showing you the change in the image. To boost the Saturation (purity of color), click and drag to the right on the Saturation slider. Dragging to the left lowers saturation. To increase Lightness, click and drag to the right. To decrease lightness, click and drag to the left.

Using the Adjustment Slider

As you drag the sliders, you'll notice that the range of the change is restricted by the gray adjustment slider that appears between the two color bars. The percentage change allowable appears above the slider. The adjustment slider controls the range of change and the fall off (how quickly change occurs). The middle (dark area) of the adjustment slider is the actual range of colors affected by the adjustments. The lighter areas to the left and right of the darker part represent the fall off. As you read through the following, try clicking and dragging the different parts of the slider. Here are the four ways to adjust the slider:

☐ To choose a different color area in your image to adjust, click and drag in the middle of the gray slider.

☐ To adjust the width of the range of color correcting, click and drag the white bar to the left or the right.

☐ To adjust the range for color correction but not the fall off, click and drag on the lighter area of the bar.

☐ To adjust the fall off but not the range of color correcting, click and drag on one of the white triangles.

REMEMBER: *The Hue/Saturation command is available when you create an adjustment layer.*

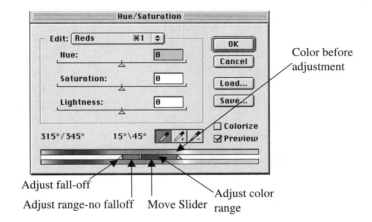

If you select the Colorize check box option, the colors in the image change to one color (the currently selected foreground color, if it isn't black or white). In this case, adjusting the slider controls lets you tint the image with the color controlled by the Hue slider. To review image colorization using the Hue/Saturation dialog box, turn to Chapter 12.

 TIP: *If you wish to colorize a grayscale mode image, change the image's mode to RGB or CMYK color.*

Replacing Colors with the Replace Color Command

Another helpful color-correcting option that works hand in hand with the Hue, Saturation, and Lightness sliders is the Replace Color command. You might think of this command as being a type of Search and Replace feature for color. The command creates a mask around a specified color, then allows you to change the hue, saturation, and lightness of the areas within the mask.

To try out the Replace Color command, load any color image, or try using an image from the Adobe Samples folder. After the image is loaded, choose Replace Color from the Image | Adjust submenu.

18

To view your image in the Replace Color dialog box, click on the Image radio button. You'll use the Selection radio button to see the mask Photoshop creates in the image. Currently there is no mask.

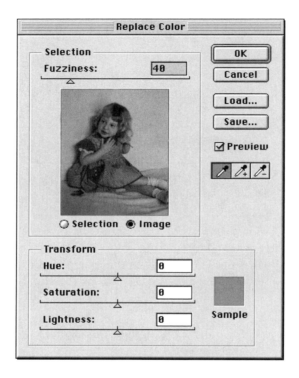

To start creating the mask, you must choose a color in your image that you want masked. Start by clicking on the first Eyedropper in the dialog box. Move the Eyedropper tool over a color in the image you wish to replace. Click on the Eyedropper in the image. To see how Photoshop creates the mask based on the color, click on the Selection radio button in the Replace Color dialog box. The white area in the Preview box is the area within the mask.

You can expand or contract the mask by clicking and dragging on the Fuzziness slider, or by entering a value between 0 and 250 into the Fuzziness field. The Fuzziness slider extends the edges of the color range within the mask.

If you wish to add colors, click on the Eyedropper+ or Eyedropper–, then click on the mask in the dialog box or in the image. Try extending the range of the mask by clicking on the Eyedropper+ and then clicking on another color in your image. After you click, the color will be added to the mask.

TIP: *When the Eyedropper is selected, you can switch to the Eyedropper+ by pressing SHIFT or switch to the Eyedropper– by pressing OPTION (Windows users: ALT). You can temporarily switch between the mask and the image in the Preview area of the dialog box by pressing CTRL, regardless of whether the Selection or Image radio button is selected.*

Once the mask shows the desired area of your image, use the Hue and Saturation sliders to correct or alter the colors. Notice that the sample color swatch previews the colors you create.

If you wish to use your settings again so that they can be reloaded at a later time, click on the Save button so that you can name your settings and save them to disk. The Load button will allow you to load the settings when you need them again.

If you're happy with the changes you made, click OK to close the dialog box; otherwise, choose Cancel.

Changing Ink Percentages with the Selective Color Command

Once you begin to color correct RGB or CMYK files, you may wish to fine-tune color your images by using Photoshop's Selective Color command, which allows you to add or subtract the percentage of inks used in colors. For instance, you could make an apple redder by removing a percentage of cyan, red's complement, and/or adding magenta.

 REMEMBER: *The Selective Color command can be used in an adjustment layer.*

 NOTE: *When using the Selective Color command, you might wish to set the Eyedropper so it displays Total ink percentages. To do this, click on the Info palette's pop-up menu and choose Palette Options. In the Info Options dialog box, set First or Second color to Total ink. After you make changes in the Selective Colors dialog box, move the Eyedropper over your image to view the total percentages for all CMYK inks. You can also SHIFT-CLICK in your image to set Color Sampler points, and view the ink percentages of the points.*

18

Before trying out the Selective Color command, load an image on screen. To use the Selective Color command, choose Selective Color from the Image | Adjust submenu. In the Selective Color dialog box, click the Preview button so you will be able to see the changes in your image as you experiment with the Selective Color command. Next, choose a color from the Colors pop-up menu. This is the color in your image that you wish to change. Note that you can also change whites, grays, and blacks.

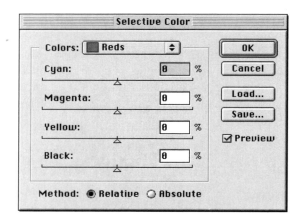

The percentage of ink added or subtracted is calculated differently depending on whether you select the Relative or Absolute radio button. Relative applies the percentage based upon the percentage of the original ink. Absolute just adds the percentage to the original ink percentage. For instance, assume you are adding color to a 50% Cyan pixel. If you add 5% Cyan in Relative mode, Photoshop will compute 5% of 50% (.05 × .5), which produces a 2.5% increase. Thus, the Cyan ink will be changed to 52.5%. If you add 5% of Cyan in Absolute mode, Photoshop simply adds 5% to the 50%, which results in 55% Cyan.

Try clicking on the Absolute radio button, then watch how your image changes when you drag the sliders to adjust the colors. When you're done experimenting, click Cancel or OK to accept the ink changes. If you'd like, you can also use the Save and Load buttons to Save and Load settings for use on other images.

NOTE: *A variety of third-party vendors have created plug-ins that can speed up and simplify the task of color correcting images. Vivid Details Test Strip uses an intuitive interface similar to Photoshop's Variation commands. However, Test Strip provides full screen previews, zooming controls and allows changes in 1% increments. It even allows you to save a Test Strip view to create a Test Proof. Prepress Technologies' Spectre Plug-ins sets up a color-correction table that can quickly be applied to images. Monaco Systems' MonacoCOLOR features batch processing. This allows many images to be corrected automatically while the computer is unattended. MonacoCOLOR also features scanner calibration options and provides many image correction features that can be run with one keystroke.*

Working with the Channel Mixer

As you work with color correcting you may find that correcting poorly digitized images is quite a task. Photoshop's Channel Mixer is a high-end prepress utility that allows you to edit an image's channels by adding or subtracting color to the color channels in an image. The Channel Mixer also provides a quick means for creating tinted and grayscale image effects. You can even use it to edit an image's channels to use as a mask. To use the Channel Mixer, load an image on screen. Then choose Image | Adjust | Channel Mixer to open the Channel Mixer dialog box. Make sure the Preview check box is selected so you can preview the adjustments you make to your image.

Start by choosing the channel that you wish to edit. To experiment, start by choosing an Output Channel—such as Red if you are using an RGB color image. The Output Channel is the channel that you will be changing in your image. Next, click and drag on a Source channel. As you click and drag, you add color to the Output channel. While the Channel Mixer dialog box is open, you can move the Eyedropper over the colors (or SHIFT-click to set Color Sampler points in your image) to view the color changes in the Info palette. You'll see that the color in the Output Channel is boosted when you click on one of the Source channel sliders.

18

If you wish to darken or lighten the Output channel, click and drag on the Constant Slider or enter a value into the Constant field. Dragging left or entering negative values darkens the image; dragging right lightens the image. Technically, the Constant slider adds a black channel with different opacities over the Output channel if you drag left; when you drag right, a white channel with varying opacity is added to the channel.

To create a grayscale image out of the RGB channels, click Monochrome, then adjust the sliders to produce the effect you desire.

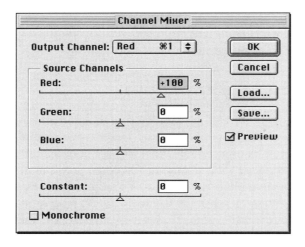

Basic Training with the Channel Mixer

If you start using the channel mixer with an RGB or CMYK image, you may find it somewhat difficult to predict exactly what is happening when the colors in your image change. If so, try out through the following example which step by step shows you how colors can change when channel values are added or subtracted in a simple RGB image. Before you begin, create a new RGB file, 5 inches by 5 inches with a White background. Next open up the Channels palette by choosing Window | Show Channels.

1. In order to fully understand the Channel Mixer, it's helpful to change the Color Channels so that they display their thumbnails in color. To do this, choose File | Preferences | Display & Cursors. In the Preferences dialog box, select the Color Channels in Color option.

2. Notice that each color channel in the Channels palette is filled with color. This tells you that the white background you see on screen is created from Red 255, Green 255 and pure Blue 255.

3. Next, create three different overlapping shapes on screen: make one shape Red, one Green, one Blue. Use the Rectangular Marquee tool to create a rectangular selection on screen. Fill the Selection with pure Red. Use the Elliptical Marquee to create a circle on screen. Fill the Selection with Green. Use the Polygon Lasso tool to create a triangle. Fill the Triangle with Blue. (To fill, choose Edit | Fill or press Option-Delete (Windows users: ALT-BACKSPACE) to fill with the foreground color.

4. Open the Channel Mixer dialog box by choosing Image | Adjust | Channel Mixer.

   Start by setting the Output Channel to Red. This means that the changes you make in the the Channel Mixer will edit the Red channel in your image.

5. In the Source Channels section, remove red from the red channel by clicking on the Red slider and dragging it to the left until the Red slider readout is 0. Notice that the Red square on screen changes to black. Why? You've removed all red from the red channel. Thus in the square image area on screen, there is no red, no green and no blue. Red 0, Green 0 and Blue 0 produce black. To confirm this look at the Red channel in the Channels palette. The channel is completely black because there is no color in the channel.

   Now take a look at the background of your image. Notice that it changed from white to Cyan. The color change occurred because the background of your image is now composed entirely of Blue and Green. If you create a color from Blue 255 and Green 255, you create Cyan.

6. Now click and drag the Green slider in the Source channels to the right to the 100 percent point. The green circle on your screen now changes to Yellow, and the background changes to White. This may seem a bit confusing: Why does green change to yellow when you output green to the red channel? Here's the explanation: First, take a look at the Channels palette. Notice that you can see the shape of the circle in both the Red and Green channels. The circle is yellow in the composite RGB image because it is composed of Green from the Green channel and 100 percent Red

18

(which you added with the Channel Mixer). If you create a color with Red 255 and Green 255, you create Yellow. The background changed to white because you added 100 percent color to the red channel. This means that the background area of the screen is composed of Red 255, Green 255 and Blue 255—which makes white.

7. Now change the Output Channel to Blue, then drag the Green Source slider to 100 %. The Circle area on screen changes to white. It changes because you added 100 % Green to the Blue channel. This means that the Circle area on screen is now composed of 100% Red, 100% Blue and 100% Green. In other words the White area is created from Red 255, Blue 255, Green 255.

The foregoing exercise should help get you started with the Color Mixer. At this point, feel free to change the Output Channel and Source percentages to analyze other changes in the image.

 NOTE: *You can easily recreate this exercise to analyze how the Color Mixer affects CMYK images. Start with a CMYK Color file and make sure that the Channels palette displays the channels in color. Create four different shapes, each filled with a different CMYK color. (Fill the shapes with Cyan 100%, Magenta 100%, Yellow 100% Black.) Set one of the CMY Channels as the Output channel, then drag one of the Source Channels to the right. Note how the colors change in the Channels palette, then observe the change on screen.*

Conclusion

As you've seen, Photoshop provides enormous possibilities and many different options when you need to retouch or color correct an image. As you gain more experience with retouching and color correcting, you'll be better able to predict how changes in the relevant dialog boxes will affect your image on screen. You'll also be better able to judge the best retouching and/or color-correcting tool for the job at hand.

CHAPTER 19

Calibration and Output

No matter how exquisite your Photoshop images, all of your design and image-editing work may be in vain if the final printed (or other) output does not match the onscreen image. To get sharp and vibrant printed images, you need to have a clear understanding of how they are produced and how system calibration affects output quality.

This chapter focuses on two subjects: the printing process and system calibration. Most Photoshop users do not need to have a thorough knowledge of the printing and calibration processes because the prepress house or print shop can take care of these complicated issues. On the other hand, even if you don't output your own proofs and film separations, and even if you don't have to set screen frequency in the Halftone Screens dialog box, understanding the prepress concepts covered in this chapter will make for a smoother and more efficient production process. With that goal in mind, this chapter provides an overview of the printing process, explains how proofs can be used to predict color accuracy, and shows you how to calibrate your system to a proof. It concludes with step-by-step instructions for printing separations.

Once you grasp the printing process, you'll understand how output resolution, screen frequency, paper stock, and halftones affect the output quality of your images.

The Role of Halftones in Image Output

When an image is printed on a printing press, it consists of many small dots called *halftones*. The size and shape of these dots and the angle at which they are printed create the visual illusion of continuous grays or continuous colors. In traditional printing, halftones are created by placing a glass or mylar screen containing a grid of dots between an image and the film or negative paper on which the image is printed. This photomechanical process re-creates the image as a pattern of dots. Dark areas have large dots, and light areas have small dots.

In color publishing, cyan, magenta, yellow, and black screens are used in the traditional halftone process. The print quality depends on how close together the lines are. The finer the lines, the better the quality. The final result also depends upon the screen angles at which the halftones were created. Specific angles must be used in order to provide clear and consistent color. The traditional screen angles are 105 degrees for cyan, 75 degrees for magenta, 90 degrees for yellow, and 45 degrees for black. When screen angles are not corrected, a mottled and undesirable pattern, called a *moiré,* may appear. (An example of a moiré pattern can be seen in Chapter 10, Figure 10-1(a).)

Commercial printers use the halftone screens to create plates for each of the four process colors. In the printing process, paper is printed with patterns of different-sized cyan, magenta, yellow, and black dots to create the illusion of countless colors. Take a magnifying glass and look closely at a printed color image, and you'll see the pattern of dots in various colors and sizes.

Digital Halftones

As in traditional printing, digital images that are output to a printer or imagesetter are also separated into halftone dots. The output device creates the halftone dots by turning groups of smaller dots, often referred to as *pixels,* on or off.

If the output device is an imagesetter, it can output to film as well as paper. An imagesetter producing output at a resolution of 2,450 dots per inch (dpi) creates over 6 million dots per square inch. At 300 dpi, a standard laser printer creates images with 90,000 dots per square inch. The more dots an image has, the better its resolution and the higher its printed quality.

It's important to remember that these pixels are *not* the halftone dots. In the printing process, the pixels are organized into a system of cells, and it is within these cells that the halftone dots are created. For instance, the dots from a 1,200-dpi imagesetter might be divided into 100 cells per inch. By turning the pixels off or on inside each cell, the printer or imagesetter creates one halftone dot.

The number of halftone dots per inch is called the *screen frequency, screen ruling,* or *line screen* and is measured in lines per inch (lpi). A high-screen frequency, such as 150 lpi, packs the dots very closely together, producing sharper images and distinct colors. When the screen frequency is low, the halftone dots are spread out and produce coarser images with less refined colors.

 REMEMBER: *For the highest-quality reproduction of digital images, image file resolution generally should be one and a half to twice the screen frequency (measured in lines per inch). Also, remember that quality often depends on the paper stock used. To review the relationship between image resolution and screen frequency, see Chapter 8.*

Calculating Gray Levels

The number of pixels that the imagesetter turns off or on to create a halftone determines the maximum number of gray levels that can be printed in an image. The number of gray levels determines the quality of continuous-tone images and whether a gradient blend prints properly. If you print at a screen frequency of 150 and a resolution of 2,450 dpi, you produce output with the maximum number of grays possible (256). Most continuous-tone images require at least 150 shades of gray for acceptable printed results.

 TIP: *If you need to eliminate banding due to insufficient gray levels in a blend, try applying the Add Noise filter to each channel containing color in your CMYK color image. Filters are explained in Chapter 10. Selecting the Dither check box in the Gradient Options palette can also eliminate banding.*

In order to ensure the image quality you desire, you can calculate the number of gray levels (including white) that will be printed, using this formula:

Number of Grays = (Output Resolution ÷ Screen Frequency)^2 + 1

On an output device printing at 1,200 dpi and with a screen frequency of 100, each cell is a 12-by-12 matrix of pixels (1,200 ÷ 100 = 12). The pixels in each cell produce one halftone dot. In this 12-by-12 cell, the different combinations of pixels being turned on or off produce 145 levels of gray, including white (12^2 = 144 + white = 145).

Figure 19-1 illustrates how a halftone is created from pixels and how the number of pixels in the cell determines the number of gray levels. In a 5-by-5 cell, 26 combinations of gray (5^2 + white) are possible. White is created when no pixels

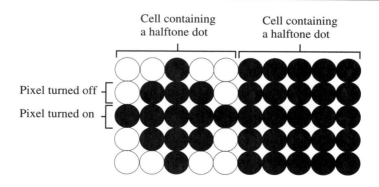

FIGURE 19-1   Pixels turned off and on create halftone dots and determine gray levels

are turned on, 50% black is created when half the pixels are turned on, and 100% black is created when every pixel is turned on.

Conversely, if you know your output resolution and the number of grays desired, you can compute the required screen frequency with the following formula:

Screen Frequency = Output Resolution ÷ Number of Grays

If more grays are desired, the screen frequency can be reduced. For instance, if the screen frequency drops to 80 lines per inch (lpi) and the resolution remains at 1,200 dpi, the halftone cell size is increased to a 15-pixel square ($1,200 ÷ 80 = 15$), which produces 226 grays ($15^2 + 1$). This can create a dilemma: The greater the number of grays, the lower the screen frequency; the greater the screen frequency, the sharper the image, yet the fewer the gray levels. The simple solution to this predicament is to always print at the highest resolution with the highest screen frequency, ensuring sharp images, crisp colors, and 256 shades of gray.

Unfortunately, printing at the highest possible resolution and screen frequency may not always be possible, because of two factors: paper stock and printing presses. Not all printing presses can handle high-screen-frequency output, and not all paper is suitable for high-screen-frequency printing. For instance, when you print at a high screen frequency on newspaper stock, it absorbs the dots, causing too much ink to spread, and produces a muddy output. Thus, paper stock is often the determining factor in deciding what screen frequency to use. American magazines printed on coated stock often use a screen frequency of 133 or 150 lpi; European magazines often use a higher screen frequency. A glossy magazine or art book may be printed at 200 lpi. Newspapers are usually printed at 85 lpi.

Resolution, screen frequency, and paper stock are all issues that should be discussed with your print shop, prepress house, or service bureau. You should also decide whether you want your output on paper or film. Although film is more expensive than paper, it provides sharper output, which is especially important at screen frequencies over 100 lpi. This is the reason color separations are output to film.

If you are producing color separations, the imagesetter will produce four different film separations. The four pieces of film will not be in color, but rather four grayscale versions of the cyan, magenta, yellow, and black components of your image. The print shop will use the four pieces of film (for each of the four process colors) to create plates for use on a printing press.

19

Printing Proofs of Your Images

Before you actually go to press with a Photoshop project, you should view a printed sample, or *proof*, of your image. The proof will help you judge the anticipated quality of the final printing job. Proofs can warn you that colors will not print correctly or that moirés may appear, and will tell you the degree of dot gain to be expected. (*Dot gain* is the expansion or contraction of halftone dots, usually due to ink spreading on paper.)

If you are printing a grayscale image, you may feel that your 300- or 600-dpi laser printer output is sufficient as a proof. If you are creating color images, there are a variety of choices available for color proofs: digital proofs, off-press proofs, and press proofs.

 NOTE: *No matter how good your proofs look, various problems can occur on press that affect the quality of your images.*

Digital Proofs

A *digital proof* is output directly from the digital data in your Photoshop file. Most digital proofs are created by printing to a thermal-wax printer, color laser printer, or dye-sublimation printer. Digital proofs can also be output on a high-end inkjet printer, such as the Scitex IRIS, or on other high-end printers, such as the Kodak Approval Color Proofer. Digital proofs are often very helpful as the design process proceeds.

Because digital proofs are not created from an imagesetter's film, color output may not be highly accurate, although high-end printers from Kodak, Scitex, and 3M can come close to matching film output. Commercial printers generally will not accept a digital proof as a *contract proof* that they will contractually agree to match.

 NOTE: *If a service bureau will be creating a digital proof of your image, you may be asked to save your file in EPS format. For more information, see Appendix A.*

Off-Press Proofs

These proofs are created from the imagesetter's film, which will eventually be sent to the print shop. Thus, an off-press proof is considered more reliable than a digital proof as an indicator of how the image will print. The two major types of off-press proofs are *overlay proofs* and *laminated proofs*.

The overlay proof comprises four different images exposed on acetate sheets that are overlaid. An overlay proof is generally considered not as accurate as a laminated proof, where each colored layer is developed and laminated to a base material. Apart from providing a reliable indication of color, laminated proofs can be very helpful in predicting if moirés will appear in your final output. Dupont's Chromalin and 3M's Matchprint are two well-known laminated systems. When analyzing a Matchprint, be aware that it can make colors look more intense than actual colors produced by inks on a printing press. This is often because the proofs don't represent ink seepage into certain paper stocks.

Press Proofs

A press proof is considered the most accurate proof because it is made from the actual plates the printer will use, and it is printed on the stock that has been chosen for the job. Thus, the press proof will be a good indicator of dot gain, and it will also provide an accurate assessment of final color.

Bear in mind that press proofs are often printed on sheet-fed presses, which may be slower than the press used for the actual print job. The cost of creating printing plates and inking the press make the press proof the most expensive proofing process. For this reason, most clients have traditionally opted for off-press proofs. However, press proofs are becoming more popular in direct-to-press print jobs, where no film is used. Most direct-to-press print jobs are used for short-run printing.

 NOTE: *Many artists do not need their images printed on printing presses, yet desire high-quality fine art prints of their work. To satisfy this demand, several digital printmaking studios have pioneered outputting digital images using long-lasting inks and printmaking papers. Most of these printmakers create high-quality prints by outputting images on a Scitex IRIS printer. Using the IRIS, these service bureaus can output images to a variety of substrates such as canvas, rice paper, linen, and silk. Three companies that provide these services are Cone Editions in East Topsham, Vermont; Digital Pond in San Francisco; and Nash Editions in Manhattan Beach, California.*

Why You Should Calibrate Your System

You will want to proof your images as often as possible during a project—the earlier you catch problems with color and design, the easier and cheaper it is to fix them. Another way to help avoid problems in attaining color accuracy is to properly *calibrate* your monitor and system. Calibration helps ensure that the image you see on screen portrays your final output as accurately as possible. Calibration is necessary because monitors, scanners, printers, and printing presses vary in the way they render color.

 REMEMBER: *Jobs that are sent to different printers may require different calibration settings. You may need to change the options in the RGB, CMYK or Grayscale Setup dialog boxes. See Chapter 1 for more details.*

Monitor Calibration and Color Setup

Calibration is discussed in several places in this book. In Chapter 1, instructions for running the Adobe Gamma utility and choosing an RGB color space are discussed in detail. Although the setup may seem confusing to some users, we placed the instructions in the first chapter of this book to emphasize the importance of calibrating your system as soon as possible, particularly before you start using Photoshop for color image work. Ideally, you've been working through the exercises in this book with the Photoshop's color options properly set.

If you have neglected to investigate Photoshop's color settings options, you may be working with onscreen colors that are tainted by color casts. Images may appear lighter or darker on screen than they will print. Also, don't forget that the settings in the RGB Setup and CMYK Setup dialog boxes are used when Photoshop converts from RGB color to CMYK color.

If you have not run the Adobe Gamma utility or selected appropriate options in the RGB, CMYK, or Grayscale Setup dialog boxes, return to Chapter 1 now and follow the instructions provided. Once your monitor is calibrated and you've chosen the proper color space for your system, you can fine-tune it further using a printed proof as a guide.

Calibrating to a Proof

Certainly the best way to help calibrate your system is to use a press proof—a sample from a printing press. However, for most users the most efficient and affordable method is to use an off-press proof, such as a Matchprint. This is a sample printout created from the imagesetter's film generated from your Photoshop files. The following sections give an overview of calibrating a system to grayscale and color proofs. If you have questions regarding calibration, consult your prepress house—many use Photoshop every day and may be able to help out.

Calibrating to a Grayscale Proof

If you are printing a grayscale image, calibrating to a proof is quite simple. When calibrating, you can compensate for dot gain that occurs "on press." (As mentioned earlier and discussed in detail in Chapter 12, dot gain is a change in the size of a halftone dot, usually caused by ink absorption. Dot gain may also be caused by a miscalibrated imagesetter.)

Your first step in calibrating to a grayscale proof is to obtain a proof of a grayscale image that is printed at the resolution, screen frequency, and (hopefully) on the paper stock you will use for printing. Try to use an image that spans a large tonal range, from highlights to shadows. You might wish to add an 11-step gray bar in an area in the image. Also, be sure to have your prepress house or commercial printer output the image with a grayscale calibration bar, which steps through grayscale levels. For more information about printing calibration bars, see the section "The Page Setup Dialog Box" later in this chapter.

When you are ready to calibrate to the proof, open the grayscale image from which the proof was created. Before continuing, make sure that your system is setup for grayscale printing. To do this, choose File | Color Settings | Grayscale Setup. In the Grayscale Setup dialog box select the Black Ink option, and make sure the Preview check box is selected. Close the dialog box, then open the CMYK Setup dialog box. From the Ink Colors pop-up menu, choose the printer or inks that you will be using. Note that some of the options are for coated paper, others for uncoated paper. After you make your selection, a corresponding

19

percentage is automatically entered into the Dot Gain field. This means that the display of your image on screen will reflect the Dot Gain percentage specified in the dialog box. If the Preview box is selected in the CMYK Setup dialog box, you'll see your image darken or lighten depending upon the choice in the CMYK Setup dialog box.

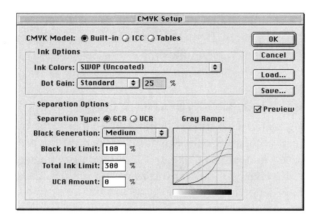

 REMEMBER: *For Grayscale and Duotone images, the Dot Gain setting in the CMYK Setup dialog box only affects screen display. The setting does not affect the data in the Grayscale image itself.*

If the image on your monitor is lighter or darker than the proof, you may want to change the percentage in the Dot Gain field so that the display matches your image. Before you make changes, however, be sure to consult with your commercial printer and find out if Photoshop's default Dot Gain setting is sufficient. If you do wish to change the value in the Dot Gain field, entering a higher percentage will make your screen display darker, and a lower percentage will make it lighter. Click OK to see the results in the image on screen. Once your screen image matches the printed proof, click the Save button so that you can name and save your settings.

When you work on a grayscale image, load the saved CMYK Setup settings. Then use the Image | Adjust command's Curves and Levels dialog boxes to lighten or darken your image. Since the CMYK Setup Dot Gain settings only affect screen display, changes in the Curves and Levels dialog boxes will compensate for dot gain. (To review the Curves and Levels dialog boxes, see Chapter 18.)

Calibrating to a Color Proof

For a color images, the calibration process is a bit more complicated. If you will be converting images from RGB Color to CMYK Color, your calibration settings will affect the color data in the CMYK color file. As discussed in Chapter 12, when you switch RGB color to CMYK color mode, Photoshop utilizes the settings in the RGB and CMYK Setup dialog boxes to create the color data for the CMYK color image.

When you calibrate to a color proof, you attempt to match screen colors in a CMYK image to printed color output. As mentioned earlier, before beginning the calibration process, make sure that your have run the Adobe Gamma utility and have entered the proper settings in the color setup dialog boxes. If you are using Photoshop's Built-in color model (specified in the CMYK Setup dialog box), you can make a variety of different adjustments to make a screen image match the proof of the image.

 NOTE: *If you are using ICC profile (in the CMYK Setup dialog box), your image on screen should match the printer proof. If it doesn't, you may need to contact your printer's manufacturer to obtain a different ICC profile, or you may need to create a new ICC profile using software and hardware that creates ICC profiles. If your printer is miscalibrated, onscreen colors may not match printed proofs. Finally, you may be able to match your proof by adjusting dot gain settings using Photoshop's Transfer Functions (in the Page Setup dialog box, described later in this chapter). If you are using ICC profiles, you cannot adjust dot gain in the CMYK Setup dialog box.*

To begin the calibration process, use a CMYK color image as your proofing image—it should not be an image that you converted to CMYK color from RGB color. It also should be an image that is saved as a CMYK color file and that does not have an embedded ICC profile. If desired, you can create a test image from CMYK color swatch combinations. The swatch combinations should include swatches of 100 % of each of the CMYK colors, as well as swatches from a combination of the CMYK colors, and swatches that create black (creating a test document is described in Photoshop's Help files.) Rather than create a test image from scratch, it's probably easiest to use the calibration file that is provided with Photoshop.

 NOTE: *Before you open an image to use as a proof, you must prevent Photoshop from converting the CMYK color space of the test file. To do this, choose Color Setup | Profile Setup. In the Profile Mismatch Handling section, open the CMYK pop-up menu and choose Ignore. (Be sure to change the dialog box to its original settings later.)*

If your prepress house or commercial printer creates the proof, load the image from which the proof was created on screen. Your next step is use the CMYK Setup dialog box to calibrate the image onscreen to the proof.

Compensating for Dot Gain

To compensate for dot gain, open the CMYK Setup dialog box (File | Color Settings | CMYK Setup). To access the Ink Colors pop-up menu, the Built-in color model must be selected. In the Ink Colors pop-up menu, shown in Figure 19-2, choose the correct printer or ink colors. The Dot Gain percentage will change according to your choice for Ink Colors, and represents expected dot gain in image midtones. Photoshop uses the Dot Gain percentage to create a dot gain curve for the entire image's tonal range, from highlights to shadows. (As mentioned earlier in this chapter, the Dot Gain field changes the image display to compensate for dot gain on press.)

Adobe recommends that you use a densitometer to take a reading at the 50 area on the proof's calibration bar (a color bar of CMYK and CMY color combinations). A *densitometer* is a device that measures densities of colors and can provide a precise reading of dot gain. If you do take readings and wish to manually set the dot gain, choose Standard in the Dot Gain field. Subtract the dot gain percentage from 50 percent, and enter that value into the Dot Gain field. Alternatively, you can choose Curves, and enter the dot gain percentage into the 50% field in the Dot Gain Curves dialog box.

Custom...
Other
AD-LITHO (Newsprint)
Dainippon Ink
Eurostandard (Coated)
Eurostandard (Newsprint)
Eurostandard (Uncoated)
✓ **SWOP (Coated)**
SWOP (Newsprint)
SWOP (Uncoated)
Toyo Inks (Coated Web Offset)
Toyo Inks (Coated)
Toyo Inks (Dull Coated)
Toyo Inks (Uncoated)

FIGURE 19-2   The Ink Colors pop-up menu

If you don't want to incur the expense of purchasing a densitometer or don't know how to use one, your next best choice is to adjust Dot Gain so that the image on screen looks like the proof. The higher the percentage you enter in the Dot Gain field, the darker the image will become. Click OK to see the results on screen. Once you have found the best setting, return to the CMYK Setup dialog box so that you can name and save your settings. To save your settings, click the Save button.

 NOTE: *If you are uncertain about the effects of changing the Dot Gain setting, consult your commercial printer.*

If you notice color casts in your image, you should contact your printer or prepress house which may be using different curve settings for the CMYK inks. If desired, you can adjust Photoshop's dot gain curve by choosing Curves in the Dot Gain pop-up menu. In the Dot Gain Curves dialog box, you can select an ink Color radio button, then enter the dot gain percentage in the appropriate field. If you prefer, you can also click and drag on the curve to specify a change in the dot gain settings.

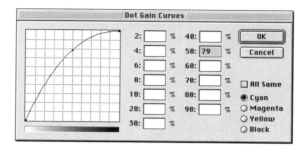

> **NOTE:** *As mentioned earlier, dot gain can also occur because of a miscalibrated imagesetter. Photoshop allows you to compensate for miscalibration in the CMYK Setup dialog box by choosing the Transfer Functions option in the Page Setup dialog box. Nevertheless, when dot gain appears in film separations due to miscalibrated equipment, compensating for it is probably better left to the service bureau or prepress professionals. See the "Transfer Functions" section later in this chapter.*

Adjusting for Custom Ink Colors

In addition to adjusting dot gain, the CMYK Setup dialog box allows you to adjust for custom ink colors. This might be necessary when you use ink sets that do not appear in the Ink Colors pop-up menu. To open the Ink Colors dialog box, choose Custom in the Ink Colors pop-up menu. The values you see are for the different CMYK color combinations and CIE coordinates. The CIE coordinates are internationally defined color standards. If you have a color measuring device such as a spectrophotometer or a colorimeter, Adobe suggests that you take color readings from your proof and enter the readings in the Y, x and y fields.

NOTE: *To access the Ink Colors dialog box, the Built-in option must be selected in the CMYK Setup dialog box.*

If you do not have color-reading equipment, you can click on the color swatches to open the Color Picker. In the Color Picker dialog box, you can adjust the colors to match your proof. When you are finished, click OK. Save your settings in the CMYK Setup dialog box by clicking the Save button and then clicking OK to exit.

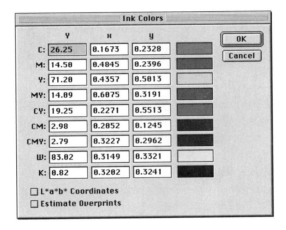

 REMEMBER: *As discussed in Chapter 12, changes made in the CMYK Setup dialog box do not affect the color data in a CMYK file, but only the screen display of the image; the settings are used when Photoshop converts from RGB color to CMYK color. The settings in the CMYK Setup dialog box do not affect the display of RGB color images.*

 NOTE: *A product that can prove helpful when calibrating is Colortron, which sells for about $1,000. This hand-held device for measuring color can serve as a monitor calibrator, file/ink densitometer, or a light meter. Accompanying software can determine a match of a sample color to a color-matching system such as PANTONE, and can determine the best CMYK approximation of a sample color.*

19

Saving Separation Tables

Now that you have compensated for dot gain and adjusted for custom ink colors, your system is calibrated. Once the information in the CMYK Setup dialog box is correct, you can save the settings as a separation table. In the CMYK Setup dialog box, click the Tables option. Click on the Save button; name your table after Photoshop creates it. When you wish to use the separation table, open the Tables section of the CMYK Setup dialog box and load the table by clicking on the Load button. Photoshop will use this table when you convert from RGB color to CMYK color.

For more information about using Separation Tables dialog boxes, see Chapter 12.

Trapping in Photoshop

When calibration is completed and you are ready to produce your output, your next consideration is whether you'll need to correct for registration problems that might occur during the printing process. Photoshop's Image | Trap command can help.

 NOTE: *The Image | Trap command only appears in CMYK color images.*

As paper passes through a printing press, misalignment or movement of the printing plates may cause thin white gaps or color halos to appear around adjoining areas of colors. *Trapping* fixes these discrepancies by slightly overlapping the colored areas so that the gaps won't appear during on-press printing.

When Photoshop traps, it spreads lighter colors under darker ones. Pure cyan and pure magenta, however, spread equally under each other.

 NOTE: *Before you begin to adjust trap settings, bear in mind that trapping is primarily needed when solid tints adjoin. Since most Photoshop images are continuous-tone images with gradual color transitions, trapping is usually unnecessary.*

After consulting with your print shop on the width of the trap adjustment, select Trap from the Image menu. In the Trap dialog box, select a measurement unit from the pop-up menu, and in the Width field enter the width for the trap.

Here's an example of how trapping works: Suppose you entered a value of 2 pixels for the trap width. When a portion of an image with a high percentage of yellow adjoins a dark color, the yellow (because it is the lighter color) will spread out 2 pixels. Thus, if a gap existed between the two plates that was 2 points or less, the yellow ink would fill the gap.

If you wish to see the Trap command in action, create a CMYK file with a swatch of a dark color overlapping a swatch of yellow. Execute the Trap command. Then use the Channels palette to view only the yellow channel. To see the difference—before and after applying the trap—use the Edit | Undo command.

 CAUTION: *Discuss trapping issues with your prepress house, which may use a specific software package to trap, before outputting your image to film.*

Photoshop's Printing Options

Now that you have an understanding of the printing and calibration processes, you'll probably want to explore all of the options available in Photoshop's Page Setup and Print dialog boxes. The Page Setup dialog box provides numerous output features, several of which fall into the realm of the prepress house or service bureau. If you are not printing to a color printer or imagesetter, you may never need to access these options; nonetheless, getting familiar with them will help complete your knowledge of the printing process.

19

NOTE: *When Photoshop prints, it prints all visible layers. If you only wish to print a specific layer, see Chapter 15 to learn how to hide layers.*

The Page Setup Dialog Box

As discussed in Chapter 2, the Page Setup dialog box allows you to specify whether labels, registration marks, and crop marks will be printed on a page. As you'll see in this section, this dialog box also contains prepress options that govern screen frequency and halftone angles.

Figure 19-3 shows a composite output of an image with a label, crop marks, registration marks, calibration bars, a caption, and a 1-pixel-wide border around the image.

To access the Page Setup dialog box, choose Page Setup from the File menu. Mac users will pick a printer using the Chooser in the Apple menu; the Chooser

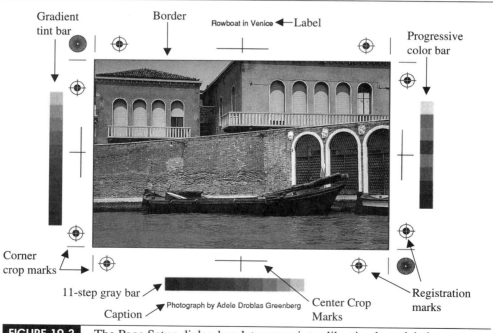

| **FIGURE 19-3** | The Page Setup dialog box lets you print calibration bars, labels, a caption, a border, and registration and crop marks for your image |

cannot be accessed while the Page Setup dialog box is displayed. Windows users will choose a printer from the Page Setup dialog box.

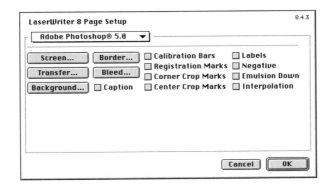

Here is an overview of the Page Setup dialog box:

☐ For both Mac and Windows users, the Paper and Orientation settings work much the same as in any Mac or Windows program.

 TIP: *In Photoshop, it's faster to use the Image | Transform | Rotate Canvas command to rotate an image before printing rather than changing orientation when printing.*

☐ **Calibration Bars** This option prints an 11-step gray bar, a progressive CMYK color bar, and a CMY gradient tint bar (if the image is a CMYK color image) on each page. The calibration bars are used to match a proof to the screen image; you can see how closely screen grays or colors match the printed output. The gray bar on the page prints from 0 to 100% gray in 10% increments.

☐ **Registration Marks** Registration marks are used to align pieces of film for printing color separations or duotones. Turn on Registration Marks when you want these marks printed around the edges of the image.

☐ **Corner Crop Marks** Crop marks indicate where paper should be trimmed. Turn on Corner Crop Marks to print these marks at the edges of your image.

19

☐ **Center Crop Marks**   Select Center Crop Marks to place crop marks around the center of your image.

☐ **Labels**   Select Labels to print the document name and channel name on the page with the image.

☐ **Negative**   Negatives are often used for film output. Most commercial printers in the United States require a film negative to create plates, although other countries create plates from positives, rather than negatives. Ask your printer whether a film positive or negative is required. If you are printing to paper, do not select the Negative option.

☐ **Emulsion Down**   Both film and photographic paper have a photosensitive layer called *emulsion*. When examining film, the emulsion side is the dull side. When the emulsion side is up in a film negative, type will be readable and not reversed. Your print shop may require the emulsion to be up or down. Usually, printing on paper is Emulsion Up; this is Photoshop's default setting.

☐ **Interpolation**   Some PostScript Level 2 printers can improve the appearance of low-resolution files by interpolating pixels when printing. If you do not have a PostScript Level 2 printer, this option will not change output quality.

The Page Setup dialog box also includes buttons that open up additional dialog boxes with more printing options; these buttons are described in the paragraphs that follow.

Printing with a Border

Select the Border button if you wish to have a black border printed around your image. In the Border dialog box, you select a unit of measurement and a width for the border.

Printing with a Caption

Select the Caption check box if you wish to print the information entered in the Caption field of the File Info dialog box. To access the File Info dialog box, choose File Info from the File menu. If the caption information does not appear in the dialog box, choose Caption from the Section pop-up menu. For more information about the File Info dialog box, see Appendix A.

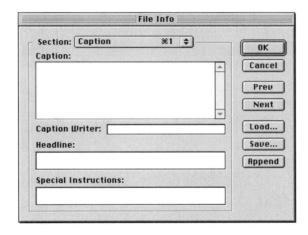

Printing with a Background Color

If you are outputting to slides, you may wish to have a colored background printed to fill in the area surrounding the image. When you select the Background button, the Color Picker will appear. Choose the color that you wish to have as your background and click OK.

Transfer Functions

As mentioned earlier in this chapter, when an image is output to film, dot gain can occur due to miscalibration of the imagesetter. The Transfer Functions are used to compensate for this. Photoshop's Transfer Functions can also be used to create a custom dot gain curve if you are using ICC profiles specified in the CMYK Setup dialog box.

19

To open the Transfer Functions dialog box, click on the Transfer button. In the Transfer Functions dialog box, enter compensating values in fields that correspond to the dot gain percentages in the image. For instance, if dot gain is higher than it should be, subtract the desired dot value from the dot gain caused by the miscalibration, then enter the value in the appropriate field. Here's an example: Assume that an imagesetter is printing halftone dots at 60%, when they really should be printed at 50%. The difference between the two figures is 10%. Subtract 10% from 50% and you get 40%. Thus, you enter **40** in the 50% field of the Transfer Functions dialog box.

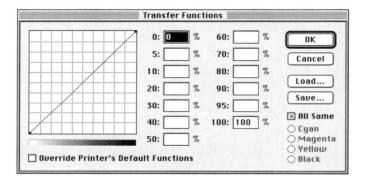

 NOTE: *If you check the Override Printer's Default Functions option in the Transfer Functions dialog box, and you export an EPS file with Include Transfer Function selected in the EPS Format dialog box, the transfer information is used in the exported file.*

 CAUTION: *Don't change any of the settings in the Transfer Functions dialog box without first consulting your service bureau.*

Setting Halftone Screens

The Screen button presents a Halftone Screens dialog box, in which you can specify elements such as screen frequency, screen angle, and halftone dot shape.

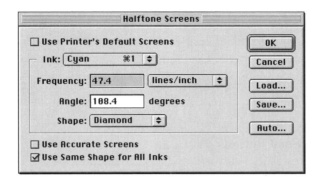

 CAUTION: *Before changing the default settings in the Halftone Screens dialog box, consult with your service bureau or print shop.*

☐ **Use Printer's Default Screens option**   If you select this option, any dialog box settings are overridden, and output will be based upon halftone screen settings built into the printer. When this check box is selected, most of the options in the Halftone Screens dialog box are disabled.

☐ **Ink pop-up menu**   If you are working with a CMYK color image, click on this pop-up menu to select the channel. Enter the screen frequency and angle for each channel. If you are printing color separations, the angle for each screen must be set properly to prevent the appearance of moiré patterns. To access these options, deselect the Use Printer's Default Screens check box.

☐ **Auto button**   If you wish to have Photoshop calculate the screen angles, click the Auto button. In the Auto Screens dialog box, enter the printer resolution and screen frequency. Click OK to have Photoshop calculate the best screen angle for all four halftone screens.

19

☐ **Shape pop-up menu** This pop-up menu in the Halftone Screens dialog box offers a list of custom halftone shapes that you can select from to create various printing effects. If you wish all four inks to have the same halftone shape, select the Use Same Shape for All Inks check box.

☐ **Use Accurate Screens option** If you are sending output to a PostScript Level 2 printer or an Emerald controller, Adobe recommends that you turn on this option.

☐ **Save and Load buttons** Use these buttons to store and use your halftone screens settings. If you wish to change the default settings, press OPTION (Windows users: ALT), and the Load and Save buttons will change to Default buttons. To create new default settings, click the ->Default button; to return to the original default settings, click <-Default.

Producing a Bleed

The Bleed button allows you to print crop marks inside your image. These crop marks provide the printer with a guide for trimming so that the image can extend (or bleed) to the edge of the page.

 NOTE: *Even though you enter a value for a bleed, crop marks will not appear unless you select the Corner and/or Center Crop Marks options.*

After you click on the Bleed button, a dialog box appears, allowing you to enter a value up to 3.18 mm (.125 inches). This is the distance from the edge of your image that will be trimmed away.

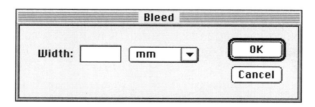

The Print Dialog Box

After you have selected all the desired options in the Page Setup dialog box, your next step in printing an image is to open the Print dialog box by choosing Print from the File menu. Most of the options in the Print dialog box will be familiar to Mac and Windows users, except for the options at the bottom of the dialog box. These options vary depending on the image mode (RGB, CMYK, etc.). The following options are important to understand when printing Photoshop images.

- **Encoding** Binary is Photoshop's default encoding format for outputting files. However, some networks and spoolers will not process binary data. If this is the case for your spooler or network, select ASCII. Bear in mind that an ASCII file is approximately twice as large as a binary file, so transferring data to the printer will take longer. The JPEG encoding options should only be used with PostScript Level 2 output devices. JPEG encoding compresses output files, which means data is downloaded faster. When outputting using JPEG encoding, Photoshop utilizes the highest quality compression. Nevertheless, since JPEG is a "lossy" compression format, output quality may be reduced.

- **Print Selected Area** If you wish to print an area you have selected on screen, choose Print Selected Areas. (This option is always available no matter what image mode your file is in.)

- **Space** This option allows you to convert color spaces during printing. For instance, you may wish to print an RGB image to a CMYK color printer; you may wish to print a CMYK color image to an RGB printer; or you may wish to print a color file to a grayscale printer. If you choose a mode other than the current image mode, Photoshop applies the settings in the appropriate Color Setup dialog box to produce the color conversion.

- **Separations** If you wish to print separations, choose Separations from the Space pop-up menu. Printing Separations is described in the next section. The Separations option is only available when you are working with a CMYK color or duotone image.

◻ **Printer Color Management** Choose this option if you wish the printer to convert the file to the printer's own color space. If you are using a postscript printer, Printer Color Management changes to Postscript Color Management. Note that you would normally select this option if you were printing to an RGB printer, or if you have already made the conversion to the printer's color space. If you wish to print a CMYK file on a PostScript Level 2 printer with PostScript Color Management, Adobe recommends choosing Lab in the Space pop-up menu.

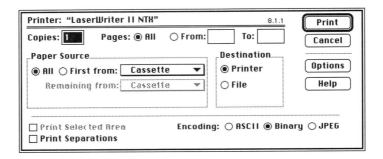

Printing Separations

This section leads you step by step through the process of printing a CMYK separation. Even if you're producing output to a 300-dpi laser printer, you may find it educational to see the separation process in action.

To print separations, you will need a CMYK color image or an RGB color image converted to CMYK color. When converting, Photoshop uses the settings in the RGB Setup and CMYK Setup dialog boxes. Before you convert an image from RGB color to CMYK color, make sure these settings are correct. And always use the File | Save As or Save a Copy command to rename your file before converting, so you'll have a copy of your original image. After converting to CMYK color, apply the Unsharp Mask filter to sharpen your image. For a complete discussion of converting from RGB color to CMYK color, see Chapter 12.

Photoshop 5 ▶ In Action

A scanned photograph of the World Trade Center was selected with the Marquee tool. Then Kai's Power Tools were applied to create the fisheye effect. It was then copied and pasted into the final image.

A linear blend from dark to light violet was created with the Gradient tool.

To create spheres, the Elliptical Marquee tool, Gaussian Blur filter, Fill command, and an alpha channel were used.

The New York City skyline was created in Adobe Illustrator and then placed into the final image in Photoshop.

Artist: Loren Ruderman   Client: The Port Authority of New York and New Jersey

Loren created this image for the panels in the Observation Deck elevator in the World Trade Center in NYC. The image was separated and output to film. The film was given to a porcelain enamel fabricator who output the image on porcelain enamel sheets. Loren started by making a selection with the Rectangular Marquee tool, filling it with a blend using the Gradient tool, then duplicating it twice. After all three linear blends were completed, he proceeded to make the largest shaded sphere by creating a selection with the Elliptical Marquee tool in a black alpha channel. After the circular selection was created, he filled it with white. He then created a smaller circular selection in the top-left side of the circular selection and filled it with black. Then the Gaussian Blur filter was applied before filling the circular selection with black. Next, the spherical selection was loaded onto the final image and filled with black using a low opacity setting. In order for the sphere to have four rings (four levels of shading), Loren repeated these steps three more times, but each time he increased the size of the circular selection and increased the opacity value. By duplicating the large shaded sphere five times and scaling each duplicate, Loren created the smaller shaded spheres. The final step was to apply the Add Noise filter to each channel in the file to compensate for banding.

19

Suppose you want to print your CMYK color image with registration marks, the image's filename, and crop marks. Follow these steps:

1. From the File menu, choose Page Setup.

2. In the Page Setup dialog box, select the Registration Marks, Labels, and Crop Marks check boxes. Click the Screen button.

3. In the Halftone Screens dialog box, click the Auto button to have Photoshop automatically set the halftone screen angle.

4. In the Auto Screens dialog box, enter your printer's resolution. If you are printing to your laser printer, type **300**. Enter **53** as the screen frequency, and make sure lines/inch is set in the corresponding pop-up menu. If you are using a PostScript Level 2 printer, select the Use Accurate Screens option. Click OK to return to the Halftone Screens dialog box.

5. Select the Use Same Shape for All Inks option. Click OK.

6. In the Print dialog box, select Separations from the Space pop-up menu, then click OK.

When the separations print, four images will be output, one for each of the CMYK colors.

 NOTE: *Second Glance LaserSeps Pro is a Photoshop export filter that creates process separations without halftone screens. It creates the separations using a process called "stochastic screening."*

The Future

The printing and prepress industries are constantly seeking ways to improve color reproduction and speed up turnaround time. The past few years have brought new developments that could change how Photoshop users work with images that must be output to printing presses. Two of the most important developments are direct-to-plate digital printing and stochastic screening.

Direct-to-Plate Digital Printing

Direct-to-plate printing is a process in which images are printed directly from digital files. No filmed negatives are needed in direct-to-plate printing. Theoretically, the process is similar to printing directly to a standard laser printer. Direct-to-plate printing has proven most effective in small print runs because quality color output can be produced quickly and at a low cost.

Stochastic Screening

In traditional four-color printing, the overlaying of different-sized CMYK halftone dots creates the illusion of countless colors. *Stochastic screening* (sometimes known as *FM,* or *frequently modulated screening*) creates colors by producing similar-sized dots that are smaller than halftone dots. The precise distribution of the dots creates the illusion of continuous-tone color. In many respects, the process is similar to dithering (the way Photoshop creates the illusion of many colors in an image that is composed of 256 or fewer colors).

Proponents of stochastic screening contend that the process produces finer detail and can reproduce colors better than traditional color printing. Those who have already begun using stochastic screening say that they can scan images at lower resolutions than those needed for traditional color printing.

In general, stochastic screening produces a grainier look in areas with light tones, but as improvements are made in stochastic screening technology, many predict that a majority of commercial printers will adopt the system by the end of the decade.

Conclusion

This chapter has shown how Photoshop allows you to enter into a technical realm once open to prepress professionals only. Undoubtedly, many Photoshop users would rather not worry about calculating gray levels, compensating for dot gain, and choosing between GCR and UCR (covered in Chapter 12). Although these prepress tasks can be avoided to some degree, you'll find that the more you work with Photoshop, the less daunting they will become. If you establish good relations with prepress houses and commercial printers, you'll have an easier time overcoming problems and getting your questions answered.

19

CHAPTER 20

Outputting to the Web, Multimedia, and Digital Video

Why has the popularity of the World Wide Web skyrocketed? Graphics is undoubtedly one major reason. Graphics and creative design are the keys to an attractive and successful Web site. Just think how many people would be using the Web if there were no graphics, if all Web sites were purely text. Who is creating much of the graphics on the Web? Photoshop artists.

 NOTE: *If you have an Internet connection and a Web browser installed on your computer, you can access information from Adobe's Web site directly from Photoshop: Simply click on the eye icon at the top of the Tool box palette (or choose File | Adobe On Line). When the Adobe On-Line dialog box appears, click on Configure to set up your browser. You can also choose whether you wish to update the Adobe Online dialog automatically and how often you want it updated.To manually update the dialog box, click Update. Adobe's Web address is www.adobe.com.*

Photoshop's power as both a creative tool and production tool has made it virtually essential to any artist interested in outputting sophisticated images to the Web. This chapter provides a detailed look at how to output images to the World Wide Web. Also discussed are several Web utilities that can help you build Web pages and make your graphics dazzling. Since many of the same issues that arise when creating graphics for the Web are relevant to multimedia production, this chapter also reviews outputting files to multimedia programs such as Macromedia Director, Adobe Premiere, and Adobe After Effects.

Web and Multimedia Color Calibration

If you are designing images for the Web or multimedia, you'll undoubtedly want the colors you see on screen to match the colors your audience sees on their own computer monitors. Unfortunately, as discussed in Chapter 1, different monitors and different computer systems display colors differently. As a first step in attempting to minimize the differences between systems, Web and multimedia producers should calibrate their monitors.

If you haven't already done so, run Adobe's Gamma utility, then choose an RGB color space (see Chapter 1 for details). If you are creating images for the Web and most multimedia programs, you'll probably want to stick with sRGB, (which stands for Standard RGB), sRGB is Photoshop's default RGB color space and represents how most computer monitors display colors. However, if you will be outputting to video, you may wish to open the RGB Color Setup dialog box (File | Color Settings | RGB Setup) and choose either SMPTE-C (for NTSC color, the U.S. television standard) or SMPTE-240M (for high-definition television), instead of sRGB.

GrayScale Color Settings

If you are working with Grayscale mode images for the Web and multimedia, you do not want Photoshop to change the display of your image to compensate for dot gain (which occurs during the printing process). To specify how Photoshop displays grayscale images choose (File | Color | Settings | Grayscale). In the Grayscale Setup dialog box, make sure that the RGB choice is selected. If you choose the Black Ink option, Photoshop uses the Dot Gain setting in the CMYK setup dialog box to compensate on screen for dot gain. For more information about dot gain see Chapter 12.

Turning Off Embedded Color Profiles

If you need the colors in Photoshop to match colors in a multimedia program, your best bet may be to simply load an image in Photoshop and compare how it looks in your multimedia program. You may even wish to turn off Photoshop's color management options. Why turn them off? If you load and resave different images using different RGB color spaces, you may find that the color values in your image change. This can be particularly troublesome if you are trying to save images using Web-safe colors. You also might wish to turn off Photoshop's color profile tagging to help ensure file sizes are as small as possible.

You can turn off Photoshop's profile tagging feature by choosing File | Color Setup | Profile Setup and deselecting the RGB option in the Embed Profile section. You can also save any image without an embedded color tag by selecting the Exclude Non-Image Data after choosing Photoshop's File | Save a Copy command. If you turn off Photoshop's color management system, you should also turn off the Display Monitor Compensation in the RGB Setup dialog box (File | Color Settings | RGB Setup).

Choosing Image Resolution for the Web and Multimedia

If you are outputting for either the Web or multimedia, one of your first concerns should be to ensure that you are creating your graphics at the correct resolution. If image resolution is too high, viewing your Web site or multimedia production could prove to be a frustrating experience for even the most patient viewer. When resolution is too high, an image's file size increases, which means it takes longer to download to a Web browser and longer to redraw on screen.

If you are creating images for the Web or a multimedia program, the resolution of the images need only be as high as the resolution of a computer display (usually 640 × 480 pixels, 72 ppi). Creating images at higher resolutions only results in larger file sizes; it doesn't result in better quality. (Of course, you may need to create images at a higher resolution if you will be enlarging them or using them in video applications for film.)

The monitor you use may not be set to a higher resolution than 72 ppi. However, since virtually all computer monitors can display images at 72 pixels per inch, most Web designers create images at 72 ppi. This ensures that all Mac and Windows users can view images properly. If someone is viewing an image created at 72 ppi on a monitor set to a higher resolution, the image looks smaller than its creation size. Nevertheless, it should still be sharp.

Resizing Digitized Images

If you are adding scanned images to a Web page or to a multimedia production, you can digitize the image at 72 pixels per inch (if you are not going to enlarge the image). If you need to reduce the image, simply use Photoshop's Image Size command (Image | Image Size). In the Image Size dialog box, make sure that the Resample Image check box is selected. Enter the new dimensions for your image. When you click OK, the image will be resized and the 72-ppi resolution will be maintained.

 TIP: *Always try to keep the file size of your Web and multimedia graphics as small as possible. When you reduce image size in Photoshop with the Resample Image check box on, the file size of the image is reduced. Most Web page-building programs and page-layout programs do not reduce file size when you reduce your image's dimensions.*

NOTE: *Resizing low-resolution images that contain text may distort the text or make the text unreadable.*

If you will be enlarging images, you should multiply your enlargement scaling factor by 72 ppi to calculate your scanning resolution. For instance, if you will be enlarging an image that you want to be twice its original size, multiply 2 × 72 to calculate your scanning resolution, 144 ppi. To enlarge your image, open up Photoshop's Image Size dialog box (Image | Image size). To avoid adding pixels when you enlarge, deselect the Resample Image check box, then enter the new dimensions for your image. Immediately, the resolution drops to 72 ppi. Click OK to complete the adjustment.

 REMEMBER: *When you enlarge an image with the Resample Image check box on, the file size of your image does not grow, because you haven't added any pixels to the image. For more information about choosing resolution and resizing images, see Chapter 8.*

Choosing Image Size

As you begin to create images for the Web or multimedia, it's important to remember that most users viewing your Web images will be downloading them from modems and may be viewing your work on systems not as powerful as yours. (You should also remember that some Web browsers don't even show any graphics on screen.) To help ensure that your viewers won't get frustrated and surf off to other locations, keep the file size of your graphics small. The larger an image is, the longer it takes to download. Thus, try not to stuff too many graphics on a page. If you need to display large images on screen, give the user a choice. Show the image as a thumbnail. Allow the user to click on the thumbnail to go to another page to see the image full screen.

 NOTE: *A 48K file takes about 16 seconds to download on a 28,800 baud modem.*

 NOTE: *Text on the Web takes less time to download than graphics. Be aware, though, that text appears in Web browsers based on the fonts installed on the user's system. If you need text to appear in a specific font as a logo or with special effects, you should probably create the text as a graphic in Photoshop (you may also want to use Adobe Illustrator or Meta Creations Painter).*

20

Web and Multimedia File Formats

The quality of images that appear on the Web and in multimedia productions is often determined by how they are converted to Web or multimedia file formats.

Most multimedia programs on the Mac accept PICT as a file format; on the PC, BMP is the standard. Before converting file formats, many multimedia producers reduce the number of colors in their images to reduce file size and to ensure that they can be viewed on systems that only display 256 colors at a time. (See the color table discussion later in this chapter and in Chapter 12 to learn more about using Indexed Color mode to reduce the number of colors in your images.)

 NOTE: *Macromedia Director loads JPEG images, as well as PICT and BMP.*

If you are going to be outputting images to the Web, you can save your image in several file formats: CompuServe GIF (often pronounced "jiff "), JPEG, and PNG (often pronounced "ping"). Most Photoshop artists use the most common Web file formats: GIF and JPEG. The following sections provide a brief review of the formats, followed by instructions on how to save in each format.

 NOTE: *Many Webmasters predict PNG will eventually be the standard Web file format because it is supposed to be royalty-free, and because it provides better file compression than GIF and better color fidelity. PNG is covered in Appendix A.*

JPEG File Format

JPEG (Joint Photographic Experts Group) is a file format commonly used to output scanned images to the Web. It is primarily used when images need to display transitional colors, often when images must display thousands or millions of colors. JPEG is used for Web images because it can reduce file size by compressing images. It does this by subtracting image data from files, which means that image quality may be degraded. When you output your file as a JPEG image you can specify whether you need a high-, medium-, or low-quality image. The higher the quality, the larger the file's size; the lower the quality, the smaller the file's size.

If you decide to save your files in JPEG format, remember that users with 8-bit color boards can only view 256 colors on screen at a time. If you save a 24-bit color file in JPEG format, it may look ragged and the color quality may appear poor to viewers using 8-bit systems. To preview your image in 8-bit color depth, change your color display to view 256 colors. Mac, Windows 95/98, and Windows NT users can easily do this by changing settings accessed through their operating systems' Control Panel settings.

Saving in JPEG Format

If your image has no layers, you can save in JPEG format by simply choosing File | Save As, then choosing JPEG from the File Format (Windows users: Save As) pop-up menu. If your image contains layers, you must choose File | Save a Copy, which flattens the exported image. In the JPEG dialog box, choose a quality setting. For the best color quality, choose BaseLine Optimized.

 NOTE: *The JPEG dialog box is shown in Appendix A.*

If you want your Web audience to see the image gradually become more detailed through the use of progressive image scans, choose the Progressive option in the JPEG dialog box. Next, enter the number of scans desired. (Note that this feature requires more RAM and is not supported by all Web browsers.)

GIF File Format

The most common file format for outputting images to the Web is GIF (Graphic Interchange Format). GIF file format requires that the number of colors in an image be reduced to 256 or less. This a major factor in reducing file size. Since the number of colors in an image can only be 256 or fewer, GIF is commonly used for images that don't display many color transitions. Web buttons and logos are commonly saved in GIF file format. Furthermore, many Web artists who use GIF files create their images or convert them using a Web-safe palette of 216 colors (using this palette is described later in this chapter).

 NOTE: *Images with 256 colors are generally about three times as small as images with millions of colors.*

GIF also allows you to control image transparency. For instance, assume you want to place a logo from Photoshop text on your Web page, and you want the background color of the Web browser to show through the letters. Photoshop's

20

File | Export | GIF89a command allows you to do this. The GIF89a export module also allows you to convert RGB files with or without layers to GIF format. Photoshop's GIF89a plug-in also provides options for choosing a Web-safe color palette and interlacing images. *Interlaced images* are images that gradually sharpen into focus as they are being downloaded to a Web browser.

NOTE: *This chapter covers Photoshop's File | Export | GIF89a command because it provides more options than using File | Save As to save in CompuServe GIF format. Saving in CompuServe GIF format is covered in Appendix A. If you do wish to save your file using CompuServe GIF, convert the file to Indexed Color first. Also, note that you can use an alpha channel to create transparent areas in your GIF file. For more information, see Appendix A.*

The following table summarizes the differences between saving in JPEG format and saving in GIF format using the GIF89a export command.

File Format	Advantages	Disadvantages
GIF89a	Small file size, good for flat color	May not produce good results from scanned images with colors
	Transparency can be controlled using layer transparency (from an RGB file) or alpha channel or using Eyedropper (indexed files)	Must reduce color palette to 256 or fewer colors
	Allows interlacing	
	Allows animated GIF	
JPEG	Can control image quality and display millions of colors	Cannot control transparency
	Good for continuous-tone scanned images	Images viewed on 256-color systems may not look correct
	Allows progressive scans in which images gradually become sharper	

Exporting Using GIF89a

The following sections show you how to convert RGB color images and Indexed Color to GIF format using Photoshop's File | Export | GIF89a command. If you export from RGB color, you can specify that transparent areas in a layer be the transparent areas in your GIF file. If you are exporting from an Indexed Color file to GIF, transparent areas are created by clicking with the Eyedropper in your image, or they can be based on the masked area in an alpha channel.

 NOTE: *For information about converting to Indexed Color, see Chapter 12.*

 TIP: *Photoshop's Help menu can lead you, step-by-step, through the process of saving a file in GIF format. Choose Help | Export Transparent Image. Just answer the questions on screen and click the Next button. Choose Online instead of Print to proceed to save your file in GIF or PNG format.*

1. If you want the GIF file to include only part of an image, select the portion of the image you wish to include. To create smooth transitions between the image and the background of the Web browser, you may wish to feather the edges of the selection. After you select the image, copy it into a new layer, then hide all underlying layers. The transparent portion of the layer (checkerboard pattern), as shown below, will be transparent in the final GIF image.

2. To export the file, choose GIF89a from the File | Export submenu.

 NOTE: *You will not be able to make any portion of your image transparent if your image is not in a layer on a transparent background.*

The Transparency Index Color swatch allows you to specify the transparency color. For instance, if you are using Netscape and would like the browser's gray background to show through the transparent area in your image, you can leave the transparency color set to the default color. Netscape gray is 204 red, 204 green, 204 blue.

3. If you wish to change colors, click on the transparency color swatch. This opens the Photoshop, Apple, or Windows system's Color Picker. Choose your color by clicking in the Color Picker or by entering values in the fields.

4. Your next step is to choose a color palette for your image. GIF89a restricts you to 256 or fewer colors.

☐ If your image contains 256 colors or less, choose Exact. This means that the GIF image will contain exactly the same colors as your original.

☐ If your image contains more than 256 colors, your best bet is to choose Adaptive. When you choose Adaptive, Photoshop samples colors in your image and makes a color table out of the sampled colors.

☐ Choose System if you wish your image to create a color table from the Windows or Macintosh default color palette. If you choose this option, you may find that users on different computer systems will not view the images as you intended them to be.

☐ To choose a color palette that you've created in Photoshop, click the Load button, then load the palette from disk. Then click OK. Using the Load button, you can load Photoshop's Web-safe palette from the Color Palettes folder (located in the Goodies folder). If you choose a Web-safe palette, colors are converted to those that are used by both Netscape's browsers and Microsoft's Internet Explorer. Thus, clicking on the Preview button should give you a good idea of how the image will appear in some Web browsers (you may find that new versions of some Web browsers handle colors differently than older versions).

▫ If you choose the Adaptive option and wish to restrict the colors to fewer than 256, enter the number. Reducing the number of colors in a large image can make a significant difference in file size.

▫ If you choose System or use a custom color palette, make sure that the Use Best Match check box is selected.

5. To see how your image will appear in a Web browser, click Preview.

 NOTE: *The Preview option in Photoshop's Indexed Color dialog box provides a better preview of the image with its reduced color palette.*

In the Preview window, seen in Figure 20-1, you can reposition the image by selecting the Hand tool and clicking and dragging on the image. Double-click on the Hand tool if you want to fit the entire image in the window.

FIGURE 20-1   The GIF89a Export Preview window

20

To zoom in, select the Zoom tool. Click and drag over the image areas that you wish to zoom into. Press OPTION (Windows users: ALT) and click to zoom back out. Click OK to close the Preview window.

6. Select Interlaced if you wish to have your image gradually come into view as it is loaded into the Web browser. If you are using your image as background or text, deselect Interlaced.

   If you didn't like the preview, press OPTION (Windows users: ALT) and click Reset. You can then try a different palette or different number of colors.

7. To export the file to disk, click OK. In the Save As dialog box, name your image, and click Save.

 NOTE: *Images saved using the GIF89a export command appear as CompuServe GIF files in the Format (Windows users: Save As) pop-up menu.*

Exporting Indexed Color Images to GIF

If you export an Indexed Color file to GIF format, you can click on areas in your image that you would like to appear transparent or you can use an alpha channel to create transparency in an image. Note that these options are not available when you export an RGB file using Photoshop's File | Export | GIF89a command.

   If you want the background of your image to be transparent, you must create an alpha channel masking out the part of your image that you want transparent. If you wish to create an alpha channel, first create a selection on screen. Then choose Select | Save Selection. The area within the selection will be included in your image (if Masked Areas is selected in the Channels palette; otherwise the area outside the selection will be included). The area outside of the selection will be transparent. You can also use Quick Mask mode to create the selection. For more information about Quick Mask mode using channels, see Chapter 14).

 TIP: *To create an intricate selection you may wish to first create a path around your image with one of the Pen tools, then convert the path to a selection by choosing Make Selection in the Path palette menu.*

1. Open an Indexed Color file, or convert your file to Indexed Colors, by choosing Image | Mode | Indexed Color.

2. To open the GIF89a dialog box, choose GIF89a from the File I Export submenu.

3. Click the Interlaced check box if you wish to have the image gradually appear on screen when seen in a Web browser.

4. If you want to use an alpha channel to create transparent areas in your file, choose the alpha channel in the Transparency From pop-up menu. (In the image shown below, we created a selection around the paintbrush, then chose Select I Save Selection to create the alpha channel. By choosing this option, all areas surrounding the paintbrush are transparent on our Web page.) If you want to leave the transparency color set to the Netscape gray, do not click on the Transparency Preview color box. Otherwise, click on the Transparency Preview check box to choose the color you wish to use for transparent areas and continue to step 7.

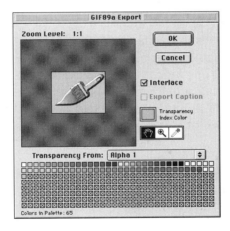

5. If you do not want to control transparency with an alpha channel, make sure that Selected Colors is selected in the Transparency From pop-up menu. Select the Eyedropper Plus tool, then click on the image areas (in the Preview box) that you want to be transparent, or click on the small color swatches at the bottom of the dialog box to choose the colors that you want to be transparent.

6. Next, you must decide if you want to set the background color of your browser or Web page. If you want to leave the transparency color set to Netscape gray, do not click in the Transparency Preview color box. If you

wish to change the color used for transparency, click on the Transparency Preview color box, then choose a new color in the Color Picker dialog box. After you pick a color, you can still click on the Eyedropper Plus tool or the color swatches to add to the image areas that you want to be transparent.

7. If you wish to zoom into your file, select the Magnifier tool on screen and click in the preview box. To zoom out, press OPTION (Windows users: ALT) and click. If you wish to reposition the image in the Preview box, select the Hand tool, then click and drag in the Preview area.

8. To close the GIF89a dialog box, click OK, then name your file in the Save As dialog box.

Choosing Color Tables for the Web and Multimedia

One of the most troublesome issues facing designers who create images for the Web and multimedia is how to effectively create attractive images with the fewest number of colors. Images that look great with thousands or millions of colors may look spotted or ragged when reduced to 256 or fewer colors. If you're designing images for 8-bit computer systems it's important to remember that these systems can only display 256 colors at a time. This means that every button, as well as every image, on a Web page or a multimedia screen should use the same 256-color palette.

One technique for ensuring that all elements share the same color palette is to copy all elements into one Photoshop file, and then use the Image | Mode | Indexed Color command to create a type of "super palette." If you are creating a multimedia project for one computer platform, you may be able to convert every image you use in your presentation to Indexed Color by simply choosing the Mac or Windows system palette.

Another problem faced by Web designers, particularly those designing on the Macintosh, is the difference between the Mac and Windows system palettes. Windows reserves the first and last 20 colors in its palette for system operations, meaning only 216 colors are available. Web browsers such as Netscape have their own palette of colors—both Netscape Navigator and Microsoft Explorer use a

216-color palette. You can convert your image to this palette by choosing the Web palette when converting to Indexed Color (Image | Mode | Indexed Color).

The Web palette creates 216 colors using different combinations of six evenly spaced color values. The color values of the six colors are: 0, 51, 102, 153, 204, and 255.

 TIP: *The easiest way to paint with Web-safe colors is to load Photoshop's 216-color Web palette into the Swatches palette, then choose your colors by clicking on swatches. To load the palette, choose Replace Colors from the Swatches Palette pop-up menu, then load the Web-Safe Palette from the Color Palettes folder (inside the Goodies folder).*

 TIP: *System 8 for the Mac includes a Web Color Picker. You can switch to this Color Picker by choosing File | General Preferences. In the General Preferences dialog box, choose Apple. When you activate the Color Picker in Photoshop (you can click on the foreground or background color icon), you can choose Apple's HTML Color Picker to pick Web-safe colors. In order to use this option, the Color Picker System extension must be installed in your System folder's Extensions folder.*

If you use a color in your image that the browser's color palette can't match on an 8-bit color system, the browser tries to provide the best match for the missing color by dithering. The results, however, may not be appealing. How can you make your images look as good as possible on the Web? You can convert your images to Indexed mode using Photoshop's Web palette. You can also turn to other programs, such as Adobe ImageReady, Equilibrium DeBabelizer and Pantone ColorWeb, which specialize in palette conversions.

Using ImageReady

Photoshop users who want to squeeze every last byte out of their Web graphics should definitely consider Adobe's ImageReady Web graphics package. ImageReady provides a Photoshop-like environment with selection and cropping tools similar to Photoshop's. ImageReady's Actions, Layer, and History palettes are almost identical to Photoshop's. Furthermore, many of the commands used to transform graphics and images are similar to Photoshop's. So why use ImageReady if you already have Photoshop?

One of ImageReady's most attractive features not found in Photoshop is animation. Using ImageReady, you can convert images in separate Photoshop layers into an animated GIF file. ImageReady also includes a command called Folder as Frames which automatically loads a folder full of images and creates an animated sequence out of them. We used this technique to populate the animation palette shown in Figure 20-2. Once the images appear in the animation palette, they can be edited using ImageReady's own image-editing tools.

ImageReady also includes many features that optimize the process of Web-color management and file size reduction. Web designers will also appreciate ImageReady's ability to selectively alter specific colors in an image to make them Web safe. It can also lock specific colors to prevent them from being altered. Mac users will particularly appreciate ImageReady's View | Windows Gamma command, which previews how an image will appear on a Windows monitor.

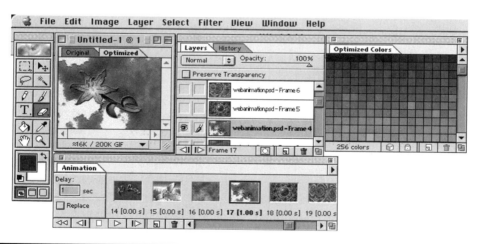

FIGURE 20-2 Photoshop's images used to create GIF animation using Adobe ImageReady

Using DeBabelizer

DeBabelizer (available on Mac, Windows 95, and UNIX platforms) has long been the answer to the prayers of multimedia producers. DeBabelizer does an excellent job of reducing the colors in an image, usually with visually pleasing results. One of DeBabelizer's most powerful features is its Superpalette command, which can batch-convert images to GIF or PICT format and apply a palette sampled from all images to the converted images. This means that images presented on one Web page or one screen in a multimedia presentation will appear as desired when viewed on an 8-bit system.

DeBabelizer can flatten Mac QuickTime movies so that they can be viewed on the Web and on the Windows platform. DeBabelizer also allows you to apply a filter to a series of frames in a QuickTime movie. The program is compatible with many Photoshop third-party plug-ins' images.

The current version of DeBabelizer allows you to use a 216-color Netscape palette. Using DeBabelizer scripts, you can batch-convert many images at one time to this palette. Equilibrium has found that bright colors work best with the Netscape palette. Brown colors and flesh tones are not handled well.

For more information about Equilibrium DeBabelizer, see Equilibrium's Web page: www.equilibrium.com.

Using Pantone ColorWeb

The Pantone Internet Color system is a program created to help Web designers achieve the best possible cross-platform output. The focal point of the program is a cross-platform 216-color palette. The palette is accessible from any program that can access the Apple system palette. Using the palette, you can ensure that you are not choosing colors that a Web browser needs to dither. ColorWeb can be used to control colors for backgrounds, text, the currently active link, and visited and unvisited links. The program includes a printed source book of colors which simulates the onscreen colors. The numbered guide includes RGB values that enable you to recreate the colors using Photoshop's Color palette. For more information, see Pantone's Web page at: www.pantone.com.

20

NOTE: *Digital Frontier's HVS Color is another highly recommended utility for downsizing the colors in an image and converting to GIF format. HVS functions as a Photoshop plug-in. It not only does an excellent job of reducing colors in an image, but it is usually more effective than Photoshop at squashing image file size.*

Web Page and Graphics Creation Programs

Despite the tremendous power and versatility of Photoshop, the program won't automatically output a Web page for you or instantly create 3-D text and images. The following sections review several programs that can jumpstart your Web site and help create eye-popping graphics for the Web and multimedia.

Using Adobe PageMill

If you want to start designing your own Web pages and don't want to spend time learning or writing HTML code, Adobe PageMill will prove to be a valuable investment—one that quickly pays for itself.

Adobe PageMill allows you to easily create and prototype Web pages. Essentially, the program is a page layout program for the Web. Like page layout programs, it allows you to place graphics on the screen and add rules and text to lay out a page. You can also drag GIF and JPEG images from Photoshop directly into PageMill. Once you have your text and graphics loaded, you can change type size and colors and add clickable image maps or hot spots. Many formatting commands that normally require careful typing in HTML code can be created by simply clicking buttons on a toolbar at the top of the screen. The HTML code is created automatically.

Figure 20-3 shows images and 3-D text that we imported into PageMill as part of our own Web site. (Visit our Web site at: www2.infohouse.com/~addesign.) The images and text were created using Adobe Photoshop, Adobe Illustrator, Fractal Design Painter, and Strata StudioPro. As we worked on the page, we simply clicked a button to preview the page to see how it would appear in a Web browser. Figure 20-4 shows the HTML code automatically generated by PageMill. (We did need to edit the file paths in the HTML code when we sent the files to our Web provider from another computer.)

The latest version of PageMill allows you to create tables, frames, and forms in your Web pages. You can easily link one page to a button by clicking and dragging a page icon from one page to the button image. If you want to add a bit

FIGURE 20-3   Images created in Photoshop and other programs placed into Adobe PageMill

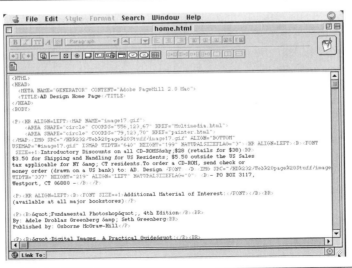

FIGURE 20-4   HTML code created automatically by PageMill

20

of animation, you can use the File | Place command to place QuickTime movies directly into your page. PageMill also allows you to easily embed Acrobat PDF files into your Web pages.

One of the more interesting features of PageMill is its Download Statistics feature. Using this option, you can predict just how long it will take for an image to appear when viewed on a browser using a specific modem speed.

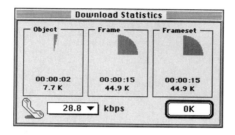

 TIP: *If your GIF files take too long to download, try reducing the number of colors in an image. You may be surprised how good images that use 128 or fewer colors can look.*

Using Virtus 3-D Website Builder

Many Web pundits predict that future Web sites will be 3-D environments that allow you to walk through three-dimensional space. If you want to get a jump on the competition and quickly start creating 3-D Web environments, you should investigate 3-D Website Builder (for both Mac and Windows platforms). Using 3-D Website Builder, you can allow viewers to click buttons to walk through a simulated store, art gallery, or outdoor location.

Creating 3-D environments is very simple. The program includes a gallery of objects and shapes that can be dropped into the scene that you are creating. Figure 20-5 shows a simple 3-D interior scene that we created in just a few minutes by dragging objects from gallery libraries and positioning them in the viewing window. As we positioned the objects, the actual 3-D scene was created in the Walkthrough window. We added the brick texture by clicking on wireframe shapes near the fireplace and selecting from a texture library.

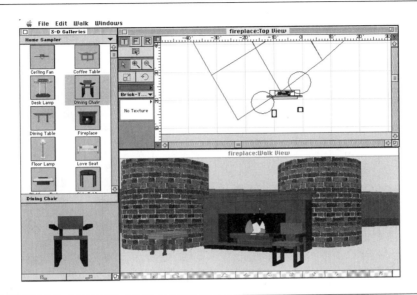

FIGURE 20-5   Walkthrough environment created in Virtus 3-D Website Builder

3-D Website Builder also allows you to create hot spots out of objects, which means that you send a Web surfer to another page or Web site when a 3-D object is clicked. 3-D Website Builder exports files in VRML (Virtual Reality Markup Language) and JPEG (Mac users can also save in PICT format; Windows users can save in BMP format). VRML formats can be read by virtual reality browsers. The program's manual includes instructions for configuring HTML browsers, such as Netscape, so that they will open up a helper file to read VRML files. For more information, point your browser to the Virtus Web site: www.virtus.com.

Outputting to Multimedia Programs

Photoshop is one of the most commonly used tools to prepare images for multimedia programs such as Macromedia Director, Adobe Premiere, and Adobe After Effects. As mentioned earlier, many Mac-based multimedia programs read PICT and JPEG images; Windows-based multimedia programs use BMP and

20

JPEG. Using Photoshop, you can easily convert images to these formats. (See Appendix A for more details.) The following sections provide a look at several cross-platform multimedia programs and utilities.

 TIP: *If you are working on multimedia projects that will be viewed both on Macs and in Windows, you'll find that images appear darker in Windows than they do on the Mac. If you are designing on the Mac and your images are going to appear in the Windows environment, you might wish to make them a little brighter. All multimedia producers should test their work on both platforms. You can get an idea of the difference between the two platforms by choosing File | Color Settings | RGB Setup. In the RGB setup dialog box, choosing Apple RGB with the Preview check box selected approximates Mac color monitors; changing the setting to sRGB shows how PC users may view the image.*

Using Macromedia Director

Macromedia Director is undoubtedly the most popular multimedia authoring tool in the world. Using Director, you can import Photoshop files saved in JPEG format as well as PICT (on the Mac) or BMP (for Windows users) formats. Each Photoshop image that is imported in Director becomes a cast member. Cast members can then be placed on a score and animated. Figure 20-6 shows the table of contents screen for a CD-ROM we created in Macromedia Director: "The Ultimate Interactive Guide to Painter 5."

Most of the elements for this screen were created in Photoshop. We added beveling effects using both Photoshop and Alien Skin's Eye Candy filters. The 3-D buttons at the bottom of the screen were created in Strata StudioPro. The "rollover" effect, showing the chapter number in white, was programmed in Director. To create the effect, we needed to create a separate white overlay for each chapter. Each chapter overlay was created in a Photoshop layer to ensure proper registration. Once the graphics were created, we converted them to Indexed Color. In this particular screen, all elements were converted to Indexed Color using the Mac system palette. When the image is viewed in the Windows environment, it is slightly darker. You can see this image in color at www2.infohouse.com/~addesign.

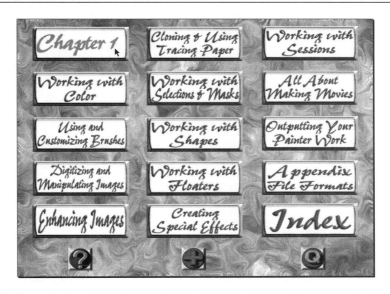

FIGURE 20-6   CD-ROM table of contents screen created in Photoshop and other programs, then imported into Director

Using MediaLab's PhotoCaster and AlphaMania

MediaLab's PhotoCaster and AlphaMania provide the missing link between the Adobe Photoshop and Macromedia Director programs. PhotoCaster and AlphaMania are plug-in programs (called "Xtras") that add to the capabilities of Director when it imports cast member files.

PhotoCaster allows you to import Photoshop layers as separate Director cast members, an invaluable aid to multimedia designers. If you have PhotoCaster, you can design an entire multimedia screen, buttons and all, in one layered Photoshop image. When the file is imported into Director, the layers are separated, each appearing as a separate cast member, each with the correct registration point. If you have PhotoCaster you do not need to convert your file from Photoshop to another file format or convert from RGB to Indexed Color mode.

Using PhotoCaster is quite simple. After you install it into Director's Xtras folder, you can access it by choosing Insert | Media | PhotoCaster. This loads the PhotoCaster Open dialog box, which displays Photoshop files.

The dialog box options allow you to load all layers from a Photoshop file or selected layers. When you drag the cast members on stage, they are automatically registered in their proper positions. Additionally, PhotoCaster's white reduction feature alters the imported cast members so that Director can distinguish between which areas you want transparent and which you want white. Note that PhotoCaster can also create a super palette out of all the layers in the file, and reduce the number of colors in images as it imports them.

As a simple example, we created a button in Web Edition TextureScape, then embossed text for the button in a Photoshop layer. We then duplicated the text into another layer and darkened it in that layer. We wanted the dark text to be the on state of the button and the light text to be the off state of the button. Figure 20-7(a) shows the Layers palette for the background of our button and the text. Figure 20-7(b) shows the results after opening the Photoshop file in Director using Photo-caster. Notice that the three layers arrived in Director as separate cast members. We then selected two of the cast members and dragged them on stage to create the off state of the button, and set the Ink property of the text to transparent. Now, using Director's programming language, Lingo, we could easily switch between the on button state and the off button state.

AlphaMania is another MediaLab Xtra specifically designed to work with Photoshop images. AlphaMania reads the transparency of Photoshop layers and Photoshop alpha channels. This means that you can create a gradient in an alpha channel in Photoshop and use it in Director to create transparency. When the

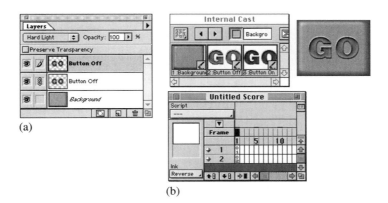

FIGURE 20-7   (a) Photoshop's Layers palette showing button text and background; (b) layers imported by PhotoCaster as separate cast members

image is imported into Director using the AlphaMania Xtra, it becomes an AlphaMania cast member. When you place the cast member on stage, the transparent areas are determined by the luminosity values of the alpha channel. The transparency remains in effect even if you make the object draggable by the user.

AlphaMania also helps solve a major annoyance for Photoshop/Director users: jagged edges. Images that are smooth in Photoshop often appear jagged in Director. Since Photoshop anti-aliasing is handled by layers, AlphaMania can preserve feathered edges that would normally look jagged in Director. (For instance, the CD-ROM image shown in Figure 20-1 would appear as a smooth image, maintaining the transparent hole and its feathering if it were imported into Director using AlphaMania.)

Figure 20-8 provides an example of how AlphaMania can utilize a Photoshop alpha channel. Notice that our Go button is now partially transparent. We created this effect by creating a blend in an alpha channel in Photoshop. We then saved a copy of our file as a PICT image (Windows users can save in TARGA file format). This flattened our file, but maintained our alpha channel. After we loaded the button into Director, it appeared as an AlphaMania cast member. We then created a blend and dragged this to the stage. Next, we dragged our button over the blend. AlphaMania allowed the colors of the blend to show through the transparent areas of the button. The results look great, but Director users must realize that PICT files that accept alpha channels are 32-bit (24-bit color; 8-bit alpha channel), which means the file size of AlphaMania cast members is much larger than 8-bit PICT files.

 FIGURE 20-8   AlphaMania used the alpha channel in Photoshop to create a transparent effect in Director

NOTE: *You can download demo versions of both PhotoCaster and AlphaMania from MediaLab's Web site: http://www.medialab.com*

Working with Adobe Premiere

Adobe Premiere turns your computer into a digital movie editing studio. Premiere is used to create multimedia presentations from digital images, digital movies, and sounds.

You can create interesting and unusual backgrounds with Adobe Photoshop, and then import these images into Adobe Premiere to animate them by applying filters, transitions, and motion. The current version of Premiere is completely cross-platform: both Mac and Windows versions can create animated GIF movies and QuickTime digital movies; the Windows version can create AVI (Video For Windows) movies as well.

Photoshop files can be loaded directly into Premiere. Files with layers can be loaded as merged images, or the individual layer can be loaded as a separate image. Figure 20-9 shows the Premiere window with Photoshop images imported into video Tracks A and B, and a transition, Track T. Once the Photoshop file is imported, it appears in the Project window. Next, you need to drag the Photoshop file to video Track A of the Time Linewindow. You can easily duplicate the image into multiple frames and apply a filter to them, apply a transition between two images, or use the Motion command to set an image in motion over time.

In order to apply a transition, you drag a Photoshop file to video Track A and another to video Track B, then drag a transition from the Transition palette to video Track T. Applying a transition allows you to have one Photoshop file gradually dissolve into another with an effect being applied to it as it dissolves. Note that there are over 50 transitions in Premiere's Transition palette.

Photoshop 5 In Action

Artist: Eve Elberg

Multimedia artist Eve Elberg created this screen for a Macromedia Director multimedia production. Since most multimedia screens are designed for 640 × 480 pixels, she created a 640 × 480 RGB document in Photoshop.

In Photoshop, Eve created each element in separate layers: the background, the panel, the title, and the button elements. The bevel around the buttons was created using the freeware "Sucking Fish" filters. The drop shadows behind the buttons were created by duplicating the button layers, filling them with black, running a Gaussian Blur, adjusting the layer opacity to varying percentages, and setting the compositing method to Multiply.

She saved the elements by first hiding layers she didn't want; then she chose the File | Save A Copy command. Eve used this process to flatten four different files in PICT format for the Macintosh. She created four different files so that she could use the four elements as separate Director cast members. Then she chose Image | Mode | Indexed Color and set the palette to Adaptive, the Color Depth to 8 bits per pixel, and the Dither to Diffusion. Next she used the Actions palette to record an action for a palette conversion. When she recorded the action, she set the palette choice to Previous. Setting the choice to Previous ensured that all conversions used by the action would use the same palette.

Next, she converted the palettes for the rest of the files by using the Actions palette's Batch command. She set the source folder to Conversions and the Destination file to Converted. After the process was complete, each PICT file was converted to the same 256-color palette.

20

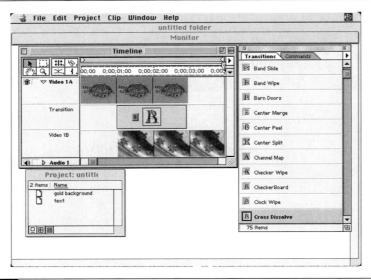

FIGURE 20-9   Adobe Photoshop files imported into Premiere

To apply a filter to a Photoshop image that is extended over several frames in Premiere, you need to choose Clip | Filters. In the Filters dialog box, you can choose a filter to be applied to the image at a certain amount or have the filter applied at different increments at the start and end of the image by clicking on the Start and End buttons in the Filter dialog box.

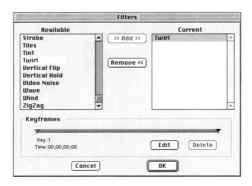

To preview an animation in Premiere, you must save the file. After you save the file, Premiere creates a preview, which is displayed in the Monitor window. If you like the preview and want to save your your digital movie, you choose File | Export | Movie.

Working with Adobe After Effects

Adobe After Effects is one of the most sophisticated digital editing and special effects programs available for both Macs and Windows. It's especially valuable to multimedia producers who use Photoshop, because of Photoshop's ability to import a file with layers directly into After Effects. When the file appears in After Effects, all of the Photoshop layers are intact, ready to be animated. Using After Effects, you can integrate your Photoshop files into a multimedia production composed of digital video images, still images, and sounds. Like Photoshop, After Effects' layers provide numerous blending effects. However, unlike Photoshop, blending effects and filters can be applied to frames of a digital video over time. Layers can be blurred, sharpened, or beveled. Using After Effects, you can put several digital movies in different layers and run them in different sections of your screen.

After you are done animating all your files and footage, you can save your project as a QuickTime movie, Photoshop 3.0 sequence, PICT sequence, Electric-Image IMAGE, Diquest DDR, or Filmstrip file. Images can also be output to videotape as well as to digital video.

Figure 20-10 shows an animated sequence we created out of Photoshop files. In it, each image gradually appears on screen and then moves into position.

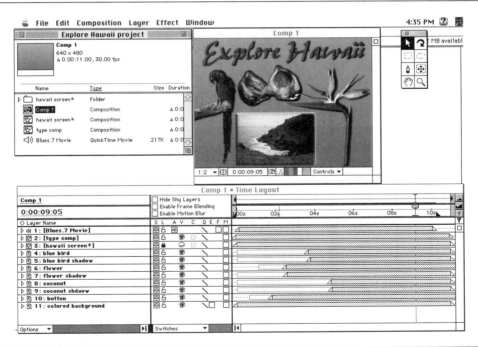

FIGURE 20-10 Adobe Photoshop files with layers imported into Adobe After Effects

20

Conclusion

The Web and CD-ROM multimedia productions have necessitated new software tools for digital artists. Despite the arrival of these new software tools, none replaces Photoshop as a tool for creating and editing digital images. You might even go so far as to say that the Web and multimedia were made popular because of Photoshop.

CHAPTER 21

Watermarking Your Images and Copyright Information

The popularity of image-editing programs like Photoshop and the availability of digitizing equipment like scanners and digital cameras have sparked new concerns about copyright protection. Artists are justifiably worried about unauthorized use of their images. Many designers are concerned that they might inadvertently publish an image that they don't have permission to use.

This chapter provides a basic overview of copyright laws and offers some tips about how you can protect yourself against unauthorized use of your images. If you create or use digital images, a working knowledge of copyright laws can be as important as knowing how to use the latest features of Photoshop 5.

Understanding the Copyright Laws

The copyright laws of the United States were written to protect an artist's right of expression. Works created by artists, photographers, and writers are all covered under the copyright laws, which specify who has the right to copy a work. A copyright owner has the right to:

- Copy his or her work
- Create derivative works (new versions based on the original)
- Perform the work
- Exhibit the work or control who exhibits it

For Photoshop users, several aspects of the law are important to understand: The copyright law protects all works as soon as they are created—even if they are not registered with the U.S. copyright office, and even if they do not display the familiar copyright symbol.

Independent Contractors and Work for Hire

As a Photoshop user, it's important for you to understand how the copyright law distinguishes between works created by full-time employees and works created by independent contractors. If you are an employee at a design studio, publishing house, or photography studio, the copyright of your work is owned by your employer. Under current copyright laws, your employer owns the copyright for 75 years after the work is published or 100 years after the work was created, whichever comes first.

Independent contractors, such as freelancers, are generally considered to be the copyright owners of their own works. If you are an artist and are hired on a freelance basis, you probably own the copyright of the works you create, even if others at the company supervised you. However, the person who hires you may require that you transfer, or assign, the copyright to him or her. If you sign such a contract, you no longer own the copyright.

Copyright Terms

If you create a work of art, you may be surprised to learn that you don't own the copyright forever. The copyright of any work you create belongs to you throughout your entire life, and lasts 50 years after your death. Prior to 1978, different laws were in effect. From 1909 to 1977, a copyright was only granted for 28 years. Copyrights could be renewed once after 28 years. In 1976, Congress changed the law and extended both the first term and second term of a work's protection. To anyone using copyrighted images, these figures can be important. An old-time image that you think is no longer covered by copyright laws may actually be covered. In order to be safe, assume that any work created after 1922 is copyrighted. Mathematically, copyrights on works created before 1922 should have expired. For instance, if a work was created in 1921, its copyright could have been extended in 1949. Twenty-eight years later, in 1977, the work should have entered the public domain. When a work is in the public domain, it can be freely copied and distributed.

Watermarking Photoshop Files

Despite the fact that images are copyrighted as soon as they are created, you still may feel the need to provide extra copyright protection. Photoshop's Digimarc filters can add the protection you seek. The Digimarc filter adds a watermark to your Photoshop file.

Digimarc watermarks are imperceptible to most viewers. The content of the watermark alerts users as to the creator's copyright ID, whether the image is restricted or royalty free, and whether the image contains adult content. Digimarc claims that the watermark survives "normal" editing, including sharpening, blurring, rotating, cropping, printing, scanning, color separation, and file format conversion.

 TIP: *If you wish to watermark an Indexed Color image, convert it to RGB color first, embed the watermark, then reconvert the file to Indexed Color.*

Whenever an image is opened or scanned into Photoshop, the Digimarc software can automatically look for the digital Digimarc watermark (if the Detect Watermark filter is installed). If a watermark is found, a copyright symbol is added to the image's title bar. The software can automatically open up your Web browser and send you to Digimarc's Web site with information about the watermarked image.

The Digimarc Web site (www.digimarc.com) allows consumers to look up information about images. If you want to start registering your images, you can register for a year's free subscription, or pay $99.00 for a professional subscription. A professional subscription provides more advantages than the free "lite" subscription and allows you to designate as many as three different photo- or stock-imaging agents. Both subscriptions are available on-line at the Digimarc Web site. Once you obtain a membership, you can obtain a Creator ID, which can be looked up by someone who wants to use one of your images.

 NOTE: *Watermarks only appear in images that have a minimum size of 256 by 256 pixels.*

Creating a Watermark

To create a watermark in your image, choose Filter | Digimarc | Embed Watermark. In the Embed Watermark dialog box, you can choose whether you wish the image to be restricted or royalty free. You can also use the slider to make the watermark more or less durable. The more durable the watermark, the more likely it will survive many reproductions. If the image contains adult content, you can also check the adult content check box.

```
┌─────────────────────────────────────────────────────┐
│ ▓▓▓▓▓▓▓▓▓▓▓▓▓▓▓▓ Embed Watermark ▓▓▓▓▓▓▓▓▓▓▓▓▓▓▓▓ │
│ ┌─ Copyright Info ──────────────────┐               │
│ │                                    │  ┌─────────┐ │
│ │ Creator ID:  PictureMarc Demo  [ Personalize... ]│   OK    │ │
│ │                                    │  └─────────┘ │
│ │ Type of Use: ● Restricted          │  ┌─────────┐ │
│ │              ○ Royalty Free        │  │ Cancel  │ │
│ │                                    │  └─────────┘ │
│ │ □ Adult Content                    │               │
│ └────────────────────────────────────┘               │
│                                                       │
│              Watermark Durability:  [ 4 ]             │
│   less visible               more visible            │
│   ├──────────────────────────────────△───┤           │
│   less durable               more durable            │
└─────────────────────────────────────────────────────┘
```

To register your image with Digimarc, click Personalize in the Embed Watermark dialog box. You can then access Digimarc's Web site to obtain a registration ID.

```
┌─────────────────────────────────────────────────┐
│ ▓▓▓▓▓▓▓▓▓▓ Personalize Creator ID ▓▓▓▓▓▓▓▓▓▓▓ │
│                                                  │
│        Creator ID: [              ]  ┌────────┐ │
│                                       │   OK   │ │
│                                       └────────┘ │
│   ┌──────────────────────────────┐   ┌────────┐ │
│   │     Click the Register button to obtain │   │ Cancel │ │
│   │ [▨] your own Creator ID via the Internet, │  └────────┘ │
│   │     or contact Digimarc Corporation at: │   ┌────────┐ │
│   │                                  │   │Register│ │
│   │ URL: [http://www.digimarc.com/register]  └────────┘ │
│   │ Phone: U.S. +1-800-664-8277     │ │
│   │        Intl. +1-503-223-0127    │ │
│   └──────────────────────────────┘ │
└─────────────────────────────────────────────────┘
```

After you embed the watermark in your image, a tiny copyright symbol appears in the title bar and in the lower left part of your screen.

Checking Copyright Status

If you want to check the status of an image created by another artist or check the status of an image that you have created, open the image and choose Filter | Digimarc | Read Watermark. If there is no watermark in the image, you will receive a message informing you that no watermark exists; otherwise, the Watermark Information dialog box appears, as shown below.

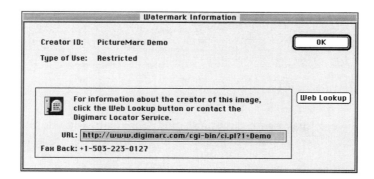

The dialog box shows you the status of the image. If the image is registered and you have a Web browser installed, you can click on the Web Lookup button. This opens up your Web browser and automatically connects you to the Digimarc Web site, so that you can see who the registered owner of the image is.

Conclusion

As you work with digitized images, always play it safe by ensuring that you are not violating copyright laws. If you want more information about U.S. copyright laws, you might want to read the pamphlet: *Intellectual Property Rights in an Age of Electronics and Information*, published by the Office of Technology, U.S. Government Printing Office, Washington, D.C.

If you are interested in learning more about recent developments in copyright law, check this site on the Internet: gopher://marvel.loc.gov/11/copyright. You can also examine the details of the copyright law at http://www.law.cornell.edu/uscode/17.

APPENDIX A

Importing and Exporting Files

Y ou will often use Photoshop as part of a team of graphics applications. This
appendix covers file formats and the techniques for exporting files created in
Photoshop to other programs, and importing files created in other programs into
Photoshop.

Using File | Save As and File | Save a Copy

When you need to save a file in another format, you can use the File | Save, File |
Save As, or File | Save a Copy commands. If you've already saved the file, you
must use File | Save As or File | Save a Copy to switch formats. Both the Save As
dialog box and the Save a Copy dialog box (shown in Figure A-1) allow you to
pick a specific format from the Format pop-up menu (Windows users choose from
the Save As pop-up menu.). Figure A-2 shows the Format pop-up menu that
appears in the Save a Copy and Save As dialog boxes when saving an RGB image.
However, if you've created layers in your document, you will only be able to save
in another file format by using the File | Save a Copy command. File | Save a Copy
allows you to flatten any existing layers of an image. If layers are not flattened,
you can save only in Photoshop's native format, Photoshop. File | Save a Copy

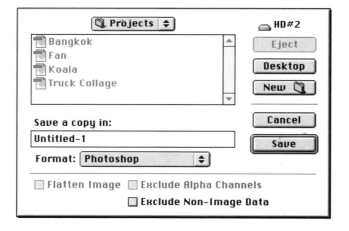

FIGURE A-1   The File | Save a Copy dialog box allows you to flatten an image and
exclude paths and color tags

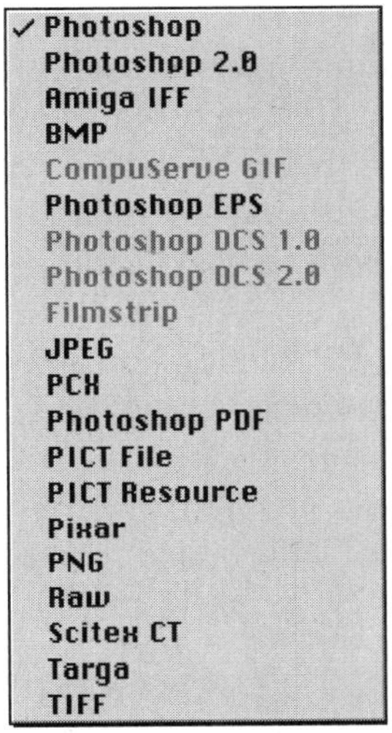

A

Photoshop ✓
Photoshop 2.0
Amiga IFF
BMP
CompuServe GIF
Photoshop EPS
Photoshop DCS 1.0
Photoshop DCS 2.0
Filmstrip
JPEG
PCX
Photoshop PDF
PICT File
PICT Resource
Pixar
PNG
Raw
Scitex CT
Targa
TIFF

FIGURE A-2   File formats available when saving Photoshop files

also allows you to save an image without its alpha channels. This is necessary when you wish to save in EPS, JPEG, and Scitex CT formats. File | Save a Copy also allows you to save "Exclude Non-Image Data" when saving a file. This option saves without color tags, paths, and file information. It can be helpful when you wish to reduce file size.

 NOTE: *Saving a file without alpha channels makes the file size smaller.*

After you choose a new file format and click the Save button, a File Format dialog box often appears, which allows you to specify conversion options.

 REMEMBER: *After executing the File | Save As command, you will be working in the document you just saved. After you execute File | Save a Copy, you will not be working in the file you just saved.*

Working with EPS Files

The EPS (encapsulated PostScript) format is widely accepted by graphics and page-layout programs in Mac and PC environments. The format was originally created as an output format for printing graphic images. If you need to output your files to programs such as QuarkXPress, Adobe Illustrator, or Adobe PageMaker, you can use the EPS format. If you are producing your file to be output by a service bureau, you may need to convert your file to EPS format.

The DCS 1.0 version of the EPS dialog box allows you to save color separations for CMYK and multichannel files. The DCS 2.0 format is used for exporting Photoshop CMYK images that include spot color channels and one alpha channel. If you are working in a bitmap mode file, the EPS format also allows you to save white areas of your image as transparent areas.

Saving an EPS, DCS1.0 or DCS 2.0 Format

To save a file in Photoshop EPS, DCS 1.0 or DCS 2.0 format, choose Save As or Save a Copy from the File menu. If you choose Save As and your image includes alpha channels, you will not be able to access the Photoshop EPS or DCS 1.0 file formats. If you choose Save a Copy instead, Photoshop will automatically turn on the Exclude Alpha Channels check box. If you are saving a CMYK file with an alpha channel with no layers, you will be able to save it in DCS 2.0 format. If you are using File | Save As, rename the file so that you don't overwrite the previous version. In the Format pop-up menu (Windows users: Save As pop-up menu), choose Photoshop EPS, Photoshop DCS 1.0 or Photoshop DCS 2.0. (Windows users will see the filename extension change to .EPS.) To continue the conversion process, click on the Save button (Windows users: OK).

Photoshop next opens the EPS Format dialog box. The dialog box that appears depends upon the mode of the file you are exporting. For instance, the dialog box for saving an RGB file is different from the dialog box that appears when you are saving a CMYK file. If you are exporting a CMYK Color file, for example, the Photoshop EPS Format dialog box looks like this:

Many programs, Adobe Illustrator included, allow previews of the EPS file. If you choose the 1 bit/pixel option in the Preview pop-up menu, the preview will be in black-and-white. The 8 bits/pixel choice allows 256 colors or shades of gray. Mac users can create previews for the PC by choosing either the TIFF (1 bit/pixel) or TIFF (8 bits/pixel) option. Mac users can also choose Macintosh (JPEG) to save the preview using the JPEG compression format.

The Encoding pop-up menu options allow you to choose whether the EPS file will be a binary or ASCII file or compressed using the JPEG compression format. JPEG removes image data from your file, which can produce a loss in quality. The binary and ASCII formats do not remove data from your file. A binary file is more compact than an ASCII file. Photoshop provides both formats because some applications cannot read the binary format.

In general, you will want to avoid using the Include Halftone Screens and Include Transfer Function check box options; both of these options may override the settings of an imagesetter or a page-layout program. Check with your service bureau before you turn on these options. Here is what they do:

- With Include Halftone Screens enabled, Photoshop sends the halftone screen angles and screen frequency settings that are entered into the Halftone Screens dialog box (accessed from the Page Setup dialog box). Enabling this option may override an imagesetter's or other application's halftone screen settings.

- With Include Transfer Function enabled, Photoshop sends its Transfer Functions information to the EPS file. The Transfer Functions dialog box (accessed from the Page Setup dialog box) allows you to specify dot gain settings to compensate for miscalibrated imagesetters. A well-run service bureau keeps its imagesetters properly calibrated; thus, any Transfer Functions settings you make can adversely affect the quality of the final color separations.

If you have a PostScript printer and wish to have the printer convert your file to the printer's color space, choose PostScript Color Management. (Only select this option if you didn't already convert the file in Photoshop.) For CMYK images, this option is only supported by PostScript Level 3 printers.

If you are saving a file in Photoshop DCS 1.0 format you can create separate EPS files for use with programs that utilize Quark's Desktop Color Separation (DCS) format. When you choose one of the Multiple File choices in the pop-up menu, Photoshop creates a file for each CMYK component. A fifth file, called a master file, contains a preview of the composite image. If you want a color preview file, choose the 72-pixels/inch color option; for a grayscale preview, choose the 72-pixels/inch grayscale option. If you choose one of the No Composite options, you cannot print a composite from the file. Note that all five DCS files must be in the same folder if you wish to reload the composite file.

As mentioned earlier, Photoshop DCS 2.0 is used to save files that include spot color channels and one alpha channel. Like the DCS 1.0 dialog box, the DCS 2.0 dialog box allow to save your separated file as multiple files or as a separate file with grayscale or colored previews. These options are shown below and described in the previous paragraph.

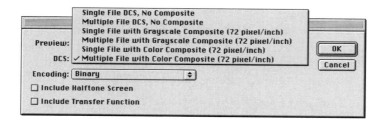

 NOTE: *IN SOFTWARE's Platemaker is a Photoshop plug-in that allows you to export DCS files that can include channels for spot colors, varnishes, foil stamping, or even embossing plates.*

 NOTE: *If you wish to export a clipping path, the Photoshop file should be saved in EPS format. For more information about clipping paths, see Chapter 13.*

Opening an EPS File

Photoshop's EPS format is designed to read files EPS files created by different graphics applications.

1. To open an EPS file created in another application, choose Open from the File menu. If you don't see the file, click on the Show All Files check box.

A

2. Select the file you wish to open. Notice that the file format name is displayed in the File | Open dialog box. Click OK.

If the file was exported by Adobe Dimensions and many other programs, the Rasterize Generic EPS Format dialog box appears which aids you in converting from a drawing or vector program to Photoshop's pixel-based or raster format. In the dialog box, you can change the image's Width, Height, Resolution, and Mode. You can also choose whether to use anti-aliasing. If you want Photoshop to soften the edges of the imported file, click the Anti-aliased check box.

Turning on the Constrain Proportions option ensures that Width and Height will remain at the same ratio in the converted file. When Constrain Proportions is enabled, a change in either the Width or Height measurement forces a proportional change in the other dimension.

3. When you're ready to load the file, click OK. In a few moments, the file opens into Photoshop.

Although the EPS file is now open in Photoshop, it has not been converted to Photoshop's native format. If you intend to edit the file and save and reload it, it's best to convert (save) the file to Photoshop format. Otherwise, you will be met by the Rasterize Generic EPS Format dialog box each time you load the file.

4. To save the file in Photoshop format, choose either Save, Save As, or Save a Copy from the File menu. Before continuing to save the file in another format, Mac users should rename the file; this prevents overwriting the previous file on the disk. (On the PC, when you change file formats,

Photoshop changes the filename extension of the file to .PSD; thus, the original file is not overwritten. It's a good idea to rename the file anyway, however, to avoid confusion between versions.) To switch to Photoshop format, choose Photoshop from the list in the Format (Windows users: Save as) pop-up menu. Click Save to execute the conversion.

Placing an EPS File into a Photoshop Document

At times you may want to place an Adobe Illustrator document into a file that is already open in Photoshop. If you want the image to be anti-aliased, select the Anti-alias PostScript check box in the General Preferences dialog box. This dialog box is accessed by choosing General from the File | Preferences submenu.

Here are the steps to place an EPS file into a Photoshop file:

1. Open the Photoshop file into which you intend to place the Illustrator file.

2. From the File menu, choose Place.

3. From the list of files that appears, select the file that you wish to place, and click Open.

4. The EPS file appears within a bounding box in a layer. If you wish to move the imported image, position the mouse pointer on the border box. (The selection pointer should be the arrow pointer.) Click and drag the image to the desired location.

 NOTE: *If you don't see an image on screen, no preview may have been saved with the file. You can still complete the steps in this section. After you press ENTER you should see the image on screen*

If you wish to resize the image and change the width-to-height (aspect) ratio, click and drag on one of the image corners. If you wish to change the image size but maintain the aspect ratio, press SHIFT and then click and drag the mouse. If you wish to rotate the image, click and drag outside of the image borders in the direction that you wish to rotate.

To rotate, click and drag outside of the bounding box. To skew the placed EPS file, press COMMAND (Windows users: CTRL), then click and drag on a handle.

Once you are satisfied with the size and placement of the imported image, press ENTER (Mac users can also press RETURN).

GIF89a

GIF (often pronounced "jiff") is one of the most widely used formats for outputting images to the World Wide Web. You can export files to GIF format by choosing File | Export | GIF89a. When you export your file, you can save the file under a new name and thus preserve the original file. Using GIF89a, you can export an RGB file to GIF format, and you can control which image areas appear transparent when viewed on a web browser. If you convert an Indexed file to GIF format using the GIF89a command, you can designate an alpha channel to control transparency in an image. For detailed information about using the GIF89a format, see Chapter 20.

CompuServe GIF

CompuServe GIF is a common format used to output images to the Web. Since CompuServe GIF allows only 256 or fewer colors, images must be converted to Indexed Color before saving in this format. When you save your file in CompuServe GIF, a dialog box appears, allowing you to choose whether to save your image in Normal or Interlaced Row format. If you choose interlaced, the image gradually comes into focus when viewed on the Web.

If you are working with images that will output to the Web, you may prefer to use Photoshop's File | Export | GIF89a command. GIF89a allows you to export RGB Color images in GIF format, and allows you several options to designate which image areas are transparent.

 NOTE: *When you are exporting to GIF format, alpha channels mask your image. This can cause the final image to be cropped according to the mask.*

PNG Format

PNG is a new file format specifically designed to compress images that will be output to the Web. Many Web experts predict that PNG (often pronounced "ping") will eventually replace GIF as the preferred Web file format. Unlike GIF, PNG files are not limited to 256 colors. Web browsers that support PNG include Internet Explorer 4.0 and higher. Netscape Navigator 2.0 and higher support PNG with a plug-in.

Images saved in PNG format maintain all color and all alpha channels—which allows you to blend image edges with web page backgrounds. Images saved in PNG format are compressed using a lossless filtering process. When you save in PNG format, a dialog box appears allowing you to choose a compression algorithm and choose whether you want the image to gradually come into focus when viewed on the Web. If you want the image to gradually come into view, choose the Adam 7 interlacing method.

 NOTE: *You cannot save a CMYK Color mode file in PNG format*

Working with TIFF Files

TIFF format is frequently used for both Mac and PC graphics files. TIFF, which stands for "tagged-image file format," was introduced by the Aldus Corporation as a format for saving scanned images. Although the format is used by most page-layout programs, it is not accepted by all drawing programs.

TIFF files can be loaded directly into Photoshop. When you save a TIFF file in Photoshop, the TIFF Options dialog box appears.

Here you can specify whether the document is for the Macintosh or IBM PC-compatible computers. Just choose the appropriate radio button under Byte Order.

One valuable feature of exporting files in TIFF format is that TIFF files can be compressed. In the TIFF Options dialog box is a check box you can select to enable LZW (Lempel-Ziv-Welch) Compression. LZW is a "lossless" compression format; the file is compressed without removing image data from it. Most page-layout programs can read compressed TIFF files.

If you have created alpha channels in your Photoshop file, the alpha channels will automatically be saved with the file. Alpha channels are generally used to save masks, as explained in Chapter 14.

Working with PICT Files (Macintosh Only)

PICT is one of the most common data-file formats available on the Macintosh. Most multimedia programs, such as Macromedia Director, can import PICT files, and most 3D programs, such as Strata Studio Pro, Macromedia Extreme 3D, MetaCreations Infini-D, can import PICT files. Most Macintosh graphics applications, such as Canvas and Claris Draw, can save files in this format. Some PC programs, including CorelDRAW, also accept the format. Both PICT and PICT2 (colored PICT) images can be loaded directly into Photoshop.

When you are saving files in PICT format, the PICT File Options dialog box appears, which allows you to designate the Resolution (pixel depth) of the image. Which dialog box you see depends upon whether you are saving a grayscale or color file.

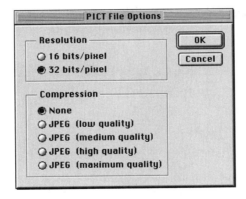

- If you are saving a grayscale file, specify 2 bits/pixel for 4 colors, 4 bits/pixel for 16 colors, and 8 bits/pixel for 256 colors.

- The choices for color images are 16 bits/pixel or 32 bits/pixel. If you are exporting a 24-bit color image, choose the 32 bits/pixel option. This 32-bit option appears because the Macintosh includes an extra 8-bit channel (an alpha channel). If you are not using 24-bit color in Photoshop, choose the 16-bits/pixel option; this keeps file sizes smaller.

When QuickTime is installed, the Compression section allows you to reduce file size with JPEG compression. (See the section "Compressing Files Using JPEG" later in this appendix.)

 NOTE: *You cannot save CMYK Color or Lab Color images in PICT format. You cannot save images with more than one alpha channel in PICT format.*

Importing PICT Images Using the Anti-Aliased PICT Command

Although PICT images load directly into Photoshop using the File | Open command, you may prefer to use the File | Import command to import PICT images. With File | Import, you can select the Anti-Aliased PICT option; this activates a plug-in that offers options similar to those in the Rasterize Generic EPS Format dialog box. (See "Opening an EPS File" earlier in this appendix.)

```
┌─────────────────────────────────────────┐
│░░░░░░░░░░░░░░Anti-Aliased PICT░░░░░░░░░░░░│
├─────────────────────────────────────────┤
│                                          │
│   Image Size: 532 K                      │
│                               ┌────────┐ │
│        Width:  504  (pixels)  │   OK   │ │
│                               └────────┘ │
│        Height: 360  (pixels)  ┌────────┐ │
│                               │ Cancel │ │
│   Mode:          ☑ Constrain  └────────┘ │
│                    Proportions           │
│      ○ Gray Scale                        │
│      ● RGB Color                         │
│                                          │
└─────────────────────────────────────────┘
```

The Anti-Aliased PICT dialog box lets you change Width and Height proportionally and choose to open the document as a Gray Scale or RGB Color file. When you execute the Acquire command and import the PICT file, Photoshop uses anti-aliasing to soften image edges.

Using BMP Format

BMP (Windows Bitmap) format is commonly used by many Windows graphics programs. Most multimedia programs require you to save images in BMP format before you can import them. When you export an image, you can choose to export the image for Windows or OS | 2. You can also choose to export your image as a 1-, 4-, 8-, or 24-bit image. 4- and 8-bit images can use RLE (Run-Length Encoding) compression. This is a lossless compression format, and thus doesn't result in a degradation of image quality.

 NOTE: *CMYK files cannot be converted to BMP format.*

Compressing Files Using JPEG

The JPEG file format is commonly used to compress files before outputting them to the Web. Web designers often use JPEG file format to save scanned images to the Web—images for which color gradations are important. For more information about the Web, see Chapter 20. Also, see Saving in JPEG Format, discussed later in that chapter. JPEG (Joint Photographic Experts Group) is a "lossy" standard, which means information is removed from the file during the compression process. Usually the absence of the subtracted information is not noticed if the image is compressed using a high-quality setting. When the file is reopened, the lost information is not returned to the file. If you've opened any of Photoshop's tutorial files, you may have already worked with JPEG files. JPEG files can be opened directly into Photoshop.

When saving a file in JPEG format, use the File | Save As or File | Save a Copy command and choose JPEG from the Format pop-up menu. The JPEG Options dialog box appears, allowing you to choose a Quality option and include paths in the image. To obtain the best fidelity, select BaseLine Optimized.

If you are outputting your image to the Web and want to have it gradually come into focus on screen as it is downloaded from the Web, choose Progressive (note that not all browsers support this feature). When you choose this feature, you can also specify how many "scans" are made as the image is downloaded. Note, however, that more RAM is required for Progressive JPEG images.

Photoshop 5 ▶ In Action

The 3 D shapes were created in Infini-D.

The TBN logo was created in Adobe Photoshop.

The icons were created in Freehand.

The robot was created in Infini-D.

The pattern was created in Adobe Photoshop.

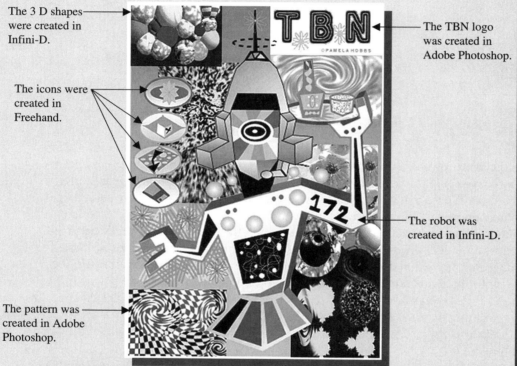

Artist: Pamela Hobbs

Client: ACSII Magazine Tokyo

Pamela created this magazine cover using Adobe Photoshop, Macromedia Freehand, and MetaCreations Infini-D (a 3-D program). She started by creating the TBN logo and patterns in Photoshop. Once these images were completed, she saved the files as EPS images so they could be placed into Freehand.

The 3-D shapes in the top left-hand corner of the cover and the robot were created with Infini-D. Once these images were completed, she saved the files as EPS images and placed them into the final image in Freehand. With Freehand, she created the icons on the left side of the cover.

Remember, JPEG files cannot contain alpha channels.

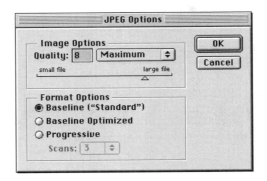

Scitex CT Files

Scitex workstations are often used at prepress houses for image editing and color correction. Files created by Scitex workstations using the Scitex CT (continuous tone) format can be loaded directly into Photoshop and can be used with Photoshop's File | Import | Quick Edit command.

Only Grayscale, RGB Color, and CMYK Color Photoshop files may be saved in the Scitex CT format. Also, you can't save a file with alpha channels in Scitex CT format. If you have a Scitex system, you need special utilities created by Scitex to complete the transfer process.

Photo CD Files

Photo CD files can be opened directly into Photoshop. Kodak's CMS CD plug-in, copied to your hard disk when you install Photoshop, allows you to open Photo CD files by choosing File | Open. This plug-in was designed to increase the color range and fidelity of Photo CD images that are loaded into Photoshop. The plug-in helps color reversal or slide film formats look similar to their appearance when viewed on a light box.

After you execute the File | Open command, a dialog box appears, allowing you to choose how you want the Photo CD file to load:

```
┌─────────────────────────────────────────────┐
│  Image:  IMG0001.PCD;1                       │
│                                              │
│  Resolution:  [ 2048 by 3072 ▼ ]            │
│                                              │
│  File Size:  18.0M                           │
│                                              │
│  ☒ Landscape (faster)                        │
│                                              │
│  ┌──────────┐                                │
│  │  Source  │  Kodak Photo CD                │
│  └──────────┘                                │
│  ┌─────────────┐                             │
│  │ Destination │  Adobe Photoshop RGB        │
│  └─────────────┘                             │
│  ┌────┐  ┌────────────┐  ┌────────┐  ┌─────┐ │
│  │Kodak│ │ Image Info │  │ Cancel │  │  OK │ │
│  └────┘  └────────────┘  └────────┘  └─────┘ │
└─────────────────────────────────────────────┘
```

🞏   Specify the desired Resolution for the file to be imported.

🞏   Click on the Source button to open a dialog box in which you can choose a Precision Transform option for conversion—Ektachrome (color reversal/ slide), Kodachrome (color reversal/slide), or Photo CD Color Negative. If the film "term" is not known but the medium is color reversal/slide, choose Ektachrome. Choose Kodachrome only if K-14 film processing was used to create your negatives. Click OK to accept the Source setting.

🞏   To specify the Destination color space, click the Destination button to open another dialog box. In the Device pop-up menu, select Adobe Photoshop CIELAB if you wish to have images opened in Lab color mode. Images that will later be converted to CMYK Color should be opened in this format. To open an image in RGB Color mode, select Adobe Photoshop RGB. You will see the words "RCS to Adobe Photoshop" or "RCS to Adobe RGB." Don't be confused by the abbreviation RCS, which stands for Reference Color Space. This is an interim color space used in the conversion from Photo CD color space to the destination color space. When you're ready, click OK to accept the settings.

To load the image, click OK in the dialog box.

If you are working on images that will be converted to CMYK, check with Kodak to see whether you can use one of their profiles that converts a file from Photo CD's color space (Photo YCC) into a CMYK color file.

For more details on using Photo CD technology with Photoshop, refer to Chapter 8.

A

 NOTE: *Photoshop cannot save files in Photo CD format.*

PDF Files

PDF (Portable Document Format) is a file format created by Adobe Systems. If you save your file in PDF format, users can view it with Adobe's Acrobat Reader software (provided on the Adobe Photoshop CD-ROM), even though they may not own Photoshop. Using Adobe Acrobat software (not the Acrobat reader), users can embed navigation and hypertext features in PDF files. PDF files can also be embedded into Web HTML documents.

To open a PDF File in Photoshop choose File | Open. If you don't see the file choose select the Show All Files check box (Windows users: All Formats). Select the file, then click open. If the PDF file includes more than one page, a dialog box appears on screen allowing you to pick the page that you wish to open. After you choose a page, the Rasterize Generic PDF Format dialog box appears. The choices in the dialog are same as the Generic EPS format dialog box described above. Select the appropriate options in the dialog box, then click OK.

To place a PDF file into an existing Photoshop file, choose File | Place. The placed image appears in Photoshop in a new layer within a bounding box. You can move the image by clicking and dragging in the bounding box. You can also scale the image by clicking and dragging on a handle, pressing SHIFT while clicking and dragging scales proportionally. To rotate, click and drag outside of the bounding box. To skew the placed PDF file, press COMMAND (Windows users: CTRL), then click and drag on a handle. Press Enter when you have completed moving or transforming the image.

 NOTE: *You can open a multi-page PDF file into separate Photoshop files by choosing File | Automate | Multi-Page PDF to PSD.*

Filmstrip Files

Filmstrip files are used in animation programs such as Adobe Premier. Filmstrip files can be loaded into the Macintosh version of Photoshop and resaved using Filmstrip format. You cannot, however, convert a file created in Photoshop into a Filmstrip file.

From Mac to PC and Back Again

If you are using a Mac and wish to load a Photoshop file created on the PC, or vice versa, you need only use the standard File | Open command. No special conversion procedures are necessary to load and save files between these two platforms.

To use a PC file on the Mac or to save a file on the Mac for use on the PC, you need to save the file on a medium formatted for the PC (a disk or removable hard drive). Several utility programs, including Dataviz's MacLink Plus and Apple's PC Exchange allow PC files to be displayed on the Mac.

If you are saving a file on a Mac that will be loaded onto a PC, you must give the file a name that is no more than eight characters long and contains no spaces. When you name the file, include a period at the end, followed by a two- or three-letter filename extension. The extension is a "code" that alerts Photoshop for Windows what file format to expect. The following is a list of acceptable file formats and their filename extensions.

Format	Filename Extension
Amiga	.IFF
CompuServe Graphics	.GIF
Encapsulated PostScript	.EPS
Illustrator	ASCII EPS	.AI
JPEG (Compressed)	.JPG
MacPaint	.MPT
PC Paintbrush	.PCX
Photoshop standard	.PSD
Pixar	.PXR
PixelPaint	.PXI
Raw	.RAW
Scitex CT	.SCT
Targa	.TGA
TIFF	.TIF
Windows Bitmap	.BMP

TIP: *Mac users: To make Photoshop automatically add a PC file extension to a file name, press OPTION when you choose from the Format pop-up menu. If you wish to always save your files with PC file extensions, choose File | Preferences | Saving Files. In the Append File Extension popup menu, choose Always.*

The following is a list of PC-compatible filename extensions for palettes and settings:

Palette	Setting	Filename Extension
Arbitrary	.AMP
Brushes palette	.ABR
Color table	.ACT
Colors palette	.ACO
Curves	.CRV
Custom filters	.ACF
Displacement maps	.PSD
Duotone options	.ADO
Halftone screens	.AHS
Hue	Saturation	.HSS
Levels	.ALV
Printing inks	.API
Separation setup	.ASP
Separation table	.AST
Transfer functions	.ATF
Variations	.PSV

Saving PC Files on Mac Disks

Many service bureaus accept data on Syquest and Iomega removable hard disks. If you use Photoshop for Windows and need to load and save files on Mac-formatted disks, you might wish to purchase DataViz Mac Opener (www.dataviz.com).

APPENDIX B

Using the File Info Command

A dobe Photoshop allows you to tag image files with captions, descriptions, and photo credits. Photoshop uses a format adopted by The Newspaper Association of America and the International Press Communications Council to identify images. Although this section of the program is primarily designed for the press, other users can take advantage of the entry screens to enter historical information about images. You might even include a brief description of how your images were created, and what (if any) stock images appear.'

To enter identifying information about an image, choose File Info from the File menu. In the File Info dialog box, use the Section pop-up menu to navigate through five different screens: Caption, Keywords, Categories, Credits, and Origins. You can either use the pop-up menu to navigate through the different sections or click on the Next button. The following is a brief description of each section.

Each dialog box features Save, Load, and Append buttons that allow you to save the information from all sections to a File Info file, load them on screen, or append the information if necessary. The files saved from the File Info dialog boxes are saved not in Photoshop's native image format, but in a special file format that can be correctly loaded only from the File Info dialog box.

Caption

The Caption section allows you to enter a caption of up to 2,000 characters. The name of the caption writer, a headline, and special instructions can also be entered into this section.

NOTE: *To print the Caption field beneath an image, select the Caption option in the Page Setup dialog box (choose File | Page Setup). Then choose File | Print.*

Keywords

The Keywords section allows you to enter different search categories for images.

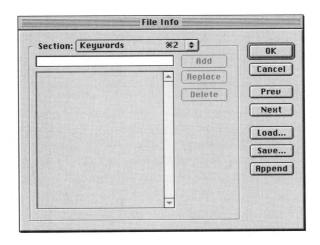

The Keyword field allows up to 31 characters. After you type the word, click on the Add button to add the word to the Keyword list. You can enter as many keywords as you like. If you wish to delete a keyword, select the word by clicking on it, then click on the Delete button. To replace a keyword, enter a new word in the Keyword field, then click on the Replace button.

 NOTE: *Both the Caption and Keyword entries can be searched with third-party image database software such as Extensis Portfolio.*

Categories

The Categories section allows you to enter a category code, enter supplemental categories, and tag the file with an Urgency value.

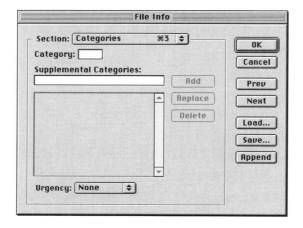

The Category field is designed to hold a three-digit Associated Press category code. To add supplemental categories, enter a word in the Supplemental Categories field, then click on the Add button. After supplemental categories are added, they appear in a list in the middle of the screen. To delete a category, click on it; next, click on the Delete button. To replace a supplemental category, enter a new supplemental category, then click on the Replace button. To set editorial urgency, click on the Urgency pop-up menu and choose from the list of choices. The lower the value, the greater the urgency.

Credits

Use the Credits section to enter a byline, a byline title, a credit, and source information.

Origin

Use the Origin section to enter historical information about the image. In the Object Name field, type a description of the image. To enter the date, click on the Today button (the date set on your computer will be entered). Enter information in the appropriate fields for city, state, country, and transmission reference.

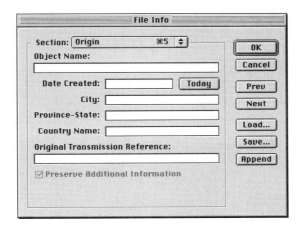

Copyright & URL

This section allows you to provide copyright information about your file. You can select Mark As Copyrighted to indicate that the image is copyrighted, and you can include your own copyright notice. You can also add a URL (Universal Resource Locator), which is essentially a Web address where information can be obtained about the image or creator. When the Photoshop user clicks on the Go To URL button, Photoshop loads the user's browser and sends the browser to the Web page designated in the URL field.

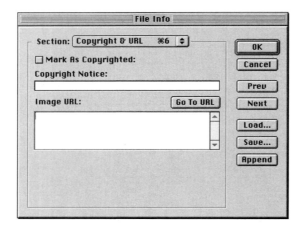

 NOTE: *Check this dialog box section to find the copyright and URL information for images in Adobe Photoshop's Samples folder.*

APPENDIX C

Vendor List

The following is a vendor resource list. The information is provided so that you can easily get answers to your questions about different products you might be interested in purchasing or using. The companies have been divided into three groups: hardware; software; and stock images, footage, and music.

Hardware

AGFA Corporation
Division of Bayer
200 Ballardvale St.
Wilmington, MA 01887
508-658-5600 or
800-685-4271
www.agfa.com

Apple Computer Inc.
One Infinite Loop
Cupertino, CA 95014
408-996-1010 or
800-538-9696
www.apple.com

APS Technologies
6131 Deramus Ave.
Kansas City, MO 64120-0087
816-483-1600 or
800-233-7550

ATI Technologies, Inc.
33 Commerce Valley Dr. E.
Thornhill, Ontario
Canada L3T 7N6
905-882-2600

CalComp
14555 N. 82nd St.
Scottsdale, AZ 85260
602-948-6540 or
800-458-5888
www.calcomp.com

Canon USA, Inc.
1 Canon Plaza
Lake Success, NY 11042
516-488-6700
www.canon.com

Connectix
2655 Campus Dr.
San Mateo, CA 94403
415-571-5100 or
800-950-5880
www.connectix.com

DayStar Digital, Inc.
5556 Atlanta Hwy.
Flowery Branch, GA 30542
770-967-2077
www.daystar.com

Dell Computers
One Dell Way
Round Rock, TX 78682
888-325-4265
www.dell.com

Eastman Kodak Co.
343 State St.
Rochester, NY 14650-0405
800-242-2424
www.kodak.com

EPSON America, Inc.
20770 Madrona Ave.
Torrance, CA 90509
310-782-0770
www.epson.com

Hewlett-Packard Co.
11311 Chinden Blvd.
Boise, IN 83714
208-396-2373 or
800-752-0900
www.hp.com

IBM
1133 Westchester Ave.
White Plains, NY 10604
914-642-3000 or
800-426-3333
www.ibm.com

Iomega
1821 West Iomega Way
Roy, Utah 84067
800-mystuff
www.iomega.com

IRIS Graphics
6 Crosby Dr.
Bedford, MA 01730
617-275-8777 or
800-947-4712

C

LaCie
8700 S.W. Creekside Place
Beaverton, OR 97008
800-999-0143

Leaf Systems
250 Turnpike Rd.
Southborough, MA 01772
800-685-9462

Linotype-Hell Company
425 Oser Ave.
Hauppauge, NY 11788
516-434-2000

Microtek Labs, Inc.
3715 Doolittle Dr.
Redondo Beach, CA 90278
310-297-5000

NEC Technologies, Inc.
1414 Massachusetts Ave.
Boxborough, MA 01719
508-264-8000 or
800-388-8888
www.nec.com

Newer Technology
4848 West Irving
Wichita, KS 67209
316-943-0222
www.newertech.com

Nikon Inc.
1300 Walt Whitman Rd.
Melville, NY 11747-3064
516-547-4200 or
800-645-6635
www.nikon.com

Optronics
7 Stuart Rd.
Chelmsford, MA 01824
508-256-4511 or
800-454-5490

Olympus America Inc.
Two Corporate Center Dr.
Melville, NY 11747
516-844-5000
www.olympus.com

Polaroid Corp.
575 Technology Square
Cambridge, MA 02139
617-386-6204
www.polaroid.com

QMS, Inc.
One Magnum Pass
Mobile, AL 36618
334-633-4300 or
800-523-2696

Radius Inc.
215 Moffett Park Dr.
Sunnyvale, CA 94089-1374
408-541-6100 or
800-227-2795
www.radius.com

Scitex America Corp.
Eight Oak Park Dr.
Bedford, MA 01730
617-275-5150
www.scitex.com

Silicon Graphics Inc.
2011 N. Shoreline Blvd.
Mountain View, CA
94043-1389
415-960-1980
www.sgi.com

Sonnet Technologies, Inc.
18004 Sky Park Circle
MS:260
Irvine, CA 92614-6428
949-261-2800
www.sonnettech.com

Sony Electronics Inc.
One Sony Dr.
Park Ridge, NJ 07656
201-930-1000 or
800-352-7669
www.sony.com

Storm Software, Inc.
1861 Landings Dr.
Mountain View, CA 94043
415-691-6600 or
800-275-5734

Summagraphics Corp.
8500 Cameron Rd.
Austin, TX 78754
512-835-0900 or
800-337-8662

SyQuest Technology Inc.
47071 Bayside Pkwy.
Fremont, CA 94538-6517
510-226-4000 or
800-249-2440

Tektronix, Inc.
26600 SW Pkwy.
Wilsonville, OR 97070-1000
503-685-3150 or
800-835-6100

3M Company
3M Center 225-3S-05
St. Paul, MN 55144-1000
612-733-4895 or
800-328-9438

TrueVision RasterOps Corp.
2500 Walsh Ave.
Santa Clara, CA 95051
408-562-4200 or
800-411-8229
www.truevision.com

UMAX Technologies, Inc.
3353 Gateway Blvd.
Fremont, CA 94538
510-651-8883

Wacom Technology, Inc.
501 S.E. Columbia Shores
Blvd., Ste. 300
Vancouver, WA 98661
360-750-8882 or
800-922-6613
www.wacom.com

X-Rite, Inc.
3100 44th St. S.W.
Grandville, MI 49418
616-534-7663
www.xrite.com

Software

Adobe Systems
345 Park Ave.
San Jose, CA 95110-2704
1-408-536-6000
800-879-3219
www.adobe.com

Aladdin Systems, Inc.
165 Westridge Dr.
Watsonville, CA 95076
408-761-6200

Alien Skin Software
1100 Wake Forest Rd.
Ste. 101
Raleigh, NC 27604
919-832-4124
www.alienskin.com

Andromeda Software Inc.
699 Hampshire Rd., Ste. 109
Thousand Oaks, CA 91361
800-547-0055

Arrivo, Inc.
409 Main St.
Amherst, MA 01002
413-259-1093/413-256-8941
www.arrivo.com

AutoDesk, Inc.
111 McInnis Pkwy.
San Rafael, CA 94903
415-507-5050 or
800-445-5415

Autodessys Inc.
2011 Riverside Dr.
Columbus, OH 43221
614-488-9777

Avid Technology
222 Third St.
Cambridge, MA 02142
www.avid.com

Caligari Corp.
1955 Landings Dr.
Mountain View, CA 94043
415-390-9600

Canto Software Inc.
330 Townsend St., Ste. 212
San Francisco, CA 94107
415-905-0300
www.canto-software.com

Claris Corp.
5201 Patrick Henry Dr.
Santa Clara, CA 95052-8168
408-987-7227 or
800-325-2747
www.claris.com

Corel Corp.
1600 Carling Ave.
Ottawa, ON Canada K1Z 8R7
613-728-8200 or
800-772-6735

DataStream Imaging Systems
P.O. Box 2148
Lexington, KY 40595
www.datastrem.com

C

DataViz, Inc.
55 Corporate Dr.
Trumbull, CT 06611
203-268-0030 or
800-733-0030
www.dataviz.com

Electric Image Inc.
117 E. Colorado Blvd.,
Ste. 300
Pasadena, CA 91105
818-577-1627
www.electricimage.com

Electronics For Imaging,
Inc. (EFI)
2855 Campus Dr.
San Mateo, CA 94403
415-286-8600

Equilibrium
475 Gate Five Rd., Ste. 225
Sausalito, CA 94965
415-332-4343
www.equilibrium.com

Extensis
1800 SW First Ave., Ste. 500
Portland, OR 97201
503-274-2020
www.extensis.com

Human Software Co.
14407 Big Basin Way
Saratoga, CA 95070-0280
408-741-5101

Letraset USA
40 Eisenhower Dr.
Paramus, NJ 07652
201-845-6100 or
800-343-8973

Macromedia
600 Townsend St.
San Francisco, CA 94103
415-252-2000 or
800-326-2128
www.macromedia.com

Media Lab, Inc.
400 S. McCastlin Blvd.
Louisville, CO 80027
303-499-5411
www.medialab.com

MetaCreations, Inc.
Formerly MetaTools, Inc. &
Fractal Design Corp.
6303 Carpinteria Ave.
Carpinteria, CA 93013
805-566-6200
www.metacreations.com

MicroFrontier
3401 101 St., Ste. E
Des Moines, IA 50322
515-270-8109

Microsoft Corp.
One Microsoft Way
Redmond, WA 98052-6399
800-426-9400
www.microsoft.com

Pantone, Inc.
590 Commerce Blvd.
Carlstadt, NJ 07072-3098
201-935-5500
www.pantone.com

Quark, Inc.
1800 Grant St.
Denver, CO 80203
303-894-8888

Strata, Inc.
2 West St. George Blvd.,
Ste. 2100
St. George, UT 84770
801-628-5218 or
800-6STRATA
www.strata3d.com

Symantec
10201 Torre Ave.
Cupertino, CA 95014-2132
408-253-9600
www.symantec.com

The Valis Group
2270 Paradise Dr.
Tiburon, CA 94920
800-VALIS04

Vertigo Technology, Inc.
Suite 300-842 Thurlow St.
Vancouver, BC
Canada V6E 1W2
www.vertigo3d.com

Virtus Corp.
118 MacKenan Dr., Ste. 250
Cary, NC 27511
919-467-9700
www.virtus.com

Xaos Tools
600 Townsend St.,
Ste. 270
San Fransisco, CA 94103
415-487-7000 or
800-833-9267

Stock Images, Footage, and Music

Acuris, Inc.
931 Hamilton Ave.
Menlo Park, CA 94025
415-329-1920

ArtBeats
P.O. Box 709
Myrtle Creek, OR 97457
503-863-4429 or
800-444-9392

Classic PIO Partners
87 E. Green St., Ste. 309
Pasadena, CA 91105
818-564-8106 or
800-370-2746

ColorBytes, Inc.
830 Kipling St., Ste. 200
Lakewood, CO 80215
303-989-9205 or
800-825-2656

Comstock
30 Irving Place
New York, NY 10003
800-225-2727
www.comstock.com

DIAMAR Interactive
600 University St., Ste. 1701
Seattle, WA 98101
206-340-5975

Digital Stock, Inc.
400 South Sierra Ave.,
Ste. 100
Solana Beach, CA 92075
619-794-4040 or
800-545-4514

Digital Zone Inc.
P.O. Box 5562
Bellevue, WA 98006
206-623-3456

D'pix, Inc.
Division of Amber
Productions, Inc.
414 West 4th Ave.
Columbus, OH 43201
614-299-7192

Fotosets
4104 Twenty-Fourth St.
San Francisco, CA 94114
415-621-2061 or
800-577-1215

Killer Tracks
6534 Sunset Blvd.
Hollywood, CA 90028
213-957-4455

Neo Custom Painted
Environments
2000 W. Fulton St.
Chicago, IL 60612
312-226-2426

New Vision Technologies Inc.
P.O. Box 5486
Station F
Nepean, ON, Canada
K2C-3M1
613-727-8184

Periwinkle Software
7475 Brydon Rd.
La Verne, CA 91750
909-593-5062 or
800-730-3556

Photodex
1781 Barcelona St.
Livermore, CA 94550
510-449-9079

PhotoDisc Inc.
2013 4th Ave., Ste. 200
Seattle, WA 98121
206-441-9355 or
800-528-3472
www.photodisc.com

C

Picture Network International
2000 14th St. North, Ste. 600
Arlington, VA 22201
800-764-7427

Planet Art
505 S. Beverly Dr., Ste. 242
Beverly Hills, CA 90212
213-651-3405 or
800-200-3405

PressLink
11800 Sunrise Valley Dr.,
Ste. 1130
Reston, VA 22091
703-758-1740
http://corpweb.
krmediastream.com

T/Maker Co.
1390 Villa St.
Mountain View, CA 94041
415-962-0195

Viewpoint DataLabs
625 South State St.
Orem, UT 84058
801-229-3000 or
800-328-2738

Vivid Details
8228 Sulphur Mtn. Rd.
Ojai, CA 93023-9372
805-646-0217
www.vividdetails.com

Wayzata Technology
21 N.E. 4th St.
Grand Rapids, MN 55744
218-326-0597 or
800-735-7321

Work For Hire
P.O. Box 121
Pleasantville, NY 10570

APPENDIX D

How the Photoshop Portfolio Images Were Created

933

In the color insert of this book we've included interesting, diverse, and professional works of Photoshop art. As you examine the images and read through the explanations of how the images were created, you may notice similarities of approach and execution.

To all of the artists, two of the most important stages in creating these images were conceptualization and planning. All of the artists had a central idea or concept they wished to portray in their images. Most of them began developing their ideas with rough sketches on paper. Many times the artists showed and discussed these sketches with clients and art directors.

A crucial step in the planning stage was to ensure that all images needed in the final artwork could be obtained and digitized. Obtaining images could mean searching through stock photo albums and CD-ROM collections or scheduling photography sessions. A few of the artists took the photographs themselves. When the artists digitized their work, all were very careful to ensure that it was digitized at the correct resolution. (To learn more about digitizing your images, see Chapter 8.) As they planned their work, the artists analyzed whether they should be working in RGB or CMYK color mode. They also kept in mind whether they would be outputting to a transparency, a commercial printing press, or video. (For more information about outputting your artwork, see Chapters 19 and 20.) As part of the conceptualization/design process, some of the artists created low-resolution versions of their images. By using low-res files, they could work faster, and quickly show their clients "comps" of what the final images might look like.

Following the conceptualization and planning stages, the artists focused on their artistic vision. None of the artists used simple special effects to make their images as wild as possible. Instead of relying on special effects, they relied on ability, intuition, and a firm knowledge of fundamental Photoshop techniques. The artists created selections or masks using the selection tools, the Pen tool, alpha channels, layers, and layer masks. (For more information on selections, see Chapter 4. For information on using the Pen tool, see Chapter 13. For more information on using alpha channels, see Chapter 14. For more information on working with layers, see Chapters 15 and 16.) They copied and pasted the selections to blend image elements together. They also used blending modes in the Layers palette and changed Composite Control settings in the Layers Options dialog box.

After reviewing the images in the color insert sections of this book, you're certain to agree that Photoshop offers unlimited design possibilities. Yet despite the freedom Photoshop provides, don't forget the importance of conceptualization, planning, and knowledge of ba'''sic Photoshop skills. As you gain more proficiency in Photoshop from reading this book and working on your own Photoshop projects, you might wish, every now and then, to return to the color insert section for inspiration and ideas. In the meantime, have fun learning Adobe Photoshop.

2   This fantastic image won an APA Gold Award for Special Effects and Kodak's VIP Image Search '91 awards for Best in Show and Best in Digital Photography. The image was created as a self-promotion piece for R/GA Print, a division of R/Greenberg Associates, which is well known for its creation of a Diet Coke television commercial featuring Paula Abdul dancing with Gene Kelly.

The dove, the parrot, and the sky in this image were photographed by New York City photographer Ryszard Horowitz. The cone was created using R/GA Print's own proprietary 3-D computer software and was rendered twice, once with the sky and once with "wild" colors. In order to create the opaque blue sky and the clear sky, a linear blend was applied using the Gradient tool in an alpha channel. All of the images were then composited together using the Image | Calculations (Image | Apply Image in Photoshop 5.0) and Edit | Paste commands. The mirrored image of the cone was created by copying, pasting, and then changing Composite Control slider settings in the Layers Options dialog box.

Alpha channels and the Apply Image commands are covered in Chapter 14. The Composite Control sliders are covered in Chapter 16.

3   J.W. Burkey, a Dallas photographer, created this image as a personal experiment. He wanted to learn more about working with MetaCreations Bryce, MetaCreations Poser, Strata StudioPro, and Adobe Photoshop. J.W. created the 3-D figure using Poser and the Cadeusis insignia using Strata StudioPro. He created the background using Bryce and composited the image together using Photoshop.

J.W. began planning the image by going to the library to look through 2-D samples of insignias. J.W. found that some insignias had the twirling snake-like cylinder look and some didn't. After sketching what he wanted, artist Jim Qualia used StudioPro to create two cones with rounded tips and twirled them around the staff's center part. Jim Qualia also created the rest of the insignia using StudioPro. J.W. tweaked the 3-D wireframe insignia so that it had a good falling angle, but so that you could still see the face of it.

Once all the 3-D elements were created, they were rendered as separate files. Since the shadow of the Cadeusis did not render exactly the way he wanted it to (it didn't fit perfectly pixel per pixel), J.W. also rendered another scene; the Bryce background with the Poser figure and the Cadeusis insignia with the shadow. Next, J.W. imported all the rendered elements into a Photoshop file. J.W. used a layer mask to airbrush parts from one layer to another to create the perfect shadow.

To see more of J.W.'s art, visit his Web site: http://www.jwburkey.com.

D

4 Columbus, Ohio artist, Larry Hamill, started creating this image by photographing a still life with plexiglass cylinders and spheres, and a six-inch tall cast bronze figure created by artist Eric Marlowe. The unusual quality of light was created by placing multicolored neon tubes around the still life.

After Larry shot the scene, he scanned it and used it as the foreground. The gray clouds in the background came from a photograph he took of a northern Ohio storm. He made a selection and pasted the clouds behind the foreground. The 3-D objects were created using MetaCreations Bryce. The 3-D images were pasted into the spheres and the Twirl filter (Filter | Distort |Twirl) was applied to provide the spiral effect.

5 Kenneth Gore, a New York City artist, used both MetaCreations RayDream Studio and Adobe Photoshop to create this image. Using RayDream Studio, he created several 3-D objects which he rendered with alpha channels. Next, he assembled the 3-D images in Photoshop using layers for placement, retouching, and creative enhancement.

The lettering in the pipes was rendered separately. Then, in Photoshop, he floated the image and used a path to create shadows.

For the finishing touches, Kenneth used the Airbrush tool to create details in the shadow areas. He also used the Airbrush to refine the edge glows and the beam of light from above down the head of the figure, then he used the Noise filter to break it up to create a particle effect. For these areas where he used the Airbrush, he created a path, which he converted to a selection using a feather for a soft edge. Kenneth also used the Smudge tool to blend pixels together for a subtle effect.

To see more of Kenneth's artwork, visit his Web site: http://www. grandeillusionsart.com.

6 Nik Kleinberg created this imaginative magazine cover for *Sports Illustrated for Kids.* It is composed of a variety of photographs which were scanned and placed into one file. The first image to be digitized was the wide-eyed child at the table. After the three images of the standing players were scanned, they were outlined using the Pen tool, converted to selections, then scaled using the Scale command. The player images were also rotated using the Edit | Transform | Rotate command. Then they were copied and pasted into the file with the child, and their shadows were created using the Pen tool and the Image | Adjust | Levels command.

The players on the cards were also outlined with the Pen tool, converted to selections, then filled with white. For the finishing touch, a football was scanned in, selected, scaled, copied, and then pasted into the final image. Finally, the Motion Blur filter was applied to the football to make it look like it was flying through the air.

7 This image was created from a set designed by Santa Barbara Studios for the movie "500 Nations" (from Pathways Productions; Jack Leustig, owner and producer; Kevin Costner and Jim Wilson, executive producers), which aired on CBS as a miniseries. Christopher started creating this image by scanning a slide of the sky. After retouching the image, he added rays of light using the Airbrush and Gradient tools and the Rubber Stamp tool's Cloning option. He also used the Airbrush tool to create the sky's haze. To paint the trees, he used the Paintbrush tool with a one-pixel-wide brush. Based upon the staff archaeologist's design, he created an oil painting of the pyramids on canvas. He photographed it and then scanned and synthesized it into the final image. The images of the Indians, who were actors in costumes, were digitized using a video camera, then frame-grabbed. Christopher then scaled down the actors in Photoshop using the Scale command, and color-corrected the images using commands in the Image | Adjust submenu.

8 Thetford Hill, Vermont artist John Stephens created this image, "A Rolls Royce Silver Ghost at the Shore" (a series of illustrations for a proposed new book, *Amelia's New Car*), by first using Photoshop to conceive, edit, and enhance photographs. When the "right" photograph is unobtainable, John sometimes sets up a scene in a 3-D program such as Fractal Design Ray Dream Designer. However, just as in a photograph, there is much work left to do in Photoshop. The car in the background was created using MetaCreations Ray Dream Designer.

The figure of Amelia in front of the car was a photograph. Because of poor lighting, the dress and the face were very uninteresting in the photograph. The dress was edited using an egg tempera technique, commonly used during the Renaissance, of cross hatching the folds. John blurred them with the Blur tool using a Gaussian Blur. John generally prefers this technique (instead of the Airbrush tool) because it gives him incredible control of small amounts of color and shadow. John cannot overemphasize the importance of using the Quick Mask. He used this to add a gradient to obtain the subtle shimmering effects of the silver paint as well as the reflections in the water.

9 New York City artist Christopher Ching created this image for an article on computer memory. To create the image, Christopher scanned a paper texture which he used as the character's skin and pattern. The pattern is from a printed fabric, which he darkened in a layer over the background and changed the opacity.

Christopher also scanned the circuits. After he scanned, he adjusted the Hue and Saturation (Image | Adjust | Hue/Saturation). The head is scanned from a watercolor he painted traditionally. Christopher used the Lasso tool to select the eyes and adjust brightness and contrast.

10   San Francisco artist Marcos Sorenson created this image for *Juice Magazine*. The art director for the project was Fred Dodsworth. Marcos starts his images by first creating a hand sketch. Then he faxes the sketch to the client for approval. Marcos faxes the sketch from the computer so that it is cleaner and has more contrast than from a regular fax machine.

To create his images, Marcos often uses video grabs for reference material. In this case he resized a video grab to 300 ppi and used it for the background. After resizing the video grab, Marcos converted the file to Grayscale and then back to RGB color so he could color it in Photoshop. He then blurred it using the Gaussian Blur filter and added color with the Edit | Fill command using the Color blending mode.

After the background was complete, Marcos scanned a ginger root by placing the root directly on the scanner bed. (Before scanning the right ginger root, Marcos looked for a ginger that had just the right gestures, so that he could create the right shape for the character). After the ginger was scanned, he duplicated it and flipped it a few times to create the character.

Marcos first created a sketch of Fred with a pencil. He scanned the sketch and then used the Pen tool so that he could create a sharper version. With the path created, he converted it into a selection and filled it with black. He used the Airbrush to create volume in the foot, shoulder, etc. To create the reflection of both Fred and Ginger, Marcos duplicated the image he had created. He then flipped it vertically and reduced the opacity to 10% to create a ghost version.

To see more of Marco's artwork, visit his Web site: http://WWW.astrocat.com.

11   Yardley, Pennsylvania artist John Ennis created this image, called "Brand New Cherry Flavor," for the jacket sleeve for a novel written by Todd Grimson and published by Harper Collins. Described to John as a hard-core, hard-rock Hollywood thriller, the book needed a cover that looked modern, sensual, disturbing, and pop.

The composition began in Photoshop, with a combination of photographed and hand-drawn elements. The face was first painted to look like flesh. This was kept on a separate layer to isolate it from the rest of the composition. The red lips were selected and copied to yet another layer. Working with layers is covered in Chapters 15 and 16.

Kai's Power Tools filter, Texture Explorer, was applied to the face layer to create the psychedelic effect. To keep the lips from having the psychedelic effect, they were reapplied. When the image was complete, John flattened the file for final output.

12 This image, created by artists Rico Lins and Mauricio Nacif, was used as the cover illustration for an issue of the *Washington Post Magazine* that featured an article titled "What's Wrong with Newspapers?" To digitize the image, Rico and Mauricio used a camcorder. After the pens were digitized, they were individually scaled and distorted using commands in the Edit | Transform submenu commands. The artists then created the target by scanning different newspapers and applying tinted rings using circular selections filled at a low-opacity setting. The borders of each separate ring were enhanced with the Select | Modify | Border, Select | Feather, and Edit | Fill commands. The shadows were created with the Lasso tool's Feather option and the Edit | Fill command. Finishing touches were applied with the Airbrush and other painting tools. Finally, the Dodge and Burn tools were used to balance specific areas of shadow, textures, and light sources.

The Dodge and Burn tools are discussed in Chapter 7.

13 Long Beach, New York artist Peter Jivkov created this illustration using Adobe Photoshop, Macromedia Freehand, MetaCreations Bryce, MetaCreations RayDream Designer, and scanned line art. The mouse, the road signs, and the ostrich were inked with a brush and scanned in as line art. In Photoshop he set up two layers, one for the line art and one for the color. This allowed him the freedom to make quick color changes. This also allowed him to paint only the line art if the Preserve Transparency option was checked in the Layers palette.

In Bryce Peter created the sky and rocks seen in the background. Using Bryce's advanced sky generation controls, Peter easily got the sky he wanted. In MetaCreations RayDream Designer, Peter modeled and rendered the road. The lanes were drawn in Freehand and then imported to Photoshop for compositing over the road. Peter scanned a small piece of desert which he manipulated in Photoshop to create the desert for the illustration. The entire illustration was composited in Photoshop.

To see more of Peter's artwork, visit his Web site:http://www.peterjivcov.com.

14 New York City artist Sanjay Kathari began this cover for a children's dictionary by creating the three-dimensional interior of the "sky" box from a digitized image of a sky. To create the top, bottom, and sides of the box, he copied and pasted the sky, then used the Edit | Transform | Scale and Perspective commands. Along the edges and corners, he used the Dodge and Burn tools to add shadows and contrast to enhance the sense of depth.

To increase contrast in the zebra, Sanjay used the Curves command. Next, he needed to add detail because the original zebra's underside was too dark. To lighten the dark areas, he copied and pasted different white areas using partial opacities. To lighten the shadow areas in the neck, he used the painting tools. To produce the shadow for the zebra, he first used the Pen tool to create a path around the zebra, then converted the path into a feathered selection. He shifted the zebra selection to the position where he wanted the shadow. Then he darkened the selected area slightly by using the Curves command. Next, he silhouetted the apple using the Pen tool. Then he copied and pasted the apple into the final image. Using the Dodge tool, he lightened the edges of the right side of the apple to simulate a light source. The shadow for the apple was created in the same way as the shadow for the zebra.

The last step was to create the text. The flat planes around the text were created in alpha channels, where they were scaled and rotated. Selections were then loaded from the alpha channels and filled with the appropriate colors to produce yellow and red flat planes around the type. The Dodge and Burn tools were used to produce the beveled edge effect for the type. Both Sanjay and Clifford Stolze worked together on the type usage.

15 Although it may not be apparent, much of the power of this fascinating image comes from placing one layer on top of another, then erasing parts of the different layers. New York City artist Sanjay Kathari started by creating a low-res version of the image to show the client, Adobe Systems, Inc. To build this image, he placed different scanned images of photographs he had taken into layers. The sky, brick wall with ivy, a building with windows and an alley, the inner arch, the outer arch, and a car with wheels are all separate layers. To build the final image, Sanjay carefully blended the layers together by hiding or revealing elements from each layer. For more information on blending layers together, see Chapter 16.

Sanjay started with the Background layer, a flat brick wall with ivy on it. To add more ivy to the brick wall, he first selected the ivy using the Select | Color Range command; then he copied and pasted the ivy selection. When editing the sky, Sanjay created a channel, then used the Gradient tool to create a blend in the channel. Next, he loaded the selection from the channel. Then he darkened and added yellow to the sky with the Image | Adjust | Curves command. Finally, he added motion to the sky by using the Motion Blur filter. The outer arches that appear in the brick wall are really the same arch that was copied and pasted several times. Visible within each arch is another image appearing from a different layer.

The wheels were originally part of an image of a road and a car. Sanjay spread out the distance between the wheels by cutting and pasting. Then he selected the wheels and the road, and pasted them into a new layer in the final image.

16 New York City artist Adam Cohen started this image by creating an abstract background using the Pen tool, the selection tools, and the Gradient tools. Next, he scanned in some topographical land textures. He shaped these textures into the United States shape and cut and pasted them on a new layer above the colored background. Using Image | Adjust | Hue and Saturation, he colored the textured shapes to fit with the background. Adam also added some transparency to other areas. At this point, Adam began to paste in images according to his original sketch. Adam always keeps images in different layers so he can edit and adjust the composite, angle, and scale. Finally, the artwork was output onto posters and T-shirts, to advertise the Community Development Block Grant.

17 This humorous animal balancing act was created from several photographs taken by Howard Berman. With the assistance of a professional animal handler, Howard took at least two photographs each of the dog and the cat in different positions. Separate photos were taken of the fish and the fish bowl. The fish were shot in a calm, stable fish tank and the fish bowl was shot while water was being splashed in it. The two birds that look like parrots are actually one bird, a canary, whose image was enlarged in the computer to look like a parrot. The bird and the wheel, which was made by a model maker, were photographed separately. The ball under the dog was shot and then enlarged in Photoshop. After the photographs were taken, they were scanned, then copied and pasted by Bob Bowen and Frank Lance at R/GA Print using the selection tools and alpha channels. The shadow was created using the selection tools and the Image | Adjust submenu's Levels and Curves commands.

18 Eric Kunzendorf, a Dunwoody, Georgia artist who co-heads the Electronic Art Department at The Atlanta College of Art, created "Aperture" using Photoshop, which he output at 25" × 25" using a LaserMaster inkjet printer.

Eric says that this piece represents the first large-scale color piece he has attempted. He can't say that there is any deeper meaning; he was simply experimenting with Photoshop. He started with an Adobe Illustrator piece that he had created for *Orlando Magazine* a few years earlier (it consisted of a very stylized head with a book growing out of it). Eric rasterized it into Photoshop and started adding scanned photographs. He included a photo of himself (just the eyes and glasses) which he placed at the bottom center. He used a gradient mask to let some of the stylized head show through. He then created a mask for the entire head and book. After selecting the head and book, he inverted the selection (Select | Inverse) to select the background. Eric used the Edit | Paste Into command to place the photos of the clouds and mountains behind the head. He then created two gradient masks for the effects at the top of the piece. He filled one with white, which resulted in the gradient at upper right; and he applied the Pointillist filter to the gradient at upper left.

19 Thetford Hill, Vermont artist John Stephens based this image, "The Lady of Shalott," on a poem by Alfred Lord Tennyson. To create the image, he scanned an ornate gilt picture frame. Then, using the Edit | Transform | Skew command and Filter | Distort | Shear command, he bent the image around the gunwale. The dress was smeared with the Smudge tool. The water by the bow was created using Quick Mask mode with various filters from Xaos Tools. As he worked, he loaded selections and applied color to the selections. Quick Mask was used extensively to get the shimmering effect on the young woman, especially in her hair. The Smudge tool helped created the water by the water lilies.

20 Yardley, Pennsylvania artist John Ennis created "Savage Longings" for the cover art for a romance novel by Cassie Edwards, published by Leisure Books. John created the Indian village scene using MetaCreations Bryce and imported it into Photoshop. The figures were painted using Photoshop's brushes, and the still life elements were added. The transitional texture between the still life elements and the village scene was created in MetaCreations Painter by assigning a custom texture to one of the brushes.

To see more of John's art, visit his Web site: http://www.voicenet.com/~ennis.

21 Yardley, Pennsylvania artist John Ennis created this fantasy image. Using a model as a reference, "Pixie" was created as a logo for a series of novels published by Leisure Books involving romantic themes based on fairy tales.

After scanning in the photo of the model, John re-drew and painted using Photoshop's brushes. The final stage of the illustration involved creating an outline around the art. The white background was transparent at this stage. By pressing COMMAND (Windows users: CTRL) and clicking on the target layer in the Layers palette, he created a selection around the image. Then he stroked the selection and added color.

22 Bellevue, Washington artist Henk Dawson created this sleek image for a cover of Motorola's internal publication "One Voice." The feature article, depicted on the cover, was called "SPS is on Track: Toward Challenging Destinations." Thus, the bullet train is ready to head to a new destination, or at least, off the page. The subtle, yet important imagery in the background hints at some of the challenges discussed in the cover article: complex internal mechanisms, restraints of time, and expanding global communications. The contrast of using old world elements such as the antique maps and gears to communicate a high-tech idea makes new ideas seem more approachable. Henk especially enjoyed using Photoshop to create the rich textures of this piece.

Once advertising agency Pressley Jacobs Design, Inc. created the initial concept and art direction (Art Director: Beverly Lo), Henk began to work. After the agency presented Henk with the concept, he refined it in a sketch. Although the main element is a 3-D image created in Strata StudioPro, the background is entirely a Photoshop collage which adds greatly to the texture and complexity of the piece. In his creative process, Henk has found that combining surreal 3-D elements with photos and organic colors adds to the allure of the piece. People want to see things that they are familiar with, yet don't mind if a new idea or object is presented in the familiar midst. Henk found it useful to use Photoshop for the background textural elements because it is easier to create complex textures in Photoshop than in a 3-D program.

To see more of Henk's artwork, visit his Web site: http://www.d3d.com.

23 The Warner Bros. Marketing Department, in conjunction with their in-house design department, The Idea Place, hired Imagic, Inc. to help design and create this image for the "Batman and Robin" domestic movie poster. Initially, The Idea Place provided several artists at Imagic with pencil sketches and raw photography to create a number of ideas to be presented to Warner Bros.

After an extensive testing and refining process over several months, three images were selected as a series to be recreated and finished in high resolution for 8×10 transparency output. Myra Wood and Page Wood worked together to create this image using 4×5 transparencies for the stars' heads and unit and stock photography for the other elements in the poster.

To keep the file size manageable, the image was created in three sections: the background, the heads, and the "x" effect. After color correcting each element, layer masks were used to blend the images together to create the base for the background. The Airbrush tool in the layer mask mode was used to isolate each head from its original background. To create the "x" effect, white dots were painted in the form of an "x." Next, the Gaussian Blur and Radial blur in spin mode were applied. A final file was created by blending the three merged files using gradations in layer masks to allow portions of each to fade from one to the other. Once everything was in position, extensive illustration, retouching, and color correction followed to complete this poster.

24 Henk Dawson, a Bellevue, Washington artist, created this piece of art called "Vision 30/30" for a central promotional image for the Graphic Artists Guild 30th Anniversary Event.

This image was used in conjunction with three other images to promote the Graphic Artists Guild 30th Anniversary. Four panels, each with a different era's glasses, were used to communicate the topic of the "Past, Present, and Future" of the graphics industry. Henk's panel, depicting the year 2,000 and beyond, explores the various mediums expected to explode in the graphics industry. Around and behind the futuristic glasses, subtle, undefined elements protrude then fade, achieving a neo-cubist effect.

Henk says he has always been inspired and intrigued by photocollage illustrations, and he wanted to apply it to his medium, 3-D. So, he took collage elements and applied them to simple 3-D shapes to create a collage with dimension. It all started with a very loose sketch which he scanned into Photoshop. After he touched up the scan, he started experimenting by applying textures.

To see more of Henk's artwork, visit his Web site: http://www.d3d.com.

25 New York City artist/author Adele Droblas Greenberg created this image for a children's CD-ROM game. Adele started by first using the Pen tool to create four paths that defined the area for the walls and floor. After all of the paths were created, each was turned into a selection. With a selection on screen, Adele pasted a texture into the selection using the Edit | Paste Into command. The textures were all created with Kai's Power Tools. Next, a photograph of two angels (taken with an Eastman Kodak digital camera) was placed into a new layer and blended with the back wall using a Layer Mask. Lastly, the dog (also photographed with a digital camera) was placed in a new layer. The shadow below the dog was created using the Airbrush tool. After the image was completed, it was imported into Adobe After Effects, where it was used as part of an animation in a QuickTime movie. The movie was later imported into Macromedia Director, where the project is being authored.

26 Pamela Hobbs, a San Francisco artist, created this image, "Top Ten," using both Adobe Photoshop and Macromedia Freehand. Pamela started by first creating black line art for the premise of the composition. She created the line art by using traditional ink and brush techniques.

Pamela used Freehand to produce the striped colored background area to go behind the main podium to create the illusion of space. Pamela added circles of light over the colors using the Freehand Intersect filter. Pamela then imported the Freehand background to Photoshop as an EPS file. Next she scanned the inked line art at 300 dpi and placed it into the Photoshop composition.

Pamela finalized the artwork for reproduction by using various painting techniques in Photoshop, utilizing the Actions palette, Layers palette, and several custom brushes with custom gradations.

To see more of Pamela's artwork, visit her Web site: http://www.pamorama.com.

27 Wendy Grossman, a New York City artist, starts most of her images in a similar fashion. After the client calls and gives her an assignment over the phone or faxes it, Wendy has the client describe the assignment as if it were a story. She then asks the client to give her six words and six icons that best illustrate the concept they are trying to portray. Next, Wendy creates a pencil sketch, which she scans into Photoshop then e-mails to the client. She does not fax it, because faxing loses some of the shading in the image. Next the client approves it or makes changes to the content and placement.

Once Wendy has approval from the client, she gathers all her photo references together. Then she starts to build the illustration. To create this image, Wendy primarily used the Pen tool in Illustrator and Photoshop. She used the Pen tool in Illustrator to create the electronic device, because it required more precision. Wendy also used Illustrator's Pen tool to create the buildings.

Wendy used Photoshop's Pen tool to create the hand that holds the electronic device. To create the shading in the hand, Wendy used both the Dodge and Burn tools to create shading. Wendy also selected a portion of the hand and copied it to a layer using Layer | New | Layer Via Copy. Then she chose the Difference mode in the Layers palette's blending mode pop-up menu.

To create the airplane, Wendy retouched a photograph of an airplane using the Airbrush, Dodge, and Burn tools. Wendy used the Airbrush to create the lights of the plane. She also used various brushes with different fade outs. To create the stars, Wendy inverted a photo of stars, then she airbrushed the clouds with white and gray.

To create the stripes passing through the globe, Wendy first created various paths. Wendy turned the paths into selections, and inverted the selections. Next, she used the Airbrush tool and airbrushed the outside of the selections. To mask out a piece of the globe, Wendy used layer masks.

The Ship was also created using paths, which she turned into selections and filled with color. She then used the Burn tool to darken areas within the selections.

28 Dallas photographer J.W. Burkey wanted to create a collage about sound. So, he began look though his large collection of photographs for appropriate images. J.W. has a large resource of photographs, because whenever he travels, he always takes an extra day to photograph images that have visual metaphors, such as doorways and bridges.

J.W. already had the ear, CD, stairs, and oboe and hand. The ear was a prosthetic ear to which he applied an Artistic filter to make it painterly. For the oboe and hand, he shot the person with a black cloth around him so that it would be easier to isolate the items he wanted. The arch, which looks like a tuning fork, was on a building on a doorway. The banner going across the arch was created using Strata StudioPro. The words on the banner are in French. They aren't supposed to mean anything. J.W. made them in French so that it would not detract from the image. The notes were created using the typeface Sonata. The shell he shot and blended with the background, which is a photograph of water in a pool. To create the collage, J.W. combined the various photographs using different layers and layer masks. To create the jagged edge on the image, J.W. painted edges on white paper with black paint. He then scanned the edge. In fact, he has a few edges he has created and scanned and placed in a folder for future reference.

Check out J.W.'s Web site: http://www.jwburkey.com.

29 To create this image, Larry Hamill, a Columbus, Ohio artist and photographer, combined both his artistic and photographic skills. Larry has a degree in painting and drawing, but with the help of Photoshop, he has been able to use photography as an extension of his fine arts talent. Larry feels that his photography is also an extension of his painting skills. When he photographs an object, he carefully examines the way light falls on it, just as if he were painting.

Larry began this image by first creating a painting with geometric elements. The painting was an acrylic on an 8 × 10 canvas, which he had scanned on a flatbed scanner. Once the painting was scanned, he loaded it into Photoshop, where he made selections with the Lasso tool and pasted in photographs he had taken in Jerusalem, Milan, Death Valley, Germany, and a steel mill in West Virginia. When Larry pasted the images into the painting, he used the Edit | Transform command to fit the images into place. He also used layer masks to blend the copied images into the painting. After he was finished pasting in the images, Larry tweaked the colors using the Curves command.

30 New York City artist Adam Cohen began creating this image (called "Internet") by creating a color palette based on a Pantone process color book. Next, he created an original abstract painting of shapes and colors. Adam created the shapes using the Pen tool, the Elliptical Marquee tool, and layers. This abstract piece became the background of the illustration. Adam continued work on this background with lights and darks forming the large computer monitor. After the completion of the monitor, many rendered images were pasted into a new layer. Then he scaled and rotated these images into the composition. Finally, the large car, telephone, and paper money shapes were airbrushed in a top layer.

31 New York City artist Robert Bowen created this image, called "Fabric Woman," as a prototype advertisement for a perfume manufacturer. The source image was made from a sheer silk fabric that was carefully rigged with preliminary folds to resemble as much as possible a human figure. However, photography alone couldn't create the full effect. Bob added the human features by compositing with various image-processing options, particularly the Dodge and Burn tools, which can lighten and darken while at the same time maintaining the fabric texture. No scanned image was used. As Bob worked, he used the Pen tool to create selections that were copied into different layers. He often used layer masks and the Edit | Transform commands to add to the final effect.

32 New York City artist Sanjay Kathari photographed this model on a loveseat with a very soft, flat light. When developing the image, he had transparency film processed using color negative chemistry. This made all the colors very saturated. It also, however, added a yellow cast to the highlights and the film grain tended to get a little coarse. After the film was processed, Sanjay scanned the negative on a Scitex scanner. Using the Scitex scanning software and Photoshop, he removed the yellow cast with the Curves command. To reduce the grainy effect, Sanjay used Photoshop's Airbrush tool to soften the skin texture. He then used the Dodge and Burn tools to accentuate the model's eyes and lips.

To enhance the red in the loveseat, Sanjay first created a selection using the Lasso tool. Then he used the Image | Adjust | Curves command to push yellow and magenta to 100%, which removed all of the cyan. The changes applied to the Curves dialog box made the sofa redder. Sanjay also made curve adjustments to lower the black, leaving only enough for the shape and detail.

The background was originally red. Sanjay applied a huge feather radius of 100 pixels to the selection around the sofa. After the selection was feathered, he then used the Hue/Saturation sliders to shift the red color to cyan. What appears to be a glow is merely the red that is left over from the background appearing as it was before the feathered selection was applied. The last step was to add noise to the green background.

33   Dallas photographer Bob Shaw created this image as a learning exercise—he was experimenting with various compositions using Photoshop. To create the image, Bob started by photographing a bank vault (he created it using HO scale model railroad gears for one of his clients) on a checkerboard background. He also made and photographed a glass ball with a miniature model of a house in it. Before photographing the glass ball, he frosted it with an airbrush. The sky was shot from an airplane, looking down on clouds. The wall doors are inset into a photograph of a darker sky.

Once Bob has photographed all the scenes he needs for an image, he has them scanned using the Kodak Photo CD process so that he can easily archive the images. After the images are digitized Bob uses the Lasso tool to select the images and place them in different layers in one file. When selecting the bubbles, Bob applied a feather to the selection so that when he copied and pasted the image, the edges would be soft and not hard.

As Bob works he creates layers which allow him to easily make changes to the image. If he needs to isolate an area within a layer (such as to change a color of an item), he selects it once and then saves the selection to an alpha channel. When he needs the selection again, he simply loads the selection using the Select | Load Selection command.

To see more of Bob's artwork, visit his Web site: http://www.powhouse.com.

34   John Craig, a Soldiers Grove, Wisconsin illustrator, created this image for a Stanford University brochure designed by Gordon Mortensen. John began by setting up a grid on paper, which he uses as a template. John created this graph paper, blue-grid style, to use when working on various images. The grid consists of 60-degree angles and is similar to isometric drafting grids.

With the grid, John started drawing in black with the Line tool and the Pencil. John set the Line tool so that it didn't create anti-alias lines, and thus would retain the jagged edges. When using the Pencil he set the Brushes palette to a 1-pixel hard-edged brush. When he used the Pencil, he pressed the SHIFT key so that the Pencil would draw straight lines. Once John had created a few lines, he built more lines by using the Lasso tool to clone and flip the lines. Once the black and white lines were complete, John got approval from his client before continuing. After the approval process, he filled in the image with color—placing the color in another layer. He used the Paint Bucket to add color, with the help of the Pencil to add detail and highlights. John also added color using the Gradient tool. To create the background, John filled the area with a gradient, then he applied the Mosaic filter (Filter | Pixelate | Mosaic). To create the image in the frame, John also filled the area with a gradient, then applied the Mosaic filter.

35 To create this intriguing book cover, England artist Dave McKean started with a 4-by-5-inch transparency of the boy in the chair, the collaged tower, and the puppet. At first, the image didn't look lively enough, so Dave scanned the transparency and about 30 other images along with fragments of photos, textures, and type. Then he rebuilt the entire image from scratch, giving it more of an "out of kilter" feel. When working, Dave used every one of Photoshop's selection tools, copying and pasting the various elements into the final image. To adjust the colors, he used the Image | Adjust submenu commands: Curves, Levels, Color Balance, Hue/Saturation. When blending the different elements together, he changed Composite Control settings so he could control just what range of pixels would appear in the final image. Finally, to add depth and energy, he applied sharpening and blurring filters to different image areas.

Dave says, "Although I love photography, this gravity-less digital space has become my favorite reason to use a computer."

36 John Craig, a Soldiers Grove, Wisconsin illustrator, created this image for Informix (a software company) for a promotional brochure. Gordon Mortensen was the designer of the project. To create this engraving-type collage, John started by cutting up copies of old black and white engravings and pasted them to make a collage. Then he scanned the collage using Photoshop in Grayscale. Next, John refined and cleaned up the scanned collage by adjusting the contrast, taking gray out of the image and making the blacks blacker. Next, John converted the file to Bitmap mode, making it a black-and-white image. With the image as a bitmap, John had a crisp engraving, so next he converted the file to Grayscale and then next to RGB color mode. In RGB color mode, John used the Select | Color Range command to select and copy the image. He pasted it in a new layer. He put the base color for the background (usually a natural color) in this layer. Then he created another layer and put all the pastel colors in this layer. He created yet another layer with the image in it for all the dark colors. When working with colors, John used a limited palette of only seven solid colors and seven tints—which resembles the way he used to work, using Pantone overlays on acetate. When all was complete, John flattened the image.

37 New York City artist Marcio Pereira started by creating the background texture, using the Difference Clouds filter (Filter | Render | Difference Clouds). He enhanced the effect by creating a gradient in a layer mask. To create the fire, he sketched a path with the Pen tool, then used the KPT Texture Explorer's Fiery Plasma option to light up the pen selection. To bring out the flame effect, he used the Smudge tool with a small brush, smudging it outward. To create the dragon, he blended various objects together with the Airbrush tool and layer masks. He used the Screen blending mode to make it look as though the body is in smoke. He added muscles to the body by creating paths and cloning different parts of the body into the paths. To create the recessed type, he created white type in a channel and created black type in a layer. He then applied the Gaussian Blur and Emboss filters with different blending operations to produce the final effect.

38 Santa Rosa, California artist James Dowlen generally starts all his images by sketching his ideas out in pencil on grid paper. After consulting with art director Charles Drucker, James turned to the computer to create the Globe image. James created the globes by first rendering each element separately in Crystal Topas (a PC 3-D program) against a black background. He used a black background so that he could easily eliminate extraneous edge pixels in Photoshop with the Layer | Matting | Remove Black Matte command. (To learn more about the Remove Black Matte command, see Chapter 4.) In Topas, he rendered each globe using a scanned photo texture map of the computer products seen in the globes. Then he wrapped the texture maps around the globe models. The tile floor was also created in Topas. The sky was painted in MetaCreations Painter. After creating the separate elements, James placed the images into Photoshop, where he carefully trimmed away extraneous black edge pixels. Then he selected the elements with different selection tools before pasting them into the background image. To soften the image and create an early morning misty effect, he applied the Diffuse Glow filter (Filter | Distort | Diffuse Glow). After applying the filter, he pasted in the globes so that they would remain crystal clear.

39 Santa Rosa, California artist James Dowlen started creating the Droid in the same manner as the Globes image (Image 38), by sketching his ideas in pencil and consulting with art director Charles Drucker. Both James and Charles tried out different versions until they arrived at a solution they both agreed upon. When time permitted, color comps were created, but often the colors were discussed on the phone as the image developed. He started the image by creating the 3-D background airport scene in Topas. The sky, the city, and the tarmac were created in Painter. Since the Droid was to be the focus of the image, it required the most attention. James started by scanning a sketch, then painted over it in MetaCreations Painter. He dropped the Droid and other images into the background by selecting with the Magic Wand tool with a low tolerance setting. Next, he copied and pasted the Droid into the destination image. To blend extraneous colored pixels, James used the Layer | Matting | Defringe command, then touched up the blending work around image edges with the Paintbrush tool. To learn more about the Defringe command, see Chapter 4.

40 This photograph (also shown in Chapter 18) of a beautiful New England town was taken by Gene Ahrens for the cover of a proposed Reader's Digest book, *Back Roads of America*. The image was almost perfect; however, the power lines and telephone wires running through the town marred the landscape. The art director of Reader's Digest General Books, David Trooper, felt that areas of the sky were too dark and would conflict with the color of the book's title. He also wanted the road signs in the foreground removed. To make the changes, the image was scanned and saved as a CMYK file, then retouched and color-corrected by Adele Droblas Greenberg.

41 This image (also shown in Chapter 18) shows the final cover for the proposed book after retouching and color-correcting. To remove the road signs, telephone wires, and power lines, Adele cloned using the Rubber Stamp tool. Before color-correcting, several masks were created using the selection tools and Quick Mask mode. To make the water bluer, she added cyan using the Levels command in the Image | Adjust submenu. The clouds behind the title were lightened using the Curves command in the Image | Adjust submenu. The colors on the hills across the water were made to look more autumn-like and the foliage in the town was made more vibrant. For a full discussion of the steps involved, see Chapter 18.

42 This photograph (also shown in Chapter 18) was taken in the late 1800's of a 24-year-old French nobleman who came to the United States in hopes of fulfilling his dream of raising cattle. The photograph was selected for the Reader's Digest book *Discover America's Past*, where it appears as a sepia. Notice that the lower part of his left leg and his left foot are badly faded and barely noticeable. In addition to restoring the leg and foot, the book's art editor, Ken Chaya, asked Adele Droblas Greenberg to paint in the left elbow, add tone to the pistol, and enhance the detail in the rifle and hat.

43 Here is the image (also shown in Chapter 18) after retouching. Adele began restoring the lower-left leg and left foot by copying, pasting, and flipping part of the right leg and foot into a new file. She then used the Rubber Stamp tool to clone the foot back into the image, and the Airbrush tool to provide a seamless transition between the restored and original areas. Before painting the left elbow, Adele used the Eyedropper tool to set the foreground color so it matched the tone of the original. Next, she used the Airbrush and Paintbrush tools to paint in the left elbow. For complete details on how this image was retouched, see Chapter 18.

APPENDIX E

Conclusion

We hope this book has truly opened up the wonders of the Photoshop world to you. Now that you've worked through the chapters, examined the beautiful images in the Photoshop Portfolio color inserts, and studied the excellent Photoshop in Action examples, you can see the almost unlimited design choices that Photoshop offers. We hope that you've already begun to use the examples in this book as a springboard for your own creativity and design ideas, and are planning projects that might once have seemed difficult or even impossible. We're sure you already agree that after you've experienced the magic of Photoshop, you'll never want to turn away from it. Tomorrow's more powerful computers and improved versions of Photoshop are sure to be even more exciting and enticing. We hope this book will help bring you into that future.

For updated information on Photoshop, visit our Web site: www2.infohouse.com/~addesign.

We hope you've enjoyed your journey through *Fundamental Photoshop*.

Adele & Seth

Index

955

H